Trotsky and the Problem
of Soviet Bureaucracy

Historical Materialism Book Series

The Historical Materialism Book Series is a major publishing initiative of the radical left. The capitalist crisis of the twenty-first century has been met by a resurgence of interest in critical Marxist theory. At the same time, the publishing institutions committed to Marxism have contracted markedly since the high point of the 1970s. The Historical Materialism Book Series is dedicated to addressing this situation by making available important works of Marxist theory. The aim of the series is to publish important theoretical contributions as the basis for vigorous intellectual debate and exchange on the left.

The peer-reviewed series publishes original monographs, translated texts, and reprints of classics across the bounds of academic disciplinary agendas and across the divisions of the left. The series is particularly concerned to encourage the internationalization of Marxist debate and aims to translate significant studies from beyond the English-speaking world.

For a full list of titles in the Historical Materialism Book Series
available in paperback from Haymarket Books, visit:
www.haymarketbooks.org/category/hm-series

Trotsky and the Problem of Soviet Bureaucracy

Thomas M. Twiss

Haymarket Books
Chicago, IL

First published in 2014 by Brill Academic Publishers, the Netherlands
© 2014 Koninklijke Brill NV, Leiden, the Netherlands

Published in paperback in 2015 by
Haymarket Books
P.O. Box 180165
Chicago, IL 60618
773-583-7884
www.haymarketbooks.org

ISBN: 978-1-60846-478-4

Trade distribution:
In the US, Consortium Book Sales, www.cbsd.com
In Canada, Publishers Group Canada, www.pgcbooks.ca
In the UK, Turnaround Publisher Services, www.turnaround-psl.com
In Australia, Palgrave Macmillan, www.palgravemacmillan.com.au
In all other countries, Publishers Group Worldwide, www.pgw.com

Cover design by Ragina Johnson.

This book was published with the generous support of
Lannan Foundation and the Wallace Global Fund.

Printed in Canada by union labor.

10 9 8 7 6 5 4 3 2 1

Library of Congress Cataloging-in-Publication data is available.

Dedicated to the memory of my mother,
Ruth Ann Twiss, and to my father,
James Albert Twiss

∵

Contents

Preface

The author of any book incurs many debts – scholarly, financial, and emotional. Here, I can only mention a few of the contributions others have made to this work. I hope that those I have omitted will forgive me.

First, I want to thank a number of people who have contributed important recommendations and critical evaluations. I owe a special debt to Jonathan Harris, chair of my dissertation committee. Throughout the writing of my dissertation, he was a constant source of support and valuable criticism. Other committee members included Bill Chase, who generously shared his expertise in the Stalin era, and Ron Linden and Ilya Prizel, who both assisted greatly with their probing questions. Among friends who contributed, I especially thank Paul Le Blanc for his thoughtful observations and for providing a model of how to combine serious scholarship with engaged political commitment. I thank the reviewers at Brill for their invaluable comments and criticisms, which were crucial to the process of transforming a dissertation into a book. Also, I want to thank my editors – Sebastian Budgen, David Broder, Nathaniel Boyd, Danny Hayward, and Debbie de Wit – for their assistance and their patience.

Many people have helped me locate and obtain crucial resources for this work. In particular, I thank Naomi Allen for providing copies of documents that were especially important for this project, and Carmine Storella for his many useful suggestions. I also want to express my appreciation to Karen Rondestvedt and Dan Pennell, the former and the current Slavic bibliographers in the University Library System at the University of Pittsburgh, as well as to Patricia Colbert, Patricia Duff, and Vicki Redcay in the Interlibrary Loan department of Pitt's Hillman Library for their assistance.

I thank the University Library System at the University of Pittsburgh for professional development leaves that made it possible for me to finish both the original dissertation and the revisions for this book. Related to that, I thank my colleagues in Hillman who had to shoulder extra responsibilities during my absences.

Most of all, I want to thank my family. I am grateful to my parents for their encouragement during this long process. I thank my wife Pamela for her love and support, and for creating an environment in which it was possible to do productive work. I recognise that her own scholarly work often took a back seat, and I deeply appreciate her sacrifices. I also want to acknowledge her invaluable editorial advice. Finally, I want to thank my son Noah, a young admirer of Trotsky, who has frequently raised critical questions of his own regarding this project.

Throughout, I have employed the Library of Congress system for transliteration, making exceptions only for a very few of the best-known names. Thus, this work refers to Rakovskii, Osinskii, and Sosnovskii, but also to Trotsky rather than Trotskii, and Zinoviev rather than Zinov'ev.

Introduction

For most of the last two decades of his life, the political and theoretical issue that concerned Leon Trotsky more than any other was the problem of Soviet bureaucracy. Even in the years immediately after the Bolshevik Revolution he criticised manifestations of bureaucratic inefficiency in the military and economic organs of the Soviet Union. By late 1923 he had begun to detect the corrosive presence of bureaucratism – understood as authoritarianism, excessive centralism, and conservatism – in the Soviet state and the Bolshevik Party. He continued to analyse that problem during the party struggle of 1926–7 and afterwards, defining it in terms of policies that he perceived as increasingly repressive and highly responsive to bourgeois pressure. Finally, in his last years – most notably in his classic work *The Revolution Betrayed* – he denounced the privileged bureaucratic caste that he believed had usurped power, attaining an unprecedented degree of autonomy from all social classes of Soviet society.

An examination of the development of Trotsky's views on this question is important for a number of reasons, including for explaining the actions and perspectives of one of the most important political figures of the twentieth century. For example, a familiarity with his views on *glavkokratiia* in the early 1920s is necessary for understanding his early preoccupation with central economic planning. A grasp of what he, as well as Lenin, meant by the term *bureaucracy* in late 1922 is required in order to appreciate the significance of the 'bloc' that the two leaders forged at that time. A comprehension of Trotsky's theory in 1926–27 is needed for grasping the relationship between the political, economic, and international demands he raised in the party struggle of those years. It also is essential for understanding his refusal to form a broad alliance with the party right in 1928–9, his readiness to accept at face value the accusations in the show trials of the First Five-Year Plan, his perpetual anticipation of a sharp turn to the right in economic and Comintern policy in the early 1930s, and his hesitation to break with the Comintern in mid-1933. Finally, some knowledge of his later theory is important for understanding his analysis of the Moscow Trials of 1936–8.

Beyond that, a study of Trotsky's views on bureaucracy is important in terms of the history of ideas. Martin Krygier has noted the impact of Trotsky's post-1923 writings on students of bureaucracy, observing that Trotsky's writings 'had a considerable influence on the reception of the concept of bureaucracy by later Marxists and by many non- or ex-Marxists'.[1] Perhaps even more significantly, a number of scholars have commented upon the influence of

---

1   Krygier 1979a, p. 89.

Trotsky's writings on serious examinations of the phenomenon of Stalinism. For example, in 1958 John Plamenatz asserted, 'As an indictment of Stalinism, Trotsky's account of Soviet Russia is formidable. So much so, indeed, that some version or other of it has been adopted by nearly all of Stalin's more plausible critics'.[2] More recently, Duncan Hallas has observed that whatever criticisms can be made of Trotsky's analysis of Stalinism, 'it has been the starting point for all *serious* analysis from a Marxist point of view', and Henry Reichman has asserted that 'it is Leon Trotsky's critique that continues to shape key elements of what many scholars – including some otherwise hostile to Marxism – regard as Stalinism'.[3]

Finally, a clarification of Trotsky's later theory of Soviet bureaucracy is essential for anyone who would attempt to apply it to a study of Soviet history or to the contemporary process of capitalist restoration in Russia and Eastern Europe. Various scholars have commented not only on the past influence, but also on the contemporary significance of Trotsky's analysis of Stalinism. Along those lines Baruch Knei-Paz asserted in 1979 that no one had done more than Trotsky 'to show the social and historical roots of Stalinism', and that his explanation 'was, and in many ways still is, one of the most perceptive theoretical accounts of it'.[4] And in 1983 Perry Anderson depicted Trotsky's general interpretation of Stalinism as continuing to be 'the most coherent and developed theorization of the phenomenon within the Marxist tradition'.[5] Furthermore, a number of writers have noted the value of Trotsky's later theory for comprehending the process of capitalist restoration in Russia and Eastern Europe. For example, in 2001 the British Trotskyist Alan Woods asserted that Trotsky's analysis of Stalinism, 'with a delay of 60 years', had been 'completely vindicated by history'.[6] And more recently Western social scientists such as Stephen White and Allen C. Lynch have turned to Trotsky's 1936 observations to illuminate the dynamics of capitalist restoration.[7] But to apply a theory presupposes an intimate familiarity with it, and that, in turn, requires an understanding how it was created and applied over time. As Trotsky observed in a preface to a Greek edition of his writings on bureaucracy in 1933, 'It is impossible to understand

---

2 Plamenatz 1954, p. 303.

3 Hallas 1984, p. 28; Reichman 1988, p. 67. Along these same lines, Ticktin has asserted that Trotsky's articles on the Soviet Union written between 1923 and 1936 'have provided the theoretical basis for practically every serious Marxist analysis of the Soviet Union' (Ticktin 1995b, p. 65).

4 Knei-Paz 1978, p. 369.

5 P. Anderson 1984, p. 118.

6 Woods 2001. See also C. Edwards 1998; Miles 1994–5; Miles 1998.

7 S. White 2000, p. 291; Lynch 2005, p. 77.

correctly either scientific or political ideas without knowing the history of their development'.[8]

Although a number of other works have addressed this topic in various ways, in each case the focus, the scope, or the depth of the study has differed from that of this book. Some have had broader or significantly different concerns; some have concentrated more narrowly on a single aspect of Trotsky's theory or on one work; others have attempted to sketch the development of Trotsky's views on bureaucracy or Stalinism only briefly.

Studies with a broader or differing focus that have included discussions of Trotsky's analysis of bureaucracy have included biographies, general examinations of his political thought, works that have compared his views with those of another theorist, and studies of other aspects of his thinking that overlap with his analysis of bureaucracy. To date, probably the most extensive examination of the evolution of Trotsky's thinking regarding bureaucracy is contained in Isaac Deutscher's classic biography, and especially the second and third volumes.[9] Other biographical works that are noteworthy in this regard include Robert Wistrich's *Trotsky: Fate of a Revolutionary* and the last two volumes of Tony Cliff's *Trotsky*.[10] General studies of Trotsky's political thought that present outlines of his main, and especially his later, ideas on bureaucracy are Duncan Hallas's *Trotsky's Marxism*, Baruch Knei-Paz's *The Social and Political Thought of Leon Trotsky*, Ernest Mandel's *Trotsky as Alternative* and *Trotsky: A Study in the Dynamic of His Thought*, and John Molyneux's *Leon Trotsky's Theory of Revolution*.[11] Books of a comparative nature that discuss Trotsky's views on this topic are Michael M. Lustig's *Trotsky and Djilas: Critics of Communist Bureaucracy* and Emanuele Saccarelli's *Gramsci and Trotsky in the Shadow of Stalinism*.[12] Works focusing upon other aspects of his thought but that also contain significant examinations of his analysis of bureaucracy include several unpublished doctoral dissertations, but most notably David Law's 'Trotsky in Opposition: 1923–1940'. Published monographs in the same category are *The Evolution of Trotsky's Theory of Revolution* by Curtis Stokes and *Trotsky, Trotskyism and the Transition to Socialism* by Peter Beilharz.[13]

---

8   Trotsky 1972f, p. 87.

9   Deutscher 1954; Deutscher 1959; Deutscher 1963.

10 Wistrich 1979; Cliff 1991; Cliff 1993. Other significant biographies that discuss Trotsky's views on bureaucracy to varying degrees include Broué 1988; Thatcher 2003; Volkogonov 1996.

11 Hallas 1984; Knei-Paz 1978; Mandel 1995; Mandel 1979; Molyneux 1981.

12 Lustig 1989; Saccarelli 2008.

13 Law 1987a; Stokes 1982; Beilharz 1987. See also Braun 1993; Egan 1973.

Yet other studies have concentrated more narrowly on a particular aspect of Trotsky's theory, or exclusively on Trotsky's most important work on the subject, *The Revolution Betrayed*. Among the former are works on the class nature of the Soviet Union that include discussions of Trotsky's 'workers' state' position, such as *The Bureaucratic Revolution* by Max Shachtman, *State Capitalism in Russia* by Tony Cliff, *Marxism and the U.S.S.R.* by Paul Bellis, *Trotskyism and the Dilemma of Socialism* by Christopher Z. Hobson and Ronald D. Tabor, and *Western Marxism and the Soviet Union* by Marcel van der Linden.[14] Additionally, Jay Bergman, David Law, and Robert Warth all have published articles dealing with Trotsky's use of the Thermidor analogy, while Robert McNeal has written on Trotsky's perception of Stalin.[15] Since 1936 many authors have also written essays, reviews, articles, chapters, and pamphlets explaining, interpreting, extolling, criticising, or testing the arguments of *The Revolution Betrayed*.[16]

A fairly small number of works have focused directly on the evolution of Trotsky's theory of Soviet bureaucracy. The most significant of these are Perry Anderson's 'Trotsky's Interpretation of Stalinism', Siegfried Bahne's 'Trotsky on Stalin's Russia', Martin Krygier's 'The Revolution Betrayed? From Trotsky to the New Class', David W. Lovell's *Trotsky's Analysis of Soviet Bureaucratization*, Robert McNeal's 'Trotskyist Interpretations of Stalinism', and Hillel Ticktin's 'Leon Trotsky and the Social Forces Leading to Bureaucracy', and his 'Leon Trotsky's Political Economic Analysis of the USSR, 1929–40'.[17] All of these, including David W. Lovell's monograph, are relatively brief essays.

Many of the publications cited here have included insights that are incorporated in this work. However, none has systematically and comprehensively examined the history of the evolution of Trotsky's theory of the Soviet bureaucracy. For some, a broader or differing focus has diverted their attention from that particular story. For others, the narrower concentration upon one aspect of Trotsky's theory or just one of his works has limited their contribution to the larger picture that is examined here. Finally, the brevity of all the previous works directly devoted to the development of Trotsky's views on this topic has

---

14   Shachtman 1962; Cliff 1974; Bellis 1979; Hobson and Tabor 1988; Linden 2007.

15   On Trotsky's views regarding Thermidor, see Bergman, 1987, pp. 73–98; Law 1987b, pp. 4–15; Law 1982, pp. 433–49; Warth 1985. On Trotsky's perception of Stalin, see McNeal 1982, pp. 377–87; McNeal 1961, pp. 87–97.

16   Arthur 1972; Burkett 1987; Day 1987; T. Edwards 1958; Foxcroft 1938; James 1964; Katz 1977; Kolakowski 2005, pp. 934–52; Michail 1977; Milenkovitch 1987; Plamenatz 1950; Plamenatz 1954, pp. 281–305.

17   Anderson 1984; Bahne 1962; Krygier 1979a; Lovell 1987; McNeal 1977; Ticktin 1995a; Ticktin 1995b. See also Krygier 1978. For still more works that deal with Trotsky and the 'Russian Question', see W. Lubitz and P. Lubitz 1999, pp. 134–47.

meant that major aspects of that development have been missed, important writings have been overlooked, and the significance of some of Trotsky's writings has been misjudged.

The goal of this work is to explain the development of Trotsky's thinking on the problem of Soviet bureaucracy from shortly after the Bolshevik Revolution in 1917 through the writing of *The Revolution Betrayed* in 1936 and the application of his theory to the Moscow Trials of 1936–8. As already suggested, Trotsky did not always employ the word *bureaucracy* [*biurokratiia*] when dealing with this problem. Sometimes he used other terms such as *bureaucratism* [*biurokratizm* or *kantseliarshchina*], *officialdom* [*chinovnichestvo*], or *red tape* [*volokita*]. Throughout this study there is an attempt to note the specific word Trotsky utilised at each point. However, the term *bureaucracy* is also used here in a generic sense when discussing Trotsky's understanding of the 'problem of bureaucracy' or 'Trotsky's theory of bureaucracy' – even when *biurokratiia* was not the precise term employed. The book begins with 1917, rather than 1923 as most other works on this topic commonly do, in order to show the important ways Trotsky's views on bureaucracy shaped his positions and behavior from the time of the revolution through 1922, and also to shed new light on the origins of his struggle against 'bureaucratism' in the New Course controversy of 1923. It culminates with Trotsky's *The Revolution Betrayed* and his analysis of the Moscow Trials because that work represents the most complete statement of his later theory, and his analysis of the trials represents his most extensive application of that theory.

While examining the development of Trotsky's general understanding of Soviet bureaucracy, this study also attempts to identify the sources of those views. Special attention is paid to how his most pressing concerns shaped his thinking on the problem. Also, the influence of other thinkers is examined. At the same time, this work looks at how Trotsky's general perspective influenced his perceptions of unfolding developments, and how it guided his political behavior. The primary focus here is explanatory, not evaluative. However, the conclusions of each chapter as well as the concluding chapter of the book contain evaluations of his theory and of his policy analyses at each point.

For a systematic comparison of ideas across time, a standard set of analytical categories is essential. However, Trotsky's perceptions of the problem changed so dramatically over the years that it is impossible to apply any highly specific set of categories to all periods. Consequently, for each period the following general categories are applied: his *conception* of the problem of bureaucracy, his understanding of the major *characteristics* of bureaucracy, his explanation of the *causes* of the problem, his beliefs regarding its *consequences*, and his conclusions regarding the *cure* for the problem.

In each period the *conception* of bureaucracy employed was Trotsky's general understanding of the problem. In the first years after the revolution he consistently associated bureaucracy with inefficiency. By late 1923 he had begun to view the phenomenon of 'bureaucratism' as a variety of political alienation involving excessive centralisation of authority in the apparatuses of the state and the party, but also the susceptibility of those apparatuses to alien class pressures. This conception received an even sharper expression in 1926–7 when Trotsky denounced the problem of 'bureaucratism', and the Soviet 'bureaucracy', in terms of the growing centralism, authoritarianism, and repression in all Soviet political institutions, and also in terms of the responsiveness of the party leadership to increasingly powerful bourgeois interests. In the early 1930s, although he began to depict the bureaucracy as a social formation that had usurped power, he continued to view it as highly receptive to bourgeois pressures. However, by the mid-1930s he had concluded that the bureaucracy was an exceptionally autonomous and self-sufficient 'caste' – an image he would utilise for the remainder of his life.

The *characteristics* category involves the most salient features of bureaucracy for Trotsky at any given time. For example, characteristics of bureaucratic inefficiency in the early years of the revolution included the centralist domination by the industrial *glavki* of regional and local economic organs and enterprises, combined with the inadequate coordination of the activities of the different *glavki* with each other. In later years Trotsky frequently discussed such features as the bureaucracy's size, its privileges, its attitudes, its political composition and patterns of recruitment, its internal divisions, and especially its policies.

The *causes* heading covers all of Trotsky's explanations of the origins of the problem. In the early years he attributed the phenomenon of *glavkokratiia* to mistakes made in constructing socialist economic institutions with no historical precedent. By 1926–7 he perceived the fundamental source of bureaucratism to be a shift in the balance of class forces that had pushed state and party apparatuses to the right, thereby promoting restrictions on workers' democracy. In the mid-1930s he explained the usurpation of power by the bureaucracy by reference to various factors that had contributed to the demoralisation of the proletariat, as well as to the function of the bureaucracy in mediating social conflict. Finally, in *The Revolution Betrayed*, while continuing to discuss factors that had weakened the Soviet working class, he defined the essential function of the Soviet bureaucracy in terms of the distribution of scarce resources in a backward, transitional society.

The *consequences* category includes Trotsky's understanding of both the immediate and the longer term effects of bureaucratisation. In his earlier writings he concentrated upon the relatively short-term effects of bureaucratic inefficiency in disrupting industrial production and military supply. Beginning with 1923 he became more concerned with the larger and longer-term prospect that bureaucratism might result in capitalist restoration. This remained a major concern of Trotsky's until his death, though his position varied regarding both the immediacy of the danger and the path that such a restoration might take. Throughout this work, the criteria by which Trotsky concluded that the Soviet Union remained a workers' state are discussed in the section on consequences.

Most broadly, Trotsky's views regarding the *cure* for the problem of bureaucracy fall into three approaches. During the years 1917–22 he focused especially on the structural reorganisation of the Soviet economy. Roughly from 1923 until 1933 he advocated political reform of Soviet institutions, beginning with the party. Then, in the period 1933–40 he called for force or revolution to overturn bureaucratic rule. Throughout the years 1923–40 his thinking also shifted and evolved regarding such issues as alliances, tactical demands, and the role of the international oppositional movement.

As far as sources are concerned, all of the primary materials utilised for this study have been published at one time or another. At a very early stage of work on this project, a number of previously unpublished documents from the Trotsky Archives at Harvard University were examined. However, Pathfinder Press subsequently published translations of those documents, including several translations by this author. Since that time, a large number of documents by Trotsky have been published in Russian on the Web or in print. Materials employed for this project include books, pamphlets, resolutions, and articles written for public consumption, but also 'circular letters', private letters, and a diary.

For the most part, Russian and English versions of Trotsky's writings were used. The English translations utilised were mainly those produced by political publishers – Pathfinder and Monad in the U.S., and New Park in the U.K. – plus a few titles issued by academic and commercial presses.[18] Wherever possible,

---

18   In roughly chronological order (by date written) those titles include: *Leon Trotsky Speaks* (Trotsky 1972a); *Report of the Siberian Delegation* (Trotsky 1980a); *Leon Trotsky on the Paris Commune* (Trotsky 1970a); *The Permanent Revolution and Results and Prospects* (Trotsky 1969); *1905* (Trotsky 1972b); *The Trotsky Papers 1917–1922* (Trotsky 1964–71); *From October to Brest-Litovsk* (Trotsky 1919); *How the Revolution Armed: The Military Writings and Speeches of Leon Trotsky* (Trotsky 1979–81); *Terrorism and Communism: A Reply to Karl Kautsky* (Trotsky 1972c); *The First Five Years of the Communist International* (Trotsky 1972d); *Kronstadt* (Lenin and Trotsky 1979); *The Position of the Soviet Republic and the Tasks of Young Workers* (Trotsky 1972e); *Social Democracy and the Wars of Intervention in Russia*

existing translations were checked against the Russian originals. Russian language sources used include two series originally published in the Soviet Union:
Trotsky's *Kak vooruzhalas revoliutsiia: na voennoi rabote* and his *Sochineniia*. In
this latter series, volume 15, *Khoziaistvennoe stroitel'stvo Sovetskoi respubliki*,
and volume 21, *Kul'tura perekhodnogo perioda* were especially important
sources for Trotsky's early views on bureaucracy.[19] Additional Russian language
sources used include the original Russian texts of his book *The Stalin School of
Falsification*, his autobiography, his book *The Revolution Betrayed*, and his biography of Stalin;[20] collections of his oppositional writings published in print
and on the web;[21] and facsimile print and Web editions of Trotsky's journal
Biulleten' oppozitsii.[22]

Numerous memoirs and secondary sources were also employed. Secondary
sources included surveys of the history of Soviet politics, economics, and foreign policy; histories of the Comintern; more specialised monographs and
articles on Soviet and Comintern history; biographies of Trotsky, Lenin, Stalin,
and Bukharin; and works that deal directly or indirectly with Trotsky's analysis
of bureaucracy.

     (Trotsky 1975a); *Lenin's Fight against Stalinism* (Lenin and Trotsky 1975); *Problems of
     Everyday Life and Other Writings on Culture & Science* (Trotsky 1973a); *The Challenge of the
     Left Opposition* (Trotsky 1975b; Trotsky 1980b; Trotsky 1981); *Leon Trotsky on Britain*
     (Trotsky 1973b); *Leon Trotsky on China* (Trotsky 1976a); *The Stalin School of Falsification*
     (Trotsky 1971a); *The Third International After Lenin* (Trotsky 1970b); *My Life: An Attempt at
     an Autobiography* (Trotsky 1970c); *The Writings of Leon Trotsky* (Trotsky 1971b; Trotsky
     1972f; Trotsky 1972g; Trotsky 1973c; Trotsky 1973d; Trotsky 1973e; Trotsky 1974; Trotsky 1975c;
     Trotsky 1975d; Trotsky 1976b; Trotsky 1977a; Trotsky 1978; Trotsky 1979a; Trotsky 1979b); *The
     History of the Russian Revolution* (Trotsky 1977b); *The Struggle Against Fascism in Germany*
     (Trotsky 1971c); *Leon Trotsky on France* (Trotsky 1979c); *Trotsky's Notebooks, 1933–1935:
     Writings on Lenin, Dialectics, and Evolutionism* (Trotsky 1986); *Trotsky's Diary in Exile, 1935*
     (Trotsky 1963f); *The Serge-Trotsky Papers* (Serge and Trotsky 1994); *The Revolution Betrayed:
     What is the Soviet Union and Where Is It Going?* (Trotsky 1937); *The Case of Leon Trotsky:
     Report of Hearings on the Charges Made Against Him in the Moscow Trials* (Preliminary
     Commission of Inquiry 1968); *Portraits: Political & Personal* (Trotsky 1977c); *The Spanish
     Revolution, 1931–39* (Trotsky 1973f); *The Transitional Program for Socialist Revolution*
     (Trotsky 1973g); *In Defense of Marxism (Against the Petty-bourgeois Opposition)* (Trotsky
     1970d); *Stalin: An Appraisal of the Man and His Influence* (Trotsky 1941).
19   Trotsky 1991a; Trotsky 1963d; Trotsky 1963e.
20   Trotsky 1990; Trotsky 1991b; Trotsky 1972h; Trotsky 1985.
21   Fel'shtinskii 1988; Fel'shtinskii 1999–2002; Fel'shtinskii 1990; Trotsky 1989; Trotsky 1995.
22   *Biulleten oppozitsii* 1973; *Biulleten oppozitsii* 2002.

CHAPTER 1

Bureaucracy before October

When Bolsheviks, including Trotsky, first began to address the issue of bureaucracy soon after the October Revolution of 1917, they derived their understanding of that problem from various sources. One of these was popular usage of the word *bureaucracy* in both Russia and Western Europe. As commonly used in the early twentieth century, the primary understanding of the term remained close to its original meanings: the rule of officials, or a body of officials who ruled. Secondary definitions and connotations included an excessive degree of formalism and paperwork, as well as the apathy, ignorance, and inefficiency of state officials. An additional influence for the Bolsheviks was the traditional Marxist analysis of bureaucracy. Consistent with the primary popular meaning, Marx and Engels perceived bureaucracy as related to the problem of political alienation. That is, they identified bureaucracy with the independence of the state apparatus from the control of society as a whole, and with the domination of that apparatus over society. Furthermore, they believed that, in normal periods, this alienation was directly related to control of the state by an exploitative class. Finally, they predicted that the problem of bureaucracy would be greatly reduced by the coming socialist revolution, and that eventually it would wither away altogether. In the years and months preceding the Bolshevik Revolution both Trotsky and Lenin reaffirmed this traditional Marxist analysis.

1.1 Evolving Meanings of Bureaucracy

Scholars have identified a variety of meanings of the term *bureaucracy* in current Western usage. Martin Albrow has counted seven, and Fred Riggs has identified eleven contemporary uses of the word.[1] Although it had not yet acquired quite as many meanings in either Western European or Russian discourse at the time of the Bolshevik Revolution, bureaucracy already had accumulated a wide range of denotations and connotations. Still, the most common popular understanding of that word remained close to its original meaning.

By most accounts the term *bureaucratie*, or bureaucracy, was first coined in 1745 by the French Physiocrat Jacques Claude Marie Vincent de Gournay, who

---

1 Albrow 1970, pp. 84–105; Riggs 1979.

was also responsible for inventing the expression *laissez faire*.[2] Gournay created it by combining the French *bureau*, which referred to a writing desk but also to an office where officials worked, with the Greek word *kratein*, meaning 'to rule'. His intent was to identify a form of rule comparable to systems such as democracy and aristocracy. From the beginning the word was used as a pejorative to indicate the excessive power of state officials, while also suggesting their tendency to meddle in areas beyond their proper concern. Gournay's friend the Baron de Grimm observed in a letter to Diderot in 1764:

> We [in France] are obsessed by the idea of regulation, and our Masters of Requests refuse to understand that there is an infinity of things in a great state with which a government should not concern itself. The late M. de Gournay...sometimes used to say: 'We have an illness in France which bids fair to play havoc with us; this illness is called bureaumania'. Sometimes he used to invent a third or fourth or fifth form of government under the heading of bureaucracy.[3]

Along the same lines, the following year Grimm remarked, 'The real spirit of the laws of France is that bureaucracy of which the late M. de Gournay...used to complain so greatly; here the offices, clerks, secretaries, inspectors, and *intendants* are not appointed to benefit the public interest, indeed the public interest appears to have been established so that offices might exist'.[4] The term *bureaucratie* soon began to appear in French literary and popular discourse. In 1789 the dramatist and writer Louis Sébastien Mercier explained in his *Le Tableau de Paris* that bureaucracy was a 'word recently coined to indicate, in a clear and concise manner, the overgrown power possessed by simple clerks who, in the various offices of the administration, make up and push forward all sorts of projects, which they find most often in dusty drawers in the offices, and which they favor for reasons of their own, good and bad'.[5] More neutrally, the 1798 supplement to the dictionary of the French Academy defined bureaucracy simply as 'Power, influence of the heads and staff of governmental bureaux'.[6]

In the following years, the word with its original meaning began to find its way into other Western European languages. One of the earliest German uses of the term was the observation by Kant's colleague Christian Klaus in 1799

---

2   See Albrow 1970, p. 16 (where Gournay is mistakenly called 'Jean'); Krygier 1979b, pp. 21–2.

3   Quoted in Albrow 1970, p. 16. See also Krygier 1979b, p. 22.

4   Quoted in Albrow 1970, p. 16. See also Krygier 1979b, p. 22.

5   Mercier 1999, p. 172. See also Krygier 1979b, p. 22.

6   Quoted in Albrow 1970, p. 17.

that the Prussian state, 'far from being an unlimited monarchy . . . is but a thinly veiled aristocracy . . . which blatantly rules the country as a bureaucracy'.[7] Consistent with this usage, an 1813 edition of a German dictionary of foreign expressions defined bureaucracy as the 'authority or power which various government departments and their branches arrogate to themselves over fellow citizens'.[8] The earliest uses in English also corresponded with this understanding. In 1818 the English writer Lady Morgan referred to 'the *bureaucratie* or office tyranny by which Ireland had been so long governed'.[9] Similarly, articulating a theme that would become common in English writing on the subject, the writer Thomas Carlyle in 1850 condemned bureaucracy as a distinctly 'continental nuisance', and observed that there was no risk that it would arise in England, since 'democracy is hot enough here'.[10]

As the term traveled geographically, its meaning began to evolve. One early important development involved the extension of the term's referent beyond the rule by officials to include also the body of officials who ruled. For example, in his 1821 book *Europe and the Revolution* the German writer Johann Joseph von Görres described the bureaucracy as a civil institution comparable to the standing army.[11] Likewise, in his 1848 work *Principles of Political Economy* the English philosopher John Stuart Mill opposed the concentration of all management skill and power of organised action 'in a dominant bureaucracy'.[12]

Meanwhile, a host of secondary characteristics related to the image of a ruling body of officials also came to be attached to the term. Bureaucracies were seen as concerned primarily with their own group interests. This was the case, for example, in the description in 1821 by Prussian statesman Freiherr vom Stein of the *Bureaulisten* as 'a class for themselves – the clerical caste'.[13] The internal hierarchy of state apparatuses was viewed as related to the domination they exerted externally. Thus, an anonymous Hamburg pamphlet of 1844 compared the hierarchy of the Prussian bureaucracy to that of the military, asserting that in both, hierarchy was designed to maintain the 'divine right of despotism' through 'blind devotion and the eternally unchangeable acknowledgement of its infallibility'.[14] Furthermore, bureaucracies were perceived

---

7   Quoted in Krygier 1979b, p. 23.
8   Quoted in Albrow 1970, p. 17. See also Krygier 1979b, p. 23.
9   Quoted in Krygier 1979b, p. 23.
10   Quoted in Albrow 1970, p. 21. See also Krygier 1979b, p. 29.
11   Albrow 1970, p. 20.
12   Mill 1994, p. 347. See also Albrow 1970, p. 22.
13   Quoted in Krygier 1979b, p. 24. See also Albrow 1970, p. 19.
14   Quoted in Krygier 1979b, p. 25.

as unproductive and parasitical upon society. The same Hamburg pamphlet described bureaucracy as 'a powerful cancer' which 'feasts voraciously, insatiably, and lives off the marrow and blood of the people'.[15]

At the same time, bureaucracy also began to be identified with other characteristics less clearly related to the original meaning, but associated in the public consciousness with the internal operations of state apparatuses or the personal characteristics of state officials. Robert von Mohl, professor of political science at Heidelberg, recorded a number of these in 1846, noting that they varied with the social group making the complaint. He observed, for example, that nobles condemned the inconsiderateness of officials, industrialists bemoaned their 'indolence and apathy', scholars derided bureaucratic ignorance, and artisans deplored unnecessary paperwork.[16] A trait mentioned in von Mohl's own definition that also came to be recognised as one of the hallmarks of bureaucracy was the tendency of officials to be 'satisfied with purely formal conduct'.[17] Another popularly perceived feature of bureaucracy was its inefficiency. Thus, an article published in *Blackwood's Edinburgh Magazine* in 1836 complained of the bureaucratic organisation of the French education system that it was not only despotic but also inefficient.[18] Similarly, in 1867 British essayist Walter Bagehot unfavorably contrasted the inefficiency of bureaucracy with the efficiency of the business world and with public administration controlled by democracy.[19]

At times there was also a tendency to identify bureaucracy with a particular form of administration. After 1806, the Prussian system in which a *collegium* of officials took collective responsibility for a government function was replaced by the bureau system in which responsibility at each level was placed in an individual. Since the bureau system resulted in faster decisions and greater unity and decisiveness of action, it was widely perceived that it also enhanced the power of officials. Thus, the 1819 edition of the Brockhaus encyclopedia observed, 'This bureaucracy becomes increasingly dangerous as the previous custom of conducting business through *collegia* falls into disuse'.[20] It was not long before bureaucracy began to be identified, especially in Germany, with the bureau system itself. For example, in 1845 the socialist Karl Heinzen defined bureaucracy as 'an administrative structure where a single official controls the

---

15   Quoted in Krygier 1979b, p. 25.
16   Albrow 1970, p. 29. Krygier 1979b, pp. 25–6.
17   Quoted in Krygier 1979b, p. 26.
18   Krygier 1979b, pp. 26–7.
19   Albrow 1970, pp. 23–4.
20   Quoted in Albrow, 1970, pp. 27–9. See also Krygier 1979b, pp. 28–9.

administration, as opposed to a collegial structure'.[21] At least for some, this suggested that bureaucracy was not inefficient, but highly efficient.[22]

A further development worth mentioning was the application of bureaucracy to bodies of functionaries outside of the state. This innovation is sometimes associated with the 1911 work *Political Parties* in which the German sociologist Robert Michels diagnosed the 'oligarchical tendencies' within the Social Democratic Party of Germany (SPD).[23] However, by the first decade of the twentieth century leaders of the left wing of the socialist movement, including Rosa Luxemburg and Lenin, were already referring to bureaucracy and bureaucratism within the labour and socialist movements.[24]

1.2   Bureaucracy in Russia

The term *bureaucracy* [*biurokratiia*] seems to have arrived in Russia somewhat later than in Germany or Britain, but it was in use there at least by the mid-nineteenth century. References to bureaucrats [*biurokraty*] appeared in 1856 in 'Russkie voprosy', Nikolai Ogarev's series of articles on the peasantry, and in Nikolai Dobroliubov's 1857 review article of Mikhail Saltykov's *Gubernskie ocherki*.[25] By the end of the nineteenth century, *bureaucracy* and related words were commonly employed in Russia. From the beginning, the connotations there were at least as pejorative as in the West, and perhaps even more so. Contemporary writers have noted that in Russia today the meaning of bureaucracy is consistently negative, never neutral or positive as it sometimes is in the West.[26] The same was true in the decades preceding the Russian Revolution.

In the late nineteenth and early twentieth centuries the primary meaning attached to bureaucracy in Russian remained closely tethered to Gournay's original understanding of the term. For example, in 1891 the Brockhaus and Efron *Entsiklopedicheskii slovar'* provided as the first meaning of *biurokratiia* 'the direction which state administration assumes in the countries where all matters are concentrated in the hands of the organs of a central governmental

---

21   Quoted in Albrow 1970, p. 28.

22   See Krygier 1979b, p. 28; Albrow 1970, p. 31.

23   Michels 1962. See Albrow 1970, pp. 36–7.

24   See, for example, Lenin 1960–70, vol. 7, pp. 364, 396–7; Lenin 1960–70, vol. 8, p. 307; Lenin 1958–65, vol. 8, pp. 351, 384–5; Lenin 1958–65, vol. 10, p. 36; Luxemburg 1970, pp. 196, 204, 214, 216; Luxemburg 2012.

25   '*Biurokratiia*' in Evgen'eva 1981.

26   See Hamilton 2007, p. 258; Tarasov n.d.

power, acting on orders (of authorities) and through orders (by subordinates)'.[27]
The first definition offered by the *Slovar' russkago iazyka*, published by the
Imperial Academy of Sciences in 1892, included 'command by officials'
[*chinonachalie*].[28] Along the same lines, the 1903 *Tolkovyi slovar' zhivogo
velikorusskago iazyka* defined bureaucracy as 'administration where official
command [*chinonachalie*] rules'.[29] Finally, the *Entsiklopedicheskii slovar'* published a few years later by Granat explained that *biurokratiia* meant 'an administrative structure which is characterized by its complete alienation from life
and by the despotic attachment to society of principles of government alien to
its real interests'.[30]

Beyond that, the connotations and secondary definitions of *biurokratiia*
provided by these reference works also corresponded closely to the associations and meanings that had evolved in Western Europe. In 1891 the Brokhaus
and Efron *Encyclopedic Dictionary* provided an extensive discussion of these.
It asserted that under bureaucracy 'officialdom [*chinovnichestvo*] assumes
a special, exceptional position – it feels itself the leading center of all social
life and it forms a special caste outside of the people'. In fact, this dictionary
identified 'the alienation of officialdom from the rest of the population . . ., its
caste exclusiveness' as one of the distinctive features of bureaucracy. The same
work included among the disadvantages of bureaucracy the fact that matters
requiring state intervention usually were conducted badly, that bureaucracy
involved the unnecessary intervention of authorities, and that contact with
bureaucratic organs of authority often occurred at the expense of the dignity
of the average person. Also, it asserted that, in contrast with 'healthy administration' that subordinates form to essence, 'bureaucracy observes form for the
sake of itself and sacrifices the essence of the matter to it'.[31]

Another common association with *biurokratiia* was the notion of internal
hierarchy suggested by the frequently offered synonym *chinovnichestvo* – often
translated into English as 'officialdom'.[32] As Alan Kimball has explained, within
the nineteenth century tsarist state,

27   '*Biurokratiia*' in Andreevskii et al. 1890–1904.
28   '*Biurokratiia*' in Imperatorskaia akademiia nauk 1982.
29   '*Biuro*' in Dal' 1994.
30   '*Biurokratiia*' in Zhelieznov et al. 1993.
31   '*Biurokratiia*' in Andreevskii et al. 1890–1904. Bureaucratic formalism was closely related to
      the 'paper-pushing' [*bumazhnoe mnogopisanie*], listed by Dal' as a defining characteristic
      of bureaucracy. '*Biuro*' in Dal' 1994.
32   See, for example, 'bureaucracy' in Aleksandrov 1899; 'bureaucracy' in Aleksandrov 1909;
      '*biurokratiia*' in Imperatorskaia akademiia nauk 1982; '*biurokratiia*' in Pavlenkov 1913;
      '*biurokratiia*' in Zhelieznov et al. 1993.

The word *chinovnichestvo* referred to the formal system of comprehensive national administration by state servitors holding rank – *chin* – up and down the 'Table of Ranks'. The Table of Ranks established appropriate, hierarchical rungs for civilian, military, church, and royal court servitors.[33]

Again, this emphasis upon hierarchy was noted explicitly in Vladimir Dal's 1903 *Tolkovyi slovar'*, which defined *biurokratiia* in part as 'graded subordination; the dependence of every official person on the next higher'.[34] Furthermore, the association of *biurokratiia* with the German bureau system was evident in Pavlenkov's 1918 dictionary of foreign words, which depicted bureaucracy as a 'system of administration by which the main head executes all orders under his own responsibility; it is contrasted with a collegial system'.[35]

Reference works included many of these same associations in their definitions of the related term *bureaucratism* [*biurokratizm*]. For example, Pavlenkov's 1913 *Entsiklopedicheskii slovar'* defined bureaucratism as 'a system of conducting business by administration by office means, on the basis of the reports of subordinates in accordance with the instructions of higher superiors, not taking into consideration the wishes of the population or its representatives, with the observance of official secrecy'.[36] Additionally, Pavlenkov's 1918 dictionary of foreign words noted that bureaucratism 'signifies a completely formal, clerical carrying out of business, the subordination of truth and fact to form; the useless multiplication of files and business correspondence, and the abuse of power by a superior'.[37]

Both in Russia and in exile, leaders of the Russian socialist movement such as Trotsky and Lenin absorbed and utilised all of these denotations and connotations current in Russia and in Western Europe. This wide range of meanings can be seen reflected in an article by Lenin written in April 1905. There, he responded to Menshevik accusations that the Bolsheviks advocated 'bureaucratic centralism' in the party and the implementation of a 'formal *bureaucratic* principle'. First, Lenin based his argument upon various secondary meanings of bureaucratism common in both Russia and Western Europe:

Bureaucratism [*biurokratizm*], taken in general, may denote officialism [*kantseliarshchina*], red tape [*volokita*], formalism [*bumazhnost'*], paper

---

33 Kimball 1998. See also *'chin'* in Wade 1996.
34 *'Biuro'* in Dal' 1994.
35 *'Biuro'* in Pavlenkov 1918.
36 *'Biurokratizm'* in Pavlenkov 1913.
37 *'Biurokratizm'* in Pavlenkov 1918.

answers [*otpiski*]. This sort of bureaucratism is evil … It is clear to every reader who is at all conscientious that this is the kind of bureaucratism meant by the Bureau of Committees of the majority, so that to accuse [Lenin's paper] *Vperyod* of contradicting itself is utter childishness.

Continuing, Lenin employed an understanding of bureaucratism more closely related to the primary meaning of bureaucracy as rule by officials:

Bureaucratism [*biurokratizm*] may [also] mean infringement of the legitimate and, if we may say so, of the 'natural' rights of every opposition, a fight waged against a minority by unfair means. Such bureaucratism is possible … but there is no principle involved in it. It must be combated by the establishment of constitutional guarantees of the rights of minorities.[38]

However, in the years before the October Revolution the thinking of Trotsky and Lenin about the question of bureaucracy was not just shaped by popular understanding of that issue. To a large extent it was also influenced by the writings of Marx and Engels on the subject.

1.3   Marx and Engels on Bureaucracy

Comments on bureaucracy can be found scattered throughout the writings of Marx and Engels on the state. Although they never explicitly defined the term, their understanding of the problem coincided closely with the popular usage. Consistently, they employed it as a pejorative for a state apparatus that had come to stand over and dominate society as a whole. That is, for both Marx and Engels, bureaucracy was an embodiment of what may be called political alienation.[39] While they saw this problem as especially pronounced in certain

---

38 Lenin 1960–70, vol. 8, p. 307; Lenin 1958–65, vol. 10, p. 36 (translation modified). See also Lenin 1960–70, vol. 7, pp. 364, 396–7; Lenin 1958–65, vol. 8, pp. 351, 384–5.

39 'Political alienation' is used here in preference to 'alienated social power' (utilised by Tucker 1969) and 'parasite state' (employed by Hunt 1974, Hunt 1984, Sanderson 1963, and Plamenatz 1954). 'Alienated social power' is too cumbersome to be used conveniently, and, as Draper has pointed out, 'parasite state' is inexact. See Tucker 1969, pp. 56–60; Tucker 1973a, pp. 127–30; Hunt 1974, 125–30; Hunt 1984, pp. 3–6, 126–8, 231–9; Sanderson 1963, pp. 951–3; Sanderson 1969, pp. 55–74; Plamenatz 1954, pp. 144–51; Draper 1977, bk. 2, pp. 622–8.

abnormal state forms, in their mature writings Marx and Engels described it as characteristic of all class states. Furthermore, they believed it would only begin to disappear in the proletarian state of the future. Many of these themes first appeared in embryonic form in Marx's 1843 polemics against Hegelian political philosophy, *The Critique of Hegel's Philosophy of Right* and 'On the Jewish Question'.

1.3.1   *The Young Marx on Bureaucracy*

In his *The Philosophy of Right* Hegel had contrasted two spheres of Prussian society – civil society and the state. In civil society, according to Hegel, men pursued their individual needs and self-interests. Although Hegel viewed the egoism of civil society as beneficial in some respects, he argued that it had engendered an eternal war of each against all that threatened to tear society apart. Fortunately, however, in Prussian society the conflicting private interests of civil society were reconciled by the second sphere, the state, which promoted the universal interests of society. Hegel believed that three Prussian political institutions participated in this mediation: the monarch, the legislature, and the civil service. As opposed to all other classes of civil society, the civil service was a 'universal class', seeking only the common good.[40]

The young Marx contemptuously rejected Hegel's claim that the Prussian state was motivated by universal interests. In his *Critique*, Marx argued that the central institution of the modern state, the 'bureaucracy', was just one more self-seeking corporation, 'a *particular, self-contained* society within the state'.[41] Rather than representing the true interests of society, the bureaucracy simply defined the common good to correspond with its own particular interests. As Marx put it, 'The bureaucracy appears to itself as the ultimate purpose of the state ... The bureaucracy holds the state, the spiritual essence of society, in thrall, as its *private property*'.[42] The bureaucracy hid this reality from the outside world by the veil of secrecy with which it surrounded all its operations. Internally, it disguised the truth from its own members by a 'hierarchy of knowledge' in which 'the apex entrusts insight into particulars to the lower echelons while the lower echelons credit the apex with insight into the

---

40   Hegel 1973, pp. 179–208. For useful summaries of Hegel's views and Marx's 1843 response, see Hunt 1974, pp. 53–92; Avineri 1972, pp. 1–15; Avineri 1968, pp. 8–64; O'Malley 1970, pp. ix–lxii; Liebach 1982, pp. 77–93.

41   Marx 1974a, p. 107.

42   Marx 1974a, pp. 107–8.

universal, and so each deceives the other'.[43] In the pursuit of its particular interests the bureaucracy attempted to control all aspects of society:

> Its crass spiritualism is revealed in its wish *to do everything*. That is to say, it makes *will* the prime cause because it is nothing but active existence and receives its content from outside itself, and can therefore only prove its own existence by moulding and limiting that content. For the bureaucrat the world is no more than an object on which he acts.[44]

Against Hegel's claim that the state resolved the conflicts of civil society, in his essay 'On the Jewish Question' Marx asserted that the state, rising out of these conflicts, depended upon their continued existence for its legitimacy: 'Far from abolishing these *factual* distinctions, the state presupposes them in order to exist . . . It is only in this way, *above* the *particular* elements, that the state constitutes itself as universality'.[45] In fact, according to Marx, the state only emerged as an institution fully distinct from society in the modern era. Only in modern society, with the abolition of all ties between individuals, was it possible for the state to appear as the sole repository of the general interest. Having arisen out of the conflicts between particular interests, the state continually sought to perpetuate them. Consequently, although the state initially attacked the corporations in the pursuit of its own aims, ultimately it was compelled to ensure their survival by force.[46]

In his early writings Marx was still vague about how the political alienation characteristic of modern society could be overcome. However, two conclusions already stood out. First, in 'On the Jewish Question' Marx argued that the separation of the state and its bureaucracy from civil society would have to be abolished through the elimination of the contradictions that divided civil society.[47] Second, in the 'Introduction' to his *Critique* he explained that this could only be achieved by a *true* universal class with interests that coincided with those of society as a whole. By late 1843 Marx had discovered this class in the proletariat.[48]

Although Marx and Engels periodically referred to the problem of bureaucracy in later years, they never again dealt as extensively with this term as Marx

---

43   Marx 1974a, p. 108.
44   Marx 1974a, pp. 108–9.
45   Marx 1974a, pp. 219–20.
46   Marx 1974a, pp. 106, 232–3.
47   Marx 1974a, p. 234.
48   Marx 1974a, p. 256. On this point see Avineri 1968, pp. 57–61; and Avineri 1972, pp. 8–9.

had in 1843. Nevertheless, from their scattered references it is clear that they continued to associate it with the problem of political alienation. Furthermore, in some respects they continued to describe and explain this alienation in terms quite similar to Marx's 1843 analysis.

1.3.2   *The Class State and Political Alienation*

Not long after Marx explained the conception of the state as a manifestation of political alienation he, together with Frederick Engels, began to develop another conception of the state: as an instrument used by the dominant economic class to defend and extend its own interests. This view of the state appeared as early as 1844 in *The Condition of the Working-Class in England*, where Engels spoke of 'the bourgeoisie as a party, as the power of the State', and observed, 'It is quite obvious that all legislation is calculated to protect those that possess property against those who do not'.[49] Marx adopted the class state conception by the following year when he and Engels collaborated on their first joint work, *The German Ideology*. At that time they wrote that the state is 'nothing more than the form of organisation which the bourgeois are compelled to adopt, both for internal and external purposes, for the mutual guarantee of their property and interests'.[50] Perhaps the best-known expression of this view can be found in the *Communist Manifesto* (1848) where Marx and Engels asserted, 'The executive of the modern State is but a committee for managing the common affairs of the whole bourgeoisie'.[51] More generally, Engels later described the state as being 'as a rule, the state of the most powerful, economically dominant class, which, through the medium of the state, becomes also the politically dominant class, and thus acquires the means of holding down and exploiting the oppressed class'.[52]

Two contemporary scholars, Richard Hunt and Robert C. Tucker, have emphasised the contradiction they have perceived between the conception of the state expressed in these passages and that contained in Marx's 1843 writings. Furthermore, they have argued that Marx and Engels resolved this contradiction by analysing the state in normal periods in terms of their class conception, while reserving Marx's 1843 analysis for 'abnormal' state forms

---

49   Marx and Engels 1962, p. 318. See also Marx and Engels 1962, p. 247. On Engels's paternity of the class state notion, see Draper 1977, bk. 1, pp. 182–4; Hunt 1974, pp. 107–9.
50   Marx and Engels 1998, p. 99.
51   Marx 1974b, p. 69.
52   Engels 1972, p. 160.

such as Bonapartism.[53] It is true that Marx and Engels discarded aspects of Marx's 1843 analysis when they first developed their class conception of the state. However, Hunt's and Tucker's argument obscures the fact that, throughout the remainder of their lives, Marx and Engels retained Marx's 1843 view that *all* state bureaucracies manifested political alienation.

Of course, the adoption of the class conception of the state clearly entailed a modification of Marx's earlier position. Most importantly, Marx and Engels abandoned the view that the state apparatus or bureaucracy was driven primarily by self-interest in normal periods. For example, in 1849 Marx explained that in modern bourgeois society, 'It inheres...that bureaucracy and army, instead of being masters of commerce and industry, be reduced to their tools, and be *made* into mere organs of bourgeois business relations'.[54] Similarly, in 1852 Marx explained that in the period between the two Bonapartes the French state bureaucracy 'was the instrument of the ruling class, however much it strove for power in its own right'.[55]

At the same time, however, Marx and Engels continued to view the state and its bureaucracy, as Marx had in 1843, in terms of the problem of political alienation. They still described the state as an institution that had established its independence from society and that ruled over it, falsely claiming to represent the general interest. For example, in *The German Ideology*, even while noting the role of the state in enforcing the interests of the bourgeoisie, Marx and Engels characterised the state as 'a separate entity, alongside and outside civil society', and explained that this 'illusory community, in which individuals have up till now combined, always took on an independent existence in relation to them'.[56] In *The Eighteenth Brumaire of Louis Bonaparte* (1852) Marx described the French 'bureaucratic and military organization' as it had developed from the period of absolute monarchy up to the time of Napoleon III as a 'frightful parasitic body, which surrounds the body of French society like a caul and stops up all its pores'. Under this state machinery, 'every *common* interest was immediately detached from society, opposed to it as a higher *general*

---

53   Hunt 1974, pp. 125–30; Hunt 1984, pp. 3–6; Tucker 1973a, pp. 127–39; Tucker 1969, pp. 56–60. Both Plamenatz and Sanderson have also argued that Marx and Engels held two conceptions of the state that were incompatible (Plamenatz 1954, p. 151; Sanderson 1963, p. 947). Other works that have noted the persistence of certain themes from Marx's 1843 analysis in the later writings of Marx and Engels include Avineri 1968, Avineri 1972; Evans, M. 1975, p. 113; Hobsbawm 1982, p. 230.
54   Quoted in Draper 1977, bk. 2, p. 498.
55   Marx 1974c, p. 238.
56   Marx and Engels 1998, pp. 99, 86.

interest, torn away from the self-activity of the individual members of society and made a subject for governmental activity'.[57] Years later, in his *Anti-Dühring* (1878) Engels spoke of the 'political force [which] has made itself independent in relation to society, and has transformed itself from society's servant into its master'.[58] Furthermore, in an 'Introduction' (1891) to Marx's *The Civil War in France* Engels contended that the 'transformation of the state and the organs of the state from servants into masters of society' had been 'an inevitable transformation in all previous states'.[59]

These passages clearly indicate that the mature Marx and Engels saw *all* states as manifesting political alienation comparable in some respects to that observed by Marx in Prussia in 1843. Marx and Engels never explicitly explained how they reconciled the notion that the state stands above and dominates the whole of society with the idea that the state is subordinate to a part of society. However, it is likely they would have asserted that, in serving a privileged minority, the class state dominates 'society', understood as the vast majority of a society's members. Besides that, they might have argued that the class state stands above and dominates even individual members of the dominant economic class.

1.3.3   *Engels on the Origin of the State*

An examination of the account by Engels of the origin of the state further demonstrates that he, at least, saw the original alienation of the state from society and its subordination to dominant class rule as simultaneous and interdependent processes. According to Engels, the first public authority, the ancestor of the modern state, was created by pre-class society to carry out certain essential functions on behalf of society as a whole. In his *Anti-Dühring* Engels explained that these functions included irrigation, defense against external enemies, the 'adjudication of disputes', the 'repression of encroachments by individuals on the rights of others', and religious functions.[60] He noted in *The Origin of the Family, Private Property, and the State* (1884) that this authority was not yet properly a state for it was not 'separated from the totality of those concerned'.[61] Over time this authority, as a distinct institution, developed its own particular interests and was able to elevate itself above the control of the rest of society. In a letter to Joseph Bloch in 1890 Engels explained,

---

57   Marx 1974c, p. 237.
58   Engels 1939, p. 202.
59   Engels in Marx 1966, p. 16.
60   Engels 1939, pp. 165, 198.
61   Engels 1972, pp. 99, 117.

The persons appointed for this purpose form a new branch of the division of labour *within society*. This gives them particular interests, distinct,
too, from the interests of those who empowered them; they make themselves independent of the latter and – the state is in being.[62]

However, the primitive public authority was not able to effect this transformation simply by an act of will. Rather, this was only made possible by the simultaneous expansion of the functional significance of its power. In particular, the
authority became increasingly indispensable as a mediator of the conflicts that
arose between communities with the growth of productive forces and the division of labour.[63] With the emergence of social classes, the mediating function
of the authority became even more necessary in order to prevent class struggle
from tearing society apart. In *The Origin* Engels explained that the state

> is a product of society at a certain stage of development; it is the admis-
> sion that this society has become entangled in an insoluble contradic-
> tion with itself, that it is cleft into irreconcilable antagonisms which it
> is powerless to dispel. But in order that these antagonisms, classes with
> conflicting economic interests, might not consume themselves and soci-
> ety in sterile struggle, a power seemingly standing above society became
> necessary for the purpose of moderating the conflict, of keeping it within
> the bounds of 'order'; and this power, arisen out of society, but placing
> itself above it, and increasingly alienating itself from it, is the state.[64]

Up to this point Engels's account of the emergence of the state closely paralleled Marx's 1843 analysis of the origin of the modern state. In the context
of a society rent by conflicting particular interests, the state arose as a body
claiming to represent the general interest; in reality, it was nothing but one
more particular institution, 'placing itself above' society and 'increasingly
alienating itself from it'. However, Engels further argued that, even as the state
raised itself above the control of society as a whole, it became the instrument
of the dominant economic class. In fact, as indicated in his 'Ludwig Feuerbach
and the Outcome of Classical German Philosophy' (1888), Engels saw a direct
relationship between these processes:

---

62   Marx and Engels 1972a, p. 644.
63   Engels 1939, p. 198.
64   Engels 1972, p. 159.

> Society creates for itself an organ for the safeguarding of its general inter-
> ests against internal and external attacks. This organ is the state power.
> Hardly come into being, this organ makes itself independent in regard to
> society; and indeed, the more so, the more it becomes the organ of a par-
> ticular class, the more it directly enforces the supremacy of that class.[65]

Engels suggested two different ways in which the class state may have come
into being. In his *Anti-Dühring* he described a tendency for the rulers of the
emergent state to establish *themselves* as the dominant economic class.[66] On
the other hand, in *The Origin* it appears that, even where the state remained
somewhat distinct from the dominant class, it became the servant of that
class: 'As the state arose from the need to hold class antagonisms in check,
but as it arose ... in the midst of the conflict of these classes, it is, as a rule, the
state of the most powerful, economically dominant class, which, through the
medium of the state, becomes also the politically dominant class, and thus
acquires new means of holding down and exploiting the oppressed class'.[67]
By this, Engels may have simply meant that the function of ensuring social
harmony most benefited the class that had the most to gain from the existing
order. However, this passage also suggests that, as the state freed itself from
general societal control, it became more vulnerable to conquest by the most
powerful of the contending classes.

Conversely, for Engels the transformation of the state into the servant of
the dominant class also increased the state's alienation from society. As the
emergent state began to serve the interests of the dominant class, its activities increasingly precluded communal participation and control. In *The Origin*
Engels described this tendency in ancient Greece:

> This special public power is necessary, because a self-acting armed orga-
> nization of the population has became impossible since the cleavage into
> classes ... The people's army of the Athenian democracy was an aristo-
> cratic public power against the slaves, whom it kept in check; however,
> a gendarmerie also became necessary to keep the citizens in check, ...[68]

In the account of Engels, then, the transformation of the original public
authority into an institution standing above and dominating society was

---

65 Marx 1935, p. 463.
66 Engels 1939, p. 198.
67 Engels 1972, p. 160.
68 Engels 1972, p. 159.

directly related to its conversion into a tool of class domination. The fundamental cleavages between particular interests gave rise to the state as an institution alienated from society as a whole. This process was facilitated by, and simultaneously encouraged, the subordination of the state to the interests of the dominant class.

However, Marx and Engels also believed that in certain exceptional periods the state attained not only an extreme degree of independence from society, but also a large measure of autonomy from class control.[69] For Marx and Engels such exceptional state forms included Oriental Despotism, Caesarism, Absolute Monarchy, Tsarist Autocracy, and Bonapartism.[70] Of these state forms, the two thinkers devoted the greatest attention to Bonapartism.

1.3.4   *Bonapartism*

Although Marx and Engels spoke of the 'Bonapartism' of Napoleon Bonaparte and of Bismarck, their most extensive analyses of that phenomenon dealt with the regime of Louis-Napoleon Bonaparte, or Napoleon III.[71] Following his election as President of France in December 1848, Louis Bonaparte proceeded to extend his control over the state apparatus and army at the expense of the Legislative assembly. Then, in December 1851 he staged a successful coup against the Second Republic and the following year had himself proclaimed emperor of France. Beginning with Marx's 1852 work *The Eighteenth Brumaire of Louis Bonaparte*, Marx and Engels repeatedly attempted to define Louis Bonaparte's regime and explain its origins.

Consistent with other writings by Marx and Engels on the state in normal periods, Marx described the French state bureaucracy *prior* to Bonaparte's coup as both an organ of class rule and as a manifestation of political alienation. On one hand, the bureaucracy had, since its inception under the absolute monarchy, tended to advance the interests of the bourgeoisie, and in the period between the two Napoleons it had become the mere instrument of the

---

69   Nicos Poulantzas has used 'relative autonomy' to indicate the degree of separation of the state from the direct control of the dominant economic class. Hal Draper has distinguished between the 'independence' of the state from society as a whole and the 'autonomy' of the state with regard to every other section of society (Poulantzas 1975; Draper 1977, bk. 1, p. 312n).

70   For discussions of the views of Marx and Engels on Caesarism, Oriental Despotism, Absolute Monarchy, and Tsarist Autocracy, see Draper 1977, bk. 2, pp. 464–83, 515–87; and Hunt 1984, pp. 27–63.

71   For a discussion of the views of Marx and Engels on the Bonapartism of Napoleon I and Bismarck, see Draper 1977, bk. 2, pp. 427–37.

capitalist class.[72] On the other hand, Marx characterised the pre-Bonapartist bureaucracy as a 'parasite' that had risen above society and extended its control into all areas of social concern while legitimising its power in terms of the general interest.[73]

However, according to Marx, Louis Bonaparte's coup inaugurated two important changes in the character of the French state. First, the state became even more independent from society as a whole:

> The state parasite received only its last development during the second Empire. The governmental power with its standing army, its all directing bureaucracy, its stultifying clergy and its servile tribunal hierarchy had grown so independent of society itself, that a grotesquely mediocre adventurer with a band of hungry desperadoes behind him sufficed to wield it.[74]

At the same time, through Bonaparte's coup the state was able to attain such an unprecedented degree of autonomy from the bourgeoisie that it appeared 'that all classes fall on their knees, equally mute and equally impotent, before the rifle butt'.[75] Marx described Bonaparte as being 'only where he is because he has broken the political power of this middle class, and breaks it again daily'.[76] In the Bonapartist state, then, Marx and Engels saw an exception to the normal pattern of a direct relationship between the state's independence from society and its subordination to the dominant economic class.

Marx and Engels offered varying accounts of how the Bonapartist state had attained such a high degree of autonomy from class control and an extreme degree of independence from society. At one point Marx represented this as an *unintended* consequence of conscious bourgeois policy. According to this interpretation, the bourgeoisie had strengthened the state as a sword against the proletariat. Then, with Bonaparte's coup the bourgeoisie discovered that the sword was two-edged: the state had become autonomous enough to turn against its master.[77] In a second explanation Marx contended that the capitalist class *purposefully* established a state independent of its direct control in order to defuse the political struggle of the proletariat. The French bourgeoisie

72   Marx 1974c, p. 238.
73   Marx 1974c, pp. 186, 237.
74   Marx 1966, p. 164.
75   Marx 1974c, p. 236.
76   Marx 1974c, p. 245. See also Marx 1966, pp. 230–1.
77   Marx 1966, pp. 65–6.

'realized instinctively that although the republic made their political rule complete it simultaneously undermined its social foundation, since they had now to confront the subjugated classes and contend with them without mediation, without being concealed by the Crown, without the possibility of diverting the national attention by their secondary conflicts amongst themselves and with the monarchy'. Consequently, they began 'to yearn for the return of the previous forms of this rule, which were less complete, less developed, and precisely for that reason, less dangerous'.[78]

However, it was Engels who, in *The Origin*, provided the best-known explanation for the extreme autonomy of the state – not only under Louis Bonaparte, but also under Napoleon I and the previous absolute monarchs. In each case the state had been able to utilise the 'balance' achieved in the class struggle to enlarge its own power and independence:

> By way of exception, however, periods occur in which the warring classes balance each other so nearly that the state power, as ostensible mediator, acquires, for the moment, a certain degree of independence of both. Such was the absolute monarchy of the seventeenth and eighteenth centuries, which held the balance between the nobility and the class of burghers; such was the Bonapartism of the First, and still more of the Second French Empire, which played off the proletariat against the bourgeoisie and the bourgeoisie against the proletariat.[79]

This balance made it impossible for either class to establish its own direct control over the state. Consistent with this account, Marx in *The Civil War in France* (1871) described the Bonapartism of the Second Empire as 'the only form of government possible at a time when the bourgeoisie had already lost, and the working class had not yet acquired, the faculty of ruling the nation'.[80]

Beyond offering these general interpretations of the origins of Bonapartism, Marx and Engels attempted to identify the various social groups that Louis Bonaparte relied upon in establishing and consolidating his rule. First and most important was the French peasantry. At one point Marx even asserted that Bonaparte 'represents the most numerous class of French society, the *small peasant proprietors*'.[81] However, as a number of commentators have noted, Marx seems to have meant by this that Bonaparte *portrayed* himself

---

78   Marx 1974c, p. 175. See also Marx 1974c, p. 224.
79   Engels 1972, p. 160.
80   Marx 1966, p. 66.
81   Marx 1974c, p. 238.

as the champion of the peasants and *relied upon* their electoral and military support.[82] Second, Marx explained that the lumpenproletariat organised in the Society of 10 December provided Bonaparte with the shock troops necessary for his conquest of power, staging demonstrations on his behalf and beating up his republican opponents.[83] Third, according to Marx, Bonaparte solidified his rule with the support of the state bureaucracy. Although it was already bloated and powerful when Louis Bonaparte assumed the Presidency, he granted it further privileges to ensure its allegiance:

> An enormous bureaucracy, with gold braid and a fat belly, is the 'Napoleonic idea' which is most congenial of all to the second Bonaparte. It could not be otherwise, for he has been forced to create, alongside the real classes of society, an artificial caste for which the maintenance of his regime is a question of self-preservation. One of his first financial operations was therefore to raise officials' salaries to their old level and to create new sinecures.[84]

Finally, Marx and Engels described how Bonaparte relied upon the passivity of the French workers in his struggle with their class enemy, and how he even attempted to win their support by granting universal suffrage and promising 'socialist' social programs.[85]

Although Marx and Engels saw Bonaparte as courting and obtaining the support of all sectors of French society, and although they argued that he was the servant of no class, in their view there was no doubt about which class benefitted most from his rule. Even while breaking the *political* rule of the capitalist class, he continued to preserve and strengthen its 'social power'.[86] In the pursuit of his own self-interests and those of his state, Bonaparte found himself compelled to promote the coincident interests of the capitalist class. In 1852 Marx explained,

> Bonaparte is the executive authority which has attained power in its own right, and as such he feels it to be his mission to safeguard 'bourgeois

---

82   Draper 1977, bk. 2, pp. 401–2; Hunt 1984, p. 54; Miliband 1973, pp. 165–6; Plamenatz 1954, pp. 144–5. On the other hand, Tucker 1973a, pp. 138–9 has taken this statement by Marx at face value.

83   Marx 1974c, pp. 197, 204, 206, 234.

84   Marx 1974c, p. 243.

85   See Draper 1977, bk. 2, pp. 404–6; Hunt 1984, p. 56.

86   Marx 1974c, p. 190.

order'. But the strength of this bourgeois order lies in the middle class. He therefore sees himself as the representative of the middle class and he issues decrees in this sense.[87]

1.3.5 Proletarian Dictatorship and the End of Bureaucracy

In their mature works as in Marx's 1843 writings, Marx and Engels clearly believed that the coming socialist revolution would eliminate the problem of bureaucracy, understood in terms of political alienation. They anticipated that the proletarian state emerging from the revolution would immediately abolish the worst aspects of the problem, and that ultimately even this relatively 'de-alienated' state would disappear along with class domination. However, between the revolution and the withering of the state, the proletariat would need its own state – a 'dictatorship of the proletariat' – to enforce its own immediate interests and to lay the basis for a classless society.[88]

As Hal Draper has demonstrated, the term *dictatorship* as used by Marx and Engels meant 'a *domination*, a *social rule*', and was not opposed to democracy.[89] In fact, throughout their writings Marx and Engels stressed the necessarily democratic character of the workers' state. The draft of the *Communist Manifesto* by Engels predicted that the revolution would establish 'a democratic constitution implying directly or indirectly the political rule of the proletariat'.[90] Similarly, the *Communist Manifesto* proclaimed that 'the first step in the revolution by the working class, is to raise the proletariat to the position of ruling class, to win the battle of democracy'.[91]

However, it was the experience of the Paris Commune of 1871 – the first 'dictatorship of the proletariat'[92] – that dramatically reinforced their conviction that the proletarian state would, of necessity, be radically democratic. Marx and Engels fully approved of the Commune's attempts to institutionalise democracy. In *The Civil War in France* and in an introduction to that work, Marx and Engels commended the steps taken by the Commune to fill all posts by election on the basis of universal suffrage, and to provide for the immediate

87   Marx 1974c, p. 245. See Marx 1966, p. 66 for his 1871 summary of the benefits that the bourgeoisie derived from the Second Empire.
88   See Draper 1962a; Draper 1962b; Draper 1987, pp. 11–41 for exhaustive studies on the use of the term *dictatorship of the proletariat* by Marx and Engels.
89   Draper 1962a, p. 93.
90   Marx and Engels 1972b, p. 332.
91   Marx and Engels 1972a, p. 352.
92   The assertion by Engels that the Paris Commune was a 'dictatorship of the proletariat' appears in Marx 1966, p. 18. Draper has demonstrated that Marx also held this view (Draper 1987, pp. 31, 37).

recall of all officials. They supported the Commune's limitation of the salaries of state officials to the level of 'workmen's wages', and the election of a majority of 'naturally working men, or acknowledged representatives of the working class' to the Commune. They applauded the 'suppression of the standing army and the substitution for it of the armed people', and acclaimed the elimination of 'the whole sham of state-mysteries and state pretensions' through the Commune's publication 'of all its doings and sayings'. Finally, they endorsed the democratisation of the state through the abolition of the distinction between the executive and legislative branches.[93]

On the basis of this experience Marx and Engels concluded in 1871 that 'the working class cannot simply lay hold of the ready-made state machinery, and wield it for its own purposes'.[94] Rather, the capitalist state bureaucracy would have to be smashed and a more democratic one substituted in its place. According to Engels, the democratic measures taken by the Commune had brought about both the 'shattering of the former state power and its replacement by a new and truly democratic one'.[95] For Marx the Commune was the 'political form at last discovered under which to work out the economic emancipation of labour'.[96]

In part, the endorsement of radical democracy by Marx and Engels was derived from class considerations. That is, they viewed the democratic measures of the Commune as a means of restricting bourgeois political power and subordinating the state to the proletariat. Engels explained in 1891 that 'in order not to lose again its only just conquered supremacy, this working class must, on the one hand, do away with all the old repressive machinery previously used against it itself, and, on the other, safeguard itself against its own deputies and officials'.[97] The concern of Engels here seems to have been that, without such democratic norms as those established by the Commune, the state apparatus might break away from working-class control and reestablish capitalist rule.

At the same time, Marx and Engels viewed the democratic measures of the Commune as a way to reduce the independence of the state from society, to begin to overcome the ancient problem of political alienation. Engels described the election and recall of officials and the payment of 'workmen's wages' as steps taken 'against this transformation of the state from servants of

---

93   Marx 1966, pp. 16, 67, 68, 80, 170.
94   Marx 1966, p. 64; Marx and Engels 1972a, p. 332.
95   Engels in Marx 1966, p. 16.
96   Marx 1966, p. 72.
97   Engels in Marx 1966, p. 15.

society into masters of society'.[98] In *The Civil War in France* Marx characterised these measures as the beginning of 'the destruction of the State power which claimed to be the embodiment of that unity independent of, and superior to, the nation itself, from which it was but a parasitic excrescence'.[99]

Similarly, Marx and Engels viewed the functions of the post-capitalist state as both advancing the class interests of the proletariat and reducing the level of political alienation. Initially, the dictatorship of the proletariat would attempt to satisfy the immediate interests of the working class by abolishing class exploitation and defending the conquests of the workers.[100] At the same time, through its nationalisation of the means of production, the state would be transformed from an institution standing above society into 'the representative of society as a whole'. By the appropriation of bourgeois property, Engels wrote in *Anti-Dühring*, the proletariat

> puts an end to itself as the proletariat, it puts an end to all class differences and antagonisms, it puts an end also to the state as the state ... The first act in which the state really comes forward as the representative of society as a whole – the taking possession of the means of production in the name of society – is at the same time its last independent act as a state.[101]

Eventually, even this 'state' – which was not quite a state – was expected to vanish as class domination dissolved and scarcity was abolished. In a famous passage from his *Anti-Dühring* Engels described this process:

> As soon as there is no longer any class of society to be held in subjection; as soon as, along with class domination and the struggle for individual existence based on the former anarchy of production, the collisions and excesses arising from these have also been abolished, there is nothing more to be repressed which would make a special repressive force, a state, necessary ... The interference of the state power in social relations becomes superfluous in one sphere after another, and then ceases of itself ... The state is not 'abolished', it *withers away*.[102]

---

98   Engels in Marx 1966, p. 16.
99   Marx 1966, p. 69.
100   See, for example, Marx and Engels 1972a, pp. 352–3, 664–5; Draper 1962a, p. 101.
101   Engels 1939, pp. 306–7.
102   Ibid.

This did not mean that under socialism there would be no authoritative coordinating bodies. As Hal Draper has pointed out, the withering of the state for Marx and Engels meant the disappearance of official coercion, not of public authority itself.[103] In an 1872 essay Engels predicted that after the coming social revolution, 'public functions will lose their political character and be transformed into the simple administrative functions of watching over the true interests of society'.[104] Political – that is, repressive – functions would disappear, but 'administrative functions' and, presumably, an administrative authority, would persist. Similarly, in *The Civil War in France* Marx wrote of the 'legitimate functions' that the Paris Commune would have 'wrested from an authority usurping pre-eminence over society itself, and restored to the responsible agents of society' if the Commune had survived.[105] Furthermore, in his (1874–5) 'conspectus' on Bakunin's *Statism and Anarchy* Marx apparently assumed that elections of a non-coercive public authority would continue to occur under socialism: 'As soon as the functions [of public authority] have ceased to be political ones, there exists (1) no government function, (2) the distribution of the general functions has become a business matter, that gives no one domination, (3) election has none of its present political character'.[106]

In the absence of class conflict, however, there was little danger that such an authority would elevate itself above societal control. Furthermore, lacking the means of repression, it would never again be able to dominate society. Thus, socialist society would finally eliminate the problem of bureaucracy.

1.4   After Marx and Engels

Leaders of the socialist movement who came later continued to accept the conclusion of Marx and Engels that bureaucracy would cease to be a problem after the socialist revolution. However, at the same time the leadership of the Second International consistently blunted the anti-bureaucratic, anti-statist thrust of Marx's and Engels's doctrine, particularly regarding the dictatorship of the proletariat. Although some figures in the left wing of the International, including Trotsky, challenged this 'orthodox' view prior to 1917, it was Lenin who in that year most clearly and sharply reaffirmed the expectations of Marx

---

103   Draper 1970, p. 288.
104   Marx and Engels 1972a, p. 664.
105   Marx 1966, p. 69.
106   Marx 1974d, p. 336.

and Engels regarding the anti-bureaucratic and radically democratic character
of the revolutionary state.

1.4.1   *The Socialist Movement and Post-Revolutionary Bureaucracy*

The continuing tendency within the socialist movement to minimise the threat
of post-capitalist bureaucracy is illustrated by the writings of Karl Kautsky, the
best known leader and foremost theoretician of the Social Democratic Party
of Germany and the Second International. In his 1908 work *The Foundations of
Christianity* Kautsky briefly considered the potential for the bureaucratisation
of the socialist movement and for the emergence of a bureaucratic class after
the revolution. Neither, he concluded, was a serious danger, for 'we may maintain not only that Socialism will not develop any internal contradictions in the
period preceding this victory [of the proletariat], that will be comparable with
those attending the last phases of Christianity, but also that no such contradictions will materialize in the period in which the predictable consequences of
this victory are developed'.[107] Kautsky based the latter conclusion on the premise that class differences traditionally have been generated by private ownership of the means of production, and by military and scientific needs. Private
property would be abolished soon after the revolution. Furthermore, Kautsky
argued that the economic preconditions already existed for overcoming the
tendency on the part of the military and science to promote class differentiation. The development of productive forces had eliminated the necessity of
confining military training to a small 'aristocracy of warriors', while the growing economic integration of nations had made war 'a piece of ruthless folly'. At
the same time capitalism, by creating a greater demand for intellectuals and
the potential for mass education, had reduced the need for a scientific elite.[108]

   However, even while sustaining the traditional Marxist optimism regarding
the withering of state and bureaucracy, the leaders of the Second International
ignored or rejected major aspects of the views of Marx and Engels on the dictatorship of the proletariat. Most importantly, they minimised the depth of
the radical democracy envisioned by Marx and Engels and the distance that
separated this democracy from even the most democratic bourgeois republic. As early as the 1890s and consistently afterwards, Kautsky endorsed *existing* parliamentarism, both as a means by which the proletariat could come
to power and as the specific form of the dictatorship of the proletariat.[109] He

---

107   Kautsky 1972, pp. 468–9.
108   Kautsky 1972, pp. 469–72. For a discussion of Kautsky's views on bureaucracy, see Mandel
      1984, pp. 70–1.
109   Salvadori 1979, pp. 35–8.

repeated the call by Marx and Engels for the 'conquest of political power', but made no reference to their views on the need to smash the bourgeois state.[110] Furthermore, he rejected the idea of a 'government of the people and through the people in the sense that public affairs should be administered not by functionaries but by popular masses working without pay during their spare time'. This, he said, was 'a utopia, even a reactionary and anti-democratic utopia'.[111] Although Marx and Engels had assumed the existence of paid functionaries, their emphasis had been precisely upon the 'utopian' idea of 'government of the people and through the people'.

Kautsky's response in 1912 to criticisms by the Dutch left-socialist Anton Pannekoek reveals even more sharply the contrast between his views on the revolutionary state and those of Marx and Engels. Pannekoek had rejected the SPD's and Kautsky's parliamentary orientation and had revived the call by Marx and Engels for the destruction of the bourgeois state machine. In reply, Kautsky conflated the two issues, dismissing Pannekoek's views as semi-anarchist while reaffirming the SPD's perspective: 'The goal of our political struggle remains the same as it has been up to now: the conquest of state power through winning a majority in parliament and raising parliament to be the master of government. Not, however, the destruction of state power'.[112] None of the existing ministries of bourgeois governments, Kautsky argued, could be eliminated by a revolution. Rather than calling for the destruction of the state, the SPD strove for its subordination to the working class through the election of high officials.[113]

At this point nearly all Russian socialists, including Lenin, accepted Kautsky's position as authoritative. However, there was little reason for them even to consider the question for most were unified in the view that the coming revolution in Russia would be bourgeois-democratic, not socialist, in nature. Only after the completion of the democratic revolution, Lenin argued in the summer of 1905, would it be appropriate to address the question of the dictatorship of the proletariat.[114] Furthermore, Lenin explicitly rejected the slogans of the Paris Commune as inapplicable to the Russian situation.[115]

---

110   See, for example, Kautsky 1971; Kautsky 1907. See also Lenin's later critique of Kautsky in Lenin 1960–70, vol. 25, pp. 476–91.
111   Quoted in Salvadori 1979, p. 161.
112   Quoted in Sawer 1977, p. 211.
113   Salvadori 1979, p. 161.
114   Lenin 1960–70, vol. 9, p. 86.
115   Lenin 1970, p. 14.

Nevertheless, anticipating his later views on the revolutionary state, during the turbulent year 1905 Lenin suggested that a revolutionary government in Russia could be based upon 'soviets'. The soviets or workers' councils that appeared in cities throughout Russia during the revolution of 1905 were institutions composed of delegates elected by the workers to direct the revolutionary struggle. In the course of their development they approached the status of alternative governments. Lenin first commented on the soviets in November 1905 while still in exile. Already at that point he had concluded that the St. Petersburg Soviet 'should be regarded as the embryo of a *provisional revolutionary government*'.[116] Assessing the role of the soviets in early 1906, Lenin characterised them as 'embryonic forms of a new revolutionary authority' and 'embryos of a new, people's, ... revolutionary government'.[117]

Meanwhile, one of the few Russian Social Democrats who already held a position to the left of Lenin's was Leon Trotsky. In the summer of 1905 Trotsky arrived at a conclusion that would become central to his theory of permanent revolution: that a successful revolutionary struggle in Russia would bring to power a dictatorship of the proletariat which, in the process of completing the democratic revolution, would be compelled to undertake socialist measures. As early as July 1905 Trotsky predicted that the future revolutionary government in Russia would not be a 'dictatorship of the proletariat and the peasantry' as Lenin held, but rather a 'dictatorship of the proletariat supported by the peasantry'.[118]

The imminent prospect of a Russian dictatorship of the proletariat suggested to Trotsky the relevance of the experience of the first dictatorship of the proletariat, the Paris Commune. In December 1905 he wrote, 'For us, the history of the Commune is now not just a great dramatic moment in the international struggle for liberation, not a mere illustration of some sort of tactical situation; it is a direct and immediate lesson'.[119] In turn, Trotsky's study of writings of Marx and Engels on the Commune led him to a vision of the dictatorship of the proletariat that was far more anti-bureaucratic and anti-statist than Kautsky's. Trotsky proclaimed that the first tasks of the proletariat in power would be 'to consolidate its position, arm the revolution, disarm reaction, widen the base of

116   Lenin 1960–70, vol. 10, p. 21.
117   Lenin 1960–70, vol. 10, pp. 155, 243.
118   Trotsky 2009, p. 444; also quoted in Trotsky 1972b, p. 310. For Trotsky's full exposition of this theory, see his 1906 work *Results and Prospects* in Trotsky 1969, pp. 36–122. For the history of the development of Trotsky's theory of permanent revolution, see Löwy 1981, pp. 30–69; and Day and Gaido, pp. 1–58.
119   Trotsky 1970a, pp. 10–11.

the revolution, reconstruct the state'.[120] All of these required the same radically democratic measures that had been enacted by the Commune: 'The abolition of the standing army and the police, the arming of the people, the dispersion of the mandarin bureaucracy, the establishment of the principle of election of all functionaries, the equalization of their salaries, the separation of church and state – these are the measures which, from the example of the Commune, it is necessary to carry through at the very beginning'.[121]

Like Lenin, Trotsky also believed that the 1905 soviets had the potential to become institutions of a revolutionary state. In 1905 he characterised the soviets as 'indisputably future focal points of support for a provisional government'.[122] Four years later he asserted that the St. Petersburg Soviet had been 'a workers' government in embryo' and 'the first embryonic organ of revolutionary power'.[123] However, Trotsky went beyond Lenin in observing direct parallels between the democratic and anti-bureaucratic character of the soviets and that of the Paris Commune. He described the St. Petersburg Soviet of 1905 as 'the organized power of the mass itself over its separate parts. It constitutes authentic democracy, without a lower and an upper chamber, without a professional bureaucracy [*biurokratiia*], but with the voters' right to recall their deputies at any moment'.[124] Beyond that, Trotsky predicted that future soviets would dismantle the tsarist state and abolish absolutism, destroying its 'material structure' by reform and by 'dissolution of the army, annihilation of the police and bureaucracy'. Furthermore, the soviets would transform public authorities into 'agents of municipal self-government'.[125] Years later, on the eve of the Bolshevik Revolution, Lenin would arrive at similar conclusions.

1.4.2   *The State and Revolution*

In the summer of 1916 the young, left-wing Bolshevik Nikolai Bukharin submitted an essay for inclusion in a collection of programmatic articles edited by Lenin. There, Bukharin repeated the anti-statist heresies of left-Marxists such as Pannekoek that the Marxist goal was the 'revolutionary destruction' of the bourgeois state, and that 'the difference between Marxists and anarchists is not

---

120   Trotsky 1970a, pp. 20–1.

121   Trotsky 1970a, p. 21. Compare these passages with Sawer 1977, p. 213 who claims that in 1905 Trotsky, like Lenin, 'saw no particular institutional significance in the structure of the Commune'.

122   Trotsky 1970a, p. 25.

123   Trotsky 1972b, pp. 251, 253.

124   Trotsky 1972b, p. 253; Trotsky 1963a, part 2, p. 188.

125   Quoted in Anweiler 1974, p. 90.

at all that the Marxists are statists and the anarchists are anti-statists, as many assert' but only that socialists support economic centralisation. Lenin at first dismissed Bukharin's views as 'semi-anarchism' and accused him of ignoring the need for a post-revolutionary state.[126] However, Bukharin prompted Lenin to reconsider the theory of the state. By February 1917 Lenin's rereading of Marx and Engels led him to the conclusion that, despite 'small errors', Bukharin was '*closer* to the truth than Kautsky'.[127] Lenin now agreed that the task of the proletarian revolution was to smash the old bourgeois state machine and to replace it with a new one. At the same time he accepted a conclusion Trotsky had reached years earlier – that the form of the dictatorship of the proletariat had manifested itself not only in the Paris Commune, but also in the soviets of 1905. In his notes on the state in early 1917 Lenin wrote,

> Marx's fundamental idea: the conquest of *political power* by the prole-
> tariat does **not** mean the taking over of a 'ready-made' state machin-
> ery, *but*... its 'smashing' and destruction, and its *replacement* by a **new**
> one... One could, probably,... express the whole matter thus: *replace-*
> *ment* of the old ('ready-made') state machine and parliaments by *Soviets*
> *of Workers' Deputies* and their trustees.[128]

Not long after Lenin wrote these lines he had the opportunity to apply them to living soviets. In one of his first statements after the February Revolution Lenin noted the dual power that had emerged in Petrograd between the Provisional Government and the Soviet of Workers' Deputies. As in 1905 Lenin described the Petrograd Soviet as 'an organisation of the workers, the embryo of a work-ers' government, the representative of the entire mass of the *poor* section of the population'. Now, however, he went beyond his old slogan of the 'democratic dictatorship of the proletariat and peasantry', calling for the preparation of the second stage of the revolution. By implication, this was to involve the estab-lishment of a dictatorship of the proletariat exercised through the soviets.[129] During the following months he repeatedly explained that the characteristics of soviet power would be those admired by Marx in the Paris Commune.[130]

Lenin developed these themes most fully in his pamphlet *The State and Revolution* written in August–September 1917 and published the following

---

126   Sawer 1977, pp. 214–16; Cohen 1980, pp. 39–40; Harding 1983, vol. 2, pp. 92–3.

127   Lenin 1958–65, vol. 49, pp. 388, 390–1. Quoted in Cohen 1980, p. 42.

128   Lenin 1978, pp. 49, 51.

129   Lenin 1960–70, vol. 23, p. 304.

130   Lenin 1960–70, vol. 23, pp. 324–8; Lenin 1960–70, vol. 24, pp. 23–4, 38–9, 67–71, 145–6.

January. In that work Lenin again explained that, for a certain transitional period after the seizure of power, the proletariat would need a state 'both to crush the resistance of the exploiters and to *lead* the enormous mass of the population – the peasants, the petty bourgeoisie, and the semi-proletarians – in the work of organising a socialist economy'.[131] However, the type of state needed by the proletariat was not the same as that created by the bourgeoisie. The old state was unsuitable because it had been created for a different purpose, 'to maintain exploitation, i.e., in the selfish interests of an insignificant minority against the vast majority of the people'.[132] Furthermore, the main institutions of the old state machine, the bureaucracy [*chinovnichestvo*] and the standing army, were connected 'by thousands of threads' with the bourgeoisie.[133] Consequently, Lenin described as the most fundamental point of the Marxist theory of the state that 'all previous revolutions perfected the state machine, whereas it must be broken, smashed'.[134] In its place the proletariat would substitute a state designed 'to completely abolish all exploitation, i.e., in the interests of the vast majority of the people, and against the insignificant minority'.[135]

The smashing of the old state was to be accomplished '"only" by fuller democracy'. In fact, Lenin noted, this meant the replacement of the old institutions by fundamentally different ones.[136] He asserted that the repressive functions of the state could be carried out directly by the armed people 'with a very simple "machine", almost without a "machine"'. Thus, the standing army could be abolished.[137] Regarding the other post-revolutionary function of the state, the construction of a socialist economy, Lenin believed that this would temporarily require the continued existence of some form of bureaucracy:

> Abolishing the bureaucracy [*chinovnichestvo*] at once, everywhere and completely, is out of the question. It is a utopia. But to *smash* the old bureaucratic [*chinovnichii*] machine at once and to begin immediately to construct a new one that will make possible the gradual abolition of all

---

131   Lenin 1960–70, vol. 25, p. 404.

132   Lenin 1960–70, vol. 25, p. 403.

133   Lenin 1960–70, vol. 25, p. 407; Lenin 1958–65, vol. 33, p. 29.

134   Lenin 1960–70, vol. 25, p. 406.

135   Lenin 1960–70, vol. 25, p. 403.

136   Lenin 1960–70, vol. 25, p. 419.

137   Lenin 1960–70, vol. 25, pp. 419, 463.

bureaucracy – this is *not* a utopia, it is the experience of the Commune, the direct and immediate task of the revolutionary proletariat.[138]

However, this new bureaucracy would be radically different from that of the bourgeoisie. At the outset the 'specific "bossing" of state officials' would be replaced 'by the simple functions of "foremen and accountants"'. These functions, Lenin argued, had been so simplified by capitalist culture that they were 'already fully within the ability of the average town dweller'.[139] Thus, it was 'quite possible, after the overthrow of the capitalists and the bureaucrats [*chinovniki*], to proceed immediately, overnight' to replace them with the control and supervision 'by the armed workers, by the whole of the armed population'.[140] Thus, '*all* may become "bureaucrats" [*biurokraty*] for a time and ... therefore, *nobody* may be able to become a "bureaucrat" [*biurokrat*]'.[141]

To the extent that a distinct body of state officials was needed, it would be kept subordinate to the society as a whole through the measures implemented by the Paris Commune. All officials were to be elected and subject to recall at any time, and their salaries were to be 'reduced to the level of ordinary "workmen's wages"'. Furthermore, democratic control would be maintained over executive functions by turning them over to representative institutions – in the process, transforming these institutions 'from talking shops into "working" bodies'.[142] To the extent this occurred, functionaries would 'cease to be "bureaucrats" [*biurokraty*], to be "officials" [*chinovniki*]'.[143] Lenin also foresaw that the proletarian state would continue to need a 'scientifically trained staff of engineers, agronomists, and so on'. However, he believed the use of these experts posed no threat to popular control over the state: 'These gentlemen are working today in obedience to the wishes of the capitalists, and will work even better tomorrow in obedience to the wishes of the armed workers'.[144]

For Lenin, as for Marx and Engels, the dictatorship of the proletariat was only to survive during the transition to communism. In the final analysis the state was only a tool for the suppression of one class by another. When classes ceased to exist a 'systematic struggle against a definite section of the population' would no longer be necessary. Although Lenin saw the withering of the state

---

138   Lenin 1960–70, vol. 25, p. 425; Lenin 1958–65, vol. 33, p. 48.

139   Lenin 1960–70, vol. 25, p. 426.

140   Lenin 1960–70, vol. 25, p. 473; Lenin 1958–65, vol. 33, pp. 100–1.

141   Lenin 1960–70, vol. 25, p. 481; Lenin 1958–65, vol. 33, p. 109.

142   Lenin 1960–70, vol. 25, pp. 421, 423.

143   Lenin 1960–70, vol. 25, p. 487; Lenin 1958–65, vol. 33, p. 115.

144   Lenin 1960–70, vol. 25, p. 473.

as a lengthy process, he believed it would begin with the abolition of the bourgeois state and its replacement by the dictatorship of the proletariat. He recalled that even the short-lived Paris Commune was already ceasing to be a state because it had replaced repression of the majority by the minority with repression of the minority by the majority.[145]

However, in one passage Lenin indicated that some sort of state would continue to exist for a period, even after the threat of capitalist restoration had disappeared. This would be during the lower stage of communism when goods would be distributed according to work performed. Following Marx, Lenin pointed out that such a system involved the application of an equal measure of compensation to individuals who had unequal needs. As such, the principle of 'equal right' was 'a violation of equality and an injustice' and was, in fact, a form of 'bourgeois right'. Until the economic prerequisites were created for distribution according to need, a state would be necessary for the regulation of labour and the distribution of goods.[146]

According to Lenin, when the higher stage of communism was reached the state would wither away completely. At that point production and distribution would be organised according to the principle: 'From each according to his ability, to each according to his needs'! Then, when both class rule and bourgeois norms of distribution had ceased to exist, the state with its bureaucracy would no longer be necessary.[147]

1.5   Conclusion

In the years immediately after the revolution, Bolshevik views on bureaucracy were shaped by various influences, including popular uses of the term and classical Marxist writings on that issue. From popular Russian and European discourse the Bolsheviks derived a primary understanding of bureaucracy as referring to rule by officials, or to a body of officials who ruled. Secondarily, they perceived bureaucracy in a variety of other negative phenomena that included excessive formalism, paperwork, and inefficiency. From Marx and Engels they inherited an analysis that identified the problem of bureaucracy with political alienation, that associated it with bourgeois control of the state, that anticipated it would be reduced by the dictatorship of the proletariat,

---

145   Lenin 1960–70, vol. 25, pp. 44, 457, 464.
146   Lenin 1960–70, vol. 25, pp. 465–8.
147   Lenin 1960–70, vol. 25, p. 469.

and that predicted it would disappear altogether in the socialist society of the future.

Despite expectations derived from the classics, shortly after the revolution many Bolsheviks detected the resurgence of phenomena that they viewed as manifestations of bureaucracy or bureaucratism. Some, such as the opposition groupings that flourished within the party from 1918 to 1922, continued to define and analyse the problem in traditional Marxist terms. At times, Lenin also characterised the problem of Soviet bureaucracy this way – although on other occasions, drawing heavily upon the secondary meanings and associations of bureaucracy, he identified the problem quite differently as one of inefficiency. In those years Trotsky's position was distinctive in that he defined the problem of Soviet bureaucracy *exclusively* in terms of factors promoting inefficiency. However, in later years Trotsky, too, would come to perceive the relevance of the classical Marxist analysis of bureaucracy for the Soviet situation.

Revolution and the Problems of Bureaucracy

Soon after the October Revolution, many Bolsheviks began to assert that the problem of bureaucracy had not died with the old regime. Although there was a consensus that bureaucracy was a growing problem, there was little agreement on exactly what that problem was or how to account for its reappearance. A series of opposition groups, employing traditional Marxist analysis, defined the problem in terms of political alienation, and perceived bureaucracy in the elevation of Soviet political, economic, and military institutions above the control of the working class. Furthermore, in keeping with the classical Marxist analysis, they argued that this problem was related to the degree of political power or influence exercised by the exploiting classes. Lenin spoke similarly at times, warning of the bureaucratising influence of the bourgeois specialists, and denouncing the 'bureaucratic' centralism and authoritarianism of some of his comrades. However, on other occasions he employed bureaucracy in a wholly different sense to characterise the enormous inefficiency of the Soviet state and party apparatuses. In later years Trotsky, too, would come to define the problem of Soviet bureaucracy in terms of extreme political alienation. However, in the first period of Soviet power his analysis was unusual in that it rejected both the view that Soviet bureaucracy involved the rule of officials and the notion that it was related to the use of bourgeois specialists. Instead, Trotsky identified the problem exclusively with the sources of inefficiency in Soviet military, economic, and political organs.

2.1   The Dream Deferred

On the eve of the Bolshevik insurrection Lenin confidently predicted that the coming revolution would resolve the age-old problem of bureaucracy. In *The State and Revolution* he argued that the socialist revolution would establish a dictatorship of the proletariat modeled after the Paris Commune. Through the soviets the masses of workers and, following them, the peasants would take power into their own hands. Popular control over the state would be assured by the dissolution of the standing army, the elimination of the distinction between the state's executive and legislative branches, the introduction of election and recall of all officials, and the limitation of officials' salaries to the level of 'workmen's wages'. In time, as the need for a repressive apparatus faded, even this radically democratic state would disappear.

During the first six months of power the Bolshevik leaders had reason to believe that their utopian dreams were about to become a reality. The insurrection itself, though planned and directed by the party leadership, enjoyed the ardent support of industrial workers. The day after the insurrection the Bolsheviks handed power over to the Second All-Russian Congress of Soviets, composed in the majority of Bolshevik delegates. In the following weeks and months workers and peasants throughout Russia continued to establish soviets as organs of local government. At all levels elected soviet deputies received only minimal wages and exercised both executive and legislative powers.[1] Outside of the soviets as well, the new regime was characterised by a high degree of popular participation. In the early months of Soviet power the factory committees first introduced workers' control over the factories and then began to nationalise them outright, workers in Petrograd organised their own tribunals to dispense revolutionary justice, and peasants spontaneously seized the property of the large landowners.[2]

On the crest of this revolutionary wave the Bolsheviks continued to proclaim the dream of a radically democratic and anti-bureaucratic state. In this regard no one was more optimistic than Lenin. Immediately after the insurrection he repeated to the Petrograd Soviet the central refrain of *The State and Revolution*: 'The oppressed masses will themselves create a power. The old state apparatus will be smashed to its foundations and a new administrative apparatus set up in the form of the Soviet organisations'.[3] At the Seventh Party Congress in March 1918 he elaborated, 'Soviet power is a new type of state without a bureaucracy, without police, without a regular army, a state in which bourgeois democracy has been replaced by a new democracy, a democracy that brings to the fore the vanguard of working people, ... makes them responsible for military defence and creates state machinery that can re-educate the masses'.[4] In the same period he further argued that other mass institutions such as the trade unions, factory committees, militia groupings, and peoples' courts, could facilitate popular participation in the affairs of state.[5] Finally, he continued to predict that under socialism the state would disappear altogether.[6] At the Seventh Party Congress Lenin noted that the withering of

---

1   Liebman 1975, p. 218; Anweiler, 1974, pp. 206, 220; Carr 1950–3, vol. 1, pp. 154–5; Serge 1972, p. 95.
2   Liebman 1975, pp. 216–17, 326; Anweiler 1974, pp. 220–1; Serge 1972, pp. 95–6.
3   Lenin 1960–70, vol. 26, p. 239.
4   Lenin 1960–70, vol. 27, p. 133.
5   See Harding 1983, vol. 2, pp. 177, 183–6.
6   Lenin 1960–70, vol. 26, p. 466.

the state had already begun, though he added more cautiously, 'We shall have managed to convene more than two congresses before the time comes to say: see how our state is withering away'.[7]

Trotsky also emphasised many of these same democratic and anti-bureaucratic themes. In March 1918 he observed, 'Yesterday the mass-man was nobody, a slave to the Tsar, the nobles and the bureaucracy'.[8] In July of that year he described the revolution as a 'revolt of the peasants against the landlords, of the workers against the capitalists, of the whole people against old tsarist bureaucratism and against the Tsar himself'.[9] Furthermore, on the day of the insurrection he expressed confidence that the new state would serve only working people: 'We, today, we, the Soviet of Soldiers', Workers', and Peasants' Deputies, are going to undertake an experiment unique in history, the establishment of a government that will have no other aim than the satisfaction of the needs of the soldiers, workers, and peasants'.[10] A few months later he explained that the representation of the interests of working people was guaranteed by the right to elect and recall all officials of the soviets. Because of this, in comparison with the old dumas and zemstvos, there were 'in the Soviet incomparably more serious, more profound guarantees of the direct and immediate relation between the deputy and the electors'.[11]

However, by early 1918 the dream of immediately realising the commune state had already begun to fade. Increasingly, the policies adopted by the party leadership and the emergent structures of power diverged from the aspirations of *The State and Revolution*. During the civil war that raged from the spring of 1918 until late 1920, highly paid 'bourgeois specialists' continued to occupy positions of authority throughout Soviet political, economic and military institutions; working-class initiative gave way to centralism in all spheres; the state apparatus expanded enormously; the Soviet leadership found itself resorting to coercion, not only against its enemies, but also against the classes it claimed to represent; and opposition parties were harassed into impotence. Finally, the power of the soviets indeed 'withered', but in its place grew the power of a hierarchically organised party. During these years the goal of a commune state

---

7   Lenin 1960–70, vol. 27, pp. 126, 148.
8   Trotsky 1979–81, vol. 1, p. 39.
9   Trotsky 1979–81, vol. 1, p. 413; Trotsky 1991a, vol. 1, p. 304 (translation modified). See also
      Trotsky 1979–81, vol. 1, p. 132; Trotsky, 1991a, vol. 1, p. 105.
10   Trotsky 1972a, p. 72.
11   Trotsky 1919, pp. 28–9; Trotsky 1963b, p. 278.

did not disappear entirely from the pronouncements of the party leaders, but it receded further and further into the distance.[12]

It is debatable whether the Marxist vision of the commune state could have been realised under the best of circumstances. However, the Bolsheviks never had the opportunity to find out. From the beginning they were beset by difficulties that had not been anticipated in the classics. Marx and Engels had expected that the proletariat would first come to power in the most economically advanced countries. Instead, the revolution triumphed in the most backward country of Europe. Russia lacked not only the social surplus necessary to begin socialist construction, but also the degree of literacy required for mass political participation, and even a proletariat large enough to constitute a stable base for the revolutionary regime. Furthermore, Marx and Engels assumed the revolution would be international in scope. In the early years of Soviet power the Bolsheviks continued to count upon the world revolution to rescue them from the effects of backwardness and imperialist intervention.[13] Yet, despite the revolutionary wave that swept over Europe in the wake of the world war, Russia remained an isolated outpost of socialism surrounded by hostile capitalist powers. Finally, there was no anticipation before 1917 of the transformative effects of a brutal civil war that would necessitate the militarisation of all aspects of public life, inflict devastation upon the proletariat, and bring the economy of the revolutionary state to the brink of collapse. At the same time, subjective factors also eroded the vision of the commune state. In the heat of polemics and the desperation of the moment, Bolshevik leaders sometimes characterised policies dictated by necessity as manifestations of revolutionary virtue, while justifying policies that were merely expedient in terms of dire necessity. In doing so, they accelerated the drift toward authoritarianism, and helped to perpetuate it even after the worst dangers had receded.

The first deviation from the Marxist vision involved the recruitment of large numbers of bourgeois specialists to serve in the institutions of the Soviet state. Although in 1917 Lenin had recognised that the dictatorship of the proletariat would need to utilise experts from the old regime, he had not anticipated that the Soviet state would be compelled to pay these 'spetsy' more than 'workmen's wages' or to entrust them with major decision-making powers.[14] However, by the spring of 1918 the deteriorating economic situation convinced Lenin that 'without the guidance of experts in the various fields of knowledge, technology

---

12   See Liebman 1975, pp. 222–7. See also Lih 1995a.

13   See in particular Marx and Engels 1972b, pp. 334–5. For Lenin's statements on this, see Harding 1983, vol. 2, pp. 199–200; Liebman 1975, pp. 360–5.

14   Lenin 1960–70, vol. 25, p. 473; Lenin 1960–70, vol. 26, pp. 105–7.

and experience, the transition to socialism will be impossible'. Admitting it was a departure from the principles of the Paris Commune, he now proposed the payment of very large salaries to attract the services of the *spetsy*.[15] This inducement was an immediate success. By August over half the officials in the commissariats – the ministries of the new government – and nearly 90 percent of the upper-level officials had held administrative posts before the revolution.[16]

The influx of bourgeois specialists into industrial administration and the military was comparable. In December 1918, 57 percent of the membership of the most important 'chief committees' [*glavki*] of the Supreme Council of the National Economy (vsnkh) in charge of Soviet industry consisted of former employers and employers' representatives, technicians, and officials from various departments, while 43 percent were workers or representatives of workers' organisations. By 1921, at least 80 percent of the 'most responsible posts' in vsnkh and 74 per cent of the members of the administrative collegia of the industrial *glavki* consisted of specialists and ex-officials.[17] At the factory level the managers appointed by the *glavki* during the civil war were, for the most part, bourgeois specialists.[18] Meanwhile, Trotsky, the new Commissar of War, insisted that the Soviet armed forces be commanded by the most competent 'military specialists' available – the former tsarist officers. By the end of 1918 these constituted 76 percent of the command and administration of the Red Army.[19]

The civil war years also witnessed a growing centralisation of all political, military, and economic institutions. One form this took in the soviets was the widespread delegation of powers to executive committees. In the centre it soon became clear that the All-Russian Congress of Soviets, consisting of more than a thousand deputies, was too large to direct policy effectively or even to convene regularly in the context of a civil war. In its place the 15-member Council of Peoples' Commissars (Sovnarkom) emerged as the dominant state institution. At lower levels, too, soviet executive committees increasingly assumed the powers of the local soviets.[20] Meanwhile, the local soviets and their organs came to be dominated more and more by those of the centre. In the early months of power the autonomy of the regional soviets often assumed extreme

---

15   Lenin 1960–70, vol. 27, pp. 248–9.

16   Rigby 1979, p. 62.

17   Azrael 1966, p. 46.

18   Carr 1950–3, vol. 2, pp. 186–7; Bettelheim 1976, pp. 155–6.

19   Trotsky 1941, p. 279.

20   Carr 1950–3, vol. 1, pp. 220–1; Liebman 1975, pp. 229–30; Sakwa 1988, pp. 174–5, 176 (describing the situation in Moscow).

and disruptive forms.[21] This regionalism was partly overcome with the adoption of the 1918 constitution, which placed soviets and their executive committees at each territorial level under the control of the corresponding institutions at the next higher level.[22] Subsequently, the need for a unified direction of resources for the war effort accelerated the drift toward centralism. During the civil war local soviets were subordinated not only to higher soviets, but also to the local arms of such institutions as VSNKh, the Extraordinary Commission for Combating Counter-Revolution and Sabotage (Cheka), and the Military Revolutionary Committee.[23]

The most centralised institution to emerge in the civil war was the Red Army. In the first months after the revolution the military forces at the disposal of the Soviet government consisted mostly of militia and partisan detachments composed of worker volunteers and commanded by elected officers. Upon assuming the post of Commissar of War, Trotsky set about reconstructing an army along more traditional lines, insisting that this was necessary for the successful prosecution of the war.[24] He reinstituted conscription and the appointment of officers, defending this last measure on the grounds that the election of officers had been introduced by the Bolsheviks simply as a means 'to break the class resistance of the commanding personnel'. Furthermore, he asserted that, with the establishment of Soviet power, 'there can be no antagonism between the government and the mass of the workers ... and, therefore, there cannot be any grounds for fearing the *appointment* of members of the commanding staff by the organs of the Soviet power'.[25]

Meanwhile, a similar process of centralisation was occurring in the economy. To reverse economic disintegration, in late 1917 and early 1918 the powers of the factory committees and councils of workers' control were transferred to the more centralised trade unions and VSNKh.[26] By late 1918 the intensification of the war led to the establishment of war communism, a rigidly centralist command economy subordinated to the needs of war. With the diminishing supply of consumer goods, trade relations between the cities and the countryside broke down. In order to feed the Red Army and the starving cities, the Bolsheviks sent armed detachments from the urban centres to confiscate grain. Private trade was outlawed and price controls and rationing were instituted.

---

21   See Liebman 1975, p. 228.
22   Carr 1950–3, vol. 1, p. 144.
23   Carr 1950–3 , vol. 1, p. 223; Liebman 1975, p. 229.
24   Trotsky 1979–81, vol. 1, pp. 28–48.
25   Trotsky 1979–81, vol. 1, p. 47.
26   Carr 1950–3, vol. 2, pp. 78–9.

At the same time nearly all industry was nationalised and placed under the direction of VSNKh and its organs – the *glavki* and *tsentry* [centres].[27]

Centralisation also proceeded in the management of individual factories. Against the resistance of the trade unions, Lenin waged a successful campaign to replace collegial boards with individual factory managers. As Lenin saw it, 'large scale machine industry – which is … the foundation of socialism – calls for absolute and strict *unity of will*'. This could only be achieved by 'thousands subordinating their will to the will of one'.[28] Both Lenin and Trotsky brushed aside objections that one-man management [*edinonachalie*] subverted proletarian direction of the economy, arguing that working-class rule was assured through the abolition of private ownership and through the power of the soviets, not by the form of industrial management.[29]

The attempt under war communism to centralise all aspects of economic and social life was undoubtedly one of the reasons for the enormous growth of the state apparatus during these years. From the first half of 1918 until the first half of 1919 membership rolls for the trade union of Soviet officials quadrupled, expanding from 114,539 to 529,841.[30] Within Moscow, in May 1919 approximately 16 percent of the population and 31 percent of those employed were office workers; despite decreases in the total number of office workers in Moscow, by 1920 they still comprised nearly a third of the working population.[31] One factor besides centralisation that contributed to the growth of the state apparatus was the pressure on the state to provide jobs for the unemployed. As Gregory Zinoviev commented in December 1920, 'We can make as many resolutions as possible but if, at the same time … tens of thousands of people press upon us in many cities, seeking to find some kind of work for themselves, we cannot by any means fight against the swelling of bureaucracy in our apparatus'.[32]

Related to economic centralisation was the escalation in state coercion, not only against the class enemy and the peasants, but also against the working class. At Lenin's insistence, piece work and the hated Taylor system of industrial administration were reintroduced in the factories. Furthermore, labour courts

---

27   On war communism, see Carr 1950–3, vol. 2, pp. 151–268; Dobb 1966, pp. 97–124; Malle 1985; Nove 1976, pp. 59–78.

28   Lenin 1960–70, vol. 27, pp. 268, 269.

29   Lenin 1960–70, vol. 30, p. 456; Trotsky 1972c, p. 162.

30   Serge 1972, p. 356.

31   Sakwa 1988, p. 192. According to Liebman 1975, p. 321, citing Pietsch 1969, p. 137, by the end of 1920 the total number of Soviet officials had reached at least 5,880,000.

32   Quoted in Liebman 1975, p. 321.

were established to punish violators of labour discipline. Lenin explained that *'those* who violate labour discipline ... are *responsible* for the sufferings caused by the famine and unemployment'. We 'must know how to find the guilty ones', he insisted, 'to bring them to trial and ruthlessly punish them'.[33] During the civil war the trade unions were induced to adopt a productionist orientation and to play an active role in enforcing labour discipline. As Trotsky asserted in 1920, 'The further we go,... the more do the unions recognize that they are organs of production of the Soviet State, and assume responsibility for its fortunes – not opposing themselves to it, but identifying themselves with it'. Thus, they were becoming 'organizers of labor discipline' and 'the apparatus of revolutionary repression against undisciplined, anarchical, parasitic elements in the working class'.[34]

Under Trotsky's inspiration economic authoritarianism reached its peak in 1920. By then most of the White Armies were in flight, but the civil war and the inefficiency of war communism had brought the Soviet economy to a state of ruin. To resuscitate industry, Trotsky proposed a scheme for the 'militarisation of labour'. Aspects of this policy included the conversion of military units into labour armies and the assignment of industrial workers to specific enterprises. As an initial step in implementing this plan, the Third Army of the Urals was transformed into a labour army. According to Trotsky, such methods were not simply necessitated by difficult circumstances; rather, they were 'the inevitable method of organization and disciplining of labour-power during the period of transition from capitalism to Socialism'.[35] For this reason – and not simply because of bourgeois resistance – the state could be expected to intensify its repressive powers for a period of time after the revolution: 'Just as a lamp, before going out, shoots up in a brilliant flame, so the State, before disappearing, assumes the form of the dictatorship of the proletariat, *i.e.*, the most ruthless form of State, which embraces the life of the citizens authoritatively in every direction'.[36] In early 1920 Trotsky was assigned the task of reviving the transport system. He reorganised the Chief Political Administration of the People's Commissariat of Communications (Glavpolitput'), giving it powers to draft party workers and assign them throughout the country. In August he also established the Central Transport Commission (Tsektran), which placed all transport workers under his control, and dismissed railroad union leaders who had criticised his policies. Furthermore, he threatened to 'shake up' all

33   Lenin 1960–70, vol. 27, p. 266.
34   Trotsky 1972c, p. 111.
35   Trotsky 1972c, p. 143.
36   Trotsky 1972c, p. 170.

the trade unions as he had the transport unions. Finally, at the end of the year Trotsky elaborated a plan for the complete subordination of the unions to the state.[37]

Meanwhile, the ideal of soviet democracy also was undermined by the escalating repression of all opposition parties, including those of the left. *The State and Revolution* had not explicitly discussed the question, but the radically democratic system projected in that work seems most consistent with a system of competing parties. Furthermore, there is evidence to suggest that Lenin initially anticipated some degree of political pluralism in the soviets. For example, in January 1918 he commented that 'if the working people are dissatisfied with their party they can elect other delegates, hand power to another party and change the government without any revolution at all'.[38] However, in late 1917 Bolshevik efforts to establish a multi-party coalition government of the left foundered on what Marcel Liebman has characterised as the 'hostility, contempt and refusal to compromise' of the Mensheviks and the Socialist Revolutionaries.[39] Then, in 1918 one opposition party after another, or sections of them, rose in armed revolt. In turn, each was repressed, its leaders arrested, and its newspapers banned. When sections of these parties drew closer to the Soviet government during the civil war, the Bolsheviks permitted them a degree of freedom. Still, they remained under suspicion, and for their semi-loyalty enjoyed at best semi-legality.[40]

In 1920 Trotsky offered a defence of one-party rule in terms far more sweeping than the necessities of the moment. It was, he claimed, the only means by which the interests and desires of a heterogeneous proletariat could be unified:

> The exclusive role of the Communist Party under the conditions of a victorious proletarian revolution is quite comprehensible. The question is of the dictatorship of a class. In the composition of that class there enter various elements, heterogeneous moods, different levels of development. Yet the dictatorship pre-supposes unity of will, unity of direction, unity of action. By what other path then can it be attained? The revolutionary supremacy of the proletariat pre-supposes within itself the political supremacy of a party, with a class programme of action and a faultless internal discipline.[41]

---

37   Daniels 1960, pp. 124, 129–30; Day 1973, pp. 35–9; Deutscher 1954, pp. 501–2, 507.
38   Lenin 1960–70, vol. 26, p. 498. On this point, see Le Blanc 1990, pp. 297–8.
39   Liebman 1975, p. 241.
40   See Liebman 1975, pp. 242–57.
41   Trotsky 1972c, pp. 107–8.

Trotsky argued that the historically progressive character of the repression of opposition parties was demonstrated by its effect: 'Noske [the conservative German Social Democrat and minister of military affairs] crushes the Communists, but they grow. We have suppressed the Mensheviks and the S.R.s – and they have disappeared. This criterion is sufficient for us'.[42]

During these years perhaps the most important deviation from the vision of direct, soviet democracy proclaimed in Lenin's *The State and Revolution* was the usurpation of the powers of the soviets by the Communist Party. It seems that several factors were responsible for this. First, it proved far more difficult than Lenin had anticipated to enlist the masses in the administration of the state. By March 1919 Lenin was forced to admit that 'the Soviets, which by virtue of their programme are organs of government *by working people*, are in fact organs of government *for the working people* by the advanced section of the proletariat'.[43] In effect, this meant the soviets were organs of government by the party, for that was where the 'advanced sector of the proletariat' was concentrated. Second, in the context of the civil war the Bolshevik leadership actively sought political hegemony in the soviets and other mass institutions in order to ensure their political reliability. In line with this, party domination of these organisations at the lower levels was assured by the formation of disciplined party 'fractions' within each of them, and by the appointment of party members to important non-party posts.[44] Third, the difficulties of the war combined with the requirements of efficiency to strengthen the party's role. As local soviets atrophied during the war, party committees were forced to step in to assume their coordinating functions.[45] At the summit of power the Central Committee filled the need for a central arbiter and final court of appeal for disputed questions in the soviets and other mass organisations.[46] Trotsky explained, 'This affords extreme economy of time and energy and in the most difficult and complicated circumstances gives a guarantee for the necessary unity of action'.[47] Finally, with the growing size of Sovnarkom meetings, the most pressing matters were resolved by the Politburo.[48]

One consequence of these developments was that party leaders increasingly tended to equate proletarian rule with party rule. In 1919 Lenin made a

---

42   Trotsky 1972c, pp. 109–10. See also Trotsky 1972d, p. 121.
43   Lenin 1960–70, vol. 29, p. 183.
44   See KPSS 1970a, pp. 72, 76, 134, 232.
45   Rigby 1979, p. 184.
46   Carr 1950–3, vol. 1, p. 225; Rigby 1979, p. 182.
47   Trotsky 1972c, p. 107.
48   Rigby 1979, pp. 182–3.

virtual slogan of the phrase 'dictatorship of the party': 'Yes, the dictatorship of one party! We stand upon it and cannot depart from this ground, since this is the party which in the course of decades has won for itself the position of vanguard of the whole factory and industrial proletariat'.[49] The following year he characterised any attempt to distinguish between the dictatorship of the proletariat and the dictatorship of the party as evidence of 'an unbelievable and inextricable confusion of thought'.[50] Along the same lines, in 1920 Trotsky remarked,

> We have more than once been accused of having substituted for the dictatorship of the Soviets the dictatorship of our party. Yet it can be said with complete justice that the dictatorship of the Soviets became possible only by means of the dictatorship of the party.[51]

Even as it usurped the powers of the soviets, the party was transformed by the same processes of centralisation that were occurring in the state. At all levels the party experienced the concentration of power in fewer and fewer hands. Local party committees shrank as their members were mobilised for the war, and their authority was assumed by party chairmen, renamed 'secretaries' in 1920.[52] At the centre, party congresses, like meetings of the All-Russian Congress of Soviets, soon proved to be too large and too infrequent to define policy. The Central Committee, consisting of fifteen full and seven candidate members in 1918, quickly assumed this role. However, its ascendancy was only temporary, for military responsibilities often forced its members to be absent from Moscow. By 1919 the oppositionist V.V. Osinskii was complaining that 'even the Central Committee as a collegiate body does not, properly speaking, exist', for 'comrades Lenin and Sverdlov decide current questions by way of conversation with each other or with individual comrades in charge of this or that branch of Soviet work'.[53] That same year this concentration was codified by the creation of three new subcommittees of the CC: a five-member Politburo responsible for urgent policy decisions; a five-member Orgburo entrusted with the overall direction of party work; and a Secretariat, consisting

---

49   Quoted in Carr 1950–3, vol. 1, p. 236.
50   Ibid.
51   Trotsky 1972c, p. 109. For similar statements by Zinoviev and Kamenev, see Liebman 1975, p. 280; and Draper 1987, p. 140.
52   Service 1979, pp. 100–1, 121, 140, 147.
53   Quoted in Carr 1950–3, vol. 1, pp. 199–200. See also Service 1979, pp. 101–2.

of one secretary and five assistants, which was later placed in charge of day-to-day organisational tasks.[54]

Meanwhile, power in the party, as in the state, was gravitating to the centre. This tendency grew especially pronounced as the practice of electing local party officials declined. It became common for local party committees to co-opt new members to replace those lost to the war, and for higher level committees to appoint committee chairmen at lower levels. The Politburo and Orgburo frequently appointed officials in the provincial party institutions, often without consulting these bodies. The powers of the local party committees were further weakened by the creation, at Trotsky's insistence, of centrally appointed 'political departments' in charge of all political work in the Red Army and in various local factories and industries.[55]

The conclusion of the civil war brought to the surface all the pent-up frustrations that had accumulated since 1918. In the face of an outpouring of popular discontent, the party leadership was forced to institute economic and political reforms. It scrapped the system of war communism and promised to decentralise the party. Beyond that, it took steps to curb the party's control over state institutions and to revive the soviets. After the detour of the civil war, it seemed that the Soviet state was about to emerge again on the road charted in *The State and Revolution*.

One indication of the growing dissatisfaction with war communism was the response within the party to Trotsky's plan to 'statify' the trade unions. Trotsky's proposal touched off an explosion among party union leaders and oppositionists who were fed up with industrial authoritarianism. Even Lenin turned against Trotsky's authoritarian measures at this point. Lenin agreed with Trotsky that the unions should encourage labour discipline and productivity, but now he placed greater stress on persuasion than coercion. Furthermore, he argued that the unions needed to preserve their independence from an increasingly 'bureaucratic' state. The trade union question was resolved at the Tenth Party Congress in 1921 with the adoption of Lenin's perspective.[56]

However, the party was confronted with even more serious manifestations of discontent. In the early months of 1921 a wave of strikes swept the factories of Petrograd while peasants rose in open revolt throughout the country. In March the sailors of the Kronstadt naval garrison mutinied in solidarity with

---

54   Carr 1950–3, vol. 1, pp. 200–1.

55   Service 1979, pp. 121–2, 127, 136, 140; Daniels 1960, p. 114.

56   On the trade-union debate see Daniels 1960, pp. 129–36; Day 1973, pp. 37–43; Deutscher 1950, pp. 42–58; Harding 1983, vol. 2, pp. 256–74; Schapiro 1977, pp. 273–95; Service 1995, pp. 152–6; Tsuji 1989, pp. 31–100.

the rebelling workers and peasants.[57] The uprisings were quickly crushed, but the party also began to institute reforms to undercut the economic sources of discontent. The Tenth Party Congress replaced forced requisitioning of grain with an agricultural tax in kind. In the following months the other features of the New Economic Policy (NEP) began to take shape: monetary wages replaced rationing, domestic private trade and small-scale private industry were encouraged, and the state began leasing enterprises to their former owners or to producers' cooperatives. Also, the centrally controlled *glavki* were dismantled and replaced by autonomous 'trusts' as the basic unit of industrial production.[58]

In late 1920 and early 1921 efforts were also made to reverse the centralisation that had transformed the party during the war. This was the thrust of the resolution on party construction adopted by the Ninth Party Conference in September 1920. The resolution called for the frequent convening of local party meetings to discuss important issues, outlined measures to encourage members to criticise party institutions, demanded an end to the practice of appointing party functionaries, and urged the abolition of political departments. Additionally, it established a hierarchy of control commissions to investigate alleged violations of party democracy.[59] Similarly, the Tenth Party Congress announced the end of the 'militarisation' of party life, and called for the restoration of 'workers' democracy' within the party.[60]

Finally, after the civil war attempts were made to revive the soviets as institutions of power. A series of laws enacted in 1921–2 strengthened the soviets and restricted the authority of the 'extraordinary organs' such as the Cheka that had flourished during the war. Sovnarkom ceded much of its power to the Central Executive Committee (CEC) of the Congress of Soviets and its Presidium. Also, beginning with the Eleventh Party Congress in 1922, Lenin increasingly insisted upon extricating the party from its direct involvement in state affairs and increasing the responsibilities of soviet institutions at all levels.[61]

However, anyone who believed that the commune state was about to become a reality was quickly disillusioned. The revival of soviet democracy presupposed the existence of a powerful and self-confident proletariat. But the war years had taken a heavy toll upon the working class: approximately 60,000

---

57   See Avrich 1970.

58   On the early period of NEP, see Carr 1950–3, vol. 2, pp. 269–357; Dobb 1966, pp. 125–48; Nove 1976, pp. 83–92.

59   KPSS 1970a , pp. 189–95; Service 1979, p. 145.

60   KPSS 1970a, pp. 206–18; Carr 1950–3, vol. 1, p. 209.

61   Rigby 1979, pp. 173–6, 211.

industrial workers had died on the battlefield, hundreds of thousands more perished from hunger and disease, others fled to the countryside to escape starvation, and thousands were absorbed into the swelling state apparatus. Consequently, by 1922 the industrial working class was less than half of its size in 1917.[62] With little exaggeration, Lenin observed in October 1921 that 'the proletariat has disappeared'.[63]

Another precondition for the revival of soviet democracy was the easing of restrictions on opposition parties. However, from the perspective of the Bolsheviks, this too was impossible. Dissatisfaction with the regime was so widespread at the end of the civil war that it was unlikely the Bolsheviks could have won a genuinely democratic election. But the Bolsheviks had no intention of surrendering power to the Mensheviks and S.R.s, for doing so would have sacrificed the goals for which they had just fought a bloody civil war. At the Tenth Party Congress Trotsky asserted the 'historic birthright of the party, which is obliged to defend its dictatorship, in spite of temporary vacillation of elements, in spite of temporary vacillation even in the midst of the workers'.[64] This attitude was reinforced by the fear that bourgeois political activity would revive with the partial restoration of capitalism under NEP. Instead of loosening their restrictions on opposition parties, the Bolsheviks now banned them altogether. Lenin bluntly expressed this intolerance at the Eleventh Party Congress in 1922:

> And when a Menshevik says, 'You are now retreating; I have been advocating retreat all the time, I agree with you, I am your man, let us retreat together', we say in reply, 'For the public manifestations of Menshevism our revolutionary courts must pass the death sentence, otherwise they are not our courts, but God knows what'.[65]

The increasing repression of anti-Bolshevik dissent had an immediate impact upon democracy within the party as well. Isaac Deutscher has described the dynamic involved:

> If the Bolsheviks were now to engage freely in controversy, if their leaders were to thrash out their differences in public, and if the rank and file

62   Service 1979, p. 136; Liebman 1975, pp. 346–7; Deutscher 1959, pp. 5–7. For a qualified version of this picture, see Koenker 1985, pp. 424–50.
63   Lenin 1960–70, vol. 33, p. 65.
64   RKP(b) 1963, p. 351.
65   Lenin 1960–70, vol. 33, p. 282.

were to criticize the leaders and their policy, they would set an example to non-Bolsheviks who could not then be expected to refrain from argument and criticism. If members of the ruling party were to be permitted to form factions and groups in order to advance specific views within the party, how could people outside the party be forbidden to form their own associations and formulate their own political programmes?[66]

Consequently, for the first time in Bolshevik history, the Tenth Party Congress imposed a ban on party factions. Afterwards, the 1921 purge of 'undesirable elements' was used to eliminate rank and file oppositionists, while opposition leaders were reassigned to obscure outposts.[67]

Meanwhile, the flow of power from the state to the party continued unabated. This process was accelerated by the steady deterioration of Lenin's health from mid-1921 until his death in 1924. Lenin's had been the most powerful voice for restricting the prerogatives of the party, and in his absence Sovnarkom referred even more disputed questions to the Politburo.[68] At the same time, the Orgburo and Secretariat were amassing ever greater powers through the appointment of party personnel. Partly, this was simply a continuation of practices initiated during the civil war; partly, it grew out of the attempt after the war to reorganise the party in order to direct the machinery of state more effectively; and partly, it was a product of institutional self-aggrandisement by the Orgburo and Secretariat. At any rate, the individual who benefitted most from the growing powers of these bodies was Stalin – the leading figure in the Orgburo and, after April 1922, General Secretary of the party.[69]

2.2   The Oppositions and Political Alienation

During the period 1918–22, some of the most vocal and consistent critics of Soviet bureaucracy were a series of opposition groupings within the Russian Communist Party. Although they differed on many questions, they were united in characterising the problem in terms of the deviation of Soviet practice from the radically democratic and proletarian ideals expressed in the writings of Marx and Engels on the Paris Commune and in Lenin's *The State and Revolution*. Each group denounced the growing authoritarianism and

---

66   Deutscher 1959, p. 16.
67   Service 1979, pp. 163–5, 180–1; Daniels 1960, pp. 159–65.
68   Rigby 1979, pp. 207–8, 211–12; Service 1979, p. 178.
69   Service 1979, pp. 176–7; Rigby 1979, pp. 185, 212.

centralism of Soviet institutions. Also, each linked this problem with the growth of bourgeois power and influence.

The Left Communists came together in early 1918 to oppose the signing of a peace treaty with Germany, and as proponents of a policy of revolutionary war. However, even after the ratification of the Brest-Litovsk treaty in March, they continued to function as a faction, shifting their focus to economic policies.[70] At the time, Lenin was attempting to reverse the progressive deterioration of the economy by halting further nationalisation of enterprises, curbing the powers of the factory committees, imposing labour discipline, and recruiting bourgeois specialists to serve as industrial managers. For the Left Communists these policies represented an impermissible departure from the revolutionary socialist principles that Lenin himself had expressed. Nikolai Bukharin, one of the leaders of the Left Communists, observed, 'It is good ... that the cook will be taught to govern the state; but what will there be if a Commissar is placed over the cook? Then he will never learn to govern the state'.[71]

For the Left Communists the danger of Lenin's policies was that they would promote 'bureaucratic centralist' methods in politics and might result in the transfer of economic power to a section of the bourgeoisie. By 'bureaucratic centralism', they seem to have understood any measure that removed direct control of production from the workers and that imposed labour discipline from above. The Left Communists believed that these measures, like the signing of the Brest-Litovsk treaty, had originated in the willingness of the party leadership to compromise principles for the sake of survival. If taken to their logical conclusion, such policies raised the prospect of the degeneration of the revolution by undermining the independent initiative of the working class.

> With the policy of administering enterprises on the basis of broad participation by capitalists and semibureaucratic centralization it is natural to combine a labor policy directed toward the institution among the workers of discipline under the banner of 'self-discipline', toward the introduction of obligatory labor for workers..., piecework payment, lengthening of the working day, etc.
>
> The form of government administration will have to develop in the direction of bureaucratic centralization, the rule of various commissars, the deprivation of local soviets of their independence, and in practice the rejection of the type of 'commune state' administered from below.[72]

---

70   Cohen 1980, pp. 62–3.
71   Quoted in Cohen 1980, p. 75. For a similar remark by Osinskii, see Daniels 1960, p. 86.
72   Daniels 1984, p. 100.

Ultimately, the Left Communists predicted, the result would be the collapse of the dictatorship of the proletariat and the restoration of some form of capitalism. As Osinskii warned,

> The stick, if raised against the workers, will find itself in the hands of a social force which is either under the influence of another social class or in the hands of the soviet power; then the soviet power will be forced to seek support against the proletariat from another class (e.g. the peasantry), and by this it will destroy itself as the dictatorship of the proletariat.[73]

The only way out of the danger for the Left Communists was through economic measures that continued the offensive against capital while expanding workers' democracy. Along these lines they advocated nationalisation of all large-scale industrial and financial enterprises and the extension of the principle of workers' control. Each enterprise was to be managed by a board, two-thirds of which would be composed of elected workers' representatives. In turn, the factory boards were to be subordinate to a network of elected economic councils. Although the Left Communists did not entirely reject the use of bourgeois specialists, they insisted that these were to be nominated only by worker-dominated factory boards and subject to removal from below.[74]

The Left Communists were decisively defeated in May at the Congress of Councils of the National Economy, and by June they had collapsed as an organised opposition. However, soon afterwards they saw part of their programme implemented in a Sovnarkom decree that nationalised all large-scale industry.[75] In later years many of the leaders of the Left Communists continued to be active in other opposition groupings that combated bureaucracy and fought to limit the power of the specialists.

From the moment when Trotsky first announced his plans for the construction of a Red Army, his policies encountered resistance within the party. By the Eighth Party Congress in March 1919 this discontent had crystallised into what later became known as the Military Opposition. This was a heterogeneous grouping that included, in addition to former Left Communists, leaders of the partisan detachments that had formed in late 1917 and early 1918. Among these, local military leaders of the city of Tsaritsyn supported by Stalin played a prominent role. Like the Left Communists, the Military Opposition

---

73   Quoted in Daniels 1960, p. 85.
74   Daniels 1960, pp. 83, 86–7; Siriani 1982, pp. 143–9.
75   For the reasons behind this decree, see Schapiro 1977, pp. 140–1.

also resisted the use of bourgeois specialists – in this case, former tsarist officers. Furthermore, it opposed Trotsky's efforts to introduce a high degree of
centralism in the Red Army, his elimination of the election of officers, and his
introduction of political departments to organise all party work in the army.[76]
The Military Opposition did not develop a general analysis of the problem of
bureaucracy, but their views on this question seem consistent with those of
the Left Communists. At the Eighth Party Congress the former Left Communist
V.M. Smirnov decried Trotsky's centralisation of all political work in the
army 'according to a completely bureaucratic model'.[77] Although the Military
Opposition's views were rejected by the Eighth Congress, some of its leaders
were already espousing a broader platform in a new opposition grouping – the
Democratic Centralists.

The Democratic Centralists appeared early in 1919, and reached the high
point of their influence and activity in 1920–1. They were composed largely of
intellectuals who were alarmed by the decline of democracy and the growth of
centralism and authoritarianism within the institutions of the economy, state,
and party. These were tendencies that, according to the Democratic Centralist
Osinskii, stifled 'the creative initiative of the conscious workers'.[78] Like the
Left Communists, the Democratic Centralists saw these as manifestations of
'bureaucratism' or 'bureaucratic centralism'. For example, at the Ninth Party
Congress in 1920, V.N. Maksimovskii declared,

> We are defending that democratic centralism which is inscribed in
> the statutes of the party adopted at the December conference. We are
> defending democratic centralism in the construction of the organs
> of Soviet power…The Central Committee is guilty of bureaucratic
> centralism. … It is said that a fish begins to rot from its head. At the top
> the party is beginning to fall under the influence of this bureaucratic
> centralism.[79]

Even more sharply, T.V. Sapronov denounced the concentration of power in
the hands of a few leaders as the 'dictatorship of the party bureaucracy'.[80] Also,
Osinskii noted the expansion of military at the expense of civilian culture.[81]

---

76   On the Military Opposition, see Daniels 1960, pp. 104–7; Schapiro 1977, pp. 235–52.
77   RKP(b) 1959, p. 158.
78   Daniels 1984, p. 125.
79   RKP(b) 1960, p. 49.
80   RKP(b) 1960, p. 51.
81   RKP(b) 1960, p. 115.

The solution to the problem for the Democratic Centralists was through proletarian democracy and decentralisation. They vigorously defended collegial
management of enterprises as a method of training workers in administration
and eliminating the need for bourgeois specialists, and they resisted Trotsky's
efforts in 1920 to militarise the economy. As far as the state was concerned,
they attempted to revive the power of the soviets, proposing a change in the
composition of the Central Executive Committee of the All-Russian Congress
of Soviets to make it more representative, and the restoration to the CEC of the
legislative powers that had been assumed by Sovnarkom. Also, they demanded
the return of power from the central state institutions to the local soviets. The
Democratic Centralists advocated similar measures against bureaucratism in
the party. They proposed an expansion and proletarianisation of the Central
Committee, and the institution of the 'collective principle' for decision making
at all levels of the party. Against the flow of power from the local party organisations to the centre, they called for an end to the Secretariat's practice of
appointing local party officials and issuing directives to provincial party organisations, and they urged the abolition of the special political departments.
Finally, they argued that the entire party should have the opportunity to consider all important matters, and that oppositionists should be able to air their
differences freely.[82]

Meanwhile, yet another dissident group, the Workers' Opposition, appeared
in late 1920. As its name suggests, this group was composed almost entirely
of industrial workers. The Workers' Opposition condemned the power of the
bourgeois specialists, the introduction of one-man management in industrial
enterprises, and also Trotsky's appointment of trade-union leaders. The most
distinctive contribution of the Workers' Opposition was its advocacy of the
rapid transfer of the industrial management to the trade unions. Nationally,
this was to be exercised by a central organ elected by the unions grouped
according to branches of production; locally, enterprises were to be controlled
by elected workers' committees.[83]

The Workers' Opposition's views on bureaucracy were most clearly articulated by Aleksandra Kollontai in a pamphlet published in early 1921. According
to Kollontai, bureaucracy was a pervasive phenomenon in both the state and
party. In both cases the problem was the excessive centralisation of decision
making:

---

82   Daniels 1960, pp. 109–11, 114, 116; Schapiro 1977, pp. 223–4, 230; Service 1979, pp. 108, 130.
83   Daniels 1960, pp. 125–29, 133; Holmes 1990, pp. 5–7; Kollontai 1977, pp. 164–7, 176–89;
      Schapiro 1977, pp. 221–3, 284–6; Shliapnikov 2004.

The harm in bureaucracy does not only lie in the red tape...The harm lies in the solution of all problems, not by means of an open exchange of opinions or by the immediate efforts of all concerned, but by means of formal decisions handed down from the central institutions. These decisions are arrived at either by one person or by an extremely limited collective, wherein the interested people are quite often entirely absent. *Some third person decides your fate: this is the whole essence of bureaucracy.*[84]

For Kollontai, this hyper-centralism was one example of the deviations of Soviet policy from the 'class-consistent principles of the communist programme'.[85] She also singled out Trotsky as one of the most blatant of the 'defenders and knights of bureaucracy'.[86]

Kollontai attributed the growth of bureaucracy to bourgeois and petty-bourgeois influence in the state and party. This influence was exerted in two ways. First, the state and party had been forced to reconcile the often antagonistic interests of heterogeneous classes – the proletariat, the peasantry, the petty owners, and the bourgeoisie. In doing so, the Soviet leaders had adapted their policies to bourgeois and petty-bourgeois pressures and had begun to distance themselves from the proletariat.[87] Second, out of necessity the Soviet state been compelled to rely upon the skills of the specialists, and to incorporate these bourgeois and petty-bourgeois elements into state institutions. According to Kollontai, 'These are the elements that bring decay into our Soviet institutions, breeding there an atmosphere *altogether repugnant to the working class*'.[88]

For Kollontai, the elimination of the problem of bureaucracy had to begin in the party. 'As soon as the party...recognises the self-activity of the masses as the basis of our state', she predicted, 'the Soviet institutions will again automatically become living institutions, destined to carry out the communist project'.[89] To reform the party, the Workers' Opposition demanded the expulsion from the party of all non-proletarians who had joined after 1919, the elimination of all non-proletarian elements from party administrative positions, the

84   Kollontai 1977, pp. 191–2.
85   Kollontai 1977, p. 159.
86   Kollontai 1977, p. 190.
87   Kollontai 1977, pp. 159, 163, 166, 167, 169.
88   Kollontai 1977, p. 164.
89   Kollontai 1977, p. 192.

reinstitution of the elective principle for all posts, and the submission of all major policy questions to the rank and file.[90]

The Democratic Centralists and the Workers' Opposition participated in the winning of important reforms such as the reversal of the growing militarisation of labour and the measures adopted by the Ninth Party Conference and Tenth Party Congress for the democratisation of the party. However, like the Left Communists, they failed in their efforts to realise the traditional Marxist vision of a commune state. While both groups continued to be active into the mid-1920s, after the Tenth Party Congress they quickly declined in influence under the repression of the party leadership.[91]

Although the opposition groups within the party were quite vocal in their criticisms of bureaucracy, they were not alone in raising these concerns. During the years 1918–22 central party leaders such as Lenin and Trotsky also spoke out against the dangers of bureaucracy. Of the two, Lenin was in many ways closer to the views of the oppositionists.

2.3 Lenin on Political Alienation and Inefficiency

By the spring of 1918 Lenin had concluded that the danger of economic collapse and the difficulties of involving the masses in the administration of the state temporarily necessitated significant departures from the principles of the commune state. From that point until his death Lenin endorsed measures that were widely denounced by the party oppositions as 'bureaucratic': the employment of bourgeois specialists, the payment of salaries far exceeding workmen's wages, the introduction of economic and political centralism, and the use of economic and state coercion to increase labour productivity. Yet, during these years he also frequently expressed his concerns about the growth of the problem of bureaucracy. As early as April 1918 he noted the 'shadow of a possibility' of the 'bureaucratic distortion of the Soviet form of organisation'.[92] In the following years this shadow lengthened and deepened in Lenin's mind until it began to darken his entire outlook on the prospects for socialism in Soviet Russia.

Despite Lenin's profound differences with the party oppositionists, his concerns about the dangers of bureaucracy at times coincided to a considerable

---

90   Kollontai 1977, pp. 193–6.
91   On the repression of the Democratic Centralists and Workers' Opposition, see Daniels 1960, pp. 159–65; Schapiro 1977, pp. 325–37; Service 1979, pp. 163–5, 181–2.
92   Lenin 1960–70, vol. 27, pp. 274–5.

degree with theirs. Like the oppositionists, he feared that departures from the ideals expressed in *The State and Revolution* might ultimately subvert the Soviet state. Lenin, too, saw this problem as related to the steady influx of bourgeois elements into the state apparatus. Also, at times he deplored the bureaucratism displayed by other party leaders in advocating policies that he viewed as excessively centralist or authoritarian. In all of these cases he remained close to the primary meaning, and the traditional Marxist understanding, of bureaucracy. However, there were many other occasions when he utilised secondary meanings of the term when speaking of administrative inefficiency in the state and party apparatuses.

Often when Lenin spoke of bureaucracy and bureaucratism he had in mind the former tsarist officials and their attitudes. In early 1919 he warned that the struggle with bureaucracy was far from over, for the old tsarist bureaucracy was 'trying to regain some of its positions'.[93] Shortly after this, at the Eighth Party Congress, he elaborated:

> We dispersed these old bureaucrats, shuffled them and then began to place them in new posts. The tsarist bureaucrats began to join the Soviet institutions and practise their bureaucratic methods, they began to assume the colouring of Communists and, to succeed better in their careers, to procure membership cards of the Russian Communist Party. And so, they have been thrown out of the door but they creep back in through the window.[94]

The problem with the tsarist officials was that they were 'imbued with bourgeois views' and had retained their 'thoroughly bourgeois outlook'.[95] In part, this meant that they were exclusively concerned with their own narrow interests. Thus, on one occasion Lenin denounced those 'petty officials, petty bureaucrats accustomed to the old and selfish way of doing things'.[96] Beyond that, out of hostility to the workers and the goals of socialism, the old bureaucrats unconsciously subverted Soviet policy, or consciously engaged in sabotage. In November 1920 he spoke of the 'hundreds of thousands of old officials whom we got from the tsar and from bourgeois society and who, partly

---

93   Lenin 1960–70, vol. 29, p. 109.
94   Lenin 1960–70, vol. 29, pp. 182–3. See also Lenin 1960–70, vol. 29, p. 32; Lenin 1960–70, vol. 33, p. 428.
95   Lenin 1960–70, vol. 31, p. 421; Lenin 1960–70, vol. 29, p. 179.
96   Lenin 1960–70, vol. 31, p. 402.

deliberately and partly unwittingly, work against us'.[97] The greatest danger was that the tsarist officials would be able to redirect policy toward the restoration of capitalism. At the Eleventh Party Congress in 1922 Lenin suggested this was a real possibility:

> If we take Moscow with its 4,700 Communists in responsible positions, and if we take that huge bureaucratic machine, that gigantic heap, we must ask: who is directing whom? I doubt very much whether it can truthfully be said that the Communists are directing that heap. To tell the truth, they are not directing, they are being directed.[98]

Lenin also observed that the bureaucratising effect of the old officials was not confined to the state apparatus. In November 1920 he noted the growth of bureaucratic tendencies in the party as well, explaining,

> It is natural that the bureaucratism that has reappeared in Soviet institutions was bound to have a pernicious effect even on Party organisations, since the upper ranks of the Party are at the same time the upper ranks of the state apparatus ... Since the evil is the old bureaucratism which has been able to show itself in the Party apparatus, it is obvious and natural that all the symptoms of this evil are in the Party organisations and institutions.[99]

Similarly, at the Eleventh Party Congress Lenin asked whether the 4,700 Communists in responsible positions in Moscow had not 'come under the influence of an alien culture'.[100]

If the officials from the old regime were so unreliable, why had they been employed by the Soviet state? According to Lenin, this had been necessitated by the lack of effective participation by the masses in state administration. In late 1917 and early 1918 he blamed the low degree of involvement by the proletariat and poor peasantry on their lack of self-confidence.[101] By 1919 and 1920 he was concentrating on another factor: the lack of culture [*kulturnost'*] – that is, of literacy and the knowledge of basic organisational and office procedure –

---

97   Lenin 1960–70, vol. 33, pp. 428–9.
98   Lenin 1960–70, vol. 33, p. 288.
99   Lenin 1960–70, vol. 31, pp. 421–2; Lenin 1958–65, vol. 42, pp. 32–3 (translation modified). See also Lenin 1960–70, vol. 31, p. 435.
100   Lenin 1960–70, vol. 33, p. 288.
101   Lenin 1960–70, vol. 26, pp. 409, 469.

among the masses.[102] For Lenin, the absence of these skills prevented workers and peasants from getting involved in state administration, and lowered the effectiveness of those who did.

Once employed by the Soviet state, the tsarist bureaucrats had little trouble evading the control of their Communist bosses, for the culture of Communists was hardly higher than that of the masses. Lenin explained at the Eleventh Party Congress,

> Their [the old bureaucrats'] culture is miserable, insignificant, but it is still at a higher level than ours. Miserable and low as it is, it is higher than that of our responsible Communist administrators, for the latter lack administrative ability. Communists who are put at the head of departments... are often fooled.[103]

Yet, despite the risks in employing the tsarist officials, Lenin could not agree with the oppositionists that the use of specialists should be curtailed. With all their defects, the specialists were a resource that the Soviet government could not afford to waste. 'We cannot live without this apparatus', Lenin confessed at the Eighth Party Congress in March 1919; 'every branch of government creates a demand for such an apparatus'.[104] Instead, for the time being it was necessary to carefully supervise and control their activity. Just as the army had installed commissars to oversee the tsarist generals, so other state institutions needed to attach 'worker commissars' to its experts. In time, it could even be hoped that the specialists would be won over, or 'conquered *morally*'.[105]

Ultimately, however, Lenin's solution to the problem was to draw workers and peasants into the work of running the state in order to replace the bourgeois specialists. Again, at the Eighth Party Congress Lenin contended, 'We can fight bureaucracy to the bitter end, to a complete victory, only when the whole population participates in the work of government'.[106] Although Lenin ultimately concluded that it would take years for the masses to acquire the skills necessary to participate in state administration, he believed they could begin immediately to learn these skills by watching the work of the bourgeois

---

102   Lenin 1960–70, vol. 31, p. 421. See also, for example, Lenin 1960–70, vol. 29, pp. 109, 178–9, 184; Lenin 1960–70, vol. 33, pp. 395, 428, 488.
103   Lenin 1960–70, vol. 33, p. 288.
104   Lenin 1960–70, vol. 29, p. 182. See also Lenin 1960–70, vol. 29, pp. 178–9, 265.
105   Lenin 1960–70, vol. 29, pp. 179–80. See also Lenin 1960–70, vol. 29, pp. 33, 265; Lenin 1960–70, vol. 30, p. 351; Lenin 1960–70, vol. 33, p. 442.
106   Lenin 1960–70, vol. 29, p. 183. See also Lenin 1960–70, vol. 31, pp. 425–6.

specialists.[107] In January 1919 he argued, 'We must appoint more workers of average qualifications to the government offices, who would learn their jobs from the specialists and be able to replace them eventually and do the practical work independently'.[108] Thus, while Lenin saw the specialists as part of the bureaucratic problem, he believed that they could contribute to its solution.

From 1920 onward, Lenin believed that the masses could best be drawn into the administration of the state by participating in the work of the Commissariat of Workers' and Peasants' Inspection (Rabkrin). Rabkrin was formed in 1920 through the reorganisation of the Commissariat of State Control, and was specifically entrusted with the task of fighting bureaucracy in the state apparatus.[109] Soon, it replaced the soviets in Lenin's thinking as the institution most conducive to mass political participation. In January 1920 Lenin advised Stalin, the head of Rabkrin, that '*all* working people, both men and *particularly women*, should serve in the Workers' and Peasants' Inspection'.[110] In a speech delivered in November of that year he urged that 'hundreds of thousands and millions of working people should pass through the school of the Workers' and Peasants' Inspection and learn to administer the state (which was something nobody had taught us), so that they might replace hundreds of thousands of bourgeois bureaucrats'.[111] Other institutions through which Lenin hoped the masses would learn administrative skills were the trade unions and the producers' and consumers' cooperatives. He also expressed the hope that the expansion of the school system would create 'a large body of young people capable of thoroughly overhauling our state apparatus'.[112]

Meanwhile, Lenin proposed that bourgeois elements who had managed to worm their way into the party, and others infected with bourgeois attitudes, should be purged from the party. In 1919 he suggested an indirect 'purging' of the party by making 'steadily *increasing demands*' upon its members. One of these demands included 'subbotniks', or unpaid days of work. Faced with such demands, Communists who were not committed revolutionaries

---

107 For comments indicating that it would take a long time before workers and peasants could replace the specialists, see, for example, Lenin 1960–70, vol. 29, p. 183; Lenin 1960–70, vol. 33, p. 429.

108 Lenin 1960–70, vol. 28, p. 406. See also Lenin 1960–70, vol. 30, p. 351.

109 On the formation of Rabkrin, see Tucker 1973, pp 207–8; Rees 1987, pp. 12–24.

110 Lenin 1960–70, vol. 30, p. 300.

111 Lenin 1960–70, vol. 31, pp. 434–5. On Rabkrin, see also Lenin 1960–70, vol. 30, pp. 327–8, 351–3, 414–6; Lenin 1960–70, vol. 31, pp. 434–5; Lenin 1960–70, vol. 32, p. 191.

112 Lenin 1960–70, vol. 28, pp. 418–19, 428; Lenin 1960–70, vol. 30, pp. 328–9. Quotation from Lenin 1960–70, vol. 33, p. 429.

would leave the party of their own accord.[113] In 1921, Lenin recommended a more direct method of purging the party – the expulsion of 'those who have lost touch with the masses', and 'those who have "attached" themselves to us for selfish motives...those who have become "puffed-up commissars" and "bureaucrats"'.[114]

Although Lenin accepted the oppositionist view that the problem of bureaucracy was related to the use of the bourgeois specialists, he did not frequently agree with the oppositionist definition of the problem as one of excessive centralism or authoritarianism. However, on at least two occasions Lenin used the term *bureaucracy* in precisely this sense. In each case, the relevant policies had already provoked, or were threatening to provoke, popular discontent. Also, in each case Lenin concluded that centralism had outlived its usefulness or had gone too far.

This was the meaning behind Lenin's denunciation in late 1920 and early 1921 of Trotsky's trade-union policies as 'bureaucratic'. Lenin had endorsed Trotsky's 'shake up' of the rail union leadership earlier in the year as a necessary measure to revive transport. But with the growth of oppositionist and trade-union discontent, Lenin drew back from authoritarian measures while Trotsky pressed ahead.[115] Even then Lenin did not entirely reject the measures that Trotsky had employed as head of Tsektran. He explained that the problem was not that Tsektran had brought pressures to bear, but that it had indulged in pressures to excess, and had failed to switch to normal trade-union methods at the proper time.[116] Trotsky's persistence in the use of coercion now drew heavy fire from Lenin. He denounced Trotsky's 'shaking up' of the trade unions as 'irregularities and bureaucratic excesses', he characterised Trotsky's further proposals to reorganise the unions as a 'real bureaucratic approach', he predicted that workers would view Trotsky's scheme for replacing 'workers' democracy' with 'industrial democracy' as a 'bureaucratic set-up', and he derided Trotsky's pamphlet containing his trade-union proposals as nothing but 'bureaucratic projecteering'.[117]

Lenin believed that Trotsky's bureaucratic tendencies derived from his application of a military perspective to economic problems. Thus, he denounced the 'degeneration of centralism and militarized forms of work into bureaucratic practices, petty tyranny, red-tape'.[118] According to Lenin, there were two

113   Lenin 1960–70, vol. 29, p. 432.
114   Lenin 1960–70, vol. 33, pp. 39–40.
115   See Harding 1983, vol. 2, p. 259.
116   Lenin 1960–70, vol. 32, pp. 37, 56.
117   Lenin 1960–70, vol. 32, pp. 44, 41, 34, 30.
118   Lenin 1960–70, vol. 32, p. 45.

aspects of military experience: a 'positive side' consisting of 'heroism, zeal, etc.', and a 'negative side of the experience of the worst military types' which included 'red-tape and arrogance'. Trotsky's theses played up to the worst in military experience.[119] Because of 'excesses' such as those committed by Tsektran, Trotsky's characterisation of the Soviet Republic as simply a 'workers' state' was wrong. More precisely, it was 'a workers' state *with a bureaucratic twist to it*'. In light of this distortion, Lenin observed, 'We now have a state under which it is the business of the massively organised proletariat to defend itself'.[120] Although the dispute was resolved by the Tenth Party Congress, this episode continued to color Lenin's view of Trotsky. It was at least partly for this reason that Lenin referred in his 'Testament' to Trotsky's 'excessive preoccupation with the purely administrative side of the work'.[121] By that time, however, Lenin had begun to perceive Stalin as perhaps the most bureaucratic of the Soviet leaders.

The issue that evoked this characterisation was Stalin's handling of a dispute with the Georgian party leadership in late 1922. In September Lenin clashed with Stalin over a proposal for a new Soviet constitution to be adopted the following year. Stalin had pressed for the direct incorporation of the Ukraine, Byelorussia, Azerbaijan, Georgia, and Armenia into the Russian Republic as 'autonomous republics'. Concerned about the sensibilities of the traditionally oppressed nationalities, Lenin argued for the creation of a new, federalist structure. Although Lenin easily won this dispute, Stalin proceeded with other plans to incorporate Georgia, Armenia, and Azerbaijan into a Transcaucasian Federation – a proposal that was especially offensive to the leaders of the Georgian party. Near the end of November Lenin grew alarmed over reports of repression directed by Stalin and executed by Sergo Ordzhonikidze against the Georgian Central Committee. By the end of the year Lenin had come to fully endorse the Georgian position.[122]

At that point Lenin described the behavior of Stalin, Ordzhonikidze, and Feliks Dzerzhinskii – who headed an investigating commission that whitewashed the situation – as typically bureaucratic. Their centralist and authoritarian actions, Lenin observed, were characteristic of 'that really Russian man, the Great-Russian chauvinist, in substance a rascal and a tyrant, such as the typical Russian bureaucrat is'.[123] Lenin seems to have viewed this as a special

---

119   Lenin 1960–70, vol. 32, p. 37.

120   Lenin 1960–70, vol. 32, pp. 24–5.

121   Lenin 1960–70, vol. 36, p. 595.

122   For accounts of the 'Georgian affair', see Lewin 1970, pp. 43–103; Service 1995, pp. 274–82; Smith 1998.

123   Lenin 1960–70, vol. 36, p. 606.

problem in Stalin's case, given his enormous power as General Secretary. In his 'Testament' written at the end of December, Lenin remarked that he was 'not sure whether [Stalin] will always be capable of using that authority with sufficient caution'.[124] A few days later in notes on the Georgian situation, he criticised 'Stalin's haste and his infatuation with pure administration, together with his spite against the notorious "nationalist-socialism"', and he denounced Stalin as a 'Great-Russian bully'.[125]

Aside from supporting constitutional guarantees of the rights of the national republics, Lenin attempted to combat this bureaucratic authoritarianism through the demotion and exemplary punishment of those responsible for the repression of the Georgians. In an addendum to his 'Testament' Lenin urged that Stalin be replaced as General Secretary by someone 'more tolerant, more loyal, more polite, and more considerate to the comrades, less capricious, etc.'[126] Furthermore, Stalin and Dzerzhinskii were to be publicly condemned for their handling of the Georgian affair, and Ordzhonikidze was to be expelled from the party for at least two years.[127]

Like the oppositionists, then, when Lenin addressed the problem of bureaucracy after the revolution, he often spoke in terms of a classical Marxist account of political alienation – either referring to the excessively centralist and authoritarian policies of his comrades, or warning of the influence of exploitative classes over the Soviet state apparatus. However, these were not Lenin's only concerns. As head of state, he was more focused than the oppositionists on the possibility that, due to simple inefficiency and incompetence, the Soviet state would prove unable to cope with vital military, economic, and political tasks. This fear, too, was reflected in many of his comments on the problem of bureaucracy. Consistent with popular secondary understandings of the term, Lenin frequently employed bureaucracy as well as red tape when describing the inefficiency, waste, sluggishness, and excessive size of the state apparatus.

Lenin first attacked the inefficiency of the state apparatus as early as December 1918 at the Second Congress of Economic Councils. There, he angrily announced that he had received reports of warehouses filled with goods kept under lock and key while peasants clamoured for commodities. In an apparent swipe at party oppositionists, he explained that the origin of this 'red tape' was to be found in collegial management, and the consequent decline of

124   Lenin 1960–70, vol. 36, p. 595.
125   Lenin 1960–70, vol. 36, pp. 606, 608.
126   Lenin 1960–70, vol. 36, p. 596.
127   Lenin 1960–70, vol. 36, p. 610; Trotsky 1970c, p. 487.

individual responsibility.[128] A few weeks later he described the Soviet state as 'ground down by red tape'. Explicitly rejecting the accusations of opposition-ists that this was caused by excessive centralism, Lenin argued instead that it was 'because we have not got strict centralisation'.[129]

During the following years, Lenin waged a successful campaign to replace collegial administration with one-man management. However, the waste and inefficiency continued and even increased. At the beginning on March 1922 Lenin painted a bleak picture of the bureaucratic wasteland of the state apparatus:

> We have huge quantities of material, bulky works, that would cause the heart of the most methodical German scientist to rejoice; we have moun-tains of paper, and it would take Istpart [Commission for Collecting and Studying Materials on the History of the October Revolution and the History of the Russian Communist Party] fifty times fifty years to go through it all; but if you tried to find anything practical in a state trust, you would fail; and you would never know who was responsible for what. The practical fulfillment of decrees – of which we have more than enough ... is never checked. Are the orders of the responsible Communist officials carried out? Can they get this done? No.[130]

Later in the month, at the Eleventh Party Congress, Lenin continued his assault on bureaucratic inefficiency. There, he informed the delegates of a recent case in which a French capitalist wanted to sell the Soviet government a large sup-ply of badly needed canned meat. Because of the red tape of the Commissariat of Foreign Trade, the transaction was not completed for several weeks – and then only because of Lenin's initiative. Lenin summed it up as 'simply the usual inefficiency of the Russian intellectuals to get things done – inefficiency and slovenliness'.[131]

In the same report Lenin also noted the excessive size of the state appara-tus, 'that huge bureaucratic machine, that gigantic heap'.[132] Part of this prob-lem was reflected in the number of state commissions: there were 120 of these when, in Lenin's view, only sixteen were needed.[133] By November of 1922 Lenin

---

128 Lenin 1960–70, vol. 28, pp. 378–9.
129 Lenin 1960–70, vol. 28, pp. 405–6.
130 Lenin 1960–70, vol. 33, p. 224.
131 Lenin 1960–70, vol. 33, pp. 292–6.
132 Lenin 1960–70, vol. 33, p. 288.
133 Lenin 1960–70, vol. 33, p. 308.

was complaining that since 1918 the number of state officials just in Moscow had grown from 231,000 to 243,000, even after reductions, and he asserted the state apparatus was more than twice the necessary size.[134]

Lenin explained the growth of bureaucratic inefficiency primarily as a consequence of the incompetence of former underground revolutionaries as state administrators.[135] Again, what Communists lacked was 'culture'. This was, for example, the problem with the officials in the Commissariat of Foreign Trade who were incapable of purchasing canned meat from the French capitalist.[136] Lacking culture, Communist officials were constantly drawing up schemes, but were incapable of practical work.[137] Lenin complained that many Communists were of no use in combating red tape, and some were even a hindrance in this respect.[138] One consequence of this incompetence was that officials were afraid of taking responsibility for their work. In turn, this promoted the proliferation of commissions that could shelter bureaucrats, and it constantly led state bodies to refer petty administrative questions to the highest party institutions.[139]

Over the years Lenin suggested a number of measures to improve state efficiency. First, he advocated raising the level of individual and departmental responsibility – for example, through the use of individual instead of collegial management. Lenin emphasised the same principle in April 1922 in a recommendation concerning the responsibilities of the newly created Deputy Chairmen of Sovnarkom. The Deputy Chairmen were to 'demand more self-reliance and more responsibility from every Peoples' Commissar and every government department', and to see that the responsibilities of Soviet officials were precisely defined.[140] Second, he hoped to improve state administration through the appointment of competent Communists to responsible posts. In April 1922 Lenin proposed that the Deputy Chairmen supervise the placement of Communists in Soviet offices. They were to become acquainted with Soviet officials 'so as to test and choose men, and also to really improve the machinery of Soviet government'.[141] Furthermore, Lenin recommended that the Deputy Chairmen supervise the distribution of Communists to guarantee

134   Lenin 1960–70, vol. 33, p. 394.
135   Lenin 1960–70, vol. 33, p. 224.
136   Lenin 1960–70, vol. 33, p. 295.
137   Lenin 1960–70, vol. 33, p. 223.
138   Lenin 1960–70, vol. 33, pp. 75, 225.
139   Lenin 1960–70, vol. 33, pp. 306–8.
140   Lenin 1960–70, vol. 33, p. 336.
141   Ibid.

that they occupied posts in which they could 'combat bureaucracy and red tape' and improve the lot of citizens who had to deal with 'our utterly inefficient Soviet machinery of administration'.[142] Third, Lenin proposed punishing those who were guilty of inefficiency. For example, Lenin threatened jail for the officials involved in the canned meat affair, and he recommended the same treatment for other officials responsible for red tape.[143] He also urged the Deputy Chairmen to impose penalties for 'bureaucratic methods, red tape, inefficiency, neglect, etc.' These were to include dismissal and legal prosecution in widely publicised trials.[144] Fourth, Lenin believed that efficiency could be improved through proper supervision over the methods used in the state institutions. Again, the most important tool in this regard was the Workers' and Peasants' Inspectorate. Rabkrin's duties included studying the methods of 'a given office, factory, department, and so forth' and introducing practical changes.[145] Another form of guidance in administrative methods was the reorganisation of one or a few departments that could serve as models for the rest. In 1922 Lenin charged the Deputy Chairmen with this task.[146] Similarly, in early 1923 he suggested Rabkrin do the same, starting with the most poorly organised state institution – Rabkrin itself.[147] Finally, Lenin proposed to cut the number of government commissions severely, reduce the staffs of departments, and eliminate 'unproductive expenditure'. The sole exception to this last measure was to be the Commissariat of Education – perhaps partly because Lenin saw it as so important in fighting bureaucracy.[148]

2.4 Trotsky and Bureaucratic Inefficiency

Although Trotsky's later writings on bureaucracy have received significant attention, little has been written about his views on this question during the period 1917–22. In these years Trotsky, like other Bolsheviks, frequently raised concerns about the growth of bureaucracy in the Soviet state apparatus.

---

142 Lenin 1960–70, vol. 33, p. 338. For other comments on the need to put 'the right man in the right place', see Lenin 1960–70, vol. 33, pp. 300, 304; Lenin 1960–70, vol. 36, p. 566; Lenin 1960–70, vol. 45, p. 498.

143 Lenin 1960–70, vol. 33, pp. 295–6; Lenin 1960–70, vol. 36, p. 562.

144 Lenin 1960–70, vol. 33, p. 340.

145 Lenin 1960–70, vol. 33, p. 42.

146 Lenin 1960–70, vol. 33, p. 337.

147 Lenin 1960–70, vol. 33, p. 492.

148 Lenin 1960–70, vol. 33, pp. 307, 444, 463.

However, in contrast with party oppositionists and Lenin, in this period he did not address the problem of Soviet bureaucracy in terms of a Marxist analysis of political alienation. That is, he did not define it in terms of the tendency of a political apparatus to stand over and dominate society; nor did he see it as related to the influence of exploitative classes on the Soviet state. Rather, he identified the problem exclusively with the sources inefficiency of Soviet institutions. More specifically, he employed variations of the term *bureaucracy* in reference to three distinct though overlapping problems: he condemned as bureaucrats [*biurokraty*] officials who, out of self-interest, opposed the implementation of policies he viewed as efficient; he criticised as bureaucratism [*biurokratizm, kantseliarshchina*] or red tape [*volokita*] the inefficient work habits of officials; and most importantly, he denounced the bureaucracy [*biurokratiia*] embodied in the inefficient organisation of entire areas of work.

Disagreements within the party over the meaning of bureaucracy occasionally generated confusion when Trotsky, under attack for his 'bureaucratic'-authoritarian methods, responded by hurling the charge of 'bureaucracy' back at his critics. In fact, however, these semantic differences were a reflection of vastly different concerns. No doubt, Trotsky's almost exclusive preoccupation with efficiency in this period was largely a product of his responsibilities as head of the largest department of the Soviet apparatus, the War Commissariat.

2.4.1   *Bureaucratic Obstructionism*

On several occasions in the years immediately after the revolution, Trotsky – like the opposition groups and Lenin – utilised the term *bureaucracy* to characterise groups of officials who were distorting Soviet policy. However, in each case he explicitly rejected the view that the problem was one of excessive centralism or capitalist influence. Rather, Trotsky's concern was that the officials were obstructing the implementation of efficient policies. While he sometimes suggested that there was a class basis to the problem, he described this merely in terms of the 'petty-bourgeois' outlook that guided the actions of the bureaucrats.

Trotsky's first discussion of Soviet bureaucracy took place in late 1918 and early 1919, in reaction to the Military Opposition's resistance to the use of former tsarist officers in the Red Army.[149] In Trotsky's view such hostility to the specialists was irrational from a military point of view and could only be explained in terms of ignorance or concern for personal well being. In August 1918 he described one part of the Military Opposition as 'people infected with

---

149   See Deutscher 1954, pp. 427–8 for a brief discussion of Trotsky's remarks on the Military Opposition.

panic or those who are remote from the entire work of the military apparatus'.[150] However, the more important part of the opposition for Trotsky consisted of 'bureaucrats' [*biurokraty*] – party members assigned to military work who were mainly preoccupied with their own status and privileges. Clearly, by this Trotsky was referring to the military leadership in Tsaritsyn, supported by Stalin.

Trotsky's sharpest denunciation of this group appeared in a letter of 10 January 1919. There, he observed, 'Only a wretched Soviet bureaucrat [*biurokrat*], jealous for his new job, and cherishing this job because of the personal privileges it confers and not because of the interests of the workers' revolution, can have an attitude of baseless distrust towards any great expert, outstanding organiser, technician, specialist, or scientist – having already decided on his own account that "me and my mates will get by somehow"'.[151] Behind this preoccupation with narrow self interest, Trotsky perceived a worldview shaped by unspecified 'petty-bourgeois traditions and influences', as well as by the petty-bourgeois background of some officials:

> The heritage of the past, petty-bourgeois traditions and influences, and finally, just the demand of strained nerves for a rest, all do their work. In addition, there are fairly numerous representatives of the intelligentsia and semi-intelligentsia who have sincerely rallied to the cause of the working class but internally have not yet fused with it, and have retained many qualities and ways of thought which are characteristic of the petty-bourgeois milieu. These, the worst elements of the new regime, are striving to become crystallised as a Soviet bureaucracy [*biurokratiia*].[152]

Besides denouncing members of this bureaucracy as selfish, Trotsky also derided them as incompetent, self-satisfied, lazy, and conservative. For example, in August 1918 he ridiculed certain party military figures who 'are incapable of keeping an eye on anything, behave like satraps, spend their time doing nothing, and, when they meet with failure, shuffle off the blame on to the General Staff officers'.[153] On 10 January he elaborated:

150 Trotsky 1964–71, vol. 1, pp. 106–9.
151 Trotsky 1979–81, vol. 1, p. 223; Trotsky 1991a, vol. 1, p. 171. See also Trotsky 1979–81, vol. 1, pp. 201–2. For a description of the Military Opposition written by Trotsky years later, see Trotsky 1941, pp. 297–8.
152 Trotsky 1979–81, vol. 1, p. 222; Trotsky 1991a, vol. 1, pp. 170–1 (translation modified).
153 Trotsky 1964–71, vol. 1, pp. 108–9.

Our own bureaucracy [*biurokratiia*], ... is real historical ballast – already
conservative, sluggish, complacent, unwilling to learn and even expressing enmity to anyone who reminds it of the need to learn ... [This trend]
is nourished by the moods of limited, envious, complacent (and yet at
the same time unsure of itself) philistine-bureaucratic [*biurokraticheskii*]
conservatism ...[154]

Although Trotsky did not believe that these bureaucrats actually sought capitalist restoration, he was convinced that their oppositional activities were
increasing the likelihood of that outcome. Pioneering a theme later used
against Trotsky and his supporters, he condemned his critics as 'worse than
any saboteur', a 'genuine menace to the cause of communist revolution', and
'genuine accomplices of counter-revolution'.[155]

During the party controversies of 1920, Trotsky returned to the notion that
the problem of bureaucracy consisted of officials who opposed efficient policies out of self interest. As we have seen, in that year Trotsky was attacked for
'bureaucratic' authoritarianism for advocating one-man management and the
'shake up' of the trade unions. In both cases, he dismissed the accusation and
countercharged that it was his opponents who were the true bureaucrats.

Early in 1920 Bolshevik oppositionists and trade unionists joined the
Mensheviks in challenging attempts by Lenin and Trotsky to replace collegial management of enterprises with one-man management. *Edinonachalie*,
the critics claimed, was inherently bureaucratic in that it restricted the self-
activity of the proletariat. Trotsky responded by rejecting the view that the
supremacy of the proletariat was related to the form of industrial management, and by arguing for the greater efficiency of individual authority.[156] He
further observed that a large part of the opposition to one-man management
originated in the trade-union bureaucracy:

But the question of 'threes' and 'fives' [that is, the collegial boards] interests, not the laboring masses, but the more backward, weaker, less fit-
ted for independent work, section of the Soviet labor bureaucracy. The
foremost, intelligent, and determined administrator naturally strives to
take the factory into his hands as a whole, and to show both to himself
and to others that he can carry out his work. While if that administrator
is a weakling, who does not stand very steadily on his feet, he attempts

154   Trotsky 1979–81, vol. 1, pp. 223–4; Trotsky 1991a, vol. 1, pp. 171–2 (translation modified).
155   Trotsky 1979–81, vol. 1, p. 223; Trotsky 1964–71, vol. 1, pp. 108–9.
156   Trotsky 1972c, pp. 162–3.

to associate another with himself, for in the company of another his own
weakness will be unnoticed.[157]

No doubt, Trotsky's reference to the 'labor bureaucracy' was intended to con-
jure up associations with the conservative and self-seeking trade-union and
socialist bureaucracies of the advanced capitalist countries.[158]

Later in that year Trotsky defended himself once more against charges
of bureaucratism for his authoritarian methods in running Tsektran and his
threat to impose similar measures in other unions. While admitting there was
bureaucratism in Tsektran, Trotsky suggested it was less advanced there than
in unions that had not completed their economic tasks and, 'losing ground
under their feet become bureaucratized [*biurokratiruiutsia*]'.[159] Trotsky's
meaning was obscure, but he seems to have been saying that in such unions
the leadership simply gave up on fulfilling its productive responsibilities and
concentrated instead on defending its own narrow interests.

2.4.2   *Bureaucratic Work Habits, Attitudes, and Incompetence*
Another understanding of bureaucracy that appeared in Trotsky's statements
during the years 1919–22 involved the work habits, attitudes, and capabilities of
Soviet officials. Understood in this sense, bureaucracy referred to various secondary characteristics popularly associated with that term, including an excessive preoccupation with formalities and paperwork, an attitude of apathy and
indolence, and simple incompetence on the part of officials. Trotsky's remarks
in this regard were not always consistent or clear. Thus, at times he spoke as
if these were *defining* characteristics of bureaucracy or bureaucratism, and at
times as if they were *sources* of that problem. Also, while he sometimes *identified* these traits with bureaucracy, on a few occasions he *contrasted* them with
the 'good sides' of bureaucracy. However, in each case he blamed these characteristics for some of the inefficiency of state institutions.

On a number of occasions Trotsky sharply criticised the bureaucratic formalism and apathy that permeated the Soviet state apparatus. For example,

---

157   Trotsky 1972c, p. 164; Trotsky 1963c, p. 156.
158   Trotsky also may have had this analogy in mind in his response to the critics of his
       militarisation of labour in early 1920. Then, Communist oppositionists joined Mensheviks
       in denouncing Trotsky as 'the new Arakcheev' after the authoritarian Minister of War
       who had set up military farming colonies under Alexander I and Nicholas I. Trotsky
       characterised this as evidence of his critics' 'petty-bourgeois intelligentsia and trade-
       unionist prejudices' (Trotsky 1963d, p. 113).
159   Trotsky 1963d, p. 410.

during Kolchak's White offensive in April 1919, Trotsky complained that reinforcements were too slow in coming to the front, and in general the 'necessary effort is not observable in the tempo of work of Soviet institutions'.[160] Decisions, urgent measures, and the transmission of orders from one institution to another were frequently delayed, and the responsible local workers often failed to check on the fulfillment of decisions. Part of the problem for Trotsky was excessive formalism – the 'routine' and 'red tape' [*volokita*] that had 'accumulated already in our Soviet mechanism'.[161] At the same time he spoke of a 'new Soviet Oblomovism', suggesting that local Soviet officials were as slothful as the character Oblomov in Goncharov's novel. What was needed, in Trotsky's estimation, was greater effort on the part of provincial and *uezd* [county] soviet executive committees and party committees. Furthermore, he insisted that workers in the provinces who had 'become overgrown with the cobwebs of bureaucratism [*kantseliarshchina*] must be removed from their posts'.[162]

Trotsky observed an even more blatant example of passivity in local state institutions in June 1919. At Liski on the Southern Front, he encountered a trainload of wounded and sick Red Army soldiers who had not been fed during the entire twelve hours the train had been sitting in the station. He partially blamed the medical apparatus of the Southern Front, which had failed to notify the station about the train. Even more appalling for Trotsky was the failure of local authorities to respond to the situation: 'Can one conceive any worse example of obtuse heartlessness and shameless bureaucratism [*kantseliarshchina*], even in the foulest times of foul Tsardom!' Trotsky promised a thorough reorganisation of the army medical and communication apparatuses and a 'vigorous shake-up of local Soviet institutions that shut their eyes when, under their very noses, soldiers of the Red Army are suffering and dying'. This 'shake-up' was to be achieved through the exemplary punishment of apathetic officials: 'We must show in practice to idlers and saboteurs that an indifferent attitude to wounded and sick Red Army men will be punished by the Soviet Republic in the same way as treason to the socialist fatherland'.[163]

Trotsky's own economic work was disrupted by the bureaucratic apathy of local officials in February 1920. En route to the Urals to direct the organisation of the First Labour Army, his train buried itself in the snow and was partially derailed. For nineteen hours Trotsky fumed while the train lay helpless. Although he raged against 'sabotage and kulak-type self-seeking', it seems the

160   Trotsky 1979–81, vol. 2, p. 520.
161   Trotsky 1979–81, vol. 2, p. 521; Trotsky 1991a, vol. 2:1, p. 367.
162   Trotsky 1979–81, vol. 2, p. 528; Trotsky 1991a, vol. 2:1, p. 374.
163   Trotsky 1979–81, vol. 2, p. 299; Trotsky 1991a, vol. 2:1 pp. 204–5.

real problem was a pattern of negligence.[164] Local soviets had sent an inadequate number of men to clear the tracks after a major snow storm; then,
on the night of the accident the local railway administration had failed to
warn Trotsky's train about the drifts. After the accident, it took ten hours for
a work team to arrive and more than fifteen hours for a representative from
the next station to show up, while some local railway officials failed to appear
at all. Subsequently, the head of the Transport Cheka at Sasova, attempting to cover for the local officials, did nothing but summon the head of the
sector and the senior track foreman to 'present a report on the snowdrifts'.[165]
Trotsky denounced both the negligence of the local officials and the formalist
response of the Cheka as examples of bureaucratism. In the end, 'the bureaucrat [biurokrat] from the Cheka took the transport bureaucrats away from their
work in order to submit a useless bureaucratic [biurokraticheskii] report'. In
this case Trotsky's solution was to place 59 kilometers of the rail line under
martial law and to threaten those responsible with the 'maximum punishment' at the hands of a Revolutionary Military Tribunal.[166]

By the end of 1920 and early 1921 Trotsky began to focus upon yet another
concern related to bureaucracy: the woeful ignorance of Soviet officials regarding the most efficient methods of organising work. At first he characterised
this as an example of their failure to master the 'good sides' of bureaucracy.
However, by the beginning of 1921 he was including ignorance of organisational technique as a major source of red tape.

Trotsky first raised this issue at the height of the trade-union controversy
in late 1920. At that point he was confronted with accusations of bureaucratism for his attempt to 'shake up' the trade unions and fuse them with
state institutions. In an article in December Trotsky evaded the accusation
by redefining bureaucracy, this time filling it with a *positive* content. To the
extent he had been responsible for the bureaucratisation of the trade unions,
he asserted, this was not a reproach. In almost Weberian terms Trotsky now
defined bureaucracy [biurokratiia] as an *efficient* system of administration
which included such positive qualities as 'a more special acquaintance with
particular branches of administration and the economy, a precise hierarchy
of interrelationships, definite methods of work elaborated by long practice,
etc.'[167] Similarly, in a speech delivered to the expanded plenum of Tsektran
in December, his list of the 'good sides' of bureaucracy included methods of

164   Trotsky 1979–81, vol. 3, p. 74.
165   Trotsky 1979–81, vol. 3, p. 76.
166   Trotsky 1979–81, vol. 3, pp. 75–7; Trotsky 1991a, vol. 2:2, pp. 52–4.
167   Trotsky 1963d, p. 218.

work developed by 'German and American bureaucracy [*biurokratiia*]', such as
'rationalization, Taylorism, distribution, forms of responsibility, supply, plan,
bookkeeping, etc.'[168] Bureaucratism in this sense was not an invention of tsarism, but 'an epoch in the growth of humanity, when humanity passes from the
medieval mist to the bourgeois order and creates certain skills and methods of
administration, creates good and more precise offices with good typewriters . . .
along with correct bookkeeping and management'. These were skills the Soviet
state needed to acquire, Trotsky warned, if it did not want ' "to become lice
ridden" ' and 'retire from the scene'.[169]

Trotsky never again spoke in such glowing terms about bureaucracy –
perhaps because it was too risky to employ this rhetorical device when so
many comrades were already complaining about his bureaucratic proclivi-
ties. Nevertheless, he continued to berate the incompetence of Soviet officials, along with their apathy, as *manifestations* of bureaucratism. In a speech
delivered in January 1921 Trotsky asserted that red tape in the Soviet apparatus
was at least three-fourths a product of low culture and poverty. This clumsi-
ness and red tape [*volokitnost'*], he argued, could only be overcome 'by raising the quality of work, the accumulation of material wealth, and the raising
of culture'.[170] Consequently, he called for a 'struggle against bureaucratism
[*biurokratizm*], which now means struggle against laxity, ignorance, and slack-
ness in all spheres of our life'.[171]

Along these lines, in the fall of 1921 Trotsky launched a campaign to raise
the level of culture in the Red Army. There, the task was to instil discipline in
the fresh recruits who had replaced the demobilised veterans of the civil war.
Trotsky repeatedly attempted to inspire his troops in the mundane tasks of
greasing their boots and cleaning their rifles, while chastising them for spitting
and dropping cigarette butts in the barracks.[172] Predictably, the campaign elicited complaints about his nagging over 'trifles', and about his 'bureaucratism'.
Just as predictably, Trotsky responded by redirecting the charge back at his
critics, implying that *they* were the ones guilty of a bureaucratism that combined formalism, laziness, and ignorance. 'The slovens and sluggards', he complained, loved 'to hide themselves behind the struggle against bureaucratism',
but they failed to understand the term's true meaning:

---

168   Trotsky 1963d, pp. 419–20.
169   Trotsky 1963d, p. 420.
170   Trotsky 1963d, p. 233.
171   Trotsky 1979–81, vol. 4, p. 13; Trotsky 1963d, p. 248.
172   See Trotsky 1979–81, vol. 4, pp. 22–5, 32–3, 74–81, 84–106.

Bureaucratism [*biurokratizm*] means attention to empty form at the expense of content, of the matter actually in hand. Bureaucratism wallows in formalities, in nonsensicalities, but does not concern itself at all with businesslike details. On the contrary, bureaucratism usually sidesteps the practical details of which the matter itself is composed, being concerned merely to ensure that everything adds up on paper.[173]

2.4.3 Glavkokratiia

Although Trotsky denounced bureaucrats who opposed efficient policies out of self interest, and condemned bureaucratic inefficiency in the defective characteristics of state officials, the most important notion of bureaucracy for Trotsky during these years involved another concern – the inefficiency that he believed was built into the very structure of Soviet military, political, and, especially, economic institutions. In particular, he criticised the excessive centralism of these institutions as well as the inadequate coordination between them. From late 1919 through 1922 Trotsky wrote more extensively and coherently about this form of bureaucracy than any other.

In the spring of 1919 Trotsky first began to denounce the bureaucratism inherent in the inadequate coordination of local soviet institutions. During the Kolchak offensive in April, he complained that reinforcements were slow in arriving at the front because of delays in the supply of uniforms at the local level. The problem was not that there were no uniforms available; rather,

Local Soviet institutions work, as often as not, in isolation from each other. Uniforms held by the National Economic Council or by the supply committee [of the local soviet] are not available when required by the military commissariat of the province or the *uyezd*.[174]

At the time, he simply urged that it was 'necessary to finish decisively with red tape [*volokita*] and disparity between departments, in every *uyezd* and provincial town'.[175]

However, supply problems continued to plague the Red Army. In July Trotsky asserted that deficiencies in supply were largely responsible for recent military setbacks. 'We must eliminate, at all costs, the criminal red tape [*volokita*] of the army supply organs and the barren bureaucratism [*kantseliarshchina*] which has succeeded the chaos which previously prevailed, not replacing but merely

---

173   Trotsky 1979–81, vol. 4, pp. 23–4; Trotsky 1991a, vol. 3:1, p. 16.

174   Trotsky 1979–81, vol. 2, p. 513.

175   Trotsky 1979–81, vol. 2, p. 514; Trotsky 1991a, vol. 2:1, p. 363.

supplementing it', he insisted. Trotsky explained that, given the slowness of Soviet rail transport and the mobile character of the war, the supply service was too centralised. By the time requisition orders reached the supply organs of the front and the supplies were dispatched, the units that requested them had been dissolved or transferred. 'As a result', he observed, 'the boot never reaches the soldier's foot'. To eliminate the problem, he proposed to decentralise supply distribution, shifting the responsibility from organs of an entire front to those of individual armies and to supply chiefs on each supply train.[176]

By the end of the year, Trotsky's responsibilities as War Commissar had led him to examine similar problems of inefficiency in war-related production. There, he again discovered a pattern of excessive centralism and inadequate local coordination. At the Seventh Congress of Soviets in December and at a meeting of the Moscow party committee in January, he reported that frequently one institution in a province would have cloth; a second, thread and buttons; and a third, spare sewing shop workers. Yet in the same province there were soldiers who were inadequately clothed. The problem was that the transfer of materials had to be approved by the centre, and orders from the centre did not always correspond to the local situation. To have overcoats sewn, the centre would sometimes instruct that cloth be shipped from one province that had buttons to another that had none.[177] In the previous year, Trotsky reported to the Moscow party committee, he had sent hundreds of telegrams protesting against such 'superfluous centralism' to VSNKh.[178]

As Trotsky shifted his attention from specifically military concerns to broader economic questions, he immediately perceived similar problems in all branches of the economy. At a meeting of the party fraction of the Central Council of Trade Unions in January 1920 Trotsky related the findings of the Moscow provincial economic council. In Moscow one local factory was inactive for over two months while it waited for the replacement of a driving belt, another had to shut down several times because it had run out of canvas, and a third could not produce silicate brick because it had failed to receive an armature for its steam engine. In each case the necessary parts and materials were available locally, but the existing regulations did not permit them to be transferred to the factory in need.[179] The following month Trotsky witnessed comparable problems in the distribution of grain in the Urals. There he saw workers eating oats or starving, while in other areas the horses were eating

---

176   Trotsky 1979–81, vol. 2, pp. 70–3; Trotsky 1991a, vol. 2:1, pp. 54–5 (translation modified).
177   Trotsky 1963d, pp. 96–7.
178   Trotsky 1963d, p. 97.
179   Trotsky 1963d, p. 39.

wheat or supplies were rotting. The problem was that the provincial supply committees were not allowed to transfer wheat from one province to another, but were required to send all grain west of the Urals from which it was to be centrally redistributed. However, rail transport had broken down to such an extent that grain could not be shipped. 'One cannot imagine greater idiocy passing under the name of centralism', Trotsky complained. 'A stop must be put to this monstrous bureaucratism [*biurokratizm*]'.[180]

Summarising the problem before the Ninth Party Congress at the end of March 1920, Trotsky argued that 'the question of red tape [*volokita*] and bureaucratism [*biurokratizm*] in the sphere of our economy is not at all reducible to a struggle with isolated bureaucrats [*biurokraty*], with the bureaucratic [*biurokraticheskii*] practices of some specialists, etc'. Although this notion was 'fairly widely held', it was 'extremely superficial'. Rather, bureaucratism and red tape were based 'in the very structure of our economic institutions'.[181] At the time, fifty or so *glavki* and *tsentry* under VSNKh dominated all industrial production and distribution.[182] Each *glavk* controlled a separate branch of industry down to the level of the enterprise. The problem, as Trotsky saw it, was the rigid central control exercised by the *glavki* over the various industrial trusts and local enterprises, combined with an inadequate degree of coordination between separate *glavki*, trusts, and enterprises. Since 1918 the Democratic Centralists had denounced the excessively centralist control of local industry by the *glavki*, calling the system '*glavkism*'. Now, Trotsky renamed it '*glavkokratiia*', defining it as 'the rule of separate, vertically centralized *glavki*, which are not linked organizationally and which are badly coordinated in their work'.[183]

For Trotsky, the lack of coordination was evident from the foundations of industry all the way to the summit. At the Ninth Party Congress Trotsky complained that at the local level there were 'no cross-sectional connections, no canals which would combine the trusts or the enterprises of the various trusts with one another'.[184] Regarding the summit, he noted in an article written in December 1920 that, although VSNKh had been established to direct the

---

180 Trotsky 1964–71, vol. 2, pp. 56–7, 46–7 (translation modified). See also Trotsky 1963d, pp. 148–9.

181 Trotsky 1963d, pp. 146–7.

182 See Remington 1984, p. 68; Carr 1950–3, vol. 2, p. 182.

183 Trotsky 1963d, p. 217. Trotsky's first use of *glavkokratiia* appears to have been in a conversation of 23 March 1920 (Trotsky 1963d, p. 337). In a speech of 2 December 1920 he took credit for coining the term (Trotsky 1963d, p. 415). For another discussion of Trotsky's views on *glavkokratiia*, see Lih 2007, pp. 129–32. For Democratic Centralist criticisms of 'glavism', see Carr 1950–3, vol. 2, pp. 183–4; Malle 1985, p. 225; Remington 1984, pp. 70–2.

184 Trotsky 1963d, p. 147.

economy in accordance with a single plan, this goal had never been realised. Instead, VSNKh had become, in effect, just one more commissariat – the 'People's Commissariat of Industry' – among many, and had even failed to establish coordination between the *glavki* under its direction: 'Even within the Supreme Council of the National Economy…the separate branches of the economy (fuel, metal, textile production, etc.) developed into independent, centralized *glavki*, the coordination of whose work is still, to a significant degree, a task of the future'.[185]

According to Trotsky, this system had created a host of difficulties, especially for local institutions. In December 1920 he argued that whenever a local organ wanted to get any practical results out of a decree, it had to 'climb up to the summit of a *glavk*, descend, climb again to the summit of another *glavk*, and so on without end'. The local institution was confronted with a choice: it could either wander through the maze of red tape in an attempt to fulfill decrees, or it could 'break the front of red tape [*volokita*]' by the 'violation or circumvention of decrees'.[186] The ultimate result was the disruption of industrial production, especially that which was locally based. In a speech at an all-city party conference in Moscow at end of March 1920, Trotsky asserted, 'At the present time *glavkokratiia* prevents economic growth in the local areas: the programs of the center are fulfilled poorly, in dimensions of three or five percent'.[187]

In various statements Trotsky indicated that numerous factors had contributed to the formation of the system of *glavkokratiia*. Originally, it had arisen as a necessary and healthy reaction against the extreme decentralisation of the first period of Soviet power. However, mistakes had been made because there had been no historical precedent to serve as a guide. Also, the vastness of the country, the ruined state of the economy inherited form the old regime, and the devastation of the civil war had greatly complicated the task of planning.[188] Thus, Trotsky concluded in December 1920, *glavkokratiia* had been 'a transitional moment in the construction of a socialist economy', but now it was 'a transitional form which it is necessary to get over'.[189]

Clearly, Trotsky's analysis of bureaucracy differed substantially from Lenin's, both in his exclusive preoccupation with the problem of inefficiency and in his focus on the structural inadequacies of the Soviet economy. Consequently, it is not surprising that Trotsky also rejected Lenin's panacea for bureaucracy – the

---

185   Trotsky 1963d, pp. 217–18.
186   Trotsky 1963d, pp. 221–2.
187   Trotsky 1963d, p. 105.
188   Trotsky 1963d, pp. 105, 118, 215–17, 218, 416–17.
189   Trotsky 1963d, pp. 416, 417.

Workers' and Peasants' Inspectorate. In part, Rabkrin had been set up to institute control over the tsarist experts. To the extent that this was Rabkrin's purpose, Trotsky argued in December 1920, it was irrelevant to the struggle against
bureaucracy:

> If the problem were conscious criminality or vices brought in from the
> outside, the Workers' and Peasants' Inspectorate could, probably, fulfill
> its designated task. But the methods of the Inspectorate have turned out
> to be invalid precisely because the problem is not at all one of exposing
> and abolishing, but of establishing a correct and coordinated economic
> organization on new bases.[190]

That is, for Trotsky the real struggle involved introducing greater efficiency into
Soviet economic organs. To the extent that this was the goal of Rabkrin, it was
at least on the right track. But in this case, its methods were faulty: 'It is impossible to create a separate department which would combine in itself . . . all the
state wisdom and would actually be able to check on the work of the other
departments, not only from the point of view of the honesty and efficiency
of their work, but also from the point of view of the expediency and correctness of the organization of the work as a whole'.[191] In fact, Trotsky claimed, the
departments saw Rabkrin as less than useless, for Rabkrin itself was a source of
red tape [*volokita*] and arbitrariness.[192]

   Trotsky's own solution to the problem was to begin to restructure the entire
Soviet economy from the enterprises to the summit. What was needed first of
all was a degree of economic decentralisation. Thus, at the Seventh Congress
of Soviets in December 1919, and again at the Eighth in December 1920,
Trotsky supported the slogan of 'powers in the local areas'.[193] Specifically, he
advocated granting greater autonomy to individual enterprises and local economic organs with regard to the exchange of local resources and products. He
asserted in March 1920 that, although it was necessary to preserve and develop
vertical centralism in the *glavki*, this had to be combined with 'the horizontal
coordination of enterprises along the lines of the economic *raiony* [districts],
where the enterprises of the various departments of industry and of diverse
economic significance are compelled to live on the same sources of local raw

---

190   Trotsky 1963d, p. 222.
191   Trotsky 1963d, pp. 222–3. See also Trotsky 1963d, p. 412; Rees 1987, pp. 29–30.
192   Trotsky 1963d, pp. 223–4.
193   Trotsky 1963d, p. 225.

materials, means of transport, labor power, etc'.[194] In line with this, in January 1920 he supported a proposal that would allow nationalised enterprises to supply requests from other institutions in the same locality when these were approved by a *gubsovnarkhoz* (provincial council of the national economy).[195]

Simultaneously, Trotsky fought for the creation of new institutions to coordinate regional resources. In December 1919, Trotsky proposed the organisation of labour armies along the lines of 'territorial and production districts' in his original plan for the militarisation of labour. He envisioned that these labour armies would be able to assist the revival of local economic centres by helping to coordinate the local exchange of resources.[196] By the following March he was able to report to the party congress that, wherever labour armies had been established, regional economic centres had crystallised around them. Each of these, he argued, could unite representatives of local economic institutions with those of the centre and take upon itself the tasks of transferring raw materials, labour power, etc. within a region.[197]

Finally, Trotsky urged greater coordination of the *glavki* and economic commissariats from the top. He anticipated that ultimately this would occur through a single economic plan that would replace *glavkokratiia* with 'authentic socialist centralism'.[198] At the Eighth Congress of Soviets in December 1920 he suggested that the recent creation of various interdepartmental economic organs was a step in this direction.[199] The next step, he argued, would be to hand over the task of coordinating all economic departments to one institution. VSNKh had proven incapable of playing this role. Now it was necessary to try again, entrusting the job to the Council of Labour and Defense, a body created to coordinate resources for the war effort.[200]

In early 1921 Trotsky had cause to celebrate his successes in the struggle against *glavkokratiia*.[201] The Eighth Congress of Soviets had just endorsed his call for both greater local economic autonomy and a single economic plan, and had assigned the task of working out such a plan as well as the coordination of the work of the economic commissariats to the Council of Labour and

---

194   Trotsky 1963d, p. 119. See also Trotsky 1963d, pp. 151, 226, 243.

195   Trotsky 1963d, p. 39.

196   Trotsky 1979–81, vol. 3, pp. 48–9.

197   Trotsky 1963d, pp. 151–2, 119.

198   Trotsky 1963d, pp. 40, 151.

199   Trotsky 1963d, pp. 220–1, 239–40.

200   Trotsky 1963d, pp. 227–8.

201   See Trotsky's 4 January report on the Eighth Congress of Soviets, Trotsky 1963d, pp. 232–48, especially p. 235.

Defense.[202] In February, Sovnarkom decided to create a 'state general planning commission' (Gosplan) attached to the Council of Labour and Defense – a decision that was fulfilled on 1 April.[203] However, Trotsky soon discovered that the struggle was far from over. While he had won significant reforms within the context of war communism, in the following months this entire system was scrapped with the introduction of the New Economic Policy.

Trotsky watched the unfolding of NEP with mixed emotions. On one hand, he welcomed the fact that NEP had dealt a serious blow to the hyper-centralism of war communism. A series of measures adopted during 1921 released industry completely from the grip of the *glavki*: the growth of small and medium-scale private and cooperative enterprises was permitted, industrial enterprises administered by the state were grouped into new 'unions' or 'trusts' with the right to buy and sell on the open market without interference from the centre, and the *glavki* themselves were abolished.[204] In an address to the Fourth Congress of the Comintern in November 1922 Trotsky praised this NEPist reversal of the 'policy of a centralized bureaucratic [*biurokraticheskii*] management of industry'.[205] On the other hand, he was increasingly concerned about the simultaneous retreat from economic planning.[206] Although in his speech to the Fourth World Congress of the Comintern he argued that NEP was one of the 'transitional stages' between capitalism and 'complete socialism, with its socially planned economy', he had already begun to criticise the slow pace of that transition.[207]

Trotsky no longer used the term *glavkokratiia*, but he continued and intensified his struggle against the bureaucratic inefficiency that he saw as arising from the lack of planning and central coordination. As early as 3 May 1921, just one month after the establishment of Gosplan, he complained to Lenin, 'Unfortunately, our work is being done as hitherto without any plan and without any understanding of the need for one, and the planning commission is more or less a planned negation of the need for a practical business-like economic plan for the near future'.[208] He returned to this theme in a letter to the Central Committee on 7 August 1921 in which he pointed out that NEP had already evoked 'practical muddle and ideological confusion' because of the unsystematic

202   Chernenko and Smirtiukov 1967–88, vol. 1, pp. 192–3.
203   Carr 1950–3, vol. 2, p. 373; Deutscher 1959, p. 41.
204   Dobb 1966, pp. 131–2; Nove 1976, pp. 87–8; Carr 1950–3, vol. 2, pp. 296–306.
205   Trotsky 1972d, p. 230; Trotsky 1963c, p. 311.
206   For a discussion of this retreat, see Carr 1950–3, vol. 2, pp. 374–7.
207   Trotsky 1972d, p. 233.
208   Trotsky 1964–71, vol. 2, pp. 450–1.

way it was being introduced. Again, the problem was that there was no centre that could direct the economy. He reminded the Central Committee that under war communism, 'The constant clashes between economic, trade union, and Party organs, especially over the matter of individual appointments and transfers, were capable of ruining the most thriving industry'. Now the problem was compounded by the fact that three-fourths of the business of administrating the economy consisted of selecting and teaming officials – a task requiring some 'community of purpose' in administration. Furthermore, Trotsky anticipated that new conflicts would emerge under NEP between state enterprises, enterprises under contractual obligation to the state, and enterprises leased to private capital. Without an authoritative economic centre, he predicted, the relationship between these enterprises and state institutions (especially Rabkrin) would 'inevitably become a new source of red tape [*volokita*], carping and abuse'.[209]

Although he continued to recommend 'a degree of decentralization, transferring the initiative and the responsibility to the institution on the spot', this was already a lesser concern. With greater emphasis Trotsky argued again for the intervention of a single economic centre 'to ensure that *the central economic apparatus does function in such a way as to ensure the genuine and uninterrupted regulation of economic life by actively eliminating bureaucratic* [biurokraticheskii] *hindrances and assisting in the establishment of straightforward relationships between interdependent organs and establishments*'. He now believed that, given its planning responsibilities, the newly created Gosplan was best suited to play this role. However, for it to do so Gosplan would have to be totally reorganised in its composition, redirected from theoretical to practical methods of work, and guided by the needs of large-scale industry.[210]

2.4.4   *Party Bureaucratism and Glavkokratic Inefficiency*

In December 1921 and through the following year Trotsky began to address a new concern: the issue of bureaucratism in the party. In some of his statements there were also indications that he was beginning to perceive the problem of bureaucracy as one of political alienation. However, his brief remarks on this subject only hinted at themes that would later figure prominently in his analysis. For the time being, the focus of Trotsky's remarks regarding bureaucracy remained concentrated upon the issue of glavkokratic inefficiency. In fact, it was this concern that was largely responsible for bringing Trotsky into an alliance with Lenin in late 1922.

---

209   Trotsky 1964–71, vol. 2, pp. 578–83.
210   Ibid.

It seems that the first statement in which Trotsky alluded to the problem of party bureaucracy was in a note to Lenin of 21 December 1921. Two days before, Lenin had solicited reactions from the Politburo to a proposal to restrict admissions to the party in the wake of a recent purge of 'unsuitable elements'. Specifically, Lenin supported a draft resolution that would have instituted a probationary period of a year and a half for workers and three years for everyone else.[211] In his response, Trotsky raised 'big hesitations' about the plan: 'While keeping the inevitable tendency to charge party members with any important and semi-important posts', he observed, 'we will get a closed party of administrators'. For Trotsky, this meant 'a party of those who enjoy privileges'. Consequently, he urged the Politburo to make it as easy as possible for real industrial workers to join the party, reducing their provisional membership to a half year.[212] Lenin immediately acceded to Trotsky's recommendation.[213]

This note contains seeds would later emerge as prominent themes in Trotsky's analysis of political alienation within the party. These include Trotsky's vague reference to 'administrative' characteristics in the party – evocative of hierarchy and overspecialisation, his observation that administrative authority was becoming associated with privilege, and his suggestion that the best way to combat these developments was by increasing the party's proletarian composition. At this point these were only undeveloped anticipations of his later thinking. However, one idea here that Trotsky continued to raise in 1922 was the notion that involvement in state administration was having a negative impact upon the party.

Trotsky returned to the issue of party-state relations at the Eleventh Party Congress in March 1922. In his political report to the congress, Lenin sharply criticised the tendency of high state officials to drag even minor problems before the Politburo or the Central Committee of the party.[214] This was a theme Trotsky could readily endorse, for it seems to have been inspired by a memorandum he had written to the Politburo earlier in the month.[215] In the Congress discussion, Trotsky elaborated on Lenin's point, observing that the practice criticised by Lenin occurred at the local level as well as the summit.

---

211 Lenin 1960–70, vol. 33, p. 138; also reproduced in Trotsky 1964–71, vol. 2, pp. 648–51.

212 Quoted in Pantsov 2000, pp. 20–1.

213 Lenin 1960–70, vol. 42, pp. 369–70. See also Lenin 1960–70, vol. 33, pp. 254–5.

214 Lenin 1960–70, vol. 33, p. 307.

215 For this memorandum, see Pipes 1996, pp. 148–9. For evidence that Lenin was influenced by Trotsky on this question, see Lenin 1960–70, vol. 45, pp. 517, 730n627; and Rigby 1979, p. 208. In contrast, Pipes 1996, p. 148 claims that 'Lenin dismissed [Trotsky's proposal] without discussion'. See also van Ree 2001, p. 91.

The problem, Trotsky argued, was that it was commonly believed that any complex state question suddenly became simple when it was introduced into a party committee:

> It is believed that the same economist who could not cope with his economic work when he was in charge of a provincial economic council is anointed with grace when he is appointed gubkom secretary. Precisely by force of such 'anointment' he decides, without hesitation, all economic, military, administrative, and all other questions.[216]

One consequence of referring such questions to party committees was that state institutions lost all sense of responsibility. Even more important was the effect this had on the party apparatus: 'That which is the worst in bureaucratism [*biurokratizm*], that is, a relationship to matters without knowledge of the essence of things, but an approach only from the point of view of the forms of things, inevitably infiltrates into the party apparatus'.[217] Here, Trotsky was addressing the old issue of bureaucratic formalism – though he now saw this as a concern in the party as well as the state. Finally, he hinted at an idea that he would develop more fully the following year – that through its preoccupation with details, the party risked losing its revolutionary perspective: 'I repeat that, given such a summary resolution of all questions, not principled, but routine and practical, bureaucratism inevitably takes over party apparatuses'.[218]

Although it has been suggested that in these remarks Trotsky was raising obliquely the question of party democracy, this reads too much of Trotsky's later position into his comments.[219] Rather, the fundamental question for Trotsky was still the need for centralised coordination of the economy. In the absence of economic leadership by an authoritative state body, economic questions were resolved on an ad hoc basis by party committees. Later, in a letter to the Politburo on 15 January 1923, he would explicitly attribute the constant referral of questions to the Secretariat, Orgburo, and Politburo to the lack of a real planning and coordinating body for the economy.[220] However,

216 RKP(b) 1961, p. 133.

217 Ibid. Similarly, in his military report to the Eleventh Party Congress, Trotsky defined bureaucratism as 'an approach which is not practical and concrete but formal: dealing not with the substance of a matter but with circulars and bits of paper' (Trotsky 1979–81, vol. 4, p. 183).

218 RKP(b) 1961, pp. 133–4.

219 Hough and Fainsod 1979, p. 121.

220 Trotsky 1964–71, vol. 2, pp. 816–17.

having been rebuffed by the Central Committee in August 1921 in his attempt to have coordinating powers assigned to Gosplan, he evidently felt constrained to confine himself at the Eleventh Party Congress to mere allusions to this issue.

Nevertheless, Trotsky raised this question again shortly afterwards. A few weeks after the congress, Lenin circulated to the Politburo his proposal to create two Deputy Chairmen of Sovnarkom to combat state bureaucratism. Trotsky's response was quite critical. First, he predicted that the selection of two Deputy Chairmen would only generate new difficulties. Furthermore, he argued that Lenin's proposal did nothing to address inefficiency rooted in the structure of the Soviet economy, and in some ways even compounded it. 'The main thing', Trotsky complained, 'is that I still cannot envision the sort of organ, which will in practice be able to control economic work on a day-to-day basis'. Again, he argued that, while Gosplan outwardly approximated such an organ, in practice it had become simply an 'academic institution'. Meanwhile, controversies that continually erupted between state economic departments were referred to the Council of Labour and Defense or the Politburo, and were 'resolved by rule of thumb ... when the water is reaching our throats'.[221] One of the tasks envisioned for the Deputies in Lenin's proposal was the 'reduction of the establishment of Soviet institutions'. But in Trotsky's view, the tendency to create new bodies was due to the absence of a real planning and coordinating organ. Without a 'forward-looking, controlling economic organ', the CC had been forced to set up 'an economic commission, a budgetary commission, a gold commission, and so on and so forth'.[222]

Trotsky was equally critical of the role Lenin's plan envisioned for Rabkrin. Lenin had proposed that the Deputy Chairmen would utilise Rabkrin to combat inefficiency in the work habits of state officials. Reiterating his own 1920 critique of Rabkrin, Trotsky contended that the attempt to introduce better methods by means of a separate department was deeply misguided:

> This work cannot in any event be done at second hand through the medium of a special department which peeps in from time to time and takes note of everything that is needed. This is Utopia. There never has been such a department anywhere on earth, and in the logic of things there cannot be one.[223]

---

221 Trotsky 1964–71, vol. 2, pp. 730–3.

222 Trotsky 1964–71, vol. 2, pp. 734–5. In November, after a third Deputy was added, Trotsky listed the 'troika' of Deputies as another extraneous commission (Trotsky 1964–71, vol. 2, pp. 748–9; see also Trotsky 1964–71, vol. 2, pp. 816–17).

223 Trotsky 1964–71, vol. 2, pp. 732–3.

Officially, he asserted, instructions to the departments were carried out, but
they failed to produce results because of material shortages as well as 'ignorance, incapacity and so forth'. The way to rectify this problem was not by a
'swoop from without', but through the long and difficult process of raising the
level of Soviet education, and enhancing the organisational competence of
officials through a system of schools and training courses for the masses and
for office workers. Furthermore, Trotsky judged Rabkrin to be an unsuitable
instrument because it had proven itself unfit for serious work of any type. In a
possible indication that he was aware of Stalin's maneuvering, Trotsky noted
'the extraordinary growth of intrigue in the organs of the People's Commissariat
of Workers' and Peasants' Inspection, which has become proverbial throughout the country'.[224]

It is not surprising then that when Lenin's proposal was approved over
Trotsky's objections, Trotsky repeatedly declined Lenin's request that he
become a Deputy Chairman. It may be, as Isaac Deutscher has suggested, that
Trotsky's pride was hurt 'by an arrangement which would have placed him formally on the same footing as the other vice-Premiers who were only Lenin's
inferior assistants'.[225] However, evidence supports Deutscher's other explanation: 'He could not, without contradicting himself, accept a post in which he
would have had to give effect to an economic policy which in his view lacked
focus, and to guide an administrative machinery which he held to be faultily
constructed'.[226] This, in fact, was what Trotsky asserted.[227]

Lenin's last attempt to convince Trotsky to take on the job occurred in a
discussion with Trotsky in late 1922.[228] In the course of the conversation, Lenin
'spoke of the terrible growth of bureaucratism [*biurokratism*]' in the state apparatus and once more urged Trotsky to become a Deputy Chairman in order to
address the problem.[229] In reply, Trotsky reviewed his initial objections to the
creation of the position, and again suggested that bureaucratism was related
to the lack of planning. He pointed out that over the previous two years the

---

224   Trotsky 1964–71, vol. 2, pp. 730–1.
225   Deutscher 1959, pp. 36–7.
226   Deutscher 1959, p. 48.
227   See Trotsky 1964–71, vol. 2, pp. 818–21.
228   Trotsky later provided at least four separate accounts of this meeting, differing from
        each other in some details. See Trotsky 1964–71, vol. 2, pp. 818–21; Trotsky 1971a, pp. 73–4;
        Trotsky 1970c, pp. 478–9; Trotsky 1941, p. 365. The version suggested here places greatest
        weight on Trotsky's first two accounts of this conversation and on points that appear in
        multiple accounts. For a different version of this meeting, see van Ree 2001, pp. 92–4.
229   Trotsky 1964–71, vol. 2, pp. 818–19; Trotsky 1971a, p. 73; Trotsky 1990, p. 85; Trotsky 1970c,
        p. 479; Trotsky 1991b, pp. 454–5; Trotsky 1941, p. 365.

Orgburo, the Secretariat, and the Politburo repeatedly had made decisions 'without reference to the interested department and even behind its back'. These included 'piecemeal reductions in the army, instead of planned reductions...; similar phenomena as regards budgetary expenditure and analogous occurrences in the domain of individual appointments'. In Trotsky's view, this had 'utterly destroyed the possibility of proper work, selection and training of officials and of any sort of correct assessment or any sort of anticipation of a planned economy'.[230]

At this point, according to his later account, Trotsky's comments went beyond the issue of efficiency and began to address political concerns. Evidently, Trotsky had noticed the efforts of Stalin, Zinoviev, and Lev Kamenev to promote their own people and to block his succession to the leadership. Noting that bureaucratism [*biurokratizm*] was a problem in party as well as state institutions, he reported that in the provinces, the districts, the party locals and the Central Committee, he had observed 'a special selection of functionaries and specialists, party and non-party, around certain party personalities and groups'. Among these officials, a 'mutual shielding' was taking place: 'Attacking a functionary you run into the party leader'.[231]

After a moment's reflection, Trotsky recalled, Lenin responded, 'That is, I propose a struggle with Soviet bureaucratism [*biurokratizm*] and you are proposing to include the bureaucratism of the Organization Bureau of the Party?' 'I suppose that's it,' replied Trotsky. Lenin then invited Trotsky to join him in a 'bloc' against bureaucratism in general, and against the Organisational Bureau in particular.[232] Trotsky agreed. Specifically, the bloc was to fight for the creation of a committee attached to the Central Committee that would 'look into the question of the more correct selection, training, and promotion of officials and of more correct organizational relationships'. At the end of the meeting Lenin promised to give the organisational details further thought.[233]

It is probable that Lenin and Trotsky viewed the agreement somewhat differently, but it marked the beginning of the convergence of their views on bureaucracy. No doubt Lenin partly saw it as a way to begin to address, through 'more correct selection, training, and promotion', state inefficiency that was

230   Trotsky 1964–71, vol. 2, pp. 820–1. See also Trotsky 1970c, p. 479.

231   Trotsky 1971a, pp. 73–4; Trotsky 1990, p. 85; Trotsky 1970c, p. 479; Trotsky 1991b, p. 455; Trotsky 1941, p. 365.

232   Trotsky 1971a, p. 74; Trotsky 1990, p. 86. See also Trotsky 1970c, p. 479; Trotsky 1941, p. 365.

233   Trotsky 1971a, p. 74. See also Trotsky 1964–71, vol. 2, pp. 820–1; Trotsky 1941, p. 365. In *My Life* Trotsky says that Lenin asked him to think over the organisational details (Trotsky 1970c, p. 479).

a product of the lack of culture of Communists. Also, he must have hoped to use the committee to curb the bureaucratic authoritarian exercise of power by Stalin, the head of the Orgburo. Trotsky wanted to use the committee primarily to promote centralised planning and coordination, but also to neutralise his opponents who obstructed the implementation of planning for selfish political reasons. The bloc never fully materialised due to the rapid deterioration of Lenin's health. However, shortly afterwards the dying leader came to accept two of Trotsky's earlier conclusions: that Rabkrin, as it was then constituted, was virtually useless; and that it made sense to grant greater powers to Gosplan.[234] At the same time, in early 1923 Trotsky began to embrace many of Lenin's views regarding bureaucracy.

2.5   Conclusion

Although Trotsky shared the broad agreement within the Bolshevik Party that bureaucracy continued to be a problem after the revolution, his approach was distinctive in defining bureaucracy exclusively in terms of factors that promoted inefficiency in Soviet institutions. For Trotsky, these factors included the obstructionism of self-interested officials; characteristic work habits, attitudes, and inadequacies of Soviet officials; and inefficient approaches to the organisation of broad areas of work. Trotsky's disparate remarks on bureaucratic inefficiency during these years hardly constituted a theory. Nevertheless, his comments regarding the obstructionism of officials, as well as the problem of *glavkokratiia*, are of some interest.

In a number of his statements about bureaucratic obstructionism, it is hard to avoid the conclusion that Trotsky was merely utilising the term *bureaucracy* as a swear word against his opponents. However, his denunciation of the 'bureaucratic' component of the Military Opposition is noteworthy for its apparent similarities to his later analysis of Soviet bureaucracy. As Trotsky's biographer Isaac Deutscher observed, his writings on the Military Opposition contained 'in a nutshell... the leitmotif of Trotsky's later struggle against Stalin'.[235] In both cases Trotsky denounced a conservative, petty-bourgeois bureaucracy that threatened to derail the revolution in the pursuit of its own narrow interests; in both cases Trotsky's central opponent was Stalin. Still, it is important to recognise that Trotsky's earlier and later views in these controversies were far from identical. For Trotsky, the issues in the later debates

---

234   Lenin 1960–70, vol. 33, pp. 481–6; Lenin 1960–70, vol. 36, pp. 593, 598–9.
235   Deutscher 1954, pp. 427–8.

were broader than military policy, and much deeper than mere obstruction-ism. Furthermore, there was no direct continuity between Trotsky's condem-nation of the military bureaucracy and his later disagreements with Stalin. To the extent that, following his debate with the Military Opposition, he contin-ued to identify bureaucracy with a self-seeking layer of officials, his denuncia-tions were directed against members of the trade-union apparatus, not Stalin. Also, for years after the defeat of the Military Opposition, Trotsky's primary understanding of bureaucracy involved, not the obstructionism of selfish offi-cials, but the inefficient organisation of broad areas of work.

More specifically, Trotsky's most important statements about bureaucracy during these years were devoted to the issue of *glavkokratiia*. His analysis of that problem constituted a persuasive critique of the inefficiency of Soviet indus-try under war communism. For that reason, as Lars Lih has noted, Trotsky's statements on that topic struck a responsive chord in the popular conscious-ness, and the term *glavkokratiia* 'rapidly became a byword in 1920'.[236] Even Zinoviev, Trotsky's fiercest opponent at the time, cited his analysis approvingly at the Ninth Party Conference in September 1920; as did the anti-Communist, Russian-American economist, Leo Pasvolsky in 1921.[237] Furthermore, Trotsky's critique of *glavkokratiia* remained relevant even after the introduction of NEP, for it highlighted real and serious economic problems related to the inade-quate coordination of the trusts.[238] At least partially due to the persuasiveness of Trotsky's analysis, Lenin ultimately endorsed his proposal to grant legisla-tive powers to Gosplan.

However, it is also apparent that Trotsky's entire approach to bureaucracy in this period was severely limited and misdirected in its exclusive concentration upon inefficiency. Due to his 'preoccupation with the purely administrative side of the work', Trotsky ignored the mounting problems of political alien-ation documented by opposition groups during these years. In this respect, the analyses of Soviet bureaucracy by the oppositionists, and even by Lenin, were superior to Trotsky's – despite their excessive focus on the bourgeois special-ists. Beyond that, as Lenin and various oppositionists noted, Trotsky's preoccu-pation with efficiency impelled him to introduce centralist and authoritarian policies that contributed to the weakening of the vestiges of workers' democ-racy in the Soviet Union.

Nevertheless, in 1923 Trotsky's concern about inefficiency began to lead him in a different direction. At the end of 1922 Trotsky was still defining the

---

236 Lih 2007, pp. 129, 131.

237 RKP(b) 1972, p. 141; Pasvolsky 1921, pp. 207–11.

238 On the lack of coordination of industry under early NEP, see Nove 1976, pp. 101–2.

problem of bureaucracy much as he had in previous years. By that point his struggle against bureaucratic inefficiency had brought him into conflict with the majority of the party leadership. In the following year this conflict would intensify, inspiring Trotsky to redefine the central problem of Soviet bureaucracy as one of political alienation.

From Inefficiency to Political Alienation

The year 1923 represented a watershed in the development of Trotsky's thinking. When Trotsky addressed the issue of bureaucracy in the first years after the revolution, he described it almost exclusively in terms of factors responsible for inefficiency, especially in the military and economic organs of the state. In 1923 he began to characterise the problem as one of political alienation in all political institutions in the Soviet Union. Although in later years his views continued to develop and change, his understanding that the fundamental problem was one of political alienation would remain constant. This shift in focus brought his thinking into line with the dominant tradition in the Marxist analysis of bureaucracy. Marxists writing in this tradition commonly identified bureaucracy with the tendency of the state to rise above and dominate society. Furthermore, they viewed political alienation in normal periods as closely related to the inclination of the state to fall under the sway of exploitative classes. In 1923 Trotsky began to perceive both characteristics in Soviet political institutions.

While a number of factors contributed to this shift in Trotsky's thinking, one that was especially significant was the leadership majority's continuing resistance to measures viewed by Trotsky as necessary for eliminating economic problems he had associated with *glavkokratiia*. From this, Trotsky concluded that the mistaken orientation of Soviet economic policy originated in the elevation of the party and state apparatuses above the control of the ranks and the masses, and in their consequent deviation from the needs of the masses and the goals of socialism.

3.1   Conflicts within the Party Leadership

The winter and spring of 1922–3 were marked by widening differences within the party leadership around three main questions: economic policy, policy regarding the minority nationalities, and the organisational reform of central party institutions. While these issues brought Trotsky and Lenin closer together, they contributed to the mounting tensions between Trotsky and the leadership majority, headed by Zinoviev, Kamenev, and Stalin.

The greatest cleavage involved broad differences in economic orientation. The New Economic Policy had been adopted in 1921 to achieve a variety of goals. The Bolsheviks had hoped that that the partial restoration of free enterprise would promote short-run economic revival, that elimination of forced requisitioning of grain would overcome the disaffection of the peasantry, and that the growing success of agriculture would subsidise the gradual expansion of industry. By the winter of 1922–3 the first two of these objectives were being met. The harvest of 1922 yielded as much as three-fourths of a normal pre-war crop, and the volume of both internal and foreign trade was increasing. Also, the peasants seemed to be generally satisfied. However, industry lagged far behind agriculture, turning out only one-fourth of its pre-war output, and this industrial production was concentrated largely in light industry.[1]

In this context the leadership majority opposed any policy change that might endanger the *smychka* [link] between the proletariat and the peasantry. Consequently, they resisted all efforts to increase the peasant's tax burden. Majority spokesmen such as G.Ia. Sokol'nikov, the Commissar of Finance, emphasised stabilisation of the currency to protect the peasants against inflation. To achieve this goal, the majority pursued conservative policies of financial orthodoxy: attempting to establish a gold-based ruble, allocating credits to industry primarily on the basis of short-run profitability, and encouraging grain exports in order to build up Soviet reserves of foreign currency. At the same time, majority leaders resisted an increase in state economic planning, for this sounded suspiciously like a call for a return to war communism.[2]

However, within the upper ranks of the party leadership a minority, which included Trotsky, Iuri Piatakov (the vice president of VSNKh), and the economist Evgenii Preobrazhenskii, was growing increasingly concerned over the slow pace of industrial recovery.[3] The minority insisted that a faster pace of industrialisation was necessary for balanced, short-run economic development, for strengthening the proletarian base of the Soviet regime, and for the ultimate attainment of socialism. In line with this, in late 1922 and early 1923 Trotsky began to call for a program of 'primitive socialist accumulation', analogous to the early stages of capital accumulation described by Marx.[4] Although Trotsky agreed with the majority that it was necessary to stabilise the currency, he saw this concern as subordinate to the need for more rapid

---

1   Carr 1954, pp. 3–11; Deutscher 1959, p. 38; Dobb 1966, pp. 154, 161.

2   Carr 1954, pp. 17–19; Deutscher 1959, p. 39.

3   On the economic views of Trotsky and this minority, see Carr 1954, pp. 14–15, 20–4; Daniels 1960, pp. 202–3; Day 1973, pp. 72–3; Deutscher 1959, pp. 39–46.

4   For references to 'primitive socialist accumulation', see Trotsky 1972e, p. 9; Trotsky 1972d, p. 270; RKP(b) 1968, p. 351. According to Trotsky, the term was first coined by Vladimir Smirnov (RKP(b) 1968, p. 351.).

industrialisation. Consequently, he proposed an increase in state subsidies to industry, arguing that these should be granted on the basis of long-term economic need, not short-run profitability.[5]

Trotsky suggested a number of methods for financing this industrialisation program. He stressed the need for greater sacrifices on the part of the working class, even going so far at the Twelfth Party Congress as to tell the Soviet proletariat that 'there may be times when the state does not pay wages in full or only pays them by half, and you, the worker, will credit the state at the expense of your wages'.[6] He also suggested using the proceeds from grain exports to purchase foreign industrial machinery. Finally, he asserted that large sums could be saved for reinvestment by reducing overhead expenses in existing industry and by concentrating industrial production in a smaller number of more efficient enterprises. For Trotsky, the key to the implementation of all these recommendations was, once again, economic planning.[7]

In late 1922 and early 1923 these differences provoked a number of clashes between Trotsky and the Politburo majority. The first conflict erupted in late 1922 around the question of the state monopoly of foreign trade. In an attempt to promote foreign trade, the October plenum of the Central Committee voted to free the import and export of various commodities from state control. Lenin and Trotsky were absent from the meeting, but, when they heard of the decision, both vigorously protested against this weakening of the state monopoly. Trotsky, perceiving the issue as related to central planning, utilised the opportunity to raise that concern again, arguing that Gosplan should be granted powers to regulate foreign trade. Although at this point Lenin still rejected Trotsky's idea of strengthening Gosplan, he proposed that Trotsky assume the defence of their common position on the trade monopoly at the December plenum. By 13 December Lenin was able to congratulate Trotsky on their victory in overturning the October decision 'without a single shot'. Soon afterwards, Lenin accepted in part Trotsky's position on Gosplan, recommending that the party congress 'on certain conditions invest the decisions of the State Planning Commission with legislative force'.[8]

While Trotsky's economic views were converging with Lenin's, his differences with the leadership majority continued to widen. In January Stalin suggested the creation of a new supreme economic authority that was to include the Finance Committee, while excluding both VSNKh and Gosplan, the two

5   RKP(b) 1968, p. 333. Also, see Day 1973, pp. 72–3, 80, 82.
6   RKP(b) 1968, p. 345. See also Deutscher 1959, p. 44; Carr 1954, pp. 23–4.
7   Trotsky 1972a, pp. 144–6; RKP(b) 1968, pp. 323, 324–6, 336–43.
8   See the correspondence between Lenin and Trotsky in Trotsky 1964–71, vol. 2, pp. 774–89.

institutions most likely to articulate the needs of industry. Trotsky succeeded in blocking this proposal, complaining in the discussion about this further confirmation of the 'financial dictatorship', and reasserting the need to strengthen industry and the powers of Gosplan.[9] The following month Trotsky, as the head of a new committee on industrial policy, came up with a plan for extending credits to the industrial trusts. However, the committee majority – which ultimately included Stalin, Aleksei Rykov, Sokol'nikov, Kamenev, and Dzerzhinskii – rejected Trotsky's proposal. The final draft of the committee's theses represented an uneasy compromise between the views of Trotsky and the majority.[10]

Despite his disagreements with the majority, Trotsky was permitted to deliver the report on industry to the Twelfth Party Congress in April. Again, Trotsky's theme was the urgent need to devote greater resources to industry and greater attention to economic planning. The most noteworthy aspect of the address was his contention that more rapid industrialisation was necessary in order to maintain the *smychka* with the peasantry. Trotsky explained that the slow development of industry, combined with the rapid revival of agriculture, had resulted in a dramatic increase in the prices of industrial goods and a decline in the prices of agricultural commodities. He illustrated the situation with a diagram in which the lines representing agricultural and industrial prices crossed in September 1922 and then steadily widened like a pair of scissors. His conclusion was that the 'scissors crisis' threatened to deprive the peasants of the benefits of their surpluses. Unable to purchase the goods they needed from the state, the peasants would turn increasingly to local village industry, and away from the cities.[11] However, the informed observer easily could have discerned significant differences between Trotsky's perspective and that of the leadership majority. At various points in the congress, Zinoviev, Sokol'nikov, and Kamenev insisted upon the priority of peasant agriculture under NEP, criticised the notion of 'the dictatorship of industry', and poked fun at comrades who had obsessed over planning under war communism.[12] Nevertheless, majority spokesmen did not challenge Trotsky's conclusions directly, and the congress adopted the theses on industry with only minor amendments.

A second issue dividing the leadership in early 1923 was the nationalities question. By early 1923 Lenin had come to believe that the integration of the national republics into the Soviet Union needed to be slowed, and perhaps reversed, out of consideration for the sensibilities of nations that were system-

9   Trotsky 1964–71, vol. 2, pp. 816–23. See also Day 1973, pp. 77–8.
10   Day 1973, pp. 79–81; Fel'shtinskii 1988, vol. 1, pp. 23–5, 35–48.
11   RKP(b) 1968, pp. 319–22.
12   See Carr 1954, pp. 17–19; Day 1973, pp. 81–6.

atically repressed under the old regime. At the same time, Lenin concluded that the Great Russian chauvinism evident in actions of Stalin, Ordzhonikidze, and Dzerzhinskii reflected the attitudes of the 'truly Russian bureaucrat'. In a letter to the party congress Lenin singled out these individuals in particular for punishment.[13] On 5 March 1923, with his health failing rapidly, Lenin turned to Trotsky with the request that he take upon himself the defense of the Georgian case 'now under "persecution" by Stalin and Dzerzhinsky'.[14] At the February plenum of the Central Committee Trotsky had expressed serious reservations about Stalin's handling of the Georgian conflict. Now, citing reasons of ill health, Trotsky declined to accept responsibility for the defence of the Georgians. Nevertheless, he asked to review the relevant documents, and promised to look into the question if his health permitted.[15]

Soon afterwards, Trotsky later recalled, he presented Kamenev with a series of demands for Stalin. Trotsky did not support Lenin's proposal for the exemplary punishment of Stalin, Ordzhonikidze, and Dzerzhinskii. However, he demanded a radical change in nationalities policy, an end to the persecution of Stalin's Georgian opponents, a termination of 'administrative oppression' within the party, a stronger emphasis on industrialisation, and 'honest cooperation in the highest centres'.[16] Fearing an open confrontation with Lenin and Trotsky, Stalin accepted Trotsky's terms. Meanwhile, however, Lenin's health continued to deteriorate, and a few days after his communication with Trotsky he suffered another stroke that ended his political career. With Lenin incapacitated, Stalin's confidence returned. At the Georgian party conference in mid-March, the Georgian nationalists were pushed further back by Stalin's supporters.[17]

In the following weeks Trotsky continued to press for a change in policy on the national question. On 19 March he wrote an article for *Pravda* denouncing Great Russian chauvinism; in the Central Committee on 22 March he demanded the recall of Ordzhonikidze from Georgia, attacked the idea of a Transcaucasian Federation, and endorsed the position of the Georgian Central Committee; and in a speech delivered in Kharkov on 5 April he again took up the defence of the oppressed nationalities.[18] Still, he did not make public

13   Lenin 1960–70, vol. 36, pp. 596, 606, 610. For accounts of the 'Georgian affair', see Lewin 1970, pp. 43–103; Service 1995, pp. 274–82: Smith 1998, pp. 519–44.

14   Lenin 1960–70, vol. 45, p. 607.

15   Trotsky 1970c, p. 483; Smith 1998, p. 538; Buranov 1994, p. 50.

16   Trotsky 1970c, p. 486.

17   Daniels 1960, pp. 183–4.

18   Lenin and Trotsky 1975, pp. 140–8; Fel'shtinskii 1988, vol. 1, p. 51; Trotsky 1972a, pp. 162–7.

Lenin's last article on the Georgian situation. The day before the congress convened, Kamenev, learning of Lenin's article, urged the Central Committee to publish it. Trotsky justified his silence about the article on the grounds that he did not know what Lenin intended to do with it. Subsequently, the presidium of the Twelfth Party Congress approved a motion to withhold the article from publication.[19] At the congress Stalin delivered the report on the national question amended in accordance with Trotsky's demands. However, he also defended his own policies in Georgia, and claimed that Georgian nationalism against other oppressed nationalities was on the offensive. The debate on this report was long and heated, but Trotsky did not participate.[20]

Meanwhile, in the early months of 1923 the leadership debated Lenin's proposals to reform the central institutions of the state and the party. In a series of notes and articles dictated between late December 1922 and early March 1923, Lenin outlined two sets of recommendations for combating state and party bureaucratism. Both plans contained provisions designed to improve the efficiency of state and party bodies, increase proletarian and peasant representation in the central party institutions, and reduce the power of Stalin.

Lenin advanced his first proposals in a letter to the upcoming party congress, written in late December and early January. One section, later called Lenin's 'Testament', is best known for its descriptions of leading Bolsheviks. There, Lenin praised Trotsky as 'perhaps the most capable man in the present C.C.', while criticising his 'excessive self-assurance' and 'excessive preoccupation with the purely administrative side of the work'. Lenin was referring at least in part to Trotsky's position in the trade-union controversy of 1920–1, but he may also have been thinking of his past differences with Trotsky over the issue of bureaucracy. Regarding Stalin, Lenin noted his 'unlimited authority' as General Secretary, and questioned 'whether he will always be capable of using that authority with sufficient caution'. Later, in a post-script inspired in part by the Georgian affair, Lenin described Stalin as 'too rude', and recommended that he be replaced as General Secretary by someone 'more tolerant, more loyal, more polite and considerate to the comrades, less capricious, etc.'[21]

The same letter contained a proposal to increase the size of the Central Committee from twenty-seven full members and nineteen candidates to between 50 and 100 members. The new members were to be 'mainly workers

---

19   Fel'shtinskii 1988, vol. 1, p. 53; Carr 1954, p. 280; Daniels 1960, pp. 183–4, 186.
20   Carr 1954, pp. 280–3; Daniels 1960, pp. 185–6; Deutscher 1959, pp. 97–8. Trotsky also wrote another article on the national question for *Pravda* soon after the party congress (Trotsky 1958).
21   Lenin 1960–70, vol. 36, pp. 594–5, 596.

of a lower stratum than those promoted in the last five years to work in Soviet bodies'. For a number of years they were to go through a course in state management under the guidance of the most qualified members of the Workers' and Peasants' Inspectorate. Rabkrin itself was to be demoted to 'an "appendage" or, in certain conditions, ... an assistant to these members of the C.C.' Lenin argued that this plan would have three positive effects: it would raise the prestige of the CC – apparently in relation to the Politburo, Organisational Bureau, and Secretariat; it would contribute to the stability of the party threatened by potential antagonism between the proletariat and the peasantry and by 'conflicts between small sections of the C.C.'; and it would help the workers improve the machinery of the state.[22]

Lenin outlined further proposals for institutional reorganisation in 'How We Should Reorganize the Workers' and Peasants' Inspection' written in late January, and 'Better Fewer, But Better' written in early March. The ideas presented in these articles were clearly based on the plan he had discussed with Trotsky to form a special commission attached to the Central Committee to improve the selection, training, and promotion of officials, and organisational relationships in general. As Lenin envisioned it, this commission was to be composed of two reorganised institutions: the Central Control Commission and Rabkrin. The five-member CCC, created to combat party bureaucracy, was to be vastly expanded by the addition of 75–100 workers and peasants. It was to meet with the Central Committee once every two months in a supreme party conference – partly in order to bring the issue of bureaucratism into all important party decisions. Its activities were to include attending Politburo meetings and examining all documents pertaining to its work, theoretical study of scientific methods of organising labour, and helping to supervise and improve the state machinery.[23]

This new CCC also was to be 'amalgamated' with a refurbished Rabkrin, the organ established to fight bureaucracy in the state. In what appears at least partially to have been a swipe at Stalin, head of the Workers' and Peasants' Inspectorate from 1919–22, Lenin berated the extreme disorganisation of Rabkrin: 'Everybody knows that no other institutions are worse organised than those of our Workers' and Peasants' Inspection, and that under present conditions nothing can be expected from this Peoples' Commissariat'.[24] Lenin

22   Lenin 1960–70, vol. 36, pp. 593–4, 596–7. On Lenin's organisational proposals in early 1923, see Daniels 1960, pp. 190–1; Harding 1983, vol. 2, pp. 302–8; Lewin 1970, pp. 118–22; Rees 1987, pp. 39–49; Service 1995, pp. 295, 301–3.
23   Lenin 1960–70, vol. 33, pp. 482, 484–5, 493–4.
24   Lenin 1960–70, vol. 33, p. 490.

recommended cutting the staff of Rabkrin from over twelve thousand to 300–400 officials who were to be screened for reliability and tested for their knowledge of the state apparatus and organisational methods. Tasks of Rabkrin were to include combining and coordinating a number of higher institutions for the organisation of labour and rebuilding one model commissariat. The Peoples' Commissar of Rabkrin and its collegium were to continue to direct Rabkrin's staff, but would also assume the leadership of the new CCC.[25] One important new idea in these proposals was the merging of a state institution with a party organ. As in the case of Lenin's proposal to expand the Central Committee, this innovation appears to have arisen from Lenin's recognition of the need to involve higher party circles in any effort to reform the state apparatus.

These recommendations provoked mixed reactions within the Politburo. Stalin, perhaps recognising the potential for strengthening his base in an enlarged CC, immediately backed the expansion. On 29 January his Secretariat delivered to the Central Committee a series of amendments to the party statutes that would increase the size of that committee to 50 full members. The 'workers' to be added to the Central Committee were to consist of 'directors, leaders of oblast organizations, the most authoritative members of the national Communist parties, etc'. At the same time the power of the Central Committee was to be enhanced by requiring that the Politburo refer 'especially important political questions' to it.[26] Trotsky rejected this plan, arguing at a CC meeting on 22 February that it would disrupt efficient decision making by the Central Committee and that it 'would do very little to improve the connection [of the CC] with the masses'.[27]

Trotsky and Stalin also disagreed over Lenin's suggestion to enlarge the CCC and amalgamate it with a reformed Rabkrin, but on this question their positions were reversed. Stalin initially opposed the idea. No doubt he felt seriously compromised by Lenin's attacks on Rabkrin, and resisted the dismantling of the massive organisation he had constructed between 1919 and 1922. The Politburo majority attempted to prevent the publication of Lenin's article in which the plan was discussed, and Stalin's supporter V.V. Kuibyshev even suggested printing a dummy copy of *Pravda* to deceive the ailing leader.[28] On the other hand, Trotsky fully endorsed Lenin's proposal, the outlines of which he had agreed upon in their final conversation.[29]

---

25   Lenin 1960–70, vol. 33, pp. 482–4, 490–3.
26   Fel'shtinskii 1988, vol. 1, p. 19.
27   Fel'shtinskii 1988, vol. 1, p. 30; Daniels 1960, p. 192.
28   Trotsky 1975b, p. 62; Trotsky 1971a, pp. 72–3.
29   Fel'shtinskii 1988, vol. 1, p. 31; Deutscher 1959, pp. 88–9.

FROM INEFFICIENCY TO POLITICAL ALIENATION

Ultimately, the Twelfth Party Congress adopted modified versions of both sets of recommendations. However, the new members of both the expanded CC and the CCC were chosen, contrary to Lenin's intent, from the ranks of the party officialdom, not from the proletariat and peasantry. Lenin's idea to transform the combined CC and CCC into a supreme party conference that would oversee the work of the central party organs was dropped. Furthermore, the most important consequence of the reforms was to strengthen Stalin, for most of the new members of both the CC and the CCC were his supporters. Ironically, V.V. Kuibyshev who had proposed the dummy issue of *Pravda*, was chosen to chair the CCC.[30]

In this period discussions about bureaucratism were not confined to the leading circles of the party. In particular, two small opposition groups on the periphery of the party were especially vocal in raising this issue. The first was the Workers' Group of the Russian Communist Party, founded by the worker G.T. Miasnikov. Shortly after the Tenth Party Congress, Miasnikov began to agitate for 'freedom of the press for monarchists to anarchists inclusive', for which he was expelled from the party in 1922. Subsequently, he continued his political activities underground, forming the Workers' Group. In early 1923 the Workers' Group warned that, unless NEP was implemented by the workers and peasants, it could degenerate into rule by an elite and a 'New Exploitation of the Proletariat'. The Workers' Group demanded the removal of specialists from positions of authority, free speech for all viewpoints within the working class, and the election of new soviets centred in the factories.[31] The second group, known as the Workers' Truth, was an organisation founded in late 1921 that was composed largely of intellectuals. Workers' Truth argued that the Soviet Union had become a 'state capitalist' system dominated by a new bourgeoisie composed of NEPmen (the capitalist traders and speculators who flourished under the New Economic Policy), and of party, soviet, and trade-union bureaucrats. Furthermore, it asserted that the Communist Party itself was now nothing more than 'the party of the organized intelligentsia'. The Workers' Truth called for a new 'Workers' Party' that would fight for democratic rights and the interests of the proletariat.[32]

At the Twelfth Party Congress no one admitted supporting either group, but the criticisms of both were echoed in milder terms by several delegates. The

---

30   Daniels 1960, p. 197; Rees 1987, pp. 51–2, 60–3.

31   See especially Pirani 2008, pp. 195–6. Also, see Avrich 1984, pp. 9, 16–20; Carr 1954, pp. 80–2; Daniels 1960, pp. 159–60, 204; Deutscher 1959, p. 107.

32   Carr 1954, pp. 79–80; Daniels 1960, pp. 160–1; Daniels 1984, pp. 147–8; Pirani 2008, pp. 126–9.

two central issues in this regard were the suppression of free speech within the party and the appointment of local party secretaries. Vladimir Kosior protested against the fact that many party members were excluded from party and state work or were transferred to different parts of the country simply because they had disagreed with the Central Committee. He further urged the repeal of the 1921 resolution banning party factions. L.A. Lutovinov denounced the growing tendency to view the Politburo as an 'infallible pope' and to treat every practical criticism of the party as a manifestation of Menshevism. At the same time, Preobrazhenskii complained that 30 percent of all the secretaries of provincial committees had been 'recommended' by the Central Committee.[33] In his response to the discussion, Stalin insisted that 'never in the past six years has the Central Committee prepared for a congress so democratically as it prepared for this one'. Nevertheless, he noted that freedom of discussion was necessarily limited by the fact that 'we are surrounded by enemies'.[34] Despite his growing concerns about the party regime, Trotsky said nothing in the discussion of Stalin's organisational report.[35]

A question that has aroused considerable speculation is why Trotsky failed to attack the leadership majority at the Twelfth Party Congress on the issues of the national question and the party regime. This question is especially significant in light of his own later estimation that, if he had 'come forward on the eve of the twelfth congress in the spirit of a block of Lenin and Trotsky against the Stalin bureaucracy', he would have been victorious, even without Lenin's participation.[36] It is likely that a number of factors were involved. Quite plausibly, Trotsky later explained that he had feared independent action on his part would be interpreted as a personal bid for power, and that he had still hoped Lenin would recover sufficiently to lead the struggle.[37] Others have attributed Trotsky's silence to 'a lapse in political will power', a lack of 'political sense and acumen', or Trotsky's belief that he was still bound by his agreement with Stalin on the Georgian question.[38] Finally, it has also been suggested by Isaac Deutscher that Trotsky was intensely preoccupied with economic policy, and that he saw this as the 'key to all other problems'.[39] This last explanation is supported by Trotsky's analysis of bureaucracy during this period, for this analysis

---

33   Carr 1954, pp. 276–7; Daniels 1960, pp. 194–5, 204; Deutscher 1959, p. 96.
34   Stalin 1952–5, vol. 5, pp. 227–9.
35   See Deutscher 1959, p. 98.
36   Trotsky 1970c, p. 481.
37   Trotsky 1970c, p. 482.
38   Daniels 1960, p. 206; Carr 1954, p. 272; Deutscher 1959, p. 98; Carmichael 1975, p. 282.
39   Deutscher 1959, p. 98. See also Daniels 1960, p. 206.

largely continued to revolve around his understanding of the economic challenges confronting the Soviet Union.

3.2   Inefficiency and Political Alienation

In the first few years after the revolution Trotsky defined the problem of bureaucracy in terms of factors that contributed to the inefficiency of the Soviet military and economic institutions. He reiterated a number of these views, and especially his critique of structural economic inefficiency, in early 1923. In fact, aspects of Trotsky's analysis of *glavkokratiia* were scattered throughout his statements on bureaucracy at this time. However, at this point new themes also were beginning to emerge in his speeches and writings. To a greater degree than before Trotsky began to speak of bureaucracy within the party as well as the state. At the same time he began to associate the problem of Soviet bureaucracy with political alienation. Specifically, he denounced various modes of behaviour prevalent within the state apparatus that betrayed a fundamental lack of responsiveness to the needs and concerns of the masses. Furthermore, he condemned a conservative tendency in Soviet policy that, he believed, reflected and encouraged the responsiveness of the state and party apparatuses to alien class pressures.

In early 1923 Trotsky continued to address problems of structural economic inefficiency in the Soviet economy related to the phenomenon of *glavkokratiia* under war communism and afterwards. Just before and again at the Twelfth Party Congress Trotsky returned to the theme of the 'glavkokratic' character of the state-controlled sector of the economy under NEP. At the congress he explained that there were two basic flaws in the organisation of the state trusts: they dominated the enterprises so completely that they crushed all independence and initiative, and each operated too independently in relation to the state in general and VSNKh in particular.[40] In Trotsky's view, the trusts inevitably had assumed a 'bureaucratic [*biurokraticheskii*]' and 'red-tapist [*kantseliarskii*]' character, for they had been 'created by the methods of war communism, that is, by methods of central *glavkokratic* prediction and direction from above'.[41]

Once again, Trotsky called for a reorganisation of the trusts along the lines of his earlier proposals for reforming the *glavki*. The task, he asserted, consisted 'in establishing the necessary balance between the state, the trust and the

---

40   RKP(b) 1968, p. 331.
41   RKP(b) 1968, p. 325.

factory'.[42] In part, this involved some decentralisation of economic authority, granting greater autonomy to the economic oblasts and national republics and to individual enterprises. Trotsky argued that 'a factory has to be able to point out to the trust that it is advantageous to it to act just so and not otherwise or we will have in the trust the old *glavkokratiia*, only made up to correspond to the conditions of the New Economic Policy'.[43] Simultaneously, he proposed to coordinate the entire economy through a central economic plan. In a speech delivered at a party conference in Kharkov on 5 April he asserted: 'The policy of "from one case to the next", the practice of improvisation, economic guerilla tactics, amateurism, must more and more, under the staunch leadership of our party, yield place to planning methods and the principle of planning'.[44] Most importantly, he explained at the Twelfth Party Congress, this involved enhancing the powers of Gosplan.[45] In Trotsky's view a stronger Gosplan would not only improve the coordination of the trusts, it would also help to combat the tendency to create 'all sorts of temporary and accidental commissions: investigating, directing, verifying, preparatory, etc'.[46] He rejected the notion that an ideal plan could be created overnight, for such a course could only lead back to the economic crises of war communism and the 'comprehensive economic constipation' of *glavkokratiia*. Rather, the extension of planning was to be achieved gradually, on the basis of accumulated experience.[47]

While continuing to view the problem of bureaucracy as one of inefficiency, in early 1923 Trotsky also began to describe it in terms of political alienation. A number of factors seem to have contributed to this change. No doubt, Trotsky's own deepening sense of isolation from the leadership majority played a part. Throughout his career, Trotsky consistently identified his personal fate with that of the revolution. Now, as he became increasingly alienated from the centres of power, Trotsky became more and more aware of manifestations of political alienation he had been inclined to overlook. It is clear that Lenin's last writings influenced Trotsky's thinking as well. In his final conversation with Lenin, Trotsky accepted the offer to form an alliance against bureaucracy, and it is apparent that this agreement inspired Trotsky to reconsider and embrace

---

42   RKP(b) 1968, p. 331.
43   RKP(b) 1968, p. 332.
44   Trotsky 1972a, p. 152.
45   RKP(b) 1968, pp. 342–3.
46   RKP(b) 1968, p. 679.
47   RKP(b) 1968, p. 677; Trotsky 1972a, p. 152. R. Davies 1957, pp. 111–15 is mistaken in arguing that 'Trotsky put forward his proposals for central planning as an immediate solution to the dangerous economic situation of 1923–24'. See also Vilkova 1996, p. 154.

many of Lenin's views. Even more influential for Trotsky were policy developments that suggested the growth of political alienation in the state and party. One of these was the arrogant treatment of the Georgian Central Committee by Stalin and his supporters. However, it appears that the most important development for Trotsky was the continuing resistance of the leadership majority to economic planning. From this, Trotsky concluded that the problem was greater than economic inefficiency: it involved the political sources of the leadership's mistaken orientation.

Trotsky's most important comments on state bureaucratism during this period appeared in an article written for *Pravda* on 3 April and in his Kharkov speech of 5 April. In both, Trotsky based his remarks on Lenin's recent statements regarding bureaucracy. In Kharkov Trotsky depicted the problem of 'quality' in the state in terms of 'a state machine which begins with a young, selflessly devoted but quite inexperienced Communist, goes on through an indifferent office clerk, and ends with a gray-haired expert who sometimes, under irreproachable forms, engages in sabotage'. That is, the party 'created this clumsy, creaking machine which to a considerable degree is not "ours"'.[48]

It seems that Trotsky meant to suggest two different notions of bureaucracy here. One problem, again, was the general inefficiency of the state apparatus. In his Kharkov address Trotsky characterised the state machine as 'wretchedly bad'.[49] Similarly, in his article of 3 April Trotsky complained,

> If we could take an impression on a sensitive plate of the manners, replies, explanations, orders, and signatures of all the cells of the bureaucratic organism, be it only in Moscow for a single day, the result obtained would be one of extraordinary confusion. And it is worse in the provinces.[50]

However, in both his Kharkov speech and his *Pravda* article Trotsky was also referring to the phenomenon of political alienation. For Trotsky, this problem was evident in the growing separation of the state apparatus from the masses – a separation that had taken a variety of forms, ranging from the indifference of bureaucrats to the needs of working people, to expressions of rudeness and Great Russian chauvinism by state officials. Related to these phenomena were manifestations of bourgeois influence within the Soviet state, including acts of sabotage by specialists and the conservative drift of economic policy.

---

48   Trotsky 1972a, pp. 156, 157.
49   Trotsky 1972a, p. 156.
50   Trotsky 1973a, p. 49; Trotsky 1963e, pp. 61–2.

At its most basic level the problem was that the state officials often demonstrated a 'complete indifference to the living human being and his living work' and a 'heartless formality'.[51] When Trotsky previously criticised state officials for their apathy and excessive formalism, he presented these as isolated cases. Now, he perceived bureaucratic indifference and formalism as widespread phenomena. He insisted that 'a Soviet official ought to behave attentively and respectfully to an old, illiterate peasant woman'. Yet, all too often the peasant's experience was quite different: 'There sits our red-tapist, directing her with the tip of his finger to number so-and-so, and she hesitates, turning this way and that, in front of number so-and-so, utterly helpless, and leaves her office without achieving anything'. While Trotsky acknowledged that this was not a balanced account of the behaviour of state officials, he observed that even if it was 'only one-third true to life', there was 'a frightful abyss between the state machine and the working masses'.[52]

Political alienation was also apparent for Trotsky in the 'rudeness' of the average Soviet official. In his 3 April article he noted that, in the 'civilized' West, the state bureaucracy raises 'itself above the people as a closely united professional caste' and 'treats the workman and peasant arrogantly'. The problem was even more blatant in the Soviet Union, where 'civility, as a general rule, does not exist'.[53] It is possible that Trotsky was thinking here of Lenin's recent denunciations of 'Orjonikidze's rudeness and the connivance of Stalin and Dzerzhinsky' in the Georgian affair.[54] In another article written at the end of April, Trotsky depicted the state apparatus as deeply infected with great power chauvinism: 'In the Soviet administrative machine . . . tendencies of this kind [i.e., "Great Power" attitudes] are powerful to an extreme degree – and not only among former generals'.[55]

At the same time Trotsky increasingly noted related deviations of the state from the goal of socialist construction. One form this took was the 'conscious sabotage' carried out by 'gray-haired experts' within the state apparatus.[56] Even more worrisome was the conservative distortion of economic policy under the pressure of private capital. In an article written for *Pravda* on 13 March Trotsky described how, in both state and party work, 'departmentalism [*vedomstven-nost'*], bureaucratism [*biurokratizm*], distortion of human relations by market

51   Trotsky 1973a, p. 49; Trotsky 1963e, p. 61.
52   Trotsky 1972a, pp. 156–7.
53   Trotsky 1973a, pp. 48, 49; Trotsky 1963e, pp. 60, 61.
54   Lenin 1960–70, vol. 45, p. 608.
55   Trotsky 1958, p. 102.
56   Trotsky 1973a, p. 50; Trotsky 1972a, p. 156.

influences, all these develop a very great force, which drags at people, . . . and corrupts them'.[57] Similarly, in his Kharkov address Trotsky spoke of 'the market relations which engender of themselves currents of centrifugal force that can distract and rob the state machine in the direction of the interests of private capital, wedge the NEP bourgeoisie into it with their interests and ideas, plunder state industry, turning it inconspicuously into the channels of private accumulation'.[58]

Trotsky borrowed heavily from Lenin in his attempts to explain the causes of both state inefficiency and political alienation. In his last writings Lenin had suggested three sources of bureaucratism: the low level of Soviet culture, the difficulties of constructing the Soviet state in the midst of revolutionary turbulence, and the fact that a large part of the administrative apparatus had been inherited from the tsarism.[59] In his article of 3 April Trotsky cited all three as 'principles that maintain and nourish bureaucratism [*biurokratizm*]':

> Foremost among them, of course, is our lack of culture, backwardness, and illiteracy. The general muddle resulting from a state machinery in continuous process of reconstruction, inevitable during a revolutionary epoch, is in itself the cause of much superfluous friction, which makes up an important part of bureaucratism. It is the heterogeneity of class in the Soviet apparatus, and in particular the presence of aristocratic, bourgeois, and Counselor of State [i.e., tsarist state official] practices that is responsible for the more repulsive of its forms.[60]

Two days later in his Kharkov address he offered a similar explanation.[61] Trotsky did not attempt to sort out which factors had produced which form of bureaucratism. However, it seems he viewed low culture and the difficulties of state construction as responsible for state inefficiency, and the employment of specialists – itself necessitated by the low culture of the masses – as a major source of the alienation of the state from the masses. Although in past years Trotsky had defended the experts against charges of bureaucratism, now – perhaps because he feared the *spetsy* would ally themselves with the 'NEP bourgeoisie' – he began to take these charges more seriously. He approvingly paraphrased Lenin's last observations on the excessive power of the specialists:

57   Trotsky 1973a, p. 104; Trotsky 1923.
58   Trotsky 1972a, p. 168.
59   Lenin 1960–70, vol. 33, pp. 481, 488, 501; Lenin 1960–70, vol. 36, pp. 596–7.
60   Trotsky 1973a, p. 50; Trotsky 1963e, p. 62 (translation modified).
61   Trotsky 1972a, p. 156.

'Vladimir Ilyich writes about our state machine that it is neither more nor less than very similar to the czarist state machine, anointed, as they say, colored in the Soviet style, but if you examine it, it is the same old bureaucratic machine'.[62]

Beyond this, however, Trotsky was increasingly concerned about the distortion of policy that resulted from the anonymous 'market relations' of NEP that exerted pressure on the state from without, and the members of the 'NEP bourgeoisie' who had infiltrated the state machinery. Again, Trotsky's concern was that these would divert policy, distracting and robbing 'the state machine in the direction of the interests of private capital'.[63] Ultimately, this suggested the prospect that the state might begin to represent bourgeois interests – though in early 1923 that danger still seemed distant. At this point Trotsky's greater concern was that the separation of the state from the masses and the implementation of conservative economic policies might disrupt the *smychka* between the workers' state and the peasantry, or between Russia and the masses of the non-Russian republics. In particular, Trotsky saw the alliance with the peasantry as threatened by the formalism and indifference of the typical state official, and even more by the mistaken economic policies that were provoking the scissors crisis. In the event of such a rupture, the peasantry could 'cease to be led by the proletariat and fall under the leadership of the bourgeoisie'.[64] In the non-Russian republics the threat was greater, for there Great Russian chauvinism could provoke the rise of national opposition movements, uniting the 'bourgeoisie and the toilers, wholly directed against the revolution'.[65] In either case, Trotsky warned, the outcome of an ensuing civil war 'would be doubtful for us'.[66]

In his proposals to reduce state bureaucratism, Trotsky dissociated himself from the extreme positions of groups such as the Workers' Truth and the Workers' Group. Trotsky's view at this time was that the Soviet state was defective in many respects, but not as hostile to the goals of socialism as these groups claimed.[67] Nor could he accept the view articulated in an anonymous opposition pamphlet circulated on the eve of the party congress that called for the liquidation of the party's leading role. 'If there is one question which

---

62 Trotsky 1972a, p. 155. Trotsky also spoke of 'the organic hatred of a deposed aristocracy [employed by the Soviet state] towards the class that deposed it', and he blamed bourgeois and aristocratic officials for the most virulent forms of rudeness in the state apparatus, as well as for acts of 'conscious sabotage' (Trotsky 1973a, p. 50; Trotsky 1963e, p. 63 [translation modified]).

63 Trotsky 1972a, p. 168.

64 Lenin and Trotsky 1975, p. 141.

65 Lenin and Trotsky 1975, p. 142. See also Trotsky 1972a, pp. 162–3.

66 Trotsky 1972a, p. 164.

67 Trotsky 1972a, pp. 155–6.

basically not only does not require revision but does not so much as admit the thought of revision', Trotsky insisted, 'it is the question of the dictatorship of the party, and its leadership in all spheres of our work'. In Trotsky's opinion, any party member who challenged this should be 'unanimously dumped by all of us on the other side of the barricade [i.e., expelled]'.[68]

Instead, in a set of proposals that combined Lenin's recommendations with his own earlier suggestions, Trotsky called for sweeping reforms of the state apparatus. From Lenin, he took the idea that the principal institution for carrying out this work was a strengthened CCC combined with a reformed Rabkrin:

> Through what agency [should the state be reformed]? Through that which erected it, through the party. And for this party too we need a fresh, improved organ for sounding this machine, a probe which is not only moral but also political and practical – not on the plane of formal state inspection, which has already shown its complete bankruptcy, but on the plane of party penetration into the heart of the matter, to carry out a selection process in the most important fields of work.[69]

Evidently, it was the idea of merging Rabkrin with a party institution, in the process transforming 'formal state inspection' into 'party penetration into the heart of the matter', that enabled Trotsky to overcome his previous hostility to that body. At the same time, Trotsky added to Lenin's proposal his own frequently expressed emphasis on planning, calling for the '*systematic, planned reconstruction of the state machine*'.[70] He insisted that party leadership of the state had to 'assume a more planned character' and the state organs had to 'learn to work within the framework of a plan and a system, to construct a plan which looks to the future, not staggering from one case to the next'.[71] In other words, the combined CCC-Rabkrin was to function in relation to state institutions in general just as he hoped Gosplan would function in the economic sphere.

As Trotsky envisioned it, the new party-state institution was to concentrate its efforts on evaluating the work of state institutions, and selecting and training state functionaries. He anticipated that all of these activities could help in the struggle against both inefficiency and political alienation: the new 'central party-and-Soviet organ ... will be able to sound the state machine in a new way both from the angle of its general efficiency and from that of how

---

68   Trotsky 1972a, pp. 158, 160.
69   Trotsky 1972a, pp. 157–8.
70   Trotsky 1972a, p. 157.
71   Trotsky 1972a, p. 161.

it responds to a simple illiterate old woman'.[72] This body would focus on the 'technical improvement of the machine, the decrease of staffs, the introduction of greater order, thoroughness, and accuracy in the work, and other measures of a similar nature'. Additionally, it would begin to educate 'thousands of new workers ... in the spirit of service, simplicity, and humanity'.[73] One more measure that Trotsky probably expected would be carried out by the combined ccc and Rabkrin was the exemplary expulsion from the state apparatus of 100 civil servants 'who showed a rooted contempt ... for the working masses'.[74]

Trotsky also outlined a number of additional proposals to eliminate both inefficiency and political alienation from the state apparatus. One was to increase 'the struggle against the low conditions of culture, illiteracy, dirt, and poverty'.[75] Another was to mobilise public opinion against bureaucratic rudeness. In this regard, he believed the press could play an important role.[76] Finally, to root out bureaucratically inspired Great Russian nationalism, Trotsky called for the reeducation of the party on the national question and the punishment of chauvinist officials.[77]

While dealing with the issue of political alienation in the state, in early 1923 Trotsky began to address related phenomena in the party. He had alluded to the issue of party bureaucratism at the Eleventh Party Congress the previous March and in his last conversation with Lenin at the end of the year. On each of these occasions Trotsky's remarks were directed against the inefficiency he saw as arising from the lack of central economic planning. Trotsky returned to the subject in his article of 13 March and again in his Kharkov address. Although he continued to see a connection between party bureaucratism and the lack of planning, he now began to describe the problem in the party, as in the state, as related to the deeper problem of political alienation.

Trotsky did not yet publicly address the decline in party democracy, though it is obvious he was growing increasingly concerned about this. In his 22 February remarks to the Central Committee on the organisational reform of the leading party institutions, he spoke of the importance for the cc of 'constant, and not only periodic connections with "the people at the bottom" [nizy]' and the need for the Central Committee to have around itself 'a constant, living, and active party "encirclement"'. He argued that 'this would add

---

72   Trotsky 1972a, p. 158.
73   Trotsky 1973a, p. 50; Trotsky 1963e, p. 62.
74   Trotsky 1973a, p. 51; Trotsky 1963e, p. 64.
75   Trotsky 1973a, p. 50; Trotsky 1963e, p. 62.
76   Trotsky 1973a, p. 51.
77   Lenin and Trotsky 1975, pp. 144, 146–7.

to the C.C. the living experience of the localities and of the "people at the bottom"', and would 'exert a needed pressure on the C.C.'[78] Also, in his demands to Stalin around the Georgian question, Trotsky explicitly called for an improvement in the party regime. However, it is clear that at this point Trotsky was more immediately concerned with the conservative policies of the leadership majority, and specifically with the majority's resistance to economic planning.

Trotsky mentioned a number of factors that he believed were responsible for this conservatism, or that threatened to exacerbate it. As in his discussion of state bureaucratism, one was the 'distortion of human relations by market influences', that 'drags around people, wraps them round and corrupts them'.[79] Another was the infiltration of NEPmen into the party – although in Trotsky's estimation this was less of a problem in the party than in the state, for in the previous year the party had 'purged itself of alien elements and added to its proletarian element'.[80] However, in early 1923 Trotsky attributed the growing conservatism of the leadership largely to dynamics within the party itself, and specifically to the increasing specialisation of party officials and members who were involved in the work of state institutions:

> The officers of the party, both central and local, consist with few exceptions of comrades who are charged with most responsible state service, almost always of a specialized kind. The same applies also to a very substantial number of party members who are not formally officers of the party but who make up its fundamental cadres. The communists now bring their entire personalities into their administrative, economic, military, diplomatic, and any other sort of work.[81]

According to Trotsky, the problem with such specialisation was that it could lead to the development of a narrowly specialised outlook. Trotsky variously referred to this as the problem of 'bureaucratism', 'departmentalism', 'departmental degeneration', and 'the crystallization in the upper strata of the party along the lines of profession and department'.[82] At the Eleventh Party Congress in 1922 he had warned vaguely that the party's preoccupation with routine and practical questions could lead to the growth of bureaucratism. Now he defined this threat more sharply: 'Not a single serious party member will claim that

78   Fel'shtinskii 1988, vol. 1, p. 30.
79   Trotsky 1973a, p. 104.
80   Trotsky 1972a, p. 168.
81   Trotsky 1973a, p. 102.
82   Trotsky 1973a, pp. 102–4.

in the sphere of party leadership we have attained perfect and unchangeable forms, and that as our work inevitably becomes more complicated and subdivided the party will not be threatened with the danger of becoming dissolved in this work and losing the ability to see the forest for the trees'.[83] Trotsky clearly meant to suggest that this already had occurred to some degree. The specialisation of leading party members had narrowed their horizons to such an extent that, in dealing with economic questions, they were unable to perceive the needs of the entire economic forest.

If the growth of this conservative specialisation continued unchecked, Trotsky feared it could lead to extreme forms of political degeneration. In this respect he found the experience of the Social Democratic and trade-union leaderships of Western Europe to be instructive. In the course of their development these groups had 'retreated further and further into day-to-day, purely reformist, detailed work, in practice repudiating revolutionary struggle against capitalism, bowing to the ground before its might'.[84] However, Trotsky did not believe that specialisation *inevitably* resulted in degeneration. In each case where a socialist organisation had degenerated, the problem was not simply that the group involved itself with specialised work; it was that petty jobs were 'openly or tacitly counterposed to a great historical task'. For Trotsky, it was the 'unity of a great aim' that could elevate the details of socialist construction above 'petty-bourgeois hairsplitting', provide inspiration to those participating, and save the party from degeneration.[85]

Consequently, Trotsky's solution to the problem of party bureaucratism was not to reduce specialisation, but, again, to increase planning, particularly in the economic sphere. Trotsky envisioned that establishing a real economic plan would combat the tendency to departmentalism within the party by unifying the work of all its members:

> Socialist construction is planned construction on the largest scale. And through all the . . . twists and turns of the NEP, the party pursues its great plan, educates the youth in the spirit of this plan, teaches everyone to link his particular function with the common task, which today demands sewing on Soviet buttons, and tomorrow readiness to die fearlessly under the banner of communism.[86]

---

83   Trotsky 1972a, pp. 160–1. See also Trotsky 1973a, p. 103.
84   Trotsky 1973a, pp. 100–1.
85   Trotsky 1973a, p. 101.
86   Ibid.

Trotsky also devoted attention to the role that the new institution for political planning, the merged CCC-Rabkrin, could play in combating party bureaucratism. The creation of this new organ, like the strengthening of economic planning, would help to unify the experience of party members employed in diverse Soviet offices by establishing greater coordination between those institutions. The establishment of the combined CCC-Rabkrin, Trotsky asserted, involved 'approaching the state machine in a new way, embracing and evaluating it as a whole in respect of the most important matters and fundamentally, and along these lines subjecting it to regular influence'.[87] Additionally, the selection of seventy-five workers and peasants to serve on the CCC would enable lower levels of the party to exert a 'needed pressure' on the Central Committee.[88] Finally, Trotsky saw the new institution as an instrument for dealing with party members who had become politically unreliable. The communist who had begun to degenerate through over-specialisation was to be 'pulled up with a jerk in good time' – that is, warned to correct his behaviour. The member who had become so specialised that he had 'lost his moral link with the party' was to be expelled.[89]

Finally, Trotsky argued that bureaucratism in the party could be combated by increasing its proletarian composition.[90] In part, he saw this as an effective means of insulating the party against the corrupting pressures of the market and the NEPman. Beyond that, he believed that a large proletarian membership would serve as an anchor to prevent the specialised leadership from drifting away from its revolutionary perspective and pulling the party with it:

> It is necessary first and foremost to increase systematically the number of members working at the bench ... The more abundantly the underground springs of the party are nourished, the less the crystallization in the upper strata of the party along the lines of profession and department will threaten the party with bureaucratic ossification.[91]

---

87   Trotsky 1972a, p. 161. See also Trotsky 1973a, p. 104.
88   Fel'shtinskii 1988, vol. 1, p. 30.
89   Trotsky 1973a, p. 104.
90   Trotsky 1972a, p. 169.
91   Trotsky 1973a, p. 103. Another method for fighting departmentalism in the party, according to Trotsky, was to elevate the consciousness of the membership through an improved party press (Trotsky 1973a, p. 104).

3.3   The New Course Controversy

In the months following the Twelfth Party Congress, differences between Trotsky and the leadership majority continued to widen. One new area of conflict concerned Communist strategy in Germany. Others involved organisational manoeuvres by the majority of the party leadership against Trotsky, new developments in the party regime, and the leadership's response to a series of economic crises. Ultimately, the disagreements culminated in the explosion of the 'New Course' controversy of 1923–4, which pitted Trotsky and a new Opposition against the leadership majority.

By the summer of 1923 Germany was in the midst of a social crisis precipitated by the French occupation of the Ruhr and the ensuing hyperinflation.[92] Both factors contributed to a dramatic growth in the influence of the German far left and to a massive upsurge in working-class militancy. Uncertain how to proceed in this explosive situation, the Communist Party of Germany (KPD) appealed for guidance to Moscow, where they found the central leadership divided on a number of issues. The most radical position was advanced by Trotsky, who concluded by late August that a confrontation was imminent, and who insisted that the KPD should set the date for an insurrection and should focus all of its energies on preparations for this. Through the summer and fall of 1923 Zinoviev also advocated an aggressive approach, though in August he estimated that the German revolution was months, not weeks, away. Furthermore, he insisted that the date finally selected for the insurrection, 9 November, was nonbinding and 'for orientation' only. The most consistently conservative position was held by Stalin, who warned in July that an attempted insurrection by the KPD 'would end up in a crash', and who later suggested that the German revolution would arrive the following spring at the earliest.[93]

Ultimately, the KPD was compelled to act earlier than anticipated by the decision of the central German government to send troops against the left coalition government of Saxony. In response to this threat the KPD proposed an immediate general strike to its SPD allies. When the SPD rejected the Communist proposal, the KPD abruptly canceled its plans for insurrection. The following day only the Hamburg party organisation rose in a revolt that was quickly crushed. Subsequently, Zinoviev declared that the retreat of the

---

92   On the abortive German revolution of 1923 see Angress 1963, pp. 281–474; Broué 2005, pp. 683–816; Carr 1954, pp. 153–64, 174–89, 201–42; Harmon 2003, pp. 221–302.

93   For the positions of the Soviet leaders, see Angress 1963, pp. 392–5, 401–3; Broué 2005, pp. 757; 763–6; Carr 1954, pp. 186–7, 204–8; Daniels 1960, pp. 213–15; Harmon, *Lost Revolution*, pp. 259, 271–2.

KPD had been 'inevitable' under the circumstances. In contrast, Trotsky bitterly remarked that it was 'a classic demonstration of how it is possible to miss a perfectly exceptional revolutionary situation'.[94]

Meanwhile, through the summer and early fall of 1923 the party leadership majority took steps to consolidate its position through new manoeuvres against Trotsky, punitive transfers of its critics, and the increasing appointment of local party secretaries. In the Central Committee it was proposed that a number of CC members, including Stalin, should be added to Trotsky's Revolutionary Military Council. Although Trotsky was able to prevent this, he was forced to accept supporters of Stalin and Zinoviev on the council. Kuibyshev explained to Trotsky, 'We consider it necessary to wage a struggle against you but we cannot declare you an enemy; this is why we must resort to such methods'.[95] In the same period Khristian Rakovskii and Osinskii, who had criticised party policy at the Twelfth Congress, found themselves dispatched abroad on diplomatic assignments.[96] Finally, the appointment of party secretaries at this point reached such unprecedented levels that even supporters of the leadership majority were compelled to concede the deterioration of party democracy. Dzerzhinskii complained to the CC that 'the dying out of our party, the dying out of its internal life, the prevalence of nomination instead of election, is becoming a political danger and is paralyzing our party in its political leadership of the working class'.[97] A few months later Bukharin observed regarding Moscow, 'Our cell secretaries ... are usually appointed by the district committees', and he asserted that 'in the majority of cases the elections in our party organizations have in fact been transformed into mockery of elections, because the voting takes place not only without preliminary discussion, but ... according to the formula, "Is anyone opposed?"'[98]

At the same time, the Soviet Union was experiencing a series of economic crises. Following the Twelfth Party Congress, industrial prices continued to rise while agricultural prices dropped. The price scissors reached their widest separation on 1 October when industrial retail prices stood at 187 percent of the 1913 level, and retail prices of agricultural commodities fell to 58 percent.[99] The high prices of manufactured goods in turn generated a 'sales crisis' in

---

94   Angress 1963, p. 462; Broué 2005, pp. 809–10, 818; Trotsky 1975b, p. 201.

95   Trotsky 1975b, p. 57.

96   Carr 1954, p. 290.

97   Quoted in Daniels 1960, p. 211. On the continuing deterioration of the party regime in 1923, see Deutscher 1959, p. 105.

98   Quoted in Trotsky 1975b, p. 149.

99   Carr 1954, p. 87.

which large quantities of consumer products remained unsold in warehouses. Industries were forced to cut back in production, compounding the already serious problem of unemployment, and to reduce the level of wages or to pay them irregularly.[100] The leadership majority viewed the crisis not as a symptom of insufficient industrialisation, but as a result of exorbitant price setting by the trusts. Consequently, the policy pursued was one of directly forcing down industrial prices. In August, state credits to industry were restricted to compel enterprises to sell existing stocks at lower prices. However, this measure only exacerbated the problems of industry, leading to higher unemployment and more wage cuts.[101] Workers in various cities responded to the deterioration in their standard of living with a wave of strikes in August and September. Adding to the concern of the Soviet leadership was the fact that the strikes were encouraged and assisted by members of the Workers' Group. The leadership reacted with repression against the strikers and members of both the Workers' Truth and Workers' Group.[102]

At the end of September the Central Committee established three commissions to come up with solutions to the crises: a commission on the scissors crisis, one on wages, and one devoted to the internal party situation. The party minority, including Trotsky, boycotted the scissors commission, believing it would fail to address the underlying causes of the crisis.[103] The conclusions of Dzerzhinskii's commission on the party situation turned out to be just as unsatisfactory to the minority. Instead of addressing the decline in party democracy, the commission's most important recommendation was that all party members be required to report to the GPU any information they had about the underground groups.[104]

On 8 October Trotsky wrote a sharp response to the Dzerzhinskii commission proposal. He did not directly challenge the recommendation; in fact, he asserted instead that informing on 'hostile elements' within the party was 'so elementary a duty' that no special resolution to that effect was necessary. Rather, he argued that the need for such a resolution was symptomatic of a 'dramatic worsening of the inner-Party situation and the increased isolation' of the CC from the party. Then he proceeded to criticise the party's mistaken economic orientation and the steady erosion of party democracy since the Twelfth

100   Carr 1954, pp. 93–4; Daniels 1960, p. 209.
101   Carr 1954, pp. 97–8; Daniels 1960, p. 209.
102   Carr 1954, pp. 93–5, 292–3; Daniels 1960, pp. 209–10; Deutscher 1959, pp. 106–8; Pirani 2008, pp. 199–205.
103   Carr 1954, pp. 104–5; Daniels 1960, p. 211; Deutscher 1959, p. 111.
104   Carr 1954, p. 295; Daniels 1960, p. 211; Deutscher 1959, p. 108.

Party Congress. Trotsky concluded by declaring his intention to give his opinion on the current situation in the party 'to every Party member whom I regard as adequately prepared, mature, consistent, and therefore able to help the Party emerge from the deadlock without factional convulsions and shocks'.[105] One week later a group of 46 prominent party members – including supporters of Trotsky in past struggles and former members of the Democratic Centralists – sent their own statement to the Politburo. The criticisms of economic policy and the party regime contained in this manifesto, which came to be known as the 'Platform of the Forty-six', were essentially those leveled by Trotsky.[106]

The response of a joint plenum of the CC and the CCC was to condemn Trotsky's letter as having 'objectively acquired the character of a factional action', and to denounce the 46 as a 'factional group'.[107] However, in early November the majority leaders, under pressure from the ranks, shifted their approach from condemnation to concession. On the anniversary of the Revolution *Pravda* published an article by Zinoviev calling for more workers' democracy within the party. In a report to a district committee on 2 December, Stalin encouraged more 'open discussion' and the application of the 'principle of election . . . to all Party bodies and official posts' – barring 'insuperable obstacles', though he also noted that under conditions of NEP, with a growing bourgeoisie, it was necessary to impose limits on democracy, such as requiring that party officials have a pre-October party standing. Furthermore, he observed that it was necessary to set limits to discussion to keep the party from degenerating into a 'debating society'.[108] At the same time *Pravda* opened its pages to a debate on the question of party democracy. On 5 December this period of concessions culminated in the adoption by the Politburo and the Presidium of the CCC of a 'New Course' resolution co-authored by Stalin, Kamenev, and Trotsky.[109]

For the most part, the analysis and the recommendations of the resolution reflected Trotsky's views. It noted the need for greater coordination of all sectors of the economy and 'the exceptional importance of Gosplan' and other planning agencies. It also spoke of the 'objective contradictions' that had arisen

---

105   Vilkova 1996, pp. 46–7, 57.

106   The text of this statement can be found in Carr 1954, pp. 367–73; Trotsky 1975b, pp. 397–403; and Vilkova 1996, pp. 82–96. Trotsky further developed these themes in a second letter to the CC-CCC, dated 23 October 1923. Vilkova 1996, pp. 139–69.

107   Institute of Marxism Leninism of the Central Committee of the CPSU 1972, pp. 235, 236.

108   Stalin 1952–5, vol. 5, pp. 371, 376–8.

109   Carr 1954, pp. 301–7; Daniels 1960, p. 222; Deutscher 1959, pp. 116–19; Law 1995, p. 238. The text of the New Course resolution appears in Trotsky 1975, pp. 404–13.

from 'the prevailing market relations' of NEP, from the necessity of employing 'capitalist forms and methods of work' by the state, and from the use of non-proletarian elements in the state apparatus. These contradictions included:

> striking disparities in the material living standards of party members . . .; the growth of connections with bourgeois elements and the ideological influence of the latter; a departmentalized narrowing of intellectual horizons among officials . . .; and as a result of this, the weakening of the connections between communists working in different sectors; the danger of a loss of perspective of socialist construction as a whole and of world revolution; the danger . . . of the 'NEP degeneration' of a layer of functionaries who . . . come most into contact with bourgeois elements; the process of bureaucratization that can be observed in the party apparatus; and the resulting threat of the party becoming separated from the masses.[110]

To deal with these problems the resolution called for more 'workers' democracy', defined as 'liberty of frank discussion of the most important questions of party life by all members, and the election of all leading party functionaries and commissions by those bodies immediately under them'.[111] It outlined measures to increase free discussion within the party, to promote new functionaries from the rank and file, to expand educational work, and to convene party conferences twice yearly. The resolution also rejected the conversion of the power of superior bodies to confirm local party secretaries into a right of appointment.[112]

A few days after the adoption of the resolution, *Pravda* published an open letter by Trotsky to party meetings. There, he hailed the 'exceptional significance' of the resolution, characterising it as an 'important turning point' in the historical road of the party, but warned that 'now the bureaucrats are ready to "take note" of the "new course", that is, *to nullify it bureaucratically'*. Consequently, he urged party members to begin to implement the resolution by their own initiative.[113]

Trotsky's letter offered fresh encouragement to his sympathisers who had been leading the revolt in local party meetings during the previous month. Alarmed by these open manifestations of oppositional activity, the party leadership majority responded with a concerted attack upon Trotsky and

---

110   Trotsky 1975b, p. 406.
111   Trotsky 1975b, p. 408.
112   Trotsky 1975b, pp. 408–10.
113   Trotsky 1975b, p. 126.

the Opposition, developing many of the themes that would characterise the anti-Trotsky campaigns of subsequent years. Trotsky was accused of using democratic slogans for purely factional purposes, he was charged with seeking to drive a wedge between younger and older party generations, he was denounced for having consistently underestimated the peasantry, and the philosophy of 'Trotskyism' was depicted as inherently anti-Leninist. To buttress this last accusation, the majority leaders dragged out Trotsky's Menshevik past and reviewed his differences with Lenin over the Brest-Litovsk Treaty and the trade unions.[114] Confined to his apartment by illness, Trotsky was unable to defend his record and his views at public party meetings. (It is worth noting that this – like Trotsky's refusal to take on the defence of the Georgians the previous spring – was an early case in which illness interfered with his ability to act at a crucial political juncture).[115] Nevertheless, he responded to his antagonists in a series of articles that were republished in January in a pamphlet entitled *The New Course* in which he provided an extensive explanation of his new thoughts on party bureaucratism.

3.4   Trotsky and the New Course

In his New Course writings Trotsky continued to move beyond his previous preoccupation with inefficiency, increasingly associating the problem of bureaucracy with the phenomenon of political alienation. Again, it is possible to interpret Trotsky's sudden advocacy of 'workers' democracy' as a cynical manoeuvre inspired by self-interest. This was exactly how it was portrayed by Stalin.[116] Perhaps more sincerely, Shliapnikov, the former leader of the Workers' Opposition, also characterised it this way, asserting, 'In the present controversy the only goal of Comrade Trotsky and the Opposition is simply to seize the apparatus'.[117] In fact, it is likely that Trotsky was further sensitised to manifestations of political alienation by the manoeuvres of his opponents. However, from the description of the party situation in the New Course resolution signed by Stalin and Kamenev and from other admissions of majority supporters, it is clear that the developments in the party regime denounced by Trotsky were real enough.

---

114   Carr 1954, pp. 315–22; Daniels 1960, pp. 231–2; Deutscher 1959, pp. 125–6.
115   As Trotsky later observed, 'My high temperature paralyzed me at the most critical moments, and acted as my opponents' most steadfast ally' (Trotsky 1970c, p. 522).
116   Carr 1954, pp. 336–7; Daniels 1960, p. 231.
117   Quoted in Daniels 1960, p. 228.

Moreover, it is evident that Trotsky continued to be motivated to a large degree by his longstanding concern that the Soviet Union was devoting insufficient attention to economic planning and industrialisation. While disavowing the advocacy of democracy as an 'end in itself', Trotsky had concluded that the only way to correct the party's economic orientation was by transforming the party regime.[118] One reason he had reached this conclusion was that, in direct violation of the decisions of the Twelfth Party Congress, the leadership majority had done nothing to promote planning and industrialisation. In his 8 October letter to the Central Committee Trotsky complained that,

> after the Congress, Gosplan was in fact relegated [to the background]. Its work on reaching individual targets is useful and necessary, but has nothing in common with the planned regulation of the economy as it was passed by the Twelfth Congress. The lack of coordination in planning is especially trying in the work of central and, in general, major state economic bodies. To an even greater extent than before the Twelfth Congress, the most important economic issues are being solved in a hurry, without due preparation, regardless of their planning connections.[119]

Additionally, instead of the 'thorough personal selection of managerial personnel' mandated by the Twelfth Congress, which for Trotsky was achievable only through planning, the Orgburo had instituted the assignment of personnel 'from the point of view of their ability to support or oppose the inner-Party regime, which is being secretly though no less actually established by the Orgburo and the Secretariat'.[120]

Meanwhile, Trotsky also was beginning to view new developments in the party regime with increasing alarm. Since the Twelfth Party Congress, the party regime had deteriorated to the point that it was 'much farther from workers' democracy than the regime of the toughest periods of War Communism'. For Trotsky, as the New Course resolution had stated, worker's democracy meant the election of party functionaries and the free discussion of all important issues. 'In the most severe time of War Communism', Trotsky asserted, the 'practice of appointments was not spread at one-tenth of its present scale'. Provincial party secretaries were now almost universally appointed, and once selected, they proceeded to make all other appointments, dismissals, and other important decisions at the provincial level. Whenever anyone opposed

---

118   Trotsky 1975b, p. 64.
119   Vilkova 1996, pp. 47–8. See also Trotsky 1975b, p. 52.
120   Vilkova 1996, p. 51.

the decision of a provincial party secretary, that secretary, 'with the help of the Center', had the dissident transferred. Consequently, party members were afraid to express their views openly. Trotsky also recalled that at the height of the civil war the party organisations and the press were centres of discussion and debate. Now, there was 'no trace of such open exchange of opinions on matters of true importance to the Party'.[121]

As a number of writers have emphasised, in late 1923 Trotsky conceptualised the problem in terms of the disease of 'bureaucratism' that had infected the party, and not yet in terms of a state and party 'bureaucracy' that ruled the Soviet Union.[122] Nevertheless, while Trotsky perceived the problem of bureaucratism as merely a disease or tendency, he rejected as 'unworthy of a Marxist' the notion that it involved 'only the aggregate of the bad habits of officeholders'. At various times in the past he had spoken precisely in such terms. Now he insisted that bureaucratism was a 'social phenomenon', that is, 'a definite system of administration of people and things'.[123] By this, he was suggesting that bureaucratism involved the breakdown of collective decision making by the rank and file, and its replacement by a hierarchical system of authority. Along these lines, Trotsky described the party as 'living, as it were, on two stories: the upper story, where things are decided, and the lower story, where all you do is learn of the decisions'.[124]

For Trotsky, this gravitation of power to the 'upper story' was related to its concentration in the hands of the Old Guard – members who had joined the party before the October Revolution. He did not contest the fact that the Old Bolsheviks had contributed innumerable services to the revolution; nor did he deny that, if they had the other necessary qualities, their appointment to leading positions should be encouraged. Nevertheless, he warned that the 'growing discontent with the self-sufficient secretary's apparatus, which identifies itself with the old Bolshevism, may have the most grave consequences for the ideological hegemony and organizational leadership of old Bolsheviks in our half-million-member Party'.[125]

In passing, Trotsky commented upon a series of attitudes characteristic of members of the party apparatus. Some were features he had noted previously in his discussions of bureaucratic inefficiency. Now, he seems to have

121   Vilkova 1996, pp. 51–2.
122   See, for example, P. Anderson 1984, p. 118; Bellis 1979, p. 58; Lovell 1985, p. 21; Law 1995, p. 242.
123   Trotsky 1975b, p. 91.
124   Trotsky 1975b, p. 69.
125   Vilkova 1996, p. 53.

concluded that these traits had arisen out of the impulse of party officials to preserve their own power. One of these attitudes was excessive 'formalism', or the rigid application of formal principles, described by Trotsky as 'the essential attribute of bureaucratism'. As an example, he noted the tendency to 'consider every criticism a manifestation of factionalism'. While conceding that factions and 'every *incorrect* deviation' might become the entering wedge for alien class interests, Trotsky pointed out that this applied to bureaucratism as well.[126] Closely related to formalism was a preoccupation with tradition that served to legitimise the existing party leadership. It was true, Trotsky asserted, that 'without a continuous lineage, and consequently without a tradition, there cannot be stable progress'. Nevertheless, for Trotsky the real revolutionary tradition of Marxism was 'a method of historical analysis, . . . and not a mass of decisions prepared in advance'.[127]

Three more attitudes Trotsky depicted as common within the party apparatus were a 'complete distain for the mood, the thoughts, and the needs of the party', 'bureaucratic smugness', and 'apparatus cliquism'. The first of these was related to the indifference and hostility to the masses that, earlier in the year, he had described as characteristic of the state apparatus. 'Bureaucratic smugness' referred to the confidence of party secretaries in their ability to make decisions about matters with which they had little or no familiarity – a tendency Trotsky had noted as early as the Eleventh Party Congress. On the other hand, 'apparatus cliquism', or the 'corporatist and departmental spirit of the separate constituent parts of the party', was a trait only recently diagnosed by Trotsky. It referred to the group consciousness of the party secretaries, and was especially menacing for it implied the possibility that the apparatus might evolve into a distinct social grouping or 'bureaucracy'.[128]

Trotsky suggested that bureaucratism and its attendant characteristics were to blame for the conservative drift of policy in a number of areas. It was the absence of democracy in the party, he now claimed, and not just the lack of planning, that was responsible the development of a narrow specialised outlook among the party leaders. Without democracy,

> Leadership takes on a purely organizational character and frequently degenerates into order-giving and meddling. The party apparatus goes more and more into the details of the tasks of the Soviet apparatus, lives

---

126   Trotsky 1975b, pp. 80, 84, 85.
127   Trotsky 1975b, pp. 134, 96.
128   Trotsky 1975b, pp. 69, 75; Trotsky 2004 (translation modified).

the life of its day-to-day cares, lets itself be increasingly influenced by it, and fails to see the forest for the trees.[129]

Again, Trotsky was suggesting that this narrow departmental mentality in turn had promoted the mistaken orientation of Soviet economic policy.

Additionally, Trotsky believed that bureaucratic traditionalism was responsible for other erroneous policies. Explicitly, he blamed the recent failure in Germany on the conservative traditionalism of the KPD, which had persisted in a 'propaganda policy' when a new orientation was required.[130] However, just a few paragraphs later he noted that the 'relatively strong bureaucratization of the [Bolshevik] party apparatus is inevitably accompanied by the development of conservative traditionalism with all its effects'.[131] It is likely that Trotsky was implying that the hesitations of the KPD leadership had been reinforced by the timidity of the Russian leadership, and especially of Zinoviev, head of the Comintern. Finally, Trotsky blamed bureaucratic traditionalism for Stalin's repressive national policies: 'Only recently we saw the most official interpreters of the party's traditions on the national question take a stand in direct contradiction to the needs of party policy in this question as well as to Lenin's position'.[132]

Among Trotsky's concerns about the long-term consequences of bureaucratism was that it might weaken the internal vibrancy and unity of the party. 'Bureaucratism', wrote Trotsky, 'kills initiative and thus prevents the elevation of the general level of the party. That is its cardinal defect'.[133] Most important in this regard was the effect that it was having on the party youth. For young people to develop politically, Trotsky observed, they needed the opportunity to criticise and to think independently. By stifling initiative, the party apparatus was obstructing the education of the next generation of Bolshevik leaders.[134] Trotsky also suggested that bureaucratism threatened to promote the development of disruptive factionalism. When communists had no sense that they were able to participate actively in making decisions affecting the party, and

---

129   Trotsky 1975b, p. 77.

130   Trotsky 1975b, pp. 94–5.

131   Trotsky 1975b, p. 96.

132   Trotsky 1975b, p. 98. Trotsky also utilised the history of party differences to suggest his opponents were prone to traditionalism. He noted that the October Revolution, Brest-Litovsk, and 'the creation of a regular peasant army' had required initiative and a break with tradition (Trotsky 1975b, p. 97). Of course, Bolshevik policy regarding these issues had been opposed by Zinoviev and Kamenev, Bukharin, and Stalin, respectively.

133   Trotsky 1975b, p. 125.

134   Trotsky 1975b, p. 127.

when their questions were ignored or their criticisms repressed, many began 'looking for a substitute for independent party activity in the form of groupings and factions of all sorts'.[135]

Beyond that, Trotsky reasserted that bureaucratism could lead to the complete 'opportunistic degeneration' of the leadership:

> In its prolonged development, bureaucratization threatens to detach the leaders from the masses; to bring them to concentrate their attention solely upon questions of administration, of appointments and transfers; to narrow their horizon; to weaken their revolutionary spirit; that is, to provoke a more or less opportunistic degeneration of the Old Guard, or at the very least of a considerable part of it.[136]

Ultimately, Trotsky warned again, the bureaucratisation of the party increased the possibility of capitalist restoration. The economic preconditions for restoration could be created by the failure to reverse the leadership's erroneous economic policies. If private capital continued to accumulate at the expense of nationalised industry, the peasantry eventually would fall under its economic, and consequently its political influence.[137] Meanwhile, bureaucratism was generating the political prerequisites for restoration by weakening the party, inciting unhealthy factionalism, and promoting the degeneration of the leadership. Consequently, political paths by which counterrevolution might occur included 'the direct overthrow of the workers' party, or its progressive degeneration, or finally, the conjunction of a partial degeneration, splits, and counterrevolutionary upheavals'.[138]

Trotsky said relatively little at this time about the underlying causes of party bureaucratism. He was far more concerned with demonstrating its dangers and indicating how these could be combated.[139] Nevertheless, he stressed that party bureaucratism was 'not at all a "survival" of the war period'. If it were a mere 'survival', the problem would be diminishing, not growing. Rather, it was 'the result of the transference to the party of the methods and administrative manners accumulated [in the state] during these last years'.[140] He further

135   Trotsky 1975b, p. 72. See also Trotsky 1975b, p. 127.
136   Trotsky 1975b, p. 72.
137   Trotsky 1975b, pp. 88, 89.
138   Trotsky 1975b, p. 88.
139   This is also noted by Knei-Paz 1978, p. 374.
140   Trotsky 1975b, p. 70. Also, see Trotsky 1975b, p. 76.

asserted that the state apparatus was 'the most important source of [party] bureaucratism'.[141]

Combining ideas he had expressed earlier in the year with new and undeveloped insights, Trotsky explained the origins of *state* bureaucratism as follows:

> Its profound causes lie in the heterogeneity of society, the difference between the daily and the fundamental interests of various groups of the population. Bureaucratism is complicated by the lack of culture among the broad masses. With us, the essential source of bureaucratism resides in the necessity of creating and sustaining a state apparatus that unites the interests of the proletariat and the peasantry in perfect economic harmony, from which we are still far removed. The necessity of maintaining a permanent army is likewise another important source of bureaucratism.[142]

He did not elaborate but, consistent with his analysis earlier in the year, he undoubtedly viewed some of these factors as promoting bourgeois influence, and some as contributing to the growth of centralised, authoritarian, and hierarchical relationships within the state apparatus.

In turn, Trotsky suggested that these relationships had been transmitted into the party by communists involved in state work and by the party apparatus that had been entrusted with the oversight of the state:

> On one hand, it [the state apparatus] absorbs an enormous quantity of the most active party elements and teaches them the methods of administration of people and things, instead of political leadership of the masses. On the other hand, it largely occupies the attention of the party apparatus, over which it exerts influence by its methods of administration.[143]

In fact, he noted, a large part of the party now consisted of state and party officials who had learned the 'methods of administration' of the state apparatus. These were the 'functionaries' who constituted 'one of the fairly stable social groupings' of the Soviet regime.[144]

One factor that contributed to the political weight of these functionaries was the relative decline in proletarian membership in the party. Trotsky explained that after the seizure of power, the first concern of the proletariat

---

141 Trotsky 1975b, p. 91.
142 Trotsky 1975b, pp. 91–2.
143 Trotsky 1975b, p. 91.
144 Trotsky 1975b, p. 74.

had been to create its own state apparatus. This had required the transfer of Bolshevik workers from the factories to the state, cooperative, and other apparatuses, resulting in a weakening of the factory cells and an increase in the number of functionaries in the party.[145] Subsequently, the growth of the working class as a whole, which might have provided new proletarian recruits, had been retarded by the slow development of industry.[146] The result was that now less than one-sixth of the party membership was composed of proletarians actually working at the bench.[147]

Consequently, Trotsky's ultimate solution to the problem of party bureaucratism was to strike at its foundations by eliminating state bureaucratism and proletarianising the party. He did not even consider relinquishing party control over the state or abolishing one-party rule, for he believed that such measures would only weaken the resistance of the Soviet regime to capitalist restoration.[148] By this time he also had given up on the combined CCC-Rabkrin as an anti-bureaucratic tool since, in his view, this institution had been organised in such a way that it had been 'rendered harmless'.[149] Instead, he called for renewed efforts against state bureaucratism, urging 'the education of party youth, based upon personal initiative' so that the young people would learn to 'serve the state apparatus in a new manner and to transform it completely'.[150] Additionally, he reasserted the need to accelerate industrial expansion and to recruit more workers to the party.[151] Nevertheless, Trotsky seemed to recognise that in the short run these measures would not be effective in combating party bureaucratism. He emphasised that the struggle against state bureaucratism was 'an exceptionally important but prolonged task'.[152] Furthermore, while he judged that increasing the proletarian content of the party was 'the best guarantee that it will retain its proletarian character', he cautioned that 'the membership of the party can be altered seriously (so that, for example, the factory cells make up two-thirds of its ranks) only very slowly and only under conditions of noteworthy economic advance'.[153]

---

145   Trotsky 1975b, p. 73.
146   Trotsky 1975b, p. 75.
147   Ibid.
148   Trotsky asserted: 'We are the only party in the country, and in the period of the dictatorship [of the proletariat] it could not be otherwise' (Trotsky 1975b, p. 78).
149   Trotsky 1975b, p. 62.
150   Trotsky 1975b, p. 92.
151   Trotsky 1975b, pp. 74, 90, 92.
152   Trotsky 1975b, p. 92.
153   Trotsky 1975b, pp. 90, 74.

For the immediate future, then, Trotsky focused less on the elimination of the sources of party bureaucratism and more on the need for a direct assault against party bureaucratism itself. This required the immediate implementation of the democratic reforms embodied in the New Course resolution. In its struggle against bureaucratism, Trotsky insisted, the party could not count on the leadership. Rather, it had to rely on its own initiative and '*subordinate to itself its own apparatus* without for a moment ceasing to be a centralized organization'.[154] He called on the rank and file to begin to take control of party organisations at every level and to institute workers' democracy:

> Every unit of the party must return to collective initiative, to the right of free and comradely criticism – without fear and without turning back – and to the right of organizational self-determination. It is necessary to regenerate and renovate the party apparatus and to make it feel it is nothing but the executive mechanism of the collective will.[155]

Of course, there were limits to the degree of democracy Trotsky was ready to advocate, even within the party. Most importantly, he refrained from asserting the right of party oppositionists to organise themselves into factions. To some extent this may have been for tactical reasons. A challenge by Trotsky to the ban on factions certainly would have been seized upon by his opponents as the ultimate evidence of his 'anti-Leninism'. More importantly, it is clear that Trotsky honestly supported the ban for reasons closely related to his understanding of the problem of bureaucracy. Just as the bureaucratised party apparatus, separated from the control of the party as a whole, was falling under the influence of increasingly powerful bourgeois elements, Trotsky believed that *all* political groupings that were more or less independent of the party – especially groupings with their own internal discipline – were susceptible to the same process. As he explained in *The New Course*, 'Even episodic differences' might come to 'express the remote pressure of distinct social interests, and . . . be transformed into stable groupings', and these groupings could become 'organized factions which, opposing themselves to the rest of the party, undergo by that fact even greater external pressure'.[156] Consequently, the task

---

154   Trotsky 1975b, p. 124.
155   Trotsky 1975b, p. 126.
156   Trotsky 1975b, p. 79.

was to find the '*intermediate line*' that separated the '*calm*' of bureaucratically enforced unity from factionalism.[157]

Once the party membership asserted its power, Trotsky predicted, it quickly would find allies within the apparatus itself. Of course, there were some 'mummified bureaucrats' who would have to be removed from their posts, but in Trotsky's estimation the 'vast majority' of the members of the apparatus were not yet bureaucratised. He anticipated that the New Course controversy would 'teach a good deal to the majority of the apparatus workers and will get them to abandon most of their errors'. When these elements realised the dangers of bureaucratism, they would participate enthusiastically in implementing the New Course resolution.[158]

Still, for Trotsky this was not the end of the struggle. He had been roused to opposition largely by his concerns about the majority's economic policy. This policy had shifted the Soviet state off of tracks that led to socialism, and onto rails that led in the direction of capitalist restoration. For Trotsky, then, workers' democracy was only 'a means and not an end in itself'. The value of the new course in the coming period, he asserted, would be determined by the degree to which it helped the party resolve its 'principal economic task' – the establishment of 'centralized, planned management of the economy'.[159]

3.5   Political Defeat and Theoretical Retreat

During the debate that raged through December, the Opposition found considerable support within the party ranks. A stronghold of the Opposition was in Moscow, where the assault on the leadership was led by Preobrazhenskii, Piatakov, and T.V. Sapronov. There, the Opposition frequently dominated party meetings, and won nearly half the vote, if not a majority, at the cell level.[160] It was also able to capture various provincial party organisations that contained concentrations of dissidents transferred from the centre. The Opposition

---

157   Trotsky 1975b, pp. 79, 80. Cliff 1991, pp. 16–17 and Marot 2006, pp. 182–3 have argued, probably correctly, that Trotsky would have taken a different position on the ban on parties and factions if he had perceived the bureaucracy as a 'class enemy' or 'social force acting in its class interests'. It is likely this also would have been true if he had defined the problem in terms of a 'bureaucratic caste' that was usurping power, as he did in later years. However, is not clear how or why he would have made such a theoretical leap in 1923 when his own simpler approach seemed to address his concerns.

158   Trotsky 1975b, pp. 126–7, 69, 129.

159   Trotsky 1975b, pp. 64, 65.

160   Murphy 2001, p. 332; Murphy 2005, p. 165; Pirani 2008, p. 219.

found social bases of support among soldiers, the student youth, and, ironically, among party members employed in the heartland of bureaucratism – the state apparatus and especially the economic bodies. No doubt, this last grouping was drawn to the Opposition for its advocacy of industrialisation and central planning.[161] Additionally, recent research indicates that at least a quarter of the worker's cells in Moscow, and perhaps far more, supported the Opposition.[162]

Nevertheless, the Opposition was severely hampered by internal weaknesses. Most important was its inability to differentiate its programme clearly from that of the leadership majority. As far as the question of the party regime was concerned, the rank and file could perceive little difference between the two sides, both of which claimed to support democratic reforms. Additionally, the Opposition was unable to present any short-run solutions to the low wages and unemployment that were troubling industrial workers.[163] Besides, some workers still remembered the militarisation of labour and the trade-union 'shake-up' advocated by Trotsky and his supporters in 1920, and they distrusted the sudden conversion of many Opposition leaders to workers' democracy. Another weakness was the Opposition's leadership. Trotsky's inability to participate actively in the discussion, together with his failure to openly identify himself with the minority, left the Opposition without a representative who could match the prestige of Zinoviev, Kamenev, Bukharin, and Stalin. Also, some party members viewed many of the Opposition's leaders as compromised by their previous association with 'anti-Leninist' groupings such as the Left Communists and the Democratic Centralists.[164]

More important than the internal weaknesses of the Opposition was the overwhelming organisational strength of the leadership majority. Through its control of the party press, the majority was able to limit access to the views of the Opposition and to drown its criticisms in a flood of counteraccusations. Party members who were inclined to sympathise with the Opposition were intimidated from speaking or voting against the leadership by the fear of dismissal from their jobs, expulsion from the universities, or transfer to other locations. Finally, through the tiered system of election, the leadership was able to substantially reduce the representation of the Opposition. Consequently, although the Opposition gained nearly half the votes at the

161   Carr 1954, pp. 324, 326, 332; Cliff 1991, pp. 44–5; Daniels 1960, pp. 227–8; Deutscher 1959, p. 132; Hinks 1992, pp. 141–3; Law 1995, p. 246.
162   Hinks 1992, pp. 143–6; Murphy 2001, pp. 332–3, 346; Murphy 2005, p. 165.
163   Related to this, see Carr 1954, pp. 327–8; Pirani 2008, pp. 222, 223.
164   Carr 1954, pp. 326–8; Daniels 1960, pp. 229–30.

cell level in Moscow, it received only 36 percent at district conferences in the Moscow province, and only 18 percent at the Moscow provincial conference that elected delegates to the Thirteenth Party Conference.[165]

Ultimately, the Opposition claimed only three out of 128 voting delegates at the party conference that convened in mid-January. The conference endorsed the deepening economic orientation to the peasant market and rejected Opposition proposals to increase the degree of central planning and accelerate industrialisation. In a resolution on the discussion, the conference also branded the Opposition a 'petty bourgeois deviation', insisted on the need for discipline, and reaffirmed the party's ban on factions.[166] Trotsky's persistent fever kept him from attending the conference, and even before its final session he boarded a train for the Caucasus seeking rest and recovery. In Tiflis he received the news of Lenin's death, which finally dashed his hopes that Lenin would recover to join him in an assault on bureaucratism. Misinformed about the date of Lenin's funeral, Trotsky did not return to Moscow but continued on to the resort of Sukhum.[167]

The majority leaders quickly found new opportunities to strengthen their own positions. At Lenin's funeral they inaugurated a Lenin cult that was used to legitimate their power.[168] At about this time the CCC began to oust Oppositionists on grounds of 'opportunism' and personal defects.[169] Meanwhile, in honour of Lenin the leadership opened the doors of the party to over 200,000 industrial workers. According to Trotsky's later account, the effect of this was to swamp the party with politically unsophisticated and easily manipulated members who would back the leadership majority.[170]

Not one Oppositionist was elected as a delegate to the Thirteenth Party Congress in May, and only a few Oppositionists, including Trotsky, were permitted to speak. The theme and tone were set by Zinoviev, who called for the unity of the party against its disrupters. One after the other, delegates denounced the Opposition's factional activities and its petty-bourgeois

---

165   Carr 1954, p. 333; Daniels 1960, pp. 228–9; Law 1995, pp. 246–7; Pirani 2008, p. 219.

166   Carr 1954, pp. 125–30, 333–41; Daniels 1960, pp. 233–4.

167   Carr 1954, p. 346; Deutscher 1959, p. 133. For a critical review of the evidence regarding Trotsky's claim that Stalin deliberately misled him about the date of the funeral, see Thatcher 2009, pp. 194–202.

168   On the beginnings of the Lenin cult, see Carr 1954, pp. 347–51; Daniels 1960, pp. 236–7.

169   Carr 1954, pp. 356–7; Daniels 1960, pp. 238–9.

170   Trotsky 1937, pp. 97–8. Endorsements of this view of the Lenin Levy by Western historians include Daniels 1960, p. 238; Deutscher 1959, pp. 135–6; Hosking 1993, pp. 143–4; Pirani 2008, pp. 230–1; Schapiro 1971, pp. 313–14. For different views on this, see Carr 1958–64, vol. 1, pp. 106–7; Fitzpatrick 1982, p. 97; Hatch 1989.

FROM INEFFICIENCY TO POLITICAL ALIENATION

orientation.[171] In his address to the congress Trotsky adopted a conciliatory tone, while reasserting the correctness of the views he had expressed in *The New Course*. Although he probably already had serious reservations about the scale and pace of the Lenin Levy, his own recent statements on behalf of party proletarianisation compelled him to endorse it. In response to Zinoviev's demand that he admit he had been wrong about the situation within the party, Trotsky flatly refused. However, he simultaneously reaffirmed his own loyalty, declaring that 'if it should come to that, I will not be the least soldier on the least Bolshevik barricade'.[172]

At the Congress and in the following months the leadership took further steps to consolidate its position and to eradicate the Opposition. Once again, the CC was expanded, mostly by the addition of Stalin's supporters. The new CCC, also expanded, was directed to continue the work of weeding the party membership, particularly in educational and governmental institutions where Oppositionists were concentrated. Meanwhile, the leadership began to press the other parties of the Comintern into line behind the anti-Trotsky campaign. Since the Comintern's founding in 1919, the foreign sections had revered Trotsky as a leader of the world revolution. Now, at the Fifth Congress in June 1924, the delegates joined in his denunciation and voted to replace Trotsky on the Executive Committee with Stalin.[173]

Barred by party discipline from criticising party policies, in the summer of 1924 Trotsky turned to historical analysis to vindicate his own record and to cast a shadow over the political biographies of his adversaries. His opponents, depicting themselves as Lenin's faithful disciples, had portrayed Trotsky as an unregenerate Menshevik. Trotsky's answer appeared in 'Lessons of October', a preface to a collection of his speeches and writings from 1917. There, he described the internal party situation of 1917 as a struggle between a left wing led by Lenin – and implicitly, by himself – that had pushed for an insurrection to complete the proletarian revolution, and a right wing led by Kamenev and Zinoviev that, insisting the revolution could not go beyond bourgeois-democratic limits, had opposed the insurrection. Although Trotsky asserted that 'nothing could be more paltry' than an attempt to turn the disagreements of 1917 'into weapons of attack against those who were at that time mistaken', it was precisely as a weapon that he now wielded the history of the revolution.[174] As Trotsky saw it, the issue was not merely historical. Once more he insisted

171   Carr 1954, pp. 384–5.
172   For Trotsky's speech, see Trotsky 1975b, pp. 146–62.
173   Daniels 1960, p. 242; Deutscher 1959, pp. 146–51; Rigby 1968, p. 128.
174   Trotsky 1975b, p. 200.

that the attempted revolution in Germany in 1923 had collapsed as a direct consequence of the failure of the German Communist Party to take decisive action.[175] Again, the obvious implication was that the leaders of the Russian Communist Party who had directed preparations for the German insurrection had reiterated their errors of 1917.

The counterattack by the party leadership was massive. In the books, pamphlets, and speeches of the 'literary debate' the triumvirs and their supporters denounced Trotsky's interpretation of the events of 1917, while supplying their own accounts, which increasingly diverged from historical accuracy. At the same time they subjected Trotsky's own political record to fresh attacks. The latest allegation, made by Stalin, was that Trotsky had persistently opposed his own theory of permanent revolution to Lenin's view that socialism could be constructed in one country.[176]

In January 1925 Trotsky was forced to resign from his position as Commissar of War. A few months later he was reassigned to serve on the Supreme Council of the National Economy under Dzerzhinskii, where he chaired three commissions. In this capacity Trotsky was able to return to the economic issues raised by the Opposition. In August he wrote a series of articles for *Pravda* that utilised Gosplan figures to demonstrate the need for broadening the scope of economic planning and accelerating industrialisation.[177] Nevertheless, following the Opposition's defeat, he found it necessary to retreat from open criticism of the party leadership as well as from his explosive analysis of party bureaucratism. The Oppositionist Victor Serge later recalled how in 1925 Trotsky advised the Opposition, 'For the moment we must not act at all: no showing ourselves in public but keep our contacts, preserve our cadres of 1923, and wait for Zinoviev to exhaust himself'.[178] In this period Trotsky continued to raise the issue of bureaucracy on various occasions, but for the time being he limited himself to relatively innocuous remarks about red tape and bureaucratism in the Soviet state.[179]

---

175   Trotsky 1975b, pp. 201, 203, 230–1, 233, 249, 250, 251, 254, 256.
176   Daniels 1960, pp. 244–52; Deutscher 1959, pp. 154–60.
177   Deutscher 1959, pp. 160–3, 208–12; Stalin 1974, pp. 319–82.
178   Serge 1980, p. 209.
179   Trotsky 1973a, pp. 152, 157, 171; Trotsky 1963e, pp. 123, 129, 188, 378. However, behind some of these remarks it is possible to discern elements of Trotsky's New Course analysis. See Twiss 2009, pp. 188–90.

3.6   Conclusion

During 1923 Trotsky's critique of Soviet bureaucracy underwent a major transformation. In late 1922 he was still describing the problem almost exclusively in terms of 'glavkokratic' inefficiency in the economy. However, in the following year a variety of factors, including the continuing resistance of the leadership majority to economic planning, convinced Trotsky that the problem could be understood best in terms of the traditional Marxist analysis of political alienation. Consistent with that analysis, in 1923 he began to perceive both state and party bureaucratism in terms of the growing separation of officials from the masses or ranks, and to see this as related to deviations to the right in a number of policy areas.

Despite the merits of Trotsky's 1923 perspective, it is clear in retrospect that it contained a number of serious weaknesses. Perhaps the most basic deficiency was that it greatly underestimated the depth of the problem. At the end of December 1923 Trotsky confidently predicted that the Opposition's criticisms of the party regime would convince the overwhelming majority of the party apparatus to return to the methods of workers' democracy. Trotsky's statement in this regard may have been at least partially a rhetorical device to draw hesitant rank and file members into the struggle, and partly a product of excessive optimism about the pressure the membership would be able to exert. More importantly, it appears to have been a reflection of his failure to gauge the depth of the leadership majority's resistance to democratisation. The same failure was expressed in the very term *bureaucratism* – suggesting a disease afflicting an otherwise sound organism – utilised by Trotsky to characterise the basic problem.

Additional weaknesses already evident at this point involved his direct association of bureaucratism with alien class influence. At the time, Trotsky's assertion that the leadership's preoccupation with market mechanisms was retarding the development of industry was persuasive, and his belief that this orientation reflected bourgeois influence seemed quite plausible. However, his application of a similar analysis to Comintern policy was more problematic. Trotsky's supporter Karl Radek, the leading Comintern representative in Germany in 1923, was slower to embrace the idea of an insurrection and to set the date for it than Zinoviev, and Radek endorsed the KPD's cancellation of the insurrection even before Zinoviev.[180] Perhaps that is why neither Trotsky nor

---

180   Angress 1963, p. 394; Broué 2005, pp. 757, 764, 809–10, 818, 896–7; Harman 2003, pp. 259–60, 271–2, 287–8.

the Opposition made an issue out of the German events in the party struggle of 1923. However, Radek's behaviour called into question Trotsky's suggestion that bureaucratic conservatism was responsible for the German failure. Beyond that, Trotsky's belief that the Comintern leadership was excessively conservative implied that it would continue deviating to the right after the defeat of the Opposition. Instead, for a year and a half after the German failure the leadership pursued what Trotsky later described as an 'ultra-left' course, refusing to recognise the seriousness of the defeat in Germany and carrying out a policy of 'left mistakes and putschist experiments' in both Estonia and Bulgaria.[181] Comparable developments would challenge Trotsky's perspective even more sharply in 1928–33.

Another area of weakness in Trotsky's analysis during this period was his explanation of the origins of the problem of bureaucracy. In particular, his description of the origins of bureaucratism was vague and undeveloped. Furthermore, an important omission from Trotsky's account was any reference to the restrictions on workers' democracy adopted by the Bolsheviks in previous years. In *The New Course* Trotsky asserted that party bureaucratism was not a survival of the past, but a relatively new phenomenon. In fact, it seems that in late 1923 the party regime really *was* considerably less democratic than in previous years. Still, Trotsky ignored the degree to which party democracy had been eroded by measures such as the 1921 ban on factions and the punitive transfer of oppositionists. Nor did he did comment on the role that measures such as the outlawing of opposition parties or his own 'shake up' of the transport unions had played in weakening workers' democracy outside of the party. While it would have been politically counterproductive for Trotsky to have argued along these lines, there is no indication that in 1923 he even perceived past Bolshevik practices as having contributed to the problem. These were topics he would only begin to address in the mid-1930s.

Finally, during this period there were a number of problems with Trotsky's strategic orientation for the struggle against bureaucracy. Most generally, his approach was to promote workers' democracy as a means of enhancing proletarian control and countering bourgeois political influence over policy.

---

181   Trotsky 1970b, pp. 103–7, 116–24. For Trotsky's explanation of this ultra-leftism, see Trotsky 1970b, p. 124. On the communist uprising in Talinn, Estonia on 1 December 1924, see Carr 1958–64, vol. 3:1, pp. 284–6. On the bombing of the Sveta Nedelya Cathedral in Sofia on 14 April 1925, characterised by Trotsky as a 'terrorist adventure', see Rothschild 1959, pp. 259–64.

However, there were strong tensions between and within each of the elements of this strategy.

One of these was the tension between Trotsky's goal of establishing a proletarian line for the party and his method of party democratisation. As Trotsky himself indicated, in 1923 only one-sixth of the party membership was made up of factory workers. The remainder was composed of administrators, students, and agricultural workers. The most that the enhancement of party democracy could have achieved in the short run was some increase in the degree of proletarian *influence* over policy. Of course, for Trotsky, the ultimate resolution of this dilemma required the gradual re-proletarianisation of party. Yet, by Trotsky's own account, in the form it was implemented in 1924 this actually reinforced the position of the leadership majority.[182]

Equally, there was a tension between Trotsky's advocacy of greater proletarian control of the party and his economic alternative to the policies of the majority. In fact, it is doubtful that Trotsky's industrialisation program held much appeal for the Soviet working class in late 1923.[183] Just a few months before the New Course controversy, Trotsky asserted that primitive socialist accumulation would require greater sacrifices from the proletariat. However, the strike wave of the summer of 1923 suggests that Soviet workers were in no mood to listen to demands for new sacrifices. In light of this, it is remarkable that the Opposition performed as well as it did in the voting in workers' cells.

Finally, as described by Trotsky, the effects of democratisation as a means of combating bourgeois influence were themselves contradictory. Although Trotsky emphasised the value of democracy in this regard, he also believed that *too much* democracy – in the form of toleration for competing oppositional parties and factions – would provide opportunities for the reviving bourgeoisie to re-exert their influence. While the Opposition probably would have gained little immediate advantage by demanding the repeal of either ban, Trotsky's support for these restrictions hardly enhanced the long-term struggle for democracy.[184]

Despite these problems, Trotsky's shift of focus to political alienation represented an important development in his thinking. While the concept of *glavkokratiia* had been useful for identifying the economic problems of previous years, even then it had been irrelevant for understanding the deeper political concerns addressed by Lenin and the party opposition groups. Viewing

182   On this point, see Cliff 1991, p. 38; Deutscher 1959, pp. 128–9.

183   This point is suggested in Deutscher 1959, p. 131.

184   See Cliff 1991, pp. 17, 38. This point is expressed more sharply in Marot 2006, pp. 181–3.

bureaucracy in terms of political alienation, in 1923 Trotsky was able to paint a convincing and devastating portrait of the state of the party regime, to begin to explain the emerging dynamics of Soviet politics, and to formulate an initial programmatic alternative. Building on this analysis, in subsequent years Trotsky was able to construct an elaborate but coherent theory of Soviet bureaucracy.

A Coherent Theory of Bureaucracy

By 1926, realignments within the party permitted Trotsky to return to the political offensive. In 1925 Zinoviev and Kamenev broke with Stalin and the leadership majority over a wide range of issues. Implicitly, the arguments of the New Opposition confirmed Trotsky's warnings about the dangers of party bureaucratism and of a resurgent right within the country. The following year Trotsky and his supporters joined forces with the Zinovievists to form the United Opposition, which challenged the economic, international, and political policies of the party leadership throughout 1926 and 1927. In the fire of this struggle, Trotsky was able to forge a coherent theory of Soviet bureaucracy based upon the classical Marxist analysis of bureaucracy.

4.1   The Formation of the United Opposition

In early 1925 the ruling bloc of Zinoviev, Kamenev, and Stalin began to crumble. The alliance had been a shaky one from the outset, but tensions latent within the triumvirate only increased once Trotsky was neutralised as a political force. The first issue to divide the leaders was the question of what was to be done with their defeated opponent. At the Central Committee meeting of January 1925, Zinoviev and Kamenev, stung by Trotsky's recent criticisms of their behavior in 1917, proposed that he be expelled from the party, or at least from the Politburo. The majority, including Stalin, rejected these recommendations, voting only to accept Trotsky's resignation as Commissar of War. Meanwhile, the leaders initiated organisational skirmishes against each other. In late 1924 or early 1925 Zinoviev and Kamenev attempted to enlist N.A. Uglanov, the secretary of the Moscow provincial party committee, in their manoeuvres. Although Uglanov had been appointed at Zinoviev's and Kamenev's initiative, he now defected to the Stalinist camp. From that point on, the dispute assumed the form of a contest between the Moscow party organisation and the organisation of Leningrad where Zinoviev remained dominant.[1]

---

1   Carr 1958–64, vol. 2, pp. 31, 52; Daniels 1960, p. 254; Deutscher 1959, p. 241. Daniels argues that Uglanov was already a Stalin supporter at the time of his appointment.

During the summer of 1925 the struggle evolved into a debate over policy and doctrine. The most important issue concerned the party's orientation to the peasantry. Since 1923 the leadership had been united in promoting the acquisitive tendencies of the peasantry. The rationale for this approach was most clearly articulated by Bukharin, who asserted that economic concessions to the peasantry were essential for the maintenance of political stability. Beyond that, Bukharin believed that a prosperous peasantry was the main prerequisite for continued economic recovery. The future of Soviet industry, he insisted, depended upon the increased production of industrial crops and grain to feed the urban workers and to trade on the world market. Furthermore, he argued that the expansion of agricultural production would stimulate industry by fueling rural demand for consumer goods and agricultural tools. Bukharin anticipated that resources for industrialisation could be obtained through progressive taxation of the prosperous peasants and the investment of peasant savings held by Soviet banking and credit institutions. Consequently, he insisted that every incentive must be utilised to assist production and accumulation by the most productive sectors of the peasantry – the middle and well-to-do peasants.[2] He expressed this idea most forcefully in a speech in April 1925, in which he called upon peasants to '*Enrich yourselves*, develop your farms, and do not fear that constraint will be put on you'.[3]

This orientation to the well-to-do peasant received its sharpest policy expression in the spring of 1925. At that point, fearing the growth of peasant disaffection, the leadership offered new concessions to the peasantry, and especially to its wealthier strata. These concessions were codified in decisions of the April plenum of the CC that discouraged the practice of periodic land redistribution, reduced restrictions on the leasing of land and the hiring of labour, recommended the elimination of price controls on grain, and cut agricultural taxes.[4]

Until then, Zinoviev and Kamenev had been among the most vocal proponents of the party's agricultural orientation. However, in the spring of 1925 they began to back away from the policies they had helped to inspire. To a large degree this change can be explained in terms of factional considerations. As E.H. Carr has suggested, once Zinoviev and Kamenev lost their influence in the Moscow party organisation, they began to adapt their views to the sentiments of Leningrad, where industrial workers resented the grow-

---

2   For discussions of Bukharin's economic views during this period, see Cohen 1980, pp. 160–212; Lewin 1968, pp. 135–42; Nove 1979, pp. 81–99.
3   Quoted in Carr 1958–64, vol. 1, p. 260.
4   Carr 1958–64, vol. 1, pp. 266–9; Daniels 1960, pp. 258–9.

ing power of the kulaks.[5] In early May Zinoviev and Kamenev objected when the Politburo majority decided not to publish an article by Lenin's widow, Nadezhda Krupskaia, attacking Bukharin's pro-kulak philosophy. A few weeks later Zinoviev delivered a speech in Leningrad in which he argued that the slogan 'face to the countryside' meant 'face to the middle and poor peasant', not 'a turning towards the well-to-do strata in the countryside'.[6] He continued to press the issue in September in an article and a book in which he denounced the views of the émigré Russian economist N.V. Ustrialov, who had expressed his approval of NEP as a policy that could ultimately lead to the phased restoration of capitalism. In the course of his argument, Zinoviev warned that the growth of the power of the kulak and the NEPman could lead to the political degeneration of the proletarian dictatorship.[7]

In the same period Zinoviev also began to raise objections to the theory of 'socialism in one country', first advanced by Stalin in 1924. Stalin's argument was that the Soviet Union possessed the necessary means for constructing socialism, even if the world revolution failed to materialise. Perhaps Zinoviev was genuinely alarmed by this revision of doctrine; or perhaps he simply feared it would undermine the significance of his Comintern. At any rate, in September he challenged Stalin's innovation, demonstrating with abundant quotations that Lenin viewed the successful construction of socialism as dependent upon international revolution.[8]

Zinoviev, Kamenev, Krupskaia, and the Finance Commissar, Sokol'nikov, presented the case for the New Opposition at the October plenum of the CC. Their central proposals were for an end to the conciliation of the kulak and for an open discussion of the disputed issues. Although the CC majority rejected the proposal for a party-wide discussion, it was prepared to make concessions regarding agrarian policy. Even within the majority there were concerns, arising out of difficulties in grain procurement, over the orientation to the kulak. The CC now unanimously adopted a resolution on 'party work among the village poor' that condemned the underestimation of the importance of the middle peasant and of the *smychka* between the proletariat and the peasantry, but also criticised the underestimation of the kulak threat. After the plenum, the Moscow leadership stressed the former danger, while the Leningraders emphasised the latter.[9]

---

5   Carr 1958–64, vol. 2, pp. 59–60. See also Deutscher 1959, pp. 240–1.

6   Carr 1958–64, vol. 1, pp. 285–6.

7   Carr 1958–64, vol. 1, pp. 300–4; Daniels 1960, p. 259; Deutscher 1959, p. 245.

8   Carr 1958–64, vol. 1, pp. 304–5; Deutscher 1959, pp. 245–6.

9   Carr 1958–64, vol. 1, pp. 290–5, 307–8; Carr 1958–64, vol. 2: pp. 66–8, 111–15; Daniels 1960, p. 255.

Meanwhile, Zinoviev and Kamenev began to extend the debate to industrial policy. Although the leadership had vacillated over the question of industrialisation, in early 1925 it agreed that the time had come to begin replacing
worn-out machinery and constructing new factories. Consequently, the April
plenum of the CC voted substantial increases in allocations and credit to industry, especially heavy industry. Optimism regarding industrialisation reached
its high point in the Gosplan control figures issued in August that projected
a 33 percent increase in industrial production for 1925–6. At that point many
within the leadership began to balk at such an ambitious proposal. In contrast, in the fall of 1925 Zinoviev and Kamenev pressed forward as advocates of
industrialisation, arguing that no further industrial growth was possible without new machinery and new factories. Still, the debate between the minority
and the majority did not take the form of a clear struggle between supporters
and opponents of industry. One opposition leader, Sokol'nikov, continued to
resist 'excessive enthusiasm' for industrialisation out of fear that it could lead
to uncontrolled inflation, while Stalin proclaimed the need to transform the
Soviet Union 'from an agrarian into an industrial country'.[10]

The simmering tensions exploded at the provincial party conferences in
December. In Moscow a number of the speakers made insulting remarks about
the Leningrad leadership, and the conference adopted a resolution that implicitly criticised its sister organisation. Outraged, the Leningraders removed all
majority supporters from their delegation to the party congress and voted to
send a letter of protest to the Moscow conference. The Moscow provincial
party committee responded with an even more sharply worded denunciation
of Zinoviev and Kamenev. In an attempt to avert an open rupture, the majority
offered a truce in exchange for concessions by Leningrad, but the proposal was
rejected by Zinoviev, who described the terms as 'a demand for our capitulation without any guarantees for the future'.[11]

Leaders of the Leningrad Opposition repeated their objections to the
majority's agricultural policies and theoretical positions at the Fourteenth
Party Congress. At the same time they denounced the majority for its violations
of party democracy. Zinoviev complained of the persecution of Leningrad by
Moscow and urged the CC to offer all minority groupings the opportunity to
participate in party work. Kamenev's most noteworthy contribution was his

---

10   Carr 1958–64, vol. 1, pp. 329–52; Stalin 1952–5, vol. 7, p. 364.
11   Carr 1958–64, vol. 2, pp. 119–29.

denunciation of Stalin's growing power and his assertion '*that comrade Stalin cannot perform the function of uniting the Bolshevik general staff*'.[12]

In his report to the congress Stalin reasserted the need for struggle against both the kulak deviation and the underestimation of the alliance with the middle peasant. However, he argued that, since the party was already better prepared to deal with the kulak threat, it should concentrate its fire on the second deviation. He also charged that anyone who did not accept the doctrine of socialism in one country was a 'liquidator who does not believe in socialist construction'.[13] Other majority speakers depicted the New Opposition's attacks upon Stalin as motivated by personal jealousy. In reply to Zinoviev's complaints of persecution, they reminded him of his own campaign against Trotsky.[14]

Ultimately, the Leningrad Opposition was defeated by a vote of 559 to 65.[15] In the following weeks the majority began to remove minority leaders from positions of power. Kamenev was forced to relinquish his presidency of the Council of Labour and Defence, chairmanship of the Moscow Soviet, and deputy chairmanship of Sovnarkom; and he was demoted from full to candidate member of the Politburo and was temporarily assigned to the post of Commissar of Trade. Zinoviev forfeited his chairmanship of the Leningrad Soviet, but remained a full member of the Politburo and head of the Comintern.[16]

Throughout this contest, Trotsky remained silent. As Isaac Deutscher has suggested, part of the reason may have been that, wrapped up in his scientific and literary work, he was oblivious to the tensions within the leadership.[17] However, to the extent that he was aware of the conflict, he was inclined to view it as irrelevant to the struggle against bureaucratism. Up to this point he had regarded Zinoviev and Kamenev as the most consistent supporters of the party's right wing, and the most anti-democratic of the leaders, and developments in the early phases of the struggle between Leningrad and Moscow had done little to change this view. Furthermore, until late 1925 Trotsky seems to have viewed the New Opposition's concerns regarding differentiation in the countryside as exaggerated.[18] More importantly, in the early phases of the debate there was no clear difference between the New Opposition and the

12   Carr 1958–64, vol. 2, p. 138; Daniels 1960, pp. 267–8.
13   Stalin 1952–5, vol. 7, pp. 345–6, 358.
14   Deutscher 1959, p. 254; Schapiro 1971, p. 298.
15   Carr 1958–64, vol. 2, p. 144.
16   Carr 1958–64, vol. 2, pp. 151, 153–60; Daniels 1960, p. 270; Schapiro 1971, p. 300.
17   Deutscher 1959, pp. 248–9.
18   Day 1973, p. 114.

majority on the question that he still viewed as paramount – the need for planned, accelerated industrialisation.

By late 1925 Trotsky began to see the struggle in a new light. Just before the Fourteenth Party Congress he described Kamenev's new position on industrialisation as 'a step forward'.[19] At the same time, difficulties in grain procurement seem to have convinced him that the kulak threat was a real one.[20] Now, behind the demagogy of the New Opposition, he detected the 'bureaucratically distorted expression of the political anxiety of the proletariat', and an 'element of truth' in the majority's accusation that the Leningrad Opposition represented a continuation of the Opposition of 1923–4.[21] Still, he was unwilling to come to the aid of the New Opposition, for he felt that the issues were not yet clearly defined. Most importantly, he believed that the New Opposition did not recognise the central importance of industrialisation and planning.[22] Nevertheless, Trotsky anticipated that the continued development of the discussion could lead to a broader regrouping of forces and to the further clarification of the issues. For this reason, he insisted that the democratisation of the internal life of the party organisations of both Leningrad and Moscow was a necessary precondition for a struggle against the 'peasant deviation'. Also, he expressed hope that the removal of the Leningrad leaders responsible for some of the worst abuses of party democracy would contribute to this process.[23]

It was the debate over economic policy at the April CC plenum that finally united Trotsky with Zinoviev and Kamenev. There, Trotsky presented a series of amendments to Rykov's draft resolution on the economy. Basing his proposals on the decisions of the Fourteenth Party Congress that vaguely endorsed industrialisation, Trotsky again asserted that a more rapid tempo of industrialisation was essential for maintaining the *smychka* and increasing agricultural productivity. He urged that the CC instruct the Politburo to draw up a concrete plan for industrialisation for the next five to eight years. The resources were to come from various sources, including a higher tax on the upper strata of the villages. Kamenev rejected Trotsky's criticisms of the economic policies of previous years, but endorsed his demand for higher taxation of the kulaks and then presented his own amendments to combat differentiation in the countryside. Although Trotsky also criticised Kamenev's amendments, he ended up

---

19   Trotsky 1975b, p. 391.
20   See Day 1973, p. 153.
21   Trotsky 1975b, pp. 386, 393.
22   Trotsky 1975b, pp. 388–90, 391–3.
23   Trotsky 1975b, pp. 394–6. See also Deutscher 1959, p. 256.

voting for them after his own were rejected. The convergence was so apparent that at one point Stalin interjected, 'What is this? A bloc?'[24]

Around the time of the plenum Trotsky met with Kamenev and Zinoviev to discuss the possibility of an alliance. In Trotsky's first meeting with Kamenev since early 1923, Kamenev declared, 'It is enough for you and Zinoviev to appear on the same platform, and the party will find its true Central Committee'. Dismissing this 'bureaucratic optimism', Trotsky reminded Kamenev of the 'disintegrating effect' of the activities of the triumvirate. In further meetings he cautioned Kamenev and Zinoviev they needed to 'prepare for a long and serious struggle'.[25]

4.2   The Struggle of the United Opposition

Near the end of May, Trotsky, Zinoviev, and Kamenev began to unite the factions. While working to allay the misgivings of their supporters, they also hammered out the platform around which the United Opposition would struggle.[26] Combining views previously articulated by the two factions, they produced the most comprehensive programme ever created by a Bolshevik opposition group, addressing issues related to the economic, international, and regime policies of the leadership.

The United Opposition's critique of official economic policy concerned the rate of industrialisation, the growth of an exploitative layer in the countryside and towns, and the condition of the Soviet proletariat. Regarding industrialisation, the Opposition complained that the pace set by the majority was far too slow. Trotsky had raised this issue repeatedly since the introduction of NEP, and Zinoviev and Kamenev had taken it up by the end of 1925. Now, with one voice they asserted that state industry was 'lagging behind the economic development of the country as a whole'.[27] As Trotsky previously had emphasised, this was the source of the chronic 'goods famine' that discouraged peasants from selling grain to the state. Without grain to export, the state was unable to purchase industrial equipment abroad.[28] The Opposition warned that the

24   Carr 1958–64, vol. 1, p. 326.
25   Quoted in Trotsky 1970c, pp. 521–2.
26   See Serge 1980, pp. 212–13, Trotsky 1971a, pp. 92–5.
27   Trotsky 1980b, p. 78. See also Trotsky 1980b, pp. 96, 103, 122, 132, 331.
28   Trotsky 1980b, pp. 50, 122, 132, 331.

persistence of the goods famine could undermine the *smychka* between the proletariat and peasantry.[29]

A second economic criticism was that official policy was promoting the growth of an exploitative layer of kulaks and NEPmen and the further impoverishment of the poor peasant. Although this was first raised by the Leningrad Opposition, it was a concern that Trotsky now fully shared. In part, the Opposition attributed this differentiation to the low level of Soviet industry. Often, poor peasants who needed tools or other industrial goods were forced to purchase them from NEPmen at inflated prices. To pay for these goods, they had to borrow from kulaks at usurious rates, or lease their own plots or sell their labour to kulaks.[30] The Opposition further charged that the differentiation was reinforced by tax, credit, and price policies. It observed that the single agricultural tax and the increasing use of indirect taxes fell hardest on the poor peasant, and that state credits for agriculture most often went to the better-off strata of the villages. Meanwhile, the maintenance of high retail prices for industrial goods, combined with the reduction of wholesale prices, had enriched the private trader at the expense of the consumer and state industry.[31]

A third set of economic issues involved the deterioration in the level of employment, standard of living, and working conditions of the proletariat. Again, the Opposition saw these problems as partially derivative of the slow tempo of industrial development. For the worker, slow industrialisation translated into mounting unemployment – approximately two million and increasing in the summer of 1927, a decline in real wages due to rising industrial prices, and a growing housing shortage. All of these developments, the Opposition pointed out, fell hardest on the woman worker and the young worker.[32]

Against the leadership's policies the Opposition demanded a more rapid tempo of industrialisation, economic restrictions on the kulak, and greater assistance for the worker and for the poor and middle peasant. *The Platform of the United Opposition*, written in the summer of 1927, proposed net budget appropriations to industry of between 500 and 1,000 million rubles per year for the following five years, instead of the 90 to 200 million projected by Gosplan. Regarding agriculture, the Opposition called for a diversion of credit from the kulaks to the poor and middle peasants, and proposed to free the poorest 40 to 50 percent of peasant households entirely from the burden of taxation. At the same time, the Opposition suggested that the expansion of industry could

29   Trotsky 1980b, pp. 49–50, 79, 80, 103–4, 110, 117, 191, 323, 331, 385.

30   Trotsky 1980b, pp. 80, 104, 142, 230, 231, 322–6, 331–2.

31   Trotsky 1980b, pp. 304–5, 324–8.

32   Trotsky 1980b, pp. 78, 103, 121, 154–5, 230, 232, 234, 306, 312, 313–14, 315–16, 318, 330, 331.

pave the way for the gradual introduction of collective farming. On behalf of the proletariat, the Opposition demanded an increase in wages, beginning with the lowest paid workers, to a level at least commensurate with rising labour productivity. Beyond that, it appealed for an increase in unemployment benefits and an expansion in housing construction.[33]

The Opposition envisioned that the resources for this programme could be obtained from a variety of sources. Most importantly, it argued that the taxes of the kulak and NEPman should be raised by 150 or 200 million rubles. Furthermore, it demanded the imposition of a forced loan of no less than 150 million puds (2,700,000 tons) of grain from the most prosperous 10 percent of the peasantry. A large part of this grain was to be exported to the West to finance the import of industrial machinery. Although the Opposition endorsed the reduction in retail prices of industrial goods initiated by the majority, it demanded a simultaneous narrowing of the gap between wholesale and retail prices in order to maintain a greater share of the mark-up in the hands of state industry. The reduction in retail prices was to be achieved mainly by an increase in the volume of production and by cutting the costs of production and overhead.[34]

While denouncing the orientation of official economic policy, the United Opposition also launched an attack on the leadership's international policies. The Opposition charged that, just as the majority based its internal economic policies on the kulak and the NEPman, externally it relied upon alliances with petty-bourgeois elements at the expense of the world revolution. For the Opposition, the clearest example of this in 1926 involved the Anglo-Russian Trade Union Unity Committee.[35] The Anglo-Russian Committee (ARC), composed of leading representatives of the trade-union federations of Britain and the Soviet Union, was established in the spring of 1925 to promote international working-class unity in order to create an 'impregnable force against capitalist oppression' and an 'unbreakable pledge of peace and economic security'.[36] The hope of the Soviet leadership was that the committee might push the British labour movement in a revolutionary direction and also serve as a bulwark against British intervention.[37] The test of the efficacy of the committee regarding the first of these goals was not long in coming. On 3 May 1926, the General Council of the British Trades Union Congress (TUC) declared a

---

33   Trotsky 1980b, pp. 318–20, 333, 337, 326–30.
34   Trotsky 1980b, pp. 337–40.
35   The most thorough history of the ARC is Calhoun 1976. For the Opposition's views on the
      ARC, see also Cliff 1991, pp. 167–86; Deutscher 1959, p. 278.
36   Carr 1958–64, vol. 3: 1, p. 577. See also Calhoun 1976, p. 145.
37   Calhoun 1976, p. 192.

general strike in solidarity with the striking British coal miners. This action was greeted with enthusiasm in the Soviet Union where hundreds of thousands of workers participated in sympathy demonstrations and contributed millions of rubles to support the strikers. However, the enthusiasm soon gave way to dismay when the General Council rejected the Soviet offer of financial support. The sense of betrayal was further compounded when the council called off the general strike on 12 May.[38]

Soon afterwards, the Anglo-Russian Committee became an issue in the struggle within the Soviet Union. Six days after the termination of the general strike, Trotsky called on the party leadership to repudiate the ARC.[39] In July, leaders of the Opposition asserted that the General Council had betrayed the general strike and were preparing to betray the miners. Meanwhile, they charged, the General Council continued to use its association with the Bolsheviks to cover itself from the criticisms of British workers. The Opposition demanded that the Politburo convene a session of the ARC in order to expose the role of the General Council. After that, the Soviet delegation was to dissolve the committee. Such a course, the Opposition claimed, would contribute to the radicalisation of the British workers and facilitate their break with reformism. Against the argument that the committee was still useful for preventing war, the Opposition predicted that the betrayers of the British proletariat would 'betray the British proletariat even more outrageously – and with them the Soviet Union and the cause of peace – the moment a war threatens'. Finally, the Opposition warned that if the Soviets did not dissolve the ARC, the British would do so when the break was most favorable to them – a prediction that was fulfilled in September 1927 when the TUC voted to disband it.[40]

While criticising the majority's economic and international policies, United Opposition also condemned the continuing decline of democracy in Soviet political institutions. In the spring of 1926 Trotsky noted that more than five years had passed since the Tenth Party Congress had proclaimed a 'course toward party democracy' that was to include 'constant control on the part of the public opinion of the party over the work of the leading bodies'. Furthermore, over two and a half years had elapsed since the New Course resolution had defined workers' democracy as 'the liberty of frank discussion of the most important questions of party life by all members, and the freedom to have

---

38   Carr and Davies 1976–8, part 2, pp. 318–321; Calhoun 1976, pp. 232–6, 239–40; Cliff 1991, pp. 179–80.

39   See Calhoun 1976, p. 247.

40   Trotsky 1973b, pp. 253–8; Trotsky 1980b, pp. 84–5.

organized discussions on these questions, and the election of all leading party functionaries and commissions from the bottom up'. Although the intervening period had been years of peace, economic growth, working-class revival, and party proletarianisation, never before was the party regime 'so permeated by the practice of appointments from above, habits of command, suspicion, and administrative pressure, i.e., by an all-embracing principle of apparatus rule'.[41]

Instead of encouraging the free exchange of views essential to workers' democracy, the Opposition charged, the majority had stifled all critical discussion to the point that all who were dissatisfied or who had doubts or disagreements were afraid to raise their voices.[42] Throughout 1926–7 the Opposition complained that its views were withheld from the party by the refusal of the majority to publish its documents and speeches.[43] When Oppositionists tried to address party gatherings, they were shouted down and their meetings were broken up violently by 'fascist gangs' organised by the party leadership. Meanwhile, the party ranks were subjected to a one-sided and slanderous discussion of the issues.[44] At the same time, prominent Oppositionists were removed from leading party bodies, while rank and file Oppositionists were threatened with exile, expulsion from the party, or loss of employment.[45]

The Opposition also charged that the power of the central party institutions had continued to grow at the expense of the 'constant control . . . of the party over the work of its leading bodies'. In the summer of 1927 the Opposition asserted that 'the real rights of one member of the party at the top (above all, the secretary) are many times greater than the real rights of a hundred members at the bottom'.[46] Most important in this regard was the continuing practice of appointing party secretaries.[47] Beyond that, the Opposition noted similar practices in the soviets and the trade-union organisations.[48]

Connected with all these developments was the growth of the majority factionalism condemned by the 1923 Opposition. At the time the United Opposition was formed, Zinoviev and Kamenev revealed that from 1923 to 1925

41   Trotsky 1980b, pp. 64, 66.
42   Trotsky 1980b, p. 76.
43   See Trotsky 1980b, pp. 118, 123, 235, 247, 353, 383, 384, 410.
44   On the whistling, shouting down, and 'fascist' attacks, see Trotsky 1980b, pp. 393, 446. On the one-sided and slanderous discussion, see Trotsky 1980b, pp. 118, 123, 247, 249–53, 265, 353–4, 383–4, 411, 413.
45   See Trotsky 1980b, pp. 83–4, 87–8, 90–1, 107, 118, 237, 242, 246, 352, 353–4, 355, 403, 408, 410, 411, 413, 440, 448.
46   Trotsky 1980b, p. 353.
47   Trotsky 1980b, pp. 66, 352.
48   Trotsky 1980b, pp. 342–3, 352.

the party had been controlled by a secret factional 'Septemvirate' consisting
of the chairman of the CCC and all of the members of the Politburo except
Trotsky. Now the Opposition asserted that 'a similar factional grouping at
the top has no doubt existed since the Fourteenth Congress as well'. Its purpose was 'to deny the party the chance to use the normal means, provided
by the party rules, to make changes in the personnel and policies of the party
apparatus'.[49] Echoing the Leningrad Opposition, Trotsky warned that the
growing practices of appointment, repression, centralisation, and majority
factionalism were leading 'fatally toward one-man rule' in the party.[50]

The United Opposition called for a return of the soviets, trade unions, and
the party to the principle of 'workers' democracy' as defined by the Tenth Party
Congress and the New Course resolution. As a first step in this direction the
party leadership needed to end the repression of Oppositionists and to ensure
the free discussion of all contested questions. The Opposition demanded the
opening of a discussion at least three months prior to the next party congress,
where it would present its programme. Against the growing separation of
leading bodies of the party from the working class, it called for the election of
all officials, further proletarianisation of the party and its apparatus, and the
assignment of a large number of the members of the party apparatus to work
in industry. The budget and the size of the party apparatus were to be cut, and
limits were to be imposed on the length of time that any individual could hold
a party post. Additionally, the Opposition demanded the restoration of collective leadership and the implementation of Lenin's proposal to remove Stalin
from the post of General Secretary.[51]

Although the United Opposition was quickly joined by remnants of the
Workers' Opposition and the Democratic Centralists, it still had few adherents. To rectify this situation, in the early summer of 1926 it sent organisers
throughout the country to scour party cells for prospective adherents. In every
city clandestine meetings were held in workers' apartments or on the outskirts
of town. One such gathering – presided over by a Comintern official named
G.Ia. Belen'kii, and addressed by M.M. Lashevich, the Deputy Commissar of
War – became an issue in the party struggle when it was reported to the party
leadership.[52] In early June a commission of the CCC investigating the incident concluded with a stern condemnation of Lashevich, Belen'kii, and five
other participants in the 'illegal conspiratorial meeting' and recommended the

49   Trotsky 1980b, p. 87. See also Trotsky 1980b, pp. 106, 114.
50   Trotsky 1980b, p. 72. See also Trotsky 1980b, p. 116.
51   See Trotsky 1980b, pp. 75, 88, 89, 110, 115, 123–4, 236, 247–8, 255, 294, 358–61, 414.
52   Carr 1971–8, vol. 2, p. 4; Deutscher 1959, pp. 273–4.

removal of Lashevich from his post as Deputy Commissar of War and from the Central Committee. Finally, the CCC warned both Lashevich and Belen'kii that further factional activities would result in their expulsion from the party.[53]

The Opposition counterattacked at the July plenum. Early in the proceedings Zinoviev and Kamenev admitted that the 1923 Opposition had been correct in warning of the dangers of party bureaucratism, and Trotsky asserted that he had made a 'gross mistake' in accusing Zinoviev and Kamenev of opportunism. Then the Opposition presented a series of documents that included its indictment of Soviet economic policy, Soviet policy in Britain, and the party's internal regime.[54]

However, the majority refused to give ground on any of these issues. It rejected the demand for a break with the ARC, arguing that it could still contribute to the radicalisation of the British working class and the movement against intervention, and charging that the Opposition had abandoned Lenin's policy of working in the most reactionary trade unions.[55] Equally, the majority repudiated the Opposition's economic proposals, asserting that the policy of industrialisation adopted by the Fourteenth Party Congress already was being implemented, and that in the coming year industry would be in a better position to supply the peasantry with goods. Regarding taxation of the kulak, the majority rejected a course that, it claimed, would undermine the peasant's incentive to produce. The majority also opposed the demand for wage increases, insisting that these, if not tied to rising productivity, would be inflationary and would hurt the standard of living of the workers. Finally, it dismissed as nonsensical the accusation of majority factionalism, asserting that the majority could not have any factional views distinct from those of the party since it was the majority that determined the party's line.[56] Rather, it was the Opposition that had violated party discipline. For his conspiratorial activities, Lashevich was expelled from the CC and stripped of his post in the War Commissariat, and all who had participated in the meeting with Lashevich were banned from party office for two years. Most importantly, Zinoviev, who had been implicated, was removed from the Politburo.[57]

Undaunted, the minority continued its offensive, taking its case to the ranks. Increasingly, the Opposition circulated its theses among the party membership, and in late September and early October, its leaders addressed a series

---

53   Carr 1971–8, vol. 2, p. 5.
54   Stalin 1952–5, vol. 8, pp. 248–9. See Trotsky 1980b, pp. 73–92; and Trotsky 1973b, pp. 253–8.
55   Stalin 1952–5, vol. 18, pp. 185–7; Calhoun 1976, p. 271.
56   Carr and Davies 1969, part 1, pp. 6–7; Deutscher 1959, p. 279; Rykov 1970, pp. 953, 955.
57   Carr 1971–8, vol. 2, pp. 5–8; Daniels 1960, p. 279.

of factory cell meetings. There they were met by majority supporters who attempted to shout them down. On 2 October the Moscow party committee denounced the appearance of Opposition leaders the previous day as 'a crime against the party' and an attempt 'to fasten a discussion on the party'. In turn, the Politburo condemned the Opposition for violating party discipline, and referred the matter to the CC and CCC.[58]

Meanwhile, most of the party membership observed the struggle in silence. Aside from the effects of the majority's campaign of intimidation, the failure of the Opposition to arouse the party ranks may have been partly due to the economic situation. The harvest that year was especially good; and contrary to the predictions of the Opposition, the grain collection was proceeding well. Also, in August and September the party leadership, reversing its earlier position, suddenly promised a wage increase for industrial workers, undercutting a central demand of the Opposition.[59]

Faced with defeat and the prospect of reprisals, the United Opposition petitioned for a truce. Stalin agreed, but dictated severe terms: the Opposition was to accept the decisions of the party organs, admit that its factionalism had been harmful to the party, and disavow its domestic supporters who advocated a new party and its foreign sympathisers who had been expelled from their respective parties.[60] Reluctantly, the dissidents complied, promising to defend their views 'only in the forms established by the statutes and decisions of the congresses and the CC'.[61] However, soon after the conclusion of the truce, the majority moved against the Opposition. Within a week after the minority's surrender, the Politburo commissioned Stalin to prepare theses on the Opposition for the upcoming party conference. Embittered, Trotsky protested against this treachery and denounced Stalin as 'the grave-digger of the revolution'. Subsequently, the CC removed Zinoviev from the Executive Committee of the Comintern and revoked Trotsky's membership and Kamenev's candidate membership on the Politburo.[62]

Although the leadership majority clearly had broken the truce, the Opposition leaders understood that any renewal of the struggle would be met by expulsions. Consequently, at the Fifteenth Party Conference in late October and early November, they attempted to fulfil the conditions of their surrender

---

58   Carr 1971–8, vol. 2, pp. 13–14.

59   Carr and Davies 1969, part 1, pp. 16–17; Carr and Davies 1969, part 2, pp. 522–3; Deutscher 1959, pp. 282–3.

60   Stalin 1952–5, vol. 8, pp. 220–4.

61   Trotsky 1980b, pp. 127–9.

62   Carr 1971–8, vol. 2, pp. 16–17; Deutscher 1959, pp. 296–7.

by remaining silent during the discussion of the economic situation, rising to
defend themselves only after Stalin presented his report on the Opposition. In
that report Stalin denounced the Opposition as a 'Social-Democratic deviation within the party', and explained that its 'principal error' was its refusal to
acknowledge that socialism could be constructed in one country. He admitted
that the victory of socialism in the Soviet Union could not be considered 'final'
until the danger of imperialist intervention had been eliminated by revolutions 'in at least several other countries'. Nevertheless, he insisted that, even
without a world revolution, 'the proletarian dictatorship ... by its own efforts'
was 'capable of overcoming the bourgeoisie of the u.s.s.r.', and of building
a 'complete socialist society'. The Opposition's failure to recognise this truth,
Stalin asserted, explained both its pessimistic forecasts about degeneration
and its economic and international adventurism.[63]

Trotsky responded to these arguments at the party conference and again
one month later at the plenum of the Executive Committee of the Communist
International (ECCI).[64] He asserted that there was no doubt the Soviet Union
was constructing socialism. The issue was whether or not this could be completed in one country. To insist that it could, one had to assume that the world
revolution would not materialise for thirty to forty years and that the Soviet
Union would not succumb to external pressures in the meantime. For Trotsky,
both premises were groundless. Internationally, capitalism would continue to
decay, presenting the proletariat with the possibility of seizing power in a number of countries. However, if capitalism managed to avert revolution through
rising prosperity, the Soviet Union would surely be strangled – if not through
military intervention, then through competition on the world market.[65] Trotsky
also condemned Stalin's theory for its implications regarding economic policy.
He argued that, even though contemporary history demonstrated the growth
of international interdependence, the majority glorified the ideal of national
self-reliance. However, Trotsky warned, attempting to make everything domestically would slow the rate of economic development, and would reduce the
ability of the Soviet Union to compete with world capitalism.[66] In the end the
party conference unanimously endorsed Stalin's theses and threatened further
disciplinary action if the Opposition resumed its struggle. ECCI confirmed this

---

63   Stalin 1952–5, vol. 8, pp. 245, 258–94.
64   Trotsky 1980b, pp. 142–62, 182–8.
65   Trotsky 1980b, p. 161.
66   Trotsky 1980b, p. 183.

decision in early December, asserting that the Opposition represented 'a Right danger within the C.P.S.U., screened by Left phrases'.[67]

The winter of 1926–7 brought a lull in the party struggle. Following the party conference, the Opposition curtailed its factional activities. Internally, it found itself demoralised and divided over how to proceed. Trotsky utilised this 'breathing-space' to delve into a number of theoretical questions.[68] However, in the spring of 1927 the struggle resumed with even greater intensity over developments in China.[69]

Since 1924 the entire Chinese Communist Party (CCP) had been part of Sun Yat-sen's nationalist organisation, the Guomindang (GMD). The CCP had entered the GMD reluctantly, and only under pressure from the Comintern leadership. Initially, the entire Central Committee of the CCP had opposed the merger on the grounds that the GMD was a bourgeois political party, and that the fusion would obstruct the pursuit of an independent proletarian line by the CCP.[70] In the following years, the growth of the revolutionary movement and of Communist influence, rightward shifts by the Guomindang, and the tightening of GMD control over the CCP continued to strain the alliance. Repeatedly, Chen Duxiu, general secretary of the CCP, appealed to the Comintern for permission to leave the GMD, but each time his appeals were rejected. As the Comintern leadership perceived the situation, China was undergoing a bourgeois-nationalist revolution to unite the country and free it from imperialist control. Furthermore, from this perspective the GMD was not a bourgeois party, but an organisation representing the broad masses. Consequently, the leadership insisted that it was the duty of the CCP to subject itself to GMD discipline.[71]

By early 1927 China was in the midst of a revolutionary upheaval precipitated by Chiang Kai-shek's Northern Expedition against the warlord regimes in central China and Manchuria. In the wake of Chiang's armies, peasants seized land from their landlords, rose in revolt against local warlords, and entered the newly-formed peasant associations that were taking control of the villages.

---

67 Popov 1934, p. 308.

68 Deutscher 1959, pp. 308–11; Trotsky 1970c, p. 529.

69 The following account of the Chinese revolution and its relationship to the struggle within the AUCP(b) is based on Deutscher 1959 Harrison 1972; Isaacs 1961; Pantsov 2000; Peng 1976; and Ch'en 1976.

70 See Ch'en 1976, pp. 599–600; Harrison 1972, p. 49; Pantsov 2000, pp. 46–7.

71 See Deutscher 1959, p. 320; Harrison 1972, pp. 80, 86–7; Isaacs 1961, pp. 85, 87. Stalin seems to have anticipated that the CCP ultimately would seize power within the GMD. See Pantsov 2000, pp. 84–98, 129.

Meanwhile, workers engaged in acts of economic sabotage and political strikes against the warlords, seized concessions from the British, and organised mass trade unions in liberated cities and towns. Frightened, Chiang attempted to repress the upsurge, banning strikes and demonstrations, disarming workers, and closing down trade unions and peasant associations. When Chen Duxiu responded by suggesting again that the Communists leave the GMD, the ECCI emphatically rejected his proposal. In October 1926 the Soviet party leadership further urged the CCP to restrain 'peasant excesses' in order to avoid antagonising the GMD generals, and when Chen requested permission to arm the workers of insurgent Shanghai in preparation for the imminent clash, the CCP was instructed to bury its weapons and avoid conflict.

Meanwhile, Trotsky was growing increasingly critical of the Comintern's Chinese policy. Years later, he asserted that he had opposed the entry of the CCP into the Guomindang as early as 1923.[72] At least by April 1926 he was demanding in the Politburo that the CCP be allowed to withdraw from the GMD.[73] Although until September 1927 he accepted the view that China was experiencing a bourgeois-democratic revolution, for Trotsky this did not imply that the proletariat would play a subordinate role. He observed that as the revolution unfolded, the bourgeoisie who controlled the GMD were shifting rapidly to the right. Only the proletariat, supported by the peasantry, would be able to lead the revolution to victory. To do so, it had to be free to organise its own independent Communist party.[74] At Trotsky's insistence the Opposition as a whole took up the China question in the last days of March 1927. When Zinoviev and his supporters, along with the Trotskyists Piatakov and Radek, refused to abandon the GMD, Trotsky agreed to refrain from raising this demand.[75] Nevertheless, the Opposition urged the party leadership to encourage the CCP to adopt a more independent line. In particular, Trotsky proposed that the CCP begin to form soviets of workers, peasants, and soldiers in order to block a coup by Chiang Kai-shek, to organise workers and peasants, and to prepare for the seizure of power. At the same time he denounced the subordination of the CCP to the bourgeois GMD as analogous to the Menshevik line in 1917.[76]

---

72   This claim has never been independently confirmed. See Trotsky 1976a, p. 490; Pantsov 2000, pp. 102–7; Benton 1996, p. 10.

73   Soon afterwards, Zinoviev supported this view in the Politburo, but he quickly retreated from this position. See Pantsov 2000, pp. 92, 110–11, 118; Benton 1996, p. 10.

74   See Trotsky 1976a, pp. 113–255.

75   See Trotsky 1976a, p. 490.

76   See Trotsky 1976a, pp. 128–48.

Trotsky's fears of a coup were confirmed on 12 April when Chiang Kai-shek launched a reign of terror against workers and communists in Shanghai and other cities. Soon afterwards, Stalin drafted theses proclaiming a new line for the CCP. Chiang's coup, Stalin argued, signified the 'desertion of the national bourgeoisie from the revolution' and marked the beginning of a new stage in the struggle. The Chinese communists were to remain within the Guomindang, but now they were to cooperate with its left wing against Chiang. In particular, they were to support the left GMD government in Wuhan, which was destined to become 'the organ of a revolutionary-democratic dictatorship of the proletariat and the peasantry'.[77]

For the Opposition, the new line was little better than the old. Trotsky noted that, while the theses vaguely advised the CCP to 'preserve its independence', they said nothing about the need for the CCP to issue its own daily paper, or for 'relentless criticism' of the left GMD. Although the theses called for the arming of the workers and peasants, they opposed the formation of the soviets that could coordinate the struggle. Furthermore, Trotsky argued that the theses were mistaken about the character of the left GMD government. He predicted that it would soon unite with Chiang and would inflict 'a new and perhaps even more serious defeat' upon the Chinese revolution.[78] Again, Trotsky's predictions were quickly confirmed. In May and June, troops of the Wuhan government carried out widespread massacres of peasants, and on 15 July the left GMD expelled all communists from its ranks and began a campaign of arrests and executions of communists and trade unionists. In September, the remnants of the Wuhan government reunited with Chiang Kai-shek.

Embarrassed by the debacle, in the spring and summer of 1927 the leadership attempted to silence the Opposition. The Politburo rejected Trotsky's request for a special closed session of the Central Committee to discuss the Chinese question, and the Soviet press refused to publish any statements by Oppositionists on the issue. When Zinoviev protested against this boycott of the Opposition's views at a mass public meeting on 9 May, the CC denounced Zinoviev's speech as a violation of the October truce, and referred the matter to the CCC. Unable to obtain a hearing within the party, Trotsky appealed to the Executive of the Comintern for a chance to present his position.[79] Meanwhile, the conservative British government had broken off diplomatic relations with the Soviet Union on the basis of alleged evidence of Soviet espionage – a development that immediately gave rise to fears of imminent war with Britain. At the

77   Stalin 1952–5, vol. 9, pp. 229–31.
78   See Trotsky 1976a, pp. 158–248.
79   Carr 1971–8, vol. 2, p. 24.

May plenum of the ECCI Stalin employed this concern against the Opposition, denouncing Trotsky's 'attacks on the Party and the Comintern' as an example of 'something like a united front from [British foreign secretary] Chamberlain to Trotsky'. In the end, the ECCI approved Stalin's report on China and condemned the Opposition's factionalism.[80]

Aroused by developments in China, the Opposition renewed its offensive on a broad range of issues. While the ECCI plenum was still in session, it presented the Politburo with a comprehensive statement of its views on the economic, political, and international situation, concluding with the demand for a discussion of all contested questions in preparation for the Fifteenth Party Congress.[81] Meanwhile, it also organised a series of mass meetings of industrial workers in Ivanovo-Vosnesensk, Leningrad, and Moscow.[82] The majority retaliated by subjecting the Opposition to a new wave of punitive transfers. When I.T. Smilga was assigned to a post on the Manchurian border, both Trotsky and Zinoviev made brief remarks to a large number of Oppositionists who gathered at the railway station in Moscow to see him off. Immediately, the leadership charged the Opposition with organising an unlawful demonstration. In subsequent weeks, rank-and-file Oppositionists who had been present at the station were expelled from the party, and *Pravda* ran an editorial accusing the Opposition of disloyalty in the face of the imperialist threat.[83]

In late June the CCC met to consider the expulsion of Trotsky and Zinoviev from the Central Committee for Trotsky's speech before the ECCI and for their organisation of the 'demonstration' at the Iaroslavl station. Addressing the CCC, Trotsky argued that the real significance of the proceedings was to use the war scare 'to hound the Opposition and to prepare for its physical annihilation'. Although the CCC again condemned the factional activities of the Opposition, it balked at expelling the Opposition's leaders from the CC, and referred the matter to the upcoming plenum of the CC and CCC.[84]

The July–August plenum again took up the question of Trotsky's and Zinoviev's expulsion from the Central Committee. The Opposition was able to avert the removal of its leaders by a conciliatory statement that proclaimed its loyalty to the Soviet Union, rejected the view that the leadership was reinstituting capitalism, criticised efforts by German oppositionists to set up a new

---

80   Stalin 1952–5, vol. 9, p. 318; Carr 1971–8, vol. 2, p. 25.

81   See Trotsky 1980b, pp. 226–39.

82   Reiman 1987, p. 22.

83   Carr 1971–8, vol. 2, pp. 26–7; Deutscher 1959, p. 339.

84   Trotsky 1971a, p. 130; Carr 1971–8, vol. 2, p. 28. On the war scare of 1927, see Meyer 1978;
      Sontag 1975, pp. 66–7.

party, and repudiated factionalism and the formation of a new party in the Soviet Union.[85] However, the rift was now too deep to be papered over, even temporarily. Soon after the plenum, both sides resumed the struggle. While the majority continued to persecute oppositionists, the Opposition began drafting a platform in preparation for the party congress.

4.3   Trotsky and the Opposition on Bureaucratism

In 1923 Trotsky first began to perceive the relevance of the classical Marxist analysis of bureaucracy for comprehending the major political and economic developments in the Soviet Union. Again, according to that understanding, the problem of bureaucracy was one of political alienation – that is, the tendency of political institutions in class societies to separate themselves from the control of, and to rule over, society as a whole. In normal periods this tendency was seen as closely related to the domination of the state by an exploitative economic class. Trotsky did not yet develop these insights and concerns into a systematic theory in 1923. However, with the formation of the United Opposition he returned to, and began to amplify upon, many themes from his writings on the New Course controversy. Since 1923 events in the Soviet Union had further convinced Trotsky that the classical Marxist analysis of bureaucracy provided the key to understanding the current Soviet situation. Utilising this analysis, he proceeded to construct a coherent theory of Soviet bureaucracy.

4.3.1   The Conception of Bureaucracy

Consistent with classical Marxist analysis of bureaucracy, during the years 1926–7 Trotsky's conception of the problem of Soviet bureaucracy focused on two general concerns. Throughout these years he and the Opposition denounced as 'bureaucratism' the continuing centralisation of decision making and growth of authoritarianism within the party, state, and other important Soviet institutions. Simultaneously, they condemned the developing links they perceived between Soviet political institutions and capitalist elements within Soviet society, and the responsiveness of Soviet institutions to those elements. More clearly than before, Trotsky and the Opposition argued that these class shifts within Soviet institutions were, in themselves, manifestations of bureaucratism.

During the New Course controversy Trotsky had deplored the growing separation of the party apparatus from the control of the rank and file party members. In particular, he criticised the tendency of party officials to decide all questions, including the selection of lower-level officials, as well as the efforts of party leaders to repress the free discussion of important issues. In 1926–7 Trotsky and the Opposition asserted that centralisation of decision making within the party had continued to increase in further violation of the principle of workers' democracy. In a document submitted to the Politburo in June 1926 Trotsky denounced the 'unlimited domination of the party apparatus', and the establishment of a 'regime based on the absolute authority of the apparatus', asserting that these tendencies constituted the 'essence of bureaucracy [*biurokratiia*]'.[86] However, as Trotsky perceived it, this process had gone far beyond the concentration of power in the apparatus. In the same statement he described the 'concentration of the all-powerful party apparatus in the hands of an ever more restricted leadership core'.[87] Of course, by this he was referring to the growing authority of the Stalin faction, depicted by Trotsky in October 1926 as '*a faction within the ruling faction*', which, through one-sided discussions and organisational measures, was establishing 'a ruinous regime of one-man rule in the party'.[88]

Trotsky and the United Opposition also viewed the authoritarianism of the leadership as considerably worse than it had been in 1923. At the time of the New Course controversy, Trotsky and the Opposition were mainly concerned about the stifling of free discussion in the party cells. While the United Opposition complained that this practice had become even more widespread by 1926–7, it further asserted that the party leadership was now engaged in the active repression of party dissidents. Again, the methods denounced by the Opposition ranged from the suppression of Opposition documents, to the breaking up of meetings by 'fascist gangs', to the firing of Oppositionists from their jobs. As the party struggle approached its climax in the summer of 1927, Trotsky predicted that this course could only culminate in the attempt by Stalin to achieve the 'physical destruction' of the Opposition.[89]

Meanwhile, the Opposition noted the similar development of centralist and authoritarian norms in state institutions. In 1923 Trotsky had devoted considerable attention to the problem of state bureaucratism. In the *Platform of the Opposition*, submitted in September 1927, the Opposition described the regime in the soviets as comparable to that in the party:

---

86   Trotsky 1980b, p. 65; Fel'shtinskii 1988, vol. 1, p. 233.
87   Trotsky 1980b, p. 69.
88   Trotsky 1980b, p. 118. See also, for example, Trotsky 1980b, p. 72.
89   Trotsky 1980b, pp. 36, 45–6, 233, 246, 266, 267, 354–5, 393, 446.

The soviets have had less and less to do with the settling of fundamental political, economic, and cultural questions. They have become mere appendages to the executive committees and presidiums. The work of administration has been entirely concentrated in the hands of the latter...

The elected leaders in important spheres of soviet administration are removed at the first conflict with the chairman of the soviet. They are removed still more quickly in cases of conflict with the secretary of the regional committee of the party. In consequence of this the elective principle is being reduced to nothing, and responsibility to the electors is losing all meaning.[90]

Beyond the state and party, Trotsky and the United Opposition detected the pervasive symptoms of bureaucratism in all social institutions and 'all ... non-party mass organizations'. Within the factory, the 'administrative bodies are striving more and more to establish their unlimited authority. The hiring and discharge of workers is actually in the hands of the administration alone'.[91] In the unions 'the established regime obstructs the development of activism by the workers and prevents them from setting about the construction of socialism to the fullest extent'.[92] Even the Comintern had been infected with the disease of bureaucratism. In January 1927 Trotsky wrote of the 'hidden and disguised ... bureaucratic apparatus regime in the Comintern itself' and the growth of 'bureaucratism within the foreign Communist parties' under pressure from Moscow.[93]

Although when Trotsky and the United Opposition spoke of bureaucratism in the party, state, etcetera, they usually had in mind the growth of centralism and authoritarianism, this was not always the case. In line with the traditional Marxist analysis, in 1923 Trotsky had described bureaucratism as related to the growth of alien (i.e., non-proletarian) class influence within the state and party. Now he and the Opposition expanded upon this analysis, at times explicitly *defining* bureaucratism in terms of this influence. For example, the *Platform* asserted,

The question of Soviet bureaucratism [*biurokratizm*] is not only a question of red tape [*volokita*] and swollen staffs. At bottom it is a question

---

90   Trotsky 1980b, p. 343.
91   Trotsky 1980b, pp. 363, 316.
92   Trotsky 1980b, p. 233.
93   Trotsky 1980b, pp. 196–7.

of the class role played by the bureaucracy, of its social ties and sympathies, of its power and privileged position, its relation to the NEPman and the unskilled worker, to the intellectual and the illiterate, to the wife of a Soviet grandee and the most ignorant peasant woman, etc., etc. Whose hand does the official grasp? That is the fundamental question which is daily being tested in life's experience by millions of working people.[94]

Besides extending and expanding upon Trotsky's earlier critique of Soviet bureaucratism, in 1926-7 Trotsky and the Opposition also introduced terminological changes that reflected the beginning of deeper conceptual shifts. One of these was their increasing reference to the 'bureaucracy [*biurokratiia*]' within each of the major political and social institutions of the Soviet Union. In 1923 Trotsky and his supporters had directed their attacks exclusively at the problem of 'bureaucratism [*biurokratizm*]' in the state and party. While they continued to use that term most frequently in 1926-7, at times they now characterised the problem in terms of a 'bureaucracy' in the state and a 'bureaucracy' in the party. In such passages it seems that they were suggesting that the problem was more than a disease infecting these institutions; it was a social formation that dominated each of them.[95]

There are various possible explanations for this shift. First, as manifestations of bureaucratism multiplied quantitatively, it was perceived that the problem had changed qualitatively. That is, bureaucratism was viewed as so pervasive in Soviet political institutions that it began to seem inseparable from the bodies of officials within each of them. Perhaps another contributing factor was the growth in size of the state and party apparatuses. By the end of 1925 the number of paid party officials had reached approximately 25,600, while by 1926 the number of employees of state institutions exceeded two million.[96] This growth

---

94   Trotsky 1980b, p. 341; Fel'shtinskii 1988, vol. 4, p. 139. See also Trotsky 1971a, pp. 148, 149; Fel'shtinskii 1988, vol. 3, p. 117.

95   Law 1995, p. 242 has correctly observed, 'In 1923 the Opposition was discussing bureaucratism, the growth of bureaucracy as a system of administration; by 1926 it was beginning to assert the existence of a bureaucracy as an ossifying Party leadership, maintaining itself by the exercise of power'. However, during this period the Opposition also spoke of the state bureaucracy, as well as of the (combined) bureaucracy of the state, party, trade unions, etc. For references to the party bureaucracy, see, for example, Trotsky 1980b, pp. 115, 356; Fel'shtinskii 1988, vol. 2, p. 79; Fel'shtinskii 1988, vol. 3, p. 134; Fel'shtinskii 1988, vol. 4, p. 151. For references to the state bureaucracy in this period, see Trotsky 1980b, pp. 81, 341; Fel'shtinskii 1988, vol. 2, p. 16, Fel'shtinskii 1988, vol. 4, p. 139.

96   Carr 1958-64, vol. 2, pp. 199-200; Carr 1971-8, vol. 2, p. 489.

encouraged the perception that these apparatuses were large enough to be considered distinct groupings.

Even while referring increasingly to the bureaucracy of the party, the bureaucracy of the state, etc., Trotsky and the Opposition also began to speak as if the apparatuses of all Soviet political and social institutions were really just parts of one large social formation: the apparatus or 'bureaucracy'. In previous years Trotsky had distinguished clearly between the apparatuses of the state and party. Now he and the Opposition began to blur these organisational distinctions. For example, in May 1927 the 'Declaration of the Eighty-Four' complained that the 'whole official apparatus, both party and soviet [*ves' ofitsial'nyi apparat, i partinyi i sovetskii*]', was striking out at the left wing of the party.[97] Similarly, the *Platform* spoke of the (single) 'layer [*sloi*] of "administrators"' in the party, the trade unions, the economic organs, the cooperatives and the state apparatus.[98]

Again, various factors may have contributed to this development. It may have been promoted by the perception of important similarities in the various apparatuses. According to Trotsky, all of them had come to be characterised by the same centralisation of authority.[99] Furthermore, in every one of them personnel were selected and promoted on the basis of their hostility to the Opposition, and each participated directly in the persecution of the party Opposition.[100] Consequently, from the standpoint of the Opposition, the specific institutional affiliations began to seem less and less significant. Yet another contributing factor may have been the Opposition's evolving explanation of the source of the problem. In 1926–7 the Opposition increasingly described bureaucratism as originating in the shifting relationships between the fundamental classes of Soviet society. As it did so, it began to view the bureaucracy as one more social grouping, situated among and responding to the conflicting pressures exerted by the social classes.

However, neither the shift from 'bureaucratism' to the 'bureaucracies' of various institutions, nor the identification of a single social layer, 'the bureaucracy', should be exaggerated. For the time being, in 1926–7 Trotsky and the

97   Trotsky 1980b, p. 231; Fel'shtinskii 1988, vol. 3, pp. 64–5 (translation modified).
98   Trotsky 1980b, p. 356; Fel'shtinskii 1988, vol. 4, p. 151 (translation modified). See also Trotsky 1971a, pp. 172–3; Trotsky 1990, pp. 175–6; Fel'shtinskii 1988, vol. 4, p. 40.
99   Trotsky observed in December 1927 that 'in the party the apparatus is all-powerful; behind the back of the soviet organisations high-ranking bureaucrats give all the orders; and so on' (Trotsky 1980b, p. 489).
100   See, for example, Trotsky 1980b, pp. 246, 352–3.

United Opposition still most frequently characterised the problem as one of bureaucratism within all Soviet institutions.

4.3.2 Characteristics: Composition, Policies, and Doctrines

In this period Trotsky and the Opposition identified various characteristics of bureaucratism that were closely related to their overall conception of the problem, and especially to their new emphasis upon alien class influence. These included their observations regarding the class and the political compositions of the state and party apparatuses, as well as their general assessment of the policies and doctrines of the leadership.

As noted, in 1927 Trotsky defined bureaucratism in terms of the increasing fusion of the ruling circles 'with the upper layers of the Soviet-Nep society'. This and related passages indicate that for Trotsky and the United Opposition at least part of the problem involved the changing class composition of the leading bodies of the state and party. In this regard they viewed the situation as especially bad in the state apparatus. In the 'Declaration of the Thirteen' written in July 1926, leaders of the Opposition observed, 'It is quite obvious that the state apparatus in its social composition and standard of living is bourgeois or petty bourgeois to a great extent, and is drawn away from the proletariat and poor peasantry and toward, on the one hand, the comfortably fixed intellectual and, on the other, the merchant, the renter of land, the kulak, and the new bourgeois'.[101] Although the party apparatus was more proletarian than the state apparatus, the *Platform* deplored the fact that only one-tenth of the members of the 'decision-making bodies of the party' were workers in industry, compared to one-third of the party membership as a whole.[102]

A related concern for the Opposition was the political composition of the party apparatus. In 1923 Trotsky had criticised the virtual monopoly of power of members of the 'Old Guard' who joined the party before the revolution. His point was that the Old Bolsheviks in the apparatus should make room for younger party members and new ideas. However, in 1927 the *Platform of the Opposition* described the problem quite differently, warning of the 'sapping of the influence of the proletarian and Old Bolshevik nucleus of the party' and noting the rise in the percentage of party officials who formerly had been members of 'petty-bourgeois' organisations such as the Mensheviks and the Social Revolutionaries. The *Platform* pointed out that, at the time of the Fourteenth Party Congress, '38 percent of those occupying responsible and directing positions in our press were persons who had come to us from other parties'. Now,

---

101 Trotsky 1980b, p. 81. See also Trotsky 1980b, pp. 304, 342, 353, 390, 489.
102 Trotsky 1980b, p. 351.

the political composition of the directing organs of the press was even worse, and 'about a quarter of the higher cadres of the active elements in the party' were former SRs and Mensheviks.[103] Aside from actual changes in the composition of the leading organs, one factor that certainly facilitated this shift in the Opposition's critique was the changed composition of the Opposition itself. The fusion of Zinoviev's group with Trotsky's 1923 supporters had brought into the United Opposition a large number of Old Bolshevik leaders. Consequently, by 1927 the Opposition was able to criticise the apparatus from the politically advantageous standpoint of Old Bolshevism.

However, the most distinctive characteristics of Soviet bureaucratism for Trotsky and the Opposition were the political, economic, and international policies and doctrines of the party leadership. In the summer of 1927 the Opposition began to identify these policies and doctrines with the preeminent leader of the party apparatus, depicting them as the policies of 'Stalinism'. Trotsky's first written use of that term seems to have been in an oppositional declaration written on 28 June 1927 in response to Stalin's recent denunciation of the formation of a 'united front from Chamberlain to Trotsky'.[104] For Trotsky, this – as well as the earlier accusations that the Opposition wanted to 'rob the peasants' and 'to cause a war' – were 'slogans of Stalinism [*stalinizm*] in its fight with Bolshevism, in the person of the Opposition'.[105]

In other statements over the next few months, Trotsky and the Opposition clarified what they meant by the term, identifying it with the two types of policies and doctrines they viewed as characteristic of the leadership. In part, when they spoke of Stalinism they were referring to the undemocratic and repressive practices the leadership had substituted for Leninist norms,

---

103   Trotsky 1980b, pp. 308, 351.
104   The basis for this conclusion is a computer search for the term *stalinizm* in two collections of Opposition documents on the Web, *Kommunisticheskaia oppozitsiia v SSSR, 1923–1927* (Fel'shtinskii 1990) and *Arkhiv Trotskogo* (Fel'shtinskii 1999–2002). Robert McNeal has suggested that 'an essay ... entitled *The Declaration of the 83 and Our Tasks*, dated April 27, 1927', was perhaps the first occasion on which Trotsky spoke of Stalinism. McNeal explains that Trotsky wrote there 'of the errors of the "Stalinist group" and of an approaching crisis "in its Stalinist sense"' (McNeal 1982, p. 378). In fact, according to a note by Trotsky, this statement – which actually seems to have been written in June 1927 – was probably written by Zinoviev. Also, the term *stalinizm* does not appear there; rather, the term used was *stalinskii* – sometimes translated as the adjective *Stalin* and sometimes as *Stalinist* (Fel'shtinskii 1988, vol. 3, p. 82). The term *stalinskii* had been used by Trotsky at least as early as June 1926 (Fel'shtinskii 1988, vol. 1, p. 237). For a discussion of the evolution of Trotsky's views on Stalinism, see Twiss 2010, pp. 545–63.
105   Fel'shtinskii 1988, vol. 3, p. 214.

especially within the party. Along these lines, on 4 August 1927, Trotsky, with a dozen other Opposition leaders, signed a statement to the CC and the CCC noting the radical difference between the 'profound party spirit and methods of Leninism' and those of 'Stalinism'.[106] At least equally distinctive of Stalinism for Trotsky and the Opposition were the economic and international policies and doctrines of the leadership that deviated to the right of Leninism. In an address to the CC on Oct. 23, 1927 Trotsky observed that the line of the leadership had shifted in recent years 'from left to right: from the proletariat to the petty bourgeois, from the worker to the specialist, from the rank-and-file party member to the functionary, from the farmhand and the poor peasant to the kulak, from the Shanghai worker to Chiang Kai-shek, . . . etc.' In that, Trotsky asserted, 'lies the very essence [*sut'*] of Stalinism'.[107]

At times, Trotsky and the Opposition attempted to define more precisely just how far to the right the leadership's line had shifted. In 1923 Trotsky had warned of the prospect of the 'opportunistic degeneration' of the apparatus. Now, to indicate the degree of degeneration that had occurred, he and the Opposition utilised Lenin's analysis of opportunism in the Second International. When a majority of the parties of the Second International endorsed the military efforts of their respective countries at the outbreak of World War I, Lenin had denounced this 'opportunist' betrayal of revolutionary socialism. Opportunism, Lenin and Zinoviev explained in the pamphlet *Socialism and War*, 'expresses bourgeois policies within the working-class movement, expresses the interests of the petty bourgeoisie and the alliance of a tiny section of bourgeoisified workers with their "*own*" bourgeoisie, against the interests of the proletarian masses, the oppressed masses'.[108] Lenin was even more critical of socialists such as Karl Kautsky, leader of the 'Marxist Centre' of the SPD, who attempted to maintain an intermediate position between complete opportunism and revolutionary internationalism. Kautsky stated that the war had rendered the Socialist International temporarily irrelevant, that all workers should fight to defend their own fatherlands, but should be prepared to reunite in the International when the war ended. In Lenin's view the 'Kautskyites', the 'Kautskyan Centre', or simply the 'Centrists', were even more harmful than the open chauvinists in the International, for they hid 'their advocacy of an alliance with the [chauvinists] under a cloak of plausible, pseudo-"Marxist" catchwords and pacifist slogans'. These centrists vacillated 'between opportunism and radicalism', that is, between opportunism and

---

106   Fel'shtinskii 1988, vol. 4, p. 49; Trotsky 1980b, p. 266.
107   Fel'shtinskii 1988, vol. 4, p. 221; Trotsky 1980b, p. 442 (translation modified).
108   Lenin 1960–70, vol. 21, pp. 309–10.

revolutionary socialism, but in the final analysis they were only 'only a fig-leaf for opportunism'. In contrast to both revolutionary Social-Democracy and blatant opportunism, centrism was not an independent trend for it had no social roots, 'either in the masses or in the privileged stratum which has deserted to the bourgeoisie'. In fact, it was this absence of social roots that accounted for its inconsistent, vacillating behavior.[109]

Although Trotsky and the United Opposition at times criticised specific policies of the party leadership as 'opportunist' or 'Menshevik', they did not view the general line of either Soviet domestic or international policy as fully opportunist.[110] Echoing Lenin, the *Platform* explained,

> Opportunism in its fully developed form – according to the classic definition of Lenin – is a bloc formed by the upper strata of the working class with the bourgeoisie and directed against the majority of the working class. In the conditions now existing in the Soviet Union, opportunism in such fully developed form would express the desire of the upper strata of the working class to compromise with the newly resurrected native bourgeoisie (kulaks and NEPmen) and with world capitalism, at the expense of the interests of the broad mass of the workers and poor peasants.[111]

Instead, Trotsky and the Opposition perceived the general line of the party leadership as centrist, occupying a political space between the revolutionary politics of the Opposition and the complete opportunism of the Second International and the Mensheviks. At times, Trotsky spoke of the leadership's centrism regarding international policy, as in September 1926 when he referred to 'the centrist deviation on questions of the world labour movement (the Anglo-Russian Committee, the Kuomintang, etc.)'.[112] Elsewhere, he denounced 'the gradual Centrist back-sliding with respect to *internal policies*'.[113] In both cases he viewed the leadership's centrism as characterised by political vacillation.[114]

---

109 Lenin 1960–70, vol. 21, p. 326; Lenin 1960–70, vol. 22, p. 108; Lenin 1960–70, vol. 23, pp. 84, 119.
110 For references to the 'opportunist' or 'Menshevik' policies of the leadership, see, for example, Trotsky 1980b, pp. 196–7, 388; Trotsky 1973b, pp. 265, 283, 284, 288; Trotsky 1976a, pp. 165–6, 180.
111 Trotsky 1980b, pp. 388–9.
112 Trotsky 1980b, p. 104. See also Trotsky 1973b, p. 265; Trotsky 1976a, p. 274.
113 Trotsky 1971a, p. 171.
114 See especially Trotsky 1971a, p. 173. See also Trotsky 1980b, pp. 442–3; Trotsky 1976a, p. 274.

4.3.3   *Causes of Bureaucratism*

In 1923 Trotsky offered several different explanations for the growth of state and party bureaucratism. State bureaucratism, he explained, arose out of a variety of factors that included the low level of Soviet culture, the difficulties of state construction, the need to utilise tsarist experts, the growth of market relations under NEP, the influx of members of the NEP bourgeoisie into the state apparatus, and the 'heterogeneity of society'. Bureaucratism in the party derived from the specialised work of its members employed in state or party offices, was transmitted from the state apparatus, and was exacerbated by the relative decline in the level of proletarian membership.

Although Trotsky retained and expanded upon a number of these themes in the years 1926–7, he explicitly or implicitly discarded others. Most importantly, he moved away from the notion inherited from Lenin that the continuing growth of bureaucratism was due to the low level of Soviet culture. In June 1926 Trotsky explicitly rejected the majority's argument that party bureaucratism was a product of low culture, combined with the leading role of the party in the state. First, he observed, the lack of culture was declining, while party bureaucratism was rising. Second, he reasoned that 'if the party's role as a ruling party inevitably entailed its increased bureaucratization, that would imply the destruction of the party' – a conclusion Trotsky was not prepared to accept. He conceded that lack of culture 'in the form of illiteracy and the absence of the simplest necessary skills, leads mostly to bureaucratism in the state apparatus'.[115] However, even as far as state bureaucratism was concerned, Trotsky accorded this explanation a far smaller role than previously. In the same statement he also appears to reject the idea that party bureaucratism was due to a shortage of workers in the party. He noted that, owing to the Lenin Levy, the party had become proletarian in its basic composition; yet it was further from workers' democracy than ever before.[116] Finally, by September 1926 Trotsky appears to have abandoned his earlier notion that bureaucratism in the party was a product of the specialisation of its members. In his New Course writings Trotsky had begun to imply that the overly specialised mentality of the party leadership was more a consequence than a cause of bureaucratism.[117] Now he made this explicit:

> Ideological near-sightedness is always bound up with bureaucratism. The leaders of the ruling faction, who are isolating themselves to an ever

---

115   Trotsky 1980b, p. 67.
116   Trotsky 1980b, p. 66.
117   Trotsky 1975b, p. 77.

greater extent, prove incapable of assessing the situation as a whole, fore-
seeing the future, and issuing broad directives to the party. The policy
becomes small-minded or tail-endist.[118]

Meanwhile, Trotsky and the Opposition retained and expanded upon Trotsky's
earlier explanations that stressed the impact of market forces and bourgeois
pressures on Soviet economic and political institutions. These forces and
pressures were now placed within the context of a clearer and more elaborate account of the evolving character of class relations in Soviet society. In
1926–7 Trotsky's most basic explanation for the growth of bureaucratism was
the change he believed had occurred in the relative strength of social classes
within the Soviet Union. He expressed this analysis concisely in a statement to
the Politburo in June 1926:

> The fundamental cause of bureaucratization must be sought in the rela-
> tions between classes... The bureaucratization of the party... is an
> expression of the disrupted social equilibrium, which has been and is
> being tipped to the disadvantage of the proletariat. This disruption of the
> equilibrium is transmitted to the party and weighs upon the proletarian
> vanguard in the party.[119]

According to Trotsky, since the revolution Soviet proletariat had grown demoralised, and had retreated into passivity. Meanwhile, bourgeois elements had
grown in size and economic influence and had become more self-confident.
This shift in the relation of class forces had exerted a rightward pressure upon
the apparatuses of the major political and social institutions of Soviet society.
Under this pressure, the state and party had adopted policies beneficial to the
bourgeois elements, contributing to the further disruption of the class equilibrium. Meanwhile, to implement its conservative course in domestic and international policy, the party leadership had resorted to repression against the
section of the party that had retained its revolutionary, proletarian perspective. In turn, the resultant defeats of the Opposition promoted further shifts in
the balance of class forces.

In Trotsky's estimation the years since the revolution had been a period of
demoralisation and disillusionment for the Soviet proletariat. At least in the
early phase of Soviet power, the decline of proletarian self-confidence was
largely inevitable. In part, it had been a result of the 'terrible exertions of the

118   Trotsky 1980b, pp. 102–3.
119   Trotsky 1980b, p. 68.

revolution' and the 'sufferings of 1917–1921' that had resulted in the 'nervous exhaustion' of the working class.[120] Besides that, the gap, inevitable in any revolution, between the hopes and expectations of the masses and the realities of revolutionary power had contributed to the problem:

> The hopes engendered by the revolution are always exaggerated ... The conquests gained in the struggle do not correspond, and in the nature of things cannot *directly* correspond, with the expectations of the backward masses awakened for the first time in the course of the revolution. The disillusionment of these masses, their return to routine and futility, is as much an integral part of the postrevolutionary period as is the passage into the camp of 'law and order' of those 'satisfied' classes or layers of classes that had participated in the revolution.[121]

Although the proletarian masses had 'greatly improved their lot' since 1921, this improvement had been gradual. Consequently, workers had 'grown more cautious, more skeptical, less directly responsive to revolutionary slogans, less inclined to place confidence in broad generalizations'.[122] At the same time, the defeats of the international revolution also had promoted demoralisation. Trotsky explained that the Soviet proletariat had expected that 'the European revolution would follow immediately after 1917'. Instead, the period since 1917 had been years of great setbacks for the European proletariat. As a result, the 'tense, highly concentrated expectation' among the Soviet proletariat in the period of revolutionary upheaval had given way to 'deep discouragement'.[123]

Meanwhile, recent years had also witnessed the growth of self-confidence and political activity on the part of the bourgeois elements of Soviet society. Partly, this had occurred as a direct consequence of the demoralisation of the working class.[124] Added to this was the effect of the New Economic Policy. Although Trotsky and the Opposition accepted the fact that NEP was 'necessary as a road toward socialism', they noted that it had 'revived forces hostile

---

120   Trotsky 1980b, pp. 491, 170.
121   Trotsky 1980b, p. 166. See also Trotsky 1980b, pp. 170, 206–7. The *Platform* also gave a perhaps contradictory explanation of working class passivity when it spoke of the illusions among the masses engendered by a 'rapid betterment in the conditions of the workers' after the civil war (Trotsky 1980b, p. 392).
122   Trotsky 1980b, p. 170.
123   Trotsky 1980b, p. 206. See also Trotsky 1980b, pp. 246, 295, 390.
124   Trotsky 1980b, pp. 166, 208, 255.

to socialism', resurrecting a layer of peasant exploiters (the kulaks) and a layer involved in 'trading capital' that dreamed of a restoration of capitalism.[125]

For Trotsky and the Opposition, the combined effect of these shifts in class strength and mood upon Soviet political institutions had been profound. Lenin had warned that the kulak, NEPman, and bureaucrat would 'strive to unite, introduce their own "amendments" into our plans, exercise an increasing pressure on our policy, and satisfy their interests through our apparatus'.[126] Now, it seemed that Lenin's fears were materialising. The kulak and NEPman were exerting a growing pressure upon the state and party apparatuses, both from without and within. The state apparatus, penetrated by bourgeois elements, had been most directly affected. However, because the Communist Party maintained a necessary monopoly of political power, the state apparatus had fed 'much that is bourgeois and petty bourgeois into the party, infecting it with opportunism'.[127] The most important result of this process had been a 'backsliding from the proletarian class line' in economic and international policy.[128]

At the same time, for the party leadership the implementation of its conservative course had necessitated ever-sharper deviations from the principle of workers' democracy. In particular, it had required the use of repression against the Opposition, which remained true to the principles of revolutionary Marxism and which most clearly articulated the orientation of the proletarian vanguard. The 'Declaration of the Thirteen' written in July 1926 explained,

> It is quite clear that it is more and more difficult for the leadership to carry out its policies by methods of party democracy, the less the vanguard of the working class perceives these policies as its own. The divergence in direction between economic policies and the thoughts and feelings of the proletarian vanguard inevitably strengthens the need for high-pressure methods and imparts an administrative-bureaucratic character to all politics. All other explanations for the growth of bureaucratism are of a secondary nature and do not grapple with the heart of the problem.[129]

---

125   Trotsky 1980b, pp. 168–9, 306, 390.
126   Trotsky 1980b, p. 303.
127   Trotsky 1980b, pp. 390–1.
128   See, for example, Trotsky 1980b, pp. 103–4.
129   Trotsky 1980b, p. 76. See also Trotsky 1980b, pp. 103, 254, 256, 299, 355, 403, 407, 445, 452, 474.

Once initiated, the bureaucratisation of the party quickly acquired its own internal dynamic. This helped to explain both the continuing escalation of repression and the further constriction of the sphere of power within the party. As Trotsky asserted in June 1926, 'Any regime develops its own internal logic, and a bureaucratic regime develops it more rapidly than any other'. He explained that the wave of repression unleashed against party dissidents had led to 'the fragmentation of the party cadres, the removal from the party leadership of valuable elements representing a significant portion of its accumulated experience, and the systematic narrowing down and ideological impoverishment of the leadership core'. In turn, this process had generated a new contradiction 'between the growing might of the apparatus and the ideological enfeeblement of the leading center'. 'Under these conditions', Trotsky predicted, 'fear of deviations is bound to grow progressively, with inevitable consequences in the form of so-called organizational measures, which narrow down still further the range of those called upon to be part of the leadership and which push them even further down the road of bureaucratization of the party regime'.[130]

While Trotsky and the Opposition believed that the rightward drift in policy and the assault upon workers' democracy were ultimately *caused* by the shift in the relationship of class forces in the Soviet Union, they also argued that these manifestations of bureaucratism had contributed in turn to the further disruption of the class balance. This was especially true of the economic policies of the party leadership. In a memorandum written in October 1926 Trotsky explained,

> Industry lags behind the overall growth of the economy; socialist accumulation lags behind accumulation in the economy as a whole; wages lag behind the generally higher level of the economy. This means that the economic role of the proletariat is not growing rapidly enough and is even shrinking in relative terms. And this cannot help but have political repercussions.[131]

Regarding international matters, the Opposition believed that the errors of the party leadership had produced major new defeats of the world revolutionary movement, exacerbating the demoralisation of the Soviet proletariat. It was this analysis that governed Trotsky's attitude concerning the prospects for the party struggle in the wake of Chiang Kai-shek's coup in Shanghai. At that

---

130   Trotsky 1980b, pp. 69–70.
131   Trotsky 1980b, p. 122. See also Trotsky 1980b, pp. 76, 96.

point many Oppositionists were hopeful that the transparent failure of the leadership's policy in China would strengthen the Opposition. As Trotsky later recalled, his own approach was different:

> I tried to show them that the opposition could not rise on the *defeat* of the Chinese revolution. The fact that our forecast had proved correct might attract one thousand, five thousand, or even ten thousand new supporters to us. But for the millions, the significant thing was not our forecast, but the fact of the crushing of the Chinese proletariat.[132]

Finally, the Opposition also argued that the deterioration of the party regime had weakened the proletariat and further reduced its ability to influence policy. The 'Declaration of the Eighty-Four' in May 1927 explained that the policy of repression against dissidents had promoted the growing apathy within the party and the working class:

> The internal regime established for the party in recent times has caused an immense decline in the activity of the party, this leading force of the proletarian revolution. For the broad layers of rank-and-file members the opportunities for discussing and helping to solve the essential problems of the revolution in a fully conscious way have been restricted and minimized in the extreme. This could not help but affect the attitude of the working class toward the party and the level of activism of the working class as a whole – and it has affected them in the most negative way.[133]

At the same time, the decline of workers' democracy had cut off the party apparatus from rank-and-file and proletarian influence. As it grew more and more free from the control the working class, the apparatus had found itself increasingly drawn into orbit around the bourgeois elements within the Soviet Union. In June 1926 Trotsky explained that 'a class with a disorganized vanguard (and the lack of free discussion, of control over the apparatus, and of election rights means a disorganized vanguard) cannot help but become a mere object in the hands of a centralized apparatus, which in turn removes itself further and further from the party and is more and more bound to come under the pressure of hostile class forces'.[134]

---

132   Trotsky 1970c, p. 530. See also Trotsky 1980b, pp. 206, 241–2, 378; Trotsky 1970b, p. 246.
133   Trotsky 1980b, p. 233. See also Trotsky 1980b, p. 76.
134   See Trotsky 1980b, pp. 71–2.

Thus, according to Trotsky and the United Opposition, the party found itself trapped in an enormous vicious circle. Shifting class forces had engendered rightward lurches in policy and increasing repression, all of which had further disrupted the class balance. For Trotsky and the Opposition this circle defined the trajectory of the downward spiral of the revolution. The ultimate danger was that the process would culminate in capitalist restoration.

4.3.4   The Danger of Thermidor

As early as 1923 Trotsky had warned that mistaken economic policies and bureaucratism in the party could lead to a restoration of capitalism through one of three political paths: 'either the direct overthrow of the workers' party, or its progressive degeneration, or finally, the conjunction of a partial degeneration, splits, and counterrevolutionary upheavals'.[135] Trotsky returned to this question in the summer of 1927, suggesting now that the three scenarios ultimately resolved into two. Counterrevolution could come through either 'a decisive and sharp overturn (with or without intervention) or . . . several successive shifts [to the right on the part of the party]'. He did not attempt to predict which course the counterrevolution might take, but advised the Opposition to 'keep our eyes out for *either* of these variants . . . to weigh the odds, and to note elements contributing to either'.[136] Nevertheless, during this period he clearly placed the greatest emphasis on the possibility of the degeneration of the party through 'several successive shifts'. Most frequently, he characterised this as the danger of a Soviet Thermidor.

The term *Thermidor* was a historical reference to the ninth of Thermidor, Year II of the French Revolution (27 July 1794), the date when Robespierre and his supporters were overthrown. This event had marked a critical turning point in the revolution, inaugurating a period of sharp decline in mass political activity and a retreat on the part of the government from radical social measures. In the view of the Bolsheviks, the regime of Robespierre had represented the interests of the revolutionary *sans-culottes* – the small shopkeepers, artisans, and labourers. His fall, it was believed, had paved the way for the assumption of power by the big bourgeoisie.

Long before the formation of the United Opposition, the Bolsheviks were haunted by the prospect that the Russian Revolution might experience a

---

135   Trotsky 1975b, p. 88. In 1925 Trotsky returned to this possibility in his pamphlet *Whither Russia?* However, in that work he adopted a more optimistic tone, probably in order to avoid new accusations of 'pessimism'. See Trotsky 1975b, pp. 260–1.

136   Trotsky 1980b, pp. 260–1.

similar fate.[137] Apparently, the first Bolshevik to use the term after the revolution was Lenin in 1921.[138] Trotsky later recalled, 'Before the introduction of NEP
and during its first phase, many of us had quite a few discussions with Lenin
about Thermidor. The word itself was in great currency among us'.[139] In his
memoirs, Trotsky's supporter Victor Serge described how, at the time of the
Kronstadt rebellion in early 1921, Lenin remarked to one of Serge's friends, 'This
is Thermidor', utilising the term to refer to the phased restoration of capitalism that might occur under the cover of the radical slogans of the Kronstadt
sailors.[140] At the Tenth Party Congress Lenin explained that Kronstadt

> was an attempt to seize political power from the Bolsheviks by a motley
> crowd or alliance of ill-assorted elements, apparently just to the right of
> the Bolsheviks, or perhaps even to their 'left' ... The nonparty elements
> served here only as a *bridge*, a *stepping stone*, a *rung on a ladder*, on which
> the White Guards appeared.[141]

To avoid this eventuality, Lenin proposed that the Bolsheviks themselves institute their own 'Thermidor'. In his discussion with Serge's friend, he continued, 'But we shan't let ourselves be guillotined. We shall make a Thermidor
ourselves'. By this, Lenin clearly meant that the Bolsheviks would introduce a
shift to the right in the form of the New Economic Policy in order to *prevent* a
change of regime and capitalist restoration. Along these lines, in 1922 Trotsky
also asserted that with NEP, 'concessions to the Thermidor mood and tendencies of the petty bourgeois, necessary for the purpose of maintaining the
power of the proletariat, were made by the Communist Party without effecting
a break in the system and without quitting the helm'.[142]

However, by May 1921 Lenin was already considering another possible variant of Thermidor. In notes for a speech, he expressed his concern that the

---

137 On the history of the term *Thermidor* among the Bolsheviks, see Law 1987b; and Law 1982.
138 In 1903 Trotsky had suggested that 'thermidoreans' might take power in the party if
     centralism was compromised by Leninist excesses (Trotsky 1980a, p. 38). Also, Kautsky
     warned of a Soviet Thermidor in 1919 (Linden 2007, p. 19).
139 Trotsky 1980b, pp. 258–9.
140 Serge 1980, p. 131. For Trotsky's own later argument that the success of the rebellion at
     Kronstadt would have led to a restoration of capitalism in the Soviet Union, see Trotsky
     1980b, p. 259; and Lenin and Trotsky 1979, pp. 82, 133, 139.
141 Lenin 1958–65, vol. 43, p. 24. The translation used is from Trotsky 1980b, p. 259. See also the
     Tenth Party Congress resolution 'On Party Unity', cited in Law 1987b, p. 6.
142 Trotsky 1975a, p. 83.

revival of market relations under NEP might increase the possibilities of a gradual, 'Thermidorian' reinstitution of capitalism.[143] As we have seen, this was a concern Trotsky had come to share by 1923. In fact in later years he asserted that the 1923 Opposition had described this as a danger of Thermidor, although there is no known speech or document of Trotsky's from this period in which the term appears.[144] In his pamphlet *The New Course*, Trotsky raised the question of 'historical analogies with the Great French Revolution (the fall of the Jacobins) made by liberalism and Menshevism' only to dismiss these as 'superficial and inconsistent'. Unlike the Bolsheviks, Trotsky argued, the Jacobins had been forced to grapple with domestic economic relations that were not yet mature enough to sustain their programme, and to confront a Europe that was politically and economically more backward than their own country.[145]

According to Trotsky's later account, the term surfaced again in the summer of 1925 in a conversation between himself and E.M. Sklianskii, a former deputy in the War Commissariat. In that conversation, Trotsky claimed, he 'realized for the first time with absolute clarity the problem of the Thermidor – with, I might even say, a sort of physical conviction'. After defining Stalin as 'the outstanding mediocrity in the party', Trotsky attempted to account for the origins of his power:

> This is the reaction after the great social and psychological strain of the first years of revolution. A victorious counter-revolution may develop its great men, but its first phase, the Thermidor, demands mediocrities who can't see any farther than their noses.[146]

Shortly after this, the term became an issue in the escalating conflict between the party majority and the Leningrad Opposition. In a private conversation in October between the secretary of the Leningrad provincial party organisation, Peter Zalutskii, and a party member named Leonov, Zalutskii stated that the party leaders were creating a 'kingdom of a bourgeois state', and allegedly accused the leadership of 'degeneration' and attempting to bring about a 'Thermidor'. When Leonov reported the discussion to party leaders in Moscow, Zalutskii admitted the substance of Leonov's report, while denying that he

---

143   Lenin 1958–65, vol. 43, p. 403. This is pointed out in Law 1987b, p. 5.
144   See Trotsky 1975b, pp. 394–5; Trotsky 1975c, pp. 279, 314; Law 1987b, p. 7.
145   Trotsky 1975b, pp. 87–8.
146   Quoted in Trotsky 1970c, p. 513.

had ever accused the cc of degeneration or Thermidor. Nevertheless, he was promptly removed from his party office.[147]

Although the discussion of this incident at the Fourteenth Party Congress revived Trotsky's interest in the question, he did not raise the question publicly until 1927.[148] Perhaps he wanted to think the analogy through more carefully; or perhaps he wanted to avoid the furor that the term had provoked in 1925. However, the intensification of the party struggle in 1927 inflamed the passions and the rhetoric on both sides. In the early summer of 1927, A.A. Sol'ts, a member of the ccc, warned one of Trotsky's supporters of the implications of the latest declaration of the Opposition: 'You know the history of the French Revolution, – and to what this led: to arrests and the guillotine'. At his hearing before the ccc in June, Trotsky hurled the historical analogy back at his accusers, challenging Sol'ts, 'Do you clearly understand in accordance with what chapter [of the revolution] you are now preparing to shoot? I fear, comrade Sol'ts, that you are about to shoot us in accordance with the . . . Thermidorian chapter'.[149] From this point on, the term occupied a central place in Trotsky's polemical and theoretical arsenal.

As Trotsky defined it in the summer of 1927, Thermidor was 'a special form of counterrevolution carried out on the installment plan . . ., and making use, in the first stage, of elements of the same ruling party – by regrouping them and counterposing some to others'.[150] On the surface, Thermidor appeared to involve only a minor change in the revolutionary leadership, a 'stepping down one rung on the ladder of revolution – a slight shift of power to the right as the result of a certain crucial change or break in the psychology of the revolution. At the top, at the helm, there seem to be the very same people, the same speeches, the same banners'.[151] This, Trotsky argued, was even how it had appeared to the French Thermidorian leaders.[152] Nevertheless, beneath the surface the French Thermidor had marked a fundamental realignment of class forces.[153]

147 Carr 1958–64, vol. 2, pp. 112–13, Broué 1988, pp. 465–6. See also Daniels 1960, p. 255; Deutscher 1959, pp. 244–5.
148 Trotsky 1975b, pp. 394–5. However, Trotsky discussed the issue in a memorandum on 26 November 1926. See Trotsky 1980b, p. 172.
149 Trotsky 1971a, pp. 142–3.
150 Trotsky 1980b, p. 263.
151 Trotsky 1980b, p. 259.
152 Trotsky 1971a, p. 144. See also Trotsky 1980b, pp. 258, 389.
153 Trotsky 1980b, p. 260.

Trotsky insisted that a similar event was possible in the Soviet Union. Throughout the country he perceived the growth of 'elements of Thermidor' – particularly among the NEPmen and kulaks, but also within the party's right wing, led especially by prominent members of the state and trade union appa-ratuses.[154] He explained that, on the political level, a Soviet Thermidor could occur by means of a rightward shift of power within the Soviet state, or even within the party 'with the banner of communism in one's hands'.[155] But on the deeper level of class relations, a Soviet Thermidor would involve 'a shift from the path of proletarian revolution in a petty bourgeois direction'.[156] Although he certainly understood that the French Thermidor had not resulted in the restoration of feudalism, he was convinced that in the Soviet context an analo-gous event would inaugurate the return of capitalism.[157]

Trotsky attempted to describe the same process utilising analogies from the Russian Revolution. Between the February and October revolutions of 1917, the Bolsheviks had believed that a large measure of political power had slipped from the hands of the old ruling classes, but that complete class rule had not yet been attained by the proletariat. The situation was described as one of 'dual power' in which political control was shared by the bourgeois Provisional Government, and the proletarian soviets. Now, Trotsky observed, 'elements of dual power' were once again emerging in the country.[158] Thermidor would involve the 'legalisation ... of a dual power situation, this time with the bour-geoisie holding the upper hand', which would again 'help one class, the bour-geoisie, wrest power from the other, the proletariat'. That is, it would be 'a kind of Kerenskyism in reverse'.[159]

Some Oppositionists, especially those who had come from the Democratic Centralist and Workers' Opposition groupings, believed that the Soviet Thermidor already had occurred.[160] Despite the fact that the party leadership accused the United Opposition as a whole of sharing this view, the statements and documents of Trotsky and the Opposition repeatedly denied this. In a memorandum written in November 1926 Trotsky argued, 'It would be a crude

---

154   Trotsky 1980b, pp. 262, 267, 293, 384, 489.
155   Trotsky 1980b, p. 259.
156   Trotsky 1980b, p. 390.
157   The anarchist Peter Kropotkin, in a work cited approvingly by Trotsky in 1927, remarked regarding the period following the ninth of Thermidor in France, 'The reaction was able to destroy, up to a certain point, the political work of the Revolution; but its economic work survived' (Kropotkin 1971, pp. 430–1; Trotsky 1971a, pp. 142–3).
158   Trotsky 1980b, pp. 489, 502–3.
159   Trotsky 1980b, pp. 492–3.
160   Deutscher 1959, p. 292.

distortion of reality to speak of Thermidor as an accomplished fact. Things have gone no further than the holding of some rehearsals within the party and the laying of some theoretical groundwork'.[161] The following June he sharply rejected Ordzhonikidze's contention that he believed the revolution had perished, and later in 1927 the United Opposition as a whole disavowed the view that the party or its leadership was Thermidorian.[162]

Nor did Trotsky believe that Thermidor was *inevitable* in the Soviet Union as it had been in France. Returning to views he had expressed on this question in 1923, he pointed out the advantages of the Russian Revolution: it had been made by a developed and class conscious proletariat rather than the weaker 'pre-proletariat' of eighteenth-century France; and the Soviet Union was surrounded by industrially more advanced neighbours, each of which had a strong proletariat, not by backward feudal countries.[163] Nevertheless, Trotsky insisted that a Soviet Thermidor was *possible* as long as the European proletariat failed to take power.[164]

Beyond warning of the danger of Thermidor, Trotsky and the Opposition attempted to anticipate how it would unfold. They believed that it would probably begin with the crushing of the Opposition itself. For example, in December 1927 Trotsky asserted, 'The most important ... condition for a victory of Thermidor would be to crush the Opposition so thoroughly that it no longer needed to be "feared"'.[165] This would be followed by deeper shifts to the right in economic and social policy. Trotsky predicted what these would look like in an address to the CCC in August 1927:

> As the first step, repeal the monopoly of foreign trade. Give the kulak the opportunity of doubling the export and the import. Enable the kulak to squeeze the middle peasant. Compel the poor peasant to understand that without the kulak there is no other road. Raise and reinforce the importance of the bureaucracy, of the administration. Cast aside the demands of the workers as so much 'guildism'. Restrict the workers politically in the Soviets, reestablish last years' election decree [which restored

---

161   Trotsky 1980b, p. 172.
162   Trotsky 1971a, p. 155; Trotsky 1980b, pp. 293, 384. For similar statements made later in 1927, see Trotsky 1980b, pp. 469, 482.
163   Trotsky 1971a, p. 158; Trotsky 1980b, pp. 262–3.
164   Trotsky 1971a, p. 158; Trotsky 1980b, pp. 258, 260–1, 492.
165   Trotsky 1980b, p. 490. See also Trotsky 1980b, p. 234. On the election decree of the RFSFR of October 1925 and its impact upon the Soviet elections of 1925–26, see Carr 1958–64, vol. 2, pp. 347–51.

electoral rights to employers of auxiliary labor] and gradually extend it in favor of the property owners. That would be the road of Thermidor. Its name is – *capitalism on the installment plan*.[166]

Once implemented, these rightist policies would lead in turn to further changes in the political system. As in France, the counterrevolution eventually would be forced to remove its revolutionary mask and institute a repressive and dictatorial 'Bonapartist' regime. In June 1927 Trotsky asserted that, following a Thermidor, the Soviet bourgeoisie 'would subsequently discard completely the Soviet covering and transform its power into a Bonapartist rule'.[167] He elaborated in an analysis of the Fifteenth Party Congress written in late December, explaining that a Thermidor inevitably would provoke the resistance of the proletariat who 'would attempt to hold on to its positions or win back those it had lost'. Then, 'to beat back these attempts and to consolidate their hold in a genuine way, the bourgeoisie would soon need, not a transitional regime, but a more serious, solid and decisive kind – in all probability, a Bonapartist or, in modern terms, a fascist regime'.[168]

4.3.5   *Characteristics: Political Divisions*

During the party contest of 1926–7, Trotsky and the United Opposition repeatedly attempted to define the most important political currents and groupings within the Soviet Union, and the relationship of each to the party struggle. Broadly speaking, these efforts focused on the two major aspects of the problem of bureaucratism. At times, they identified the party groupings that were relevant to the growing centralisation of political authority. In other statements they mapped the broad range of political currents in the country along a left-right continuum and specified the role played by each in the shifting balance of class forces.

As part of its effort to establish that the leadership was undemocratically usurping authority, the Opposition sought to demonstrate that the supporters of the party 'majority' actually constituted a minority of the membership. In October 1926 Trotsky wrote a memorandum in which he explained that, due to the increasingly repressive and undemocratic internal party regime, the 'party

---

166   Trotsky 1971a, p. 172.

167   Trotsky 1971a, p. 140.

168   Trotsky 1980b, p. 493. See also Trotsky 1980b, p. 401. Trotsky's discussion of the possibility of a Bonapartist regime in the Soviet Union represented an important reversal of his earlier views. In 1918 and 1919 he explicitly excluded this possibility (Trotsky 1979–81, vol. 1, pp. 252–3; Trotsky 1979–81, vol. 2, p. 58).

has at present been artificially divided into three rather sharply marked-off parts: (1) the ruling faction, which constitutes the backbone of the apparatus selected from above; (2) the Opposition elements, fighting for a rectification of the party line and a restoration of normality in the party regime; and (3) the broad mass of the party in between, atomized, disoriented, and in effect deprived of any chance to actively affect the fate of the party'.[169] The obvious implication was that the leadership majority did not actually represent the majority of the rank and file.[170]

Trotsky and the Opposition also commented upon the extreme centralisation of authority *within* the majority faction. First, they noted the division between the lower-level supporters of the majority faction and the 'leading factional clique' at the top. In October 1926 Trotsky remarked that the latter was merely 'the tiny leading group' of the 'sealed off [majority] faction'.[171] Similarly, the 'Declaration of the Thirteen' explained, 'The ruling faction has its own [ruling] minority, which places faction discipline above that of the party'.[172] Beyond that, the Opposition observed a growing centralisation of authority within the top leadership of the majority faction. In October 1926 Trotsky argued that Stalin, 'relying on a group of comrades who always agree with him', was attempting to institute a regime of 'one-man rule' in the party. Increasingly, the pursuit of this goal was bringing Stalin into conflict with all the other prominent leaders of the ruling faction:

> One-man rule in the administration of the party ... requires not only the defeat, removal, and ouster of the present United Opposition but also the gradual removal of *all authoritative and influential figures in the present ruling faction*. It is quite obvious that neither Tomsky, nor Rykov, nor Bukharin – because of their past, their authority, etc. – is capable of playing the role under Stalin that Uglanov, Kaganovich, Petrovsky, et al. play under him. The ouster of the present Opposition would in fact mean the inevitable transformation of the old group in the Central Committee into an opposition. A new discussion would be placed on the agenda, in which Kaganovich would expose Rykov, Uglanov would expose Tomsky, and Slepkov, Sten, and Company would deglorify Bukharin.[173]

169   Trotsky 1980b, pp. 115–16.
170   See also Trotsky 1980b, p. 102.
171   Trotsky 1980b, p. 114.
172   Trotsky 1980b, p. 87.
173   Trotsky 1980b, pp. 116–17.

In other statements Trotsky and the Opposition located the various political currents within the Soviet Union, and especially those within the party, on a left-right political spectrum. In doing so, they employed the understandings of the terms *left* and *right* in use at the time. The utilisation of directional labels to identify political positions dates back to the French Revolution, when radical supporters of popular sovereignty and democracy sat on the left side in the Constituent Assembly and their conservative opponents sat on the right. By the late nineteenth century with the growth of large socialist movements, the application of the terms in Europe had extended to the economic sphere, where the left was identified with the advocacy of socialism, state intervention in the economy, and economic equality; while the right was associated with the defense of capitalism, the free market, and inequality.[174] Consistent with this usage, Trotsky and the United Opposition defined Soviet political currents in part by their attitudes toward workers' democracy, but even more by their positions regarding the market mechanisms of NEP. In international affairs, it seems they evaluated Communist currents largely in terms of their positions on alliances with parties that were pro-capitalist or conciliatory to capitalism.

For Trotsky and the United Opposition the far right of the political spectrum was occupied by Thermidorians. As previously noted, the oppositionists perceived this tendency as especially strong outside of the party among the kulaks and NEPmen. Politically, they believed its views were most clearly articulated by the economist N. Ustrialov who, according to the 'Declaration of the Eighty-Four', was 'the most logical, most principled, and most uncompromising enemy of Bolshevism'.[175] Trotsky explained that Ustrialov was 'realistic in his Thermidorianism' because he recognised that ultimately the completion of restoration would require 'a Bonapartist-fascist shift – by installments – onto bourgeois rails'.[176] As steps toward this goal, Trotsky observed in the autumn of 1926, Ustrialov supported Stalin's war against the Opposition and a 'Neo-Nep' consisting of further economic shifts to the right.[177]

Others promoting Thermidor from outside the party, according to Trotsky, were the Mensheviks. In contrast to Ustrialov, the Mensheviks feared Bonapartism, 'preferring a democracy which would give the petty bourgeoisie a chance to preserve some semblance of a political role'.[178] For that

---

174   Caute 1966, pp. 9, 26–44; 'Left' and 'right' in Bealey 1999; Daniels 1960, p. 5; 'Left' in Krieger et al. 1993, p. 531.

175   Trotsky 1980b, p. 234. See also Trotsky 1980b, p. 402; Trotsky 1971a, p. 141.

176   Trotsky 1980b, pp. 492, 402. See also Trotsky 1980b, p. 260.

177   Trotsky 1971a, p. 141. See also Trotsky 1980b, pp. 234, 446.

178   Trotsky 1980b, p. 402.

reason they advocated replacing the proletarian dictatorship with a system of bourgeois parliamentary democracy.[179] However, given the Russian heritage of revolutions and civil wars, Trotsky believed that a Bonapartist regime was 'a much more likely road for the return to bourgeois society than democracy'.[180] Consequently, he dismissed Menshevism as 'utopian through and through', and seems to have considered the Mensheviks as less of a threat than the Ustrialovists.[181]

Trotsky and the United Opposition also perceived a Thermidorian tendency composed of two groupings within the Communist Party. One of these was described by Trotsky as a 'right deviation [within the ruling faction] toward the kulak, the petty bourgeoisie, and middle class elements in general'.[182] In the words of the Opposition's *Platform*, this grouping 'to a great extent reflects the interests of the "economically strong" middle peasant, toward whom it steers its course and by whose ideals it is inspired'. Its leaders included Rykov, A.P. Smirnov, M.I. Kalinin, G.I. Petrovskii, V.Ia. Chubar, and G.N. Kaminskii. Around them was a layer of '"nonparty" politicians,...and other "business agents" of the wealthy peasantry, more or less openly preaching the doctrines of Ustryalov'.[183] A second rightist tendency within the party noted by Trotsky was 'a trade unionist deviation which is marching hand in hand with the deviation toward the peasant proprietor but which frequently comes into hostile conflict with the latter'.[184] The *Platform* described this as a grouping of 'trade union leaders who represent the better-paid class of industrial and office workers'. Its leaders included M.P. Tomskii, G.N. Mel'nichanskii, and A.I. Dogadov. [185] Although the Platform noted friction between these two rightist party groupings, it described them as united 'in the desire to turn the course of the party and the Soviet state to the right, in both international and domestic policies'.[186] According to the *Platform*, neither grouping *consciously* desired a Thermidor.[187] Nevertheless, as Trotsky explained, the objective political significance of the entire right wing of the party was that it served 'as a transmitting mechanism' for pressures from the 'bourgeois classes who are raising their heads'.[188]

---

179   Trotsky 1980b, p. 492.
180   Trotsky 1980b, pp. 402. See also Trotsky 1980b, 492.
181   Trotsky 1980b, p. 492.
182   Trotsky 1980b, p. 108.
183   Trotsky 1980b, pp. 355–6.
184   Trotsky 1980b, p. 108.
185   Trotsky 1980b, p. 356.
186   Ibid.
187   Trotsky 1980b, p. 389.
188   Trotsky 1971a, p. 141.

The clear implication was that the displacement of the Stalinist leadership of the party by the right wing would constitute the beginning of a Soviet Thermidor.

To the left of the Thermidorians were the centrists, consisting of Stalin and his supporters, who had achieved dominance within the party.[189] Unlike the right and the left wings, the centrist tendency had no roots in the fundamental classes of Soviet society.[190] Rather, its strength was to be found in the apparatuses of the party, the state, the economic institutions, and the mass organisations, which combined constituted an enormous 'layer of "administrators"'.[191] Without any solid base in either the proletariat or the petty bourgeoisie, the centrists were unable to pursue either a consistently revolutionary, or a consistently reformist policy. Instead, they followed an intermediate course, lurching to the left and right in response to the pressures of antagonistic classes. In October 1927 Trotsky explained,

> In reality the whole policy of this centrist faction is itself going forward under the blows of two whips – one from the right and one from the left ... This bureaucratic centrist faction ... staggers between two class lines, ... systematically sliding away from the proletarian to the petty-bourgeois course. It does not slide away in a direct line, but in sharp zigzags.[192]

Although Trotsky and the United Opposition recognised Stalin as the preeminent leader of the centrists, they paid little attention to Stalin's personal significance and influence. At least as far as Trotsky was concerned, this was because he believed that Stalin *had* little personal significance. In later accounts Trotsky recalled explaining to supporters that Stalin was a 'mediocrity' who owed his growing power to broader social layers. In 1924, he recalled, he had predicted to I.N. Smirnov that 'Stalin will become dictator of the U.S.S.R.' When Smirnov

---

189   Robert McNeal argues that in the late 1920s Trotsky at times equated Stalinism with German Social Democracy and Menshevism (McNeal 1977, p. 31). This is mistaken. Trotsky viewed the German Social Democrats and the Mensheviks as fully opportunist. Again, although he denounced the 'opportunist' and 'Menshevist' character of some Stalinist policies, during this period he viewed the general line of the Stalinists as centrist.

190   See Trotsky 1980b, pp. 356, 442.

191   Trotsky 1980b, p. 356; Fel'shtinskii 1988, vol. 4, p. 151 (translation modified). See also Trotsky 1980b, p. 108.

192   See Trotsky 1980b, pp. 442–3.

protested that Stalin was nothing but a 'mediocrity, a colorless nonentity', Trotsky responded,

> Mediocrity yes; nonentity no ... The dialectics of history have already hooked him and will raise him up. He is needed by all of them – by the tired radicals, by the bureaucrats, by the *nepmen*, the *kulaks*, the upstarts, the sneaks, by all the worms that are crawling out of the upturned soil of the manured revolution. He knows how to meet them on their own ground, he speaks their language and he knows how to lead them. He has the deserved reputation of an old revolutionist, which makes him invaluable to them as a blinder on the eyes of the country.[193]

Aside from Stalin, the *Platform* listed V.M. Molotov, N.A. Uglanov, L.M. Kaganovich, A.I. Mikoian, and S.M. Kirov among the leaders of the centrist tendency. Although the Leningrad Opposition had denounced Bukharin as the leading rightist in the party, the *Platform* now depicted him, too, as a centrist: 'Bukharin, wavering between one side and the other, "generalizes" the policies of this [centrist] group'. This evaluation of Bukharin may have been due to the fact that, since 1925, he had been gradually moving toward the left in his economic views.[194]

According to the *Platform*, the centrists were even less inclined to support Thermidor consciously than was the right tendency within the party. Stalin and his supporters were convinced that with their apparatus they could 'outwit all the forces of the bourgeoisie rather than having to overcome them through an open struggle'. However, in this, they were 'carrying out a typical policy of illusion, self-consolation, and self-deception'.[195] In particular, the repressive measures enacted by the Stalinists had bolstered the right. Trotsky observed that 'when Stalin makes the crushing of the left wing of the party the main focus of his work, ... he strengthens [the Thermidorians] and weakens the positions of the proletariat'.[196]

Trotsky and the United Opposition believed that both the centrist faction and its alliance with the party right were inherently unstable. As far as the centrist faction was concerned, this seems to have been due to its lack of a firm class basis. In August 1927, Trotsky noted that it was 'already splitting into a Right and a Left wing, both of which are incessantly growing at the expense of

---

193   Quoted in Trotsky 1941, p. 393. See also Trotsky 1970c, p. 513.
194   Trotsky 1980b, p. 356. For Bukharin's shift to the left, see Cohen 1980, pp. 242–52.
195   Trotsky 1980b, p. 389.
196   Trotsky 1980b, p. 267.

the center'. He predicted this process would only accelerate in the event of war when the 'Stalinist Center will inevitably melt away'.[197] Similarly, the *Platform* argued that the coalition of the centrists and the party right was held together only by a mutual animosity toward the Opposition.[198] Throughout 1927 Trotsky and the Opposition repeatedly asserted that the Opposition's defeat would bring to the surface all the suppressed tensions within the majority. For example, in the summer of 1927 Trotsky prophesied that if 'the Opposition were to be "smashed", then the majority faction backsliding to the right, would immediately begin to be split up into new factional groupings, with all the ensuing consequences'.[199]

The final grouping identified by Trotsky and the Opposition was the party left. Most importantly, this tendency was embodied in the Opposition itself, the 'Leninist wing of the party', which was 'fighting for a rectification of the party line and a restoration of normality in the party regime'.[200] Although the Opposition admitted that it was a minority within the party, it predicted that, once the *Platform* was circulated, the 'working class sections of the party and all genuine Leninists will be for it'.[201] Included among the 'genuine Leninists' were many officials within the 'agencies of administration and leadership' of the party, state, and mass organisations. In these institutions, the *Platform* claimed, 'there are to be found many thousands of sturdy revolutionists, workers who have not lost their ties with the masses but who give themselves heart and soul to the workers' cause'.[202]

4.3.6   *The Struggle Against Bureaucratism and Thermidor*
The strategy pursued by the Opposition flowed directly from the preceding analysis. Most importantly, this understanding dictated that, for the time being, the Opposition should attempt to reform Soviet political institutions, not to organise a new revolution. In December 1927 Trotsky observed that the struggle of the Opposition against the danger of Thermidor was a 'class struggle', while noting that such a struggle necessarily took different forms in different situations. He explained, 'The struggle aimed at tearing the power from the hands of another class is revolutionary'.[203] Such would be the character of

197   Trotsky 1971a, pp. 173–4.
198   Trotsky 1980b, pp. 108, 357.
199   Trotsky 1980b, p. 108. See also Trotsky 1980b, pp. 357, 497.
200   Trotsky 1980b, pp. 357, 115–16.
201   Trotsky 1980b, p. 357.
202   Trotsky 1980b, p. 356.
203   Trotsky 1980b, p. 489.

the struggle after a Thermidor when 'the Opposition would lead the revolutionary cadres of Bolshevism over to the struggle against the bourgeois state'.[204]
However, as long as the bourgeoisie had not conquered the state, political
power remained in the hands of the proletariat. Consequently, it was still possible to correct the 'political course, remove the elements of dual power, and
to reinforce the dictatorship [of the proletariat] by measures of a reformist
kind'.[205] Furthermore, since any attempt to establish a second party would set
the Opposition on the revolutionary road, the Opposition was obliged to conduct its struggle within the limits of the Communist Party. At the Fifteenth
Party Conference Trotsky asserted,

> Those who believe that our state is not a proletarian state, and that our
> development is not socialist, must lead the proletariat against such a
> state and must found another party.
>
> But those who believe that our state is a proletarian state, but with
> bureaucratic deformations formed under the pressure of the petty-
> bourgeois elements and the capitalist encirclement; . . . these must use
> party methods and party means to combat that which they hold to be
> wrong, mistaken, or dangerous.[206]

The goal of the Opposition, then, was to mobilise the working-class members
of the party to press for a correction of the party regime and political line. The
Platform declared the conviction of the Opposition that 'the fundamental mass
of the working class section of the party will prove able in spite of everything to
bring the party back to the Leninist road'.[207] As part of this struggle, the United
Opposition addressed its demands, far more than the 1923 Opposition had, to
the concerns of the Soviet working class. Throughout 1926–7 it circulated its
statements and manifestos within the party's working-class cells. Whenever
possible, its leaders directly addressed meetings of workers.

However, the Opposition found it exceedingly difficult to implement this
strategy. In particular, they discovered that it was virtually impossible to carry
its message to the proletarian core of the party while abiding by officially sanctioned party methods. Whenever leaders of the Opposition appeared before
meetings of workers, or even distributed its statements within factory cells of
the party, they were accused of factionalism and threatened with expulsion.

---

204   Trotsky 1980b, p. 496.
205   Trotsky 1980b, p. 489. See also Trotsky 1980b, pp. 267, 476.
206   Trotsky 1980b, p. 163. See also Trotsky 1980b, pp. 267, 293, 401.
207   Trotsky 1980b, p. 358. See also Trotsky 1980b, p. 473.

While continuing to recognise the legitimacy of the prohibition against factions, Trotsky and the Opposition repeatedly tried to circumvent this ban by
defining their activities as those of a 'grouping', not a disciplined 'faction', or by
explaining their violations of party rules as a response to the factionalism and
organisational measures of majority.[208] Nevertheless, to avoid expulsion the
Opposition ultimately was compelled to conduct the most important debates
of its struggle within the walls of the Kremlin. There, the best it could hope for
was to win the sympathies of the 'genuine Leninists' in the party apparatus.

On the occasions when the United Opposition was able to obtain a hearing within the proletarian cells of the party, it encountered an even greater
obstacle – the passivity of the Soviet working class. Trotsky commented upon
this phenomenon in a memo written in late November 1926, asserting that the
Soviet masses had 'grown more cautious, more skeptical, less directly responsive to revolutionary slogans, less inclined to place confidence in broad generalizations'.[209] Contemporary research suggests that this phenomenon had
grown even more pronounced by late 1927, due to the combined effects of
pressure exerted by the party leadership and the confusion engendered by the
Opposition's own repeated advances and retreats.[210] Nevertheless, Trotsky and
the Opposition repeatedly proclaimed their faith that, ultimately, the proletarian nucleus would arise and reassert its control over the party. The *Platform*
predicted,

> This working class section of the party will reawaken. It will find out
> what is really happening. It will take the fate of the party into its own
> hands. To help the vanguard of the workers in this process is the task of
> the Opposition.[211]

One development that, according to Trotsky, could contribute to the reawak-
ening of the Soviet proletariat would be an upsurge in the international
revolution.[212] Alternatively, he believed that the Soviet working class might
revive once it clearly perceived the domestic consequences of the rightist

---

208   Trotsky 1980b, pp. 69, 102, 106, 474.
209   Trotsky 1980b, p. 170.
210   For evidence of this phenomenon in Moscow's Hammer and Sickle Factory, see Murphy
       2001, pp. 337, 339–43, 347; Murphy 2005, pp. 169–70, 172–7, 180. For other discussions of the
       passivity of Soviet workers, see Cliff 1991, p. 268; Deutscher 1959, pp. 274–5, 282, 283, 287,
       376–7.
211   Trotsky 1980b, p. 393. See also Trotsky 1980b, pp. 268, 358, 447, 448.
212   Trotsky 1980b, p. 495.

economic policies of the party leadership. As he warned the CC in February 1927, 'The increased activism of the nonproletarian classes inevitably will bring the proletariat to its feet. It will arise to defend itself and, when conditions become at all favorable, will go over to the offensive'.[213]

4.4   On the Eve of Thermidor

In the fall of 1927 the internal party struggle escalated feverishly toward its climax. The Opposition, determined to proceed with the pre-Congress discussion, exerted every effort to bring its programme before the proletarian component of the party. At the same time, the party leadership, equally determined to silence the Opposition, resorted to unprecedented methods of repression, culminating in the expulsion of the leaders of the Opposition and a large number of their supporters. On the basis of this repression Trotsky concluded that the Soviet state was poised on the brink of Thermidor.

On 6 September the United Opposition again addressed the Politburo and the presidium of the CCC, protesting against the persecution of its adherents and demanding the return of banished Oppositionists to participate in a full pre-Congress debate. Furthermore, it called for the publication and distribution of its platform as part of the party discussion. The leadership rejected the demand to distribute the *Platform* on the grounds that it had no desire to legalise the Oppositional faction, offering instead only the publication of brief counter-theses to its own official theses.[214]

Short of total surrender, the only alternative left to the Opposition was to issue the *Platform* on its own. On the night of 12 September, the GPU raided a house where a handful of Oppositionists were duplicating the *Platform* on typewriters. The following day the GPU reported to the CCC that it had uncovered an 'illegal printshop, which was publishing the antiparty documents of the Opposition prohibited by the party'.[215] Involved in the affair was a former officer of Wrangel's White Guards who, the GPU alleged, was also tied to a 'military conspiracy'. Fourteen Oppositionists involved in the duplication of the *Platform* were expelled from the party, and one, S.V. Mrachkovskii, was imprisoned.[216] Meanwhile, in response to inquiries from Opposition leaders, the head of the GPU admitted that the former 'Wrangel officer' was an

---

213   Trotsky 1980b, p. 209. See also Trotsky 1980b, pp. 495, 497.
214   Carr 1971–8, vol. 2, pp. 34–5; Daniels 1960, pp. 312–13; Deutscher 1959, pp. 356–7.
215   Quoted in Trotsky 1980b, pp. 416–17.
216   Carr 1971–8, vol. 2, p. 35; Daniels 1960, p. 313; Deutscher 1959, pp. 357–8.

employee of the secret police. Immediately, the Opposition protested that an *agent provocateur* had been utilised to create the impression that it was working with White Guardists and military conspirators.[217] To this, Stalin replied, 'But is there anything wrong in this former Wrangel officer helping the Soviet authorities to unmask counter-revolutionary conspiracies'?[218]

A few weeks later, the leadership abruptly proclaimed a number of initiatives in economic policy. On 10 October Bukharin called for *'a reinforced offensive against capitalist elements and, first of all, against the kulak'*. Then, at the opening session of the Central Executive Committee of the Congress of Soviets, Rykov announced an increase in the proportion of peasant households exempted from taxation.[219] At the same time, the leadership unveiled a manifesto in honor of the tenth anniversary of the revolution announcing that the eight-hour day and six-day workweek would be replaced by a seven-hour workday and five-day week with no cut in pay.[220] To a large degree, these measures seem to have been motivated by a desire to undercut the appeal of the Opposition's *Platform* among the working class. At a subsequent session of the CC, Trotsky insisted that these measures did not fundamentally alter the rightist character of the official economic policy:

> Today's shouting about *'forced pressure'* on the kulak – that same kulak to whom yesterday they were shouting 'Enrich yourselves'! – cannot change the general line. Anniversary celebration surprises, such as a seven-hour workday, cannot change it either ... The political line of the present leadership is not defined by these individual adventuristic gestures ... .[221]

Trotsky denounced the shortening of the workday as transparent demagogy, pointing out that this had been introduced without regard for any of the existing long-term plans. Furthermore, the manifesto actually contained only vague promises to introduce the seven-hour day among certain categories of workers at some indefinite point in the future.[222]

Continuing its efforts to win adherents, the Opposition launched a campaign to get 20–30,000 signatures to its *Platform* prior to the Fifteenth Party Congress. (Ultimately, it succeeded in obtaining only 5,000–6,000.) Meanwhile, its hopes

217 Daniels 1960, p. 313; Deutscher 1959, pp. 358–9; Trotsky 1980b, pp. 416–27.
218 Stalin 1952–5, vol. 10, p. 193.
219 Carr and Davies 1969, part 1, p. 33.
220 Carr and Davies 1969, part 2, p. 496; Deutscher 1959, 363.
221 Trotsky 1980b, p. 443.
222 Trotsky 1980b, pp. 430–1.

for a proletarian resurgence were renewed by demonstrations in Leningrad on 15 October to celebrate the seven-hour day. The demonstrators filed past the main body of officials, but, recognising Trotsky and Zinoviev on a separate reviewing stand, gathered in a crowd of thousands around them, waving and shouting greetings. Zinoviev, convinced that this spontaneous demonstration indicated mass support, expressed optimism about the Opposition's chances of success. Although Trotsky shared Zinoviev's view that the demonstration indicated deep popular dissatisfaction, he warned that it would only impel the leadership to accelerate its destruction of the Opposition.[223]

The October plenum of the CC-CCC convened to approve the majority's economic theses for the Fifteenth Party Congress. However, in the course of the plenum Stalin renewed his demand for the expulsion of Trotsky and Zinoviev from the Central Committee. Both Trotsky and Zinoviev were shouted down, and books and a water glass were thrown at Trotsky while he spoke.[224] In his address Trotsky repeatedly returned to the theme of 'Thermidor', describing the incident of the 'Wrangel officer' as an example of a 'Thermidorian amalgam'. Stalin's goal, according to Trotsky, was 'to split the party, to cut off the Opposition, to accustom the party to the method of physical destruction'. To these ends, Stalin and his supporters had resorted to expelling and arresting Oppositionists, and to 'fascist methods' such as shouting down or beating up Oppositionists, and throwing books and stones. In attempting to destroy the Opposition, Trotsky warned, Stalin was carrying out the social orders of Ustrialov. However, the Opposition would not be silenced. Defiantly, he concluded, 'Expel us. You will not stop the victory of the Opposition – the victory of the revolutionary unity of our party and the Communist International'![225] Subsequently, the plenum unanimously approved the expulsion of Trotsky and Zinoviev from the CC.[226]

Once again the Opposition attempted to take its case to the masses. On the tenth anniversary of the revolution, Oppositionists marched in the official parades in Moscow and Leningrad, carrying banners with their own slogans: 'Strike against the NEPman and the bureaucrat'!, 'Down with opportunism'!, 'Carry out Lenin's testament'!, 'Beware of a split in the party'!, and 'Preserve Bolshevik unity'![227] Police and agents of the majority leadership ripped these banners from the hands of the demonstrators and beat up Oppositionists.

---

223   Carr 1971–8, vol. 2, p. 37; Deutscher 1959, pp. 365–6, 370; Trotsky 1970c, pp. 532–3.
224   Carr 1971–8, vol. 2, pp. 38–9; Deutscher 1959, pp. 366–7.
225   Trotsky 1980b, p. 448.
226   Carr 1971–8, vol. 2, p. 39.
227   Deutscher 1959, p. 373.

From these incidents, Trotsky concluded that the danger of Thermidor was imminent:

> When Bolsheviks are beaten up because they call for turning our fire to the right, against kulak, NEPman, and bureaucrat, then the danger of Thermidor is at hand. Those who do the beating, those who organize the beatings, and those who regard them with indulgence are Thermidorians or connivers at Thermidor.[228]

In reply to Trotsky's request for a special inquiry into the events in Moscow and Leningrad, the CC and CCC insisted that the Opposition cease its illegal, anti-party meetings. When Trotsky and Zinoviev stalked out of this joint session in protest, they were expelled from the party, while five more Oppositionists were removed from the CC and six were dropped from the CCC. A few days later Adolf Ioffe – a prominent Soviet diplomat and a close friend of Trotsky's – committed suicide in protest against Trotsky's expulsion. Ioffe's funeral was the occasion for the last public demonstration of the Opposition and Trotsky's final public speech in the Soviet Union.[229]

By this point the United Opposition was in disarray. While Zinoviev and Kamenev balked at further dissident activity out of fear that the expulsions would push the Opposition onto the road of a second party, Trotsky urged a continuation of the struggle. Still, the Opposition managed to close ranks in a final appeal to the Fifteenth Party Congress. In a statement signed by 121 Oppositionists, the United Opposition agreed to accept part of the responsibility for the crisis in the party, promised to renounce factionalism and abide by the decisions of the congress, and called upon the congress to readmit expelled Oppositionists and release those who had been imprisoned. At the congress, Stalin rejected the statement as inadequate, and a resolution was passed declaring adherence to the Opposition to be incompatible with party membership.[230]

Stalin's intransigence immediately provoked a split in the Opposition. On 10 December the Trotskyist and Zinovievist groupings issued separate statements – the Zinovievist being the more conciliatory of the two. Again, the congress declared both to be inadequate. Subsequently, a special commission expelled 75 more Oppositionists from the party. Finally, on 19 December Kamenev offered the congress a statement of total capitulation in which the

---

228   Trotsky 1980b, p. 464.
229   Carr 1971–8, vol. 2, pp. 43–4.
230   Carr 1971–8, vol. 2, pp. 47–8.

Zinovievists renounced their 'anti-Leninist' views. The congress then subjected the Zinovievists to the final insult by rejecting their recantation and
granting the expelled Oppositionists only the option of applying individually
for readmission after six months. Immediately after the congress, 1,500 more
Oppositionists were expelled and 2,500 signed capitulatory statements.[231]

4.5   Conclusion

During the years 1926–7 Trotsky's scattered insights from 1923 crystallised into
a coherent theory of the problem of Soviet bureaucracy. The new understanding that emerged was remarkably simple and elegant, yet able to account for
a wide range of political and social phenomena. In line with the traditional
Marxist critique of bureaucracy, Trotsky insisted that there was a direct relationship between the deepening political alienation within the USSR and the
growing power of exploitative classes. For Trotsky, this relationship was most
evident in the policies of the Soviet leadership related to world revolution, the
economy, and the regime.

   In fact, much of Trotsky's critique of Soviet policy – especially policy related
to international affairs – was persuasive. In particular, his analyses of the leadership's policies in both Britain and China were compelling, and in both cases
his predictions were remarkably prescient. Of course, there is no way to know
whether Trotsky's approach would have fared better than Stalin's, but it is hard
to imagine how it could have fared worse – especially in China.[232] Also, there is

---

231   Carr 1971–8, vol. 2, pp. 48–50.
232   For generally positive assessments of Trotsky's position on the ARC see Calhoun 1976,
         pp. 263–5, 270–1, 298, 299, 321, 415–16 (however, see also Calhoun 1976, pp. 409–10);
         Claudin 1975a, pp. 153–4, 37–9n57; For a brief statement supporting Stalin's approach, see
         Ulam 1973, p. 267. For positive evaluations of Trotsky's views on China, see Claudin 1975a,
         pp. 282, 286; Isaacs 1961, pp. 160–1, 185, 189, 315; Löwy 1981, pp. 75–82. For more critical
         evaluations, see Bettelheim 1978, p. 379; Brandt 1958, pp. ix, 98–9, 155–62; Mavrakis 1976,
         pp. 132–40. For more ambivalent evaluations, see Ulam 1974, p. 170; Daniels 1960, p. 215;
         Knei-Paz 1978, pp. 359–66; Pantsov 2000; Thatcher 2003, pp. 155–6. It may be, as Pantsov
         and Thatcher have argued, that before the spring of 1927 Trotsky and the Opposition
         underestimated Stalin's subjective 'leftist intentions' within the GMD. See Pantsov 2000,
         p. 129; Thatcher 2003, p. 155. However, Stalin's 5 April 1927 promise to discard the Chinese
         bourgeoisie like a 'squeezed lemon' did not alter the Opposition's conclusion that his
         policy represented a 'centrist deviation' under bourgeois pressure. See Trotsky 1976a,
         pp. 225–6; Trotsky 1980b, p. 389.

little doubt that Trotsky and the Opposition were on firmer ideological ground than Stalin in the doctrinal dispute over socialism in one country. It has been argued that Trotsky was greatly mistaken in suggesting during these years that Stalin 'willfully wasted revolutionary opportunities'.[233] However, there is no indication that Trotsky perceived Stalin at this point as *subjectively* hostile to the world revolution.[234] In fact, in these years Trotsky did not even perceive the Thermidorians within the party as consciously counterrevolutionary. Rather, he believed that, regardless of subjective intent, the party leadership was being pressured by larger forces into adopting policies and doctrines that were *objectively* disastrous for the revolution.

Somewhat more problematic were Trotsky's and the Opposition's economic views. The Opposition convincingly insisted upon the necessity of a more vigorous industrialisation policy to combat a broad range of economic problems, including the growing social differentiation in the countryside, difficulties in grain collection, the inability of state industry to satisfy consumer demand, the expansion of urban unemployment, and shortages in workers' housing. By 1926–7 even Bukharin had come to recognise the validity of the Opposition's views in this respect.[235] Furthermore, in the light of the later economic successes of the First Five-Year Plan, it is evident that a more rapid tempo of industrialisation was possible. Nevertheless, it is unclear whether the Opposition's program of industrialisation could have been realised as painlessly as the Trotsky and the Opposition suggested. The Opposition proposed that the resources for industrialisation could be obtained by imposing a forced grain loan and a steeply progressive tax on the top 10 percent of the peasantry, insisting that this could be done without discouraging production by the most productive peasants.[236] We cannot know if the peasant would have agreed.[237]

---

233   Thatcher 2003, pp. 153–5. See also Lih et al. 1995b, pp. 27–8. Lih correctly notes that Stalin was concerned with 'unmasking the British labour leaders as cowards' (Lih 1995b, pp. 29, 109, 119). However, Stalin seems to have been considerably more concerned with unmasking Zinoviev and Trotsky as 'liquidators' (Lih 1995b, pp. 106, 107, 110, 111).

234   Even years later, after Trotsky had concluded Stalinism was hostile to world revolution, he argued that the Stalinists had been anxious for the success of the Chinese revolution in 1927 (Trotsky 1974, p. 262).

235   On the merits of the Opposition's analysis and Bukharin's belated recognition of these, see Cohen 1980, pp. 209–11, 244–5; Lewin 1968, pp. 141–2, 151.

236   Trotsky 1980b, p. 305.

237   For criticisms of the Opposition's economic program along these lines, see Thatcher 2003, pp. 151–3.

Related to this is the question of whether the Opposition could have carried out its economic programme while implementing its democratic and anti-bureaucratic reforms. It has been suggested that, in advocating rapid industrialisation, increased pressure on the kulaks, and collectivisation, the Opposition anticipated all of the brutality and repression of Stalin's later 'revolution from above'.[238] As far as the Opposition's explicit program was concerned, this is simply false. A number of contemporary scholars have demonstrated that the economic policies promoted by the Opposition lay solidly within the gradualist framework of NEP. The tempo of industrialisation advocated by the Opposition never approached the rate later ordered by Stalin. The Opposition's call for a forced loan and increased taxation of the kulak was far different from Stalin's later de-kulakisation campaign. Furthermore, the collectivisation advocated by the Opposition was intended to be fully voluntary.[239] Nevertheless, it is conceivable that, despite the intentions of the Opposition, the extraction of surplus from the kulaks would have necessitated the use of coercion, contributing substantially to the growth of bureaucratism.[240]

In the political sphere, Trotsky and the United Opposition provided what appears to be a fully accurate critique of the continuing deterioration of the norms and traditions of the Bolshevik Party and of the Soviet state. Furthermore, they offered a real alternative to these developments in their demands for the enforcement of the electoral principle for all offices, for the right of all party members to present their views to the party, and for an end to the persecution of party dissidents. Nevertheless, there continued to be serious weaknesses in the Opposition's programme for political reform. Most importantly, there was still no admission that one-party rule and the ban on party factions could have a corrosive effect on the political activity of the working class. In fact, in June 1926 Trotsky went so far as to assert in a statement to the Politburo that it was 'absolutely unquestionable' that the ruling party of a revolutionary dictatorship could not tolerate a regime of contending factions.[241] And in 1927

---

238   See, for example, Dmytryshyn 1978, pp. 142–3; Meyer 1967, pp. 31–2, 37; Ulam 1973, p. 292n3.

239   See Carr and Davies 1969, part 1, p. 265; Cohen 1977, pp. 21–3; Knei-Paz 1978, p. 278; Lewin 1968, pp. 142, 147–8, 154–6; Mandel 1995, pp. 59–66; Molyneux 1981, p. 100; Nove 1981, pp. 88, 92; Service 2009, pp. 349–51; Tucker 1987, pp. 64, 68, 79.

240   On this point, see, for example, Molyneux 1981, p. 101. For another argument regarding contradictions between the Opposition's proposals for industrialisation and its democratic programme, see R. Davies 1957, pp. 111–15.

241   Trotsky 1980b, p. 69. See also Trotsky 1980b, pp. 75, 102.

the Opposition's *Platform* declared, 'The dictatorship of the proletariat imperi-
ously demands a single and united proletarian party as the leader of the working masses and the poor peasantry. Such unity, unweakened by factional strife,
is unconditionally necessary to the proletariat in the fulfillment of its historic
mission'.[242] Of course, it still would have been politically suicidal for Trotsky
to have advocated freedom for competing parties or factions. Also, it is quite
possible that Trotsky and the Opposition honestly continued to support these
restrictions in order to limit the activity of Thermidorians. However, acceptance of these restrictions carried a price. To maintain the fiction that they
were simply a loose grouping of like-minded party members, the Opposition
leaders repeatedly found themselves forced to retreat and abandon political
activity, creating confusion and disorientation among their supporters and
potential supporters.[243]

Beyond these programmatic points, there is the question of the validity
of Trotsky's and the Opposition's perception of the fundamental dynamics
involved in Soviet politics in the late 1920s. Was it true that the basic conflict
in the Soviet Union was between the proletariat and the exploitative layers
of Soviet society? Did the policies of the party leadership largely reflect the
prevailing balance of class forces in the Soviet Union? Was the fundamental cleavage within the party really between the party's right and left wings?
Was the Soviet Union sliding dangerously close to a Thermidorian restoration
of capitalism? All of these views were part of what has been called Trotsky's
'somewhat fantastic perception of the USSR in the late twenties and early
thirties'.[244] Yet, at the time, the analysis of the United Opposition did not
appear so fantastic. It is probably true that the Opposition exaggerated the
size of the kulak stratum.[245] However, it is clear that during the late 1920s the
economic power and influence of the kulaks and the NEPmen were on the
rise, and that this was perceived as a threat by a large part of the party leadership.[246] At the same time, intelligent conservative observers such as Ustrialov,
believing that the party majority's economic policies could facilitate capitalist
restoration, supported the majority against the Opposition. In fact, if one does

---

242   Trotsky 1980b, p. 392.
243   This point is emphasised in Cliff 1991, pp. 17, 19, 152–6, 269. See also Marot 2006, p. 181.
244   McNeal 1977, p. 32.
245   The *Platform* stated that the kulak stratum include approximately 10 percent of peasant
       households (Trotsky 1980b, p. 337). Contemporary authors place the figure at 3–5 percent
       in 1928 (Lewin 1968, pp. 72, 131, 176; Bettelheim 1978, pp. 87–8).
246   See, for example, Lewin 1968, pp. 186–8, 191–2, 198–210.

not look beyond 1927, the analysis of Trotsky examined in this chapter offered a persuasive account of the dynamics of Soviet politics in the late 1920s.

Nevertheless, later developments demonstrated that this analysis was deeply flawed. During the following six years reality seemed to run directly counter to the path mapped by Trotsky's theory. Throughout that period, Trotsky was compelled to grapple continuously with those contradictions.

CHAPTER 5

Left Turn and Theoretical Crisis

During the years 1928–9 Trotsky's theory of bureaucracy entered a period of crisis.[1] Repeatedly, unfolding events contradicted the expectations and predictions Trotsky derived from the theory he had developed in the party struggle of 1926–7. In the course of that struggle he had come to view the Opposition as the only force within the party capable of implementing a leftist course. Furthermore, he had predicted that if the Opposition was crushed and no major proletarian upsurge occurred, the centrist current would disintegrate, the party right would assume power, the party's economic and international policies would shift sharply to the right, and the capitalism would be restored.[2] In late 1927 and early 1928 the Opposition was decisively defeated and thousands of Oppositionists, including Trotsky, were exiled to remote regions of the Soviet Union. However, instead of moving to the right, the party leadership initiated a dramatic policy change – perceived by Trotsky and most of the Opposition as a shift to the left – which would continue to deepen in the following years. And instead of dissolving, the Stalinist current ultimately emerged triumphant in a power struggle with its moderate opponents.

In the face of the widening gulf between theory and reality, a growing number of Oppositionists began to reject the theory. Trotsky responded as scientists and politicians commonly do: he continued to insist upon the validity of his theory.[3] To maintain this position he repeatedly found it necessary to resort to highly strained interpretations of events, trimming and stretching reality to fit a Procrustean theoretical bed. On other occasions he attempted to explain developments by introducing ad hoc adjustments into his theory, implicitly modifying it to accommodate troublesome facts that could not be explained away.[4] Meanwhile, throughout this period Trotsky's continuing adherence to his theory led him to make additional erroneous predictions.

---

1 Tony Cliff also has written about the 'ideological crisis' of the Left Opposition during this period. See Cliff 1993, pp. 73–4.

2 For these predictions, see Trotsky 1980b, pp. 488–509.

3 For a discussion of this phenomenon among natural scientists, see Kuhn 1970, pp. 77–91. For a discussion of the 'theoretical crisis' in the world Trotskyist movement after World War II, see Callinicos 1990, pp. 23–38.

4 Callinicos notes a similar reaction within the Trotskyist movement to theoretical crisis after World War II. Following Karl Popper, he describes such reactions as ' "conventionalist stratagems", designed to protect the hard core [of a theory] from the persistent refutation of its

5.1   The Beginning of the Turn

During the weeks following the Fifteenth Party Congress, thousands of supporters of the 'Trotskyist' wing of the Opposition were arrested and exiled to
remote regions of the Soviet Union.[5] On 17 January 1928 Trotsky was apprehended and, with his wife Natalia Sedova and son Lev Sedov, deported to Alma
Ata in Kazakhstan.[6] While reestablishing contact with the scattered colonies
of exiles, Trotsky began preparing a series of documents for submission to the
Sixth Congress of the Communist International in July.[7] In the same period he
also devoted much of his attention to analysing the shifts taking place in both
Comintern and domestic policy.

The first indications of a change in Comintern policy were evident in China
as early as the summer of 1927. Following the expulsion of the Chinese
Communist Party from the Guomindang in July 1927, an Emergency Conference
of the CCP convened in Hankou on 7 August. Acting on instructions from
the Comintern, the conference blamed the recent failures of the party on the
'opportunist policy of capitulation' allegedly advocated by Chen Duxiu. Also,
it endorsed a new strategy of armed insurrection already being implemented
at Nanchang. The result of this strategic shift was a series of failed uprisings

---

auxiliary hypotheses' (Callinicos 1990, p. 29). For Popper's discussion of 'conventionalist
stratagems', see Popper 1968, pp. 78–84. On the proliferation of articulations and ad hoc modifications to a theory in periods of crisis, see Kuhn 1970, p. 78.

5   According to Victor Serge's later account, during 1928–29 there were approximately 5,000
Oppositionists under arrest (Serge 1980, p. 253). Natalia Sedova reported that in 1928 she and
Trotsky calculated that a minimum of 8,000 Oppositionists had been arrested, imprisoned, or
deported (Serge and Sedova 1975, p. 158). In 1937 Trotsky estimated that approximately 11,000
Oppositionists were imprisoned or deported in 1928 (Preliminary Commission of Inquiry
1968, 331–2).

6   Carr 1971–8, vol. 2, p. 53; Deutscher 1959, pp. 390–6, 401–2; Serge 1980, pp. 235–6. Trotsky's
other son, Sergei, accompanied his family part of the way to Alma Ata, then returned to
Moscow to continue his studies (Deutscher 1959, p. 395).

7   Two of these documents later appeared in English under the title *The Third International
after Lenin* – a work described by Perry Anderson as 'probably the most important text'
between 1923 and 1933 for Trotsky's views on the problem of Stalinism (P. Anderson 1984,
p. 119). In fact, these documents contain a clear restatement of the theory Trotsky developed
in 1926 and 1927. See especially Trotsky 1970b, pp. 243–4, 256–7, 294–6. However, aside from
their special emphasis on the problem of bureaucratism in the Comintern, these documents
contained nothing new on the general question of bureaucracy.

that culminated in the Canton Commune of 11–13 December, an abortive insurrection in which approximately 5,700 revolutionaries were killed.[8]

In the following months the turn was tentatively extended to other sections
of the Comintern. At the Fifteenth Party Congress Stalin announced that
'*Europe is now plainly entering the phase of a new revolutionary upsurge*', and
Bukharin declared that the immediate task of Communists was 'to sharpen the
struggle against social-democracy and, in particular, against the so-called
"Left" social democratic leaders'.[9] Further indications of a policy change were
evident at the ninth plenum of the ECCI in February 1928. Although Bukharin
devoted the bulk of his report to the struggle against 'the so-called Trotskyite
opposition', he introduced a new note by stressing the need for 'a struggle
against Right deviations within the communist parties'. Similarly, the resolutions on the British and French parties emphasised the themes of mass radicalisation and the importance of intensifying the struggle against social
democracy.[10]

Meanwhile, a parallel shift was occurring in Soviet economic policy. As we
have seen, in October 1927 Bukharin called for a '*reinforced offensive against
capitalist elements, and, first of all, against the kulak*'.[11] In December the
Fifteenth Party Congress endorsed proposals for a 'more decisive offensive
against the *kulak*,' and for the 'gradual transformation of individual peasant
holdings' into large-scale collective farms. However, at this point there was no
suggestion of a radical change in policy. At the party congress the leadership
continued to stress the moderate nature of the anti-kulak measures advocated,
and the necessarily gradual character of collectivisation.[12]

The issue that finally precipitated an abrupt change was a crisis in grain collection. The collections had proceeded well through the spring and summer of
1927, even running somewhat ahead of schedule. However, by the end of the
year they began to fall off so sharply that in November and December they
totaled less than half the collections of the last two months of 1926. Increasingly,
the party leadership grew alarmed over the prospect of food shortages and a
general disruption of economic plans. In December 1927 the CC issued two
directives to local party organisations urging the intensification of efforts to

---

8   Carr 1971–8, vol. 3: 3, pp. 819–45; Harrison 1972, pp. 123–39; Houn 1967, pp. 32–7; Isaacs 1961,
     pp. 278–92; Peng 1976, pp. 74–8.

9   Stalin and Bukharin quoted in Carr 1971–8, vol. 3: 1, p. 153.

10   Carr 1971–8, vol. 3: 1, pp. 163–4; Carr 1971–8, vol. 3: 2, pp. 363–6, 505–6; Daniels 1960,
     pp. 334–5.

11   Quoted in Carr and Davies 1969, part 1, p. 33.

12   Carr and Davies 1969, part 1, pp. 38–44; Lewin 1985, pp. 95–6; Lewin 1968, pp. 198–210;
     Reiman 1987, p. 40.

bring in the grain. Simultaneously, the leadership ordered an increase in the supply of industrial goods to key regions in order to stimulate grain sales. When these measures failed to produce results, on 6 January the Politburo issued another directive threatening leaders of local party organisations with severe penalties if they failed 'to secure a decisive improvement in grain procurements within a very short time'. Additionally, 30,000 party workers were dispatched throughout the country to assist in the collection.[13]

Contemporary scholars have suggested that the causes of the procurement crisis were many and complex. Contributing factors included a poor harvest in the main regions of market production, weaknesses in transport, deficiencies in the state collections apparatus, and passivity on the part of state grain collections agencies. However, much of the crisis was also due to conscious withholding by the peasants. To a large degree this had been made possible by the growing prosperity of many better-off peasants who found themselves in a position to pay their taxes and make necessary purchases out of their savings, while holding onto their grain in anticipation of higher prices in the spring. In 1927 these peasants withheld grain partially in reaction to agricultural prices. Late that year official prices of grain were lowered, while prices of livestock products and industrial crops were kept relatively high. Peasants who were in a position to do so sold livestock products, but held onto their grain as a reserve. At the same time, peasants were discouraged from selling grain by the general shortage of industrially produced goods that could be purchased with the proceeds. The war threat of 1927 compounded the problem, aggravating the chronic 'goods famine' by promoting panic buying and leading peasants to hoard grain for their own use. Finally, some peasants withheld grain simply because they anticipated that the series of good harvests since 1925 could not last another year.[14]

Despite the complexity of the situation, party leaders – and especially Stalin – placed the blame for the crisis squarely upon the kulak. As Stalin argued to party officials in western Siberia, the problem was that the kulak was engaging in 'unbridled speculation'.[15] Similarly, a *Pravda* editorial of 15 February, believed by some to have been written by Stalin, explained,

---

13   Carr and Davies 1969, part 1, pp. 30–1, 44–5, 49, 50; Lewin 1968, pp. 214, 216, 217; Stalin 1952–5, vol. 11, p. 13.

14   Carr and Davies 1969, part 1, pp. 44–8; Deutscher 1959, p. 403; Lewin 1985, pp. 91–7; Lewin 1968, pp. 236–7; Reiman 1987, pp. 41–3; Siegelbaum 1992, p. 191; Viola 1996, p. 21; Viola et al. 2005, pp. 17–18, 28, 52; Ward 1999, pp. 73–4.

15   Stalin 1952–5, vol. 11, pp. 4–5. See also Stalin 1952–5, vol. 11, p. 14; Carr and Davies 1969, part 1, pp. 51–2.

> Three good harvests have not gone for nothing. An increase in the reve-
> nues of the peasants from crops other than grain, from animal husbandry
> and from industrial earnings, together with the relative backwardness in
> general in the supply of industrial goods, have given the peasant in gen-
> eral, and the *kulak* in particular, the opportunity to hold back grain prod-
> ucts in order to force prices up.[16]

As a secondary cause Stalin asserted that the speculation had been facilitated
by local party and state officials who had been negligent in their struggle
against the kulak. He taunted the Siberian officials, 'Can it be that you are
afraid to disturb the tranquility of the kulak gentry?!'[17]

To deal with the crisis the leadership resorted to a series of 'exceptional' or
'extraordinary' measures. First, it instructed local officials to order the kulaks
to deliver all their grain surpluses immediately at government prices. If they
refused they were to be prosecuted for speculation under Article 107 of the
Criminal Code of the RSFSR, and their surpluses were to be confiscated.
Officials who resisted the application of Article 107 were to be dismissed. To
ensure the allegiance of the peasant majority, the leadership also attempted to
foster class struggle by announcing that 25 percent of the surpluses collected
would be resold to poor and middle peasants at low government prices or distributed in the form of long-term loans. None of these measures addressed the
alleged source of the crisis – the existence of a powerful kulak stratum.
However, in a portent of things to come, Stalin asserted that the final solution
to the kulak problem required the collectivisation of agriculture.[18]

In practice, the coercive measures applied in the countryside were more
severe than those officially endorsed. Local party officials quickly discovered
that the bulk of the grain surpluses were not held by the kulak, but by the
middle peasant. Faced with demands from the centre to collect large quantities of grain on penalty of expulsion from the party, they extended the extraordinary measures to middle and even poor peasants. Markets were forcibly
closed to compel peasants to sell grain to the state procurement organisations.
As in the civil war, grain quotas were assigned to individual households. Peasant hoarders were publicly ostracised, barred from purchasing goods at village
cooperative stores, and expelled from the cooperatives. Militia units set up
road blocks and conducted house-to-house searches to confiscate grain.

---

16   Quoted in Carr and Davies 1969, part 1, p. 52. For the allegation that Stalin was the author,
      see Ciliga 1979, p. 28. However, at this time Bukharin was the editor of *Pravda*.
17   Stalin 1952–5, vol. 11, pp. 15–16, 18, 5.
18   Carr and Davies 1969, part 1, pp. 50–1; Lewin, 1968, pp. 218–19; Stalin 1952–5, vol. 11,
      pp. 4–11.

Finally, in some areas peasants were forcibly collectivised. Ultimately, the harshness of the procurement campaign revived memories of War Communism to the extent that peasants were heard to observe, 'The year '19 is back'.[19]

Although the Politburo had approved the extraordinary measures unanimously, the implementation of the new policies soon generated conflict. The first sign of disagreement appears to have surfaced at the 6 February session of the Politburo, where Aleksei Rykov, president of the Sovnarkom, reportedly exchanged angry words with Stalin over his proposal to purge party organisations in Siberia. Subsequently, Rykov, together with Mikhail Tomskii, chairman of the Central Trade Union Council, and Mikhail Kalinin, president of the Central Executive Committee, were able to restrain Stalin's plans.[20] It is also likely that the moderates were responsible for pressuring the Stalinists into disavowing the more extreme measures employed in the collection. In a *Pravda* article of 12 February Stalin's supporter Anastas Mikoian denounced some of the administrative measures utilised in the campaign as *'harmful, unlawful, and inadmissible'*. The following day, while defending the emergency measures in a letter to local party officials, Stalin denied that these implied an abandonment of NEP, rejected the use of emergency measures against the middle peasants, and condemned the 'distortions and excesses' that had occurred.[21]

By April the crisis seemed to be over. Grain collections for January–March 1928 were far higher than those of the corresponding months of 1927, and the collection for 1927–8 exceeded that of 1926–7.[22] The resolution adopted by the April plenum of the CC represented a compromise between the Stalinists and the moderates. Although it continued to blame the kulak for the crisis and approved the recent use of extraordinary measures, it also criticised the 'excesses' that had occurred and pledged that the future offensive against the kulaks would be conducted in accordance with the methods of NEP.[23] However, by the end of April collections again began to fall off sharply.[24] Once more the leadership imposed the exceptional measures that had proven so successful in the winter. This time the widespread 'excesses' provoked a wave of discontent

19   Carr and Davies 1969, part 1, pp. 53–8; Carr 1971–8, vol. 2, p. 135; Lewin 1968, pp. 219–30.
20   Daniels 1960, p. 325. See also Cohen 1980, pp. 278–9; and Lewin 1968, p. 295.
21   Cohen 1980, p. 279; Lewin 1968, p. 231; Stalin 1952–5, vol. 11, pp. 12–22.
22   Carr and Davies 1969, part 1, pp. 58–9.
23   Carr and Davies 1969, part 1, pp. 58–9, 62–3; Cohen 1980, pp. 282–3; Lewin 1968, pp. 234–8, 296–7.
24   Partly, this seems to have been due to a poor harvest of winter wheat in the Ukraine and the northern Caucasus. Partly, it was because most of the peasant's grain reserves had been confiscated during the preceding three months (Carr and Davies 1969, part 1, pp. 63–4; Lewin 1968, pp. 238–9).

among the peasants, who rioted and demonstrated in villages throughout the country.[25]

The renewal of the crisis and the growth in peasant discontent fueled the differences within the leadership. Increasingly, Stalin and his supporters insisted that the ultimate source of the crisis was the private, individual character of Soviet agriculture. The only way out, Stalin argued, was through 'the transition from individual peasant farming to collective, socially-conducted economy in agriculture'.[26] At this point the moderates recoiled from both the extraordinary measures and from Stalin's proposals for collectivisation. Bukharin, who was emerging as the principal spokesman for the moderates, publicly attacked the idea of a 'class war' and 'some kind of sudden leap' in agriculture. Privately, he warned in letters to the Politburo that the emergency measures were alienating the whole peasantry, and he dismissed Stalin's proposal for large-scale collectivisation as sheer nonsense. Lesser moderates denounced Stalin's policies in even sharper terms.[27]

Meanwhile, another domestic issue that contributed to the mounting tensions within the Politburo was the 'Shakhty affair'. In March it was announced that the OGPU had uncovered a conspiracy of technical specialists to sabotage production in the Shakhty mines of the Donetsk Basin. Many of the 55 accused confessed to charges, today recognised as fabricated, of plotting with foreign powers to wreck Soviet industry. Throughout the show trial in May and June, the Soviet press, echoing Stalin's pronouncements, utilised the Shakhty affair to demonstrate the need for greater vigilance against class enemies, and especially for closer supervision of the bourgeois specialists. For the moderates, this response represented a serious challenge. Most generally, it called into question the view that socialism could be constructed through the peaceful collaboration of all sectors of Soviet society. More specifically, it tended to discredit Rykov, who headed the state apparatus that employed the specialists, and Tomskii, who led the trade unions responsible for overseeing them. In response, Rykov, Tomskii, and Bukharin publicly insisted that the Shakhty affair was an isolated incident, and warned against indulging in 'specialist baiting'.[28]

---

25   Carr and Davies 1969, part 1, pp. 64–5; Daniels 1960, pp. 327–8; Lewin 1968, pp. 239–41.

26   Stalin 1952–5, vol. 11, pp. 91–2.

27   Cohen 1980, pp. 284–6. See also Carr and Davies 1969, part 1, pp. 74–5; Daniels 1960, p. 328; Lewin 1968, pp. 298–9.

28   Bailes 1978, pp. 69–94; Carr and Davies 1969, part 2, pp. 584–7; Cohen 1980, p. 281; Conquest 1973, pp. 730–3; Daniels 1960, p. 326; Reiman 1987, pp. 58–66; Tucker 1990, pp. 76–9.

At the same time a number of scandals were exposed in the party organisations of Smolensk and Artemovsk.[29] Citing these and the Shakhty affair, on
3 June the Central Committee appealed to party members and workers to participate in the campaign of 'self-criticism' against 'bureaucratism' initiated at
the April plenum. Stalin clearly viewed this as an invitation to the masses
to criticise rightist officials. He denounced 'the bureaucratic elements...
in our Party, government, trade-union, co-operative and all other organisations'. Echoing Trotsky, he explained that 'bureaucracy is a manifestation
of bourgeois influence on our organizations'. Unable to openly oppose the
campaign, the moderates within the leadership could only warn of its potential 'abuses'.[30]

5.2   Explaining the Turn

Despite previous signs that the leadership was contemplating a turn in both
international and economic policy, Trotsky was unprepared for the events of
early 1928. His first response to the extraordinary measures was to express satisfaction over this vindication of the Opposition's programme. However, reacting to the turn in early 1928, some Oppositionists began to question Trotsky's
and the Opposition's traditional analysis and to urge reconciliation with the
leadership. In contrast, Trotsky continued to insist on the validity of his theory,
which ultimately shaped every aspect of his perception of the new situation.

Trotsky had not been at all impressed by the leadership's 'leftist' initiatives
in either economic or Comintern affairs in late 1927. In both cases he viewed
the new policies as temporary manoeuvres that soon would be followed by
deeper shifts to the right. As noted in the previous chapter, Trotsky dismissed
Bukharin's October call for an offensive against the kulaks and the anniversary
declaration of the seven-hour workday as 'individual adventuristic gestures',
and 'only a zigzag' that would not change the general line.[31] Similarly, his first
reaction to the news of the abortive Canton insurrection was to characterise it
as nothing but an *adventurist* zigzag by the Comintern to the left', in reaction
to the debacle produced by the previous 'Menshevik policy' in China.
Furthermore, he predicted that the Canton disaster would be followed quickly

---

29   See Carr 1971–8, vol. 2, pp. 136–42. On the Smolensk scandal, see also Fainsod 1958,
       pp. 48–52.
30   Carr 1971–8, vol. 2, pp. 298–9; Cohen 1980, pp. 281–2; Daniels 1960, pp. 326–7; Stalin
       1952–5, vol. 11, p. 137.
31   Trotsky 1980b, p. 443.

by 'a new and longer zigzag to the right' in Comintern, and especially Chinese, policy.[32]

Consequently, the economic turn of early 1928 took Trotsky by surprise. His first reaction to the extraordinary measures was to gloat over this tacit admission by the leadership that the Opposition had been correct in its economic analysis. Noting that *Pravda* had attributed the grain collection problems to the kulaks and officials conciliatory to the kulaks, in a 5 March letter to Lev Sosnovskii he quipped, 'Why, you know, this is an antiparty document, not an editorial'. He recalled that when the Opposition had sounded the alarm about the kulak danger in the past, the leadership had accused it of advocating war communism. But now, when the kulak was squeezing the leadership's tail, it even began to remember something from Marxism. From this, he concluded that the 'advantage' of the Opposition was that it had 'correctly foreseen'.[33] However, the reality was that neither Trotsky nor anyone else in the Opposition *had* foreseen the developments of early 1928. In fact, the new policies contradicted Trotsky's belief that only the Opposition could lead a struggle against the growing influence of the kulaks and NEPmen, as well as his expectation that the crushing of the Opposition would shift both policy and power in the Soviet Union to the right and raise the immediate prospect of Thermidor.

In the early months of 1928 a small but growing number of Oppositionists began to advocate accommodation with the party leadership. As Isaac Deutscher has suggested, these 'conciliators' were partially responding to the pressures that now confronted Oppositionists. Many had held high political office; most had sacrificed greatly for the revolution; now all found themselves expelled from the party and subjected to the humiliation and hardship of exile.[34] More importantly, as Deutscher and others have noted, the shift in policy inspired many to question their traditional analysis and political perspective.[35] Within the Opposition the turn had provoked a theoretical crisis that was soon to become a political one.

The most prominent conciliators included E.A. Preobrazhenskii, A.G. Ishchenko, and – by the summer of 1928 – Karl Radek. Early in 1928

---

32   Trotsky 1976a, p. 274. See also Trotsky 1976a, p. 275; Trotsky 1980b, p. 490. By March–April 1928 Trotsky arrived at the relatively more sympathetic conclusion that the Canton commune had contained only 'elements of adventurism' (Trotsky 1976a, p. 282).

33   Trotsky 1981, pp. 56–8.

34   Deutscher 1959, pp. 406, 413.

35   Deutscher 1959, pp. 406–7; Broué 1988, pp. 569, 571; Cliff 1993, pp. 74–85; Longuet 1994, pp. 39–41, 51–3. Already in early 1928 two prominent Trotskyists, Iu. Piatakov and V.A. Antonov-Ovseenko, had capitulated, justifying their recantation on the grounds that Stalin was carrying out the Opposition's programme (Deutscher 1959, p. 406).

Preobrazhenskii argued that the party leaders had implemented the extraordinary measures in reaction to the kulak offensive and under the pressure of the mounting class struggle in Europe. In doing so, they had acted as the unconscious agents of historic necessity. Soon, Preobrazhenskii predicted, the leadership would be forced even deeper to the left as the class struggle in the countryside escalated. He concluded that the Opposition had seriously misread the situation, misjudging the role played by the Stalinists and exaggerating the danger from the right. In line with this analysis he proposed that the Opposition request permission to convene a conference that would establish an alliance with the party centre.[36] Some months later Radek arrived at a similar view. Early in the summer he appealed to the Comintern Congress for the readmission of the expelled members of the Opposition. In his theses to the Comintern he admitted that perhaps 'a number of party leaders with whom we crossed swords yesterday are better than the theories which they defended'. Furthermore, he defined the task of the Opposition as one of 'fighting ruthlessly ... against all the evils against which the party is now mobilized'.[37]

Largely in reaction to the conciliators, by the summer another political grouping began to crystallise at the other extreme of the Oppositional spectrum. This current, which became known as the 'intransigents' or 'irreconcilables', tended to be younger, less concerned about economic questions, and more preoccupied with the issue of party democracy than the conciliators. Its leaders included Lev Sosnovskii, Boris Eltsin, and F.N. Dingel'shtedt. In contrast to the conciliators, the intransigents were inclined to deny the significance of the extraordinary measures. As Dingel'shtedt wrote to Trotsky in July, 'The measures have been provoked by the threat of famine and economic crisis ... Rising unemployment, the slowing of industrialization continue: where is it, this new course'?[38] Consequently, the intransigents angrily rejected proposals for reconciliation with the Stalinists.[39] However, they did not necessarily do so out of loyalty to Trotsky's theory. During this period some of the more extreme intransigents were drawn toward the Democratic Centralist

---

36   Broué 1988, pp. 569, 571; Carr 1971–8, vol. 2, p. 59; Cliff 1993, pp. 75–6, 77; Deutscher 1959, pp. 417–18.

37   Quoted in Trotsky 1981, p. 163; Broué 1988, p. 574. See also Deutscher 1959, pp. 421–2; Longuet 1994, p. 40.

38   Quoted in Broué 1988, p. 569.

39   Eltsin insisted in a letter to Trotsky in May, 'Centrism is twice as dangerous when it plays at a left policy' (quoted in Broué 1988, p. 571).

grouping, which had concluded that a Thermidor had already occurred and that it was time to form a new revolutionary party.[40]

Trotsky occupied a position roughly mid-way between these extremes. He was too concerned about policy issues and too much of a realist to dismiss the changes in policy as meaningless. Nevertheless, he was also unwilling to abandon his theory or to give up the struggle against the leadership because of the turn. Against the intransigents he insisted that the shifts were real and important. But against the conciliators he emphasised the limits of the turn, which he analysed from the standpoint of his theory.

Trotsky agreed with the conciliators that real and important shifts to the left had occurred in both economic and international policy. Consistent with popular usage and his own previous analysis, he characterised the leadership's offensive against the kulaks and the market and its new restrictions on alliances with Social Democratic parties abroad, as leftist initiatives. On 9 May in a circular letter to exiled Oppositionists he argued, 'The decisions on domestic matters (in regard to the kulak, etc.) and the decisions of the recent ECCI ... are unquestionably a step in our direction, that is, toward the correct path', and he further described these policy changes as 'a serious step to the left'.[41] Similarly, in a circular letter of 17 July he lectured the irreconcilables that 'it is impermissible to have a formally negative approach to the left shift, to say: nothing has happened, only machinations; everything remains as before. No. The greatest events have happened and are happening'.[42]

However, while insisting that the new policies represented an important shift to the left, throughout most of 1928–9 Trotsky was more concerned with combating the tendency he perceived among the conciliators to exaggerate their significance. His scepticism was understandable in light of the leadership's previous record. As he observed in early May, 'After the experiences we have gone through, we must be more cautious than ever when a turn comes, giving no unnecessary credit in advance'.[43] Besides that, Trotsky consistently measured the turn against the *entire* programme of the Opposition. When he did so, he noted that the changes fell far short of what the Opposition had demanded. Regarding economic matters, there had been no clear formulation of the tasks in agriculture or condemnation of the previous line. More importantly, there was still no recognition of the need for 'farsighted management of

40   Deutscher 1959, pp. 414, 431–2; Gusev 2008, pp. 166–8; Longuet 1994, p. 43; Marot 2006, pp. 196–7.

41   Trotsky 1981, pp. 77, 78. See also Trotsky 1981, p. 98; Trotsky 1970b, pp. 257, 258, 275; and Trotsky's 26 May letter to Mikhail Okudzhava, quoted in Trotsky 1970c, p. 552.

42   Trotsky 1981, p. 155.

43   Trotsky 1981, p. 78.

the state economy' and industrialisation.[44] Regarding international affairs, he complained that the draft Comintern programme continued to endorse the notion of socialism in one country, 'a program of social patriotism, not of Marxism', while sanctioning the policies of recent years.[45]

Beyond these considerations, much of Trotsky's scepticism regarding the turn was inspired directly by his theory of bureaucracy. As we have seen, his analysis posited a direct relationship between the conservatism of Soviet policy and the absence of proletarian democracy. From this, he now concluded that a serious course to the left would, of necessity, be accompanied by the profound reform of the party regime. Consequently, for Trotsky the character of the party regime – and especially the treatment of the Opposition – was a critical indicator of the seriousness of the turn. As he explained in a 23 May letter,

> For us the party regime has no independent significance – it only expresses everything else. That is why any experienced and serious politician must necessarily ask: 'If you think that a deep class shift in official policy has occurred, how do you explain the continuing 'export' of people who are guilty only of having understood earlier and demanded a class shift earlier? ... [The treatment of the Opposition] is a faultless gauge of how serious, well thought out, and deep is the shift that has occurred.[46]

Approaching the question from another angle, he endorsed Rakovskii's observation that, even if the leadership happened to 'stumble onto the tracks of a

---

44   Trotsky 1981, pp. 79–80. See also Trotsky 1981, p. 138. Perhaps an additional reason why Trotsky minimised the significance of the turn initially was that he did not have a clear picture of what was happening in the countryside. One Oppositional letter from April 1928 that appears to have been written by Trotsky characterised the left turn in the grain collections campaign as mostly a matter of 'general declarations', and asserted that the leadership actually had not gone any farther than 'violent denunciations' against the kulak. See N. 1928. This is an unpublished translation of N., 'Stalins Linderkurs und die Aufgaben der Opposition', *New Yorker Volkszeitung*, 19 August 1928. The translation was supplied to this author by Naomi Allen of Pathfinder Press.

45   Trotsky 1981, p. 130. See also Trotsky 1981, pp. 113, 161–2; and Trotsky 1970b, pp. 235, 257–8.

46   Trotsky 1981, pp. 91–2. Trotsky was quoting or paraphrasing his own earlier response to Oppositionist conciliators. See also Trotsky 1981, pp. 139, 149; N. 1928; Trotsky 1970b, pp. 299–301.

correct line', without a dramatic improvement in the party regime there was no guarantee it would be carried out.[47]

While downplaying the depth and significance of the turn, Trotsky insisted that in one respect it actually had confirmed his own predictions. In his circular letter of 9 May, Trotsky reminded the exiled Oppositionists, 'We predicted that *the tail would strike at the head* and cause a realignment of forces'.[48] Similarly, in his July 'Declaration' to the Sixth Comintern Congress he asserted that the Opposition had foretold that the right-wing 'tail' inside and outside the party 'would inevitably strike at the [centrist] head, and that such a blow could become the starting point for a profound regroupment within the party'. According to Trotsky, this was exactly what had happened: 'The bloodless kulak revolt of 1927–28, which occurred with the assistance of members of the party . . . is precisely a blow struck by the tail at the head'.[49] However, in letters written in May and September Trotsky conceded that he *had* made one error. In late 1927 he had anticipated a 'rather imminent economic shift to the right under the pressure of aggravated difficulties'. In fact, it turned out 'the next shift was to the left'.[50] But as Trotsky described it in September, this was only 'a partial mistake' and 'one of a completely secondary character, within a correct overall prediction'.[51] Furthermore, he believed that this 'partial' error hardly justified a major change in perspective.

In contrast to the conciliators, Trotsky was convinced that he could explain the turn without abandoning or significantly altering his theory. In a 10 March letter he endorsed I.N. Smirnov's view that the party leaders had instituted the domestic left turn as 'a drastic attempt to get out of the difficulties they blundered into with their eyes closed'.[52] Similarly, in a circular letter of 24 June he asserted that the turn had been 'crudely empirical and at the same time panic-stricken'.[53] But why had the party leadership turned left when confronted with

---

47   Trotsky 1981, p. 114. See also Trotsky 1981, pp. 128, 138, 153; Trotsky 1970b, pp. 299–301.
      Although some conciliators such as Radek saw Stalin's 'self criticism' campaign as a seri-
      ous attempt to reform the party regime, Trotsky did not. In his view, this campaign was
      'nothing but a way of venting rank-and-file discontent by denouncing the errors of sec-
      ondary importance and sacrificing one or two hundred bureaucrats as scapegoats'
      (Trotsky 1981, p. 145; see also Trotsky 1981, pp. 99–100, 102–3, 128, 159–60; N. 1928).
48   Trotsky 1981, p. 79. See also Trotsky 1981, p. 107.
49   Trotsky 1981, pp. 139–40.
50   Trotsky 1981, p. 98.
51   Trotsky 1981, p. 257.
52   Trotsky 1981, p. 60.
53   Trotsky 1981, p. 128.

difficulties, instead of to the right as expected? Previously, Trotsky had explained the fundamental dynamics of Soviet politics in terms of the shifting balance of class forces in the country. Now, he utilised the same approach to explain the turn.

Perhaps the clearest expression of this analysis appears in a letter by 'an outstanding member of the Russian Opposition' written in April 1928. Although it has never been verified, both the style and content suggest that the author was Trotsky.[54] According to this letter, a 'revival in the spirit of the Russian working class' had been evident since 1926. In fact, the entire struggle of the Opposition since 1926 had been 'just a reflection' of this revival.[55] Riding the crest of proletarian discontent, the Opposition had launched its offensive, 'expecting that the working class by simultaneous pressure would force the Central Committee to change its line'. Unfortunately, the working class did not come to the aid of the Opposition in time, and the apparatus was able to 'stifle the voice of the working class, postpone the effects of its pressure, and meanwhile crush the opposition'.[56]

Nevertheless, according to the letter, Stalin crushed the Opposition 'at the last possible moment'. In early 1928 the proletarian upsurge intensified in response to the difficulties in the grain collection, which 'revealed the power and influence of the kulaks', and the 'Donetsk-conspiracy', which demonstrated 'the inner rottenness of the bureaucratic regime and its counterrevolutionary character'.[57] (It should be noted that in other statements from this period, Trotsky also accepted the veracity of Stalinist accounts of both the 'kulak strike' and the Shakhty 'conspiracy').[58] The proletariat responded with the only form of protest at its disposal: strikes. The letter described how a 'mighty strike wave swept over the whole country', and how 'an even greater number of strikes were derailed at the last moment'. Confronted with this display of militancy, 'Stalin had no choice but to hastily proclaim a political turn

54   The letter discussed here is 'Stalin's Left Course and the Tasks of the Opposition'. (See note 44 above). The quotation is from an editorial note in the *New Yorker Volkszeitung*. Regarding the fact that the authorship of this letter has never been established, see Sinclair 1989, vol. 1, p. 439.

55   N. 1928. Later in the year, Trotsky argued that, to a large degree, this revival was based upon the reconstruction of Soviet industry (Trotsky 1981, p. 306).

56   N. 1928.

57   N. 1928.

58   On the 'kulak strike', see Trotsky 1981, pp. 55–8, 92, 96, 140; Trotsky 1970b, p. 293. On the 'Shakhty affair', see Trotsky 1981, pp. 96, 115, 141, 149, 218, 330; Trotsky 1970b, p. 293. Trotsky later revised his view of the Shakhty affair. See Trotsky 1977a, pp. 552–3n416.

to the left, and, in order to pacify the working class, raise the slogans of the opposition, which the day before were characterized as counterrevolutionary'.[59]

In fact, there really were widespread manifestations of labour discontent, including strikes, in a number of industries throughout the Soviet Union between late 1927 and the autumn of 1928. Some of this unrest was in response to the food shortages, while bad relations between workers and specialists may have contributed to the labour indiscipline in the coal mines and heavy industry. However, the main causes of worker unrest in early 1928 were the deep wage cuts and the sharp intensification of labour introduced at that time.[60] Also, strike figures from the period suggest that the characterisation of this as a 'mighty strike wave' may have been a bit of an exaggeration.[61]

Perhaps for these reasons in other accounts Trotsky put more emphasis on the role that the Opposition – the political current that most represented the interests of the proletariat – had played in forcing the turn in agriculture. For example, in a letter to Beloborodov in May Trotsky insisted that 'if all our previous work had not existed – our analyses, predictions, criticisms, exposés, and ever newer predictions – a sharp turn to the right would have occurred under the pressure of the grain collections crisis'. He asserted that the 'good, strong wedge' that the Opposition had driven in had made it impossible for the party leadership 'at this particular time, to seek a way out of the contradictions on the *right* path'.[62] Trotsky never explained precisely how the Opposition's criticism had blocked a right turn. Most likely, he meant to suggest that the leadership was unable to turn right following the 'grain strike' because it feared that the party ranks would perceive this as a confirmation of the Opposition's predictions and would rally to its support.

In the same period Trotsky also offered a variety of explanations of the leftward shift of the Comintern. One of these, contained in a document he

---

59   N. 1928. Similarly, in his 'Declaration' to the Sixth Congress of the Comintern, Trotsky asserted that the domestic left turn been 'carried out under pressure, as yet vague and unformed, from the proletarian core of the party' (Trotsky 1981, p. 147).

60   On labour unrest and labour indiscipline in this period and their causes, see Carr and Davies 1969, part 2, pp. 508–9; Chase 1990, p. 280; Gusev 2008, pp. 154–5; Longuet 1994, p. 36; Reiman 1987, pp. 54, 58; Rossman 2005, pp. 27–61; Murphy 2005, pp. 106–9; Murphy 2008, pp. 218–19.

61   OGPU summaries reported that the number of strikes in the Soviet Union declined from 1927 to 1928, though the number of strikers increased slightly (Murphy 2008, p. 173). Furthermore, according to an official trade union report, the number of Soviet workers involved in strikes declined during the first half of 1928 (Carr and Davies 1969, part 2, p. 567).

62   Trotsky 1981, p. 98. See also Trotsky 1981, pp. 78, 106, 258; Trotsky 1970b, p. 273.

submitted to the Comintern Congress, described the international turn as a by-product of the domestic economic difficulties.[63] However, in most of Trotsky's comments on the origins of the shift in Comintern policy he stressed international causes that paralleled the domestic factors he believed had provoked the economic turn. In circular letters and in his critique of the Comintern draft program, he argued that the previous 'right-centrist' course of the Comintern had led to serious defeats, landing the leadership in a 'blind alley'. Now, it was 'trying to find a way out ... to the left' under the impact of mounting proletarian pressure. In part, it had turned left in reaction to 'the undeniable shift that is taking place in the mood of the great working class masses, principally in Europe and especially in Germany'.[64] In part, it was the Opposition's 'four years of struggle' that had forced the ECCI to change its programme 'from one of a national type to one of an international type'. On this latter point Trotsky explained that bourgeois and Social Democratic praise for Stalin's policies had embarrassed the party leadership. Consequently, it 'became necessary to prove the Opposition was not being exiled for being leftist'.[65]

From this analysis Trotsky concluded that there was no reason for the Opposition to place confidence in the leadership as the conciliators were inclined to do. He believed that for the rightists within the leadership the turn was nothing but a manoeuvre. As he explained in his 23 May letter to Beloborodov, the rightists were afraid to engage the centrists in open conflict for they understood that 'within the framework of the party the proletarian core, even in its present condition, could crush them to bits in two seconds'.[66] However, he did not expect that the right would tolerate the left course for long. In a document submitted to the Comintern Congress he asserted that the right intended 'to pass from the defensive to the offensive and to take their revenge when the Left experiment will be terminated by a defeat'.[67] As far as the centrists and the 'wide circles of the party' that followed them were concerned, in his letter of 23 May Trotsky described the matter as somewhat more complex. Within these groupings he discerned 'all shades – from bureaucratic

---

63   Trotsky 1970b, p. 165. See also Trotsky 1970b, pp. 265–6.

64   Trotsky 1981, pp. 154, 161; Trotsky 1970b, p. 258. See also Trotsky 1970b, pp. 165–6. In this regard Trotsky noted a growing strike wave in Europe, and an increase in the Communist vote in France and Germany (Trotsky 1970b, pp. 259–60; Trotsky 1980b, p. 502).

65   Trotsky 1981, pp. 262, 258.

66   Trotsky 1981, p. 99. See also Trotsky 1970b, pp. 289–90.

67   Trotsky 1970b, p. 291. Similarly, the anonymous April letter previously discussed asserted that once 'those parts of the population whose moods they [the rightists] reflect start moving, they will ruthlessly launch an attack' (N. 1928). See also Trotsky 1981, p. 79.

tricksterism to a sincere desire to switch all policies onto the proletarian-revolutionary track'.[68] But even assuming some of the centrist leaders were sincere about the turn, he was convinced that their commitment to it would collapse abruptly unless it was reinforced by mass pressure. Again, the anony-mous April letter expressed this idea most clearly: 'As always the centrist Stalin-group will choose the course of the least resistance. Just as they are now feigning a left turn under the pressure of the working class they will quickly make a turn to the right under the combined pressure of the Kulak and the Nepman'.[69] Likewise, in July Trotsky warned the Comintern Congress, *'Never has this danger* [from the right] *been so great, so threatening, and so imminent as it is now'*.[70]

Nevertheless, given that the left 'manoeuvre' owed its origins to proletarian and/or Oppositional pressure, Trotsky was convinced that it could be trans-formed into a real turn 'with very energetic help from below'.[71] As the author of the anonymous letter put it, 'The fate of the "left course" ... depends upon the degree of activity of the working class at the decisive moment'.[72] By the late spring and summer of 1928 Trotsky detected signs that the working class was beginning to take the turn seriously, and to take an active part in the campaign against the right.[73] In July he asserted, 'The initial maneuver has grown over into a profound political zigzag, seizing in its vise ever wider circles of the party and wider class strata'. Consequently, he would not exclude the *'pos-sibility'* that the zigzag could develop 'in a direction of a consistent proletarian course'.[74]

The situation as Trotsky defined it required a carefully balanced approach on the part of the Opposition. On one hand, Trotsky proclaimed the Opposition's wholehearted support for the left turn and for the struggle against

---

68   Trotsky 1981, p. 99. See also Trotsky 1981 p. 98.

69   N. 1928. See also Trotsky 1981, pp. 139, 159.

70   Trotsky 1981, p. 139.

71   Trotsky 1981, p. 99. See also Trotsky 1981, p. 159; Trotsky 1970b, pp. 291–2.

72   N. 1928.

73   In this regard Trotsky agreed with Sosnovskii about the symptomatic significance of an incident in Kharkov, where a machinist named Bleskov, taking the turn and self-criticism campaign seriously, wrote a letter to the local party boss, Zatonskii, criticising party policy in terms borrowed from the Opposition. In turn, Zatonskii, insisted that Bleskov's letter be printed in the *Kharkov Proletarian*. Subsequently, Zatonskii was denounced for this 'petty bourgeois deviation'. For Trotsky, the episode indicated that the maneuver could be transformed into a turn 'with very energetic help from below' (Trotsky 1981, pp. 99–100, 102–3, 128).

74   Trotsky 1970b, pp. 291, 292. See also Trotsky 1981, pp. 107, 155.

the right, insofar as these were real. 'Are we ready to support the present official turn'? he asked the Opposition in May. 'We are', he answered, 'unconditionally, and with all our forces and resources'.[75] Similarly, in his 'Declaration' to the Sixth Comintern Congress he asserted, 'The Opposition supports every step, even a hesitant one, toward the proletarian line, every attempt, even an indecisive one, to resist the Thermidorian elements'.[76] On the other hand, the kind of support Trotsky had in mind was not passive endorsement. The task of the Opposition, he proclaimed to the Comintern Congress, was 'to see that the present zigzag is extended into a serious turn onto the Leninist road'.[77] To accomplish that task, it was essential for the Opposition to denounce all the weaknesses and inadequacies of the turn. In fact, Trotsky explained in a response to Radek, 'The pitiless unmasking of the half-measures and confusion of centrism ... constitutes the most important part of our support for any progressive steps of centrism'.[78]

The perspective from which he criticised the turn was the one that had been outlined in the Opposition's 1927 *Platform*. Trotsky insisted, '*A continued fight for the ideas and proposals expressed in the Platform is the only correct, serious, and honest way to support every step by the center that is at all progressive*'.[79] Beyond that, he again highlighted the connection he saw between party leadership's policies and the character of the party regime by emphasising four new democratic demands: (1) the freeing of imprisoned Oppositionists, the return of the deportees, and the readmission of the Opposition to the party; (2) the convening of a Sixteenth Party Congress in 1928 with guarantees for a full discussion and genuine elections; (3) the publication of all of Lenin's suppressed writings, including his 'Testament'; and (4) the reduction of the party budget to one-twentieth of its existing size – that is, to five or six million rubles. In Trotsky's view these demands provided 'a serious test of the sincerity and honesty of the leadership's steps toward party democracy'.[80] Furthermore, the first of these demands constituted 'the essential proof, the infallible means of verification, and the first indicator of the seriousness and depth of all the recent moves toward the left'.[81]

---

75   Trotsky 1981, p. 80.
76   Trotsky 1981, p. 142.
77   Trotsky 1970b, p. 292.
78   Trotsky 1981, p. 163. See also Trotsky 1981, pp. 70–1, 129, 143, 145; N. 1928.
79   Trotsky 1981, p. 143.
80   Trotsky 1981, pp. 149–50, 153. See also Trotsky 1981, p. 161.
81   Trotsky 1981, p. 149.

At this point in the discussion, a large majority of the Oppositionists in exile supported Trotsky's perspective over the approach of the conciliators.[82] That would change in the course of the following year.

5.3   The Stalinist Offensive

By early July tensions within the Politburo had reached the point that Stalin and Bukharin were no longer on speaking terms. However, the Politburo continued to present a facade of unity, unanimously adopting a resolution on the grain collections for the consideration of the Central Committee. The resolution, written on the basis of a declaration presented by Bukharin, largely reflected the views of the moderates. It emphasised the importance of the alliance with the middle peasant and the continuation of NEP, terminated the exceptional measures, and raised the price of grain 20 percent. Fearing a premature confrontation with the moderates – who held powerful positions in the party, state, and trade union apparatuses, and the press – Stalin had retreated.[83]

However, Stalin quickly returned to the offensive at the July plenum. In the heated debate on agricultural policy he insisted that Soviet industrialisation could only proceed on the basis of a 'tribute' paid by the peasantry. Furthermore, he predicted the escalation of class struggle in the countryside, again defended the emergency measures, and renewed his demand for collectivisation of agriculture.[84] During the discussion Kalinin and Voroshilov and the Ukrainian members of the CC unexpectedly abandoned the moderates, and the Leningrad delegation disavowed the moderate Leningrader, Stetskii.[85] In despair, Bukharin visited Kamenev while the plenum was still in session, hoping to conclude an alliance, or at least to dissuade Zinoviev and Kamenev from supporting Stalin. Bukharin seemed obsessed with Stalin's vindictiveness, describing Stalin as a 'Genghis Khan', and repeatedly predicted that Stalin 'will cut our throats'. To Kamenev, he gave 'the impression of a man who knows he is doomed'.[86] However, in public the moderates behaved like victors. Addressing

82   In a vote at this time, 105 Oppositionists supported Trotsky's position, against 5 for
      Preobrazhenskii's (Longuet 1994, p. 42). Broué reports 100 votes for Trotsky's draft declara-
      tion to the Comintern against three for Radek's (Broué 1988, p. 574). See also Cliff 1993,
      pp. 76–7.
83   Cohen 1980, pp. 287–9; Daniels 1960, p. 329; Deutscher 1959, p. 427.
84   Stalin 1952–5, vol. 11, pp. 165–96.
85   From Kamenev's report of a conversation with Bukharin in Trotsky 1981, pp. 378–82.
86   Quoted in Trotsky 1981, pp. 382–4.

the Moscow party organisation on 13 July, Rykov assured his listeners that the emergency measures were now over and would not be revived. According to one account, he also repeated the warning of Voroshilov, Commissar of War, that if the emergency measures were reintroduced, 'This will be the end of the NEP ... Then there will certainly be an uprising in the army'.[87]

Soon after this, the Sixth Congress of the Comintern from 17 July to 1 September continued the turn initiated at the ninth plenum of the ECCI. Although Bukharin delivered the main report to the Congress, his address contained major concessions to the international orientation now advocated by Stalin. Bukharin endorsed the view, first advanced by Stalin at the Fifteenth Party Congress, that the period of world capitalist stabilisation was giving way to a 'third period' of capitalist reconstruction, which was 'accompanied by the growth of the forces hostile to capitalism and by the extremely rapid development of its internal contradictions'. For communists, Bukharin asserted, this change required a shift in tactics. Most importantly, it was necessary to intensify the struggle against social democracy, which consciously defended the capitalist state and which had demonstrated *social fascist tendencies*. Consequently, he rejected the possibility of alliances between Communists and Social Democratic leaders, arguing that 'united front tactics must, in most cases, now be applied only from *below*'. Finally, he argued that now the central danger within the Comintern was the 'Right deviation'.[88]

The Comintern Congress contributed to the further weakening the right within the AUCP(b) [All-Union Communist Party (Bolsheviks)]. Although Bukharin's concessions postponed open conflict, they ultimately helped to legitimise Stalin's struggle against the moderates. At the same time, the Stalinists were able to utilise the Congress to undermine Bukharin's authority. At the beginning of the Congress the Russian delegation embarrassed Bukharin by recalling his theses in order to add twenty amendments, and throughout the Congress Stalinists conducted a whispering campaign among foreign delegations about Bukharin's 'right deviation' and 'political syphilis'.[89]

At this point new differences also began to emerge within the leadership regarding economic questions. Although the Stalinists and the moderates had clashed repeatedly about agricultural policy, through the summer of 1928 there were no clear differences over the other fundamental question of Soviet economics – the rate of industrialisation. By late September, this question, too,

---

87   Rykov 1928, pp. 3–4; Daniels 1960, p. 333. See also Lewin 1968, p. 309. For Trotsky's reaction
      to Rykov's speech, see Trotsky 1981, pp. 166–75, 275.

88   Bukharin 1966, pp. 106–20; Carr 1971–8, vol. 2, pp. 69–70; Carr 1958–64, vol. 3: 1, pp. 196–7;
      Cohen 1980, pp. 292–3; Daniels 1960, pp. 334–5.

89   Carr 1971–8, vol. 2, p. 69; Cohen 1980, pp. 293–4; Daniels 1960, pp. 335–7.

came under dispute. In December 1927 the Fifteenth Party Congress had approved the preparation of a five-year plan, stressing that industrialisation should proceed with caution and balance. Throughout 1928 Gosplan attempted to fulfil this charge, but found its efforts repeatedly challenged by VSNKh, which pressed for much higher tempos of industrialisation. On 19 September the Stalinist head of VSNKh, Valerian Kuibyshev, addressed the Leningrad party organisation in support of its ambitious industrial projections. He rejected the assertions of anonymous individuals that 'we are "overindustrial-izing" and "biting off more than we can chew"'. Furthermore, he warned that the most serious disproportion in the economy was 'between the output of the means of production and the requirements of the country'.[90]

On 30 September Bukharin responded with an article in *Pravda* entitled 'Notes of an Economist', ostensibly directed against the ' "superindustrializers" of the Trotskyist variety'. In reality, the article was a sustained polemic against the industrial and agricultural policies of the Stalinists. In the face of the mounting clamour for ever higher tempos of industrialisation and increased pressure on the peasantry, Bukharin appealed for moderation. Most impor-tantly, he explained, it was necessary to maintain the proper balance between agriculture and industry. According to Bukharin, the American example had shown that industrial growth requires the presence of a large and prosperous peasantry. Attempting to industrialise faster than the development of agricul-ture, pumping too much capital out of the peasantry, would undermine the very basis of industrialisation. At the same time, excessively forcing the pace of industrialisation would create shortages and bottlenecks, which would further retard the development of industry. Bukharin's solution was to increase agri-cultural productivity by limiting the kulaks, by encouraging the gradual and voluntary collectivisation of agriculture and spread of cooperatives, and by adopting a more correct price policy. Although he insisted that industrialisa-tion could not be accelerated beyond existing levels, he asserted that it was possible to maintain the existing tempo by increasing productivity and efficiency. Soon after the article appeared in print, the Stalinist majority of the Politburo censured it and began to promote rapid industrialisation aggressively.[91]

Meanwhile, the Stalinists were steadily encroaching upon the organisa-tional strongholds of the party right. In the late summer of 1928 they wrested control of *Pravda*, the theoretical journal *Bolshevik*, and the Institute of

---

90   Daniels 1984, p. 210. See also Carr and Davies 1969, part 1, pp. 303–17; Carr and Davies 1969, part 2, pp. 874–81; Cohen 1980, p. 295; Daniels 1960, pp. 351–2.

91   Bukharin 1982, pp. 301–30. See also Carr and Davies 1969, part 1, pp. 89–90, 317–19; Cohen 1980, pp. 295–6; Daniels 1960, pp. 352, 356–7.

Red Professors from the moderates. Even more important were their victories in the Moscow party organisation in the early autumn.

In September and October the central party leadership encouraged insurgents within Moscow to denounce the rightist errors of Uglanov, the secretary of the Moscow party committee. When the Moscow Committee met on 18–19 October, Uglanov found himself politically isolated within his own organisation. Stalin personally addressed the meeting to warn against the 'Right, opportunist danger in the Party' and against the 'vacillations and waverings in the Moscow organisation'. Despite Uglanov's recantation on 19 October, he was severely weakened by the dismissal of a number of his high-level supporters.[92]

Through October, Bukharin observed these skirmishes from a vacation retreat in the Caucasus. Hearing that Rykov was beginning to yield to Stalin's demands regarding industrialisation, he returned in early November to Moscow, where he presented the Politburo with a list of eleven economic and organisational demands. Only after Bukharin, Rykov, and Tomskii threatened to resign from the Politburo did Stalin agree to a compromise, withdrawing some of his more offensive nominations and, apparently, making concessions in economic policy.[93]

Although the resolutions unanimously presented by the Politburo to the Central Committee contained evidence of compromise, the November plenum marked another clear defeat for the moderates. The CC endorsed Stalin's demand for rapid industrialisation, justified by the need 'to overtake and outstrip' the advanced capitalist countries, and for the collectivisation of agriculture; and it condemned the right deviation as the main danger confronting the party. Finally, it approved a party purge of 'socially alien, bureaucratized, and degenerate elements, and other hangers on' – a campaign later applied to rank and file supporters of the moderates in the leadership.[94]

Following the plenum Stalin stepped up his organisational campaign against the right. On 27 November Molotov replaced Uglanov as party secretary in

---

92   Carr 1971–8, vol. 2, pp. 62–3, 76–7; Cohen 1980, pp. 296–8; Daniels 1960, pp. 337–41; Stalin 1952–5, vol. 11, pp. 231–48.

93   Carr 1971–8, vol. 2, pp. 78–81; Cohen 1980, pp. 298–9; Daniels 1960, p. 342; Schapiro 1971, p. 374.

94   Carr 1971–8, vol. 2, pp. 81, 142–3; Cohen 1980, p. 300; Daniels 1960, pp. 342–3, 353; KPSS 1970b, pp. 122–57; Gregor 1974, pp. 338–41; Schapiro 1971, pp. 374–75; Stalin 1952–5, vol. 11, pp. 255–302. J. Arch Getty has noted that, according to a report by Iaroslavskii in 1930, only one percent of the members expelled in this purge were eliminated for ' "fractional" or oppositional activity' (Getty 1985, pp. 46–7). However, Fainsod's discussion of this purge suggests that supporters of the party right were often expelled as 'alien elements,' or for their connection with 'alien elements' (Fainsod 1958, p. 212).

Moscow, and moderates were removed from office throughout the Moscow party organisation. At the Eighth Trade Union Congress held 10–24 December, Stalinists assailed Tomskii for the bureaucratism and excessive centralism in the trade unions. Furthermore, the party fraction at that Congress passed a resolution endorsing rapid industrialisation and urging an intensification of the struggle against the right danger. Five Stalinists were elected to the Central Trade Union Council on the recommendation of the party fraction, prompting Tomskii to resign as chairman. Then, when his resignation was rejected, Tomskii refused to return to his post. About this time Bukharin, finding himself unable to control *Pravda*, withdrew from his editorial responsibilities on that paper. Meanwhile, at the ECCI plenum on 19 December Stalin launched an attack on Bukharin's supporters in the Communist Party of Germany for their 'craven opportunism', declaring that 'the presence of such people in the Comintern cannot be tolerated any longer'. Soon afterwards, the KPD began a campaign of expulsions against rightists within its ranks, which in 1929 was extended to the other sections of the Comintern.[95]

In desperation Bukharin counterattacked with a series of articles containing a thinly veiled critique of Stalin's economic policies. Most important in this regard was his speech, 'Lenin's Political Testament', delivered on the fifth anniversary of Lenin's death and published in *Pravda* on 24 January. In the midst of renewed difficulties in grain collection and signs that the party leadership was reviving the exceptional measures of the previous year, Bukharin reaffirmed his understanding that Lenin's approach to agriculture involved a prolonged period of expanding market relations and peaceful collaboration with the peasantry.[96]

At this point tensions between the Stalinists and the moderates were further inflamed by two new issues, both involving the defeated Opposition. The first was the question of what was to be done with Trotsky, who had continued to engage in oppositional activity from exile in Alma Ata. In mid-January 1929 the Politburo majority, against the protests of Bukharin, Rykov, and Tomskii, voted to banish Trotsky from the Soviet Union. This decision was carried out on 10 February with the forcible deportation of Trotsky and his family to Constantinople. The second issue concerned Bukharin's July conversations with Kamenev. In late January Trotskyists issued a pamphlet containing an

---

95   Carr 1971–8, vol. 2, p. 81; Carr 1971–8, vol. 3: 2, pp. 451–4, 457; Carr and Davies 1969, part 2, pp. 556–60; Cohen 1980, pp. 300–1; Daniels 1960, pp. 344–8; Stalin 1952–5, vol. 11, pp. 307–24.

96   On the difficulties in grain collection during the winter of 1928–9 see Carr and Davies 1969, part 1, pp. 100–3; Lewin 1968, pp. 287–8. On Bukharin's articles in *Pravda*, see Carr 1971–8, vol. 2, pp. 86–7; Cohen 1980, pp. 301–4; Lewin 1968, pp. 325–9; Schapiro 1971, pp. 376–7.

account of the discussions. In 30 January Stalin convened a meeting of the Politburo and members of the CCC to discuss the party right's factional activities. There, he denounced Bukharin, Rykov, and Tomskii as a 'group of Right deviators and capitulators', and charged that they had attempted to form 'a bloc with the Trotskyites against the party'.[97]

Bukharin responded that his discussions with Kamenev were justified by the 'abnormal conditions' within the party. Then, supported by Rykov and Tomskii, he utilised the occasion to indict the growing 'bureaucratization' of the party and Stalin's economic policies. Regarding the former, Bukharin complained that 'the party doesn't participate in deciding questions. Everything is done from above'. He further condemned the replacement of 'collective control ... by the control of one person, however authoritative'. At the same time, he attacked Stalin's 'Trotskyist' program of rapid industrialisation, based on the 'impoverishment' of the country and 'the military-feudal exploitation of the peasantry'. Subsequently, the Politburo and the CCC censured Bukharin, Rykov, and Tomskii for factionalism.[98]

5.4   Explaining the Offensive

In light of the renewed offensive against the party right, during the late summer and autumn of 1928 Trotsky began to introduce a number of implicit modifications into his theory of bureaucracy, while continuing to reaffirm its principal tenets. Viewing the decisions of the July plenum through the lens of his theory, he initially concluded that the left turn was over, that the right had defeated Stalin, and that Thermidor was imminent. However, it soon became apparent that no major shift to the right was about to occur, and that Stalin had managed to retain and even enhance his organisational power. To account for these developments, Trotsky modified his theory by asserting that in certain periods the 'logic of the apparatus' influenced events more immediately than the balance of class forces. Consistent with this view, he acknowledged for the first time that the Stalinists might defeat the right without the aid of either the Opposition or the working class. Although Trotsky continued to insist that capitalism would be restored unless the proletariat intervened, his new attention to the relative autonomy of the apparatus led to a revised understanding

---

97   Carr 1971–8, vol. 2, pp. 82–4, 87; Cohen 1980, pp. 304–5; Daniels 1960, pp. 363–4; Deutscher 1963, pp. 1–2; Schapiro 1971, p. 377; Stalin 1952–5, vol. 11, pp. 332–40; Trotsky 1970c, p. 565.

98   Cohen 1980, pp. 304–8. See also Carr 1971–8, vol. 2, pp. 87–90; Daniels 1960, pp. 363–4; Schapiro 1971, p. 377.

of how this might occur. Also, it reinforced his growing emphasis upon democratic demands. When the leadership struggle intensified in the fall, Trotsky
explained the conflict primarily in terms of the logic of the apparatus. However,
on the basis of his theory he also continued to predict the imminent collapse
of the centrist current under pressure from the left and the right.

It came as no surprise to Trotsky when the July plenum decided to terminate
the exceptional measures and raise the price of grain. After all, on the basis of
his theory he had predicted that, unless the proletariat intervened, the party
right would soon seize power and implement a thoroughly rightist course.
Consequently, when the decisions were announced and the text of Rykov's
'victory' speech of 13 July appeared in *Pravda*, he concluded that the right had
soundly defeated the centre. In a statement to the Comintern on 22 July he
asserted, 'The right has issued entirely victorious from its first skirmish with
the center, after four or five months of "left" politics'.[99] Meanwhile, Stalin, 'the
vanquished', had been reduced to 'turning his back and occupying himself
with manipulating the apparatus'. Trotsky remarked, 'Stalin is losing time
under the impression that he is gaining it'.[100] Once again, the threat of
Thermidor seemed imminent to Trotsky, who warned that the increase in the
price of grain constituted 'the beginning of a deep and perhaps decisive turn to
the right'. Soon, he predicted, the right would attempt further concessions such
as the abolition of the monopoly of foreign trade. Following that, it would
unleash a wave of persecutions that would even exceed the repression Stalin
had inflicted upon the Opposition. 'One can imagine', Trotsky shuddered, 'what
persecutions the right is going to turn loose when relying openly upon the
property instinct of the kulak'. Again, he sounded the alarm, appealing to the
party to 'lift up its voice', and to the proletarian vanguard to 'take its destiny in
its own hands'.[101]

Events of the following weeks and months again failed to confirm Trotsky's
worst fears. There were neither new shifts to the right, nor any indication that
a right-wing reign of terror was about to begin. In fact, in this period Moscow
Oppositionists reported rumors that Stalin was preparing to renew his
left course, and that both he and the rightists were seeking the support of
the left.[102] Although Trotsky continued to speak of 'the right turn of July' and
the 'retreat of the centrists', by the end of the summer he recognised that the

---

99   Trotsky 1981, p. 168.
100   Trotsky 1981, pp. 172–3.
101   Trotsky 1981, pp. 173–5.
102   Deutscher 1959, p. 440. For a discussion of the hints dropped by Stalin during this period
        about a possible reconciliation with the Trotskyists, see Deutscher 1959, pp. 443–5.

right had not been able to seize control and implement a rightist course.[103] On this issue he challenged a group of intransigents who continued to claim that the right had eliminated the centre at the July plenum. Responding to the concerns of this group in a letter of 30 August, he observed that 'the centrists still have the apparatus', and warned that 'conflicts are still ahead'. The same day he cautioned a member of the Democratic Centralists that 'the important disputes are still ahead, and they are bound to come to the surface'.[104]

Trotsky seems to have modified his estimation of the plenum even further in late October on the basis of a report he had received about Bukharin's hysterical discussions with Kamenev.[105] From that report he concluded that Stalin had shifted course at the plenum, not because he was defeated, but as a manoeuvre in order to 'split the right wing'. By this temporary swing to the right, Stalin actually had enhanced his own organisational power. In other words, while policies were moving rightwards, power within the leadership was shifting to the centre. At least in this respect Trotsky was forced to recognise that reality was not unfolding in conformity with his theory. As he expressed it, 'the development of the apparatus has its own logic, which so far has not coincided with the general shifts of power in the party and the working class, and is even contrary to it'.[106] For the moment it was clear that the social classes were not actively intervening in the party struggle. In their absence, Trotsky suggested, the logic of the apparatus was able to play an unusually significant role. He observed,

> Naturally, if the classes should speak out loud, if the proletariat should pass over to a political attack, the positioning of these apparatus actors would lose nine-tenths of its meaning; in fact, they would drastically change their positions, moving in one direction or another. But we are passing through an as yet unfinished era in which the apparatus remains

---

103 For remarks on 'the right turn of July', see Trotsky 1981, pp. 252, 258, 276.

104 Trotsky 1981, pp. 177, 180. See also Trotsky 1981, pp. 276–7. On 18 September Trotsky reminded a Rykovist, Shatunovskii, who had reprimanded him for oppositional activities that Shatunovskii himself was a member of a 'right oppositional' grouping (Trotsky 1981, p. 247).

105 Both Isaac Deutscher and Pierre Broué have suggested that Trotsky was aware of the Bukharin-Kamenev discussion by early September (Deutscher 1959, pp. 447–8; Broué 1988, pp. 556, 576). However, the editors of Trotsky 1981 have noted that Trotsky's first reference to the meeting appeared in his circular letter of 21 October, and have plausibly suggested that the Moscow Trotskyists received a report about the July meeting from Kamenev in a meeting of 22 September (Ed. note, Trotsky 1981, p. 270).

106 Trotsky 1981, p. 271.

all-powerful ... Stalin and Rykov and Bukharin are the government. And the government plays a role of no little importance.[107]

Some of the more significant 'apparatus' factors that Trotsky saw as shaping the leadership contest included Stalin's control of the party machine and the passivity of the right-wing leaders. For the rightists to win, they would have 'to carry their fight against Stalin outside of the apparatus', openly appealing to the new proprietors and 'thundering ... like the Black Hundreds, like Thermidorians'. But despite Bukharin's tentative step in that direction with his 'Notes of an Economist', the leaders of the party right clearly were not prepared for such a struggle.[108] In contrast to the 'lower ranks of the right faction', Trotsky explained in November, the rightist leaders were still constrained by working-class dissatisfaction and by the traditions of Bolshevism.[109] Meanwhile, Stalin was plotting to eliminate his rivals by a series of policy manoeuvres and organisational assaults. For the first time Trotsky now perceived that the centre might defeat the right without the assistance of either the Opposition or the working class: 'As long as the classes are silent', he commented on 21 October, 'Stalin's scheme will work'.[110]

Still, Trotsky's new emphasis on the relative autonomy of the party apparatus did not alter his conviction that the logic of classes was ultimately decisive and that capitalist restoration was inevitable unless the proletariat intervened. In fact, in his circular letter of 21 October Trotsky revised his metaphor of 'Kerenskiism in reverse' to emphasise this conclusion, perhaps in reaction to conciliators who were encouraged by Stalin's new offensive. It will be recalled that in late 1927 Trotsky employed the expression 'Kerenskiism in reverse' to characterise the role that would be played by a future Thermidorian regime, that is, in a 'dual power situation, ... with the bourgeoisie holding the upper hand'.[111] Now, in his letter of 21 October Trotsky argued that the Soviet Union was already living through a 'Kerensky period in reverse'. He explained that, whereas under Kerenskii 'the power of the bourgeoisie passed over to the proletariat', under Stalin power was now 'sliding over from the proletariat to the bourgeoisie'.[112] In other words, the existing Stalinist regime was the final station on the road to capitalist restoration.

---

107   Trotsky 1981, p. 273.
108   Ibid.
109   Trotsky 1981, pp. 319–20.
110   Trotsky 1981, p. 272.
111   Trotsky 1980b, p. 492.
112   Trotsky 1981, p. 274.

As in the past, Trotsky reviewed two familiar scenarios by which capitalism might be restored. First, there was the possibility of a 'Thermidorian overturn', which would be followed by a 'Bonapartist' or 'fascist' regime. In light of the organisational weakness of the party right, Trotsky now believed this danger was less imminent than it had appeared in the summer.[113] However, Deutscher's observation that Trotsky 'virtually abandoned his conception of the Soviet Thermidor' in his 21 October letter is an exaggeration.[114] In the same letter Trotsky cautioned the Opposition that 'the conditions necessary for Thermidor to materialize can develop in a comparatively short time'. In the following weeks and months he also continued to refer to the possibility of Thermidor on a number of occasions.[115] At the same time, in his second scenario Trotsky suggested that the army or a section of it might stage a 'Bonapartist' coup and establish an authoritarian, right-wing regime. He believed Rykov had alluded to this possibility in July when he repeated Voroshilov's prediction that the army would answer a renewal of the emergency measures with an insurrec-tion. For Trotsky, this was clearly a threat, and he now concluded that the most likely candidate for the role of Bonaparte, albeit 'a third-rate type of Bonaparte', was Voroshilov.[116]

However, consistent with his growing recognition of the relative autonomy of the apparatus, Trotsky now suggested that capitalism might return by yet another route – actually a variation of the first two – through the 'independent victory of the centrists without the Opposition, without the masses'. According to Trotsky, such a centrist victory would not eliminate the 'Thermidorian-Bonapartist perspective'; it would 'only change and postpone it'. He reasoned that, without the assistance of the Opposition or the masses, the Stalinists could only hope to conquer the right 'through increased repression, through a further narrowing of the mass base of centrism', and 'through a further fusion

---

113   Trotsky 1981, pp. 274–5. Trotsky observed, 'At first glance, it seems reassuring that the polit-
         ical parties of the possessing class are shattered, that the new proprietors are politically
         atomized, that the right wing inside the party cannot decide to rely openly upon the new
         proprietors' (Trotsky 1981, p. 274).
114   Deutscher 1959, p. 458.
115   Trotsky 1981, p. 274. See also Trotsky 1981, pp. 307, 314, 316, 318–20, 321–8, 334–5, 337, 338,
         363; Trotsky 1975c, pp. 49–50.
116   Trotsky 1981, pp. 274–5. In this document Trotsky mistakenly dates Rykov's remark as hav-
         ing occurred in June. On Trotsky's prediction, see also Deutscher 1959, pp. 458–60.
         According to Roy Medvedev, in 1928–29 Voroshilov frequently objected to Stalin's offen-
         sive against the peasantry because he feared that policy would undermine the morale of
         the army. Medvedev attributes Trotsky's fears that Voroshilov might lead a 'peasant upris-
         ing' to exaggerated rumors about these objections (Medvedev 1985, p. 11).

of the centrist faction with the apparatus of governmental repression'. But Trotsky's theory suggested that such a worsening of the regime would inevitably strengthen rightist tendencies within the country. Consequently, he concluded that an independent victory of the centrists would prepare the way for a 'Bonapartist' capitalist regime. In fact, perhaps even Stalin himself would one day 'mount the white horse'.[117]

Perhaps at least partly because he had begun to fear that a victory of Stalinist authoritarianism ultimately posed as great a danger to Soviet power as a victory of rightist conservatism, in this period Trotsky began to stress democratic demands even more than before. In addition to his previous demands, he now called for the introduction of the secret ballot in the party and trade unions to help workers combat 'bureaucratic pressure'. Nevertheless, at this point, he recommended waiting 'until we have the necessary experience' before extending the experiment to the soviets 'where different classes take part in the voting'.[118]

An even more significant tactical innovation was Trotsky's proposal for a united front with the party right in the name of democracy. In the past, he had rejected the possibility of any alliance with the right.[119] However, by September 1928 he was already beginning to fear that an independent Stalinist victory was possible and potentially as dangerous as a victory by the right. At the same time, he saw an opportunity in the prospect that elements of the right would soon be willing to support democratic demands for their own self-preservation.[120] In a letter on 12 September to a 'Rykovist' named Shatunovskii, he observed that the existing party regime had 'brought the whole party into a state of illegality, so to speak'. To rectify this situation, he proposed a 'common effort' to 'restore the ruling party to a condition of legality'. Restating the Opposition's principal democratic demands, Trotsky declared, 'On the basis of these proposals we would even be willing to negotiate with the rights, because the implementation of these elementary preconditions of party principle would give the proletarian core the opportunity to really call to account not

117 Trotsky 1981, pp. 275–6.
118 Trotsky 1981, pp. 281–3. For later statements on the secret ballot, see Trotsky 1981, p. 368; Trotsky 1975c, pp. 58–9, 113–14, 291.
119 For example, in his declaration to the Sixth Comintern Congress, recalling how the left Jacobins had joined forces with the Right to overthrow Robespierre, Trotsky had observed, 'There have been such combinations between the right and the left in [past] revolutions. Such combinations have also ruined revolutions' (Trotsky 1981, p. 142).
120 Isaac Deutscher, Pierre Broué, and Tony Cliff have suggested that Trotsky's modification of his position on this question represented a response to Bukharin's July appeal for an alliance against Stalin (Broué 1988, p. 41; Cliff 1993, p. 84; Deutscher 1959, pp. 447–8).

only the rights but also the centrists, i.e., the main support and protection for opportunism in the party'.[121]

When this letter was circulated among Oppositionists in exile, many responded with dismay. In their view Trotsky had abandoned the traditional position for an unprincipled bloc. In response, Trotsky replied that, of course, a real 'bloc', involving a common platform, was still inconceivable. Nevertheless, he predicted that the rightists would inevitably come into conflict with the apparatus over the issue of the party regime. When they did so, they would be forced to repeat the Opposition's democratic demands, 'shamefacedly renouncing their theory and practices of yesterday and thus helping us to expose both themselves and the entire party regime'. All Trotsky had proposed was to support the rightists in this 'as a rope supports a hanging man'; he had only offered an agreement, like that between two duelists, 'about the conditions for an irreconcilable struggle'.[122]

By the end of the year it was clear to Trotsky that the leadership conflict had entered a new phase. He observed in a letter of 11 November, 'We are now witnesses of a new centrist campaign against the right-wingers'.[123] Yet, even more than previously he stressed the limitations of this conflict, which he saw as distinguished by an 'extraordinary amount of noise and tumult' but 'with a total absence of concrete form politically'.[124] In this regard he especially emphasised the inconsistencies of Stalin's leftism.[125] But for Trotsky the most important indication of the limitations of the official struggle was the fact that thousands of Oppositionists languished in exile while rightists continued to occupy the seats of power. From all of this he concluded that the new campaign against the right was 'unbalanced, false, contradictory, and unreliable'.[126]

Largely because he could see no programmatic differences that could be attributed to class pressures, Trotsky again explained the leadership conflict primarily in terms of apparatus dynamics. He insisted that the entire left turn, including the leadership struggle, was a result of the political revival of the working class and the pressure of Opposition. However, he immediately added that 'like all other processes in the party, the struggle of the centrists and rights

121   Trotsky 1981, pp. 248–9.

122   Trotsky 1981, pp. 340–2.

123   Trotsky 1981, p. 295. See also Trotsky 1981, pp. 302, 303–4, 336.

124   Trotsky 1981, p. 302.

125   These included Stalin's refusal to name the rightist leaders, the ambiguity of his position on industrialisation and collectivisation, his continued adherence to the doctrine of socialism in one country, and his failure to support an increase in workers' wages (Trotsky 1981, pp. 323–31).

126   Trotsky 1981, pp. 303, 363.

must be considered not only from the angle of class tendencies and ideas but also from the narrow angle of the bureaucratic regime'. Approaching the question from this point of view, he observed that the rupture between Stalin and the rightist leaders had resulted 'from the tendency of the bureaucratic regime toward personal power'.[127] The clear implication was that the current phase of the struggle could best be understood in terms of this tendency.

Of course, Trotsky had referred to the inclination of the regime toward personal power in previous years. In fact, in his November 1928 article 'Crisis in the Right-Center Bloc' he recalled that he had written about the prospect of the 'one-man rule of Stalin' as early as 1926, and had even predicted that this would require not only the defeat of the Opposition, but also 'the gradual removal of *all authoritative and influential figures in the present ruling faction*', including Tomskii, Rykov, and Bukharin. To this extent Trotsky was justified in asserting that the leadership conflict had confirmed his analysis.[128] However, the emphasis he now gave to the logic of the apparatus, including the argument that it was necessary to analyse *all* party developments from this point of view, was a new development in his thinking.

During this period Trotsky also suggested another explanation for the intensification of the leadership conflict. In the autumn of 1928 he noted that the Stalinists were stating continually that the views of the right and the Opposition were 'basically' the same. For Trotsky, such assertions were clearly nonsense if taken literally. However, he reasoned that they made perfect sense from a tactical point of view if the purpose was to prepare the party for a new assault upon the Opposition. Trotsky concluded, 'The campaign against the right serves only as a springboard for a new "monolithic" attack upon the left. Whoever has not understood this has understood nothing'.[129] He soon saw this analysis confirmed. On 16 December he was warned by a GPU official that, unless he immediately ceased all 'counterrevolutionary' activity, he would be moved to a new location and completely isolated from all political life. In his reply to the CC Trotsky repeated, 'The campaign against the right danger, undertaken with such clamor, remains three-quarters sham and serves above all to conceal from the masses the real war of annihilation against the Bolshevik-Leninists'.[130]

---

127   Trotsky 1981, pp. 306, 308.
128   Trotsky 1981, pp. 308–9. For the original statement, see Trotsky 1980b, pp. 116–17.
129   Trotsky 1981, p. 332. At the same time, Trotsky found himself subjected to an increasingly restrictive postal blockade which prompted his wife to remark to a friend, 'Things will not stop at this, of course. We are awaiting something worse'. Also, during this period rumors circulated within the Opposition that Trotsky was about to be removed to an even more isolated location than Alma Ata (Deutscher 1959, pp. 453–4).
130   Trotsky 1981, p. 363.

Despite the new campaign against the right and the new threat against the left, Trotsky remained certain in late 1928 that the strength of the centrist grouping was temporary. In the first place, he believed that the zigzags and two-fronted war characteristic of centrism would lead inevitably to a fragmentation of Stalin's own political current. In early January 1929 he confidently prophesied, 'As the fight against the right and the left goes on, centrism will extrude from its own midst both right-centrist and left-centrist elements, that is, it will undergo a political differentiation and fall apart'.[131] Furthermore, on the basis of his theory he predicted that the social classes and elements closely connected to them would continue to gravitate to the left and right of centrism. Writing in November 1928, he anticipated that the Soviet proletariat would move to the left. At the same time, he perceived that the 'proprietor and the bureaucrat' who had supported the centre-right bloc against the Opposition were already beginning to view the centrists as 'strangers, almost enemies' and to abandon them for the right. In light of this process, Trotsky reasserted that the right, in contrast to centrism, had 'great reserves of growth' which had hardly been tapped. Consequently, he foresaw 'the strengthening and clearer demarcation of the wings at the expense of centrism, despite the growing concentration of power in its hands'.[132]

5.5   Defeating the Right and Continuing the Turn

Trotsky's class-based predictions notwithstanding, in the following months Stalin completed his victory over his opponents within the leadership. At the Moscow and Leningrad party conferences and in the press, the Stalinists continued to escalate the campaign against the 'right deviation'. Within the Politburo they easily defeated attempts by Bukharin, Rykov and Tomskii to moderate the industrial projections of the five-year plan. The final showdown occurred at the April plenum of the CC. There, while professing support for rapid industrialisation, the moderates asserted that this goal was being undermined by 'ideological capitulation to Trotskyism' in agricultural policy. The extraordinary measures, they argued, had spoiled relations between the state and the peasantry and were threatening to destroy NEP. In response, Stalin rehearsed at length the sins of the party right – from their bending to kulak pressure, to their failure to attack 'conciliationists' within the Comintern, to their factional activities. In the end the CC endorsed the proposed five-year

---

131   Trotsky 1981, p. 371. See also Trotsky 1981, p. 332.
132   Trotsky 1981, pp. 333–4. See also Trotsky 1981, p. 371.

plan; reaffirmed that the right deviation was the greatest danger facing the party; voted to remove Bukharin and Tomskii from their posts in the Comintern, *Pravda*, and the trade unions; and warned that continued factionalism would result in further reprisals.[133]

Stalin continued to whittle away at the remaining power of the moderates through the remainder of 1929. At the end of the Sixteenth Party Conference in late April, Uglanov forfeited his positions as candidate member of the Politburo and member of the Secretariat, in late May the All-Union Central Council of Trade Unions formally removed Tomskii as its chairman, and on 3 July the ECCI dropped Bukharin from membership on its presidium and barred him from Comintern work. Up to this point the Soviet press had only attacked anonymous rightists within the party. However, at the end of August *Pravda* began to denounce Bukharin by name as 'the chief leader and inspirer of the right deviationists', and to portray his entire political record as anti-Leninist. Finally, at the November CC plenum Bukharin, Rykov, and Tomskii were forced to recant their errors, and Bukharin was expelled from the Politburo.[134]

Meanwhile, the defeat of the moderates eliminated a final obstacle to radical changes in policy by the Stalinists. As far as Comintern policy was concerned, indications of the change were evident in early July at the tenth ECCI plenum. There, the 'Third Period' announced by Bukharin at the Sixth Congress of the Comintern was portrayed as a general radicalisation of the world working class. The immediate task proclaimed for Communist parties was to conquer the leadership of the workers' movement in preparation for the seizure of power. More insistently than before, social democracy was equated with fascism. Otto Kuusinen, the Finnish Comintern secretary, explained that, while the slogans and 'to some extent' the methods of the two movements differed, their aims were identical. Consequently, Communists were to participate only in 'united fronts from below' with rank and file Socialists, not with Social Democratic leaders. In line with this, the ECCI suggested that in certain circumstances communists should organise revolutionary trade unions in opposition to those controlled by Social Democrats.[135]

At the same time, projected targets for industry continued to climb. In March Gosplan adopted minimal and optimal versions of the proposed

133 Carr and Davies 1969, part 1, pp. 248–52; Carr and Davies 1969, part 2, pp. 889–91; Carr 1971–8, vol. 2, pp. 90–2; Cohen 1980, pp. 308–11; Daniels 1960, pp. 364–6. Stalin's long speech in reply to the discussion appears in Stalin 1952–5, vol. 12, pp. 1–113.

134 Carr and Davies 1969, part 2, p. 562; Carr 1971–8, vol. 2, pp. 93, 95–6; Carr 1971–8, vol. 3: 1, p. 256; Cohen 1980, pp. 329–35; Daniels 1960, pp. 367–9; Schapiro 1971, pp. 380–1.

135 Carr 1971–8, vol. 3: 1, pp. 247–54; Cohen 1980, pp. 329–30. For excerpts from Kuusinen's remarks on social fascism, see Eudin and Slusser 1966, pp. 199–201.

five-year plan pre-dated to begin in October 1928. Even the minimal variant was optimistic, projecting a 250 percent increase in total investments by the end of five years, a 340 percent increase in the planned sector of industry, and a rise in total industrial output by 135 percent. However, the optimal version – based upon such unrealistic assumptions as five consecutive good harvests – was vastly more ambitious, proposing a growth of total investments by 320 percent and of investments in planned industry by 420 percent, and an expansion of industrial production by 181 percent. It was the optimal version that was adopted by the April CC plenum and the Sixteenth Party Conference. During the remainder of 1929 even these goals were steadily revised upwards. By September, *Pravda* was declaring that the five-year plan would be fulfilled in four years. Beyond that, at the beginning of November Stalin announced that the former optimum of the five-year plan 'actually turned out to be a minimum variant'.[136] In the words of contemporary historian Stephen Cohen, 'What remained was no longer a plan but a kaleidoscope of escalating figures, a rationalization of the breakneck heavy industrialization of the next three years'.[137]

Finally, throughout 1929 the party leadership continued the offensive in agriculture. One form this took was a revival of the extraordinary measures in the collection of grain. During the winter of 1928–9 grain procurements again encountered severe difficulties, partly due to a poor harvest in Ukraine and other important grain producing regions, and partly to the fact that peasants were selling grain on the free market to take advantage of the much higher prices. Again, the authorities resorted to extraordinary measures, including fines, arrests, imprisonment, internal exile, and the confiscation of the property of peasants engaged in speculation. Many peasants responded by simply reducing their sowings, while in some areas whole villages retaliated by withholding grain. In the same period there were frequent shootings of procurement agents, and even cases of peasant uprisings. Nevertheless, from July through December, over twice as much grain was collected as in the corresponding months of the previous year. Despite the poor harvest, by the beginning of December 1929 Mikoian was able to announce that the grain collections plan had been virtually completed.[138]

The second aspect of the turn in agriculture in the summer and fall of 1929 was the move towards mass collectivisation. Although the five-year plan approved by the Sixteenth Party Conference in April projected modest growth

136   Carr and Davies 1969, part 2, pp. 888–90, 894, 981; Cohen 1980, p. 311; Lewin 1968, pp. 344–7, 374–5; Stalin 1952–5, vol. 12, p. 129.

137   Cohen 1980, p. 330.

138   Carr and Davies 1969, part 1, pp. 100–5; Cohen 1980, pp. 330–1; R. Davies 1980a, pp. 56–104, 427; Lewin 1968, pp. 383–95, 414.

of state and collective farms, it did so within the context of a continuing emphasis on the long-term importance of private farming.[139] However, in the summer it became increasingly evident that the difficulties in grain collection were threatening to disrupt industrialisation. In response to this threat the leadership resolved to put an end to these difficulties by radically transforming the character of Soviet agriculture. During the summer the press began to speak of 'mass collectivization'; party members who were peasants were compelled to join the *kolkhozy*; and state agents, party members, and trade unionists were mobilised to assist in the collectivisation effort. Between June and October, the number of collectivised holdings increased from 3.9 to 7.6 percent of the total.[140] Then in the autumn the central party leadership decided to intensify the campaign even further. On 31 October a *Pravda* editorial called for the transfer of all the forces used in the procurements campaign to the collectivisation drive. A week later the paper published an article by Stalin which claimed that peasants, including middle peasants, were voluntarily enlisting in the collectives 'not in separate groups, ... but by whole villages, volosts [rural districts], districts, and even okrugs [regions]'. In the face of this 'spontaneous' movement of the peasantry, the November CC plenum passed a resolution declaring that the 'collective farm movement is already posing the objective of comprehensive collectivization of individual regions'. What has become known as Stalin's 'revolution from above' had begun.[141]

Meanwhile, the events of 1929 had continued to exacerbate the crisis within the Opposition. As in 1928, the renewal of the left course fostered the growth of conciliatory sentiments among Oppositionists in exile. This time, the impulse to reconcile with the party was even stronger than a year before. In the first place, the policy changes in industry, agriculture, and the Comintern were far deeper than those of 1928, reinforcing the perception that the Opposition's programme was about to be implemented – with or without the Opposition. Second, the abrupt shift in economic policy had created a crisis atmosphere, especially in the countryside but also in the city, giving rise to concerns within the Opposition that the revolution was in danger. Third, the months of exile had taken a toll upon many Oppositionists who had expected to be welcomed back to the party, if not to the leadership, within a short period of time. Finally, Trotsky's expulsion from the country had removed a powerful force for resistance.

---

139   Cohen 1980, pp. 311–12; Lewin 1968, pp. 352–3.
140   Cohen 1980, pp. 330–1; R. Davies 1980a, pp. 116–37; Lewin 1985, pp. 104–13.
141   Cohen 1980, pp. 333–4; R. Davies 1980a, pp. 155–74; Stalin 1976, p. 443; Lewin 1985, pp. 113–14; Lewin 1968, pp. 454–65.

Again, Preobrazhenskii and Radek led the conciliatory tendency. In April Preobrazhenskii distributed a document calling upon Oppositionists to recognise that, although Stalin might not be employing their methods, he was carrying out the industrialisation and collectivisation the Opposition had demanded. Now, he asserted, it was time for the Opposition to swallow its pride and come to the aid of the revolution, which was facing its gravest threat since Kronstadt. In May Preobrazhenskii travelled to Moscow to negotiate with the party leadership. There, he was joined in June by Radek and the former irreconcilable, I.T. Smilga. On 10 July the trio signed a document with 400 other exiles, renouncing the Opposition and appealing for reinstatement in the party.[142]

More capitulations soon followed. From June through most of October another grouping led by Trotsky's close associate I.N. Smirnov bargained with the leadership over the conditions of their return to the party. Smirnov explained his own motivations to a friend:

> I can't stand inactivity. I want to build! In its own barbaric and sometimes stupid way, the Central Committee is building for the future. Our ideological differences are of small importance before the construction of great new industries.[143]

Aside from such sentiments, it is clear that the theoretical failures of the Opposition played a part in the defection of this group. Early in their negotiations Smirnov and his supporters conceded in a draft statement that the Opposition had been mistaken in its prediction that the CC would turn right and initiate a Thermidor. Ultimately, a statement of surrender signed by Smirnov and hundreds of other Oppositionists appeared in *Pravda* on 3 November.[144]

Altogether, according to Oppositionist Victor Serge, 'The movement of surrender to the Central Committee in 1928–1929 carried off the greater part of the 5,000 Oppositionists under arrest'.[145] Still, not all Oppositionists in exile surrendered at this time. In August 1929 Khristian Rakovskii, V. Kosior, and

---

142   Broué 1988, pp. 629–32; Deutscher 1963, pp. 63–74; Longuet 1994, pp. 52–3. The Trotskyists Piatakov, Antonov-Ovseenko, and Krestinskii all capitulated in early 1928. However, all of these had been working in diplomatic assignments abroad in recent years and had not actively participated in the final phase of the Opposition's struggle (Carr 1971–8, vol. 2, p. 55; Longuet 1994, p. 33).

143   Quoted in Serge 1980, pp. 252–3. According to Pierre Broué, Smirnov's group did not really capitulate at this time, 'but were trying to fool the apparatus' (Broué 1989, p. 104).

144   Deutscher 1963, pp. 76–8. See also Broué 1988, pp. 637–8; Longuet 1994, pp. 57–9.

145   Serge 1980, p. 253.

M. Okudzhava submitted to the CC their own 'Declaration', which, by mid-September, had been signed by approximately 500 Oppositionists. The declaration, moderate in tone, also took the form of an appeal for reinstatement in the party. It expressed support for the five-year plan, for the collectivisation campaign, for the party struggle against the right, and for the turn in the Communist International. Furthermore, it asserted that events had 'in part swept away those barriers which have separated the Bolshevik-Leninist opposition from the party'. However, the declaration differed from the statements of the capitulators in its continued insistence upon several Opposition demands that had not been implemented. Above all, it stressed the need to restore democracy to the state, trade unions, and party. Also, in addition to the democratic demands previously raised, the declaration called on the CC to bring Trotsky back from his exile in Turkey.[146]

5.6   Explaining the New Turn

On 11 February 1929 Trotsky arrived in Constantinople with his wife and his son, Lev. Within a few weeks, he had settled on the Turkish island of Prinkipo in the Sea of Marmara. This would be his home for most of the next four years.[147] From the beginning of Trotsky's arrival in Turkey, his political and literary activities were more international in scope than they had been in recent years. His first priority was to explain the significance of his struggle to the world. During his first year abroad Trotsky attempted to do this through the publication of a series of articles in the international press, several volumes of Opposition documents, and an autobiography. In the same period he also utilised the freedom afforded by exile to collaborate with his international co-thinkers. He immediately established contact with scattered groupings of left communists recently expelled from their respective parties, and began working to fuse these together into a cohesive international organisation.[148]

However, throughout 1929 much of Trotsky's attention remained fixed on the unfolding drama within the Soviet Union. During his first weeks in Turkey Trotsky wrote about his own expulsion and the escalating repression of the Opposition. Soon afterwards, he turned his attention to Stalin's struggle against

---

146   For the text of the 'Declaration', see *Biulleten' oppozitsii* 1973, 6 (October 1929), pp. 3–7; Rakovsky 1980, pp. 137–44. See also Broué 1988, pp. 635–6; Deutscher 1963, pp. 78–81.

147   See Broué 1988, p. 603. For various first-hand accounts of life with Trotsky in Turkey, see Glotzer 1989, pp. 28–82; Van Heijenoort 1978, pp. 1–48; Swabeck 1977, pp. 152–9; S. Weber 1972, pp. 181–94.

148   Deutscher 1963, pp. 6–10, 21–3, 28–33.

the party right, and to the latest shifts in economic and international policy. His interest in these developments was made especially urgent by the fact that growing numbers of Oppositionists had begun to view them as grounds for surrender. In contrast to the capitulators, Trotsky continued to analyse the turn from the point of view of his theory of bureaucracy. In doing so, he reiterated much of his argument from the previous year.

Shortly after his arrival in Turkey, Trotsky wrote a series of articles for the international press in which he described his deportation from the Soviet Union and reported 'new arrests – of several hundred people, including 150 members of a so-called "Trotskyist center" '. According to Trotsky, this provided clear evidence that, despite the official struggle against the right, 'for Stalin the main enemy remains, as before, the left'. He asserted that all these events confirmed his view that the main objective behind the most recent campaign against the right was to prepare for a new assault on the left. Beyond that, he argued that Stalin had felt compelled to take these actions in response to the noticeable growth of the Opposition, 'especially at major industrial plants'.[149]

However, after his first few weeks in Turkey, most of Trotsky's writings about Soviet events were devoted to the struggle within the leadership and the deepening of the turn. In the spring of 1929 Trotsky recognised that the rightists within the party leadership had been defeated.[150] At the same time he concluded that the shift in industrial policy had brought Stalin at least 'outwardly closer to the Opposition', and by the autumn he was describing the new Comintern orientation as a 'sharp turn'.[151] Nevertheless, he continued to downplay the significance of these developments, despite the fact that both the struggle against the right and the policy shifts had gone much further than in 1928. For example, in an article written on 14 June for his new journal *Biulleten' oppozitsii*, he described the crushing of the right as 'sharp in form but superficial in content', and in an October letter to Soviet Oppositionists he spoke of the 'shrill, theatrical, harsh but not deep-going, break [of the Stalinists] with the right wing'.[152] In a 31 March letter he rejected assertions by party moderates that Stalin had adopted the Opposition's economic program, insisting that Stalin had 'made use of slivers of the Opposition's program', nothing more.[153] Then, in an open letter to Oppositionists on 25 September he described the new Comintern line as a 'combination of ultraleft conclusions with Right

---

149   Trotsky 1975c, pp. 31, 48–9, 25. See also Trotsky 1975c, pp. 60–2.
150   See, for example, Trotsky 1975c, pp. 67, 162.
151   Trotsky 1975c, pp. 85, 328. See also Trotsky 1975c, pp. 56, 367, 376.
152   Trotsky 1975c, pp. 162, 359. See also Trotsky 1975c, pp. 109, 327.
153   Trotsky 1975c, pp. 84–5.

principles', and observed that it departed 'no less, probably, from the Leninist line' than when it had backed alliances with the Guomindang and the Anglo-Russian Committee.[154]

Trotsky's scepticism continued to be grounded in his commitment to basic tenets of the theory of bureaucracy he had developed in previous years. As far as the Stalinist assault upon the party moderates was concerned, there was little reason for him to dismiss it as abruptly as he did except that it was difficult for his theory to accommodate a real struggle by the centrists against the right. Furthermore, Trotsky's theory suggested that the worsening of the regime that would accompany an organisational campaign by the centrists would ultimately strengthen the forces of the right. Consequently, in his October letter to Oppositionists, Trotsky observed that the Stalinist repression of the right was drawing 'the noose tighter around the neck of the party and the trade unions'. In his view this outweighed the 'positive features' of the struggle.[155]

As far as the new policies were concerned, Trotsky offered a variety of explanations for his critical attitude. Already he had begun to criticise some of these policies, such as the use of 'administrative pressure' against the kulaks and the rejection of alliances with 'social fascists', as ultraleft in character.[156] At the same time he complained that both economic and international policy continued to be grounded in the opportunist perspective of socialism in one country.[157] However, the character of the party regime remained the most important reason for his scepticism. Consistent with his theory, Trotsky again asserted that a healthy, democratic regime was both the best indicator of a correct line and the only guarantee that it would be maintained. Thus, when Radek, Smilga, and Preobrazhenskii asserted that the 'concrete figures of the five-year plan' expressed a programme of socialist construction, Trotsky reminded them,

> The central question is not the figures of the bureaucratic five-year plan themselves but the question of the party as the main weapon of the

154   Trotsky 1975c, p. 328.

155   Trotsky 1975c, p. 359. See also Trotsky 1975c, pp. 109–10, 184.

156   Even in the summer of 1928 Trotsky criticised the 'measures of administrative violence' and the 'emergency methods from the arsenal of war communism' that had been used against the kulaks (Trotsky 1981, p. 168; Trotsky 1970b, p. 279). In September of 1929 he spoke of the 'gradations from open opportunism to ultraleftism' in the new Comintern policy (Trotsky 1981, p. 258). For Trotsky's 1929 remark on the use of 'administrative pressure' against the kulaks, see Trotsky 1975c, p. 376. For his criticisms in 1929 of the ultraleft character of Comintern policy, see Trotsky 1975c, pp. 171–3, 223, 230, 328, 391–3.

157   See Trotsky 1975c, pp. 84–5, 233, 327–8.

proletariat. The party regime is not something autonomous: it expresses and reinforces the party's political line.[158]

More specifically, he evaluated the policy shifts again in terms of the treatment of the Opposition. In a 25 September letter to Oppositionists who had signed Rakovskii's declaration, he asserted that if all important differences between the Opposition and the leadership had been resolved, as Radek and Preobrazhenskii asserted, then the repression of the Opposition was nothing more than 'naked bureaucratic banditry'. But Trotsky was no more willing to accept that conclusion than were the capitulators. Instead, he insisted that the persecution demonstrated that the leadership, even after absorbing many of the Opposition's tactical positions, still maintained 'the *strategic* principles from which yesterday's right-center tactic emerged'.[159]

Nevertheless, to the degree that Trotsky recognised that the turn in economic and Comintern policy was deepening, he was compelled to account for it. Again, his explanation was based on the view that only the proletariat or the Opposition could initiate a turn to the left. At times, he argued that the *entire* left turn since early 1928 was one single process set in motion by proletarian/Oppositional pressure.[160] However, on a number of occasions he explicitly asserted that the *latest edition* of the turn was a direct result of continuing Oppositional pressure. For example, in an October letter to exiled Oppositionists he wrote that 'it was precisely our criticism that forced and is still forcing the centrists to go further left than they originally intended to go'.[161] And in November he explained to Oppositionists that 'every week "the master" [Stalin] threatens his Klims [Voroshilovs] with the words: "We can't deviate to the right just now – that is just what the Trotskyists are waiting for" '.[162]

Trotsky's belief that external pressure was required for any shift to the left by the leadership also continued to govern his approach to the tasks of the Opposition. Once more he urged his supporters to redouble their efforts to push the Stalinists leftwards. In July Trotsky appealed to his wavering comrades: 'The centrists will move over to the left only under our whip. That is why there is no reason to give up the whip in our hands. On the contrary, we have

---

158   Trotsky 1975c, p. 202. For other cases in which Trotsky evaluated the five-year plan in terms of the overall degree of democracy in the party, Trotsky 1975c, pp. 359–60, 376–7.

159   Trotsky 1975c, p. 327. See also Trotsky 1975c, pp. 135–6; Trotsky 1969, p. 134.

160   For this argument in relation to the turn in economic policy and the struggle against the party right, see Trotsky 1975c, pp. 109, 162, 251, 280, 281, 367. For this argument regarding Comintern policy, see Trotsky 1975c, p. 229.

161   Trotsky 1979a, p. 19.

162   Trotsky 1975c, p. 398. See also Trotsky 1975c, pp. 136, 200.

to use three whips'.[163] Conversely, he was convinced that every capitulation of an Oppositionist actually weakened the left turn. Consequently, when Preobrazhenskii and Radek justified their recantations in terms of a desire to assist the party's turn and struggle against the right, Trotsky responded that the wholesale capitulation of the Opposition would mean not only 'condemning ourselves to a Zinovievist vegetable existence', but would also result in 'an immediate swerving of the Stalinists to the right'.[164] Similarly, in November he explained to an Oppositionist who was considering capitulation, 'If the Opposition were to disappear, the Voroshilovs and their cronies would tomorrow climb into the saddle on the backs of the left centrists'.[165]

5.7   Revising the Theory

As far as his general theory of Soviet bureaucracy was concerned, throughout 1928–9 Trotsky's primary concern was to apply and defend the analysis he had developed in previous years, even when that required highly strained interpretations of events. However, as we have seen, in late 1928 the successes of the Stalinist against the party right also compelled him to revise his theory implicitly by emphasising the capacity of the apparatus to act independently of class pressures. During the years 1928–9 a number of additional developments, influences, challenges, and opportunities induced him to alter and elaborate upon his theory in other ways as well – most of which also tended to emphasise the autonomy of the bureaucracy.[166]

---

163 Trotsky 1975c, p. 211. See also Trotsky 1975c, pp. 398, 399.

164 Trotsky 1975c, p. 136. See also Trotsky 1975c, p. 201.

165 Trotsky 1975c, p. 398. Although Trotsky was adamant in rejecting capitulation, he tentatively endorsed, as a tactical manoeuvre, Rakovskii's conciliatory declaration to the Central Committee in August 1929. For Trotsky's comments on this declaration, see Trotsky 1975c, pp. 325–8, 340–4, 358–61, 397, 400; Trotsky 1979a, p. 19.

166 Important theoretical statements on the problem of bureaucracy can be found scattered throughout Trotsky's books, articles, interviews, and correspondence during late 1928 and 1929. However, the most important sources for statements of his revised theory in these years include his article 'Crisis in the Right-Center Bloc', written in November 1928; a series of articles entitled *Chto i kak proizoshlo?*, written for the international press in February 1929; a 1 May 1929 preface to a collection of his oppositional writings published in France under the title *La Révolution Defigureé*; and his autobiography, completed in the summer of 1929.

5.7.1   *Conception*

In the party struggle of 1926–7 Trotsky commonly had denounced the bureau-cratism that had infected the organisational apparatuses of the party, state, etc. However, during that struggle he also began to condemn the 'bureaucracies' within all of those institutions, or the 'bureaucracy' viewed as a single social layer, that had usurped power within all of them. Over the course of 1928–9 Trotsky essentially completed this terminological and conceptual shift.

Although he still spoke at times of 'bureaucratism', with increasing fre-quency he now denounced the 'bureaucracy' or the 'bureaucratic apparatus', especially within the party.[167] For example, in his November 1928 article 'Crisis in the Right-Center Bloc' he asserted that the party line had slid 'from the [pro-letarian] class to the apparatus [*apparat*], that is, to the bureaucracy [*biurokratiia*]'.[168] Similarly, in 'Where Is the Soviet Revolution Going?', written in February 1929, he anticipated a new party purge, not only of ' "Trotskyists" ', but also 'of the most degenerate elements within the bureaucracy [*biurokratiia*]'.[169] It is clear that Trotsky's concern now was less with the devel-opment of oppressive tendencies within the various apparatuses, and more with the autonomy of the apparatuses themselves.

No doubt, a number of factors were responsible for this shift. In part, it was a continuation of a process that began in 1926–7. The previous chapter sug-gested that at least one reason Trotsky first substituted the term *bureaucracy* for *bureaucratism* was that he came to view the problem of political alienation as so deeply embedded within the apparatuses that it seemed inseparable from them. If that was the case, then subsequent developments that indicated a worsening of political alienation, such as the exile of the Opposition and his own expulsion from the country, could only have reinforced this perception. Besides that, in the autumn of 1928 he was surprised by the organisational suc-cesses of the Stalinists against the party right. From this, he concluded that the party apparatus was capable of acting far more independently than he previ-ously believed possible – that is, as a relatively autonomous bureaucracy.

At the same time, Trotsky also increasingly employed the term *bureaucracy* not just in reference to each separate apparatus, but as a label for the single social entity that he believed had assumed power. Of course, he continued to distinguish between the different organisational apparatuses when that dis-

---

167   For continuing references to 'bureaucratism', see, for example: Trotsky 1981, pp. 245, 391; Trotsky 1995, p. 172; Fel'shtinskii 1999–2002, vol. 3: 2, p. 150; Trotsky 1975c, pp. 40, 81, 171; Trotsky 1929a, p. 31; *Biulleten' oppozitsii* 1973, 1–2 (July 1929), pp. 21, 35.

168   Trotsky 1981, p. 313; Fel'shtinskii 1999–2002, vol. 3: 2, p. 128 (translation modified).

169   Trotsky 1975c, p. 48 (where the article title is mistaken); Trotsky 1929a, p. 42.

tinction was relevant.[170] But more and more frequently he utilised the singular *bureaucracy* for the combined apparatuses of the party, state, etc. Thus, in a letter to the Democratic Centralist Borodai in November 1928 he asserted that the proletariat could 'regain full power, overhaul the bureaucracy [*biurokratiia*], and put it under its control by way of party and soviet reform'.[171] In December, in his essay 'Philosophical Tendencies of Bureaucratism', after describing the degeneration of the trade unions, party, state, etc., he characterised the situation as one in which a 'bureaucratic hierarchy [*biurokraticheshkaia ierarkhiia*]..., with all its ministries and departments', had 'raised itself over above society'.[172]

Here too, various factors may have contributed to the change. One was Trotsky's perception that the hierarchies of the various apparatuses shared personnel and similarities in outlook, and all participated in the repression of workers' democracy.[173] At the same time, Trotsky's thinking on this question was clearly influenced by the analysis of bureaucracy put forward in this period by his friend Khristian Rakovskii in his now famous 'Letter to Valentinov'. On 8 August 1928 in a letter to a fellow Oppositionist, Rakovskii traced the emergence of a single 'soviet-party bureaucracy [*sovetskaia partiinaia biurokratiia, sov-partbiurokratiia*]' or 'party-soviet bureaucracy [*part-sovetskaia biurokratiia*]' in the Soviet Union after the revolution.[174] Trotsky clearly was impressed by Rakovskii's contribution. In a letter of 18 September he described Rakovskii's letter as 'exceptionally interesting and significant' and suggested

---

170   For example, in a letter written in November 1928 Trotsky observed, 'There is no doubt that the degeneration of the Soviet apparatus [*sovetskii apparat*] is considerably more advanced than the same process in the party apparatus [*partinyi apparat*]' (Trotsky 1981, p. 293; Trotsky 1995, p. 224). Also, he sometimes used the unspecified term *bureaucracy* when referring exclusively to the party apparatus. See, for example, Trotsky 1981, p. 313; Trotsky 1975c, p. 48.

171   Trotsky 1981, p. 295; Trotsky 1995, p. 225 (translation modified). See also Trotsky's reference to the 'party-soviet bureaucracy [*partiino-sovetskaia biurokratiia*]' the same month in Trotsky 1981, p. 314; Fel'shtinskii, vol. 3: 2, p. 129.

172   Trotsky 1981, pp. 391, 392; Fel'shtinskii, vol. 3: 2, p. 151. See also Trotsky 1975c, p. 77; *Biulleten' oppozitsii* 1973, 1–2 (July 1929), p. 4; Trotsky 1970c, p. 505; Trotsky 1991b, pp. 476, 479.

173   Consistent with this view, in a 1 May 1929 preface to a collection of his oppositional writings entitled *La révolution défigurée*, he described the 'interlocking system' formed by the functionaries of the state, the trade unions, etc. 'Ultimately', he asserted, 'the party functionaries should be counted among them as well, inasmuch as they form a definitely constituted caste, which assures its own permanence more through the state apparatus than by internal party means' (Trotsky 1975c, p. 118). The original French also uses the term *caste* (Trotsky 1929b, p. 10). See also Trotsky 1981, p. 293.

174   Rakovsky 1980, pp. 131, 132; Rakovsky 1973, pp. 17, 18.

that it had mapped out 'for investigation some topics of exceptional importance'.[175] In his November article 'Crisis in the Right-Center Bloc' he echoed Rakovskii in describing the combined apparatuses as the 'party-soviet bureaucracy [*partiino-sovetskaia biurokratiia*]'.[176] Then, in a February 1929 article for the international press, he spoke approvingly of the 'remarkable letter dealing with the phenomenon of degeneration' in which Rakovskii had 'shown in a very striking fashion that, after the conquest of power, an independent bureaucracy [*samostoiatel'naia biurokratiia*] differentiated itself out from the working-class milieu'.[177]

Whatever the reasons, these terminological and conceptual changes carried important implications for Trotsky's theoretical perspective. From this point onwards, Trotsky defined the problem not as a disease infecting various institutions, but as a single social layer that had usurped power throughout the country. In turn, this raised questions related to the source of the problem, including: how had this bureaucracy arisen, what was its role in Soviet society, and how was it able to wrest power from the proletariat? At the same time, Trotsky's reformulation of the issue inspired new explorations of the characteristics of the problem, including examinations of the distinctive features of the bureaucracy as a social layer.

5.7.2 *Causes*

In his account of the origins of the problem, even more clearly than in his definition of it, Trotsky's thinking was influenced by Rakovskii's 'Letter to Valentinov'. In that letter Rakovskii offered his own explanation for the rise of despotism, corruption, and scandal within Soviet political institutions, and for the passivity of the Soviet masses. Rakovskii agreed with Trotsky that these developments were related to factors such as the shifting balance of class forces and the international isolation of the Soviet Union. However, he argued that such explanations were inadequate, for the same 'difficulties would continue to exist up to a certain point, even if we allowed, for a moment, that the country was inhabited only by proletarian masses and the exterior was made up solely of proletarian states'. Rather, the root of the problem was that 'any new directing class' encounters 'inherent difficulties' that could be described as 'the "professional dangers" of power'.[178]

Rakovskii explained that, although an insurgent class is bound together by the great aim of revolution during a revolutionary offensive, this cohesion

---

175   Trotsky 1981, p. 261.
176   Trotsky 1981, p. 314; Fel'shtinskii 1999–2002, vol. 3: 2, p. 129 (translation modified).
177   Trotsky 1975c, p. 47; Trotsky 1929a, p. 40.
178   Rakovsky 1980, p. 125.

begins to dissolve as soon as the class takes power. Some of its members assume political and administrative responsibilities and constitute themselves into a bureaucracy in order to address the new tasks of power: 'In a socialist state, where capitalist accumulation is forbidden by members of the directing party, this differentiation begins as a functional one; it later becomes a social one'.[179] At the same time, functions previously exercised by the revolutionary class or party as a whole become 'attributes of power'. According to Rakovskii, both processes occur because the revolutionary class is always uneducated and politically inexperienced. Although Rakovskii agreed with Trotsky that the French Revolution provided the classic model of revolutionary degeneration, the pattern he discerned differed somewhat from that previously described by Trotsky. According to Trotsky, the Thermidorian degeneration in France involved the transfer of class power from the revolutionary *sans-culottes* to the bourgeoisie. For Rakovskii, 'the political reaction which began even before Thermidor consisted *in this, that the power began to pass both formally and effectively into the hands of an increasingly restricted number of citizens*'.[180]

Applying this analysis to the Soviet experience, Rakovskii argued that the conquest of power had introduced a functional differentiation into the proletariat. As a result, the psychology of the officials of the state apparatus had 'changed to such a point that ... they have ceased to be a part of this very same working class'. Meanwhile, 'the same differentiation' had occurred in the party, leading to the creation of a combined party-state apparatus that was so autonomous that the 'bureaucracy [*biurokratiia*] of the soviets and of the party constitutes a new order'.[181]

For Rakovskii, this image of a highly autonomous bureaucracy helped to explain the leadership's turn of early 1928. In fact, it is likely that he developed his theory largely in response to the turn. He rejected the view put forward by the conciliator Ishchenko, but also articulated by Trotsky, that 'the collection of the wheat and the self-criticism are due to the proletarian resistance of the party'. Rakovskii argued,

> Unfortunately it has to be said that this is not correct. These two facts result from a combination arranged in high places and are not due to the pressure of the workers' criticism; it is for political reasons and sometimes for group reasons, or should I say faction, that a part of the top men in the party pursue this line. It is possible to speak of only one proletarian

179   Rakovsky 1980, p. 126; Rakovsky 1973, p. 15.
180   Rakovsky 1980, pp. 126–7.
181   Rakovsky 1980, pp. 130, 131; Rakovsky 1973, p. 17.

pressure – that guided by the opposition. But it has to be clearly said, this pressure has not been sufficient to maintain the opposition inside the party; more, it has not succeeded in changing its political line.[182]

Despite this difference on the origin of the turn, Trotsky was impressed with Rakovskii's analysis. In fact, he immediately adopted portions of it, combining them with his own account of the process of bureaucratisation. As in the past, Trotsky continued to assert that the problem of political alienation had arisen *primarily* as a consequence of class shifts in the Soviet Union since the civil war. For example, in one of his February 1929 articles for the international press, he attributed Stalin's victory over the Opposition to the 'significant shifts that have occurred in class relations in the revolutionary society'.[183] Similarly, in his 1 May 1929 preface to *La révolution défigurée* he explained that in the 'second period' of the revolution since Lenin's death the proletariat 'was pushed aside, forced into the background, as a result of a series of objective and subjective factors of both an internal and external nature'.[184]

However, at this point Rakovskii's influence became apparent. First, Trotsky accepted Rakovskii's argument that the proletariat had lost power in part because it was poorly prepared to rule. In his preface to *La révolution défigurée* he asserted that, because of 'centuries of oppression', the proletariat possessed 'neither historical traditions of rule, nor, even less, an instinct for power'.[185] More importantly, he accepted Rakovskii's view that the administrative apparatuses of Soviet institutions had actively promoted and directly benefited from the reaction following the revolution. In his February article 'Where Is the Soviet Revolution Going?' he explained how in the second period,

> Over and above the masses the centralized administrative apparatus [*apparat*] rises higher and higher ... The apparatus acquires a more and more self-sufficient character. The government official is increasingly filled with the conviction that the October Revolution was made precisely in order to concentrate power in his hands and assure him a privileged position.[186]

Finally, Trotsky also adopted Rakovskii's explanation of how the bureaucracy had taken shape in the first place. In his 'Crisis in the Right-Center Bloc' in

182 Rakovsky 1980, pp. 132–3.
183 Trotsky 1975c, p. 43.
184 Trotsky 1975c, p. 118.
185 Trotsky 1975c, p. 121.
186 Trotsky 1975c, pp. 46–7; Trotsky 1929a, p. 39. See also Trotsky 1975c, p. 118.

November 1928 he endorsed Rakovskii's argument that during the period of reaction after the revolution, 'differentiation [within the proletariat] set in with a bureaucracy [*biurokratiia*] emerging at the top and acting more and more in its own interests'.[187] Again, in his article 'Where Is the Soviet Revolution Going?' he repeated that an 'independent bureaucracy [*samostoiatel'naia biurokratiia*] differentiated itself out from the working-class milieu'. Furthermore, he noted that Rakovskii had shown that the differentiation 'at first only functional, ... later became social'.[188] In later years he would elaborate upon this idea at length.

However, commenting that 'naturally, the processes within the bureaucracy developed in relation to the very profound processes under way in the country', Trotsky quickly reverted to his previous class explanation. Parallel with the emerging independence of the bureaucracy from the working class, he argued, bourgeois and petty bourgeois elements in the Soviet Union had accumulated economic and political power. Increasingly, 'broad sections of officialdom [*chinovnichestvo*] ... drew close to the bourgeois strata and established family ties with them'.[189] A large section of the party-state bureaucracy grew responsive to bourgeois pressures and was ultimately transformed into 'the effective agent of bourgeois conceptions and expectations'.[190] In the process, the bureaucracy came to perceive popular initiative and criticism as interference, and began to exert pressure against the masses.[191]

5.7.3   *Characteristics*
As Trotsky shifted from defining the problem of bureaucratism as a disease to perceiving the bureaucracy as a thing, he also increasingly emphasised features he saw as characteristic of the bureaucracy as a social formation. Foremost among these were a number of attitudes and moral-psychological traits that emerged as the bureaucracy first began to differentiate itself from the proletariat.

Perhaps the most important attitude viewed by Trotsky as typical of the bureaucracy was the preoccupation of its members with privilege and power. As David Law has suggested, the exposure in early 1928 of various cases of corruption, such as those involved in the Smolensk affair, helped to focus Trotsky's attention on the issue of material privilege.[192] In a discussion of these scandals

---

187   Trotsky 1981, p. 305; Fel'shtinskii 1999–2002, vol. 3: 2, p. 120.

188   Trotsky 1975c, p. 47; Trotsky 1929a, p. 40.

189   Trotsky 1975c, p. 47; Trotsky 1929a, p. 40.

190   Trotsky 1975c, p. 118. See also Trotsky 1975c, pp. 47, 119–21.

191   Trotsky 1975c, p. 47.

192   Law 1987a, p. 324.

in one of the documents he submitted to the Comintern in June 1928, Trotsky noted the 'great encrustations of interests and connections around the apparatus'.[193] By 1929 he had begun to view privilege and power as the central preoccupations of the bureaucracy. In February he described how during the early 1920s the Soviet government official became increasingly convinced that the revolution had been made 'precisely in order to concentrate power in his hands and assure him a privileged position'.[194] Similarly, in his autobiography he asserted that, over time, 'the stratum that made up the apparatus of power developed its own independent aims and tried to subordinate the revolution to them'.[195]

Closely related to this preoccupation for Trotsky was the general loosening of moral standards within the bureaucracy. Again, the importance of this issue seems to have been suggested by the revelations in early 1928 of chronic drunkenness, promiscuity, and sexual exploitation by party officials in Smolensk and other cities.[196] In one of his statements to the Comintern in June 1928, Trotsky asked,

> Who is the hero, in the social sense of the term, of the Artemovsk, Smolensk, etc. affairs? He is a bureaucrat who has freed himself from the active control of the party and who has ceased to be the banner-bearer of the proletarian dictatorship. Ideologically, he has become drained; morally, he is unrestrained. He is a privileged and an irresponsible functionary, in most cases very uncultured, a drunkard, a wastrel, and a bully.[197]

In his 1929 autobiography Trotsky recalled how the decline of moral standards became typical within the bureaucracy as a whole during the 'second period' of the revolution. Although he noted that many members of the apparatus had devoted themselves selflessly to the revolution in the early years of the revolution, in the period of reaction, 'the sympathies and tastes of self-satisfied officials revived in them'. The prevalent outlook became one 'of moral relaxation, of self-content and triviality'. Members of the bureaucracy increasingly amused themselves with 'philistine gossip' and 'vulgarity', and grew especially fond of visiting one another, attending the ballet, and drinking parties. In the presence

---

193   Trotsky 1970b, p. 305.
194   Trotsky 1975c, p. 47.
195   Trotsky 1970c, p. 502. See also Trotsky 1975c, p. 77.
196   In part, he was also probably influenced by Rakovskii's and Sosnovskii's discussion of this theme. See Rakovsky 1980, pp. 126, 128.
197   Trotsky 1970b, p. 303. See Law 1987a, p. 324.

of Bolsheviks such as Trotsky who would not share their new interests, they displayed shame and resentment.[198]

5.7.4   Consequences

For years Trotsky and the Opposition had predicted that the rightward drift of policy combined with the steady deterioration of the party and state regimes might result in capitalist restoration. In 1928–9 Trotsky continued to defend this view, not only against Oppositionists who now concluded that these fears had been exaggerated, but also against those on his left who believed they had been realised. In response to the latter, Trotsky put forward a number of arguments to demonstrate that the class nature of the Soviet state had not yet changed fundamentally. Beyond that, he asserted that the left turn actually had reduced the likelihood of restoration. Nevertheless, in this period he remained convinced that, without profound party and state reform, restoration was inevitable.

In 1928 and 1929 the defeat of the Opposition convinced some left-wing communists both within the Soviet Union and abroad that a Thermidor already had occurred and that the counterrevolution had triumphed. The first to raise these views were members of the Democratic Centralist group in the USSR. In October 1928, the Democratic Centralist Borodai wrote to Trotsky from exile in Tiumen demanding an admission that the party and state had 'degenerated', that the dictatorship of the proletariat had ceased to exist, and that the situation within the party and the proceedings of the recent Comintern congress were evidence of a 'Thermidor with a dry guillotine'.[199] The following year Trotsky encountered similar arguments from Hugo Urbahns, leader of the Leninbund, a German Zinovievist organisation of several thousand members.[200] Urbahns declared that Trotsky's expulsion from the Soviet Union constituted an event analogous to the guillotining of Robespierre and his followers, implying that the dictatorship of the proletariat had been replaced by a Thermidorian bourgeois state.[201] Against these challenges, Trotsky advanced a number of arguments he would reiterate frequently in the following years to

---

198   Trotsky 1970c, p. 504.

199   Trotsky 1981, pp. 292, 293, 294, 297.

200   On the Leninbund, see Alexander 1991, pp. 407–11.

201   Trotsky 1975c, pp. 247, 282–3, 287–8, 314. Although apparently all of these positions were developed in unsigned articles in the press of the Leninbund, Trotsky assumed they were the positions of Urbahns who seems to have run that organisation in an authoritarian manner. See Trotsky 1975c, p. 273; and Alfred Rosmer's remarks about Urbahns, quoted in Alexander 1991, p. 410.

demonstrate that the Soviet state remained ultimately proletarian, despite the degeneration that had occurred.

First, Trotsky insisted that the party leadership's recent left turn demonstrated that its political line could be corrected by proletarian pressure. As he explained to Borodai, 'The functionary of the party, the trade unions, and other institutions,...in spite of everything,...depends upon the working masses and seems to be obliged in recent times to take these masses into account more and more'. For Trotsky, this clearly indicated that the proletariat was still able to 'regain full power, overhaul the bureaucracy' by reform of the party and soviets. At least to that extent, then, the proletariat had not yet lost political power.[202] In September 1929 Trotsky employed the same line of reasoning in a response to Urbahns. In his article 'Defense of the Soviet Republic and the Opposition', he observed that over the previous two years, 'Stalin found himself driven, simultaneously with the crushing of the Left Opposition, to plagiarise partially from its program in all fields, to direct his fire to the right, and to convert an internal party maneuver into a very sharp and prolonged zigzag to the left'. For Trotsky, this demonstrated that 'the proletariat still possesses powers to exert pressure and that the state apparatus still remains dependent on it'.[203]

Trotsky's second argument for the persistence of workers' power in the Soviet Union was based on the Bolshevik axiom that the transfer of class power was only possible through civil war. Trotsky first sketched this line of reasoning his November 1928 letter to Borodai. After asserting that the Soviet situation was characterised by growing elements of dual power, he observed,

> A condition of dual power is unstable, by its very essence. Sooner or later, it must go one way or the other. But as the situation is now, the bourgeoisie could seize power only by *the road of counterrevolutionary upheaval.*[204]

He developed the same idea more fully in his September 1929 polemic against Urbahns. There, he enumerated again the advantages of the Russian Revolution over the French: a larger, more homogeneous and resolute revolutionary class; a 'more experienced and perspicacious' leadership; and far deeper political,

202   Trotsky 1981, pp. 296, 295. Along these lines, Max Shachtman later argued that in his letter to Borodai, Trotsky's decisive criterion for a 'workers' state' was *'Does the working class still have political power, in one sense or another, even if only in the sense that it is still capable of bringing a straying and dangerous bureaucracy under its control by means of reform measures'?* (Shachtman 1962, p. 92).
203   Trotsky 1975c, p. 280.
204   Trotsky 1981, p. 295.

economic, and cultural changes. Given these advantages, he reasoned, how could the Russian Revolution be defeated peacefully when the French Thermidor had required a civil war? For Trotsky, such a conception of Thermidor was nothing but *'inverted reformism'*.[205]

Trotsky's third argument for the proletarian character of the Soviet state was based on property relations in the USSR. According to Trotsky, in the aftermath of Thermidor a new capitalist state would abolish the property forms introduced by the Bolshevik Revolution.[206] The fact that this had not happened indicated that the counterrevolution had not yet triumphed. It is noteworthy that this argument did not appear in his response to Borodai. According to Max Shachtman, that absence indicates that the economic criterion was relatively unimportant to Trotsky in this period.[207] However, it is at least as likely that he did not raise the issue because Borodai was claiming that the Russian Thermidor had occurred less than a year before. If that was the case, a Thermidorian state might not yet have had time to overturn property relations. At any rate, Trotsky forcefully articulated this argument the following year, insisting that 'ultraleftists' such as Urbahns focused all of their attention on the damaged 'shell' of the revolution while ignoring the surviving 'socio-economic kernel of the Soviet republic':

> The means of production, once the property of the capitalists, remain to this very day in the hands of the Soviet state. The land is nationalized. The exploiting elements are still excluded from the soviets and from the army. The monopoly of foreign trade remains a bulwark against the economic intervention of capitalism. All these are not trifles.[208]

From this Trotsky concluded that, despite its crimes and blunders, Soviet centrism still defended 'the social system that originated from the political and economic expropriation of the bourgeoisie'.[209]

Beyond arguing that counterrevolution had not yet triumphed, by 1929 Trotsky was insisting that the danger of restoration actually had diminished. As we have seen, his fear of imminent Thermidor began to subside in late 1928 in response to the Stalinist offensive against the party right. In 1929 he was further reassured by Stalin's victory over the moderates. In 'Defense of

---

205   Trotsky 1975c, pp. 283–4.

206   See, for example, Trotsky 1970b, p. 300.

207   Shachtman 1962, p. 93.

208   Trotsky 1975c, p. 284. See also Trotsky 1975c, pp. 54–5.

209   Trotsky 1975c, p. 286. In 1929 Trotsky also exposed a number of internal contradictions he perceived in the position of Urbahns. See Trotsky 1975c, pp. 248, 287, 289–92.

the Soviet Republic and the Opposition' he explained, 'By the power of its attack, the Opposition has forced the centrists to deliver a number of blows ... to the Thermidorean class forces and the tendencies that reflect them inside the party'.[210]

Nevertheless, Trotsky remained convinced that the return of capitalism was inevitable unless the proletariat succeeded in reforming the party.[211] In fact, even while noting Stalin's blows against the right in his article of 7 September, he stressed that these were 'of course by no means mortal and far from decisive', and warned that the classes had 'not yet spoken their final word'. In the same article he again emphasised the danger of capitalist restoration by reaffirming his characterisation of Stalinism as 'inverted Kerenskyism', and explaining that 'ruling centrism is, on the road to Thermidor, the *last* form of the rule of the proletariat'.[212] Similarly, in his letter to Soviet Oppositionists written in October, he asserted that the right was still strong enough within the apparatus that 'at the first serious push by the elemental Thermidorean mass, not only Bukharin and Rykov but, even before them, Kalinin, Voroshilov, and Rudzutak would overturn the Stalinists' if they tried to resist.[213]

5.7.5   *Cure*

A final area of change during this period was in Trotsky's understanding of how the problem of bureaucracy could be corrected. Despite Stalinist accusations to the contrary, in the years 1928–9 Trotsky continued to advocate a strategy of reform, not revolution. In his letter to Borodai in November 1928 he insisted that efforts for 'reviving and consolidating the October Revolution and the dictatorship of the proletariat' had not yet been 'tried to the very end'.[214] Explaining this perspective in his September 1929 polemic against Urbahns, he asserted that the left 'zigzag' had demonstrated that 'the proletariat still possesses powers to exert pressure and that the state apparatus remains dependent on it'. On this basis he concluded that it was necessary for the Russian Opposition to

---

210   Trotsky 1975c, p. 284.

211   In contrast, Robert McNeal – echoing Deutscher's claim that Trotsky abandoned his conception of Thermidor in October 1928 – has argued that in 1929 Trotsky was 'sufficiently impressed by the leftward swing of the Stalin régime to drop the matter [of Thermidor and Bonapartism] temporarily' (McNeal 1961, p. 92; McNeal 1966, p. 148).

212   Trotsky 1975c, p. 287. See also Trotsky 1975c, pp. 118, 122.

213   Trotsky 1975c, p. 359. On the prospect of Thermidor, see also Trotsky 1975c, pp. 49–51, 59, 199, 233, 338, 360–1, 400. As in the past, Trotsky continued to argue that a Soviet Thermidor would be followed quickly by the installation of a Bonapartist or even a 'fascist-imperialist' regime (Trotsky 1975c, pp. 56, 57, 279, 323, 338).

214   Trotsky 1981, p. 294.

maintain its strategy of reform.[215] Similarly, in an October 1929 letter to the Soviet Opposition published in the *Bulletin* after the Kosior Okudzhava-Rakovskii declaration was rejected by Iaroslavskii, Trotsky argued that 'our line remains as before the line of reform'.[216]

However, Trotsky quickly added that 'we are not ready to fight for these reforms within the limits of legality that Stalin and Yaroslavsky, in their struggle for self-preservation, constantly narrow'. In particular, he insisted that Bolshevik-Leninists needed to increase their efforts to organise as a 'faction within communism'.[217] In their conciliatory declaration Rakovskii et al. had reasserted the position that 'the existence of factions among communists, irrespective of whether they are inside the party or outside its legal boundaries, is always harmful'.[218] Trotsky was not yet prepared to criticise the original Bolshevik ban on factions. But by 1929 the expulsion of the Opposition and its subsequent failure to achieve readmission had convinced him that now it was appropriate and legitimate for the Opposition to organise and publicly identify itself as a disciplined party faction, fighting for party and state reform. This was the case even though the majority of the Opposition now found itself formally outside the party's 'legal boundaries'.[219]

By late 1929 Trotsky also had concluded that the only way the Opposition would be able to accomplish reform was through a major party crisis. No doubt, his pessimism in this regard represented a reaction to the defeat of the Opposition, and perhaps also to the recent wave of capitulations. According to Trotsky, the most likely form such a crisis would take would be a renewed attempt by Thermidorians to restore capitalism. He observed in his letter to Oppositionists in October,

> Short of a party crisis of the most profound kind, which would in all likelihood be the result of a subterranean push by the Thermidorean forces, a transition to a new stage is, unfortunately, no longer conceivable. Such a new stage could be either a stage of revival or the Thermidor stage. A party crisis would be accompanied by a new crystallization of the Bolshevik Party out of the present apparatus-stifled ideological chaos.[220]

---

215   Trotsky 1975c, p. 280. See also Trotsky 1975c, pp. 57, 75, 340.

216   Trotsky 1975c, p. 344.

217   Ibid. See also Trotsky 1975c, p. 361.

218   Rakovsky 1980, p. 144.

219   Thus, John Marot is mistaken in asserting that Trotsky 'did not abandon the politics of "non-factionalism" until 1933' (Marot 2006, p. 188).

220   Trotsky 1975c, p. 360.

A further development in Trotsky's reform strategy during 1929 was his redefinition of the Opposition as an international current. As we have noted, during Trotsky's first weeks and months abroad he began to establish contact with groups of international supporters, most of whom had been expelled from their own Communist parties in recent years.[221] From the beginning, it was clear that Trotsky envisioned that these groups would play a role in relation to their own parties analogous to the role played by the Soviet Opposition *vis-à-vis* the AUCP. Just as Trotsky rejected the idea of forming a new party in the Soviet Union, he similarly dismissed as 'utter rubbish' the idea that he would attempt to organise his international supporters into a 'Fourth International' rivaling the Comintern. As he explained to a Japanese correspondent in April and again to his American supporters in May, the Opposition had no intention of surrendering the banner of the Comintern, for it had been Stalin, not the Opposition, who had abandoned its principles. Besides, he again insisted, centrism was inherently unstable and would soon be 'ground away between the millstones of social democracy and communism'.[222] Instead, Trotsky now characterised the Left Opposition as an 'international ideological current' that was preparing to transform itself into a more disciplined 'international faction' of the Comintern. Its purpose was to work for the reform of Communist parties and Comintern, much as the Soviet Opposition was working for the reform of the AUCP and the Comintern.[223] In line with this, he stressed the need to begin to elaborate an international platform that could 'serve as a bridge' to a future Comintern programme. Optimistically, he explained that it was 'absolutely self-evident' that a regenerated Comintern would require a new programme.[224]

In the meantime, he stressed the need for clear ideological criteria to evaluate the groupings attracted to the Left Opposition. He viewed this as especially

---

221   According to Isaac Deutscher, during this period Trotsky established contact with groups of supporters in France, Germany, Italy, Spain, Holland, Belgium, China, Indochina, Indonesia, Ceylon, the United States, and Mexico (Deutscher 1963, pp. 31–3).

222   Trotsky 1975c, pp. 108–9, 134. See also Trotsky 1970b, p. xxxvi.

223   Trotsky 1975c, pp. 180, 233. In 1929 Trotsky believed that national organisations of the Communist Left Opposition in the USSR, Germany, and France should function as factions 'fighting for influence upon the proletarian nucleus of the official party'. However, in Belgium, where the CP was 'entirely insignificant', and in the US, where the situation was 'closer to that in Belgium than to that in Germany', he proposed that the Opposition organise itself as an independent party (Trotsky 1975c, p. 370). Trotsky changed his mind about the Belgian and US sections the following year (Trotsky, 1975d, p. 294).

224   Trotsky 1975c, p. 88. The 'instrument' for elaborating this international program, according to Trotsky, was to be a monthly or biweekly *international organ of the Opposition*. This publication, as Trotsky envisioned it in the spring of 1929, never got off the ground.

important because centrism was driving not only leftist critics of Stalinism, 'but also the more consistent opportunists' into opposition. According to Trotsky, there were 'three classic questions' that could be utilised to sort out these tendencies: '(1) the policy of the Anglo-Russian Committee; (2) the course of the Chinese revolution; (3) the economic policy of the USSR, in conjunction with the theory of socialism in one country'.[225] He intentionally omitted the issue of the 'party regime', or 'bureaucratism' from this list for, drawing again upon his theory, he explained, 'A party regime has no independent, self-sufficient meaning. In relation to party policy it is a derivative magnitude'.[226] Besides that, he noted that 'heterogeneous elements', including Mensheviks, claimed to oppose 'Stalinist bureaucratism' when their real target was 'revolutionary centralism'. As far as these were concerned, he declared, 'Obviously, they cannot be our cothinkers'.[227]

5.8   Conclusion

In retrospect it is clear that Trotsky's perception of developments in the Soviet Union during 1928–9 was severely distorted. Throughout these years he consistently accepted at face value the simplistic Stalinist account of the 'grain strike' and the false allegations regarding the 'Shakhty conspiracy'. To his credit, and in contrast with the extreme intransigents, he recognised that an important change was occurring in Soviet economic and international policy. Yet during these years, and especially in 1929, he greatly underestimated the significance of the shift in policy, even at various points refusing to describe it as a 'turn'. At the same time he continued to reaffirm his erroneous predictions from 1927 that only the Opposition could lead a turn away from the leaderships' previous market orientation, that the 'centrist' current would soon dissolve, and that without a major proletarian upsurge the leadership would soon swing to the right and a section of it would participate in the restoration of capitalism.

Although aspects of Trotsky's analysis were persuasive, his main explanation for the turn was implausible. It seems likely, as Trotsky argued, that the leadership instituted its policy shifts in 1928 in reaction to a series of economic and international crises precipitated largely by its own previous policies. Also, it is conceivable that worker unrest at home and growing working-class

---

225   Trotsky 1975c, p. 81. For a grouping to be admitted into the Left Opposition, Trotsky insisted that it accept the position of the 1927 *Platform* on all three questions (Trotsky 1975c, pp. 80–5, 86–7, 111, 232–3).

226   Trotsky 1975c, p. 81.

227   Ibid.

militancy abroad helped to push the leadership to change its orientation. Beyond that, it is clear that many of the policies adopted in this period were influenced by the Opposition's programme. However, Trotsky's claim that the Opposition was primarily responsible for blocking a turn to the right or forcing one to the left in late winter/early spring 1928 was unlikely. Although the Opposition experienced some growth in the immediate aftermath of the Fifteenth Party Congress, it remained a small grouping, seriously weakened by its recent defeat.[228] Abroad, it was virtually nonexistent. It is not surprising, then, that Oppositionists as different as Preobrazhenskii and Rakovskii seriously questioned Trotsky's assertions that pressure from the Opposition had brought about the turn.

If Trotsky's argument that the Oppositional pressure had compelled the leadership to turn left in 1928 was dubious, his assertion that it forced the *deepening* of the turn in 1929 was even more so. In the second half of 1928 the Opposition engaged in a flurry of activity, attracted a significant number of new recruits, and increased its influence within the working class.[229] However, by the middle of 1929 it found itself weakened by defections, increasingly demoralised, and on the brink of collapse. According to Victor Serge, in 1929 it was reduced to a handful of leaders, plus 'a few hundred comrades' in prison and 'in deportation a few hundred others'. Of that period, Serge remarked, 'Our intellectual activity is prodigious, our political action nil. Altogether there must be less than a thousand of us'.[230] Another Oppositionist, Ante Ciliga, subsequently described the general mood of demoralisation that swept the Soviet Opposition in 1929.[231] Meanwhile, the Opposition was only beginning to organise itself internationally. In such a state of disintegration at home and disorganisation abroad, it was hardly in a position to exert serious pressure.

As various writers have emphasised, the flaws in Trotsky's general theoretical perspective also weakened the struggle of the Opposition in various ways.

---

228   Michal Reiman, who emphasises the extent of Opposition support, has argued that after the Fifteenth Party Congress, 'sympathy for the Opposition persisted among a section of the working population'. However, 'the influence of the Opposition was gradually waning,' and 'it was fragmented by repression' (Reiman 1987, p. 55).

229   On the growth of Opposition activity and influence within the working-class in the summer and autumn of 1928, see Broué 1988, pp. 564–5; Cliff 1993, pp. 69–73; Deutscher 1959, p. 456; Gusev 2008, pp. 156–60; Gusev 1996, pp. 91–4; Longuet 1994, pp. 38–9; Murphy 2001, p. 346; Murphy 2005, pp. 107, 110–11; Reiman 1987, p. 97; Stalin 1952–5, vol. 11, pp. 288–9; Ward 1990, p. 220.

230   Serge 1980, pp. 253–4.

231   Ciliga 1979, pp. 59, 84–8.

It was, for example, one factor contributing to the disintegration of the Left Opposition in this period. John Marot's assertion that the capitulation of the majority of the Opposition in 1929 was a direct consequence of 'the political "imperatives" of Trotsky's views' is certainly an exaggeration.[232] Nevertheless, it is true that Trotsky's persistent definition of the Soviet situation in terms of a conflict between the proletariat and resurgent capitalism may have reinforced the inclination of some Oppositionists to enlist in the Stalinist struggle against the 'right'. More clearly, the repeated failures of Trotsky's theory led many Oppositionists to *abandon* the traditional orientation of the Left Opposition – with some embracing the positions of the Democratic Centralists and many more capitulating to the Stalinist leadership.[233]

At the same time, as Aleksei Gusev and John Marot have shown, Trotsky's theoretical perspective contributed to the Opposition's ambivalence regarding important struggles and sentiments within the working class during these years.[234] In late 1928 and early 1929 the Opposition responded to growing manifestations of proletarian discontent by statements and agitation against state efforts to scrap the existing collective agreements, against growing social inequality, and for wage increases and workers' democracy. Although all of these demands struck a responsive chord in the proletariat, dissatisfied workers frequently perceived them as unattainable within the existing political structures. While the Opposition admitted the possibility of economic strikes,

---

232   Marot 2006, pp. 192, 194. For Marot, that perspective included Trotsky's advocacy of accelerated industrialisation, his defence of the Communist Party's monopoly of power, and his failure to recognise the autonomy of the bureaucracy as a social formation. However, the industrialisation proposed by Trotsky and the Opposition differed in important respects from the policies implemented by the Stalinists; and, as suggested in the previous chapter, it was reasonable, both from the point of view of the Soviet proletariat and the peasantry. As far as Communist Party rule was concerned, there is no reason to believe that any of the capitulators, who disdainfully rejected proposals by the Democratic Centralists for a new party and a new revolution, would have been moved by such an appeal from Trotsky. Finally, regarding Trotsky's and the Opposition's general perception of the bureaucracy, it is noteworthy that in their conciliatory statements in 1928 Preobrazhenskii and Radek emphasised the *errors* of the Opposition's analysis. Furthermore, in July 1929 they and 500 other Bolshevik-Leninists repudiated the entire *Platform of the Opposition* in their declaration of surrender. In contrast, Trotsky continued to insist upon the continuing relevance of his and the Opposition's general theoretical perspective. Despite its defects, that perspective remained the basis for Trotsky's own political opposition until 1933.

233   As Cliff observes, 'It was the ideological crisis of the Trotskyist movement that disarmed the Oppositionists and tempted them to surrender to Stalinism' (Cliff 1993, p. 102).

234   Gusev 2008; Gusev 1996; Marot 2006, pp. 194–9.

it warned that these were damaging to 'industry and the [workers'] state and, consequently, workers themselves', and it advocated instead diverting working-class demands into channels of 'trade union and party legality'.[235] Furthermore, although the Opposition hesitantly appealed to non-party workers for support, it repudiated the idea of a new party that was gaining popularity in this period.[236] It is unclear what the long-term effects of a more aggressive approach might have been. But it seems likely that, at least in the short term, the orientation promoted by Trotsky's theory limited the Opposition's opportunities for growth and enhanced influence.

A number of writers have commented on the failure of Trotsky's analysis to anticipate or comprehend the developments discussed in this chapter and the next.[237] Of these, several have argued that Trotsky's essential problem was that he was misled by his Thermidorian analogy. For example, Stephen Cohen has asserted, 'The analogy would obsess and finally mislead Trotsky, blunting his perception of what was happening in the Soviet Union'.[238] However, this argument is mistaken if taken literally. As we have seen and will see again, the 'Thermidorian analogy' was used in various ways at different times by Trotsky and the other Bolsheviks. In each case, although the reference was always to a date in the French revolutionary calendar, the understanding of the significance of that date varied considerably. By itself, the use of the term *Thermidor* did not dictate any specific predictions or evaluations of Soviet reality.[239]

In fact, the principal source of Trotsky's errors during this period was not in the analogies he employed, but in the assumptions behind those analogies. One of the most important of these was his belief that the apparatuses of the state and party were incapable of exercising any significant degree of autonomy in relation to the main classes of Soviet society.[240] As Robert Wistrich has

---

235   *Biulleten' oppozitsii* 1973, 6 (October 1929), p. 9; Gusev 2008, p. 163.

236   Gusev 2008, pp. 162–8.

237   See Cliff 1993, pp. 45–51; Cohen 1980, p. 132; Deutscher 1959, pp. 457–68; Hallas 1984, pp. 38–44; McNeal 1977, pp. 31–2; Shachtman 1965, pp. 201–10; Tucker 1973b, pp. 390–3; Wistrich 1979, pp. 161–2.

238   Cohen 1980, p. 132. See also Wistrich 1979, p. 161; Tucker 1973b, pp. 390–2.

239   Furthermore, one could equally argue that Trotsky's errors during this period were the fault of other analogies he used to explain his analysis, including comparisons to the history of the Second International ('centrism and opportunism'); or to the history of the Russian Revolution and the Russian socialist movement ('dual power', 'Kerenskiism in reverse', and 'Menshevism').

240   A secondary problem was certainly Trotsky's unexamined understanding of the terms *left* and *right*. In line with popular political discourse, Trotsky and the majority of the Opposition perceived the economic turn to be 'leftist' because industrialisation, the emergency measures in grain collection, and collectivisation all involved expansions of

noted, Trotsky 'seriously underestimated the power of the bureaucracy and its autonomy, the degree to which it had created its own social support, independent of other class forces which it kept fragmented and powerless through terror and repression'.[241] Similarly, Tony Cliff and John Marot have attributed Trotsky's errors to his failure to recognise that the bureaucracy was 'an independent social force with its own material interests', that is, a 'class'.[242] It was Trotsky's assumption that the bureaucracy could only respond to external class pressures that lay behind his understanding of Thermidor during this period, as well as behind the entire theory of bureaucracy he developed in 1926–7. Although that theory had seemed a compelling one when first articulated, events of 1928 and 1929 began to demonstrate how flawed it really was. As Stalin's left turn continued to deepen in subsequent years, the crisis in Trotsky's theoretical perspective would become even more pronounced.

---

the economic role of the Soviet state and restrictions of the market and of capitalism. However, as the leadership began to implement policies that increasingly restricted the market but that also seriously undermined the living standards and working conditions of workers, the traditional understandings of the terms *left* and *right* seemed less and less relevant.

241   Wistrich 1979, p. 161.
242   Marot 2006, p. 187. See also Cliff 1993, pp. 49–51.

The Turn and the Theoretical Crisis Deepen

From late 1929 through early 1933 Trotsky continued his Turkish exile, living most of this period with members of his family and a few supporters on the island of Prinkipo. In these years Trotsky devoted part of his time to writing his *History of the Russian Revolution*, and another portion to resolving the myriad political and organisational questions that confronted his new international organisation, the International Left Opposition (ILO), founded in Paris in April 1930. However, he also dedicated a great deal of attention to developments in Soviet economic policy, Comintern policy, and policies related to the party-state regime of the USSR.

Throughout these years reality continued to diverge from the theory of bureaucracy Trotsky had developed in 1926–7. On the basis of that theory he predicted in 1928–9 that, without an increase in proletarian and/or Oppositional pressure, a deep turn to the right by the leadership was imminent. Instead, in 1929–33 he perceived the leadership veering even more sharply to the left than in 1928, adopting orientations in both economic and Comintern policy so radical that they fell entirely outside of the framework assumed by his theory. Furthermore, he had viewed the worsening of the state and party regime as directly related to the leadership's rightist orientation. However, even while implementing its new course, the leadership continued to institute policies that Trotsky viewed as deviating even further from workers' democracy. In this context the crisis in his theoretical perspective deepened dramatically.

In *The Structure of Scientific Revolutions* Thomas Kuhn explains that theoretical crises generally emerge in the natural sciences in response to the growing recognition of the existence of anomalies or counter instances to the current paradigm. However, Kuhn further argues that for an anomaly to evoke a crisis, it usually must be more than just an anomaly. It may call into question explicit and fundamental generalisations of the paradigm; or it may persist over a long period of time. In each case, although scientists respond by devising various articulations and ad hoc modifications to the theory, the anomaly continues to resist resolution. Ultimately, this situation results in the proliferation of competing articulations of the paradigm and the blurring of the paradigm's rules.[1]

The preceding paragraph in many ways describes the situation that confronted Trotsky and his supporters in the early 1930s. The apparent left turns

---

1 Kuhn 1970, pp. 77–91.

of the leadership, combined with the continued worsening of the regime, were anomalies that challenged basic assumptions of Trotsky's theory. Furthermore, the anomalies were persistent: they had appeared as early as 1928, and they continued into 1933. Left Oppositionists within Soviet prisons responded by creating their own articulations of the theory – a development that resulted in the proliferation of contending Trotskyist groupings. As in 1928–9, Trotsky's response to the anomalies was a series of strained interpretations of reality and ad hoc theoretical modifications. The ultimate effect was growing confusion and blurring in his writings that persisted until the revolution in his thinking that occurred in the years 1933–6.

6.1   Economic Upheaval

In late 1929 the leadership dramatically deepened the turn in economic policy initiated in 1928. In industry, this shift took the form of a frenetic campaign to fulfil ever higher production targets. In the countryside, it involved a declaration of war against the kulaks and the complete restructuring of Soviet agriculture. Together, within a few short years these policies transformed the economic face of the Soviet Union.

6.1.1   *The Soviet Industrial Revolution*

Throughout 1929 the ambitious goals for industrialisation set by the April plenum of the CC were repeatedly revised upwards. Then, at the Sixteenth Party Congress in June 1930, the General Secretary publicly endorsed the demand to 'carry out the Five-Year Plan in four years'. Even more ambitiously, he went on to declare that 'in quite a number of branches of industry, we can carry it out in three years, or even two and a half years'.[2] To achieve these goals, the leadership called upon the workers to exert themselves to the maximum. In this campaign it relied in part on moral incentives, utilising the trade unions to mobilise the latent idealism of the Soviet working class. Throughout the country young workers responded with heroic acts of self-sacrifice for the sake of industrialisation, enlisting in 'shock brigades' engaged in 'socialist competition'. However, physical coercion also played a significant role in the leadership's industrialisation drive. During these years the OGPU set hundreds of

---

2   Stalin 1933, p. 331. In February 1931 Stalin went on to proclaim the goal of completing the plan *'in three years in all the basic, decisive branches of industry'* (Stalin 1976, pp. 519–20).

thousands of prisoners to work digging canals, building roads, felling timber, and labouring in coal mines.[3]

Despite these efforts, by the summer of 1930 Soviet industry was already in crisis. A number of industries failed to meet planned targets, and production in others – such as coal, iron, steel, and copper – even began to fall. Rail transport proved incapable of meeting the demands placed on it, the overall quality of goods deteriorated dramatically, and attempts to fill the gap between revenues and expenditures by the unplanned issue of currency resulted in serious inflation. At the same time, the industrial work force expanded far more rapidly than anticipated, straining the supply of consumer goods, housing, and public services, and contributing to a sharp decline in the standard of living of Soviet workers.[4] An additional problem was the increase in labour turnover: by 1930 the average worker was changing jobs every eight months, and the average coal miner every four, seriously undermining efforts to create a skilled work force.[5]

The Soviet leadership attempted to address the deepening crisis in a variety of ways. Its initial reaction to the shortage of food and consumer goods was to extend the rationing system that had been in place since 1928. For industrial workers, the effect was to increase their level of consumption in relation to the rest of the urban population, while greatly equalising consumption among the industrial workers themselves.[6] However, in the context of the deepening crisis the leadership soon grew concerned that rationing was reducing the incentive of skilled workers to produce. On 23 June 1931, in a speech to a conference of economic executives, Stalin condemned the ' "Leftist" practice of wage equalization' for undermining the development of skilled labour and promoting the 'fluidity of manpower'. Soon afterwards, the leadership began to introduce significant wage differentials, especially in priority industries, to benefit skilled workers. 'Shock workers' who carried out obligations that exceeded the norm were also granted special privileges, including extra rations of meat and fat and preferential access to consumer goods and housing. At the same time, an extensive system of privileges was established for higher officials of the party, state, and other organisations. In line with these changes, in 1932 the leadership officially abandoned the traditional Bolshevik principle limiting the income of

---

3   See R. Davies 1996, pp. 31–7; R. Davies 1989, pp. 258–61; Filtzer 1986, pp. 69–72, 76; Kuromiya 1988, pp. 113–28, 194–7, 300; Nove 1976, pp. 190–2, 206, 209; Ward 1999, pp. 46, 57–9.

4   R. Davies 1981a, p. 11; R. Davies 1989, pp. 346–52, 372, 384; Filtzer 1986, pp. 44, 51–3, 58–9, 91–2, 116–17; Kuromiya 1988, pp. 140, 151, 157–60, 228–33; Ward 1999, pp. 55–7.

5   R. Davies 1989, pp. 279–80, 371; R. Davies 1996, pp. 75–6; Kuromiya 1988, pp. 209–10, 212, 221.

6   R. Davies 1989, pp. 289–300; Kuromiya 1988, pp. 234, 248–9.

all party members to that of skilled workers.[7] At the same time it resorted to administrative coercion to reduce rates of labour turnover and absenteeism.[8]

Yet another response to the crisis by the leadership was to place the blame for it on the wrecking activities of 'saboteurs'. In the early 1930s a number of such 'conspiracies', now recognised as fictitious, were uncovered. Two cases were especially important. In November and December 1930 eight technical specialists, mostly high officials in Gosplan and VSNKh, confessed to having organised a counterrevolutionary 'Industrial Party' of some two thousand members. The specialists were accused of sabotage in a wide variety of industries in preparation for a coup and the military intervention of France and Britain. As part of their wrecking activities, the defendants allegedly drew up economic targets that they believed to be unrealistically high, but that unexpectedly turned out to be achievable. All of the accused were convicted and five specialists were condemned to death, but their sentences were ultimately commuted to imprisonment. Another important show trial held in March 1931 involved fourteen members of a 'Union Bureau' of the Menshevik Party. Most of the accused in this case were former Mensheviks who had recently held responsible positions in Soviet economic and planning agencies. The defendants allegedly rejoined the Mensheviks in the late 1920s and then engaged in wrecking activities, including attempts to slow Soviet economic development by lowering goals. It was also charged that they had plotted a counterrevolutionary insurrection in collaboration with the Industrial Party and a 'Toiling Peasant Party'. On the basis of confessions, all fourteen were convicted and sentenced to various terms of imprisonment.[9]

Despite these responses, the economic crisis continued to deepen. By the winter of 1932–3, the entire Soviet economy seemed to teeter on the brink of collapse. Bottlenecks and shortages appeared in all branches of the economy. Labour productivity failed to rise as anticipated and, by some accounts, actually began to fall. Growth rates for industrial output declined steadily, and actual production in various industries began to drop. The quality of industrially produced goods also continued to deteriorate. Meanwhile, inflation mounted ever higher, and Soviet workers experienced what Alec Nove has described as 'the

---

7   R. Davies 1996, pp. 67, 71–2; Deutscher 1966, pp. 338–40; Filtzer 1986, pp. 96–9; Kuromiya 1988, pp. 280–5; Nove 1976, p. 209; Seigelbaum 1988, pp. 40, 44; Stalin 1976, pp. 536–40; Tucker 1990, pp. 110–14.

8   Filtzer 1986, pp. 108–15; Kuromiya 1988, pp. 221–2; Nove 1976, p. 208.

9   Bailes 1978, pp. 95–121; Conquest 1973, pp. 733–6; R. Davies 1996, pp. 26–31, 287; Kuromiya 1988, pp. 142–3, 165–8, 171–2; Medvedev 1973, pp. 113–37; Tucker 1990, pp. 98–100, 167–70.

most precipitous peacetime decline in living standards known in recorded history'.[10]

At that point, on 7 January 1933 Stalin announced that the First Five-Year Plan had been completed successfully in four years and three months. According to Stalin, the entire plan had been fulfilled by 93.7 percent, and the plan for heavy industry had been fulfilled by 108 percent.[11] In fact, during the First Five-Year Plan production in most areas increased both absolutely and relatively, and in some industries it showed considerable gains. Additionally, this plan laid the foundations for even greater industrial expansion in the mid-1930s. However, as most Western scholars have observed, the first *piatiletka* was not nearly as successful as Stalin portrayed it. Production of coal, pig iron, and steel fell far short of the targets; many branches of light industry did not grow at all; and textile production declined.[12]

Reacting to the crisis and to the overall failures of the plan, in early 1933 the leadership began to retreat from the extreme tempos of the First Five-Year Plan. During the previous year the Seventeenth Party Conference had adopted high targets for the Second Five-Year Plan. However, Stalin modified these projections at the CC plenum of January 1933, calling for 'less speedy rates' of industrialisation, and proposing as a minimum a '3–14 per cent average annual increase in industrial output' in place of the 22 percent allegedly achieved in the first *piatiletka*.[13]

6.1.2   *Mass Collectivisation and Dekulakisation*

Meanwhile, a comparable revolution was taking place in agriculture. By October 1929, 7.6 percent of peasant households had been collectivised.[14] Nevertheless, the leadership continued to press for higher levels of collectivisation. Speaking for the Politburo at the November plenum of the Central Committee, Molotov announced that the time had come for 'a decisive move in the matter of the economic rehabilitation and collectivization of millions of peasant households'. Bowing before the 'spontaneous' influx of poor and middle peasants into the *kolkhozy*, the plenum endorsed the 'continued

---

10   R. Davies 1996, pp. 362–79; Jasny 1961, pp. 104–9, 114–17; Kuromiya 1988, pp. 288–92; Lewin
        1973, p. 282; Nove 1976, p. 207; Ward 1999, pp. 47–8, 55–7.
11   Stalin 1976, p. 596. Three months had been added to the fourth year to make the economic
        and calendar years coincide.
12   R. Davies 1996, pp. 466–72; Kuromiya 1988, pp. 287–8; Nove 1976, pp. 191–5; Ward 1999,
        p. 47.
13   Nove 1976, p. 219; Stalin 1976, p. 602; Ward 1999, pp. 48–9.
14   R. Davies 1980a, pp. 109, 116–37; Lewin 1968, pp. 406–39; Tucker 1990, pp. 130, 134.

acceleration of the process of collectivization and sovkhoz construction', and resolved to mobilise at least 25,000 industrial workers for the effort.[15] During the winter collectivisation brigades managed to bring about a massive influx of peasants into collective farms, largely though coercion or threats of coercion. Many joined the collectives to avoid being persecuted as kulaks or kulak supporters. Peasants who attempted to evade collectivisation often found themselves subject to increased taxation, fines, or arrest. Some recalcitrant villages were surrounded by armed units and driven into the *kolkhozy* by force. By 1 March 1930 the total level of collectivisation had climbed to 14.6 million peasant households – 57.2 percent of the total.[16]

Closely related to the collectivisation campaign was the simultaneous intensification of the offensive against the kulaks. In December local authorities initiated 'dekulakisation' drives, expropriating kulaks and sometimes arresting or deporting them. In a speech on 27 December Stalin endorsed these measures, calling for a policy of '*eliminating* the kulaks as a class'.[17] The contemporary historian Moshe Lewin has argued persuasively that the leadership initiated the campaign against the kulaks 'to "convince" the peasants that all roads, save those that led to the *kolkhoz*, were barred to them', as well as to accumulate the property that was to be used for setting up the new *kolkhozy*.[18]

In late January and early February 1930 local authorities received their first instructions on how to implement dekulakisation. Kulaks most actively hostile to collectivisation were to forfeit their property and were to be imprisoned, sent to concentration camps [*kontslageri*], or shot; their families were to be exiled. 'Economically strong' kulaks were to be expropriated and deported with their families to remote areas of the country or remote districts within their region. Remaining kulaks who were considered loyal to the regime were to have part of their means of production confiscated and were to be resettled on inferior land within their own districts. Altogether, over a million families were to be dekulakised.[19]

---

15   Cohen 1980, pp. 333–4; R. Davies 1980b, pp. 157–74; Lewin 1968, pp. 454–64; Stalin 1976, p. 443; Tucker 1990, pp. 133–5; Ward 1999, p. 76.

16   Conquest 1986, pp. 147–53; R. Davies 1980a, pp. 203–28, 442; Dmytryshyn 1978, p. 168; Fainsod 1958, pp. 251–3; Lewin 1985, p. 112; Lewin 1968, pp. 514–15; Tucker 1990, p. 181; Nove 1976, p. 163; Ward 1999, pp. 76–9.

17   R. Davies 1980a, pp. 165, 183–5, 197–8; Lewin 1968, p. 487; Stalin 1976, p. 471; Tucker 1990, p. 138.

18   Lewin 1968, pp. 493–5.

19   Conquest 1986, pp. 120–1; Danilov et al. 2000, pp. 126–7; R. Davies 1980a, pp. 234–6; Lewin 1968, pp. 495–7; Nove 1976, pp. 167–8; Viola et al. 2005, pp. 209–10, 228–9; Ward 1999, pp. 76–7.

The drive was led by local soviet, party, and GPU officials, and was carried out by special detachments consisting of local party or Komsomol cadres, members of the militia or GPU, poor peasants, and industrial workers. As implemented, the campaign turned out to be more massive and brutal than officially projected. In violation of stated policy, local authorities often dekulakised areas not scheduled for mass collectivisation. Frequently, they applied the label of 'kulak' or 'ideological kulak' to middle or even poor peasants who resisted collectivisation. Also, officials who found themselves short of real kulaks often simply designated less affluent peasants as kulaks in order to fill their quotas. In violation of policy the brigades seized not only land, tools, and animals, but also personal property. The conditions of deportation were so horrible that large numbers of deportees died en route of exposure, starvation, and disease.

In numerical terms the campaign was a great success, by some accounts vastly over-fulfilling the original plans of the centre.[20] However, both the dekulakisation and collectivisation campaigns provoked significant resistance. In early 1930 large numbers of peasants began to leave the collective farms. At the same time, a wave of peasant demonstrations and uprisings swept the Soviet Union. Arson, sabotage, murder of Communists, and peasant suicides were common. Perhaps most significant for the future of Soviet agriculture was the widespread slaughter of livestock, which peasants assumed would be confiscated for the *kolkhozy*. From 1929 to 1934 over half of the county's horses, cattle, and pigs, and two thirds of its sheep and goats disappeared – most slaughtered in the first two months of 1930.[21]

In the face of such resistance, and reportedly under pressure from other members of the CC, Stalin sounded the retreat. In an article published in *Pravda* on 2 March 1930 he conceded that serious excesses had been committed by overzealous local officials who had become 'dizzy with success'. Although Stalin called on the party to 'consolidate' its successes, he insisted that the collective-farm movement should be 'voluntary'. Immediately, his article touched off a mass exodus from the collective farms. By 1 June only 24.8 percent of the

---

20   Conquest 1986, pp. 119, 128–43; R. Davies 1980a, pp. 245–51; Fainsod 1958, pp. 245–6; Lewin
       1968, pp. 497–506, 508; Nove 1976, p. 167; Tucker 1990, pp. 175, 177–8, 180–1. Lewin estimates
       that ten million persons or more were deported as kulaks (Lewin 1968, p. 508).
21   Cohen 1980, p. 339; Conquest 1986, pp. 154–60; R. Davies 1980a, pp. 255–61, 325, 333;
       Fainsod 1958, pp. 253–4; Tucker 1990, pp. 181–3.

total of peasant households remained collectivised, and by 1 September this figure was down to 21.5 percent.[22]

However, the leadership had no intention of abandoning plans for wholesale collectivisation. In the fall of 1930 the campaign was resumed anew. As part of this drive a massive new assault was launched against kulak and 'better-off' peasants. Also, 'hard obligations' of extraordinarily high volumes of grain were imposed on private farms in order to encourage collectivisation. Peasants who were unable to deliver the required amount of grain could have their lands sold and were subject to fines and imprisonment. By July 1932, 61.5 percent of Soviet peasants found themselves back in the *kolkhozy*.[23]

The most devastating tragedy associated with collectivisation was the famine of 1932–3. In the early 1930's agricultural production stagnated, at least partly because of the low productivity of the collective farms. Nevertheless, to collect grain needed for a growing urban population, the army, and export, the leadership continued to push procurement targets ever higher while keeping prices low. In the summer and autumn of 1932 many collectivised peasants withheld grain for personal consumption or to sell on the recently reopened markets, while others simply refused to work on the *kolkhozy*. The leadership responded with force. Refusal to deliver grain for state procurements was made a capital offence. Mass arrests were carried out in the rural areas, and large numbers of 'pro-kulak' elements were expelled from the party. Ultimately, even grain set aside for seed and fodder was taken from the peasantry. The resulting famine was especially acute in the Ukraine, the North Caucasus, the lower and middle Volga, the southern Urals, and Kazakhstan where, by all accounts, millions died from starvation.[24]

6.2   Trotsky's Response to the Turn

Not surprisingly, the new shift in economic policy generated confusion within the ranks of unrepentant Oppositionists. The Yugoslav oppositionist Ante Ciliga later described the situation he encountered among the imprisoned Bolshevik-Leninists in the Verkhne-Uralsk isolator in November 1930: 'The burning

22   Conquest 1986, pp. 160–7; R. Davies 1980a, pp. 269–83, 311–30, 443; Dmytryshyn 1978, p. 168; Medvedev 1973, pp. 87–8; Nove 1976, p. 171; Stalin 1976, pp. 483–91; Tucker 1990, pp. 183–6; Ward 1999, pp. 78–9.
23   Conquest 1986, p. 167; Nove 1976, p. 175; Tucker 1990, pp. 186–7; Ward 1999, p. 80.
24   Medvedev 1987, pp. 86–95; Nove 1976, pp. 176–81; Tucker 1990, pp. 190–5; Ward 1999, pp. 82–3, 93–4.

problems put by the revolution, and in particular by the Five Year Plan in its present stage, produced the greatest animation in this circle and a state of ideological crisis singularly favourable to the breaking up of opinion into small sections'. The small Trotskyist organisation in the isolator had split into three sections with three different programmes. The 'Right section' argued that the turn had met the essential demands of the Opposition, and that the Opposition should support it while criticising the exaggerated pace of the plan and the Stalinist regime. According to Ciliga, this group hoped for reform from above, expecting that difficulties would force the leadership to modify its policies. However, it opposed appeals to the masses because it feared the 'Thermidor front might well include the working class'. In contrast, the leftist 'Militant Bolsheviks' declared that the entire industrialisation drive was mere bluff. It insisted that reform could only come from below through a split in the party, and it called for reliance upon the working class. Between these groupings, the 'Centre section' advocated methods of reform from above and below.[25]

Trotsky was also having difficulties comprehending the new situation. Although he had not anticipated the deepening of the turn, he shifted his critique quickly, perhaps because he was becoming accustomed to abrupt policy changes by the leadership. By early 1930 he was denouncing the leadership's ultraleftism just as sharply as he had condemned its previous conservatism. Meanwhile, he struggled to understand the origins of the turn and to predict where it was heading. By veering to the left, the leadership had acted directly counter to his expectations. In an effort to understand what was happening, he turned to his theory. However, he repeatedly found himself forced to introduce implicit modifications to reconcile it with unfolding developments.[26]

6.2.1   Trotsky's Critique of the Turn

In certain respects Trotsky was inclined to view the new economic orientation positively. In the first place, he viewed it as yet further evidence that the Opposition's program had been correct. Early in 1930 he recalled that just a few years before, the leadership had attacked the Opposition as ' "romanticists," "fanatics", and "superindustrializers" ' for advocating a mere 20 percent annual growth rate in industry. When the Opposition had demanded more attention to collectivisation, 'three-quarters of the Politburo and 90 percent of the

---

25   Ciliga 1979, pp. 210–13.

26   For secondary sources that deal with Trotsky's views on the First Five-Year Plan, see Cliff 1993, pp. 45–67; Deutscher 1963, pp. 92–110; Law 1987a, pp. 110–17; Mandel 1995, pp. 66–9; Nove 1981, pp. 84–6; Nove 1979, pp. 46–52; Nove 1982, pp. 389–404; Thatcher 2003, pp. 166–75.

government apparatus had their orientation to the ... kulak'. Now, he observed, 'Experience has shown that the Opposition was right'.[27] Beyond that, throughout the early 1930s he repeatedly acclaimed the achievements of the plan as a demonstration of the superiority of socialist over capitalist methods. As early as February 1930 he spoke of the 'universal significance' of the successes of industrialisation, insisting that these had provided empirical evidence of the infinite potentialities inherent in socialist methods.[28] Subsequently, he praised Soviet industrial accomplishments as 'enormous in their historical importance', and as 'the most colossal phenomenon of contemporary history'.[29] Similarly, in April 1930 he spoke of the 'deeply progressive and creative significance of collectivization'.[30] A year later he even characterised 'the present tempos of collectivization' as signifying the birth of 'a new epoch' in human development: 'the beginning of the liquidation "of [what Marx described as] the idiocy of rural life"'.[31]

Yet, despite such statements as these, throughout the early 1930s Trotsky continued to criticise Soviet economic policy at least as sharply as he had in the past. In one respect, his critique was familiar. Echoing his earlier statements on Soviet economic policy, he denounced the plan's isolationism, which he saw as flowing inevitably from the doctrine of socialism in one county.[32] However, as Trotsky himself explicitly acknowledged, most of his critique of Soviet economic policy in these years was leveled not from the left, but from the right.[33] In this regard, he insisted, it was the party leadership that had changed positions, making a 'curve of 180 degrees' over the heads of the Opposition and adopting the extreme policies it previously had denounced as 'Trotskyism'.[34] In industrial policy this ultraleftism was evident in the tempo of the industrialisation drive and the virtual elimination of the role of the market in planning. In agricultural policy it could be seen in the leadership's attempt to eliminate the kulaks as a class, and in the tempo and scale of collectivisation.

---

27 Trotsky 1975d, pp. 169, 172–3, 106. See also Trotsky 1973c, p. 91; Trotsky 1973d, p. 36.

28 Trotsky 1975d, p. 105.

29 Trotsky 1973c, p. 99; Trotsky 1973d, p. 42. See also Trotsky 1975d, p. 193; Trotsky 1973c, pp. 183, 205; Trotsky 1973d, pp. 42, 66, 260; Trotsky 1972f, p. 96.

30 Trotsky 1975d, p. 173.

31 Trotsky 1973c, p. 205. At the same time, Trotsky contemptuously rejected some of the more fantastic claims of the party leadership regarding the goals and achievements of the plan (Trotsky 1973c, pp. 93, 96–8, 206; Trotsky 1973d, p. 260).

32 See Trotsky 1975d, p. 137; Trotsky 1973c, pp. 103, 208–9; Trotsky 1973d, p. 266.

33 See Trotsky 1975d, pp. 66, 96, 169–70.

34 Trotsky 1975d, p. 116; Trotsky 1973c, p. 58; Trotsky 1973d, p. 66.

The central theme of Trotsky's new critique of industrial policy was that the goals of the plan were insanely high. Repeatedly, he denounced the pace of the industrialisation drive, and especially the decision to fulfill the goals of the plan in four years, as economic madness. He ridiculed the leadership's 'industrialization races', its 'hazardous bureaucratic superindustrializations', its 'racetrack-gallop approach' and its *sporting* method', characterising these as manifestations of 'bureaucratic adventurism' and 'ultraleft lunacy'.[35] For Trotsky, the problem was not simply that the goals of the plan could not hope to be achieved – though he was certain they could not. Beyond that, he was convinced that the attempt to reach them would lead inevitably to *unevenness* in the plan's fulfillment. In turn, he insisted, this unevenness would result in disproportions and bottlenecks between industries and between different sectors of the economy. As early as 20 December 1929 he warned that 'we are heading for a disturbance of the total economic equilibrium and consequently of the social equilibrium'.[36] By late 1932, on the basis of reports from the Soviet press, he concluded that this prophesy had been realised. 'The whole trouble', he observed, 'is that the wild leaps of industrialization have brought the various elements of the plan into dire contradiction with each other'.[37]

Another concern repeatedly expressed by Trotsky was that excessive investment in industry was reducing the resources that could be allotted to consumption and to raising the standard of living of the working class.[38] In March 1930 he noted that the living standard of workers was falling, and the following summer he asserted that the economic position of the proletariat had 'extraordinarily worsened' in recent years.[39] Subsequently, utilising examples from the Soviet press, he painted a bleak picture of deteriorating working conditions, and of dwindling supplies of food, housing, and consumer goods.[40] Trotsky viewed this issue as intrinsically important, for he believed that the standard of living of workers, together with their role in governing the state, constituted 'the highest criteria of socialist successes'.[41] Beyond that, he insisted that improving the material and cultural level of the proletariat was necessary for

35   See, for example, Trotsky 1975c, p. 402; Trotsky 1975d, pp. 115, 116, 124, 130–1, 147; Trotsky 1973c, pp. 98, 100, 182–3, 230; Trotsky 1973d, pp. 66, 261.
36   Trotsky 1975c, p. 402. See also Trotsky 1975d, pp. 107, 170; Trotsky 1973c, pp. 98–100, 182–3, 206; Trotsky 1973d, p. 37.
37   Trotsky 1973d, p. 277.
38   Trotsky 1973d, p. 37. See also Trotsky 1973c, p. 288; Trotsky 1973d, p. 268.
39   Trotsky 1975d, p. 138; Trotsky 1973c, p. 284.
40   Trotsky 1973d, pp. 267–9; Trotsky 1972f, p. 101.
41   Trotsky 1973c, p. 228. See also Trotsky 1973c, p. 284; Trotsky 1973d, p. 269.

rapid industrialisation.[42] Along these lines he argued that the declining standard of living of industrial workers was at least partially responsible for the
labour shortage, for it had meant that fewer peasants were attracted to the
urban centres.[43] Furthermore, he asserted, low incomes and unbearable working conditions had contributed to high rates of labour turnover by forcing
workers to wander from factory to factory to improve the quality of their lives.
Finally, he observed that poor nutrition, abominable working conditions, and
nervous exhaustion were generating indifference among workers about the
proper care of machinery, the conditions within the factories, and the quality
of goods produced.[44] Ultimately, he warned in April 1930, this decline in quality
would affect not only the individual consumer, but also the rate of industrialisation, since industry itself was 'the chief consumer of products'.[45] Repeatedly,
he noted accounts in the press that confirmed this prediction as well.[46]

A further inevitable consequence of the excessive tempo of industrialisation for Trotsky was rampant inflation. As he explained in an open letter to the
party in March 1930,

> An accelerated pace which runs ahead of existing possibilities soon leads
> to the creation of imaginary resources where there are no real ones. That
> is called inflation. All the symptoms of it are already present and they are
> also the symptoms of a threatening economic crisis.[47]

Three years later he argued that inflation was a serious problem that was contributing to the decline in the standard of living of workers while distorting
planning.[48]

While condemning the excessive pace of industrialisation, Trotsky denounced
the leadership for proceeding without regard for two factors essential for
correct planning: the market and democracy. Again echoing the arguments of
the party right, he asserted that the market was necessary during the entire
transition period between capitalism and socialism. In part, it was needed for
consumers to be able to express their needs 'by the direct pressure of supply
and demand'. Besides that, it was indispensable as a means of checking by

---

42   Trotsky 1975d, pp. 115, 170.
43   Trotsky 1973c, pp. 283–4.
44   Trotsky 1975d, p. 138; Trotsky 1973c, pp. 268–9; Trotsky 1972f, pp. 97–8.
45   Trotsky 1975d, p. 170.
46   See, for example, Trotsky 1973c, p. 183; Trotsky 1973d, pp. 262–4.
47   Trotsky 1975d, p. 137.
48   Trotsky 1972f, p. 98. See also Trotsky 1973c, pp. 99, 102, 207; Trotsky 1973d, pp. 275–6.

'commercial calculation' on the efficacy of the plan.[49] However, he complained in October 1932, the Stalinists had prepared and implemented the plan without any concern for the market, abolishing NEP and replacing market mechanisms with 'methods of compulsion'.[50] The second factor missing from Stalinist planning, according to Trotsky, was proletarian democracy. Previously, he had focused on the *political* necessity of democracy. Now he began to insist that democracy was also crucial from the *economic* standpoint.[51] As he observed in February 1930, the preparation of a five-year plan was a complex task requiring participation 'by all related industries and by the working class'. In particular, popular involvement was needed not only to determine what the masses wanted to consume, but also what they were able and willing to set aside for accumulation.[52] However, he noted in October 1930, the existing plan had been 'worked out at the top, behind closed doors, and then handed down to the masses like the tablets from Sinai'.[53]

To correct the industrial policies of the First Five-Year Plan Trotsky advanced a wide range of demands. Against the isolationism of the plan, he urged the leadership to work aggressively for the integration of the Soviet economy into the world market. Toward this end he called on the leadership of the Comintern and the Soviet Union to approach Social Democratic parties of the West with a public appeal for joint economic cooperation. He argued that if Social Democratic workers successfully pressured their leaders into supporting such a plan, the Soviet Union might receive much-needed machinery and equipment. On the other hand, even if the Social Democratic leaders rejected the

49   Trotsky 1973d, p. 274. On the necessity of a market for the expression of consumer needs, see also Trotsky 1972f, p. 223. On the importance of a stable currency see also Trotsky 1972f, pp. 98, 222–5. Alec Nove has emphasised the significance of the market for Trotsky, in contrast to the common perception that he was consistently hostile to it (Nove 1981, pp. 95–6; Nove 1982, pp. 399–401).

50   Trotsky 1973d, p. 275. See also Trotsky 1975c, pp. 360, 376–7; Trotsky 1973c, p. 99; Trotsky 1973d, p. 273.

51   On this point, see Deutscher 1963, p. 101.

52   Trotsky 1975d, p. 117. See also Trotsky 1973c, pp. 100, 287; Trotsky 1973d, pp. 260, 275. In March 1933 Trotsky asserted, 'Even if the Politburo consisted of seven universal geniuses, of seven Marxes or seven Lenins, it would still be unable, all on its own, with all its creative imagination, to assert command over the economy of 170 million people' (Trotsky 1972f, p. 96).

53   Trotsky 1973c, p. 51. See also Trotsky 1975c, p. 377; Trotsky 1975d, pp. 116–17; Trotsky 1973c, pp. 100, 287, 291; Trotsky 1973d, p. 274; Trotsky 1972f, p. 96.

proposal it would be politically beneficial, for the effort would bond Western workers with the USSR while splitting them from their reformist leaders.[54]

Throughout these years Trotsky also urged the Soviet leadership to slow the pace of industrialisation, specifically imploring it to abandon the effort to complete the Five-Year Plan in four years.[55] In October 1932 he proposed that the leadership delay the inauguration of the Second Five-Year Plan for one year, using 1933 as a buffer year for correcting economic disproportions.[56] In March 1933 he suggested that the starting point for industrial growth targets in 1933 should be the 8.5 percent attained in 1932, rather than the 16 percent projected in the Second Five-Year Plan.[57] Additionally, he advocated using the resources freed by the slowing industrialisation to improve the living standards and working conditions of the proletariat.[58]

Finally, Trotsky addressed the issue of the planning process. He openly admitted that the Opposition had no 'a priori plan' that would painlessly extricate the Soviet economy from the 'mud' into which it had been driven. Rather, he insisted that the plan could only be developed through 'broad soviet democracy'.[59] As a first step in this direction, he called on the party leadership to submit the experiences of the plan for discussion by a democratically-convened party congress.[60]

Like his critique of industrial policy, Trotsky's critique of agricultural policy in these years was 'from the right'. He condemned the leadership's dekulakisation drive as unnecessarily violent and as futile. Beyond that, he denounced the campaign for mass collectivisation as hopelessly premature, and predicted it would decimate Soviet agriculture while providing cover for the regeneration of a new stratum of kulaks.

Although in previous years the Opposition had demanded increased pressure on the kulaks, it had proposed to implement this through tax increases and the imposition of a 'forced loan'. Now, on learning of the leadership's dekulakisation drive in the fall of 1929, Trotsky repudiated the brutality of

54   Trotsky 1975d, pp. 125–9, 131, 147, 175–6, 353–4; Trotsky 1973c, pp. 106–7, 209.

55   Trotsky 1975d, pp. 118, 124–5, 130–1, 147, Trotsky 1973c, p. 106; Trotsky 1975d, pp. 37, 254, 279.

56   Trotsky 1973d, pp. 280–1, 284.

57   Trotsky 1972f, p. 111. See also Trotsky 1975d, pp. 118, 131, 147; Trotsky 1973c, p. 107; Trotsky 1973d, p. 282; Trotsky 1972f, p. 112.

58   Trotsky 1972f, p. 111. See also Trotsky 1975d, pp. 130, 147; Trotsky 1973c, 231; Trotsky 1973d, p. 282.

59   Trotsky 1975d, pp. 117–18. See also Trotsky 1975d, p. 137; Trotsky 1973c, p. 291.

60   Trotsky 1975d, pp. 117, 137; Trotsky 1973c, pp. 106, 291; Trotsky 1973d, pp. 275, 284; Trotsky 1972f, pp. 78, 96.

the campaign, describing it as nothing but 'naked bureaucratic violence'.[61] However, his primary opposition to the drive was not based on ethics but on his belief that it could not hope to succeed. In early 1930 he ridiculed the attempt to liquidate the kulak 'by administrative order' as 'a bureaucratic adventure, spiced with theoretical charlatanism'. Of course, he conceded, it was technically possible to liquidate every kulak with just 'two policemen (well-armed)'. But preventing the reappearance of a kulak stratum was quite another matter: 'For that, an industrial and cultural revolution is necessary'.[62] Notwithstanding the projections of the First Five-Year Plan, he did not see such a revolution on the horizon.

At greater length he denounced the tempo and scale of the collectivisation drive. Although the Opposition had called for greater collectivisation, it had intended to accomplish this gradually and voluntarily. For Trotsky, the pace of Stalinist collectivisation, like that of industrialisation, had nothing to do with rational planning. This was clearly indicated by the fact that the plan adopted in early 1929, presumably on the basis of technical and economic considerations, had projected the collectivisation of only 20 percent of the peasantry by 1933. Yet, by early 1930 already 40 percent of the peasants were inside *kolkhozy*, and it appeared that the remainder would soon be joining them there. Trotsky viewed such a prospect as disastrous.[63]

The biggest problem with the tempo of collectivisation in Trotsky's estimation was that it was outpacing the development of industry. He repeatedly insisted that true collectivisation required the mechanisation of agriculture, and that this presupposed a strong industrial base. In February 1930 he argued,

> With the aid of peasant plows and peasant nags, even all of them put together, it is not possible to create large agricultural collectives, even as it is not possible to build a ship out of a flock of fishing boats. The collectivization of agriculture can be achieved only through its mechanization.[64]

---

61   Trotsky 1975c, p. 360. As early as the summer of 1928 Trotsky had described the exceptional methods employed in the grain collection campaign as 'methods from the arsenal of war communism', 'measures of administrative violence', and 'measures of desperation'. Furthermore, he had denied that these methods had anything in common with a correct course. However, he had also asserted that these methods had been made 'inevitable' by the 'entire preceding policy' (Trotsky 1970b, p. 279; Trotsky 1981, pp. 168, 236; see also Deutscher 1959, p. 447, Lewin 1973, p. 279).

62   Trotsky 1975d, pp. 111–12. See also Trotsky 1975d, pp. 135–6, 145.

63   Trotsky 1975d, p. 109. See also Trotsky 1975d, p. 173.

64   Trotsky 1975d, p. 109. See also Trotsky 1975d, pp. 136, 173, 200–1.

Unfortunately, he observed, Soviet industry was still quite backward, and would remain so for years to come. In fact, he calculated that if the Soviet Union remained isolated it would take at least ten to fifteen years to create the industrial base necessary for total collectivisation.[65]

One result of wholesale collectivisation under these circumstances, Trotsky predicted, would be the lowering of individual initiative and of agricultural productivity. In April 1930 he warned that 'with the artificial, i.e., too-precipitate formation of large collective farms', agricultural productivity actually could be 'inferior to that in individual peasant holdings'.[66] By October 1932, he found evidence in the Soviet press that this prediction also had been verified. It seemed that 100 percent collectivisation had 'destroyed the incentive of the small commodity producer long before it was able to replace it by other and much higher economic incentives', and had resulted in '100 percent overgrowth of weeds on the fields'.[67]

A further concern repeatedly expressed by Trotsky was that the new collectives would facilitate the regeneration of a new layer of kulaks. He suggested several ways in which this might occur. First, *kolkhozy* would necessarily provide a higher income to the peasant who brought more horses or other 'capital' into the farms. Otherwise, no peasants would surrender their horses, and the state would be faced with the impossible task of providing all *kolkhozy* with machinery.[68] Second, differentiation would occur if families with several adult workers received higher incomes than families with only one. Third, inequality from either source could grow even larger if the collective borrowed part of this income to invest in machinery and then repaid the loan with interest.[69] Fourth, Trotsky argued that Stalin's restoration of open markets in 1932 would enrich *kolkhozy* situated closest to the cities, while promoting 'differentiation within the collectives'.[70] In light of such concerns, in his March 1930 open letter to the party he charged that by depicting the collectives as socialist enterprises the leadership had provided 'camouflage for the kulaks within the collectives'.[71]

---

65   Trotsky 1975d, pp. 110, 203.
66   Trotsky 1975d, p. 201.
67   Trotsky 1973d, p. 270.
68   Trotsky 1975d, p. 113.
69   Ibid.
70   Trotsky 1973d, p. 276.
71   Trotsky 1975d, pp. 135–6. See also Trotsky 1975d, p. 96. For other predictions about the growth of a kulak stratum within the collectives, see Trotsky 1973c, p. 58; Trotsky 1972f, pp. 73, 110–11.

Throughout the First Five-Year Plan Trotsky demanded that the leadership retreat from both dekulakisation and massive collectivisation. Regarding the former, he called for an end to the 'administrative abolition of the kulak'. In its place, he proposed 'severely restricting the exploiting tendencies of the kulak', and creating a system of tough contracts that would require the kulak to surrender specific products at predetermined prices.[72] As far as collectivisation was concerned, beginning in March 1930 he demanded a retreat to '*selective collectivization*', concentrating resources in the most viable of the collective farms, and reorganising these according to the wishes of the peasants.[73] In early 1933 he suggested that this might involve a reduction of collectivised agriculture from 60 to 40, or even 25 percent.[74]

6.2.2   *Analysing the Turn*

Throughout this period Trotsky struggled to understand the turn in Soviet economic policy. As in 1928–9, he attempted to analyse it in terms of the theory of bureaucracy he had developed in previous years. Again, however, events continually challenged those views, compelling him to modify his analysis by emphasising the autonomy of the bureaucracy. This was especially the case regarding three important questions: the attitude of the state and party bureaucracy to the turn, the source of the turn, and its most likely outcome.

Throughout the First Five-Year Plan Trotsky made various statements about precisely who was responsible for the change of policy. Most frequently he depicted the turn as initiated by the individual, the individuals, or the group standing at the summit of political power. Thus, at times he attributed the turn to 'Stalin', the 'Stalinists', the 'Stalinist leadership', or simply the 'leadership', leaving undefined the attitude of the state and party apparatuses to the new policy orientation.[75] However, in a number of apparently contradictory passages he explicitly addressed this question.

In previous years he had depicted the party-state bureaucracy as a social formation greatly influenced by bourgeois pressure and therefore deeply

72   Trotsky 1975d, pp. 130, 147; Trotsky 1973c, p. 232, Trotsky 1973d, p. 284. Evidently on the basis of such remarks as these and on Trotsky's concerns about the growth of a kulak layer within the collectives, Robert McNeal has misleadingly claimed that Trotsky was 'eager to associate himself' with the 'destruction of the kulaks (which Trotsky considered insufficiently thorough)' (McNeal 1977, p. 32).

73   Trotsky 1975d, pp. 124, 130, 147; Trotsky 1973d, pp. 283–4.

74   Trotsky 1972f, p. 110.

75   For example, 'Stalin' in Trotsky 1973c, p. 63; 'Stalinists' in Trotsky 1973c, p. 215; 'Stalinist leadership' in Trotsky 1975d, p. 137; 'leadership' in Trotsky 1975d, pp. 107, 111, 112, 136.

conservative in its orientation. For that reason it was difficult for him to imagine such a formation supporting a radical shift to the left in economic policy. Consequently, on some occasions he asserted that the turn had been made *against* the desires of the bureaucracy. In an article of 17 October 1929 he stated that, after years of acting like economic Mensheviks, the 'apparatus [*apparat*]' received an order to change course, but 'the apparatus – both the Communists and the specialists – was absolutely unprepared for this assignment'. Furthermore, he predicted that implementation of the plan would encounter significant opposition within the bureaucracy – 'nine-tenths of the apparatus being more right-wing than the official right wing'.[76] Similarly, in an article written approximately a year later he explained that, although it had lifted Stalin on a wave of reaction, now the 'majority of the real Stalinist bureaucracy [*bol'shinstvo podlinoi stalinskoi biurokratii*]' felt betrayed by Stalin, who had made the turn 'in spite of the partly active, mainly passive resistance of the majority of the apparatus [*apparat*]'.[77]

Still, as a Marxist Trotsky could hardly attribute such a major shift to the autonomous actions of individuals. Rather, it was necessary to identify the social formation that was responsible for the turn. Thus, in a series of passages that, as Robert McNeal has noted, seem to contradict directly those just cited, he explicitly attributed the turn to the 'Stalinist bureaucracy', to the 'bureaucracy', or to the 'apparatus'.[78] For example, in an article of 13 February 1930 he observed that the 'Stalinist bureaucracy [*stalinskaia biurokratiia*], after its years of opportunist policy, is going through a period of brief but thorough ultraleft lunacy'.[79] In 'Problems of the Development of the USSR', his draft theses on the Russian question in April 1931, he characterised the turn as 'an attempt of the bureaucracy [*biurokratiia*] to adapt itself to the proletariat'.[80] Likewise, on 1 March 1932 he described how in 1928 'the Stalinist bureaucracy [*stalinskaia biurokratiia*] ... made a whirlwind turn of 180 degrees over our heads' and then plunged into 'monstrous economic and political adventurism'.[81]

Trotsky might have attempted to reconcile these statements by arguing that the overwhelming majority of the state bureaucracy opposed the turn, while

76   Trotsky 1975c, p. 367; *Biulleten' oppozitsii* 1973, 7 (November–December 1929), p. 3.
77   Trotsky 1973c, pp. 62, 63; *Biulleten' oppozitsii* 1973, 17–18 (November–December 1930), p. 23. See also Trotsky 1975c, p. 48.
78   McNeal 1977, p. 33.
79   Trotsky 1975d, p. 115; *Biulleten' oppozitsii* 1973, 9 (February–March 1930), p. 6.
80   Trotsky 1973c, p. 215; *Biulleten' oppozitsii* 1973, 20 (April 1931), p. 7.
81   Trotsky 1973d, p. 66; *Biulleten' oppozitsii* 1973, 27 (March 1932), p. 3. See also Trotsky 1973c, p. 58; Trotsky 1973c, p. 286; Trotsky 1973d, p. 275.

a majority of the party bureaucracy supported it. Such an explanation is suggested by his draft theses on the Russian question of April 1931. In that work he asserted that the 'bourgeois elements of the state bureaucracy' first 'gained considerable strength on the basis of the NEP'. Later, and partly by supporting itself on this 'strengthened and emboldened petty-bourgeois and bourgeois bureaucracy', the 'centrist bureaucracy [*tsentristskaia biurokratiia*]' or 'centrist apparatus [*tsentristskii apparat*]' – evidently, of the party – was able to triumph. Trotsky then went on to describe the turn as just the latest of 'the political zigzags of the apparatus' – again, apparently referring to the party bureaucracy.[82] Although this explanation seems to resolve the apparent contradiction in Trotsky's statements, it only underlines his difficulty in explaining how a 'centrist' apparatus could have initiated what he viewed as such a radical turn to the left.

During the early 1930s Trotsky also offered various explanations for precisely *why* the leadership or the bureaucracy introduced the turn in late 1929. At times, in line with his traditional theory, he attempted to account for it in class terms. On other occasions, when compelled to recognise that such statements were problematic, he depicted the turn as the subjective, emotional response of the leadership/bureaucracy to economic developments.

Previously, Trotsky had portrayed the turn of 1928 as the leadership's response, under mounting pressure from the proletariat and Opposition, to the 'kulak strike' of 1928. Now, confronted with the radical deepening of the turn, he reiterated this argument, describing the *entire* turn since 1928 as a single process set in motion by these same factors. For example, in an article published in November 1930 he asserted,

> Coming to the edge of the capitalist precipice, Stalin – even though he is no lover of jumps – made a breakneck jump to the left. The economic contradictions, the dissatisfaction of the masses, the tireless criticism of the Left Opposition, compelled Stalin to make this turn.[83]

Similarly, in his April 1931 draft theses on the Russian question he argued, 'The course of 1928–31 – if we again leave aside the inevitable waverings and backslidings – represents an attempt of the bureaucracy to adapt itself to the proletariat'.[84]

---

82   Trotsky 1973c, pp. 214–15.

83   Trotsky 1973c, p. 63.

84   Trotsky 1973c, p. 215. For additional passages largely attributing the turn to a reaction by the leadership to kulak resistance, see Trotsky 1975d, pp. 108–9, 136; Trotsky 1973c,

However, as an explanation of the leadership's general orientation in the early 1930s, this approach was even less persuasive than it had been in accounting for the policy shifts of 1928–9. Through the summer of 1929 Trotsky had insisted that an increase in proletarian or Oppositional pressure was needed just to *maintain* the existing policy orientation. In fact, no such upsurge occurred. By the autumn of 1929 all but a handful of Oppositionists had capitulated, and most of the remainder were in prison. Beyond that, even if the Opposition had remained an active force, this could not have helped explain a policy orientation that, in Trotsky's understanding, was far to the left of anything the Opposition had demanded. Finally, Trotsky was not inclined to accept responsibility on behalf of the Opposition or the proletariat for policies that he viewed as so seriously misguided. Consequently, he found himself forced to supplement his class explanations with others. In these, he stressed the autonomy of the leadership and/or the bureaucracy in relation to all social classes.

Most frequently during these years, Trotsky depicted the turn as the product of various emotional states of the leadership or bureaucracy. Repeatedly, he attributed the radical shift in economic policy largely to the *'panic'* experienced by the leadership when confronted with the disastrous results of its own previous policies. In his 23 March 1930 'Open Letter' to the party, he explained that after its first revisions of the plan, 'the leadership, alarmed at its own indecisiveness, no longer knew any restraint'.[85] In December 1930 he asserted that 'the economic turn toward industrialization and collectivization took place under the whip of administrative panic'.[86] Similarly, in April 1931 he stated that the 'abruptness' of the Stalinists' leap to the left 'corresponded to the extent of the panic created in their ranks by the consequences of their own policy'.[87]

On other occasions he explained that the leadership had been carried away with *excitement* in the face of the first achievements of the plan. For example, in an article dated 13 February 1930 he stated that, after revising the initial plan upwards, the leaders discovered to their surprise that the first-year projections really could be realised. At that point, they 'abandoned their petty doubts and rushed to the opposite extreme', trading their former 'passive possibilist

---

p. 91; Trotsky 1973d, p. 48; Trotsky 1972f, p. 97. For additional passages stressing the role of pressure by the Opposition and/or working class, see Trotsky 1975c, p. 367; Trotsky 1975d, pp. 106, 136; Trotsky 1973c, pp. 103, 227; Trotsky 1972f, p. 49.

85   Trotsky 1975d, pp. 136–7.
86   Trotsky 1973c, p. 215.
87   Trotsky 1973c, p. 91.

position' for one of 'unrestrained subjectivism'.[88] That same month he elaborated on this argument in a discussion with a visiting American supporter, Max Shachtman. When Shachtman asked how Stalin had come to adopt an economic program 'far more radical' than the Opposition's, Trotsky responded that 'requirements of the economic situation' had initially forced Stalin's faction to revise the five-year plan upwards. Then,

> The startling successes of the first year – startling to the centrists, who never really believed such a rapid tempo possible – not only demonstrated the enormous latent possibilities for industrial development under a proletarian dictatorship . . ., but immediately produced an extreme boldness born precisely out of centrism's previous timidity. Almost overnight, the initial successes of the plan gave rise to the wildest kind of exaggerations.[89]

Regarding the turn in agriculture, Trotsky occasionally offered an explanation that was slightly more complex, but that equally stressed the role of subjective emotional states in the behaviour of the leadership. First, in February 1930 he described the initial phase of mass collectivisation in 1929 as a *peasant* response to the 'hail of administrative blows' inflicted upon the top layer of peasants. According to Trotsky, the blows against the kulaks discouraged the peasantry from any hope of improving its lot through the market. Consequently, peasants began joining the collectives *en masse*: 'The gate of the market was padlocked. The peasants stood frightened in front of it awhile, and then rushed through the only open door, that of collectivization'.[90] In this, Trotsky essentially accepted the leadership's characterisation of collectivisation as a spontaneous movement by the peasantry. It is likely that his credulity in this regard was due to his continuing adherence to his traditional theory of bureaucracy. He simply could not imagine a bureaucratic leadership, highly responsive to bourgeois pressure, initiating such an assault upon private property.

However, at this point in Trotsky's account the leadership's subjective reaction became the decisive factor in the process. In the face of this spontaneous self-collectivisation by the peasantry, the leadership was overwhelmed with excitement. Anticipating Stalin's 'dizzy with success' argument in an article of 13 February 1930, Trotsky explained,

---

88   Trotsky 1975d, pp. 106–7.

89   Trotsky 1979a, pp. 24–5. Shachtman's *Militant* article was dated March 1930. Peter Drucker
      has placed Shachtman's visit in February (Drucker 1994, p. 48).

90   Trotsky 1975d, pp. 108–9, 110–11. See also Trotsky 1975d, pp. 132, 179; Trotsky 1973c, p. 84.

The leadership itself was no less surprised by the sudden rush of the peasants into the collectives than the peasants were surprised by the liquidation of NEP. After getting over its astonishment, the leadership created a new theory: the building of socialism has entered into its 'third' stage: there is no longer any need for a market; in the future the kulak as a class will be liquidated.[91]

Similarly, in April 1930 he described how, after the initial peasant influx into the collectives,

the bureaucracy not only proclaimed this policy as its greatest victory – 'If we're going for a ride, let's really ride!' cried the parrot as the cat dragged it off by the tail – but also developed a mad pressure on the peasantry under the banner of the liquidation of classes. Tail-endism was transformed directly into adventurism.[92]

Perhaps Trotsky was uncomfortable attributing such independence to the leadership or bureaucracy and with explaining a major policy shift in terms of such subjective factors as panic and excitement. At any rate, as soon as an alternative explanation more consistent with his theory suggested itself, he seized upon it. The key Trotsky discovered was in the confessions by the technical specialists convicted of sabotage in late 1930 and early 1931. Incredibly, he accepted these confessions, like those in the Shakhty affair, at face value, perceiving them as a clear confirmation of his own previous analysis.[93] In November 1930 he endorsed the confessions of Ramzin and his codefendants. He noted that the Opposition had argued that the slow pace of industrialisation and collectivisation in the period 1923–8 had been dictated by the kulak and the foreign bourgeoisie, through the agency of the bureaucracy. Now, these 'sociological generalizations' had been confirmed by Ramzin's own admission that he and his colleagues had plotted during that period to slow the tempo of development.[94] Similarly, during the Menshevik trial of March 1931 he asserted that the 'connection of the Mensheviks with the saboteurs ... and the imperialist bourgeoisie' had been 'irrefutably confirmed by the members of the Menshevik center'. For Trotsky it followed that in their struggle with the Opposition the centrists unconsciously had 'carried out the tasks of the

---

91   Trotsky 1975d, p. 111.
92   Trotsky 1975d, p. 179. See also Trotsky 1972f, p. 97.
93   On this see Law 1987a, p. 169.
94   Trotsky 1973c, pp. 66–9. See also Trotsky 1973c, p. 200.

capitalist general staff abroad'.[95] (He only repudiated this position in the summer of 1936, just before the first of the great Moscow Trials).[96]

Trotsky was convinced that these confessions also explained the ultraleft character of current economic policy. In connection with the trial of Ramzin and the Industrial Party, he reasoned that since 1928 saboteurs would not have been able to deepen Soviet economic difficulties by slowing the pace of industrialisation. Therefore, 'the opposite road was taken: an excessive acceleration of the tempo'. He concluded that the indictment demonstrated that in both the earlier and current periods the Stalinist leadership 'acted under the dictation of the saboteurs' center, that is, a gang of the agents of international capital'.[97] Trotsky also reiterated this argument in March 1931 after the trial of the 'Menshevik Centre', predicting the next trial would reveal that the saboteurs had been guilty of 'disruptive acceleration of disproportionate rates' through 'complete collectivization' and 'administrative dekulakization', and that many Menshevik economists had become 'veritable superindustrializers' in 1928 in order 'to prepare, by means of economic adventurism, the political downfall of the dictatorship of the proletariat'.[98]

Even Trotsky must have sensed the absurdity of suggesting that the entire turn was little more than a capitalist plot. Consequently, by March 1932 he returned to his 'panicky leadership' explanation, attributing the adventurism of the Stalinist bureaucracy to its having been 'hit over the head by the kulaks'.[99] One year later he asserted that the members of the Politburo launched into

---

95 Trotsky 1973c, pp. 198, 200–1. See also Trotsky 1973c, pp. 192–5. In late 1930 Trotsky also accepted the validity of the accusations in the trial of the 'Toiling Peasants' Party'. Noting that *Pravda* had revealed the 'adherence' of A.P. Smirnov and I.A. Teodorovich, both former Commissars of Agriculture, 'to the Kondratievs', he commented that the article was 'basically a paraphrasing' of the declarations of the Opposition during 1926–27 (Trotsky 1975d, p. 112). Regarding the Menshevik trial, Trotsky's sole doubt concerned the allegation that Riazanov had participated in the conspiracy along with the Mensheviks (Trotsky 1973c, pp. 192–7).

96 At that time the 'editors' of the *Bulletin* admitted they had 'greatly underestimated the shamelessness of Stalinist justice and therefore took too seriously the confessions of the former Mensheviks' [*Biulleten' oppozitsii* 1973, 51 (July–August 1936), p. 15].

97 Trotsky 1973c, pp. 67–8.

98 Trotsky 1973c, p. 201. In his 4 April 1931 draft theses on the Russian question Trotsky also spoke of the 'Menshevik-saboteur program of industrialization and collectivization' (Trotsky 1973c, p. 216). See also Trotsky 1973c, pp. 206, 219, 307.

99 Trotsky 1973d, p. 66.

'the adventure of 100 percent collectivization' because they were 'frightened by the consequences of their own negligence'.[100]

Trotsky's predictions regarding the ultimate outcome of the left turn were similarly contradictory. At times, he insisted that the new collective farms would regenerate a layer of kulaks and that a major turn to the right in both industrial and agricultural policy was imminent. However, by late 1932 his growing concerns about the economic crisis seem to have convinced him that, instead, the independent course of the bureaucracy might bring about complete economic collapse, perhaps combined with a counterrevolutionary upheaval that would unite elements of all classes against it.

Trotsky's economic forecast from this period that has received the greatest criticism was his repeated prediction that the collective farms would mask, and ultimately foster, the growth of a new stratum of kulaks.[101] In fairness to Trotsky, it should be noted that he was not the only observer who was worried about such a development within the *kolkhozy*. In November 1930 the head of *Pravda's* department of agricultural affairs warned that collective farms with a small degree of socialisation provided the conditions for the reemergence of economic inequality.[102] In fact, as R.W. Davies has observed, 'inequality between former poor peasants and former middle peasants persisted' in the years 1930–1.[103] Furthermore, in the middle to late 1930s a significant degree of differentiation actually did take place, both within and between *kolkhozy*.[104] Nevertheless, Isaac Deutscher has correctly argued that, although Trotsky grasped a real tendency when he spoke of differentiation within the collectives, he overemphasised its strength. In particular, he did not foresee that the leadership would be able to control the development of private property 'by a combination of economic measures and terror'.[105] To this we might add that, while Trotsky foresaw that mass collectivisation would lower agricultural productivity, he did not anticipate it could do so to the extent that in the early 1930s it would eliminate the surplus required for a significant growth in inequality. As Alec Nove has reasonably suggested, aside from a lack of information, at least

---

100   Trotsky 1972f p. 97.

101   See R. Davies 1980b, pp. 79–80; Law 1987a, pp. 113–14; Nove 1981, p. 94; Nove 1982, p. 395; and Nove 1979, p. 49.

102   R. Davies 1980b, pp. 279–80.

103   R. Davies 1980b, p. 161.

104   See, for example, Deutscher 1966, p. 331; Fitzpatrick 1994, pp. 139–42; Merl 1993, p. 42; Serge 1996, p. 36.

105   Deutscher 1963, p. 106.

part of the explanation for Trotsky's erroneous perspective on the *kolkhozy* was that he 'mistakenly identified the interests of the "Stalinist bureaucracy" with the village rich'.[106] Again, it appears Trotsky's perception was distorted by his continuing adherence to his traditional theory.

Another concern inspired by Trotsky's traditional theory was his belief that the leadership would inevitably revert to conservative economic policies. At times, this was expressed in his frequent characterisations of the turn as a left 'zigzag'.[107] However, it also was expressed in repeated explicit predictions about the imminence of a new right turn. For example, in February 1930 he asserted,

> The more frenzied the character of the present course, the sooner and sharper its contradictions will break out. Then to the former 180-degree curve, the leadership will add another, returning close to its starting point from the other end. So it has been, so it will be again.[108]

Soon after this, he perceived Stalin's 'Dizzy with Success' speech to be the signal for the beginning of the retreat. In an article of 14 March he asked, 'At what point will this retreat come to a halt? It is as yet impossible to tell. It is probable that this time also the retreat will go much further than the objective conditions require'.[109] Even more categorically, at about this time he predicted to Max Shachtman that 'Stalin, who is on the road leading away from the recent ultraleft zigzag in Russia, will not come to a halt until he has reached the other extreme and accepted the original program of the right wing'.[110]

In line with this view, throughout the following years Trotsky carefully scrutinised Soviet policy for evidence of the anticipated right shift. In the fall of 1930, seeing the Stalinists as 'waist-deep in trouble with the five-year plan', he observed that the renewed campaign against the party right suggested that Stalin was about to initiate 'an inevitable turn to the right'.[111] In the summer of

---

106   Nove 1981, p. 94.

107   See, for example, Trotsky 1975c, p. 284; Trotsky 1975d, pp. 15, 96, 106, 179, 208; Trotsky 1973c, pp. 64, 78, 215, 280, 291; Trotsky 1973d, pp. 42, 43, 67, 228; Trotsky 1972f, p. 49.

108   Trotsky 1975d, p. 116. See also Trotsky 1975d, p. 114.

109   Trotsky 1975d, p. 123. See also Trotsky 1975d, pp. 138–9, 174, 204.

110   Trotsky 1979a, p. 25.

111   Trotsky 1973c, pp. 51, 61.

1931, he described the reintroduction of piecework as a new turn to the right.[112] Also, in late 1932 and early 1933 he saw Stalin's restoration of open markets and his abrupt reduction of the goals of the Second Five-Year Plan as evidence of a right turn that could lead to the weakening in the state monopoly of foreign trade.[113]

However, by late 1932 Trotsky had begun to perceive an even more menacing danger. The deepening of the economic crisis convinced him that the leadership had brought the country to the brink of collapse. As early as 23 March 1930 he warned in his 'Open Letter' to the party that the policy of the leadership was propelling the Soviet Union 'full speed toward the most dangerous crisis and the worst catastrophe'.[114] In October 1932 he concluded the economy had '*suffered a rupture* from excessive and poorly calculated exertion', and the following March he asserted that the leadership had 'brought the national economy to the brink of absolute chaos'.[115] A result of this crisis, he observed in January 1933, was growing disaffection – especially among the peasantry, but also within the proletariat:

> The hungry workers are discontented with the party's policy. The party is discontented with the leadership. The peasantry is discontented with the industrialization, the collectivization, and the town. A part of the peasantry is discontented with the regime.[116]

The most ominous prospect was that a disruption of the economic *smychka* would break the political alliance between the proletariat and the peasantry. Trotsky saw this as especially dangerous because the *kolkhozy* had become 'organized formations for peasant strikes against the state'.[117] His ultimate fear was a peasant revolt, perhaps even assisted by elements of the proletariat.

---

112   Trotsky 1973c, p. 285.
113   Trotsky 1973d, p. 276; Trotsky 1972f, pp. 46, 49, 75, 80, 102–3.
114   Trotsky 1975d, p. 135. See also Trotsky 1975d, pp. 96, 114, 123, 126, 138, 172, 174, 200, 202–4; Trotsky 1973c, pp. 51, 61, 102, 183–4, 291, 295.
115   Trotsky 1973d, p. 280; Trotsky 1972f, p. 96. See also Trotsky 1973d, pp. 121–2, 259, 277–9; Trotsky 1972f, pp. 45–6, 75–7, 96–9, 100, 103.
116   Trotsky 1972f, p. 75. See also Trotsky 1975d, pp. 172, 174.
117   Trotsky 1972f, pp. 77, 75.

6.3   The Left Course in the Comintern

In these same years the Soviet leadership of the Comintern was deepening the radical international course inaugurated in 1928–9. Comintern leaders continued to assert that the world had entered a Third Period, characterised by a general sharpening of the contradictions of imperialism and by the intensification of international class conflict. For them, this prognosis was confirmed by the onset of the Great Depression following the Wall Street crash of October 1929. In this context the leadership proclaimed that the task of Communists in the capitalist world was to prepare the proletariat for an imminent struggle for power. Most immediately, it was necessary to wage a merciless struggle against the 'social fascists' of the Second International, who were instituting fascism in the name of socialism. To this end the Comintern banned all alliances of Communist parties with Social Democratic leaders, declaring that the only acceptable form of collaboration with Social Democrats was a united front 'from below' with Socialist workers.[118] The most important testing ground for the Comintern's Third Period strategy was Germany.

As the tidal wave of the Great Depression swept across Europe, it brought severe economic dislocation to Germany. The foreign loans and trade that had fueled economic prosperity since 1923 suddenly disappeared, industrial production faltered, banks were forced to close, thousands of small businesses were wiped out, and unemployment climbed from 1.32 million in September 1929 to over 6 million in the early months of 1932 and 1933.[119] In turn, the deepening economic crisis gave rise to political destabilisation. In March 1930 the coalition government led by the Social Democratic Chancellor Hermann Müller collapsed in a conflict over the unemployment insurance fund. Subsequently, President Hindenburg appointed Heinrich Brüning of the Centre Party as Chancellor. Confronted with parliamentary resistance to his austerity program, Brüning asked Hindenburg to dissolve the Reichstag. In the ensuing elections of 14 September, the Social Democratic Party as well as the traditional centre and right parties lost ground, while the parties at the extremes of the German political spectrum made significant gains. The Communist Party (KPD) improved its position with a vote of 4.6 million – up 40 percent from its totals in 1928. Even more remarkable was the success of the National Socialist Party, which increased its support from 810,000 votes in

---

118   For examples of this line during the years 1930–33, see Degras 1971, pp. 102–9, 112–14, 157–
        64, 190–2, 221–30.

119   Shirer 1960, p. 136; Bullock 1952, pp. 135–7.

1928 to over 6.4 million – making the Nazis the second strongest party in the Reichstag.[120]

However, the leadership of the KPD was not impressed by the Nazi electoral successes. The day after the elections the Communist paper *Die Rote Fahne* asserted that, although the election had been Hitler's 'greatest day', it also signaled 'the beginning of the end' for the Nazis.[121] Addressing the Eleventh Plenum of the ECCI the following April, KPD leader Ernst Thälmann similarly observed that after the elections 'we stated soberly and seriously that 14 September was in a sense Hitler's best day after which there would be no better but only worse days'.[122]

When the economic crisis deepened in late 1930 and 1931, Brüning began to institute austerity measures by emergency decree. Despite this, the SPD leadership supported Brüning as the lesser evil in comparison with the Nazis. In contrast, the KPD declared that Brüning's dictatorial rule demonstrated that fascism already had triumphed, and insisted that the SPD's support for Brüning only confirmed that the Social Democrats were truly 'social fascists'.[123]

As Communist hostility to the Social Democrats mounted through 1931, the KPD found itself promoting tactics that in certain respects mirrored those of the far right. It increasingly adapted itself to the nationalist sentiments that had been so effectively utilised by the National Socialists, calling for a 'peoples' revolution' for the social and national liberation of Germany from the unjust burden of the Versailles Peace.[124] Even more striking was its endorsement in the summer of 1931 of a Nazi-sponsored referendum, called the 'Red Referendum' by the KPD, against the SPD-led coalition government of Prussia. On 9 August the plebiscite was defeated in the polls, at least partly because large numbers of Communist workers boycotted the referendum.[125]

By the fall of 1931 pressure was building for a unified response by the KPD and SPD to the threat of Nazism. Within Germany, the most vocal advocates of such an alliance were the members of a number of relatively small splinter groupings from the KPD and SPD, including the Brandlerites – German supporters of Bukharin; the Socialist Workers Party, founded primarily by left-wing dissidents from the SPD; and the minuscule Trotskyist organisation. However, when the idea of unity also was taken up briefly by Rudolf Breitscheid of the

---

120   Deutscher 1963, pp. 129–30; James 1937, pp. 320–2; Shirer 1960, pp. 137–8.
121   Quoted James 1937, p. 329; Deutscher 1963, p. 130. See also Carr 1982, pp. 25–6.
122   Quoted in Deutscher 1963, pp. 130–1.
123   Carr 1982, pp. 26–8; James 1937, pp. 329–30.
124   Carr 1982, pp. 31–2; Deutscher 1963, p. 152; C. Fischer 1991, p. 105; James 1937, pp. 330–1.
125   Carr 1982, pp. 41–3; Deutscher 1963, p. 152; Fowkes 1984, pp. 164–5.

SPD in November, Thälmann abruptly rejected this proposal, asserting that the most serious danger confronting the Communist Party was the influence of social democracy over revolutionary workers. Furthermore, at the subsequent plenum of the Central Committee of the KPD in February 1932, he denounced local party organisations that had mistakenly interpreted the slogan 'united front from below' to include direct alliances with SPD organisations. Although it appeared that the KPD was about to reverse this position in the spring of 1932 with the formation of a broad alliance, the 'Anti-Fascist Action', a CC declaration of 5 June clarified that 'reformist organizations' were not to be included.[126]

Meanwhile, the strength and aggressiveness of the National Socialists continued to grow. In the presidential elections of March–April 1932 Hindenburg was reelected with Social Democratic support. However, Hitler took 30.1 percent of the vote in the first round and 36.8 percent in the second, more than doubling the Nazi totals of September 1930. Hindenberg then dismissed Brüning as Chancellor after Brüning attempted to outlaw Hitler's swelling organisation of storm troopers. When the new Chancellor, Franz von Papen, rescinded the ban on 15 June the SA immediately unleashed a wave of terror against the left.[127] Soon afterwards, Papen fulfilled a long-held dream of the Nazis by dissolving the Socialist-led Prussian government and placing Prussia under military rule. Although the SPD had declared its intention to resist such a coup by force, it quickly capitulated. Meanwhile, the German workers ignored the KPD's appeal to respond with a nationwide general strike. The consequent demoralisation of the left and the invigoration of the far right were reflected in the elections of 31 July in which the Nazis received 14 million votes, making them the largest party in the Reichstag.[128]

At its twelfth plenum in September 1932 the ECCI seemed oblivious to the impending catastrophe. In its official resolutions all Communist parties were instructed to direct their main blows against 'social fascism'. The ECCI also asserted that in Germany the SPD had helped prepare the way for the establishment of the 'fascist dictatorship' of the Papen government.[129] In his remarks Thälmann emphatically rejected appeals by Trotskyists and others for joint action with the SPD against the Nazis. According to Thälmann, Trotsky's

---

126   Carr 1982, pp. 50, 56–9, 61; Fowkes 1984, pp. 165–6; James 1937, pp. 333–4.

127   Deutscher 1963, p. 158; Shirer 1960, pp. 165–6.

128   Carr 1982, pp. 61–2; Deutscher 1963, p. 158; Fowkes 1984, pp. 166–7; James 1937, pp. 341–6; Shirer, pp. 165–6.

129   Degras 1965, pp. 224–6. See also James 1937, pp. 346–8.

advocacy of such an alliance merely represented an attempt by this 'utterly bankrupt Fascist and counter-revolutionary' to 'lead the working class astray'.[130]

When the new Reichstag convened on 12 September nearly all parties, including the KPD, SPD, and the Nazis, united in a vote of no confidence in the Papen government. Soon afterwards, the Reichstag recognised its own dissolution. In the elections of 6 November the Nazis polled two million fewer votes than in July, while the SPD vote also declined slightly. The vote for the KPD increased by 20 percent. The press of the Comintern and the KPD portrayed the election as a great victory and a sign that the Nazis had passed their peak.[131] However, events quickly revealed that such optimism was premature. On 2 December Hindenburg formed a new government under General Kurt von Schleicher – a development characterised by the Comintern press as 'a sharpened stage of the Fascist regime'. As Chancellor, Schleicher unsuccessfully attempted to win the support of both the trade-union movement and a dissident wing of the Nazi Party, but succeeded only in alienating influential business, financial, and land-owning interests. On 28 January, conceding his inability to obtain a working majority in the Reichstag, he resigned. Two days later, Hindenburg appointed Hitler to the post of Chancellor.[132]

6.4   Trotsky and the Comintern's New Strategy

During the years 1929–33 Trotsky denounced Comintern policy, as he criticised Soviet economic policy, primarily 'from the right'. In particular, he condemned the ultraleftism of the Comintern line in Germany, where he saw it as contributing to the growth and potentially to the victory of Nazism. Like the turn in Soviet economic policy, the shift in Comintern policy had contradicted his expectations. Here too, Trotsky attempted to utilise his traditional theory of bureaucracy to analyse the origins of the new orientation and to predict its probable outcome. However, as in his analysis of Soviet economic policy, he repeatedly found himself forced to modify that theory implicitly by emphasising the autonomy of the bureaucracy.[133]

---

130   Thälmann quoted in Deutscher 1963, p. 143 and Degras 1965, p. 213.

131   Carr 1982, pp. 74, 77; Fowkes 1984, p. 168; James 1937, p. 350; Shirer 1960, pp. 170–2.

132   Carr 1982, pp. 79–82, Comintern news-sheet quoted on p. 79; Fowkes 1984, pp. 168–9; Shirer 1960, pp. 172–82.

133   For other accounts of Trotsky's views on Comintern policy during this period, see Chattopadhyay 2006, pp. 506–15; Cliff 1993, pp. 108–38; Deutscher 1963, pp. 131–44; Hallas 1984, pp. 66–71; Knei-Paz 1978, pp. 350–8; Mandel 1971, pp. 9–46; Mandel 1979, pp. 88–98;

6.4.1   Criticising Comintern Policy from the 'Right'

Since the beginning of 1928, Trotsky had denounced various aspects of Comintern policy as 'ultraleft'. In that year he condemned the 'putschism' and 'adventurism' of the Canton Commune, as well as the Comintern's 'ultraleftism' in refusing to recognise the seriousness of the defeat in China in 1927.[134] In 1929 he further criticised the 'element of adventurism' in the KPD's May Day demonstration in Berlin for 'conquest of the streets' – a demonstration that was repressed by the police. Subsequently, he also condemned the 'adventurism' of the international demonstrations of 1 August 1929, called to avenge the victims of 1 May and to demonstrate again that the working class was capable of achieving the 'conquest of the streets'.[135]

By late 1929 Trotsky began to criticise the ultraleftism of the whole Third Period line, raising a variety of objections to the new orientation.[136] Most broadly, he rejected the methodology involved in the notion that the entire world revolutionary movement had entered its final period. He considered it absurd to suggest that a revolutionary situation could emerge simultaneously throughout the whole world. Beyond that, he insisted that the issue of whether or not the revolutionary struggle had entered its final period was 'a question of the relation of forces and the changes in the situation', factors that could only be tested through action.[137] Furthermore, he believed that the world movement actually had declined, not intensified, in the years 1928 and 1929 due to the defeats in Britain and China and in the context of a brief economic boom in several countries.[138] However, the greatest problem with the new Comintern line for Trotsky was its disastrous effect in Germany. There, he argued, it was disorienting and disarming the proletariat in the struggle with National Socialism.

According to Trotsky, the mass support enjoyed by Nazism, especially among the German petty bourgeoisie, could be explained by two factors: 'a sharp social crisis' and 'the revolutionary weakness of the German proletariat'.[139] In the face of economic ruin, the German middle classes found themselves compelled to seek radical solutions to their difficulties. Trotsky asserted that in

Mandel 1995, pp. 106–26; Molyneux 1981, pp. 151–6; Thatcher 2003, pp. 175–82; and Wistrich 1979, pp. 176–94.

134   Trotsky 1976a, pp. 275, 282–3, 317, 346, 350–3; Trotsky 1981, pp. 33, 76–7, 113, 154.
135   Trotsky 1975c, pp. 170, 224. See also Trotsky 1975c, pp. 432–3, 436.
136   See Trotsky 1975c, pp. 328, 367–8.
137   Trotsky 1975d, p. 53; Trotsky 1971c, p. 64.
138   Trotsky 1971c, p. 56. See also Trotsky 1975d, p. 53.
139   Trotsky 1971c, p. 122. See also Trotsky 1971c, p. 59.

such a situation it was possible for a revolutionary party to win the allegiance of the petty bourgeoisie. However, if the party of the working class proved incapable of inspiring such confidence, the petty bourgeoisie would blame the workers for the endless strikes and political disturbances, and would turn instead to fascism, 'the *party of counterrevolutionary despair*'.[140] This, he perceived, was happening in Germany.

Meanwhile, according to Trotsky, the big capitalists had begun financing Nazism in order to carry out a fundamental shift in their method of rule. He explained that in the pre-war era of capitalist upsurge, the capitalist classes of the imperialist countries had legitimised their rule through 'orderly, pacific, conservative, democratic forms'.[141] In doing so, they had leaned mainly on the working classes, 'held in check by the reformists'.[142] However, since the war capitalism, together with all of its democratic forms of domination, had entered an era of decline. Consequently, the capitalist class was no longer willing to grant new reforms; now it was focused on abolishing the old ones. Although German capitalists initially continued to rely on the assistance of the SPD leadership to implement social retrenchment, as the crisis intensified they had begun to view this solution as unsatisfactory. Wanting to 'rid itself of the pressure exerted by the workers' organizations', the capitalist class had begun assisting the development of a mass fascist movement.[143]

Repeatedly, Trotsky warned that the assumption of power by the Nazis would be catastrophic for the proletariat, both within Germany and internationally. Within Germany a Nazi victory would result in 'the extermination of the flower of the German proletariat, the destruction of its organizations, the eradication of its belief in itself and in its future'.[144] Internationally, a Nazi government would be free to conduct foreign policy without regard for the constraints that encumbered normal bourgeois parliamentary governments. As early as November 1931 Trotsky predicted that a Hitler government, acting as the 'executive organ of world capitalism as a whole', would launch a war against the Soviet Union.[145]

However, Trotsky insisted up until 1933, the cause was not yet lost. The German capitalist class as a whole had not yet decided to resort to fascism. Although the bourgeoisie did not doubt that Hitler would be 'a submissive

---

140   Trotsky 1971c, p. 59. See also Trotsky 1971c, pp. 59, 155, 266, 284.
141   Trotsky 1971c, pp. 143, 280.
142   Trotsky 1971c, p. 158. See also Trotsky 1971c, pp. 143, 281.
143   Trotsky 1971c, pp. 281, 144, 155. See also Trotsky 1971c, pp. 58, 158, 280–2.
144   Trotsky 1971c, p. 125.
145   Trotsky 1971c, p. 126.

instrument of their domination', they still feared the social upheaval that would accompany the installation of a Nazi regime.[146] For the time being they preferred more traditional authoritarian regimes such as those of Brüning or Papen – governments Trotsky regarded as 'Bonapartist' dictatorships, 'enforced by means of the army and the police' and basing themselves on the apparent balance between organisations of the fascist petty bourgeoisie and the proletariat.[147] He viewed it as grossly inaccurate and disorienting for the KPD to characterise these governments as fascist. Under Bonapartism, it was still possible to organise an effective defence of workers' organisations; under fascism, these would be swept away. For a working-class organisation to claim that there was no difference between Brüning or Papen and Hitler, was the equivalent of saying that 'it makes no difference whether our organizations exist, or whether they are destroyed'.[148]

Even more disorienting, according to Trotsky, was the Stalinist identification of social democracy with Nazism. He did not dispute the fact that the SPD served the interests of German capital; nor did he doubt that it shared a large part of the political responsibility for the growth of Nazism.[149] However, he sharply rejected Stalinist assertions that social democracy was simply a variant of fascism, insisting that these movements represented two very different forms of bourgeois rule. Whereas social democracy derived its support from the workers and their organisations, and was 'the chief representative of the parliamentary-bourgeois regime', fascism based itself largely on the petty bourgeoisie, and established itself in power by destroying parliamentarism and the organisations of the workers.[150] Because of this difference, Social Democratic leaders correctly viewed fascism as a mortal danger that threatened their role in the bourgeois regime and the income they derived from that role.[151] For Trotsky the theory of social fascism was an obstacle to the united front that was necessary for defeating Hitler. Because of the KPD's refusal to pursue such an alliance, he accused the 'Stalinist bureaucracy' of 'direct and immediate responsibility for the growth of fascism before the proletarian vanguard'.[152]

---

146   Trotsky 1971c, p. 278. See also Trotsky 1971c, pp. 58, 282, 285–6.

147   Trotsky 1971c, p. 160. See also Trotsky 1971c, pp. 144, 156, 161–2, 276, 277–8.

148   Trotsky 1971c, p. 161.

149   Trotsky 1971c, pp. 70, 144–5, 148–50, 152, 153–4, 275–7, 284–5, 318; Trotsky 1975c, p. 392.

150   Trotsky 1971c, pp. 154–5.

151   Trotsky 1971c, p. 288. See also Trotsky 1971c, pp. 70, 145, 155; Trotsky 1975c, pp. 391–2.

152   Trotsky 1971c, pp. 70, 285. See also Trotsky 1971c, p. 125. The KPD did, on a number of occasions, appeal to the ranks of the SPD for a united front. However, in Trotsky's view, 'in each of these instances only a purely formal, declamatory application of the united front was inaugurated' (Trotsky 1971c, p. 183).

In fact, he charged, the KPD had shown far less reluctance to joining a 'united front with Hitler' to bring down the SPD government of Prussia.[153]

The task of the Opposition as Trotsky described it was to do all that it could to pressure the Comintern and its sections to abandon its ultraleft and sectarian line, especially in Germany. With mounting desperation, he urged the KPD to drop the rhetoric about social fascism and to forge a united front with the SPD. The purpose of such a front would be the armed defense of working-class institutions against Nazi attacks. Trotsky explained in September 1930 that the united front would protect 'those material and moral positions which the working class has managed to win in the German state', including such institutions as workers' political organisations, trade unions, and newspapers.[154] Although he saw the immediate struggle in Germany as defensive, he suggested that this could change quickly. He predicted that the first repulse of a rightist attack would elicit a 'redoubled offensive on the part of fascism'. This in turn would solidify and radicalise the united front. At that point the KPD would be in a position to lead an offensive struggle for power.[155] According to Trotsky, it was this prospect that most frightened the SPD leadership. Nevertheless, he believed that it could be induced to join such a front under the pressure of its proletarian supporters and for the sake of its income and its survival. However, even if the Socialist leadership rejected a united front, the campaign for such an alliance would be valuable, for it would attract thousands, or even millions, of Social Democratic workers to the KPD for a militant struggle against fascism.[156] To achieve such a correct line in Germany, Trotsky insisted, a restoration of democracy was necessary, both within the KPD and the Comintern.[157]

6.4.2 Trotsky's Analysis of the Third Period Strategy

Trotsky's analysis of Comintern strategy, like his analysis of Soviet economic policy, contained contradictory approaches. As in his writings on economics, he attempted to explain the leadership's turn and to predict its most likely outcome in class terms on the basis of his theory of bureaucracy. However, he quickly found himself compelled to modify that theory by attributing the turn to autonomous characteristics of the bureaucracy, and he even began to fear that the autonomous policies of the bureaucracy might result in a Nazi victory.

---

153 See Trotsky 1971c, pp. 93–114.

154 Trotsky 1971c, p. 72. See also Trotsky 1971c, pp. 108–9, 138–9, 171–2.

155 Trotsky 1971c, pp. 248–9. See also Trotsky 1971c, pp. 72–3.

156 Trotsky 1971c, pp. 72–3, 137, 171–2, 179, 296, 304.

157 See Trotsky 1971c, p. 323.

Trotsky's account of the origins of the Comintern's ultraleft binge was similar to his explanation of the economic turn in the Soviet Union. In part, he suggested that it was a reaction by the Stalinist leadership to its previous defeats; in part, it was a response to the pressure exerted by the Left Opposition. For example, in August 1929 Trotsky commented that 'the Stalinist leadership, under the pressure of the growing danger of the Right and the whip of criticisms made by the Opposition, was forced to carry out its left turn' in Comintern policy.[158] Similarly, in his April 1931 theses on the Russian question he argued that the international 'left course of Stalin' had sprung 'from an attempt to undermine the roots of the Left Opposition'.[159] However, as in his writings on the economic turn, Trotsky stopped short of attributing the extremes of the new line to the pressure of the Opposition. Again, it would have been difficult to establish that connection since the new Comintern line was far more extreme than the orientation demanded by the Opposition, and again Trotsky wanted no credit for it.

Since there was no apparent basis for suggesting that the new orientation was prompted by bourgeois 'saboteurs', Trotsky's only alternative was to explain the extremes of the line in terms of the bureaucracy's own autonomous behaviour. Thus, he concluded that the leadership's repudiation of all alliances with reformists was an overreaction to the failures of its previous attempts to form a united front, and he suggested that the explanation for this overreaction was nothing more than the leadership's stupidity. In December 1929 he asserted that Molotov's recent rejection of such alliances represented a reaction by the centrists to the fact that they had 'burned their hands' in the Anglo-Russian Committee and now hoped 'to guard against scandals in the future' by avoiding *all* alliances. However, for Trotsky the problem with the leadership's policy regarding the ARC had nothing to do with an 'episodic agreement with reformists'. Rather, it was that the leadership had not confined its agreement to 'concrete practical goals' clear to the working class, and it had failed to break the alliance when the General Council turned against the general strike. Unfortunately, Trotsky concluded, the Comintern strategists still had not understood these lessons.[160] In a pamphlet written in January 1932, Trotsky similarly asserted that the bureaucracy had adopted the new international line in a mistaken reaction to the failures of its own ill-conceived attempts at alliances:

---

158   Trotsky 1975c, p. 229.
159   Trotsky 1973c, p. 227. See also Trotsky 1971c, p. 103.
160   Trotsky 1975d, p. 59.

The Stalinist bureaucracy chose to behave like the nearsighted monkey in the fable; after adjusting the spectacles on its tail and licking them to no result, the monkey concluded that they were no good at all and dashed them against a rock. Put it as you please, but the spectacles are not at fault.[161]

To a large degree, Trotsky's expectations regarding the ultimate prospects for the international turn continued to be influenced by his belief in the opportunist inclinations of the bureaucracy. One concern he repeatedly expressed was that the leadership would soon reverse itself and revert to its former rightist course. As in economic policy, this idea was clearly suggested by his persistent characterisation of the turn as merely a left 'zigzag'.[162] Trotsky suggested various ways that such a turn might materialise. In an article of 8 January 1930 he explained that in the event of a mass proletarian radicalisation it would become necessary for the party to initiate alliances with Social Democratic leaders pushed to the left. In such a situation, the leadership would be forced to abandon its current opposition to all alliances with reformists and would shift back toward the right. At that point it would overshoot the mark once again and all the 'Molotovs' would enter 'with "both feet" into a period of opportunist experiments' like the ARC and the Guomindang.[163] Alternatively, he suggested in December 1932, the leadership might turn right under the pressure of world capitalism: 'The more the Stalin faction turns its back on the international revolution, the more it will feel its dependency on world capital, the more it will cling to it convulsively "with both hands"'.[164]

However, as the Comintern persisted in its Third Period strategy, Trotsky became increasingly concerned about another very different danger: that the ultraleft course of the KPD would result in a Nazi victory. During these years Trotsky's alarm about this prospect intensified from month to month until February 5, 1933 when he pleaded for the final time with the KPD to propose a united front: 'What is at stake is the head of the working class, the head of

161   Trotsky 1971c, p. 183.
162   As Trotsky noted in an article of 17 October 1929, the left 'zigzag' based on the theory of 'the Third Period' was 'as if especially timed for sowing illusions, encouraging adventurous undertakings and preparing for the next turn to come – to the right' (Trotsky 1975c, pp. 367–8). See also, for example, Trotsky 1975d, pp. 140, 179–80; Trotsky 1973c, pp. 215–16; Trotsky 1973d, pp. 102, 167; Trotsky 1971c, pp. 111, 170, 215–16.
163   Trotsky 1975d, pp. 61–2.
164   Trotsky 1972f, pp. 22–3. Trotsky's reference here was to a recently reported interview of Stalin by Thomas Campbell, an American specialist in agricultural machinery, in which Stalin took Campbell's hand in both of his.

the Communist International and – let us not forget it – the head of the Soviet republic'![165]

6.5   Developments in the Party Regime

As far as the party regime was concerned, two developments stand out as most notable during these years. There was the continuing persecution of a variety of dissident groups and individuals – from former leaders of the party right, to unrepentant supporters of the left, to members who previously had supported the centre. At the same time there was the emergence of a new cult of public adulation for Stalin.

From late 1929 through 1930, the leadership continued its offensive against the former leaders of the right. At the end of August 1929 *Pravda* published denunciations of Bukharin marking the opening shots of a massive campaign that impugned his entire political record. Subsequently, at the November plenum of the CC, second-rank moderates led by Uglanov were pressured into repudiating the Right Opposition. At the same time, Bukharin, Rykov, and Tomskii submitted a declaration that, while recognising the 'positive results' of the majority's economic policies, continued to urge moderation. In response, Stalin and Molotov denounced the document, and on 17 November the plenum expelled Bukharin from the Politburo. Just eight days later the three moderate leaders relented and signed a statement of recantation. When required to elaborate on their confessions at the Sixteenth Party Congress in June 1930, Rykov, Tomskii, and Uglanov all complied in Bukharin's absence. After subjecting the moderates to enormous verbal abuse, the Congress dropped Tomskii from the Politburo, demoted three of his trade-union supporters from the CC to candidate status, and removed Uglanov together with three of his Moscow supporters from the CC. Subsequently, Bukharin was induced to acknowledge his own errors in a statement signed in November 1930, in a speech to a joint plenum of the CC and CCC in December 1930, at the Seventeenth Party Conference in January–February 1932, and together with Rykov and Tomskii at the CC plenum of January 1933.[166] Still, the treatment of the defeated moderates

---

165   Trotsky 1971c, p. 346.
166   Cohen 1980, pp. 334–5; 349–50, 354; Daniels 1960, pp. 368–9, 378; Getty and Naumov, 1999, pp. 45–50, 95–7; Medvedev 1973, p. 68; Schapiro 1971, pp. 380–1, 393, 395. Getty and Naumov note that these 'mandatory recantations were designed not only to show a united face to the world but also to "disarm" the lower-level followers of the leading oppositionists' (Getty and Naumov, 1999, p. 45).

was mild in comparison to that inflicted upon the left. For example, Rykov was allowed to retain both his seat on the Politburo and his position as chairman of the Sovnarkom until the end of 1930; and Bukharin, Rykov, and Tomskii all remained full members of the CC until 1934, when they were demoted to candidate status.[167] As far as their supporters were concerned, a relatively small number were expelled in the 1929 *chistka*, or purge, of the party.[168] However, it seems that no supporters of the party right were arrested immediately for oppositional activity.

Meanwhile, the leadership continued to justify its continuing repression of the Left Opposition with new accusations regarding the Opposition's 'counterrevolutionary activities'. Stalin raised these allegations first in a memorandum to the Politburo, reprinted with minor changes as an editorial in *Pravda* on 24 January 1929. There, he charged that the Opposition had transformed itself completely from '*an underground antiparty group into an underground anti-Soviet organization*', and he asserted that '*an impassable gulf* has opened up between the former Trotskyist opposition inside the ACP(b) and the present anti-Soviet Trotskyist underground organization outside the ACP(b)'.[169] He returned to this same theme in a letter to the journal *Proletarskaia revoliutsiia* in October 1931, asserting,

> Trotskyism has long since ceased to be a faction of communism. As a matter of fact, Trotskyism is the advanced detachment of the counter-revolutionary bourgeoisie, which is fighting against communism, against the Soviet regime, against the building of socialism in the U.S.S.R.[170]

The leadership accused Trotskyists of sabotaging Soviet railroads, and denounced Trotsky himself for establishing alliances with European fascism and Japanese imperialism against the Soviet Union.[171] On 20 February 1932, the Central Executive Committee (CEC) of the Soviets stripped Trotsky and his son Leon Sedov of Soviet citizenship for their counterrevolutionary activities.[172]

---

167   Cohen 1980, p. 355; Daniels 1960, pp. 378, 429–32; Schapiro 1971, p. 394.

168   Officially, one percent of the 170,000 expelled at this time were removed for oppositional activity. Probably most of these were rightists. It is possible that more supporters of the right were expelled under other criteria. See Getty 1985, p. 46. See also Daniels 1960, p. 343, R. Davies 1989, p. 134; Fainsod 1958, pp. 211–19, Schapiro 1971, p. 439.

169   Quoted Tucker 1990, p. 126.

170   Stalin 1976, p. 574; see also Tucker 1990, p. 153.

171   See Trotsky 1975d, pp. 230, 260–1, 345–6, 389–90; Trotsky 1973c, pp. 273, 279; Trotsky 1973d, pp. 32–3, 53, 62–4, 69, 122–4, 389; Trotsky 1971c, p. 222.

172   R. Davies 1996, p. 143. For Trotsky's response to this action, see Trotsky 1973d, pp. 62–72.

These accusations were also accompanied by new arrests of Oppositionists. By late 1929 the bulk of those who had remained faithful to the Opposition were in political 'isolator prisons' or Siberian exile.[173] In 1930–1 the leadership added to their number most of the Oppositionists who had managed until then to avoid incarceration. According to Victor Serge's account, 300 Oppositionists were apprehended in Moscow in January 1930, an additional 400–500 were arrested in May, several hundred more were picked up in August, and by '1931– 1932 there were no more Oppositionists at large'.[174] A report from the Soviet Union published by Trotsky in late 1930 claimed that there were over 7,000 Left Oppositionists 'in exile, under surveillance, or in prison', and the number was growing.[175] Even more ominous was the introduction of capital punishment as a method against the Opposition. The first to be executed was Iakov Bliumkin, an official of the GPU and a longtime supporter of Trotsky's. In the summer of 1929 Bliumkin visited Trotsky in Turkey where Trotsky gave him a message for Soviet Oppositionists. On his return to Moscow, Bliumkin was arrested, charged with treason, and executed.[176] Soon after this, Trotsky published reports that two lesser-known Oppositionists, Silov and Rabinovich, had been executed for industrial sabotage.[177]

Despite these developments, by 1930 many believed that peace finally had been established within the party. Following the defeat of the right, no differences were apparent within the Politburo or the CC, and none were expressed at the Sixteenth Party Congress in June–July 1930.[178] However, it was not long before new oppositional groupings began to emerge in response to the deepening economic strains. Each of these met with repression.

The first new dissident group was a collection of former Stalinists who came together under the leadership of S.I. Syrtsov and V.V. Lominadze in the autumn of 1930. Traditionally, Syrtsov had associated himself with the right wing of the Stalinist leadership, and Lominadze with the Stalinist left. The extent of their real oppositional activity is unclear. However, it seems that they at least participated in discussions in which they criticised official economic policy and

---

173   At this time, according to Victor Serge, members of the Left Opposition still at large numbered less than a thousand (Serge 1980, p. 254).

174   Serge 1996, p. 114.

175   *Biulleten' oppozitsii*, 17–18 (November–December 1930), p. 39. For descriptions of the circumstances of incarceration of Oppositionists during this period, see especially Ciliga 1979, pp. 151–2, 189, 200–2.

176   Deutscher 1963, p. 84. See Winsbury 1977, pp. 712–18.

177   Trotsky 1975d, pp. 157, 389; Deutscher 1963, p. 91.

178   This point is made in R. Davies 1981b, p. 29. See also R. Davies 1989, p. 335; Schapiro 1971, pp. 393–4.

agreed on a number of demands, including the need for a reduction in the number of capital projects and for a relaxation of pressure upon the peasantry. When their meetings were reported, Syrtsov and Lominadze were denounced for forming a ' "Left"-Right Bloc', and attacked as 'double-dealers' who had 'capitulated to right opportunism'. In December 1930 the Politburo and the presidium of the CCC dropped them from the CC. A number of their supporters were also expelled from the party or removed from their posts.[179]

As the economic crisis deepened and dissatisfaction increased throughout the country, oppositional sentiment continued to rise within the party, even among formerly staunch Stalinists. In June 1932 Aleksandra Kollontai, the former leader of the Workers' Opposition and now the Soviet ambassador to Sweden, remarked that the 'old hands' were criticising everything. And in September or October 1932 Zinoviev stated to the CCC that a 'fairly significant section of party members' had been 'seized by the idea of retreat'.[180]

Meanwhile, the crisis also was stimulating a revival among former dissidents on the party right. One grouping composed of former rightists was led by M.N. Riutin, previously a Moscow secretary closely aligned with Uglanov. In the summer of 1932 Riutin's group circulated an appeal 'To All Members of the AUCP(b)' and a 200 page platform that indicted Stalin's economic policies and the party regime. Particularly striking was the platform's denunciation of Stalin as 'the evil genius of the Party and the revolution, who, actuated by vindictiveness and lust for power, had brought the Revolution to the edge of the abyss'. The documents demanded a reduction in the rate of industrialisation, the abolition of forced collectivisation, the removal of Stalin, and the restoration of party democracy.[181] In November 1932 three other prominent rightists – A.P. Smirnov, the former Commissar of Agriculture, and N.B. Eismont and V.N. Tolmachev, officials of the RSFSR – privately criticised the rate of industrialisation and the methods of collectivisation and allegedly discussed the removal of Stalin. However, it is unclear to what extent they actually were involved in further oppositional activity.[182]

---

179   Cohen 1980, pp. 342–3; Conquest 1973, p. 51; Daniels 1960, pp. 378–9; R. Davies 1989, pp. 411–15; R. Davies 1981b, pp. 29–50; Medvedev 1973, p. 142; Schapiro 1971, p. 395; Tucker 1990, p. 209.

180   R. Davies 1996, p. 250.

181   Quoted in Cohen 1980, pp. 343–4. See also Conquest 1973, p. 52; Daniels 1960, pp. 379–80; R. Davies 1996, pp. 248–9; Medvedev 1973, pp. 142–3; Nicolaevsky 1965, pp. 28–9; Tucker 1990, p. 211. A copy of the platform was published in 1990 in *Izvestiia TsK*, numbers 8–12. A translated excerpt can be found Getty and Naumov 1999, pp. 54–8.

182   Conquest 1973, pp. 55–6; R. Davies 1996, pp. 254–5.

Even more significant stirrings were evident on the left. Scattered groupings of the Left Oppositionists had continued to be active even after 1929. However, more were roused to action by the crisis of 1932. In July of that year Left Oppositionists in Moscow and Leningrad prepared a draft programme that they smuggled out of the country to Trotsky. The document called for a reduction in state expenditures, the dissolution of nonviable collective farms, and economic cooperation with capitalist countries. It also offered collaboration with the ruling faction to defend the country from external danger and to overcome the crisis, and demanded a restoration of party democracy. In September the former Oppositionist I.N. Smirnov transmitted to Sedov an article on the economic situation with data culled from a confidential Gosplan report.[183] By this time, Smirnov also seems to have established a dissident grouping with Preobrazhenskii and N.I. Ufimtsev.[184] In December 1932 Trotsky observed, 'Many hundreds, perhaps even thousands, of former capitulators, particularly workers, have returned to the path of the Opposition'.[185] Meanwhile, the Zinovievists, were also growing restive. Reportedly, Zinoviev, Kamenev, and their supporters were especially concerned about the Comintern policy in Germany, and now regretted their surrender to Stalin. Also, a collection of former Zinovievists who had broken with Zinoviev and Kamenev at the time of their surrender formed their own oppositional group under the leadership of Safarov and Tarkhanov.[186]

A number of these disparate groupings came together to establish an alliance in the summer of 1932. Included were former left-Stalinists previously associated with Syrtsov and Lominadze and led by Ia.E. Sten and Lominadze; Zinoviev's supporters; former Left Oppositionists led by Smirnov, Preobrazhenskii, and Ufimstev; and Trotsky's own Opposition abroad. Additionally, the Safarov-Tarkhanov group and the Riutin group were considering joining the bloc. At this point the purpose of the alliance – at least from Trotsky's perspective – was to share information.[187]

---

183   R. Davies 1996, pp. 244–6.

184   Broué 1989, p. 100.

185   Trotsky 1972f, p. 33. An additional example of activity by Left Oppositionists was noted in a secret party report from the North Caucuses in September 1933. It stated that 'since Autumn 1932 a counterrevolutionary organization headed by "a group of Bolshevik-Leninists"' had existed in Krasnodar (Getty and Naumov 1999, p. 66).

186   Broué 1989, p. 104.

187   See Broué 1980, pp. 5–37; and Broué 1989, pp. 98–111. Also see R. Davies 1996, pp. 246–7; Getty 1985, p. 121; Getty 1986, pp. 28–9; Getty and Naumov 1999, pp. 62–3; Law 1987a, pp. 133–7.

However, this union was short-lived, for all of these groupings soon were decimated in a wave of arrests during the autumn and winter of 1932–33. Riutin and a group of his supporters were apprehended in September and charged with forming a 'bourgeois-kulak organization' to restore capitalism. Reportedly, Stalin demanded Riutin's execution, but the majority of the leadership balked at this. The presidium of the CCC expelled eighteen members of Riutin's group, and the OGPU subsequently sentenced Riutin to solitary confinement for ten years and the remaining seventeen members of the group to imprisonment or exile. Other sympathisers throughout the country, including Sten and Uglanov, were also expelled. Zinoviev and Kamenev, who had seen the Riutin platform without reporting it, were expelled from the party for the second time and again were exiled.[188] Betrayed by an informant, I.N. Smirnov and Preobrazhenskii were arrested in January 1933 and expelled from the party. Smirnov was sentenced to five years of imprisonment, and Preobrazhenskii was dismissed from his position and sent into exile. Hundreds of other former Left Oppositionists were also arrested.[189] Finally, in January 1933 Eismont, Tolmachev, and A.P. Smirnov were convicted of forming an underground factional group dedicated to restoring of capitalism. Smirnov was removed from the CC, and the other two were expelled from the party.[190]

Another significant development in the party regime in this period was the origin of what would become known as the 'cult of personality' around Stalin. Up until this point the only political icons to whom the party leadership paid regular homage were Marx, Engels, and Lenin. That changed abruptly on Stalin's fiftieth birthday. On 21 December 1929 the Soviet press exploded in a frenzy of adulation of Stalin, 'the most outstanding continuer of Lenin's work and his most orthodox disciple, the inspirer of all the party's chief measures in

---

188 Broué 1989, pp. 105–6; Cohen 1980, pp. 343–4; Conquest 1973, pp. 53–5; Daniels 1960, p. 380; R. Davies 1996, p. 253; Nicolaevsky 1965, pp. 29–30; Medvedev 1973, pp. 142–3; Serge 1980, p. 259.

189 Broué 1989, p. 105; R. Davies 1996, pp. 254–5n333; Medvedev 1973, p. 107; Serge 1972, p. 114. For Trotsky's discussion of the wave of arrests of Left Oppositionists in late 1932 and early 1933, see Trotsky 1972f, pp. 107–8. In October 1932 Trotsky noted that the international press was reporting 'new mass arrests among the Trotskyists'. (Trotsky 1973d, p. 253). See also Trotsky 1972f, p. 79; Trotsky 1972f, p. 107. On 3 March 1933, asserting that the new repressions had 'assumed a mass character such as did not occur even in 1928', he observed that the 'chief blows, naturally, are directed against the Bolshevik-Leninists' (Trotsky 1972f, p. 107).

190 The joint CC-CCC also reprimanded Rykov, Tomskii, and V.V. Schmidt for allegedly supporting these 'anti-party elements' (Daniels 1960, p. 380; R. Davies 1996, pp. 254–5n333; Medvedev 1973, p. 155).

its struggle for the building of socialism ... the universally recognized leader of the party and the Comintern'.[191] The flow of eulogies subsided somewhat following the Sixteenth Party Congress in the summer of 1930, but resumed again at the end of 1931. Old works were revised and new articles and books were published in ever-increasing volumes to proclaim Stalin's outstanding qualities and achievements as a revolutionary and a Marxist theoretician.[192]

6.6 Trotsky and the Regime

Throughout the years 1930–3 Trotsky vigorously attacked the party leadership's continuing deviations from proletarian democracy. As in the past, he denounced the apparatus for its ongoing usurpation of power through the enforcement of undemocratic norms and through its active, often brutal, repression of opponents to its left and right. Beyond that, he now also condemned the further concentration of power in the hands of Stalin and his closest supporters, the development of a 'cult of infallibility' around Stalin, and the use of threats and repression against members of the bureaucracy itself. In this period he offered a variety of explanations for the continuing deterioration of the regime. In the light of his traditional theory of bureaucracy, he was inclined to blame bourgeois influence for this trend. However, in this area too he repeatedly found himself forced to explain developments in terms of the autonomous behaviour the bureaucracy, or of Stalin and his faction.

6.6.1 *Trotsky's Critique of Developments in the Party Regime*

During these years Trotsky continued to criticise the leadership for introducing party norms that effectively deprived the ranks of all power. One of these was the campaign begun in 1929 for the mass recruitment of industrial workers to assist with the tasks of the Five-Year Plan. From January 1928 until January 1933 party membership climbed from 1,304,471 to over three and a half million.[193] In his March 1930 open letter to the party Trotsky castigated this drive, as he would subsequently denounce the 'Lenin Levy' of 1924, as 'nothing less than the dissolution of the party into the class, that is, the abolition of the party'.[194] His point was that the leadership had swamped the party in a mass of raw and easily manipulated recruits.

---

191   Quoted in Cohen 1980, p. 335. See also Tucker, 146–71; Deutscher 1966, p. 317.
192   R. Davies 1989, pp. 470–1; Tucker 1990, pp. 128–9; Medvedev 1973, p. 147.
193   Schapiro 1971, p. 439.
194   Trotsky 1975d, p. 144.

Another familiar practice again condemned by Trotsky was the centralised control of local party organisations. In his April 1931 draft theses on the Russian question he observed,

> Not a trace remains of party democracy. Local organizations are selected and autocratically reorganized by secretaries. New members of the party are recruited according to orders from the center and with the methods of compulsory political service. The local secretaries are appointed by the Central Committee.[195]

Additionally, Trotsky accused the apparatus of usurping power from the party by continuing to diminish the significance and authority of the party congress. Shortly before the Sixteenth Party Congress he again recalled that party congresses had convened once or even twice a year during the civil war; in contrast, the leadership had called the Sixteenth Congress after a delay of two and a half years.[196] Beyond that, on the eve of the congress he noted recent threats that had been made against members who criticised the line of the CC, and he concluded that for the first time pre-congress discussions were 'completely *forbidden*'.[197] He further charged that the delegates to the congress had been selected entirely according the principle 'whoever is for Stalin gets to go'.[198] To indicate the degree to which the party ranks had been deprived of power, Trotsky coined a new formulation, asserting that the party, as a party, had 'ceased to exist'. In a letter written in late 1929 or early 1930 he explained that the Communist Party was no longer 'a party in the literal sense of the word, for its composition and life are regulated by methods that are of a purely administrative character'.[199] Similarly, in October 1930 he wrote,

> One could say with a certain justification that the party as a party does not exist today. The essential functions of the party: collective elaboration of views and decisions, free election of functionaries and control over them – all these have definitely been liquidated.[200]

---

195   Trotsky 1973c, p. 211. See also Trotsky 1975d, pp. 145, 253.

196   Trotsky 1975d, p. 204. See also Trotsky 1973c, p. 166. Even then, according to Trotsky, it was being held against the 'wishes of "the top"' (Trotsky 1975d, p. 204). The basis for this assertion seems to have been reports Trotsky received of rumours that Stalin wanted to postpone the Congress again until the autumn. See Trotsky 1975d, p. 185.

197   Trotsky 1975d, pp. 254–6.

198   Trotsky 1975d, p. 257.

199   Trotsky 1975d, p. 15.

200   Trotsky 1973c, p. 45. See also Trotsky 1975d, pp. 145, 209; Trotsky 1973c, pp. 74, 166, 211; Trotsky 1972f, pp. 104, 112.

Meanwhile, throughout the years 1930–1 Trotsky commented upon the intensification of the repression against party dissidents of all persuasions, beginning with the right. In February 1930 he noted the recent 'extortion' of 'penitent
documents' and 'ritualist capitulations' from Bukharin, Rykov, and Tomskii. In
May he further observed that the three had been 'barred from all activity', and
(incorrectly) predicted that they would be formally removed from all positions
of authority soon after the Congress. In November 1930 he also predicted that
the mounting 'campaign against the right-wingers' would soon culminate in
their removal from the CC. (In fact, again, all remained full members until 1934,
and candidate members after that).[201]

However, with justification Trotsky clearly believed that the most extreme
repression was reserved for adherents of the Left Opposition. Throughout
these years he noted the various 'literary campaigns' against the Opposition
in the Soviet and international Communist press, especially late 1930 and early
1932.[202] He protested against the waves of arrests inflicted upon Oppositionists
in the Soviet Union and the various forms of physical abuse they were forced
to endure in Soviet prisons and deportation camps.[203] He condemned the
repeated episodes of physical attacks and even assassination attempts by
Stalinists against his international supporters.[204] Finally, he bitterly denounced

---

201   Trotsky 1975d, pp. 79, 80, 255, 256; Trotsky 1973c, p. 61; Cohen 1980, p. 355; Daniels 1960,
      pp. 378, 429–32; Schapiro 1971, p. 394.
202   See Trotsky 1975d, pp. 230, 260–1, 345–6, 389–90; Trotsky 1973c, pp. 273, 279; Trotsky 1973d,
      pp. 31–2, 40–1, 53, 62–4, 69, 122–4, 389; Trotsky 1971c, p. 222.
203   Trotsky 1972f, p. 107. Regarding physical abuse, in early 1930 Trotsky denounced the con-
      tinued detention of Rakovskii in the harsh climate of Barnaul after two heart attacks.
      The following year he accused Stalin of intentionally permitting Kote Tsintsadze to die
      of tuberculosis in the Crimea instead of transferring him to a sanatorium in Sukhumi
      as requested by his friends. And in January 1932 he reported information concerning
      'the most frightful injuries and acts of violence at the isolation camp in the Upper Urals',
      where Oppositionists on a hunger strike had been beaten and force fed. See Trotsky 1975d,
      pp. 79, 157–8; Trotsky 1973c, pp. 118–23; Trotsky 1973d, pp. 15; 358n4.
204   In October 1930 Trotsky spoke of the 'raids and beatings (as, for example in Leipzig)' to
      which the supporters of the ILO had been subjected in various countries. In fascist Italy
      the Communist Party had published names of Oppositionists, thereby 'exposing them to
      attacks by the police'; the prominent Spanish Oppositionist Andrés Nin had been expelled
      from the USSR 'to reactionary Estonia'; and in Greece and China 'assassinations are per-
      petrated in ambush' (Trotsky 1975d, p. 389–90). See also Trotsky 1975c, pp. 95, 97, 183, 408;
      Trotsky 1975d, p. 391; Trotsky 1973c, pp. 365–6; Trotsky 1973d, pp. 91, 166–8, 237. Among the
      victims of Stalin, Trotsky included his daughter Zinaida Volkova, who committed suicide
      in Berlin on 5 January 1933. Trotsky explained that Zinaida's disturbed mental condition
      was largely the result of Stalinist persecution (Trotsky 1972f, pp. 69–72).

the executions of Oppositionists in the USSR, gravely commenting regarding the execution of Bliumkin that 'Stalin is trying intimidation of the last of the Opposition still in his hands by the method of – shooting'.[205]

For Trotsky, all of these developments were familiar in that they simply represented additional examples of the usurpation of power by the apparatus, and of the bureaucracy's repression of its opponents. However, in the early 1930s he also observed that comparable developments were taking place within the apparatus itself. That is, he perceived a constriction of the circle of power *within* the apparatus, accompanied by the development of a 'cult of infallibility' around the leader. Beyond that, he noted the first threats and use of repression against Stalin's critics within the apparatus.

In these years Trotsky repeatedly commented upon the fact that Stalin and his closest supporters were amassing increasing powers within the bureaucracy. For example, in March 1930, discussing the abrupt turn in economic policy, he stated, 'The top-level Stalinist group has taken command in the most undisguised manner'.[206] The following May he predicted that the upcoming Sixteenth Party Congress would 'sanctify the system of "one-man rule"', and he asserted that the party 'has only one right: to agree with Stalin'.[207] In April 1931 he declared that a 'plebiscitary regime' had been established within the party whereby 'selection for the whole apparatus takes place around the "chief"'.[208] Similarly, he observed in March 1932, 'The apparatus, independent of the working class and of the party, has set the stage for Stalin's dictatorship which is independent of the apparatus'.[209] Accompanying this, he noted, had been the increasingly frequent proclamations of Stalin's infallibility. In May 1930 he argued that Stalin's 'official coronation as the infallible leader accountable to no one', had occurred in 1929.[210] Along these same lines, in March 1932 he remarked,

---

205   Trotsky 1975d, p. 23. For additional comments on the execution of Bliumkin, see Trotsky 1975d, pp. 22–5, 120–2, 146, 157, 160–1, 305–7, 342, 389. Shortly afterwards, Trotsky denounced the 'treacherous assassination' of the Oppositionists Silov and Rabinovich (Trotsky 1975d, p. 157). See also Trotsky 1975d, p. 389; Trotsky 1973d, pp. 38, 65. In June 1932 Trotsky also warned that Stalin 'wants to use the war danger [with Japan] for a new, and if possible, physical annihilation of the Bolshevik-Leninists' (Trotsky 1973d, p. 124).

206   Trotsky 1975d, p. 145.

207   Trotsky 1975d, pp. 232, 258.

208   Trotsky 1973c, p. 217.

209   Trotsky 1973d, p. 68. See also Trotsky 1975d, pp. 206, 253, 257; Trotsky 1973c, p. 63; Trotsky 1973d, p. 18.

210   Trotsky 1975d, p. 257. In 1929 Piatakov had asserted at the time of his capitulation, 'It is impossible to be loyal to the party without being loyal to the Central Committee:

Now to pledge loyalty to the 'Leninist Central Committee' is almost the same as to call openly for insurrection. Only an oath of loyalty to Stalin may be taken – this is the only formula permitted.[211]

In the early 1930s Trotsky also noted repeated situations in which members of the apparatus, including previously loyal Stalinists, were subjected to repression or threats of repression. He first wrote of this development in April 1930 in connection with a recent denunciation of the Opposition's economic views by Iaroslavskii. Trotsky suggested that Iaroskavskii's real intention was 'to frighten the lower ranks of the Stalin apparatus' who, under pressure from below, were beginning to lose faith in the leadership.[212] The following November he commented upon a case of actual persecution of former Stalinists in the Syrtsov-Lomindadze case. While he was inclined to believe that Syrtsov really was a 'right-winger', he dismissed the charge that Lominadze and others accused were 'Leftists'. Rather, they were nothing but 'despairing centrists', part of the 'majority of the real Stalinist bureaucracy' that felt 'doublecrossed by its leaders since 1928'.[213] In January 1932 he perceived a further threat of repression against members of the apparatus in Stalin's recent discovery of 'Trotskyist contraband' in Iaroskavskii's history of the party. For Trotsky, this was a clear indication that Stalin and his 'narrow faction' were organising a 'conspiracy against the apparatus'.[214]

Trotsky continued to advance a variety of demands to promote the restoration of workers' democracy. As in the past, he called for the gradual introduction of the secret ballot in the soviets and the trade unions.[215] However, he still viewed the issue of party reform as paramount, for as he explained in the autumn of 1932, a change in the party regime was a 'prerequisite for fundamental reform of the workers' state'.[216] In this regard he explained to his Russian supporters in March 1930 that the Opposition was demanding 'a free discussion in the party of the "general line", going back to 1923' as the basis for the preparation of the Sixteenth Party Congress.[217] And in March 1932, on

it is impossible to be loyal to the Central Committee without being loyal to Stalin' (quoted in ibid.).

211   Trotsky 1973d, p. 68. See also Trotsky 1975d, pp. 80, 144, 206, 253, 257; Trotsky 1973c, p. 63; Trotsky 1973d, p. 18.

212   Trotsky 1975d, pp. 176, 184.

213   Trotsky 1973c, pp. 56–7, 63–4.

214   Trotsky 1973d, pp. 40–1, 67, 69; Trotsky 1971c, p. 222.

215   Trotsky 1972f, pp. 113–14.

216   Trotsky 1979a, p. 171.

217   Trotsky 1975d, p. 131.

being deprived of Soviet citizenship, he urged the Presidium of the CEC to place its trust in the party, and to 'give the proletarian vanguard the possibility, through free criticism from top to bottom, to review the whole Soviet system and cleanse it ruthlessly from all the accumulated filth'.[218]

Of course, for Trotsky such a discussion necessarily required the participation of the Left Opposition. This was because, as he explained in his March 1930 open letter to the AUCP, 'Only the Left Opposition is capable in the present circumstances of fearlessly criticizing and explaining all that is happening in the country and the party, to the extent that it is the result of the whole preceding course of development'.[219] Consequently, he repeatedly demanded that the leadership cease all forms of repression against the Opposition and readmit its members to the party with the opportunity for normal work.[220] At the same time he appealed for an end to the persecution of the party right, insisting that it too be permitted to participate in a party-wide discussion. This was not because he endorsed freedom for all party currents on principle. In an article of 21 November 1930 he explained, 'What we mean by the restoration of party democracy is that the real revolutionary proletarian core of the party win the right to curb the bureaucracy and really purge the party: to purge the party of the Thermidoreans in principle as well as their unprincipled and careerist cohorts'. Nevertheless, he explained that the Opposition opposed Stalinist reprisals against the party right because it advocated 'a general demarcation along the whole party spectrum, not chicanery of the apparatus, exile, the noose'.[221]

A related demand endorsed by Trotsky in October 1930 was Rakovskii's appeal for a coalition Central Committee, including supporters of the right, centre, and left. He argued that the proletarian nucleus of the party did not yet have sufficient confidence in the Left Opposition to hand power directly over to it, and even if it did, such a change in leadership would look more like a palace coup than reform to the party ranks. In contrast, the slogan of a coalition CC as an 'organization commission for the reconstruction of the party' could

218   Trotsky 1975d, p. 71. Other important demands included Trotsky's call for an end to the dissolution of the party into the class, and an end to the Stalinist practice of 'self-criticism'. See Trotsky 1975d, pp. 131, 150; Trotsky 1973c, p. 232.

219   Trotsky 1975d, p. 150. See also Trotsky 1975d, pp. 185, 261; Trotsky 1973d, p. 254.

220   See, for example Trotsky 1975d, p. 150; Trotsky 1973c, p. 291; Trotsky 1973d, pp. 71–2, 125–6; Trotsky 1972f, pp. 112, 114, 142.

221   Trotsky 1973c, pp. 57, 58. See also Trotsky 1972f, pp. 88, 114, 166; Trotsky 1973c, p. 106.

have mass appeal within the party as the only means of saving the party from complete collapse in the existing crisis.[222]

As far as Stalin's personal power was concerned, in March 1932 Trotsky urged the CEC 'to carry out at last Lenin's final and insistent advice: remove Stalin'![223] However, as we shall see, when the slogan 'Down with Stalin' seemed to be gaining popularity within the USSR some months later, Trotsky actually rejected it.

6.6.2   Trotsky's Analysis of Developments in the Regime

Consistent with the theory of bureaucracy he had developed in 1926–7, Trotsky continued to blame bourgeois influence for the crushing of workers' democracy within the USSR and the party since the early 1920s. However, in light of the turn he was forced to provide an alternative explanation for the steady worsening of the regime. As in the spheres of economic and international policy, in this area too he found it necessary to explain the actions of the leadership in terms of the autonomous behavior of the party apparatus, or even the autonomous behavior of Stalin and his faction.

During the early 1930s Trotsky still maintained that the ultimate source of the worsening of the regime since the time of Lenin was bourgeois influence within the party apparatus. As he wrote in an article published in February 1930,

> The bureaucratization of the Communist Party, beginning in 1922, has paralleled the growth of the economic strength and political influence of the petty bourgeoisie, basing itself on NEP, and the stabilization of the bourgeois regimes in Europe and the whole world, resulting from the successive defeats of the proletariat.[224]

However, at a time when the kulaks and NEPmen were being liquidated along with the remnants of Soviet capitalism, it was clearly implausible to blame bourgeois influence for increasing violations of proletarian democracy. As in 1928–9, Trotsky found himself forced to explain the continuing deterioration of the regime in terms of the autonomous actions of the bureaucracy. Thus, he completed the preceding passage with the following observation:

---

222   Trotsky 1973c, pp. 54–5, 308. In September 1931 Trotsky rejected the idea of applying the same slogan to the European sections of the Comintern (Trotsky 1973c, p. 307).
223   Trotsky 1973d, p. 71.
224   Trotsky 1975d, pp. 85–6.

But the party regime is not merely a passive reflection of these deep-going processes. The party is a living force of history, particularly the ruling party in a revolutionary dictatorship. Bureaucratism is not without a material base. Its vehicle is the large solidified bureaucracy with a whole world of self-serving interests. In this way, like any other secondary and superstructural factor, the party regime – in certain very broad limits – acquires an independent role.[225]

Similarly, in an article dated 31 May 1930 he emphasised the role played by the 'self-sufficient' bureaucracy in the 'systematic deterioration of the regime' over the previous eight years:

> In addition to the pressure of hostile class forces from without,... the regime is under direct and heavy pressure from an internal factor of immense and continually growing strength: namely the party and state *bureaucracy*. The bureaucracy has been transformed into a 'self-sufficient' force... Making use of the means and methods with which the [proletarian] dictatorship has armed it, the bureaucracy more and more subordinates the party regime,... to its own interests.[226]

In contrast, it should be noted that there were Left Oppositionists who still believed that all deviations from proletarian democracy were a *direct* reflection of bourgeois influence. From this premise they concluded that the turn, undercutting that influence, should give rise to a healthier party regime. In April 1930 Trotsky responded to M. Okudzhava and other such 'unsteady elements of the Opposition' who were arguing that 'a more healthy regime should "hatch" by itself from the present "left" Stalinist policy'. He characterised this view as 'optimistic fatalism' and the 'worst caricature of Marxism'. Again emphasising the autonomy of the leadership, he observed, 'The present leadership is not a blank sheet of paper. It has its own history, intimately bound up with its "general line," from which it cannot be separated'.[227]

At various times Trotsky attempted to explain more specifically the nature of the challenge that the leadership and the bureaucracy were attempting to crush. For example, in April 1930 he suggested that the leadership was exerting pressure to destroy resistance within the party to its economic zigzags: 'The sharper this turn was, the more pitiless was the bureaucratic pressure so as

---

225   Trotsky 1975d, p. 86. See also Trotsky 1975d, pp. 259–60.
226   Trotsky 1975d, pp. 259–60.
227   Trotsky 1975d, p. 208.

not to give the party time to get its bearings in the contradictions between yesterday and today'.[228] By January 1932 he concluded that the bureaucracy had escalated its repression in response to the growing combativeness of the working class, which had risen as proletarian self-confidence was bolstered by the successes of the plan.[229] In this situation, he asserted, the apparatus was 'forced to turn the screws still tighter and to forbid all forms of "self-criticism" other than the Byzantine flattery addressed to the leaders'.[230] As the economic situation deteriorated, in late 1932 and early 1933 he explained the growing opposition within the party as a reflection of unrest among workers and peasants over the decline in their standard of living. In October 1932 he stated, 'The growth of economic disproportions, the worsening of the conditions of the masses, the growth of dissatisfaction among the workers and peasants, the confusion in the apparatus itself – these are the prerequisites for the revival of each and every kind of opposition'. Against this revival, 'The bureaucracy, caught in a blind alley, immediately replies with repression, in a large measure as a preventative'.[231]

Although Trotsky perceived that Stalin and the bureaucracy had begun to see *all* potential opposition as a threat, he was convinced that the bureaucracy had singled out the Left Opposition for the most severe repression because it represented the greatest threat to the bureaucracy's power and interests. In January 1932 he explained that the Opposition was especially hated because it 'talks openly about the bureaucracy, . . . thus revealing the secret that the general line is inseparable from the flesh and blood of the new national ruling stratum, which is not at all identical with the proletariat'.[232] More specifically, he believed that the bureaucracy feared the Left Opposition could become a pole of attraction for workers who were dissatisfied. In a May 1930 letter to Soviet Oppositionists he explained that the apparatus had been 'forced to start "working over Trotskyism" again' in order 'to prevent a link-up between the criticism and dissatisfaction in the party and the slogans of the Opposition'.[233] By early 1933 he was convinced that this 'link-up' had begun to occur. In an article dated 3 March he observed that the chief blows were 'directed against

228 Ibid. See also Trotsky 1975d, p. 184; Trotsky 1973c, p. 78.
229 Trotsky 1971c, p. 221. See also Trotsky 1973d, pp. 42–3, 47–8, 66–7.
230 Trotsky 1971c, pp. 221–2.
231 Trotsky 1973d, p. 253. See also Trotsky 1972f, pp. 103–4.
232 Trotsky 1971c, p. 214.
233 Trotsky 1975d, pp. 230–1.

the Bolshevik-Leninists, the only faction whose authority has grown immeasurably and continues to grow'.[234]

Regarding the continuing constriction of power within the apparatus and the threat or use of repression against previously loyal Stalinists, Trotsky explained both developments in terms of growing dissatisfaction within the apparatus itself. In November 1930 he attributed this dissatisfaction to the fact that the 'majority of the real Stalinist bureaucracy feels it has been doublecrossed by its leader'.[235] More frequently, however, he explained tensions within the apparatus in terms of the mounting unrest within the population at large. For example, in April 1930 he asserted, 'Under the pressure from below the alarm in the apparatus is growing, the doubts in the leadership are growing, and the voices condemning the latest zigzag are growing'.[236] Similarly, in early 1932 he observed, 'As the workers become more impatient with the orders of the bureaucracy, the apparatus becomes more distrustful of the leadership of Stalin; the two processes are interconnected'.[237] Faced with these divisions within its own ranks, the apparatus had responded by ceding power to a referee. In an article of 22 April 1930 he observed, 'The bureaucracy needs a superarbiter and for this it nominates the one who best meets its instinct for survival'.[238] A year later in his draft theses on the Russian question, he elaborated upon this idea, explaining that the apparatus had appointed an arbiter to stand over it in order to avoid having 'to appeal to the masses to settle the disputed questions'.[239]

Meanwhile, Trotsky argued, Stalin had begun to exercise his own autonomy by conspiring against members of his own apparatus who challenged, or even threatened to challenge, his policies and power. For example, in November 1930 he argued that Stalin's 'open and cynical establishment of the plebiscitary-personal regime' in the party had been in response to the resistance within the apparatus to the left turn. At the same time, he predicted that Stalin's imminent shift back to the right would be accompanied by blows against those within the apparatus 'who took the ultraleft zigzag seriously' and who resisted

---

234   Trotsky 1972f, p. 107. See also Trotsky 1975d, pp. 144, 260–1; Trotsky 1973d, pp. 69, 122–3;
       Trotsky 1971c, p. 222.
235   Trotsky 1973c, p. 63.
236   Trotsky 1975d, p. 184.
237   Trotsky 1973d, p. 67. See also Trotsky 1973c, pp. 63, 300; Trotsky 1973d, p. 252; Trotsky 1971c,
       p. 222.
238   Trotsky 1975d, p. 206.
239   Trotsky 1973c, p. 217. See also Trotsky 1972f, p. 104.

'the approaching turn'.[240] In March 1932, after noting that the apparatus was becoming 'increasingly distrustful of Stalin', Trotsky warned the presidium of the CEC, 'the conspiracy against the apparatus is pushed full speed ahead, while the apparatus is still in conspiracy against the party'.[241]

6.7   Modifying the Theory

In 1928–9, while emphasising the autonomy of the bureaucracy in his analyses of major policy developments, Trotsky was compelled to do likewise in his more general theoretical statements. The same pattern was replicated in his writings between late 1929 and early 1933. Trotsky's growing emphasis on the autonomy of the bureaucracy in his analyses of policy in those years constituted a significant, if implicit, modification of his theory. This compelled him to introduce explicit revisions into his more general theoretical statements. While continuing to depict the bureaucracy as responsive to bourgeois pressure, he increasingly stressed the bureaucracy's ability to act independently of social classes. Responsive yet autonomous – these opposing characterisations established a deep conceptual tension that ran throughout Trotsky's theory during this period.

6.7.1   *Conception of Bureaucracy*
In 1928–9 Trotsky had begun to depict the problem of bureaucracy in the Soviet Union primarily in terms of a single social formation, the bureaucracy, which had taken power within all Soviet political institutions. He continued to depict the problem similarly in 1929–33. For example, in May 1930 he wrote of 'an internal factor of immense and continually growing strength: namely the party and state *bureaucracy*'; and in the autumn of that year, he described how the 'Soviet and party bureaucracy' lifted Stalin on a wave of reaction.[242] There were still occasions when he utilised the term *bureaucratism* he had employed

---

240   Trotsky 1973c, pp. 62–3.

241   Trotsky 1973d, p. 69.

242   Trotsky 1975d, pp. 259–60; Trotsky 1973c, p. 62. For the most part, Trotsky simply used the term *bureaucracy*, though at various times he also spoke of the 'Stalinist bureaucracy' (see Trotsky 1975d, pp. 144, 204, 261; Trotsky 1973c, pp. 26, 46, 63, 286, 288; Trotsky 1971c, pp. 183, 208, 216); 'Stalinist apparatus' (see Trotsky 1975d, pp. 144, 204; Trotsky 1973c, p. 28); 'centrist bureaucracy' (see Trotsky 1975d, p. 259; Trotsky 1973c, pp. 46, 51, 307; Trotsky 1972f, p. 49), 'centrist apparatus' (see Trotsky 1973c, p. 75); 'Bonapartist bureaucracy' (see Trotsky 1975d, p. 261); 'workers' bureaucracy' (see Trotsky 1975d, p. 204; Trotsky 1971c, p. 214); 'bureaucratic apparatus' (see Trotsky 1975d, pp. 144, 256; Trotsky 1973c, pp. 45, 306; Trotsky 1971c,

so frequently in 1923–7. However, he now used that word only in reference to the repressive or excessively centralist organisational practices of the bureaucracy viewed as a social formation. For example, he explained in an article published in February 1930, 'Bureaucratism [*biurokratizm*] is not without a material base. Its vehicle is the large solidified bureaucracy [*biurokratiia*] with a whole world of self-serving interests'.[243]

An essential aspect of the problem as Trotsky now described it was still the responsiveness of the bureaucracy to bourgeois pressure. This was clear, for example, in an article of 25 April 1930 where he asserted that the 'workers' bureaucracy' in both the West and the Soviet Union, 'besides constituting an instrument for the proletariat to influence other classes, constitutes equally an instrument through which other classes influence the proletariat'.[244] In support of this idea, he repeatedly pointed to evidence that he believed demonstrated the infestation of the state and party apparatuses with pro-bourgeois elements. As we have seen, in 1930 and 1931 he proclaimed that this was shown by the confessions of the 'specialist-saboteurs'.[245] Similarly, he frequently cited the defections of three Soviet diplomats, Besedovskii, Agabekov, and Dmitrievskii, as further indications of bourgeois influence in the apparatuses. For example, in September 1931 he observed,

> To what extent is not only the state but also the party apparatus riddled with Bessedovskys, Dmitrievskys, Agabekovs – in general, class enemies – who stifle the Rakovskys and expel the Ryazanovs? To what extent will this apparatus prove to be a weapon of the dictatorship of the proletariat at the decisive moment?... But this means that the state apparatus of the

---

p. 213); bureaucratic 'caste' (see Trotsky 1973d, p. 227); and bureaucratic 'stratum' (see Trotsky 1973d, p. 35; Trotsky 1971c, p. 214).

243   Trotsky 1975d, p. 86; *Biulleten' oppozitsii* 1973, 9 (February–March 1930), p. 15. Similarly, in his April 1931 theses on the Russian question he observed, 'The gigantic difference between the bureaucratism [*biurokratizm*] of 1923 and the bureaucratism of 1931 is determined by the complete liquidation of the dependence of the apparatus upon the party that took place in this span of years, as well as by the plebiscitary degeneration of the apparatus itself' (Trotsky 1973c, p. 211; *Biulleten' oppozitsii* 1973, 20 [April 1931], p. 5). See also Trotsky 1971c, p. 214; Trotsky 1975d, p. 254.

244   Trotsky 1975d, p. 204.

245   Thus, in September 1931 he remarked, 'If the saboteurs were the agents of the bourgeoisie, that signifies that the state apparatus which they... directed to so significant a degree is not a reliable apparatus of the proletariat, but included within itself very important elements of the power of a different class' (Trotsky 1973c, p. 306). See also Trotsky 1973c, p. 219.

proletarian dictatorship has assumed a contradictory character, that is, is riddled with elements of dual power.[246]

It should be noted that, while remaining especially sensitive to 'bourgeois influence' in the state and party apparatuses during the First Five-Year Plan, Trotsky seems to have been oblivious to developments that tended to undermine such influence. These included the mass promotion of workers from the bench to responsible positions as technical specialists and administrators, and the massive influx of workers into technical educational institutions where they were prepared for promotion.[247]

At the same time, Trotsky also increasingly emphasised the autonomy of the bureaucracy in his statements about the bureaucracy's essential nature. No doubt largely in reaction to the deepening turns in economic and Comintern policy, he often spoke of the 'self-sufficient' character of the bureaucracy. For example, in his open letter to the party on 23 March 1920 he observed, 'The bureaucratic apparatus ... is acquiring ever more self-sufficiency'.[248] Similarly, in an article two months later he stated that 'the party and state *bureaucracy* ... has been transformed into a "self-sufficient" force; it has its own material interests, and develops its outlook, corresponding to its own privileged position'.[249] More significantly, in his April 1931 theses on the Russian question he asserted that the bureaucracy had grown so independent that it was even capable of shaping the development of social classes:

> The bureaucracy ... is not a passive organ which only refracts the inspirations of the class. Without having absolute independence, ... the ruling apparatus nevertheless enjoys a great relative independence. The bureaucracy is in direct possession of state power; it raises itself above the classes and puts a powerful stamp upon their development.[250]

---

246   Trotsky 1973c, p. 307. See also Trotsky 1975c, p. 359; Trotsky 1975d, pp. 15, 305–6, 341; Trotsky 1973c, pp. 45, 51; Trotsky 1973d, p. 67.

247   On these developments, see Bailes 1980, pp. 286–9; Bailes 1978, pp. 188–97; Fitzpatrick 1974, pp. 33–52; Fitzpatrick 1979a, pp. 181–213; Fitzpatrick 1979b, pp. 377–402.

248   Trotsky 1975d, p. 144.

249   Trotsky 1975d, pp. 259–60. See also Trotsky 1975d, p. 144. For a reference to the 'self-sufficient bureaucracy' in the Comintern, see Trotsky 1971c, p. 216.

250   Trotsky 1973c, p. 215.

6.7.2   *Causes of the Growth of Bureaucratic Power*

Ambivalence, but with a strong emphasis on autonomy, were also displayed in Trotsky's writings on the origins of the problem of bureaucracy. Since the mid-1920s Trotsky had explained the alienation of the state and party apparatuses from the Soviet proletariat primarily in terms of pressure exerted on the apparatuses by bourgeois or petty bourgeois elements. In this process, alien class elements played the active role, while the party and state apparatuses responded passively. This argument must have seemed less and less plausible after the leadership launched its all-out assault on the same alien elements.

Although in some of his comments on the origins of bureaucratic power during this period Trotsky continued to argue that bourgeois pressure had played an important role, he now demoted its significance while emphasising the independent efforts of the bureaucracy. One variant of this argument appeared in his April 1931 theses on the Russian question, where he characterised bureaucratisation as having occurred in two phases: in the first phase the weariness and disillusionment of the proletariat, combined with the revival of capitalism under NEP, had strengthened petty-bourgeois and bourgeois elements within the country and within the state bureaucracy:

> After the heroic straining of forces in the years of revolution and civil war, ... the proletariat could not but go through a lengthy period of weariness, decline in energy, and in part direct disillusionment in the results of the revolution. By virtue of the laws of the class struggle, the reaction in the proletariat resulted in a tremendous flow of new hope and confidence in the petty-bourgeois strata of the city and village and in the bourgeois elements of the state bureaucracy who gained considerable strength on the basis of the NEP.[251]

Trotsky's analysis here closely resembled his 1926–7 account of the origins of bureaucratism. However, in his discussion of the second phase of bureaucratisation he downgraded bourgeois pressure to a secondary role, arguing that the party apparatus had merely *utilised* the 'petty bourgeois and bourgeois bureaucracy' of the state for its own ends. He explained that in the context of a series of international defeats the 'centrist [party] apparatus' forged a 'bloc' with the 'forces of Thermidor'. Then, 'supporting itself on the strengthened and emboldened petty-bourgeois and bourgeois bureaucracy, exploiting the passivity of the weary and disoriented proletariat, and the defeats of the revolution

---

251   Trotsky 1973c, p. 214.

the world over, the centrist apparatus crushed the left revolutionary wing of the party in the course of a few years'.[252]

A condensed version of the same argument appeared in a document written for the preconference of the ILO in January 1933. Again, Trotsky depicted the bureaucracy as simply relying upon petty-bourgeois pressure to defeat the Opposition:

> The bearer of the reaction against October was the petty bourgeoisie, particularly the better-off elements of the peasantry. The bureaucracy, which is closely connected with the petty bourgeoisie, put itself forward as the spokesman of this reaction. Supported by the pressure of the petty-bourgeois masses, the bureaucracy won a large measure of independence from the proletariat...The left wing of the proletariat fell under the blows of the Soviet bureaucracy in alliance with the petty-bourgeois, predominantly peasant, masses and the backward strata of the workers themselves.[253]

In other accounts during this period Trotsky emphasised the autonomy of the bureaucracy even more by dropping mention of bourgeois or petty-bourgeois influence altogether. In these statements he asserted simply that the bureaucracy had usurped power in the political vacuum created by the decline of proletarian activity and enthusiasm after the revolution. For example, in a letter of 17 September 1930 to a conference of the German Left Opposition he explained, 'Only the decline in mass activity and the change from a revolutionary mood to one of apathy permitted the enormous growth of the party bureaucracy, which supported itself on the state apparatus for material means and for means of repression'.[254] Likewise, in an article from January 1932 he argued that the bureaucracy had been able to take power directly because of the passivity of the masses:

> The years of the revolutionary earthquake and the civil war left the masses in a desperate need of rest...The workers were ready to give the bureaucracy the broadest powers, if only it would restore order, offer an opportunity to revive the factories, and furnish provisions and raw material from the country. In this reaction of weariness, ... lies the chief cause of the consolidation of the bureaucratic regime and the growth of that

---

252   Trotsky 1973c, pp. 214–15.
253   Trotsky 1972f, pp. 48–9.
254   Trotsky 1973c, pp. 26–7.

personal power of Stalin, in whom the new bureaucracy has found its personification.[255]

6.7.3   Characteristics

Trotsky's comments in this period about some of the bureaucracy's more significant characteristics reveal a similar tension between his traditional emphasis on responsiveness to bourgeois pressure and a new emphasis on bureaucratic autonomy. On one hand, his perception of the bureaucracy's conservatism, its Stalinism, and its centrism were largely derived from his traditional understanding of the influence of bourgeois elements. On the other hand, revisions in his understanding of these three characteristics, his descriptions of the party regime, and his statements about the size of the bureaucracy were more closely related to his view of the bureaucracy as autonomous.

Throughout these years Trotsky frequently referred to bureaucratic characteristics that revealed the influence of bourgeois elements on the state and party apparatuses. That was the case in his continued references to the conservatism of the bureaucracy. For example, in January 1932 he wrote of the 'the policy of a conservative bureaucracy', and the following January he derided the bureaucracy's 'conservative habits of thinking'.[256] The incongruity of such statements in the context of the early 1930s has been noted by Alec Nove, who has asked, 'Is it the typical action of centrists and conservative bureaucrats to undertake a vast revolution from above'?[257] However, the obvious basis for Trotsky's observations is evident in his longer description of the bureaucracy's conservatism in January 1932: 'In the course of a number of years the Stalinist faction demonstrated that the interests and the psychology of the prosperous peasant, engineer, administrator, Chinese bourgeois intellectual, and British trade-union functionary were closer and more comprehensible to it than the psychology of the unskilled laborer, the peasant poor, the Chinese national masses in revolt, the British strikers, etc.'[258] All of these examples referred to policies in the middle to late 1920s. In fact, Trotsky's perception of the bureaucracy's conservatism was largely based on his continuing conviction, formed during that earlier period, that the bureaucracy was strongly influenced by bourgeois pressure.

At the same time, by the early 1930s Trotsky had begun to suggest that the conservatism of these earlier economic and international policies was linked to the bureaucracy's emergence as a relatively autonomous social formation

255   Trotsky 1973d, p. 39. See also Trotsky 1975d, pp. 206–7.
256   Trotsky 1973d, p. 34; Trotsky 1972f, p. 49. See also Trotsky 1973d, p. 227.
257   Nove 1982, p. 394.
258   Trotsky 1971c, p. 215.

defending its power and privileges. For example, in January 1932 he described conservatism as typical of 'a new ruling stratum with its own interests and pretensions' or a 'moderate stratum, reflecting the demand for "law and order"'.[259] In a pamphlet written the same month he again explained, 'The ruling and uncontrolled position of the Soviet bureaucracy is conducive to a psychology which in many ways is directly contradictory to the psychology of a proletarian revolutionist'.[260]

A similar tension was evident in Trotsky's statements about Stalinism. In 1927 he had explicitly identified the conservative polices of the leadership of that time as the 'very essence [*sut'*] of Stalinism'.[261] Along the same lines, in January 1932 he still defined Stalinism as 'the policy of a conservative bureaucracy'.[262] However, in other statements about Stalinism Trotsky clearly recognised that this 'essence' had changed. Recalling in December 1930 that conservative economic and international policies had 'constituted the essence [*sut'*] of Stalinism during the 1923–8 period', he now observed that these policies had been replaced by 'a policy of panic and precipitousness'.[263] Furthermore, although he still viewed Stalinism as a political tendency occupying a place between Thermidorians and the proletarian Left Opposition, in November 1930 he portrayed it as continuously conducting an *active struggle against* both:

> Stalin conducts, not an episodic, but a continuous, systematic, organic struggle on two fronts. This is the inherent character of a petty-bourgeois policy: at the right of Stalin, the unconscious and conscious capitalist restorationists in varying degrees; at the left, the proletarian Opposition.[264]

Also related to Trotsky's characterisation of the bureaucracy as conservative was his continuing description of Soviet economic and international policy as 'centrist' or, beginning in 1932, 'bureaucratic centrist'.[265] As in previous years, he often defined Stalinist centrism as a political orientation to the *right* of

---

259   Trotsky 1973d, p. 35.
260   Trotsky 1971c, pp. 214–15. See also Trotsky 1973d, p. 227. For other remarks on the privileged character of the bureaucracy, see Trotsky 1973d, p. 35; Trotsky 1972f, p. 49.
261   Fel'shtinskii 1988, vol. 4, p. 221; Trotsky 1980b, p. 442.
262   Trotsky 1973d, pp. 34, 35.
263   Trotsky 1973c, p. 91; *Biulleten' oppozitsii* 1973, 17–18 (November–December 1930), p. 2.
264   Trotsky 1973c, p. 77. See also Trotsky 1973c, p. 215.
265   For some specific references to the 'centrist bureaucracy', see for example, Trotsky 1975d, p. 250; Trotsky 1973c, pp. 46, 215, 226, 229, 307; Trotsky 1973d, p. 122; Trotsky 1972f, pp. 106, 109. For 'bureaucratic centrism' see Trotsky 1971c, p. 215; Trotsky 1973d, p. 223; Trotsky 1972f, pp. 49, 108.

communism or Marxism. For example, at times he explained that centrism was 'intermediate', or 'transitional', or that it 'vacillated', between 'reformism and communism', between 'reformism and Marxism', or between a 'proletarian revolutionary line and a national reformist petty-bourgeois line'.[266] Statements such as these were clearly based on his analysis of Soviet policy in the late 1920s, and they represented a reasonable description of policy in that period. However, they made little sense by the early 1930s when, by Trotsky's own account, Soviet policies had moved far to the *left* of those advocated by the Opposition.

There were times when Trotsky seemed to recognise this problem. In each such case he elaborated on his analysis in ways that emphasised the independence of the bureaucracy. For example, in the January 1932 pamphlet *What Next?* Trotsky addressed the question of how a 'centrist' bureaucracy could swing so far to the left. He explained that, in contrast with Western centrist groupings, Soviet centrism was 'equipped with a much more solid and organized base in the shape of a multimillioned bureaucracy'.[267] Of course, this still did not explain how a prolonged *ultraleft* policy could be described as 'centrist'. However, in a series of statements Trotsky dealt with this problem by simply repositioning the leftmost limit of centrist vacillation. For example, in *What Next?* he went on to assert, 'The oscillations of this *bureaucratic centrism*, in conformity with its power, its resources, and the acute contradictions in its position have attained an altogether unheard-of sweep', ranging from 'ultra-left adventurism' to the conservative policies pursued by the Soviet leadership in China and the ARC.[268] In a preface to a Polish edition of Lenin's *Left-Wing Communism* written in October 1932 he described 'bureaucratic centrism' as alternating 'ultraleft mistakes with opportunist practice', or 'radicalism and opportunism'.[269] Similarly, in a letter written the same month to a German left communist paper he asserted, 'In actual fact, the Stalinists are zigzagging between *ultraleftism* and *opportunism*', and explained 'it is precisely in this that is expressed the centrist character of the Stalinist faction'.[270]

A new emphasis on autonomy is also evident in Trotsky's descriptions of the leadership's organisational practices during these years. On the basis of both the general deterioration of the regime and the growing concentration of power in Stalin's hands, in early 1930 Trotsky began to compare the party

---

266   For definitions of centrism, see Trotsky 1975c, pp. 232–3; Trotsky 1975d, pp. 236, 237; Trotsky 1971c, p. 211.

267   Trotsky 1971c, p. 215.

268   Trotsky 1971c, pp. 215–16.

269   Trotsky 1973d, p. 223.

270   Trotsky 1973d, p. 228 (original italics). See also Trotsky 1973d, p. 326.

regime to the highly autonomous and authoritarian regimes of Napoleon and Louis-Napoleon Bonaparte. Thus, in February 1930 he asserted that the methods used against the party right represented 'a new stage in the process of the Bonapartist degeneration of the party regime'.[271] In his draft theses on the Russian question in April 1931, he denounced the 'Bonapartist system of administering the party'.[272] Finally, in implicit reference to Napoleon Bonaparte's and Louis Bonaparte's practice of legitimising their regimes by plebiscite, he frequently characterised the Stalin regime as 'plebiscitary'.[273] Periodically, he explained that he did not mean to imply by this that the Stalinist regime was literally Bonapartist, for that would indicate that it was capitalist. Rather, as he observed in July 1930, he only meant to indicate that the degeneration of organisational norms had completed 'the preparatory work within the party for Bonapartism'.[274]

Perhaps also related to Trotsky's new emphasis on the bureaucracy's autonomy were his comments in this period about its size. In 1927 the *Platform of the Opposition* had complained that the ' "layer of administrators" – in the party, the trade unions, the industrial agencies, the cooperatives and the state apparatus – now numbers in the tens of thousands'.[275] By late 1930 Trotsky was describing the 'Stalinist apparatus' as 'numbering millions of people'.[276] In January 1932 he estimated the number of 'functionaries' as 'a few million', and wrote of 'this ruling stratum of many millions', and the 'multimillioned bureaucracy'.[277] One possible basis for these new estimates was the rapid growth of the apparatuses of the state and party during the First Five-Year Plan. However, it is also likely that as Trotsky increasingly stressed the bureaucracy's autonomy, he began to emphasise its size and to redefine large numbers of officials as its members.

271   Trotsky 1975d, p. 82. See also Trotsky 1975d, p. 257.
272   Trotsky 1973c, p. 217. See also Trotsky 1975d, pp. 131, 207–8, 255; Trotsky 1973c, pp. 72, 76; Trotsky 1973d, pp. 20, 69; Trotsky 1972f, p. 103; Trotsky 1971c, p. 218.
273   See, for example, Trotsky 1975d, pp. 131, 325; Trotsky 1973c, pp. 63, 166, 211, 214; Trotsky 1971c, p. 218.
274   Trotsky 1975d, p. 335. On this point, see also Trotsky 1975d, pp. 258, 337; Trotsky 1973c, pp. 165, 217, 222; Trotsky 1973d, p. 68.
275   Trotsky 1980b, p. 356; Fel'shtinskii 1988, vol. 4, p. 151 (translation modified). The 'Declaration of the Thirteen', written in July 1926 estimated the number of 'office workers' in the country as numbering at least three million, and observed 'This statistical comparison, by itself testifies to the colossal political and economic role of the bureaucracy' (Trotsky 1980b, p. 81). However, Trotsky evidently did not count all of these as members of the bureaucracy.
276   Trotsky 1973c, p. 63.
277   Trotsky 1971c, pp. 213, 215. See also Trotsky 1973d, p. 227.

6.7.4 *Consequences*

Throughout these years Trotsky continued to fear that bureaucratisation would ultimately result in the restoration of capitalism. In the late 1920s he had based this prognosis on his perception of a steady, rightward drift in economic policy. However, the policy shift of 1929–30 raised serious questions: Was the turn a retreat from the brink of restoration, or had it made restoration more likely? Beyond that, what were the implications of the turn for the form a restoration might take? Trotsky's answers to these questions were confused, alternately drawing upon his images of the bureaucracy as responsive to bourgeois pressure and autonomous. Nevertheless, of one thing he remained convinced: that the counterrevolution had not yet occurred.

Through much of this period Trotsky seems to have been uncertain whether the net effect of recent events had been to increase or decrease the probability of capitalist restoration. On one hand, as he admitted in his April 1931 theses on the Russian question, the turn had in some respects substantially weakened the forces promoting capitalism:

> Through the combined effect of economic successes and administrative measures, the specific gravity of the capitalist elements in the economy has been greatly reduced in recent years, especially in industry and trade. The collectivization and the de-kulakization have strongly diminished the exploitative role of the rural upper strata. The relationship of forces between the socialist and the capitalist elements of the economy has undoubtedly been shifted to the benefit of the former.[278]

On the other hand, he insisted in the same theses, there were reasons for believing that the restorationist threat remained strong. First, although capitalist elements within the country had been liquidated, this had 'coincided with the accelerated appearance of the USSR on the world market' where it was forced to compete with imperialism. Second, though the 'Nepman, middleman, and kulak' had been weakened, the trials of the 'specialist-saboteurs' and Mensheviks had demonstrated that the bureaucracy still contained within itself a 'mighty agency of world capital'. Third, in Trotsky's view the 'elements of dual power' in the country had become even 'stronger as the plebiscitary degeneration of the apparatus . . . progressed'.[279] He expressed a similar ambivalence in an interview with the *New York Times* in February 1932 where he noted that 'active and passive Thermidorean tendencies' within the Soviet

278 Trotsky 1973c, p. 218.
279 Trotsky 1973c, pp. 218–19.

Union were 'very strong', but their victory was still 'far off'.[280] However, as the economic crisis deepened in the following months, his concern about capitalist restoration mounted until early 1933 when he warned that 'catastrophe looms over the Communist Party of the Soviet Union'.[281]

Throughout these years Trotsky continued to see two main paths by which capitalism might be restored. First, as he noted in his draft theses on the Russian question, there was the possibility of a '*Thermidorean* overthrow' that would involve 'a decisive shift of power from the proletariat to the bourgeoisie, but accomplished formally within the framework of the Soviet system under the banner of one faction of the official party against the other'.[282] In general, this variant seemed to suggest that the bureaucracy was responsive to bourgeois pressure. Second, there was the prospect of a '*Bonapartist* overthrow' – that is, a 'more open, "riper" form of the bourgeois counterrevolution, carried out against the Soviet system and the Bolshevik Party as a whole, in the form of the naked sword raised in the name of bourgeois property'.[283] Insofar as this form of restoration implied a coup against a significant portion of the bureaucracy as well as against the Soviet system, it suggested a high degree of bureaucratic independence from bourgeois influence. Finally, Trotsky occasionally repeated that a counterrevolution might combine these two variants.[284]

Trotsky was clearly undecided about which form of restoration was most likely. In fact, in the years 1930–3 he reversed his position on this question several times. At the beginning of 1930, he still believed that a counterrevolution would probably follow the Thermidorian path. As we have seen, at that point he frequently warned that the leadership was about to revise its economic policy and implement a thoroughly rightist course. However, concluding by late October that the centrists were 'waist-deep in trouble with the five-year plan', he predicted that the 'Kalinins and Voroshilovs' might try 'to get free of the trap by chewing off the paw that goes by the name of "general secretary"'. That is, he anticipated a Bonapartist coup, assisted by conscious 'Thermidoreans' such as Besedovskii, Agabekov, and Dmitrievskii.[285] The following month he

---

280   Trotsky 1973d, p. 47.

281   Trotsky 1972f, p. 95.

282   Trotsky 1973c, p. 221.

283   Trotsky 1973c, p. 221. For other passages during this period in which Trotsky defined Thermidor and/or Bonapartism, see Trotsky 1975d, p. 206; Trotsky 1973c, pp. 71, 76; Trotsky 1973d, p. 47; Trotsky 1972f, pp. 76–7.

284   Trotsky 1973c, pp. 71–2, 76. At the same time, he continued to predict that even a relatively pure Thermidor would ultimately elevate a Bonapartist regime to power (Trotsky 1973c, pp. 52, 76, 221–2).

285   Trotsky 1973c, p. 51.

changed his mind again, warning that Stalin was about to implement the 'inevitable turn to the right', and in the process, perhaps unwittingly unleash the 'Thermidorean-Bonapartist' danger – that is, a Thermidor followed closely by the introduction of Bonapartism.[286]

By 1931 Trotsky seems to have decided again that a Bonapartist coup was most likely. In mid-1931 he explicitly asserted that, while the turn had significantly *reduced* the likelihood of a Thermidor, the deterioration of the regime had greatly *increased* the chances of a Bonapartist overthrow:

> The crushing of the right wing of the party and its renunciation of its platform diminish the chances of the first, step-by-step, veiled, that is Thermidorean form of the overthrow. The plebiscitary degeneration of the party apparatus undoubtedly increases the chances of the Bonapartist form.[287]

However, by late 1932 and early 1933 he had changed his assessment once again, concluding that the danger of Thermidor was quite near. In October 1932 at the time of the discovery of the 'Riutin conspiracy', Trotsky described Riutin and Uglanov as having represented until then 'the most thoroughgoing Thermidorean wing in the camp of the Right', and he complained that the growing economic crisis resulting from ultraleftist economic policies had given rise to a 'new upsurge of the Right-Thermidorean tendencies'.[288] In this same period he also expressed concern that the slogan 'Down with Stalin!' could strengthen Stalin's 'Thermidorean' enemies.[289] Furthermore, he continued to warn in the following year of the possibility that the mounting crisis would propel the Soviet Union down the Thermidorian road. In fact, in an article of 11 January 1933 he counted three groupings that might support a Thermidor: the peasantry, a section of the proletariat, and a section of the Stalinist apparatus.[290]

Of course, all of this presupposed that the Soviet Union remained a 'workers' state'. At this time Trotsky addressed no major new challenges to his position on the class character of the Soviet Union.[291] Nevertheless, on a number of occasions he returned to the issue when considering the degree of degeneration

286 Trotsky 1973c, pp. 61, 64.
287 Trotsky 1973c, pp. 221–2.
288 Trotsky 1973d, pp. 249, 254.
289 Trotsky 1979a, pp. 168–9.
290 Trotsky 1972f pp. 77–8.
291 However, statements in this period that the Soviet Union was now 'state capitalist' appeared in a 1932 pamphlet by the former Workers' Oppositionist, Gavril Miasnikov, now

that had occurred. In doing so, he continued to base his argument that the USSR remained a workers' state on the three criteria he had put forward in previous years: that the Soviet state still defended the nationalisation of production and the state monopoly of foreign trade established by the October Revolution, that a counterrevolutionary civil war had not yet occurred, and that the party and state could still be reformed by the proletariat. He included all three criteria in a letter to his Bulgarian supporters in October 1930:

> Does the proletarian dictatorship still exist in the USSR? Yes, despite everything, it still exists. In spite of all the disastrous policies, in spite of all the turns in the economy toward the right and toward the left, the government continues to defend the nationalization of the means of production and the foreign-trade monopoly. The transition of power into the hands of the bourgeoisie can take place only by means of a counterrevolutionary insurrection. In the meantime, the regeneration of the proletarian dictatorship is still possible by peaceful means.[292]

Trotsky restated the same points in his draft theses on the Russian question in April 1931, including both the 'property forms' and the 'absence of civil war' criteria, in the first paragraph of the document:

> The character of the social regime [in the USSR] is determined first of all by the property relations. The nationalization of land, of the means of industrial production and exchange, with the monopoly of foreign trade in the hands of the state, constitute the bases of the social order in the USSR. The classes expropriated by the October Revolution, as well as the elements of the bourgeoisie and the bourgeois section of the bureaucracy being newly formed, could reestablish private ownership of land, banks, factories, mills, railroads, etc., only by means of a counterrevolutionary overthrow. These property relations, lying at the base of class relations, determine for us the nature of the Soviet Union as a proletarian state.[293]

Later in the same theses he inserted his 'reformability' criterion, asserting that the characterisation of the Soviet state as a workers' state 'not only signifies that the bourgeoisie can conquer power only by means of an armed uprising

---

in exile, and in an article by the Austrian Social Democrat, Friedrich Adler, also published in 1932 (Linden 2007, pp. 51–4).

292   Trotsky 1973c, p. 44.
293   Trotsky 1973c, p. 204.

THE TURN AND THE THEORETICAL CRISIS DEEPEN

but also that the proletariat of the USSR has not forfeited the possibility of subordinating the party to it, of reviving the party again, and of regenerating the regime of the dictatorship – without a new revolution, with the methods and on the road of *reform*'.[294]

At least as far as his third criterion was concerned, Trotsky's conviction that the Soviet Union remained a workers' state was actually reinforced during these years by the turn. Since he partially attributed the shift in policy to proletarian pressure, he was convinced that it confirmed that the party and state could still be reformed. Reiterating the argument he had previously made against Hugo Urbahns, he asserted in April 1930, 'Nowhere is it written and nobody has shown that the present party, ... capable ... of silently turning the leadership through 180 degrees, could not, given the necessary initiative, regenerate itself internally'.[295]

6.7.5   *Cure*

One area of Trotsky's theory that remained largely unaffected by the turn was his fundamental strategy for resolving the problem of bureaucracy. Trotsky had developed his approach to this question on the basis of his essential understanding of the problem. Against the growing responsiveness of the state and party apparatuses to bourgeois pressure and the growing independence of these apparatuses from proletarian control, in 1926–7 he had advocated the exertion of countervailing proletarian pressure to push the apparatuses back to the left and to subordinate them again to the working class. For Trotsky, this reform strategy remained the only appropriate course as long as capitalism had not been restored. In the early 1930s he continued to insist upon the same approach, both within the USSR and the Comintern.

Throughout this period Trotsky explicitly defined his response to the problem of bureaucracy within the Soviet Union as reformist. Since 1928 this orientation had been challenged by the Democratic Centralists within the Soviet Union and by Hugo Urbahns and his supporters in Germany. However, a reform strategy was already implicit in Trotsky's continuing characterisation of the Soviet Union as a 'workers' state', for according to Trotsky this indicated not only that the Soviet Union could still be reformed, but also that there was still something worth preserving. In a letter to Soviet Oppositionists on 31 October 1930 he asserted,

---

294   Trotsky 1973c, p. 225.

295   Trotsky 1975d, p. 209. See also Trotsky 1973c, p. 227. For the same argument in 1929, see Trotsky 1975c, p. 280.

There is absolutely no question ... that in the light of the approaching upheavals the Bolshevik-Leninists stand for preserving and maintaining the gains of the October Revolution, i.e., above all, the elements of the proletarian dictatorship and the leading role of the party. In this fundamental sense we remain on the road of *reform*.[296]

We might note that there was a degree of circularity in Trotsky's derivation of a reform strategy from his position that the USSR remained a workers' state while defining the USSR as a workers' state in part on the basis of his perception that it was still able to be reformed. However, as we have seen, in this period Trotsky's reform orientation was also partially based on the turn, for it demonstrated that the leadership could still be pressured into changing course. In fact, there was only one implicit difference between Trotsky's general reform orientation in these years and his earlier perspective – though it was a major one. Previously, for Trotsky reform had meant pushing the bureaucracy to the left; now it involved pressing it to the right.

As in the past Trotsky insisted that the only force capable of bringing about reform was the Soviet proletariat. More precisely, it was the proletarian core within the party, leading broader layers of non-party workers to reform the party and then the state. Thus, in February 1930 Trotsky stated that only 'the proletarian nucleus of the party, relying on the working class' could 'take from the usurpers' apparatus the power that has been usurped from the party'.[297] At the same time, he continued to view the Left Opposition, the 'vanguard of the vanguard', as the natural leader of this nucleus.[298]

Again in contrast to Urbahns, and despite the fact that virtually all Bolshevik-Leninists had been expelled from the party, Trotsky insisted that the Opposition define itself as a *faction* of the AUCP. In part, he saw this approach as flowing logically from his reformist orientation, since he believed any attempt to found a new party would necessarily push the Opposition onto the path of armed struggle. In a draft document for the ILO in January 1933, he explained, 'The policy of a *second party* there [in the USSR] would mean a policy of armed insurrection and a new revolution. The policy of the *faction* means steering a course toward internal reform of the party and the workers' state'.[299] Beyond that, he also feared that an attempt to construct a new party would alienate the

---

296   Trotsky 1973c, p. 53. See also Trotsky 1972f, p. 55.
297   Trotsky 1975d, p. 117. See also Trotsky 1975d, p. 146.
298   Trotsky 1973c, p. 65.
299   Trotsky 1972f, p. 55. See also Trotsky 1975d, p. 16.

masses of revolutionary workers within the Soviet Union who remained loyal to the AUCP. In an article of November 1931 he wrote,

> You, worker-communists, cling to the party, not in the name of the bureaucrats, but in the name of its great revolutionary past and its possible revolutionary future. We understand you fully. Revolutionary workers do not leap blithely from organization to organization like individual students. We Bolshevik-Leninists are fully ready to help you worker-communists regenerate the party.[300]

Nevertheless, Trotsky remained convinced that the reform of the party and state was no longer possible without a 'profound internal crisis' and 'a deep internal struggle'.[301] Again, he seems to have thought that a movement for reform would most likely develop in the course of a struggle against capitalist restoration. In his 1931 draft theses he explained that the task of the Opposition in such a crisis would be 'to assemble and push ahead the proletarian wing promptly, without letting the class enemy gain time'.[302] To prepare itself for that moment, it was necessary that the Opposition 'develop as a firm faction, that it analyze all the changes in the situation, formulate clearly the perspectives of development, raise fighting slogans at the right time, and strengthen its connections with the advanced elements of the working class'.[303]

In the meantime, Trotsky hoped to strengthen the position of the Opposition through alliances with other party groupings. In this respect, too, he continued to follow his traditional approach, advocating a 'bloc' with the party centre against forces further to its right. In November 1930 he asserted that, just as the Bolsheviks had forged a bloc with Kerenskii against Kornilov in 1917, likewise, a united front against counterrevolution with the *part* of the Stalinist apparatus that would not go over to the other side was 'self-evident'.[304] As the economic crisis in the Soviet Union worsened, he appealed to dissident Stalinists for just such an alliance.[305] In fact, it was partially for the sake of an alliance that in late 1932 he even renounced the slogan 'Down with Stalin'! Earlier that

300 Trotsky 1973c, p. 341. See also Trotsky 1973c, pp. 53–4.
301 Trotsky 1975d, p. 209; Trotsky 1973c, p. 65.
302 Trotsky 1973c, p. 225. See also Trotsky 1973c, p. 205.
303 Trotsky 1973c, p. 226.
304 Trotsky 1973c, p. 64. See also Trotsky 1971c, p. 217.
305 This point is also made by Law 1987a, p. 125. In this regard, compare Trotsky's March 1930 open letter to the party (Trotsky 1975d, pp. 135–50) to his more conciliatory March 1932 open letter to the Presidium of the CEC (Trotsky 1973d, pp. 62–72).

year he had urged the Soviet leadership to 'carry out Lenin's final and insistent advice: remove Stalin'![306] However, when he received reports that 'Down with Stalin'! was gaining popularity within party circles, he repudiated this demand. In part, he did so out of concern that, in the midst of the crisis, the slogan might strengthen Thermidorian forces for whom it signified 'Down with the Bolsheviks'.[307] Beyond that, he feared that it might become an obstacle to the formation of a left-centre alliance since it would be interpreted by Stalinists 'as a call to smash the Stalinist faction, expel its members from the party, etc'.[308]

As in the past, Trotsky's attitude to the party right remained hostile. However, because of the turn, it was becoming increasingly difficult to explain exactly what issues separated the right from the left. At this point both equally denounced the ultraleftism of Stalinist economic and international policy and the authoritarianism of the party regime. Awkwardly, in October 1932 Trotsky dismissed this coincidence as temporary and limited, explaining that, in contrast with the left, the right wing was a 'faction for permanent retreat', and that, despite its 'limited, temporary, and conjunctural "correctness"', its position remained fundamentally false.[309] Consequently, he continued to reject the idea of a 'bloc' – that is, an alliance around a broad, common programme – with the right against the centre.[310]

Still, the defeat of the right in the party struggle and his own growing emphasis on bureaucratic autonomy had increased Trotsky's willingness to consider limited alliances with the right to restore party democracy. He had first suggested such a possibility in his 1928 letter to Shatunovskii in which he proposed a 'common effort' to return the party 'to a condition of legality'.[311] In the same spirit in October 1930 he endorsed Rakovskii's appeal for a coalition Central Committee that would include the left, centre, and right. He observed

---

306   Trotsky 1973d, p. 71. Also, in February 1930 Trotsky insisted that it was 'necessary to remove the present leadership' because the Stalinist position on international questions was threatening the proletarian vanguard with disasters (Trotsky 1975d, p. 119).

307   Trotsky 1979a, p. 168. See also Deutscher 1963, p. 175.

308   Trotsky 1979a, p. 171. Similarly, Trotsky publicly repudiated the slogan in an article of 3 March 1933 (Trotsky 1972f, p. 113). As alternatives to 'Down with Stalin!', Trotsky proposed 'Down with the personal regime', 'For an honest party regime!' and 'For Soviet democracy!' (Trotsky 1979a, p. 173; Trotsky 1972f, p. 113).

309   Trotsky 1973d, p. 254. In the summer of 1930 Khristian Rakovskii also tried to explain the continuing distinction between the party left and the right, asserting that 'the difference between us and the Right is that between an army in orderly retreat and deserters fleeing the field of battle' (Rakovsky 1981, p. 50).

310   See Trotsky 1973c, pp. 58–9; Trotsky 1973d, pp. 248–9.

311   Trotsky 1981, pp. 248–9.

that, since the right was still in the CC with the centre, implementing this slogan would just mean including the left. Of course, he noted, the Stalinists were unlikely to agree to such a combination except in a crisis.[312] In such a situation, he asserted the following September, a coalition CC 'would be in essence an organizational commission for the reconstruction of the party'.[313]

Beyond this, in 1932 Trotsky participated in a more realistic attempt to work with party rightists, among others. In October 1932 Sedov wrote to his father from Germany announcing that a 'bloc' had been formed with the Zinovievists, with Trotskyist capitulators around I.N. Smirnov, and with a grouping of former Stalinists led by Lominadze and Sten. Sedov also reported that negotiations were proceeding with Safarov's dissident Zinovievists, and even with a group of rightists led by Riutin and Slepkov. In response Trotsky approved of the plan in general, while emphasising that it was to be 'a bloc and not a unification', and insisting that all participants retained the right to criticise each other freely. Although he now explicitly used the term *bloc*, this clearly was not to be an alliance around a broad, common platform. At least for the time being, the bloc was simply to provide 'mutual information' to the participating groups. In light of these limited goals, he did not reject the participation of the right – or even of a 'thoroughgoing Thermidorean' such as Riutin. However, he urged the participants not to wait for the right to join since waiting would 'mean leaving the ground to the Rightists'.[314]

At the same time Trotsky's position also remained reformist with regard to the Comintern. That is, he continued to reject the formation of a new international socialist organisation, insisting instead that his supporters in the ILO confine their efforts to reforming the Comintern and its sections.[315] As in his position regarding the USSR, his reform strategy for the Comintern was based largely on his understanding of the consciousness of the typical communist worker. Trotsky insisted that revolutionary workers would not yet understand or support the formation of a new International. In an interview in August 1932 he explained,

> The worker thinks slowly, he must mull everything over in his mind, I would say. He knows that the party has enlightened him and trained him

---

312   Trotsky 1973c, pp. 54–5. See also Trotsky 1973c, p. 65.

313   Trotsky 1973c, p. 308.

314   Broué 1989, pp. 100–1.

315   See, for example, Trotsky 1975d, pp. 18, 189; Trotsky 1973c, p. 341; Trotsky 1973d, p. 120; Trotsky 1972f, p. 54.

as a conscious worker, and therefore he does not change as easily as the intellectual. He learns not from discussions but from historical events.[316]

For this reason he remained convinced that, under existing circumstances, a new International would inevitably degenerate into a sterile sect. In an undated letter from 1930 he warned that adopting Urbahns's perspective on a new International would raise 'the danger of becoming isolated from the communist masses'.[317] In fact, in June 1932 he even speculated that the Stalinists actually wanted to push the Opposition into founding a new International since 'a fatal error of this type' would slow the Opposition's growth for years, 'if not nullify all its successes altogether'.[318]

Nevertheless, in these years Trotsky repeatedly conceded that the revolutionary proletariat would abandon all hope for the Comintern in the face of some 'great historic event' comparable to the betrayal of the Social Democratic parties in 1914. Then, it would be necessary for the Opposition to prepare for the construction of a new International.[319] For Trotsky, possible events of such magnitude included the restoration of capitalism in the USSR, and the victory of fascism in Germany. In a draft document on the tasks of the ILO in January 1933 he explained,

> Such a historical catastrophe as the collapse of the Soviet state would, of course, sweep away with it the Third International too. Similarly, the victory of fascism in Germany and the smashing of the German proletariat would hardly allow the Comintern to survive the consequences of its disastrous policies.[320]

However, for Trotsky these two possibilities were not entirely distinct. In fact, he was so convinced that a Nazi victory would inevitably entail the collapse of the USSR that he repeatedly linked the events together. In a letter published in January 1932 he asserted,

> Should the German proletariat be defeated by the fascists, then all will be lost for the Comintern and possibly also for the Soviet Union. For the world proletariat, that would be a setback for many years to come. Under

316   Trotsky 1973d, pp. 178–9. See also Trotsky 1975d, pp. 369–70; Trotsky 1971c, pp. 326–7.
317   Trotsky 1975d, p. 19.
318   Trotsky 1973d, p. 125.
319   See, for example, Trotsky 1971c, pp. 326–7.
320   Trotsky 1972f, p. 54. See also Trotsky 1971c, p. 326.

such tragic conditions, the Left Opposition will take over the task of continuing to develop the Marxist program, but certainly no longer within the formal framework of the Third International.[321]

Similarly, in a discussion in August 1932 about developments that might require the founding of a new International, he specified,

> Such an event would be the victory of fascism in Germany. But the victory of fascism in Germany does not only mean in all probability the collapse of the Comintern, but also includes the defeat of the Soviet Union. Only if that takes place ... will we have the right to talk about a new party, about a fourth international.[322]

6.8   Conclusion

During the period from late 1929 to early 1933 the gulf between Trotsky's expectations and developments in Soviet policy continued to widen. In previous years he had asserted that, without a proletarian upsurge and/or an increase in Oppositional pressure, the leadership would revert to its previous rightist course. But in late 1929, with no evident increase in pressure from the Opposition or the proletariat, the leadership dramatically changed its economic and international orientation, inaugurating policies that were far more 'leftist' than those advocated by the Left Opposition. Furthermore, in previous years Trotsky had insisted that there was a direct relationship between the leadership's rightist orientation and the repressive and undemocratic character of the party-state regime. However, between 1929 and 1933 Trotsky perceived the regime as continuing to worsen, while the leadership carried out radical shifts to the left in both economic and international policy.

As reality increasingly diverged from Trotsky's expectations, the crisis in his theory deepened. For the first time he found himself denouncing the general orientation of Soviet economic policy and Comintern policy as 'ultraleft'. His specific criticisms in both areas were compelling. However, Trotsky's attempt to force the unfolding situation into the Procrustean bed of his traditional theory resulted in a series of analyses, especially regarding the economy, that today appear fundamentally mistaken. These included his acceptance of the validity

---

321   Trotsky 1973d, p. 23.
322   Trotsky 1973d, p. 179. According to Trotsky, the conversation was quoted 'broadly correctly'.

of the charges in the show trials of specialists, his belief that in the main collectivisation was accomplished voluntarily, his explanation of the ultraleftism of
the First Five-Year Plan in terms of capitalist sabotage, his insistent predictions
that the *kolkhozy* would foster the development of a new layer of kulaks, and
his repeated forecasts that the leadership was about to veer sharply back to the
right, perhaps even instituting capitalism.

There are a number of likely reasons – theoretical, political, and personal –
why Trotsky continued to interpret reality in terms of a theory that in retrospect appears so misguided. One involved the previous successes of his
theory. In 1926–7 that theory provided a convincing account of a variety of
developments, including the conservative drift in Soviet policy and the steady
worsening of the party and state regimes. In light of those successes, it is
understandable that he was reluctant to abandon his traditional approach. At
the same time, there was no theoretical alternative that Trotsky found persuasive. Of course, other perspectives were advanced at the time. While conciliators argued that the leadership had proven to be 'better than their theories' or
more responsive to necessity than the Opposition had believed possible, some
irreconcilables and left communists insisted that a Thermidorian restoration
had already occurred. For Trotsky all of these involved theoretical problems
that were even greater than those of his own theory.

Aside from theoretical concerns, there were important political reasons
for Trotsky to continue to uphold his traditional theory. The Opposition's programme, its past activities, and its self-definition were all bound up with the
perspective he had articulated in 1926–7. If he had abandoned that perspective,
it could have called into question the meaning of the Opposition's struggle. On
the other hand, he must have hoped that by reaffirming his theory he could
strengthen the political centre of the Opposition, minimising defections to the
Stalinists and the 'sectarians'. Additionally, he was convinced that the theoretical alternatives advocated by the conciliators and the extreme intransigents all
led to political positions that precluded serious activity on behalf of reform.

A final factor that helps to explain Trotsky's ability to uphold his traditional
theory was his own personality. Trotsky was an extraordinarily strong-willed
individual. This is evident from his years of independent political activity
before the revolution, from the history of his debates with other party leaders in the 1920s, and from his persistence in isolated oppositional activity
during his final exile. It is likely that this stubborn streak reinforced his ability to maintain the essentials of a theory that was increasingly challenged by
counterevidence.

Nevertheless, the obvious discrepancies between theory and reality in these
years repeatedly compelled Trotsky to introduce a whole series of implicit

and explicit theoretical modifications and adjustments. At times he was again forced to explain major shifts in policy, not in terms of class pressure, but by factors that emphasised the autonomy of the bureaucracy such as panic, excitement, or sheer stupidity. Similarly, he attributed the worsening of the regime, not to the shifts in the balance of class forces, but to the conscious efforts by the bureaucracy or the Stalin group to advance their own interests. Along the same lines, he again found it necessary to emphasise the autonomy of the bureaucracy by a number of adjustments to his more general theoretical formulations.

Although these revisions seemed to bring Trotsky's analysis into a closer correspondence with reality, the result was a theoretical orientation that grew increasingly incoherent. On different occasions Trotsky found himself explaining the leftist economic policies of the leadership as inspired by proletarian pressure, bourgeois influence, or the emotional states of an autonomous bureaucracy. At times he asserted the turn had been made *against* the wishes of the bureaucracy; at other times he insisted it had been made *by* the bureaucracy. He variously argued that the left course had either increased or decreased the danger of capitalist restoration, and that it had increased the probability such a restoration would take either a Thermidorian or a Bonapartist form. He repeatedly described as 'centrist' the grouping that stood to the left of the Left Opposition, while criticising as 'rightist' a party current that held views indistinguishable from those of the left. Finally, he continued to denounce the 'conservatism' of a leadership that was dramatically transforming the Soviet economy while implementing what Trotsky viewed as a radical left course internationally. The result of these modifications was to stretch Trotsky's traditional theory nearly to the breaking point.

Theoretical Revolution

Although the theory of Soviet bureaucracy articulated by Trotsky in 1926–7 was badly shaken by subsequent shifts in Soviet policy, it was not overturned. Throughout the years 1928–32 Trotsky dealt with the contradictions between his theory and reality by various strained interpretations of events and a series of ad hoc revisions of the theory that emphasised the ability of the bureaucracy to behave autonomously. However, despite those revisions, he continued to depict the bureaucracy essentially as a social formation that was highly responsive to alien class pressures. That was about to change.

The dynamics of major theoretical transformations have been explored by social scientists and philosophers. In *The Image*, the economist and philosopher Kenneth Boulding has explained that sometimes a new piece of information or 'message' strikes 'some sort of nucleus or supporting structure' in a worldview or image, and then 'the whole thing changes in quite a radical way'. The result is 'revolutionary change', that is, a 'sudden and dramatic' reorganisation of the image.[1] Similarly, the philosopher and historian of science Thomas Kuhn has described a scientific revolution as 'a reconstruction of the field from new fundamentals' in which 'an older paradigm is replaced in whole or in part by an incompatible new one' in a process that is 'non-cumulative', and 'relatively sudden'.[2] During the years 1933–6 Trotsky's theory experienced a fundamental transformation comparable to that described by Boulding and Kuhn.

The event that sparked the revolution in Trotsky's thinking was Hitler's consolidation of power in Germany in early 1933 – a development that, for Trotsky, signaled the ultimate failure of Comintern policy. In response, he immediately abandoned his attempt to reform the KPD. That step initiated a chain reaction that within months toppled many of Trotsky's most important theoretical positions. There were various reasons why developments in Germany affected his theory so greatly when the earlier turns in Soviet and Comintern policy did not. In part, it was because in 1933 his theory had been severely weakened by the experiences of the preceding five years. More importantly, the implications of the German debacle struck directly at central 'nuclei' of his theory – his reform orientation for the USSR and his criteria for a workers' state – that had been unaffected by the previous policy shifts. Trotsky's change of position on

---

1   Boulding 1956, pp. 8–9.
2   Kuhn 1970, pp. 85, 92, 122.

those issues quickly led to a reassessment of the extent of the bureaucracy's autonomy, and to a revision of his views on questions such as the relevance of the concepts of Thermidor and Bonapartism and the origins of the problem of Soviet bureaucracy.

Over the course of the following two and a half years, Trotsky's new theoretical insights informed his analysis of events, while his analysis of unfolding developments led to further theoretical revisions. Even more than before, his interpretations of events stressed the autonomy of the bureaucracy. In turn, these analyses led Trotsky to revise his understanding of Thermidor and Bonapartism, to emphasise the concepts of bureaucratic caste and labour aristocracy, to drop the term *bureaucratic centrism*, to modify again his criteria for a workers' state, to redefine the international role of the USSR, and to call for a political revolution. By the middle of 1936 Trotsky had created the elements of a fundamentally new theory of Soviet bureaucracy.

7.1 Breaking with the Past

In the opening months of 1933 Trotsky concluded that the crisis in the Soviet economy had become so severe that the very survival of the USSR was endangered. On 11 January, in response to Stalin's recent economic report to the Central Committee, Trotsky drew his own balance sheet of the First Five-Year Plan. Despite some real economic successes, he observed, hungry workers were dissatisfied with the party's economic policy, the party was unhappy with the leadership, the peasants were discontented with industrialisation and collectivisation, and a section of the peasantry was hostile to the regime. In fact, Trotsky concluded, the economic policies of the leadership had 'enormously strengthened the danger of Thermidor'.[3] In the following weeks his concern over the state of the Soviet economy continued to mount. In a private letter written on 15 February he described the situation as 'tragic' and expressed the conviction that 'the months to come will be decisive'.[4] Then, in an article of 3 March entitled 'Alarm Signal!' he declared that the bureaucratic leadership had 'brought the national economy to the brink of absolute chaos' by its extreme tempos of industrialisation and collectivisation.[5]

In this same period Trotsky was also becoming increasingly concerned about events in Germany. On 30 January 1933 Hindenburg appointed Hitler as

3 Trotsky 1972f, pp. 75, 76.
4 Trotsky 1979a, p. 189.
5 Trotsky 1972f, p. 96.

Chancellor of a coalition cabinet. Although Trotsky viewed this as 'a fearful blow for the working class', he did not yet see the defeat as irrevocable since the opposing sides had not yet tested their forces in battle.[6] Anticipating a new phase of struggle, he turned again to the KPD, and then to Social Democratic workers, pleading once more for a defensive alliance.[7] Finally, on 3 March in the article 'Alarm Signal!' he advised the Comintern that it could be saved from 'further degeneration and complete collapse only by a radical change of all its policies, first of all that in Germany'.[8] Still, both the SPD and KPD resisted collaboration. While the SPD leaders now formally advocated a united front, as a precondition they demanded a 'non-aggression pact' between the two parties and refused to participate in any actions that might provoke civil war. At the same time the KPD leadership continued to aim its sharpest attacks at the Socialists, while directing appeals for a united front only to local Socialist organisations.[9]

Meanwhile, the National Socialists proceeded with their offensive, banning Social Democratic and Communist Party newspapers; dispersing Socialist, Communist, and trade union meetings; and replacing masses of government officials and police. When the Dutch anarchist Marinus van der Lubbe set fire to the Reichstag building on the evening of 27 February, the Nazis blamed Communists for the arson. At that point the KPD was outlawed, the entire Social Democratic press was shut down, thousands of Socialist and Communist officials and candidates were arrested, and constitutional guarantees of civil liberties were suspended. In the 5 March elections the Nazis won a plurality with 43.9 percent of the vote. Then on 23 March the new Reichstag granted Hitler dictatorial powers.[10]

Recognising the completeness of the Nazi victory, Trotsky abruptly shifted strategy in Germany. In previous years he had asserted that if KPD policy permitted the Nazis to come to power, it would be necessary to form a new communist party in Germany. Furthermore, he had predicted repeatedly that a 'great historic event', such as 'the victory of fascism in Germany', would shake

---

6   Trotsky 1971c, pp. 341, 343.

7   Trotsky 1971c, pp. 346, 349–69.

8   Trotsky 1972f, p. 114.

9   Braunthal 1967, pp. 381–2; Carr 1982, pp. 83–4; Degras 1965, pp. 249–50; Trotsky 1971c, pp. 352–4, 357–8, 362.

10   Braunthal 1967, pp. 381–4; Bullock 1952, pp. 233–40; R. Evans 2004, pp. 328–54; Shirer 1960, pp. 190–8; Trotsky 1971c, p. 371; 'Reichstag fire' in Zentner and Bedürftig 1991.

the confidence of workers in the Comintern and necessitate the founding of a new International.[11] Similarly, in his article of 5 February he warned the KPD,

> The party's renunciation of the united front and of the creation of local defense committees, i.e., future soviets, signifies the capitulation of the party before fascism, an historic crime which is tantamount to the liquidation of the party and the Communist International. In the event of such a disaster, the proletariat, through mounds of corpses, through years of unbearable sufferings and calamities, will come to the Fourth International.[12]

Consistent with this, in a letter to the International Secretariat of the ILO on 12 March Trotsky asserted, 'The KPD today represents a corpse'. Writing under the name G. Gourov, he explained that now the slogan of reform would seem ridiculous to German workers who had been betrayed by the KPD bureaucracy. Then, comparing the German debacle to the political collapse of Social Democracy on 4 August 1914 when the German, French and Belgian Socialist parties endorsed their respective nations' war efforts, he declared, 'The Fourth of August is an accomplished fact', and he called for the construction of a new party in Germany.[13]

Although Trotsky also held the leadership of the Comintern responsible for the disaster in Germany, he hesitated until mid-July before abandoning the International and its leading section. Subsequently, he admitted that the break with the Comintern should have come at the beginning of April, when the ECCI adopted a resolution declaring that the policies of the KPD 'before and at the time of the Hitler coup' had been 'completely correct'.[14] However, he explained that it had been important 'to bring about a decisive turn without leading to a split' with ILO comrades who disagreed with the call for a new German party. Also, it was 'necessary to see what the influence of the German catastrophe would be on other sections of the Comintern'.[15]

Other explanations also have been suggested for Trotsky's delay. The historian J. Arch Getty, dismissing Trotsky's own account as 'self-justifying', has

---

11 Trotsky 1973d, pp. 178–9. See also Trotsky 1973d, p. 23; Trotsky 1972f, p. 54; Trotsky 1971c, pp. 326–7.

12 Trotsky 1971c, p. 348.

13 Trotsky 1972f, pp. 137–9. Trotsky's main argument was that revolutionary German workers would soon abandon the KPD. See also Trotsky 1972f, pp. 140, 161, 191; Trotsky 1971c, p. 384.

14 For the 1 April 1933 resolution of the ECCI presidium on the situation in Germany, see Degras 1965, pp. 254–63.

15 Trotsky 1972g, p. 26. See also Trotsky 1979a, p. 287.

argued that the decision to abandon the Comintern and the timing of that decision were related to Trotsky's manoeuvring to regain personal power.[16] An alternative interpretation has combined Trotsky's own stated reasons with an explanation that stresses the importance for Trotsky of theory as a guide to political behaviour.[17]

According to J. Arch Getty, Trotsky's break with the Comintern and its timing can be explained by two 'secret strategies' designed to return Trotsky to the leadership of the AUCP. The first of these involved a secret letter to the Politburo on 15 March 1933 in which Trotsky allegedly promised that the Opposition would hold agitation for its programme 'in abeyance for an indefinite period' or even 'refrain from criticism' altogether if the leadership would recall him to power. According to Getty, Trotsky never published this letter because it contradicted his previous demands. Getty further claims that Trotsky's letter breaking with the KPD was a ploy to pressure the leadership of the AUCP into taking him back, and that he signed it with a pseudonym so that he could later disavow it if he was recalled to power. After waiting more than a month and a half for an answer, Trotsky gave up on this strategy and informed the Politburo of his intention to agitate among lower levels of the bureaucracy. But he continued to hesitate over the break with the Comintern, allegedly because he still had hopes for his second strategy: the opposition bloc formed in 1932. Soon afterwards, however, the bloc was 'decapitated' by the capitulations of Zinoviev and Kamenev. With all of his hopes for power dashed, Trotsky finally called on his supporters to break with the Comintern.[18]

Unfortunately, there are problems with virtually every aspect of Getty's account. There is, of course, no doubt that Trotsky wanted to return to power. In fact, in previous public statements he repeatedly called for the creation of a coalition CC with representatives from the Left Opposition, presumably including himself. If the Politburo had responded to his 15 March letter, Trotsky certainly would have raised this issue in negotiations. However, his letter to the Politburo did not mention this; rather, it requested only 'the opportunity for normal work within the party' for the Opposition.[19] Nor did Trotsky

---

16   Getty 1986, p. 27; Getty 1987, pp. 318–19.

17   Twiss 1987, pp. 131–7. This account coincides in a number of ways with that in Deutscher 1963, pp. 198–215. For other discussions of Trotsky's break with the KPD, the Comintern, and the AUCP, see Bensaïd 1988, pp. 5–10; Chattopadhyay 2006, pp. 525–33; Frank 1979, pp. 45–8; Law 1987a, pp. 155–8; Van Heijenoort 1973, pp. 3–5.

18   Getty 1986, pp. 29–31.

19   Trotsky 1972f, p. 142; Trotsky 1989, p. 45. For similar private and public statements during this period, see Trotsky 1973d, pp. 125–6; Trotsky 1979a, p. 173; Trotsky 1972f, p. 168.

propose delaying a discussion indefinitely or promise to abstain from criticism altogether. In his 15 March letter he offered only to negotiate the details of a party-wide discussion in the context of an explosive situation: 'Concerning the manner of presenting and defending this [the Opposition's] programme before the Central Committee and the party, not to mention the manner of putting it into effect, there can and must be achieved a preliminary agreement with the goal of preventing shocks or splitting'.[20] He never published the Politburo letter – probably because it was soon superseded by his break with the AUCP. But on 30 March, while still awaiting a reply from the Politburo, he wrote an article for his *Biulleten'* in which he publicly proposed an 'inner-party agreement' and 'an honorable agreement before the eyes of the party and of the international proletariat' regarding preparations for a discussion and the organisational framework within which it would occur.[21] Additionally, on 13 May 1933, three days after forwarding the Politburo letter to responsible party and government personnel, he wrote a brief note for the *Biulleten'* confirming the existence of his letter of 15 March and accurately describing its offer 'to carry out any work' in the interests of the Soviet republic 'on the condition that we retain our right to defend our point of view within the limits of the party statutes and Soviet constitution'.[22]

There are also major problems with Getty's account of Trotsky's attempt to pressure the party leadership. Trotsky could not have imagined that the threat of a 'split' would have influenced the leadership, since the vast majority of his supporters were already *outside* of the Comintern, having been expelled from their respective parties in previous years.[23] Nor did he retain the option of disavowing his break with the KPD by signing his 12 March letter with a pseudonym. Between 12 March and 10 May he published at least two statements under his own name proclaiming the death of the KPD and the need for a new

20   Quoted in Getty 1986, p. 30 (Getty's translation). For the original Russian, see Trotsky 1989, p. 45. The Pathfinder Press translation appears in Trotsky 1972f, p. 142. Challenged on this point, Getty seems to have dropped his original claim that Trotsky's letter contained an offer to hold discussion 'in abeyance for an indefinite period of time' or to 'refrain from criticism'. At that point Getty states, 'What was new in the secret letter was Trotsky's offer to defer, modify, or negotiate "the manner of presenting and defending this programme . . . not to mention the manner of putting it into effect" ' (Getty 1987, pp. 318–19).

21   Trotsky 1972f, pp. 167–8.

22   Trotsky 1972f, p. 235. The note was published in the July edition. See *Biulleten' oppozitsii* 1973, 35 (July 1933), p. 32.

23   As Trotsky observed in December 1932, 'It would be ridiculous to behave as if we belonged, in fact, to the official organizations of the Comintern' (Trotsky 1972f, p. 30).

party in Germany.[24] Furthermore, if Getty's account were correct Trotsky should have dropped the pseudonym after the failure of his 'first strategy'. However, he signed the first two articles calling for a break with the Comintern 'G. Gourov'.[25] Finally, it should be noted that there was nothing unusual about Trotsky's use of a pseudonym in his 12 March letter. From 1929 through 1934 he employed 'G. Gourov' or variations of that name at least 24 times, especially in contributions to the internal discussion of the ILO.[26]

Getty's discussion of the 'second strategy' is hardly more successful. Trotsky may have hoped that the opposition bloc would develop into a political force that could pressure the leadership into readmitting expelled Oppositionists. However, there is no reason to believe that he entered the bloc out of 'personal motives', rather than with the goal of reforming the AUCP. Since 1927 Trotsky had demanded the readmission of the Left Opposition as a necessary part of the process of reform. Aside from that, it is not at all clear that he abandoned hopes for the bloc only after hearing of the capitulations.[27] However, the biggest problem with Getty's 'second strategy' is related to timing. The whole

---

24   See Trotsky 1971c, pp. 375–84; Trotsky 1972f, pp. 189–97. Another statement making this point, signed 'L.D.' for Lev Davidovitch (Trotsky), was also published in this period (Trotsky 1972f, p. 140; Trotsky 1979a, pp. 221–2). One more statement containing this position, signed 'L. Trotsky', was published in France in May, though the date it first appeared is unclear (Trotsky 1972f, pp. 210–14; see Sinclair 1989, vol. 2, p. 685).

25   Trotsky 1972f, pp. 304–11; Trotsky 1972g, pp. 17–24.

26   See Sinclair 1989, vol. 2. Letters and articles related to the break with the KPD written between March and May 1933 and signed 'Gourov' or 'Gurov' appear in Trotsky 1972f, pp. 137–9, 161–3, 206–9 and Trotsky 1971c, pp. 385–7. Trotsky's use of a pseudonym in these cases may have had more to do with *where* he published statements than with the *content* of the statements. His concern may have been that contributing an article to an internal discussion bulletin under his own name might jeopardise his ability to obtain a visa in France or another Western European country. To obtain and keep his visa in France, Trotsky maintained that he was not directly involved in the political activity of any organisations. See Trotsky 1979a, pp. 188, 249; Trotsky 1979b, p. 564. It appears that all of the 'Gurov' statements listed here were first published in internal discussion bulletins of the ILO. On the other hand, the 14 March and 8 April statements on this topic signed 'Leon Trotsky' first appeared as articles in public newspapers of Trotskyist groups. The 27 April statement signed 'L. Trotsky' first appeared in an internal discussion bulletin, but in the form of a personal letter that was being reprinted in the bulletin.

27   Pierre Broué, who first discovered the bloc, suggests in one article that it was terminated by the arrests of Zinoviev, Kamenev, and other leading dissidents in the autumn of 1932 (Broué 1980, p. 19). In another article he suggests that the bloc withered away following the arrests and the subsequent cessation of activity by the Zinovievist group (Broué 1989, pp. 105–6).

point of Getty's discussion of the bloc is to fill the delay between Trotsky's final 10 May communication with the Politburo and his decision to break with the Comintern. Even if Trotsky abandoned hopes for the bloc on the first date he wrote of the capitulations, that accounts for just thirteen days, leaving more than seven weeks unexplained.[28]

In fact, there were several reasons for the delay, including the two offered by Trotsky. There is abundant evidence that he was quite serious about convincing his comrades of the need for a break with the KPD. Even in his 12 March letter he warned, 'This sharp turn in our policy, ... will not be absorbed all at once by all our comrades. That is why it is necessary to analyze the question in our own ranks and, above all, among the German comrades'.[29] Subsequently, he urged the International Secretariat of the ILO to open a discussion on the issue, and in the following months he submitted no less than five contributions to persuade members of the ILO of the need for a change in orientation.[30] Trotsky also explained that it was necessary to see if outrage over Germany would elicit a rebellion within the Comintern.[31] Of course, at this point he was quite pessimistic. Even while calling for a break with the KPD he declared, 'The collapse of the KPD diminishes the chances for the regeneration of the Comintern'.[32]

Nevertheless, Trotsky's explanations were not his only reasons for hesitation. Perhaps even more important was his recognition of the far reaching implications that a break with the Comintern would have for his political and theoretical positions regarding the USSR. Most immediately, it would

---

28   Trotsky 1972f, pp. 242–3.

29   Trotsky 1972f, p. 137.

30   Trotsky 1972f, pp. 140, 161–3, 189–97, 206–9; Trotsky 1971c, pp. 375–84. Trotsky clearly believed that the most effective way to convince hesitant comrades was to convince the International Secretariat first, and then to organise an international discussion. In his 12 March letter, he argued, 'This task [of analyzing the change in policy] will be made easier if the Secretariat immediately adopts a firm and resolute position' (Trotsky 1972f, p. 137). Similarly, in a letter to the International Secretariat of 28 March he explained, 'My aim in sending this article [of 15 March] to you was to reach an agreement with you before we could start a broader action' (Trotsky 1979a, p. 221).

31   See Trotsky 1972f, pp. 138, 163, 193. Trotsky's hopes in this regard were not entirely unfounded. Unbeknownst to Trotsky, even after the 1 April declaration of the Presidium of the ECCI that the line of the Comintern had been 'completely correct', there was a bitter assessment of the German debacle from Hermann Remelle of the KPD, and an appeal to the ECCI from Klement Gottwald of the Communist Party of Czechoslovakia for negotiations with the Second International for a united front. Similar sentiments were voiced within the French and Austrian sections (Carr 1982, p. 91).

32   Trotsky 1972f, p. 138. See also Trotsky 1972f, p. 305.

challenge his reform orientation toward the AUCP and the USSR and his characterisation of the Soviet Union as workers' state. Additionally, it would ultimately call into question his view of the bureaucracy as highly responsive to
external class pressure.

In previous years Trotsky had based his reform strategy for the Comintern
primarily on his perception that it still commanded the loyalty of revolutionary workers. However, his position regarding the AUCP was also grounded on
the recognition that a policy of a 'second party' would mean 'a policy of armed
insurrection and a new revolution' in the USSR.[33] In turn, he had based his
reform orientation for the Soviet Union largely on his view that it remained a
workers' state. This presented a potential dilemma: what position would he
take if a 'great historic event' demonstrated the bankruptcy of the Comintern,
but its leading section continued to rule a country that, by other criteria,
remained a workers' state? Until March 1933 the question was not sharply
posed. Since early 1932 he had suggested that *either* a victory of fascism in
Germany or the collapse of the Soviet workers' state would require the formation of a new International. However, since he believed that a Nazi victory
would greatly increase the chances of restoration in the USSR, this did not necessarily present a theoretical difficulty.[34]

Once Trotsky concluded that fascism had conquered power in Germany, he
was confronted with the dilemma. He immediately called for a break with the
KPD, which he saw as most directly responsible for the debacle. Yet, he still
baulked at the prospect of abandoning the Comintern. One of his secretaries
at that time, Jean van Heijenoort, later recalled, 'The problem of the USSR was
the greatest obstacle in Trotsky's mind before reaching the conclusion that
there remained no other alternative than to form a Fourth International'. Van
Heijenoort explained,

> The problem was: how to discard the policy of reform of the Bolshevik
> Party and at the same time retain the perspective of reforming the work-
> ers' state? How to proclaim the Fourth International before the Stalinist
> bureaucracy has led the USSR to its collapse?[35]

---

33   Trotsky 1972f, p. 55.
34   To the extent that Trotsky entertained the possibility that the Nazis could come to power
     in Germany without a resulting collapse of the USSR, he appears to have been undecided
     about how he would respond. See Trotsky 1973d, pp. 178–9; Trotsky 1972f, p. 54.
35   Van Heijenoort 1973, p. 4.

That this was a central concern of Trotsky's was also indicated by his writings. Even in his initial call for a break with the KPD he rejected a similar rupture with the Comintern in part because 'the question has not been settled for the USSR, where proclamation of the slogan of the second party would be incorrect'.[36]

For a time Trotsky attempted to avoid a decision, given the possibility that the dilemma would be resolved by reality. Most optimistically, he still hoped the USSR and/or the Comintern would be transformed under the pressure of the crises. As he wrote on 29 March, 'We do not give up our efforts to save the Soviet power from the ruin to which it is being driven by the Stalinists. We cannot know in advance what the reaction inside the other sections ... will be to the victory of fascism'.[37] More pessimistically, he feared that the economic crisis might result in the collapse of the USSR. Responding on 9 April to the question of whether or not the break with the KPD meant a break with the Comintern, he asserted that if 'the Stalinist bureaucracy will bring the USSR to ruin, ... it will be necessary to build a Fourth International'.[38]

However, by the early summer it was clear that neither Trotsky's most optimistic hopes nor his worst fears were about to materialise. His appeals to the Soviet leadership and the bureaucracy had elicited no response, and there had been no public dissent within the Comintern over the ECCI Presidium's pronouncement of the correctness of the KPD's polices.[39] Meanwhile, the Soviet economy seemed to be emerging from the worst of its crisis. In discussions with supporters he now proposed abandoning the Comintern, but, restrained by his position on the class nature of the USSR, he still rejected a rupture with the AUCP. Jean van Heijenoort later recalled Trotsky's formulation in private discussions at this time:

> Since April we have been for reform in every country except Germany, where we have been for a new party. We can now take a symmetrical

---

36 Trotsky 1972f, p. 138.
37 Trotsky 1972f, p. 163.
38 Trotsky 1972f, p. 193. Also in the same passage Trotsky again suggested that some Comintern sections could be reformed.
39 Additionally, Trotsky charged that, by failing to put up a serious struggle, in May the Austrian Communist Party permitted itself to be banned by the authoritarian chancellor, Dolfuss. This failure prompted Trotsky to extend his conclusion regarding the KPD to the Austrian section. See Trotsky 1972f, p. 276. See also Trotsky 1972f, pp. 269–70, 282–3.

position, that is, to be for a new party in every country except the U.S.S.R., where we shall be for the reform of the Bolshevik party.[40]

However, in light of Trotsky's perception that the AUCP controlled the Comintern, this position was clearly untenable and, as van Heijenoort notes, Trotsky quickly abandoned it.[41] On 15 July in the article 'It Is Necessary to Build Communist Parties and an International Anew', he concluded, 'In all our sub-sequent work it is necessary to take as our point of departure the historical collapse of the official Communist International'.[42] Five days later, while admitting it was impossible to simply ' "proclaim" a new International', he insisted that it was important 'to proclaim the *necessity* of creating a new International'.[43] As far as the Soviet section was concerned, he now reiterated with enhanced significance his previous observation that it no longer existed as a party, asserting on 15 July that the AUCP was 'not a party but an apparatus of domination in the hands of an uncontrolled bureaucracy'.[44] Then, on 20 July he removed all doubts about his position by arguing that to speak of reform of the AUCP 'would mean to look backward and not forward, to soothe one's mind with empty formulas. In the USSR, it is necessary to build a Bolshevik party again'.[45] On 19 August the International Secretariat of the ILO endorsed Trotsky's new position, voting for the creation of a new International.[46]

7.2   Revising the Theory

For Trotsky, the change of position regarding the Comintern and the AUCP coincided with a geographical relocation. After four and a half years in Turkey, he was finally granted a visa to live in France. On 24 July he arrived at Marseilles, accompanied by his wife, two secretaries, a typist, and an American supporter. Initially, he settled near the small town of Saint-Palais, a few miles north of

---

40   Quoted in Van Heijenoort 1978, p. 39; Van Heijenoort 1973, pp. 4–5. Isaac Deutscher, reporting the account of Trotsky's secretary Pierre Frank, has described Trotsky's intense, almost physical anguish while grappling with these issues during this period (Deutscher 1963, p. 202n2).

41   See Van Heijenoort 1978, p. 39.

42   Trotsky 1972f, p. 306.

43   Trotsky 1972g, p. 22.

44   Trotsky 1972f, p. 309.

45   Trotsky 1971c, p. 430; Trotsky 1972g, p. 20.

46   The text of this resolution appears as Appendix A, 'The International Opposition and the Communist International' in Breitman 1979, pp. 15–17.

Royan. There, he held frequent meetings with his own supporters and with representatives of various European left-socialist organisations in preparation for founding a Fourth International.[47]

Soon after his arrival in France, Trotsky's shift in position on party reform led him to revise his political strategy and his theoretical understanding of the USSR in a number of other important ways. First, it compelled him to modify his position on peaceful reform. In turn, this forced him to redefine his position on the class nature of the Soviet Union. In the process of responding to opponents who held divergent positions on that question, he was prompted to expand upon the notion of bureaucratic 'parasitism'. At the same time, his enhanced appreciation of the bureaucracy's autonomy suggested to him a revised understanding of Bonapartism, inspired him to reconsider his previous views on Thermidor, and induced him to develop a new account of the origins of the bureaucratic power.

When Trotsky decided to break with the AUCP, he immediately confronted the problem he had sought to avoid. If abandoning the AUCP implied the need for revolution, how could this be reconciled with his understanding that the Soviet Union remained a workers' state? Even while calling for a break with the AUCP, he attempted to reduce this dilemma by revising his view that a second party orientation assumed a revolutionary perspective. In his article of 20 July he wrote, 'We abandon the slogan of the reform of the AUCP, and we construct a new party as an instrument for the reform of the Soviet Union'.[48] Trotsky explained that the Bolshevik-Leninists, organised as a separate party, could reform the state while fighting alongside a section of the bureaucracy in the civil war that was already in progress and that would only intensify. The opponents in this battle were 'the counterrevolution on the offensive and the Stalinist bureaucracy on the defensive'. At the decisive moment, he predicted, the bureaucracy would disintegrate and its fragments would 'meet again in the two opposing camps'. Then the Bolshevik-Leninists would forge a united front with a section of the Stalinists against the forces of reaction.[49] Consequently, there was no need for force against the bureaucracy; rather, the new party was to direct its force against the counterrevolution. Of course, this position, too, was untenable. As Trotsky had always recognised, it was inconsistent to call for a new, illegal party but to limit its methods to peaceful reform. Thus, on

---

47   Van Heijenoort 1978, pp. 49–52. On this period of Trotsky's French exile, see Van Heijenoort 1978, pp. 49–91; Deutscher 1963, pp. 262–6; Broué 1988, pp. 769–73.

48   *Biulleten' oppozitsii* 1973, 36–7 (October 1933), p. 24; Trotsky 1971c, p. 431; Trotsky 1972g, p. 21. See also Frank 1979, p. 46.

49   Trotsky 1971c, pp. 430–1; Trotsky 1972g, pp. 20–1.

1 October 1933 in his important pamphlet *The Class Nature of the Soviet State*, he concluded: 'No normal "constitutional" ways remain to remove the ruling clique. The bureaucracy can be compelled to yield power into the hands of the proletarian vanguard only by *force*'.[50]

Still, it should be noted that Trotsky did not yet call for a new revolution. In *The Class Nature of the Soviet State* he again insisted that 'a real civil war' could only occur between the proletariat and supporters of capitalist counterrevolution. Against the bureaucracy, only 'measures of a police character' would be needed:

> When the proletariat springs into action, the Stalinist apparatus will remain suspended in midair. Should it still attempt to resist, it will then be necessary to apply against it not the measures of civil war but rather the measures of a police character. In any case, what will be involved is not an armed insurrection against the dictatorship of the proletariat but the removal of a malignant growth upon it.[51]

The task then was not revolution, but 'radical [*korennaia*] reform of the Soviet state'.[52]

However, Trotsky's call for a break with the AUCP and for the use of force against the bureaucracy immediately necessitated a revision of his workers' state position. Since 1928 he had insisted that the proletarian character of the Soviet state was demonstrated by the fact that it continued to defend the property forms established by October, by the fact that the counterrevolution had not yet triumphed in a civil war, and by the fact that the Soviet proletariat remained capable of peacefully reforming the state through the reform of the party. Although he minimised the force that would be required, his recognition

---

50   Trotsky 1972g, p. 118 (original emphasis).
51   Trotsky 1972g, p. 118.
52   Trotsky 1972g, p. 119. *Biulleten' oppozitsii* 1973, 36–7 (October 1933), p. 10. Various authors have described Trotsky's October 1933 position as essentially the same as his 1936 call for a 'political revolution': Deutscher 1963, p. 203; Hallas 1984, p. 41; Van Heijenoort 1973, p. 5; Law 1987a, p. 158; Molyneux 1981, p. 114. For other works that stress the difference between Trotsky's October 1933 position and his 1936 position, see Cannon 1954, p. 12; Hofla 1985, pp. 25–9. On at least one occasion Trotsky subsequently asserted that shortly after Hitler came to power the Opposition declared, 'The cadres, the bureaucracy, can be removed only by a new political revolution' (Preliminary Commission of Inquiry 1968, p. 271). However, it is likely that Trotsky was simplifying the development of his position to make it easier for the Dewey Commission to follow.

of the need for force and his call for a break with the AUCP were both clearly inconsistent with his reform criterion.

Even though concerns related to his workers' state position had delayed his rupture with the Comintern and AUCP, by the time Trotsky made that break he had already decided how he would address the larger question. In the first place, two of his previous criteria were still intact. Besides that, abandoning his workers' state position would have necessitated greater adjustments than the partial modification of a definition. Consequently, even in his first appeals for a new International and a new party, he reaffirmed the proletarian character of the Soviet Union.[53] Then, on 1 October in *The Class Nature of the Soviet State* he provided an extended defence of his view that the Soviet Union remained a workers' state, while implicitly redefining the meaning of that term.[54]

Again, Trotsky insisted upon the traditional 'methodological position' of Marxism that the class nature of a state could only be changed through civil war. For Trotsky, those who argued that capitalism had been restored gradually were just 'running backwards the film of reformism'.[55] Furthermore, he reaffirmed that the proletarian nature of the Soviet state continued to be defined by the economic relations established by the Revolution.[56] But missing entirely from his argument was any mention of his reform criterion. In light of his recent change of position, Trotsky simply omitted this argument without comment. However, the significance of the omission was enormous. As Max Shachtman observed years later, Trotsky 'found himself obliged to alter his criterion radically from what it had previous been, not only for him but without exception for the entire revolutionary Marxian movement'.[57]

Having reaffirmed his workers' state position, Trotsky proceeded in the same work to criticise the positions of opponents who previously had argued that a new revolution was necessary. Clearly, he hoped to prevent his critics from deriving political benefit from his change of position. One view examined was that of Lucien Laurat, an Austrian socialist and member of the French SFIO, who had recently advanced the theory that the Soviet Union represented an entirely new form of class society in which the bureaucracy not only ruled

---

53   Trotsky 1972f, pp. 308–9; Trotsky 1972g, pp. 19–20, 41–2, 51.

54   This work was published in Trotsky's *Biulleten'* as an article, 'Klassovaia priroda sovetsk-
      ogo gosudarstva', *Biulleten' oppozitsii* 1973, 36–7 (October 1933), pp. 1–12. It was also pub-
      lished in a number of countries as a pamphlet, *The Soviet Union and the Fourth
      International*. See Sinclair 1989, vol. 2, p. 717; Trotsky 1972g, p. 354n131.

55   Trotsky 1972g, p. 103.

56   Trotsky 1972g, p. 104. See also Trotsky 1972g, p. 115.

57   Shachtman 1962, p. 91.

politically, but also exploited the proletariat economically.[58] Trotsky, who
had spoken frequently of the bureaucracy's enormous privileges, readily
agreed that the bureaucracy devoured 'no small portion of surplus value'.
Nevertheless, he argued that it was technically incorrect to portray the bureaucracy as 'exploiting' the proletariat, since the bureaucracy derived its privileges
'not from any special property relations peculiar to it as a "class", but from those
property relations that have been created by the October Revolution and that
are fundamentally adequate for the dictatorship of the proletariat'. To the
extent that the bureaucracy robbed the people, what was involved was not
'*class exploitation*, in the scientific sense of the word, but ... *social parasitism*,
although on a very large scale'.[59]

On a few previous occasions, echoing Marx's characterisations of the French
state bureaucracy under the absolute monarchy and Second Empire, Trotsky
had referred to the 'parasitism' of the Soviet bureaucracy.[60] Now he offered a
more extended discussion of that phenomenon, utilising it to suggest the tran-
sience and dispensability of bureaucratic rule. Trotsky argued that, by virtue of
its function and for the sake of its privileges, the bureaucracy was concerned
with the cultural growth of the country. However, that development ultimately
undermined 'the very bases of bureaucratic domination' by strengthening the
proletariat. At the same time, the leadership's wasteful and disruptive policies
retarded growth, raising the prospect of economic collapse, capitalist restoration, and again, the downfall of the bureaucracy. Thus, from whatever angle
the question was considered, bureaucratic rule appeared to be ephemeral.
From this Trotsky concluded that the bureaucracy was 'not an independent
class, but an excrescence [*narost*] upon the proletariat', and while a tumor
might 'grow to tremendous size and even strangle the living organism', it could
'never become an independent organism'.[61]

In the same pamphlet Trotsky took up the views of his old adversary
Urbahns. In his most recent writings, Urbahns had characterised the systems
of Stalin's USSR, Hitler's Germany, Mussolini's Italy, and Roosevelt's United
States as 'state capitalist' – allegedly a necessary and progressive stage in the

---

58   'Lucien Laurat' was the pseudonym of Otto Maschl. For statements of Laurat's theory, see
       Laurat, 1931; Laurat 1932, pp. 113–19; Laurat 1940. See also Linden 2007, pp. 69–73.
59   Trotsky 1972g, pp. 113, 114.
60   See Trotsky 1975d, pp. 50, 202; Trotsky 1972f, p. 225; Marx 1974c, p. 237; and Marx 1966, p. 69.
       For a useful discussion of the concept of 'state parasite' in Marx, see Draper 1977, bk. 2,
       pp. 622–6.
61   Trotsky 1972g, p. 115; *Biulleten' oppozitsii* 1973, 36–7 (October 1933), p. 8. It is likely that in
       this passage Trotsky was thinking of Marx's use of 'parasitic excrescence', in Marx 1966,
       p. 69.

development of society. As far as the USSR was concerned, Urbahns claimed to have taken this position from Lenin. In response, Trotsky pointed out that in Western countries the forms of state economic intervention traditionally described as state capitalist were not progressive, but 'reactionary through and through'. Within the USSR Lenin had applied the term to the concessions and mixed companies of NEP, not the state-owned trusts that had developed into the industries of the 1930s. Consequently, none of the traditional Marxist understandings of state capitalism could be applied to the Soviet economy.[62]

However, Trotsky now saw something of value in the earlier views of Urbahns. Before developing his most recent position, Urbahns had described the Soviet regime as Bonapartist, standing between classes. Trotsky made short work of this confusion, observing that it was nonsense to speak of a 'supraclass, or an interclass' state, and insisting that historically Bonapartism was 'only one of the varieties of capitalist hegemony'.[63] Although in the past Trotsky himself had described the AUCP as 'plebiscitary', or even 'Bonapartist', he had done so only to indicate broad parallels between the features of Stalinism and Bonapartism, and to suggest that Stalinism was facilitating the establishment of a truly Bonapartist (capitalist) regime. Now, however, he abruptly announced that, as long as the class nature of the Soviet state was clearly defined, he was ready to fully accept such a 'widened interpretation' of Bonapartism. He further observed:

> It is absolutely correct that the self-rule of the Soviet bureaucracy was built upon the soil of veering between class forces both internal as well as international. Insofar as the bureaucratic veering has been crowned by the personal plebiscitary regime of Stalin, it is possible to speak of Soviet Bonapartism.[64]

Of course, Trotsky was not suggesting this change because he was only now aware of the bureaucracy's 'self-rule', its 'veering between class forces', or Stalin's 'personal plebiscitary regime'. He had commented on each of these in the past. Rather, his provisional redefinition of Soviet Bonapartism was due to a new appreciation, derived from his conclusion that force would be needed to remove the bureaucracy from power, of the extent of the bureaucracy's autonomy. Still, he hesitated in the face of this leap, too. It would be more

---

62   Trotsky 1972g, pp. 108–11.

63   Trotsky 1972g, p. 107. For an earlier criticism by Trotsky of the position of Urbahns that the USSR was a 'state standing between classes', see Trotsky 1973c, pp. 224–5.

64   Trotsky 1972g, p. 108.

than a year before he would apply the Bonapartist label consistently to the Soviet regime.[65]

Meanwhile, Trotsky's thinking was also changing regarding the relevance of Bonapartism's twin concept, Thermidor. As David Law has pointed out, in late 1933 the term virtually disappeared from Trotsky's writings. Law explains that it had 'ceased, in its old form, to be useful' because although capitalist restoration 'might still be an ultimate destination, it no longer was viewed by Trotsky as immediately proximate'.[66] To the extent that Trotsky was influenced on this question by economic developments, his concern about restoration may have diminished as the economic situation began to improve. Even more significantly, as Law also observes, Trotsky's change of position regarding the use of force implied a rejection of the view that restoration was the 'greatest immediate danger' in favour of 'a concentration upon, and greater respect for, the current political regime'.[67] In other words, Trotsky's previous concern about Thermidor made far less sense in light of his new emphasis on bureaucratic autonomy.

At this point Trotsky's change of position on reform also prompted him to rethink his explanation of the origins of the problem of bureaucracy. In the late 1920s he had attributed the growth of bureaucratism primarily to the effects of bourgeois pressure on the state and party apparatuses. In the early 1930s he partially amended this view to emphasise the role of the party apparatus in promoting its own autonomy. However, nowhere did he attempt to address the more basic issues of how the bureaucracy had come into being as a distinct social formation, and what were the objective factors that continued to enhance its autonomy. Trotsky's tentative revision on the question of Bonapartism suggested answers to both questions.

On 4 December 1933 in the bulletin of his international organisation, recently renamed the International Communist League (ICL), Trotsky responded to a sympathiser who had asserted that backwardness was irrelevant to the issue of socialism in one country. In part, Trotsky rejected this position on the grounds that Soviet backwardness had fostered social contradictions that threatened the very survival of the USSR. In his explanation of why this

---

65   In fact, in December 1934 Trotsky was still warning about the danger of Bonapartism in the Soviet Union (Trotsky 1979b, p. 545).

66   Here, Law attributes this shift to Trotsky's recognition of the transformation of the peasantry under collectivisation (Law 1987a, pp. 289, 291; see also Law 1982, p. 440; Law 1987b, p. 8). However, the extent of collectivisation had not changed significantly since the spring of 1933 when Trotsky frequently spoke of Thermidor.

67   Law 1982, p. 440.

was the case he offered a functional account of the origins of the bureaucracy and of the continuing growth of its autonomy:

> The bureaucracy in the USSR is neither a moral nor a technological factor but a social one, i.e., a class factor. The struggle between the socialist and capitalist tendencies assumed primarily the character of a struggle between the social interests represented by the state and the personal interests of the consumers, the peasants, the civil employees and the workers themselves. In the given situation, the overcoming of class antagonisms means the harmonizing of the social interests of production with the personal interest of the consumers, while during the present stage of development personal interest still remains the prime mover of the economy. Has this harmonizing been accomplished? No! The growth of bureaucratism reflects the growth of the contradiction between the private and social interests. Representing the 'social' interests, the bureaucracy identifies them to a large measure with its own private interests. It draws the distinction between the social and the private in accordance with its own private interests... This creates a still greater tension between the contradictions and consequently leads to a further growth of bureaucratism. At the bottom of these processes lie the backwardness of the USSR and its isolation in its capitalist environment.[68]

As he had since the 1920s, Trotsky insisted here that the problem of bureaucracy had fundamental social or even class roots. However, in this passage Trotsky did not identify the contending class forces with the social formations usually specified: the proletariat, various layers of the peasantry, etc. Rather, he spoke more abstractly of the competing 'socialist and capitalist tendencies' – most importantly, the 'social interests' represented by the state, and the 'personal' or 'private interests' of 'consumers', including workers. Furthermore, although he blamed contending class forces for the emergence of the bureaucracy, he no longer attributed the problem to the external pressures exerted by alien classes. Rather, he explained it in terms of the functions of a post-capitalist state in a backward and isolated society. In doing so, he gave specific content to his earlier general agreement with Rakovskii that the differentiation of the bureaucracy from the working class 'was at first functional, then later became social'.[69]

---

68   Trotsky 1972g, p. 167.
69   Trotsky 1975c, p. 47.

Drawing upon the Marxist classics, Trotsky described the essential function of the bureaucracy as the mediation of social conflict. In *The Origin of the Family, Private Property and the State*, Engels had explained how, 'in order that these antagonisms, classes with conflicting economic interests, might not consume themselves and society in sterile struggle, a power seemingly standing above society became necessary for moderating the conflict'.[70] Along these lines Trotsky now described the basic function of the Soviet state as the 'overcoming of class antagonisms' and 'harmonizing' competing social interests. In *The State and Revolution* Lenin had identified the functions of the state in the first phase of communist society as 'safeguarding the common ownership of the means of production' while protecting the 'bourgeois' norms of 'equality in labor and in the distribution of products'.[71] Similarly, Trotsky now asserted, 'In the given situation, the overcoming of class antagonisms means the harmonizing of the social interests of production with the personal interest of the consumers'.

Having come into being to represent the 'social' interests, Trotsky argued, the bureaucracy began to identify these with its own private interests, and to interpret the distinction between social and private in this light.[72] The ultimate effect had been to create even 'greater tension between the contradictions', which had necessitated even more mediation, fostering the further growth of 'bureaucratism'. Here, it is likely that Trotsky was thinking of the mediating role of the relatively autonomous state in periods of extreme class tension, described in the Marxist classics as characteristic of Bonapartism.[73] Utilising this approach, Trotsky was able to explain the continuing expansion of the autonomy of the bureaucracy in terms of the same functional imperatives that had called it into existence in the first place.

---

70   Engels 1972a, p. 159.

71   Lenin 1960–70, vol. 25, p. 467.

72   Again, Trotsky's debt to the Marxist classics is evident. In his *Critique of Hegel's Philosophy of Right*, Marx noted a tendency for the modern state to identify its own interests with those of society: 'The bureaucracy holds the state, the spiritual essence of society, in thrall, as its *private property*' (Marx 1974a, p. 108). In late 1930 Trotsky published a declaration by Rakovskii, Kosior, Muralov, and Kasparova that included a reference to this passage (*Biulleten' oppozitsii* 1973, 17–18 (November–December 1930), p. 16) For a critical response by other oppositionists to the use of this passage by Rakovskii et al., see *Biulleten' oppozitsii* 1973, 15–16 (September 1930), p. 63.

73   See especially Engels 1972a, p. 160. For similar passages, see Marx 1966, p. 66; Draper 1977, bk. 2, pp. 403, 406, 415, 425.

7.3   New Policy Shifts

The years 1933 and 1934 witnessed major changes and initiatives in all areas of
Soviet policy. In the economic sphere the leadership retreated from the
extreme tempos and excesses of the First Five-Year Plan and began to institute
market reforms. In foreign policy it sought alliances against growing threats to
the East and West, and in the Comintern it promoted alliances with other parties against fascism. Finally, within the AUCP(b) the leadership initiated a new
chistka, or cleansing operation, while welcoming the return of repentant dissidents at the Seventeenth Party Congress in 1934.
    Meanwhile, as Ian Thatcher has noted, for several years after his return to
Europe 'Trotsky wrote less on the USSR than at any other time in his career'.[74]
To a large extent this was probably because, when he gave up on peacefully
reforming the Soviet state, he concluded that the 'revolutionary center of grav-
ity' had shifted to the West, and he redirected his attention accordingly.[75] At
the same time he now was spending more time consulting with his international comrades and beginning work on a major biography of Lenin. Also, in
1933 and 1934 he found his work frequently interrupted by a series of forced
changes of residence until mid-July 1934 when he settled in the town of
Domène at the foothills of the Alps.[76] However, in a number of statements during this period Trotsky expressed deep concerns about the new direction of
Soviet policy in all areas. For the first time in years he found himself warning of
the potentially disastrous consequences of the leadership's *rightist* course in
the economy and in international affairs. At the same time, he condemned the
leadership's continuing assaults upon its critics. In each case his analysis was
significantly shaped by his growing emphasis on bureaucratic autonomy.

7.3.1   *Economic Retreat and Recovery*
Following the crisis of 1932 and early 1933, the Soviet leadership began to moderate economic policy and to introduce market reforms, introducing a period
of recovery and economic progress that would continue through the end of the
Second Five-Year Plan. In early 1933 the leadership began to retreat from the
excesses of the first *piatiletka*. At the CC plenum of January 1933 Stalin abruptly
modified the targets for the Second Five-Year Plan adopted in 1932. Now he
called for 'less speedy rates' of industrialisation and proposed as a minimum a
13–14 percent average annual increase in industrial output in place of the

---

74   Thatcher 2003, p. 190. See also Law 1987a, p. 176.
75   Trotsky 1972g p. 120. See also Trotsky 1972f, p. 309.
76   See Deutscher 1963, pp. 260, 269–75; Van Heijenoort 1978, pp. 49–78.

22 percent increase allegedly achieved in the first plan.[77] This moderating trend in economic policy continued in January 1934 when the Seventeenth Party Congress adopted relatively modest goals in a redrafted five-year plan. Regarding industry, the Congress approved Stalin's proposals to overcome the lag in iron and steel production, to expand production of consumer goods, to increase labour productivity, and to improve quality. In agriculture, it endorsed Stalin's recommendations to improve the maintenance of farm machinery; to introduce proper crop rotation; to pay greater attention to livestock farming; and to regionalise production of vegetables, dairy products, grain, and meat.[78]

Meanwhile, the economic crisis was beginning to recede. The recovery started with an improved harvest in 1933. That, combined with the impressive overall figures for industrial construction in the First Five-Year Plan, contributed to a sense of relief and optimism among the delegates to the Seventeenth Party Congress. Sergei Kirov, secretary of the Leningrad organisation, best captured this spirit when he joyously proclaimed, 'Our successes are really tremendous. Damn it all, to put it humanly, you just want to live and live – really, just look what's going on. It's a fact'![79] From 1934 to 1936 the industrial outlook grew steadily brighter. To a large degree the expansion of industrial production in this period was due to completion of the construction of plants begun during the first *piatiletka*. Machinery and metalworking industries experienced remarkable growth, coal production increased substantially, after 1934 the situation in rail transport improved significantly, and the production of consumer goods increased, though not as rapidly as projected.[80] At the same time the situation in agriculture continued its upward turn. Although crop yields remained low, the total production of grain slowly increased, while the supply of potatoes and vegetables as well as the supply of animal products climbed steadily.[81]

Much of the credit for the recovery in agriculture belonged to a series of trade and agricultural reforms. In the spring of 1932 the government legalised markets where *kolkhozy* could sell their surplus products at free prices. Subsequently, a decree of January 1934 reaffirmed this right, while forbidding the application of administrative pressure to compel collective farmers and peasants to sell their grain. The *kolkhoz* markets were such a success that the state itself soon introduced sale of its own surpluses at high prices in commer-

---

77   Nove 1976, p. 219; Stalin 1976, p. 602; Ward 1999, pp. 82–3.
78   Nove 1976, pp. 202, 224–7; Stalin 1976, pp. 704–5, 716–20; Ward 1999, pp. 48–9.
79   Nove 1976, p. 238; Kirov quoted in Tucker 1990, p. 251.
80   Dobb 1966, pp. 279–81; Jasny 1961, pp. 142–6; Nove 1976, pp. 228–31, 234; Ward 1999, p. 49.
81   Jasny 1961, pp. 139–40; Nove 1976, pp. 238–9; Ward 1999, p. 49.

cial stores. Meanwhile, in November 1934 the government announced it was eliminating rationing of bread and all cereal foods.[82] An additional reform was the abolition in late 1934 of the political departments in the machine tractor stations (MTSS), and the assumption of their duties by local party committees and by deputy MTS directors for political affairs.[83]

Trotsky wrote little in this period about Soviet economic developments. In addition to the reasons already suggested, it is likely that his earlier preoccupation with economic policy diminished when he realised the situation was beginning to improve. His awareness of the improvement was evident by at least 12 December 1933 when he referred to the 'good crop in the Ukraine', and 31 March 1934 when he remarked: 'That Kirov rejoices [at the Party Congress] over the technical successes and the mitigation of the food scarcity is understandable. There is not an honest worker in the whole world who does not rejoice over this'.[84]

However, in brief comments on the Soviet economy Trotsky expressed concern about the shift to the right he perceived in the recent policy changes.[85] On 30 January 1935 he described 'the general direction' of both the economic and international turns of the previous year and a half as 'to the *right, more to the right and still further to the right*'. He recalled that just a few years before Stalin had declared his intention to send the NEP 'to the devil' and had ridiculed insistence upon currency stability as a 'bourgeois superstition'. Now the bureaucracy found itself forced 'to apply to "the devil" ' for a return of the market, and compelled to eliminate ration cards to stabilise the *chervonetz*. Also, in 1933 Stalin had instituted political sections 'to exercise ruthless control over the collective farms'. But even this 'ripest product of the "Leader's genius mind" ' had been liquidated, almost without announcement.[86]

Trotsky did not object to the attempt to stabilise the currency. On the contrary, he saw this as another vindication of the Opposition's foresight. However, he complained that it was the working class – especially its poorest sections – that was being forced to pay for the mistakes of the bureaucracy through the abolition of rationing. Beyond that, he predicted that the regeneration of

---

82   Nove 1976, pp. 185, 247, 248; Hubbard 1939, p. 201.

83   Timasheff 1946, p. 146; Nove 1976, p. 244; McNeal 1974, pp. 153–5.

84   Trotsky 1972g, pp. 176, 276.

85   As early as 11 January 1933 Trotsky described Stalin's reduction of the goals of the Second Five-Year Plan as 'a turn to the right', and a 'new bureaucratic zigzag' (Trotsky 1972f, p. 80). See also Trotsky 1972f, pp. 85, 86, 103.

86   Trotsky 1971b, pp. 157–60.

market relations would lead to 'the strengthening of individualistic and cen-trifugal tendencies in rural economy and the growth of differentiation between the collective farms, as well as inside the collectives'. Finally, he was apprehen-sive about the significance of the shifts for the future. It could not yet be known, he warned, where the retreat would stop.[87] Although he was clearly suggesting that economic policy might shift even more disastrously to the right, it is note-worthy that he did not use the term *Thermidor*.

While perceiving the turn as a belated reaction by the leadership to the eco-nomic crisis, Trotsky also explained it, as he had explained the conservative policies of the late 1920s, in terms of external class pressure. In his 30 January 1935 article he asserted that the recent reforms were adopted 'under pressure of the peasantry' and that the bureaucracy was 'retreating before the *moujik*'.[88] The tendency to attribute Soviet policy to class pressure would never disap-pear from his writings. However, from this point onwards he increasingly por-trayed major policy developments as the product of conscious decisions made by the bureaucracy in the pursuit of its own interests.

The latter approach was evident in Trotsky's account during these years of the previous left turn in Soviet economic policy. In the past, he had most fre-quently attributed that turn to working class or Oppositional pressure, supple-mented by the 'panic' and/or 'excitement' of the bureaucracy. Although he still viewed the Opposition's pressure as one source of that shift, now he also stressed the role of bureaucratic self-interest. On 28 December 1934 he explained that the bureaucracy, in its recent 'heroic' epoch, 'found itself compelled *by the logic of its own interests* to adopt the program of industrializa-tion and collectivization'.[89] Similarly, on 1 February 1935 he wrote that 'in the struggle for its own positions', the bureaucracy found itself compelled to take from the Opposition measures that made it possible to save the Soviet workers' state.[90]

7.3.2   *The Turn in France*

In these years the Comintern also initiated a major reorientation in policy. Following the disastrous defeat in Germany, the focus of Comintern activity shifted to France, where an increasingly active right-wing movement had materialised. In the face of this threat and under pressure from Moscow, the

---

87   Trotsky 1971b, pp. 159–60.
88   Ibid.
89   Trotsky 1971b, p. 130 (original emphasis).
90   Trotsky 1971b, p. 170. See also Trotsky 1977a, p. 309.

Communist Party of France (PCF) rejected its earlier Third Period line and began to pursue a broad antifascist alliance.

In early 1934 aggressive actions by organisations on the extreme right in France shocked the left, impelling it to seek unity. On the evening of 6 February 1934 fascist and royalist groups converged in a demonstration in the Place de la Concorde in Paris, and marched on the Chamber of Deputies, meeting in the Palais Bourbon. In the ensuing battle with police, approximately 19 demonstrators were killed and hundreds of police and demonstrators were injured. The riot did not overthrow the Republic as some rightist leaders apparently hoped. However, it succeeded in bringing down the government of Édouard Daladier, leader of the left wing of the moderate left Radical-Socialist Party, and in bringing to power Gaston Doumergue of the Radical-Socialist right. The day after the riot the Executive of the French Socialist Party (SFIO) appealed to the PCF for joint action against the fascist threat, and organisations of the PCF and SFIO on the local level began to discuss collaboration. On 12 February, with the belated endorsement of the PCF, Communists participated with Socialists in a one-day general strike and a mass demonstration in Paris.[91]

Although the PCF leadership, supported by the ECCI, continued to reiterate its Third Period line for a time, it began to change its position in the spring and early summer of 1934.[92] In late May the PCF called for a national party conference on the question of a united front, and it appealed to the SFIO for collaboration on behalf of the victims of Nazi persecution. The Socialist leadership responded positively, but demanded a 'non-aggression pact' in exchange. When verbal attacks by the PCF continued, the executive committee of the SFIO terminated negotiations on 20 June.[93] However, shortly afterwards, acting on telegraphic instructions from the Comintern, the united front conference of the PCF accepted the Socialists' demand. The Communists pledged to 'refrain mutually from all attacks, insults and criticisms against each other's organizations and party members'.[94] A pact providing for joint actions in defence of democracy, against war preparations, and against fascist terror in Germany and Austria was signed by the two parties on 27 July 1934.[95]

---

91 Braunthal 1967, p. 416; Carr 1982, p. 189; Jenkins 2006, pp. 333–51; Mortimer 1984, pp. 209–11; Soucy 1995, pp. 30–3.

92 Braunthal 1967, pp. 420–5; Carr 1982, p. 189; Claudin 1975a, pp. 173–4; Degras 1965, p. 309; Mortimer, 1984, pp. 211–14.

93 Carr 1982, pp. 192–3; Braunthal 1967, pp. 424–5.

94 Carr 1982, p. 194; Braunthal 1967, p. 426.

95 Carr 1982, p. 195.

Within a few months the PCF was pushing for an even broader alliance. In a speech of 10 October 1934, Maurice Thorez, general secretary of the PCF, called for an electoral alliance that would include not only the SFIO, but also the Radical-Socialist Party.[96] In the following weeks the PCF appealed to the Radicals to join in 'a popular front of freedom, labor, and peace'; and on 25 November it presented the National Council of the SFIO with a 'Popular Front Program' of limited social reforms judged to be acceptable to the Radicals.[97] The SFIO leadership, complaining that this programme did not include 'a single measure of a socialist nature', proposed the addition of measures for the 'socialization of the main means of production and exchange'. However, the PCF, concerned that socialist demands would frighten away the peasantry and petty bourgeoisie, rejected these proposals. For the time being, negotiations between the two parties terminated in January 1935.[98]

Meanwhile, for Trotsky, the riot of February 1934 suggested that France was beginning to replay the recent history of Germany. He argued that, as in Germany, the capitalist class was using fascist bands to smash democracy and the organisations of the working class. Again, the fascists were drawing their popular support from the ruined middle classes, whose anger and frustration had been redirected against the proletariat.[99] At the moment, the sharpening class conflict had raised Doumergue to power as a Bonapartist 'savior' and 'arbiter'. Most immediately, Trotsky insisted, the situation demanded 'active proletarian self-defense', organised by a united front of working-class organisations. Beyond that, it required an audacious struggle for workers' and peasants' power.[100]

However, with the shift in PCF's orientation in 1934, Trotsky again found himself criticising it from the left. Although he welcomed the Comintern's abandonment of ultraleftism, he now condemned a policy that he believed could prove equally ruinous. Both SFIO and the PCF had rejected proposals to organise workers' militias, supporting instead the disarmament of the fascist leagues by the French government. In Trotsky's view this was an approach that strengthened the state while leaving working-class organisations defenceless against the fascists who would only be rearmed by the police.[101] At the same time he criticised the PCF's courting of the Radicals. He described the Radicals

---

96   Carr 1982, p. 197.
97   Mortimer 1984, pp. 228–9.
98   Mortimer 1984, p. 229.
99   Trotsky 1979c, pp. 30, 36.
100   Trotsky 1972g, pp. 240–4.
101   Trotsky 1979c, pp. 41–3, 49. See also Trotsky 1971b, p. 84.

as the party employed by the big bourgeoisie to preserve the hopes of the petty bourgeoisie for a peaceful improvement in their situation. In the current situation, with the petty bourgeoisie looking for extreme solutions, the Radicals were no longer able to play this role. Consequently, by tying itself to the Radicals the Communist Party was driving peasants and small shopkeepers into the arms of the fascist Leagues.[102] Finally, Trotsky denounced the PCF's agreement to refrain from criticism of the SFIO. By this, he asserted, the Communists had 'thrown overboard the revolutionary program'.[103]

For Trotsky the new line, which he perceived as originating largely in Moscow, revealed a complete lack of confidence in the working class.[104] In a letter of 10 August 1934 he argued that, having blamed its failures on the Western proletariat, the Comintern leadership had concluded, 'For the security of the USSR, we have to look elsewhere for help' – that is, to democracy.[105] Since French 'democracy' was embodied in the Radical Party, since the Radicals needed Socialist support to rule, and since the Socialists would only support the Radicals if the PCF stopped criticising it, the 'overriding plan of the Soviet bureaucracy' was to reestablish the regime of the Radical Herriot by freeing the SFIO from the criticism of the PCF.[106]

Beyond that, Trotsky attributed the policy change in France to fear on the part of the Soviet bureaucracy. In the past he consistently had explained right turns in Comintern policy in terms of external pressure from alien classes. In contrast he now asserted that *this* right turn, like the *left* turn of 1929–33, represented an overreaction by the bureaucracy to defeats. As he stated in an open letter 'To the Bolshevik-Leninists in the USSR' in August 1934, 'When the waters of fascism rose up to the Comintern's neck in France, frightened, it accomplished in several days, if not in several hours, a turn unprecedented in political history'.[107]

7.3.3 *Shifts in Foreign Policy*

During the same period Soviet foreign policy was shifting in response to growing military threats from both Japan and Germany. Since the occupation of

---

102   Trotsky 1979c, pp. 33, 36, 43.

103   Trotsky 1971b, p. 84. See also Trotsky 1971b, pp. 66, 70; Trotsky 1979c, p. 58.

104   However, Trotsky also understood that the general strike and workers' demonstrations of 12 February originated domestically: 'The workers of France forced the two bureaucratic apparatuses [of the PCF and SFIO] into a united front for twenty-four hours' (Trotsky 1972g, p. 243).

105   Trotsky 1971b, p. 65.

106   Trotsky 1971b, p. 66.

107   Trotsky 1971b, p. 70.

Manchuria in September 1931, the Soviet leadership had watched Japan with increasing unease. Lacking resources to deter Japanese expansion, the Soviets initially opted for a policy of appeasement. In December 1931 they offered a non-aggression pact to Tokyo – a proposal that was rejected. The following year they attempted to sell to Japan the Chinese Eastern Railway (CER), already partially occupied by the Japanese. Although Tokyo responded favourably, Moscow broke off negotiations in September 1933 after Manchukuo authorities arrested six Soviet employees of the CER in an effort to pressure the USSR into lowering the price.[108]

While strengthening its military forces in the Far East, the Soviet Union also began actively pursuing international alliances. The Japanese threat inspired Soviet participation in the conference of the League of Nations' preparatory commission on disarmament that convened in Geneva in February 1932. There, Maksim Litvinov, Commissar of Foreign Affairs, repeated earlier Soviet statements of support for general and complete disarmament, but also indicated Soviet willingness to endorse the proposal of U.S. President Hoover for a reduction of armaments by all nations. Another statement of significance was Litvinov's attempt at the Geneva conference the following year to provide an exact definition of aggression.[109] Finally, in the autumn of 1933 the Soviet Union seized upon the invitation from Franklin Roosevelt, newly elected President of the United States, to discuss recognition. On 16 November the two countries exchanged notes in which the United States recognised the Soviet Union and the Soviets pledged to settle its outstanding debts and to prevent activity on its territory by any organisation attempting to overthrow the U.S. government.[110]

At the same time the Soviet Union began to revise its policy in Europe in light of the German threat. Despite Hitler's self-proclaimed hostility to the USSR, the Soviet leadership initially hoped that German policy toward the Soviet Union would not change substantially under the Nazis. When on 5 May 1933 Germany ratified the Berlin protocol extending the 1926 Treaty of Berlin with the USSR, it seemed that this wish would be granted. However, in 1933 the Soviets grew increasingly concerned about Hitler's efforts to revise Versailles and about an Italian proposal for a pact that would exclude the USSR. Consequently, by late 1933 the Soviet leadership began seeking new alliances in Europe. In December 1933 the Politburo endorsed a French proposal for mutual assistance against Germany and a suggestion that the USSR join the League of

---

108   L. Fischer 1969, p. 213; Haslam 1992, pp. 5, 8, 11, 22–3; Moore 1945, pp. 7–33.
109   Davis 1977, pp. 169–83; Haslam 1983, pp. 93–6.
110   L. Fischer 1969, pp. 213–20; Haslam 1992, pp. 30–4; Ulam 1974, pp. 212–15.

Nations. Beyond that, the Politburo proposed to expand the alliance with France to include Poland, Belgium, Czechoslovakia, Lithuania, Latvia, and Finland. At the subsequent meeting of the Central Executive Committee, Litvinov justified the pact by distinguishing between the 'deeply pacifist' and the more militaristic imperialist powers. Negotiations over the expanded alliance continued through the following year. Meanwhile, in September 1934 the USSR joined the League, and on 5 December 1934 it concluded a protocol with France expressing the intention of both countries to pursue an eastern pact.[111]

By June 1934 Trotsky had concluded that Soviet foreign policy, like its economic policy and Comintern policy, was undergoing a 'sharp turn to the right', that is, a 'decidedly anti-Leninist turn'.[112] Aspects of this shift included Litvinov's 'purely formalistic presentation of the problems of war and peace' and the projected Soviet entry into the League of Nations. Again, Trotsky did not view either action as inherently wrong. In fact, he suggested that both were at least partially necessitated by the weakened position of the USSR. Nevertheless, he insisted that the Soviet leadership had gone far beyond what was permissible in its public statements. For Marxists, he observed, disarmament was ineffective in preventing war, and issues of 'defense' and 'aggression' were just 'questions of practical expediency'. To say otherwise, as the Soviet leadership had done, was 'to mislead the workers for the sake of a common front with petty-bourgeois pacifists', while providing cover for Social Democratic leaders who had a stake in the status quo. Furthermore, although it might be necessary for the USSR to enter the League, to acclaim this 'bloc of allies and vassals of French imperialism' as a centre for peace and to present the Soviet entry as a victory had 'nothing in common with the policy of the international proletarian party'.[113]

Along the same lines, Trotsky criticised the Stalinists for speaking of 'peaceful American capitalism' and for distinguishing more generally between the 'peaceful, democratic and pacifist' capitalist states, and 'warlike, fascist and aggressive' countries. Although he recognised that the purpose of such statements was to win allies against a possible attack from Germany and Japan, he believed they represented an 'anti-Marxist political philosophy'. Instead of relying on world revolution, Stalinism was counting on military alliances with capitalist countries and 'the insane theory of socialism in one country'.

---

111   Haslam 1984, pp. 6–20, 27–45; Ulam 1974, pp. 194–7. The text of the protocol appears in Degras 1953, pp. 96–7.

112   Trotsky 1972g, p. 294; Trotsky 1971b, p. 17.

113   Trotsky 1972g, pp. 294, 312–16; Trotsky 1971b, pp. 18–19.

One consequence would be to further demoralise the German masses who were being told that the USSR had concluded an alliance with France against them.[114]

Previously Trotsky had explained rightward shifts in Soviet policy as responses by the leadership to bourgeois pressure. Now, consistent with his growing emphasis on bureaucratic autonomy, he attributed the recent changes in Soviet foreign policy to the conservative nature of the bureaucracy itself. In an interview with a dissident member of the PCF in June 1934, after describing the right turn as a reaction to the defeat in Germany, he argued, 'A policy hostile to unity of action [with the Socialists] and a policy that presents the entry of the USSR into the League of Nations as a victory is one and the same policy, that of the ruling bureaucracy of the USSR, whose horizon is limited to the Soviet Union and that neglects and even fears the revolutionary struggle in other countries'.[115] Similarly, in an interview with Louise Bryant in late 1934 or early 1935, he asserted that the Soviet bureaucracy had become a 'purely national and conservative force' and that Soviet diplomacy 'defends the status quo'. He explained that the conditions of the Soviet bureaucrats' existence, 'as an uncontrolled privileged layer, accustomed only to giving orders, inevitably cause them to grow conservative'.[116]

7.3.4   Developments in the Party Regime

Regarding the party and state regime, one of the most important events within the USSR at this time was the new *chistka*, or cleansing of the party, initiated by the leadership in early 1933. According to a resolution of the April 1933 plenum of the CC, the mass admissions of 1931–2 had led to an influx of 'alien' elements and 'double dealers' into the party, while inadequacies of political education had resulted in the fact that large numbers of members were 'insufficiently stable' or 'politically almost illiterate'. Categories to be purged included class alien and hostile elements; 'double dealers' who attempted to undermine policy; violators of discipline who failed to carry out decisions; degenerates, including those who did not want to struggle against the kulaks; careerists, self-seekers, and bureaucratic elements; and morally corrupt elements.[117] Various authors have noted the clear political thrust to several of these categories.[118] However, as J. Arch Getty has emphasised, of the 18 percent of party

114   Trotsky 1971b, pp. 17, 18–20.
115   Trotsky 1972g, p. 294.
116   Trotsky 1979b, p. 565. See also Trotsky 1972g, p. 312.
117   Getty and Naumov 1999, pp. 126–7; KPSS 1971, pp. 98–100; McNeal 1974, pp. 124–6.
118   See Getty and Naumov 1999, p. 125; Rigby 1968, pp. 201–2, 204; Ward 1999, p. 109.

members expelled in the *chistka*, a majority were removed for relatively non-political reasons such as passivity and corruption.[119]

A second event with important implications for the party regime was the Seventeenth Party Congress, convened in late January and early February 1934. This congress, the first since the great offensive in industry and agriculture, celebrated the party's successes in the previous four years. Climaxing a year-long intensification of the personality cult, speaker after speaker credited one man for the party's victory.[120] If the gathering was characterised as a 'Congress of Victors', as Robert Tucker has observed, it also seems to have been designed to be a 'congress of reconciliation'.[121] The fact that former oppositionists were allowed to speak and were treated respectfully suggested that the years of party struggle were finally at an end. Stalin himself seemed to encourage this view in his address. Noting that at the Fifteenth Congress it had been necessary to struggle against the Trotskyites and at the Sixteenth, against the 'Right deviators', he observed, 'At this congress ... there is nothing to prove and, it seems, no one to fight'.[122]

However, there were also more ominous themes in the General Secretary's long address. Although the opportunists and deviators had been smashed, he warned, 'remnants of their ideology' lived on in the minds of some party members.[123] Some comrades, influenced by right deviators, believed that the advancement of the Soviet Union toward a classless society indicated that the dictatorship of the proletariat was about to wither away. Against this view, Stalin declared that a classless society could only be built 'by strengthening the organs of the dictatorship of the proletariat, by intensifying the class struggle, by abolishing classes, by eliminating the remnants of the capitalist classes, and in battles with enemies, both internal and external'.[124]

For Trotsky, there was no doubt that the primary intent of the *chistka* of 1933 was political: to shore up the 'self-rule of the Soviet bureaucracy' and 'the personal plebiscitary regime of Stalin'. This is not to say that he did not see a party purge as necessary. In fact, on 30 March 1933 he observed that there was no reason for the party to have two million members, and he offered the Opposition's assistance in purging 'the raw material, the ballast' to make the

---

119 Getty 1985, pp. 48–57; Getty and Naumov 1999, pp. 127–8. See also Rigby 1968, pp. 200–4.
120 Medvedev 1973, pp. 147–8; Tucker 1990, pp. 243–8, 250–1; Volkogonov 1991, pp. 197–8.
121 Tucker 1990, p. 248.
122 Stalin 1976, p. 734.
123 Stalin 1976, pp. 735–6.
124 Stalin 1976, p. 737.

party a more effective instrument for combating Thermidor.[125] Nevertheless, he had no confidence in any *chistka* initiated and conducted by Stalinists. On 3 March 1933 he declared, 'We do not trust the selections of Stalin-Menzhinsky-Yagoda; they have as their criteria not the interests of the proletarian revolution but the interests of the clique'.[126] Despite the variety of purge criteria, Trotsky viewed the central purpose of the *chistka* as an attempt to prevent the revival of genuine party discussion. On 20 July 1933 he explained, 'The purges and expulsions were at first intended to disorganize the party, to terrorize it, to deprive it of the possibility of thinking and acting; now the repressions are aimed at preventing the reorganization of the party'.[127] In an article on 12 December he concluded that 'the chief aim of the *chistka* was to terrorize the party prior to the congress... This time, everybody was to be kicked out who had ever evinced the slightest inclination toward party discussion'.[128]

More specifically, Trotsky saw the cleansing operation as aimed at members who shared at least some of the Opposition's views. On 4 January 1933 he asserted, 'This cleansing begins and ends,... with the repression of the comrades who share our views and with the destruction of all criticism and all Marxist thinking within the party'.[129] Later in the year he noted that press reports emphasised the role of the *chistka* in rooting out Trotskyists. On 12 December he observed, 'Through all the articles and notices on the *chistka*, there runs the red thread of "Trotskyism"'.[130] At this point he was not convinced that many, if any, of those being expelled were actually Bolshevik-Leninists. Some, he thought, were compromised bureaucrats, hated by the populace but labeled 'Trotskyists' to load onto Trotskyism 'guilt for the crimes of the Stalinists'. Additionally, he argued, the Stalinists were branding as 'Trotskyist' all 'criticism of bureaucratism in general' in order to remind everyone who was critical that they too could be treated in a manner befitting Trotskyists.[131]

However, Trotsky also perceived indications that Stalin was preparing a new wave of persecution against true Bolshevik-Leninists. In 1933 Soviet delegates to a conference in Rheims announced that a trial in the USSR would soon dem-

---

125   Trotsky 1972f, p. 167.
126   Trotsky 1972f, p. 112.
127   Trotsky 1972g, p. 20.
128   Trotsky 1972g, p. 176. See also Trotsky 1972g, p. 223.
129   Trotsky 1972f, p. 66.
130   Trotsky 1972g, pp. 176–7. See also Trotsky 1972g, p. 70. Thus, J. Arch Getty is mistaken in asserting that 'for Trotsky, the 1933 *chistka* was not a matter of ideology' (Getty 1985, p. 232n60).
131   Trotsky 1972g, pp. 176–7.

onstrate that Trotskyists had participated in counterrevolutionary activities. Soon afterwards, Western newspapers reported that a few dozen Trotskyists arrested in Ukraine had been charged with sabotage and treason. Vigorously denying the charges, Trotsky explained that Stalin urgently needed 'shootings of supposed Trotskyists for real crimes, or of real Trotskyists for supposed crimes' to justify the persecution of Oppositionists since 1928. Beyond that, the repressions represented a panicked response by the Stalinists to the popular sympathy for the Bolshevik-Leninists in the Soviet Union and to the gains of the Opposition internationally.[132]

Although the Seventeenth Party Congress was the scene of reconciliation with repentant dissidents, Trotsky did not expect that it would mark any improvement in the regime. Rather, in an article written on 20 January 1934, six days before the congress convened, he anticipated that it would again confirm that the party was dead as a revolutionary organisation. For Trotsky, this had been indicated by the delay, in violation of party statutes, of nearly four years in convening the congress.[133] Furthermore, he predicted it would be demonstrated again by the absence of any serious discussion at the congress. He concluded that the congress had not been called to determine policies, but to endorse the leadership, the economic plan, and the work of the Comintern.[134] Taken together, the violation of statutes, the elimination of criticism, the arbitrary purges, and the deification of the leader, all signified again 'the liquidation of the party as an active political whole that checks, elects and renews its apparatus'.[135]

However, for Trotsky the real question confronting the congress was 'where and why did the Bolshevik Party disappear'? In this connection he noted the discrepancy between the leadership's claims that socialist construction was

---

132 Trotsky 1972g, pp. 69–70.

133 Trotsky 1972g, p. 223. See also Trotsky 1972g, p. 20.

134 Trotsky 1972g, p. 222. See also Trotsky 1972g, p. 176.

135 Trotsky 1972g, p. 224. See also Trotsky 1972g, p. 176. One anticipated decision that would have some significance, according to Trotsky, would be the adoption of new party statutes. As passed, the new statutes created 'integral industrial-branch sections' in leading party bodies from the CC down to the oblast committees. Each of these was to be responsible in a different branch of the economy for implementation of party directives and verification of decisions by state and party organs (McNeal 1974, pp. 144–5). Apparently in reference to this, Trotsky observed that the new party statutes made 'a decisive turn towards the merging of the state and party ... by a final and formal replacement of the party as well as of the mass Soviets by the single bureaucratic apparatus'. Trotsky concluded that this was not the 'withering' away of the state as described by Engels, but 'its further bureaucratic concentration' (Trotsky 1972g, p. 225).

nearing completion, and the fact that coercion was intensifying. To explain this contradiction, he reviewed and expanded upon his recent account of the origins of bureaucratic autonomy. Once more, he insisted that the USSR was far from socialism. In an article written in 1932 his former friend Karl Radek had disputed this, asserting that socialism meant only the nationalisation of production and distribution, and that shortages of milk were due to the absence of cows, not of socialism. Trotsky now responded that, on the contrary, socialism requires the ability to meet all human needs: 'If the cows are nationalized, but their number is insufficient or their udders dry, this is still not socialism, because for lack of milk conflicts arise'. These conflicts, which inevitably took on a 'social and in their tendencies, a class character', in turn required 'powerful intervention from above, that is, state coercion'.[136]

Meanwhile, according to Trotsky, power at the national summit, as well as within every geographic territory of the USSR, continued to concentrate in the hands of leaders who were increasingly deified in the press. In the same article he restated his functional explanation for this process as well, connecting it with the emergence of 'bureaucratic omnipotence':

> Since the workers are denied the possibility of reelecting and directing their apparatus, some other instance is necessary to solve state problems. Disagreements within the uncontrolled bureaucracy must be settled from above, by the 'leader', who is but the personification of the apparatus.[137]

7.4   The Kirov Assassination

On 1 December 1934 an event occurred that would have an enormous impact upon the Soviet political regime in the coming years – the assassination of Sergei Kirov. What is known for certain is that at approximately 4:30 PM a young, unemployed, former party member named Leonid Nikolaev fatally shot Kirov at the Leningrad party headquarters. A debate still rages about other

---

136   Trotsky 1972g, pp. 226–7. For other passages containing this functional account of the origin of bureaucratic autonomy, see: Trotsky 1979b, pp. 523–4, and an alternative version Trotsky 1971b, p. 78.

137   Trotsky 1972g, pp. 224, 226. Trotsky had similarly explained the origins of Stalin's personal power repeatedly since 1930: Trotsky 1975d, p. 206; Trotsky 1973c, p. 217; Trotsky 1972f, p. 104.

aspects of the case, including the question of Stalin's complicity.[138] However, the consequences are clear. Immediately, the murder was utilised as a pretext for the arrest of Stalin's critics within the party. In later years it would become the pivotal event in a series of trials that would culminate in the Great Terror. Trotsky first put forward a preliminary analysis nine days after Kirov's death in a confidential circular letter to sections of the ICL. Subsequently, he returned repeatedly to the case, reexamining the assassination and its aftermath in five more articles and a press statement.[139] Through all of these writings, Trotsky's interpretation of events was shaped by his perception of the political context and by his emerging theory of Soviet bureaucracy.

Shortly after the arrest of Nikolaev, the Soviet leadership responded to the assassination by striking at enemies on the 'right'. From 5 to 18 December the Military Collegium of the Supreme Soviet sentenced 102 'White Guardists' in Leningrad, Moscow, Kiev, and Minsk to death on charges of preparing terrorist acts against Soviet officials. Allegedly, the accused were sent into the Soviet Union from abroad to carry out acts of terrorism.[140]

By the end of the month the focus of the investigation had shifted to the left. An indictment published on 26 December charged that Nikolaev had participated with thirteen others, including members of the Leningrad Komsomol, in an underground Zinovievist terrorist organisation that had planned the murders of Stalin, Molotov, and Kaganovich, as well as Kirov. It was also alleged that Nikolaev had received 5,000 rubles from an unnamed foreign consul, later identified as Latvian, who had offered to put the conspirators in touch with Trotsky. All fourteen were found guilty and shot on 29 December.[141] In mid-December Zinoviev, Kamenev, and other former leaders of the Leningrad Opposition were also arrested. Due to lack of evidence, a special board of the NKVD took charge of the cases of Zinoviev, Kamenev, and seven others to consider sentences of summary exile. However, on 17 January *Pravda* announced that a secret tribunal in Moscow had found the Zinovievists guilty of organising a 'Moscow Centre' that had inspired terrorist sentiments within the Leningrad group directly responsible for the assassination. Zinoviev reportedly confessed, 'The former activity of the former opposition could not, by the force

---

138   Works that argue that Stalin was responsible for the assassination include Conquest 1989; and Knight 1999. Works that challenge this view include Getty 1985, pp. 207–10; Getty 1993; Kirilina 1993; Lenoe 2002; and Thurston 1996, pp. 20–2.

139   Trotsky 1979b, pp. 543–7; Trotsky 1971b, pp. 112–56.

140   Conquest 1989, pp. 44–7; Tucker 1990, p. 297.

141   Conquest 1989, pp. 55–8; Conquest 1973, pp. 89–90; Knight 1999, pp. 218–20; Lenoe 2002, p. 354; Trotsky 1971b, p. 132; Tucker 1990, pp. 299–300.

of objective circumstances, but stimulate the degeneration of those criminals'. All defendants in this trial received sentences of 5–10 years.[142]

Subsequently, on 23 January 1935 the Military Collegium of the Supreme Court tried twelve members of the leadership of the Leningrad NKVD, including its head, Filipp Medved', for criminal negligence. It was alleged that, even though they 'had at their disposal information about the preparations for the assassination of Comrade Kirov', they 'had shown not merely carelessness, but criminal negligence in regard to the basic requirements of the defense of state security and had not taken the necessary measures'.[143] Eleven received fairly light sentences of two to three years in labour camps, while one received the heavier sentence of ten years.[144]

Meanwhile, the leadership was launching a broader campaign against the left. A press campaign against Trotskyism gained in intensity. Party organisations throughout the Soviet Union exposed and expelled 'Trotskyists' and 'Zinovievists', many of whom were then arrested. Former members of the Trotskyist Opposition, recently released, were rearrested and incarcerated or sent to remote regions, while family members and individuals more distantly connected to the Opposition were arrested and deported. At the same time, at least a thousand former supporters of the Leningrad Opposition were arrested.[145]

In his first letter devoted to the issue Trotsky rejected a variety of hypotheses regarding the motives for the murder, concluding that this was a political assassination directed against 'the party in power, its policies, and its leaders'. Although he argued that the leadership's response confirmed this interpretation, it is clear that he accepted it primarily because it coincided with his own view of the political context. Speculating on Nikolaev's intent, he observed that 'the Stalinist regime at times drives honest people into the blind alley of despair', and he blamed 'Stalinist policies and the regime' for the counterrevolutionary tendencies that were appearing 'even among elements that are not hostile to the regime'. The very existence of these tendencies, he concluded, reflected 'the profound political crisis' of the Revolution.[146]

---

142   Conquest 1973, pp. 88, 91–2; Conquest 1989, pp. 54–5, 59–66; Knight 1999, pp. 221–2; Lenoe 2002, p. 354; Tucker 1990, p. 304; Ward 1999, p. 110.

143   Quoted in Conquest 1989, pp. 69–70.

144   Conquest 1973, p. 93; Conquest 1989, p. 70; Knight 1999, p. 223; Tucker 1990, p. 296.

145   Getty and Naumov 1999, pp. 147–9, 151–6; Medvedev 1973, p. 166–7; *Biulleten' oppozitsii 1973*, 43 (April 1935), p. 15; Serge 1980, pp. 313–14; Serge 1996, pp. 199, 203.

146   Trotsky 1979b, pp. 545–6.

As David Law has noted, Trotsky's perspective on the general situation within the USSR also initially predisposed him to accept the leadership's allegations regarding a Komsomol conspiracy.[147] On 28 December Trotsky commented that there was no apparent reason to dispute this charge because the bureaucracy had 'not confessed it with an easy heart'. However, he then noted the 'great *symptomatic* significance' of the conspiracy, for it confirmed the extent of popular discontent within the Soviet Union, including within the party youth.[148] Of course, Trotsky was not willing to believe all of the leadership's accusations. In the same article he repudiated the charges that leading Zinovievists were involved, ridiculing the notion that Old Bolshevik leaders could have embraced either the goal of capitalist restoration or its terrorist means. In his estimation these accusations were part of just another 'juridical amalgam', with the obvious goal of completely terrorising 'all critics and oppositionists, and this time ... by the firing squad'.[149]

To explain why this was occurring, Trotsky drew upon his recent analysis of the origins of bureaucratic autonomy. Once more, he located the source of this autonomy in the struggle 'of each against all' for the satisfaction of 'essential elementary needs'. To regulate the contradictions, the bureaucracy assumed the necessary role of 'controller, judge and executioner', but then exploited this position to enhance its own power and material welfare. Ultimately, the bureaucracy's 'national conservatism, its appropriative instincts and its spirit of caste privilege' began to paralyse its progressive work. Unrestricted bureaucratic domination generated perpetual economic crises, which in turn created a permanent political crisis. In defence of the 'dictatorship of the bureaucracy', the ruling faction had found it necessary to utilise increasingly violent methods and to circulate ever 'more envenomed' amalgams.[150]

Although Trotsky saw this amalgam as directed at all critics, two targets in particular stood out. First, the charges against the Zinovievists suggested it was aimed at disaffected elements within the middle and lower levels of the bureaucracy, now inhabited by the former Opposition leaders.[151] As in previous years, Trotsky portrayed these strata as increasingly demoralised. Linking this assessment with his recent theoretical insights, he observed, 'When a

---

147   Law 1987a, p. 173.

148   Trotsky 1971b, pp. 121, 122.

149   Trotsky 1971b, pp. 115–17.

150   Trotsky 1971b, pp. 117–20. See also Trotsky 1971b, pp. 131, 142–3, 156.

151   Zinoviev and Kamenev were now working in the administration of the Central Trade Union Council and in the publishing house of the Academy of Sciences respectively (Medvedev 1973, p. 164; Zaleskii 2000, pp. 185, 208; 'Kamenev, Lev Borisovich' in Wieczynski 1980).

bureaucracy comes into contradiction with the necessities of development and with the consciousness of the class that has raised it to power, it begins to decompose and to lose faith in itself'. Bureaucrats who found themselves outside of the constricting circle of power were beginning to grumble and to harbour liberal thoughts. Trotsky speculated that Zinoviev and Kamenev, infected by the mood of their environment, had ridiculed the leader. When word of this reached Stalin, he decided to teach the 'vacillating and decomposing bureaucracy a lesson'.[152]

Trotsky also saw the amalgam as aimed at the Bolshevik-Leninists. Even in his circular letter of 10 December he suggested that Stalin might attempt to implicate the ICL – though at that point he still considered this 'not very probable'.[153] However, shortly afterwards Nikolaev's confession validated these concerns, while providing new insights into the assassination. To Trotsky, the story of the foreign consul indicated a frame up. In an article of 30 December he deduced that the Soviet secret police were financing Nikolaev and attempting to connect him with Trotsky through 'an actual or fake consul'. Trotsky soon saw this as confirmed by the dismissal and conviction of all the leading representatives of the NKVD in Leningrad.[154]

Beyond that, NKVD complicity suggested an even more sensational conclusion: Stalin was directly involved. On 26 January Trotsky asserted, 'Without the direct agreement of Stalin – more precisely, without his initiative – neither Yagoda nor Medved would have decided to mount such a risky enterprise'.[155] This was not to say that either Stalin or the NKVD intended to kill Kirov. 'We have no facts for such a supposition', Trotsky admitted.[156] Besides, he saw no motive for such a murder since, in his view, Kirov had 'played no independent role'.[157] Rather, he concluded that the entire objective of the conspiracy was to establish a link between the terrorists and himself. However, Nikolaev acted too quickly and, contrary to Stalin's plans, shot Kirov before the amalgam could be established.[158]

A few days later Trotsky elaborated on his explanation of the post-assassination amalgam once more. In an article of 30 January 30 1935 he noted that an increasingly virulent press campaign had begun denouncing 'Trotskyism', new

152   Trotsky 1971b, pp. 122–3.
153   Trotsky 1979b, p. 547. See also Trotsky 1971b, pp. 124–9; Trotsky 1963f, p. 26.
154   Trotsky 1971b, pp. 133–4. See also Trotsky 1971b, pp. 155–6.
155   Trotsky 1971b, p. 153. For earlier hints that Trotsky believed Stalin was involved, see Trotsky 1971b, pp. 134, 144.
156   Trotsky 1971b, p. 134.
157   Trotsky 1971b, p. 115.
158   Trotsky 1971b, pp. 144, 151, 153.

'Trotskyists' were being discovered everywhere, and arrests and exiles had again 'assumed a mass character'. Additionally, in an apparent reference to the recent *chistka* he asserted that 'about 300,000 individuals, 15 to 20 percent' had been removed from 'the many-times-purged party'. For Trotsky all of these developments, combined with the conviction of the leading Zinovievists, constituted a 'rabid attack against the left wing of the party and the working class'. He explained that the recent right turns in international and domestic policy had aroused alarm among class-conscious workers, while general dissatisfaction was rising among workers along with the cost of living. Consequently, 'for its sharp turn to the right', the bureaucracy required 'a massive amputation on the left'.[159]

7.5 Reinterpreting Bonapartism and Thermidor

On 1 February 1935, in his major article 'The Workers' State, Thermidor and Bonapartism', Trotsky dramatically revised his thinking concerning the theoretical concepts of Thermidor and Bonapartism, redefining both terms and applying them to the Soviet Union.[160] He made these changes largely in response to regime developments in the Soviet Union and rightward shifts in economic and international policy that again suggested the applicability of the label *Bonapartism* to the Soviet regime. The redefined terms would become key elements in his emerging theory of a highly autonomous bureaucracy.

---

159 Trotsky 1971b, pp. 160–2. Trotsky did not give the source of his figures on the removal of 'about 300,000 individuals, 15 to 20 percent' from the party, but he may have based these numbers on Ian Rudzutak's announcement on 1 Feb. 1934 at the Seventeenth Party Congress that, of the 1,149,000 party members examined in the *chistka* by the end of 1933, 17 percent (or 195,000) of those examined had been expelled, and 6.3 percent (or approximately 73,400) had been transferred to candidate status. Combined, these numbers totaled 23.3 percent of those who had undergone the *chistka*, or approximately 268,400 (KPSS 1975, p. 287). Years later, it was reported that 18 percent of members were expelled in this purge (Getty 1985, pp. 52, 53).

160 Trotsky's revision of his understanding of Thermidor and Bonapartism in February 1933 is one of the most frequently discussed developments in the evolution of his theory of Soviet bureaucracy. For other accounts of this, see Bellis 1979, pp. 64–6; Bergmann 1987, pp. 87–98; Deutscher 1963, pp. 314–18; Hallas 1984, pp. 41–2; Knei-Paz 1978, pp. 396–400, 402–3; Law 1982, pp. 441–2, 445–9; Law 1987a, pp. 291–2, 295–8, 302; Law 1987b, pp. 7–8, 11–12; Lockwood 2002, pp. 57–8; Lovell 1985, p. 49; McNeal 1977, p. 34; McNeal 1966, p. 148; McNeal 1961, p. 92; McNeal 1982, p. 382; Warth 1985, pp. 202–4; Wistrich 1979, pp. 166–8.

At the same time, his change on Thermidor and Bonapartism immediately led him to modify his theory in a number of other ways.

As far as past debates over Thermidor were concerned, Trotsky remained convinced that the Left Opposition had been essentially correct. He recalled that in 1926–7 the Democratic Centralists had claimed, 'Thermidor is an accomplished fact'! – meaning that a 'regenerating bourgeois regime' had already come to power in the USSR. Against this, the Left Opposition had rightly insisted that, although 'elements of dual power' had appeared within the USSR, it remained a workers' state.[161]

However, Trotsky now admitted that the analogy had 'served to becloud rather than to clarify the question', for the Opposition had been mistaken in employing the term *Thermidor* for capitalist restoration. Since the revolution of 1789–93 was bourgeois in character, he explained, a social counterrevolution would have restored feudal property relations. In fact, 'Thermidor did not even make an attempt in this direction'. Rather, in France the significance of Thermidor was to transfer 'power into the hands of the more moderate and conservative Jacobins, the better-to-do elements of bourgeois society', on the basis of bourgeois property relations.[162] He also now argued that Napoleon Bonaparte's coup of 1799 had comparable significance. After Thermidor, the rise of Napoleon represented 'the next important stage on the road of reaction'. Again, however, there had been no attempt to restore feudal property forms. Rather, Napoleon guarded bourgeois property 'against both the "rabble" and the claims of the expropriated proprietors'.[163]

In light of these reinterpretations, Trotsky had come to see both terms as highly useful for understanding the Soviet Union. Regarding Thermidor, he observed, 'Today it is impossible to overlook that in the Soviet revolution also a shift to the right took place a long time ago, a shift entirely analogous to Thermidor, although much slower in tempo and more masked in form'.[164] Specifically, he dated the beginning of the Soviet Thermidor back to 1924 when the Left Opposition was first defeated.[165] As far as Bonapartism was concerned, he noted that, just as Napoleon had struggled against both the feudal world and the 'rabble' on behalf of a new bourgeois aristocracy, Stalin now guarded the conquests of 1917 'not only against the feudal-bourgeois counterrevolution but also against the claims of the toilers, their impatience and their

161   Trotsky 1971b, p. 167.
162   Trotsky 1971b, pp. 168, 174.
163   Trotsky 1971b, p. 169.
164   Trotsky 1971b, p. 174.
165   Ibid.

dissatisfaction'. To reinforce this point about the dual nature of Stalinist policy, Trotsky emphasised that he was comparing Stalin's regime to the first Napoleon's youthful Bonapartism, which was 'not only the gravedigger of the political principles of the bourgeois revolution but also the defender of its social conquests', not to the completely reactionary 'Bonapartism of decay' typified by the regimes of Napoleon III, Schleicher, or Doumergue.[166]

Although Trotsky first explained his new understanding of both Thermidor and Bonapartism in the same article, there are reasons to believe that his decision to revise his position on Bonapartism came first. Statements by Trotsky over the preceding year and a half had made his change of position concerning this term a shorter leap than reinterpreting Thermidor. Also, in the weeks preceding the 1 February article he applied *Bonapartism* to the Soviet Union earlier and more frequently than the term *Thermidor*, suggesting that he viewed the former analogy to be more significant.[167] To the extent that his understanding of recent events evoked the revisions, these more clearly suggested Bonapartist rather than Thermidorian characteristics. Finally, it appears that, to a large degree, Trotsky arrived at his new position on Thermidor by deriving it logically from his revised understanding of Bonapartism.[168]

Of course, Trotsky did not redefine either term because he had just learned that neither Thermidor nor the reign of Napoleon I had restored feudalism in France. Rather, he did so because events suggested that these revisions would promote a better understanding of Soviet politics. As he explained in his 1 February article, 'The disclosure of the error was greatly facilitated by the fact that the very processes of the political degeneration, which are under discussion, have in the meantime assumed much more distinct shape'.[169]

Most important in this regard were developments in the state and party regime, especially those related to the assassination of Kirov, which suggested similarities between Stalinism and Bonapartism. In October 1933 Trotsky had listed the 'self rule of the Soviet bureaucracy' and the 'personal plebiscitary regime of Stalin' as two of the defining characteristics of 'Soviet bureaucratism'. Subsequently, he perceived these characteristics as reinforced by the *chistka*, by the new arrests of 'Trotskyists', and by the growing 'deification of the leader' prior to the Seventeenth Party Congress. Furthermore, he saw

---

166   Trotsky 1971b, p. 181.
167   Trotsky 1971b, pp. 120, 155, 162, 163, 164, 165; Van Heijenoort 1978, p. 75.
168   Other sources asserting that Trotsky's change regarding Bonapartism came first include: Knei-Paz 1978, pp. 396–7; Bergman 1987, p. 91. For the view that Trotsky changed his position on Thermidor first, see Law 1987a, p. 302; Lovell 1985, p. 49.
169   Trotsky 1971b, p. 184.

both characteristics as strengthened even more by the repression of bureaucratic dissidents and of the proletarian vanguard after the assassination.
Consequently, in his 1 February article he observed that the Bonapartist features of the regime were more apparent than ever before: 'The domination
of the bureaucracy over the country, as well as Stalin's domination over the
bureaucracy, have well-nigh attained their absolute consummation'.[170]

Beyond that, it is likely that aspects of the Kirov assassination and subsequent amalgams reminded Trotsky of specific parallels in Napoleon's rise
to power. As he noted on 1 February, 'One is literally hit between the eyes by
the resemblance between the present Soviet political regime and the regime
of the First Consul, particularly at the end of the Consulate when the period of
the empire was nigh'.[171] One event that played a key role in Napoleon
Bonaparte's transition from First Consul to Emperor was an assassination conspiracy in early 1804. As described by Alphonse Aulard, the prominent historian of the French Revolution whose work was known to Trotsky, the plot was
organised by a group of royalist exiles in Britain headed by Georges Cadoudal,
but secretly encouraged by Bonaparte's agents. According to Aulard, the
Consular police hoped to 'tarnish the glory' of Bonaparte's 'sole rival in point of
military honor', Moreau, by putting the conspirators in touch with him. The
conspirators were arrested in February 1804, before the attempt could be carried out. However, Bonaparte used the incident to justify the elimination of his
enemies on both the right and left. Subsequently, to discourage assassination
attempts his supporters proposed converting his life consulate into a heredi-
tary empire – a proposal that was ratified by a national plebiscite.[172] Trotsky
may have had this episode in mind in a discussion with his secretary shortly
after the Kirov murder:

> In a conversation with me at the time, Trotsky sketched his theory of
> what he called 'crowned socialism'. 'You will see, Stalin will get himself
> crowned'. He thought that, after the Kirov assassination, Stalin would
> assume some majestic title, like Bonaparte adopting the name of
> Napoleon.[173]

---

170   Trotsky 1971b, p. 169.
171   Trotsky 1971b, p. 175. See also Trotsky 1971b, p. 209.
172   Aulard 1910, pp. 261–9. An earlier incident of this kind involved an attempt on life of the
      First Consul on Christmas Eve, 1800. Although royalists were found to be responsible,
      Bonaparte also used this attempt to justify a wave of repression against opponents to his
      left (Aulard 1910, pp. 184–8). For Trotsky's citation of Aulard's history, see Trotsky 1971a,
      pp. 145–6.
173   Van Heijenoort 1978, p. 75.

Aside from regime developments, shifts in Soviet international and domestic policy also contributed to Trotsky's change of position on Bonapartism. In October 1933 he had listed the bureaucracy's 'veering between class forces' as the third characteristic of Soviet Bonapartism.[174] In the following months, he saw more examples of this 'veering' in the introduction of the economic 'NeoNEP' and the new line in international policy, turns Trotsky viewed as the sharpest and most significant since 1928–9. Consequently, on 30 January 1935 he included the *'diplomatic retreat before the world bourgeoisie and before reformism'* and the *'economic retreat before the petty-bourgeois tendencies within the country'* as two elements, along with the offensive against the proletarian vanguard, in the 'tripartite formula of the new chapter in the development of Stalinist Bonapartism'.[175]

Of course, since the late 1920s Trotsky had characterised the leadership's zigzags as an indication, not of Bonapartism, but of bureaucratic centrism. Through 1934 Trotsky continued to apply the term *bureaucratic centrism* frequently, especially to Comintern policy.[176] In fact, this designation seemed to fit the policies of 1934–5 far better than it fit the 'ultraleft' polices of previous years. As Trotsky remarked on 1 February 1935, the Comintern had returned to the 'old organic course' it had followed in the mid-late 1920s.[177] However, despite his stretching of the concept of centrism in recent years, the term still suggested that the bureaucracy stood *between* classes, passively responding to the pressures they exerted. In contrast, Trotsky now perceived the bureaucracy as an independent entity, standing *above* classes and mediating their conflicts. Although he still believed that classes could sometimes pressure the bureaucracy into changing course, he also now perceived that the bureaucracy was capable of independently choosing policies in its own self-interest – an understanding better captured by the term *Bonapartism* than by centrism. Consequently, in his 1 February article Trotsky announced that he was dropping centrism, explaining that the centrist phase of Stalinism had been superseded by the 'hypertrophy of bureaucratic centrism into Bonapartism'.[178]

---

174   Trotsky 1971b, p. 108. Trotsky may have taken this idea from Engels. Regarding Bismark's Bonapartism, Engels wrote, 'As things stood in 1871 in Germany, a man like Bismark was indeed thrown back on a policy of tacking and veering among the various classes' (quoted in Draper 1977, bk. 2, p. 425).

175   Trotsky 1971b, p. 163.

176   See Trotsky 1971b, pp. 72, 86, 108, 124; Trotsky 1972g, pp. 234–5, 328; Trotsky 1979b, p. 531.

177   Trotsky 1971b, p. 166. See also Trotsky 1971b, p. 158.

178   Trotsky 1971b, p. 180. Trotsky employed the term *bureaucratic centrism* just a few more times. See Trotsky 1979c, p. 121; Trotsky 1977a, p. 145. Perhaps on these occasions he used it out of habit. However, on 3 October 1937 Trotsky admonished 'some comrades' for

Similar reasoning suggested the need for a revision of Thermidor. If the bureaucracy was autonomous enough to choose its own policies, then it seemed less likely it could be pushed into restoring capitalism. Largely because of his new emphasis on bureaucratic autonomy, Trotsky had stopped using the term for more than a year. Now, the accumulating policy shifts to the right demanded that he address the question directly:

> Where does this course lead? The word 'Thermidor' is heard again on many lips. Unfortunately, this word has become worn from use; it has lost its concrete content and is obviously inadequate for the task of character- izing either that stage through which the Stalinist bureaucracy is passing or the catastrophe that it is preparing.[179]

At this point Trotsky might have been tempted to discard the term altogether. However, his revised understanding of Bonapartism suggested the value of a redefined Thermidor. From the conclusion that the Soviet Union was Bonapartist, he deduced that it had already gone through its Thermidorian phase:

> If we are to remain within the framework of the historical analogy, we must necessarily ask the question: Since there has been no Soviet 'Thermidor' as yet, whence could Bonapartism have arisen? Without making any changes *in essence* in our former evaluations – there is no reason whatever to do so – we must radically revise the historical analogy.[180]

Again, Trotsky noted similarities between the French and Soviet experiences. In both cases power had shifted to a bureaucracy through a political process involving repression, attrition, cooptation, and careerism.[181] In both countries the new phase of political stabilisation was based on an upsurge of productive forces that benefited a privileged stratum linked to the bureaucracy.[182] Finally, in both countries reaction brought to power functionaries who in 'their man-

---

continuing to speak of bureaucratic centrism – a characterisation he judged to be 'totally out of date'. He explained, 'On the international arena, Stalinism is no longer centrism, but the crudest form of opportunism and social patriotism. See Spain'! (Trotsky 1978, p. 478).

179   Trotsky 1971b, p. 166.
180   Trotsky 1971b, p. 173.
181   Trotsky 1971b, p. 174.
182   Trotsky 1971b, pp. 174–5.

ner of living, their interests, and psychology' differed dramatically from the revolutionaries who had struggled for power. In this regard, Trotsky emphasised the prominent role of former Mensheviks and right-wing Social Revolutionaries in the Soviet state offices, and especially in the Soviet diplomatic service.[183]

In order to explain how the regime became Bonapartist, Trotsky returned again to his functional account of the origins of bureaucratic autonomy and one-man rule. He portrayed the first phase of this process as overlapping historically with the process of Thermidor. Initially, the bureaucracy raised itself above the masses to carry out the necessary regulation of contradictions between 'the city and the village, between the proletariat and the peasantry', etc. At the same time, it used this regulatory function 'to strengthen its own domination'. During this phase the bureaucracy's mediation of conflicts had constituted the 'social base of *bureaucratic centrism*, of its zigzags, its power, its weakness and its influence on the world proletarian movement that has been so fatal'. When bureaucratic rule generated new social contradictions, the bureaucracy exploited these to create 'a regime of bureaucratic absolutism'. Meanwhile, contradictions within the bureaucracy itself 'led to a system of handpicking the main commanding staff; the need for discipline within the select order that has led to the rule of a single person and to the cult of the infallible leader'. Now, this process was nearing completion: 'As the bureaucracy becomes more independent, as more and more power is concentrated in the hands of a single person, the more does *bureaucratic centrism* turn into Bonapartism'.[184]

At the end of his 1 February article, fearing that opponents on his left would attempt to capitalise on these changes, Trotsky added a postscript in which he minimised the significance of the theoretical revisions:

> It is in no case a question of *changing* our principled position ... but only a question of rendering it more *precise*. Our 'self-criticism' extends not to the analysis of the class character of the USSR or to the causes and conditions for its degeneration but only to the historical clarification of these processes by means of establishing analogies with well-known stages of the Great French Revolution.[185]

---

183   Trotsky 1971b, pp. 174–8.
184   Trotsky 1971b, pp. 170–1, 180.
185   Trotsky 1971b, pp. 183–4.

However, the implications of Trotsky's revisions were far greater than he admitted. Most generally, they reinforced his characterisation of the bureaucracy as a highly autonomous social formation. In line with this, his change of position on Bonapartism immediately resulted in the dropping of bureaucratic centrism – a development that would have important implications for his analysis of policy. Beyond that, his revision of his position on Thermidor and Bonapartism enhanced the significance of two other concepts he had used in the past: bureaucratic caste and labour aristocracy, while requiring yet another redefinition of the term *workers' state*.

One concept affected by Trotsky's revised understanding of Thermidor and Bonapartism was the notion of a bureaucratic caste. Of course, the concept was an old one. Hal Draper has noted that, due to a 'vogue for things Indian', the term was popular in Germany in the early nineteenth century as 'a swearword directed especially against Old Regime strata seen as fossilized, such as the old nobility, officer élite, and so on, as well as the bureaucracy'.[186] Marx and Engels frequently employed the term in their descriptions of relatively autonomous state apparatuses of Bonapartist regimes. For example, in *The Eighteenth Brumaire*, Marx commented that Louis Bonaparte had 'been forced to create, alongside the real classes of society, an artificial caste'.[187] Also, in his first draft of *The Civil War in France* he described how, in the state of Louis Bonaparte, administration and governing were treated as 'mysteries, transcendent functions only to be trusted to the hands of a trained caste – state parasites'.[188] As Draper has observed, in such passages Marx and Engels utilised *caste* as 'a loose term for a social stratum which does not play the role of a separate class'.[189] The Bolsheviks used the term similarly. For example, in an important work written during the First World War, Zinoviev denounced the 'caste of labor bureaucrats' – that is, the officials of the Western Social Democratic parties and trade unions – as a major source of the opportunism and social chauvinism of the Second International.[190]

---

186   Draper 1977, bk. 2, p. 505.
187   Marx 1974c, p. 243.
188   Marx 1966, p. 169. See also Marx 1966, p. 170. The full text of this draft was first published in English and Russian in 1934. For other references to bureaucratic castes in Marx and Engels, see Draper 1977, bk. 2, pp. 415, 416, 504, 508.
189   Draper 1977, bk., 2, p. 415. For a useful discussion of the use of the term *caste* by Marx and Engels, see Draper 1977, pp. 505–10.
190   Zinoviev 1984, pp. 480–6.

No doubt Trotsky was thinking of these examples from the Marxist classics when he first applied the term to the Soviet bureaucracy.[191] It seems that his first references to a bureaucratic caste in the Soviet Union appeared in early 1929 in statements where he was beginning to stress the autonomy of the party-state bureaucracy. At that time he asserted that the bureaucrats who had exiled him were 'people who have got the power into their hands and converted themselves into a bureaucratic caste', and he characterised the party apparatus as 'a definitely constituted caste'.[192] In the following five years, he wrote of the bureaucratic caste in the USSR on just a few more occasions.[193]

However, at the end of December 1934 and in early 1935, the importance of the notion was underlined by Trotsky's emerging understanding of Thermidor and Bonapartism. By redefining the rise of the bureaucracy as a fundamental transfer of power, his new position on Thermidor and Bonapartism called into question the precise nature of the dominant social formation. His answer was that this was not a class, but a bureaucratic caste. Consequently, at this point Trotsky began using the term *caste* more frequently and insistently, and in ways that more clearly suggested a class-like degree of autonomy.[194]

---

191 Of course, Trotsky was not equating the bureaucratic caste in the Soviet Union with the social castes of India. In September 1939 he noted that the 'make-shift character of the term' was 'clear to everybody, since it would enter nobody's mind to identify the Moscow oligarchy with the Hindu caste of Brahmins' (Trotsky 1970d, p. 6).

192 Trotsky 1975c, pp. 77, 118; *Biulleten' oppozitsii* 1973, 1–2 (July 1929), p. 4; Trotsky 1929b, p. 10. Two translations of the 1927 *Platform of the Opposition* each incorrectly employ the term *caste* three times in reference to the Soviet bureaucracy (Trotsky 1980b, p. 356; Joint Opposition 1973, p. 67). In fact, in these passages the term used in the *Platform* was *sloi* (layer) (Fel'shtinskii 1988, vol. 4, p. 151). However, the *Platform* used *kast* in one passage referring to state bureaucracies in bourgeois countries (Fel'shtinskii 1988, vol. 4, p. 139; Trotsky 1980b, p. 340). One of the earliest characterisations of the Soviet bureaucracy as a caste seems to have appeared in a statement by the Democratic Centralists on 27 June 1927 (Fel'shtinskii 1988, vol. 3, p. 138).

193 In the issues of *Biulleten' oppozitsii* published after July 1929 and before January 1935, the term *caste* used in reference to the Soviet bureaucracy appeared in Trotsky's writings only three times (search of the website *Biulleten' oppozitsii* 2002; see *Biulleten' oppozitsii* 1973, 32 [December 1932], p. 28; Trotsky 1973d, p. 227; *Biulleten' oppozitsii* 1973, 35 [July 1933], p. 18 [incorrectly translated in Trotsky 1972f, p. 276]; *Biulleten' oppozitsii* 1973, 36–7 [October 1933], p. 19; Trotsky 1972f, p. 304).

194 In the issues of *Biulleten' oppozitsii* published in 1935, the term *caste*, used in reference to the Soviet bureaucracy, appears in Trotsky's writings five times (search of the website *Biulleten' oppozitsii* 2002). Trotsky's secretary Joseph Hansen noted the change in Trotsky's use of the term *caste* in this period, observing that in his 1 February 1935 article Trotsky 'brought fresh insight into the nature of the bureaucratic caste'. Hansen explained, 'In its

For example, in his 12 January 1935 article on the investigation into the Kirov assassination, he described the 'vile amalgam' of the consul as a typical measure used by the Stalinist bureaucracy 'in the struggle for its caste positions'.[195] Likewise, in his 1 February 1935 article on Thermidor and Bonapartism he asserted, 'The Stalinist bureaucracy smashed the Left Opposition in order to safeguard and entrench itself as a privileged caste'.[196] From this point on, the concept occupied an important place in Trotsky's theory.

Another term that received enhanced significance from the redefinition of Thermidor and Bonapartism was *labour aristocracy*. The Bolsheviks used this term frequently during the war in reference to a stratum within the Western working class that, with the labour bureaucracy, had been transformed by privileges into an opportunist tool of the bourgeoisie.[197] It seems that Trotsky first employed the term in writings on the Soviet bureaucracy in July 1931 when he condemned the increasing use of piecework as an attempt to create a stratum of more prosperous workers – an 'ever more privileged labor aristocracy'.[198] However, his reading of French history now suggested a new use for the concept in understanding Soviet Bonapartism. Recalling Napoleon Bonaparte's creation of the Legion of Honor, the imperial court, and a new titled nobility, he observed that Napoleon had 'concentrated the fruits of the regime in the hands of a new bourgeois aristocracy'.[199] Similarly, he noted that Stalin was now creating a 'new aristocracy by means of an extreme differentiation in wages, privileges, ranks, etc'.[200] Here, Trotsky was speaking of the growing layer of privileged Soviet shock workers, increasingly differentiated by titles such as 'best of the shock workers' and 'best of the best', and by medals such as the Order of the Red Banner of Labour and the Order of Lenin.[201] Like Napoleon,

---

      greed its reactionary conservatism, its opportunism, and its ruthless insistence on retaining power, [the bureaucracy] has the characteristics of a decayed ruling class' (Hansen 1974, p. 4).

195   Trotsky 1971b, p. 143; *Biulleten' oppozitsii* 1973, 42 (February 1935), p. 6.

196   Trotsky 1971b, p. 170; *Biulleten' oppozitsii* 1973, 43 (April 1935), pp. 4–5. See also Trotsky 1971b, p. 156 *Biulleten' oppozitsii* 1973, 42 (February 1935), p. 12 (translation corrected).

197   On the labour aristocracy see, for example, Lenin 1960–70, vol. 21, pp. 223, 243; Lenin 1960–70, vol. 23, pp. 112–13; Zinoviev 1984, pp. 486–96. For discussions of Lenin's uses of labour aristocracy, see Clark 1983–84, pp. 59–94; Hobsbawm 1970, pp. 47–56; Nicolaus 1970, pp. 91–101; Post 2010.

198   Trotsky 1973c, pp. 288–9.

199   Trotsky 1971b, p. 181. Regarding the Legion of Honor and Napoleon's new aristocracy, see for example, Aulard 1910, pp. 245–6; Conner 2004, pp. 49–53.

200   Trotsky 1971b, p. 181.

201   On shock work, see Filtzer 1986, pp. 97–100; Siegelbaum 1988, pp. 40–53.

Stalin was relying on his new aristocracy for political support: 'Leaning for support upon the topmost layer...against the lowest – sometimes vice versa – Stalin has attained the complete concentration of power in his own hands'.[202]

Despite Trotsky's claim that his 'self-criticism' regarding Thermidor and Bonapartism did not extend 'to the analysis of the class character of the USSR', it immediately resulted in a revision in this area as well. Although Trotsky now explicitly denied that either the French or the Soviet Thermidor involved a *social* counterrevolution, he still viewed Thermidor as a counterrevolution of sorts. Thus, he observed: 'Was Thermidor counterrevolutionary? The answer to this question depends upon how wide a significance we attach, in a given case, to the concept of "counterrevolution"'.[203] As a form of counterrevolution, a Thermidor necessarily required a civil war. For this reason, and perhaps thinking of comparisons to the waves of repression and White terror that followed the French Thermidor, Trotsky now depicted the violence and repression employed against the Opposition as a 'number of minor civil wars waged by the bureaucracy against the proletarian vanguard'.[204] Even though Trotsky qualified this assessment with the observation that, in comparison with the French edition, the Soviet Thermidor initially had maintained 'a comparatively "dry" character', he could no longer use the absence of a civil war to demonstrate that the Soviet Union remained a workers' state.[205] Consequently, in the section of his 1 February article in which he again defended his position on the class nature of the USSR, this criterion was absent. Trotsky's sole remaining argument was that the '*social content of the dictatorship of the bureaucracy is determined by those productive relations that were created by the proletarian revolution*'.[206]

---

202   Trotsky 1971b, p. 181.

203   Trotsky 1971b, p. 168.

204   Trotsky 1971b, p. 172.

205   Trotsky 1971b, p. 174. In a 1937 debate with the French Trotskyist Yvan Craipeau on the class nature of the Soviet Union Trotsky continued to predict: 'Without a victorious civil war the bureaucracy cannot give birth to a new ruling class. That was and remains my thought'. However, he did not argue that the proletarian nature of the USSR was demonstrated by the absence of a civil war. In fact, he perceived the USSR at the time as undergoing a 'preventive civil war opened up by the bureaucracy' (Trotsky 1976b, pp. 37–8).

206   Trotsky 1971b, p. 173.

7.6   Deeper Shifts, Repression, and a Constitution

From February 1935 into the summer of 1936 the Soviet leadership deepened
its turns in economic and international affairs, and combined elements of
repression and conciliation in its internal political policy. In the economy it
offered new economic incentives to the peasantry and to Soviet workers.
Internationally, it continued to seek military alliances with imperialist powers,
while promoting 'antifascist' alliances between Communist parties and
Socialist or liberal parties in the capitalist world. In policy related to the party-
state regime, the leadership continued the post-assassination repression of its
critics and initiated two new membership accounting operations that included
elements of repression. However, in late 1935 and early 1936 it also introduced
liberal reforms in a new constitution.

    Meanwhile, under threat of expulsion from France, Trotsky obtained a visa
for Norway, arriving in Oslo with his wife and two secretaries on 18 June.[207]
Through the remainder of 1935 and early 1936 he maintained his relative
silence about Soviet affairs. But in various statements he continued to criticise
Soviet economic and international initiatives from the left, while denouncing
the escalating repression he perceived in regime policy. In each case he utilised
his new theoretical insights to analyse these policy developments. In turn,
these policy analyses, in combination with his recent theoretical innovations,
led him to a new characterisation of Soviet international policy and to a further redefinition of the Opposition's strategic orientation.

7.6.1   New Initiatives in Economic Policy
The economic upturn of 1933–4 persisted into the first half of 1936. This period
saw an expansion of consumer industries and a relative improvement of living
standards in the city and, even more, in the countryside.[208] Meanwhile, in an
effort to enhance agricultural productivity, in February 1935 the Central
Committee convened the Second All-Union Congress of Kolkhoz Activists to
adopt a 'model' statute to be used by collective farms throughout the Soviet
Union. One of the provisions of the statute recognised the right of each *kolkhoz*
household to a private plot of land of between ¼ and ½ hectares. Once obliga-
tory deliveries to the state were met, *kolkhoz* members were free to consume or
sell the remaining produce from these plots. Additionally, to promote the

---

207   Deutscher 1963, pp. 289–92; Van Heijenoort 1978, pp. 77–9.
208   Dobb 1966, pp. 278–81, 286–9; Nove 1976, pp. 225, 228–31, 244–51.

recovery of livestock, individual households were permitted a limited number of animals for personal use.[209]

Regarding industry, the most important new development was the rise of the Stakhanovite movement. On the night of 30–1 August 1935 Aleksei Stakhanov, a pick operator in the Central Irmino mine in the Donbas region of Ukraine, managed to produce more than fourteen times the average shift output of coal. Stakhanov's feat was accomplished through division of labour, special advance preparations, and hard work. With the encouragement of the Soviet press, the movement quickly spread to other mines and industries, turning into a mass campaign to increase productivity. In December the CC plenum endorsed the movement, utilising it to justify an upward revision of technological and labour norms. Workers who were designated 'Stakhanovites' were rewarded with official acclaim, special privileges – including access to scarce consumer goods and housing, and wages up to four times or more above the industrial average.[210]

Again, in these years Trotsky devoted relatively little attention to Soviet economic matters. No doubt this was at least partially because he believed the upturn was diminishing both the danger of restoration and the opportunity for 'forcible reform'. He explicitly noted the economic improvement and the even greater perception of improvement by workers and peasants in a conversation with a Canadian supporter, Earle Birney, in November 1935.[211]

However, one major concern of Trotsky's regarding economic policy was the continuing rightward shift of agricultural policy in the market reforms embodied in the model *kolkhoz* statutes. Although there is no indication that he opposed those reforms, he worried that they were only the beginning of a deeper retreat. Still, in light of his recent theoretical revisions, he did not describe this as a danger of Thermidor. On 15 February 1935 he wrote in his diary,

> Certain further concessions to the petty bourgeois tendencies of the peasant seem to be in preparation. At this stage it is hard to predict the point at which they will manage to hold the line against the present retreat.[212]

---

209   Fitzpatrick 1994, pp. 117–18, 121–2; Medvedev 1987, pp. 102–5, Nove 1976, pp. 240–2, 248; Chernenko and Smirtiukov 1967–88, vol. 2, pp. 519–30.

210   See Dobb 1966, pp. 468–76; Filtzer 1986, pp. 179, 182–7; Nove 1976, pp. 232–4; Seigelbaum 1988, pp. 3–6, 63–98, 184–90, 301–2.

211   Trotsky 1979b, pp. 627–8.

212   Trotsky 1963f, p. 20. See also Trotsky 1963f, p. 90.

Trotsky's explanation in this period of the origins of Soviet agricultural policy seems to have been influenced by his recent theoretical changes. His diary statements about 'holding the line' against 'concessions to the petty bourgeois tendencies of the peasant' indicated that he saw the current turn as largely inspired by external class pressures. However, his simultaneous characterisation of the retreat as a reaction 'brought on ... by the extremely crude bureaucratic illusions of the preceding period' suggests a greater degree of bureaucratic autonomy than he had admitted in his accounts of earlier right turns.[213] This shift of emphasis was even clearer in Trotsky's description of the origins of collectivisation. Now he explicitly repudiated his earlier understanding that collectivisation was the result of 'elemental pressure from the masses'. Rather, it was a product of 'bureaucratic bungling' in which 'the frightened bureaucrats began to drive the frightened muzhiks into the collective farms with the knout'.[214]

Trotsky's second major economic concern in these years, related to his recent remarks about the development of a new Soviet aristocracy, was the growth of economic inequality. This was evident in his November conversation with Birney where he noted that, with the recent economic improvement, 'the privileged sections secured more privileges and the bureaucracy added new top layers'.[215] It was also suggested in his letter of 31 December to sections of the ICL endorsing the 'totally correct picture' of the Stakhanovite movement provided in an article by Leon Sedov published under the pseudonym 'N. Markin'.[216] A main conclusion of Sedov's article was that the Stalinist leadership was creating a privileged grouping of workers not only to promote productivity, but also to foster the development of a 'labor aristocracy' as a political base of support for the bureaucracy. The result of this 'accentuated differentiation', Sedov noted, was an extreme sharpening of 'internal antagonisms' within the working class.[217] Similarly, in *The Revolution Betrayed*, completed in 1936, Trotsky depicted the stratum of Stakhanovites as a 'workers' aristocracy', arguing that the movement had been created by the bureaucracy as a means of intensifying labour, but also 'to introduce sharp antagonisms in the proletariat' in accordance with the maxim ' "Divide and rule" '! Furthermore, he observed

213   Trotsky 1963f, p. 20.
214   Trotsky 1963f, p. 21.
215   Trotsky 1979b, p. 627.
216   Trotsky 1977a, p. 222. See also Trotsky 1976b, p. 173.
217   Markin 1936, pp. 11–12. For additional brief remarks on the Stakhanovite movement by Trotsky, see Trotsky 1977a, pp. 233–4.

that the formation of this stratum was providing a useful 'reserve for the replenishment of the bureaucracy'.[218]

7.6.2   *Further Shifts in International Policy*

Meanwhile, the shifts in Soviet foreign policy and Comintern policy initiated in the previous two years continued to deepen. As part of the continuing Soviet efforts to obtain a defensive alliance against Germany, on 2 May 1935 V.P. Potemkin, the Soviet ambassador to France, signed a treaty of Material Aid with Pierre Laval obliging each nation to assist the other in the event of an attack by a third party.[219] Two weeks later Stalin explicitly endorsed French rearmament for national defense in a communiqué issued jointly with Laval, which noted that 'Comrade Stalin expressed complete understanding and approval of the national defense policy pursued by France with the object of maintaining its armed forces at a level consistent with its security requirements'.[220] The statement elicited mixed reactions within the French left. The PCF endorsed both the alliance and the Stalin-Laval communiqué, and in a speech of 17 May Thorez explained that if an imperialist state sided with the USSR in war, 'the war would not be a war between two imperialist camps'.[221] On the other hand, Leon Blum of the SFIO asserted that the communiqué was 'a slap in the face' of all who had campaigned against French militarism.[222]

At the same time, the PCF continued to pursue an electoral alliance that would include both Socialists and Radicals. Although the PCF's new support for a strong national defence repelled the Socialists, it impressed the Radicals positively.[223] Subsequently, the benefits derived by all three parties from an informal bloc in the municipal elections of May 1935 generated new support for the alliance.[224] Ultimately, the efforts of the PCF were rewarded with the formation of the Popular Front on 14 July 1935 at a mass demonstration on the anniversary of the storming of the Bastille.[225] Despite continuing disagreements between the Communists and Socialists, the following January the PCF, the SFIO, and the Radical Socialists negotiated an agreement for the mutual

---

218   Trotsky 1937, pp. 124, 80, 128, 138–9.

219   Braunthal 1967, p. 430; Carr 1982, p. 150; Ulam 1974, pp. 223–4.

220   Degras 1953, p. 132.

221   Thorez quoted in Carr 1982, p. 204. See also Braunthal 1967, p. 432.

222   Braunthal 1967, p. 431.

223   Braunthal 1967, p. 433; Mortimer 1984, p. 234.

224   The PCF and SFIO both made substantial gains, and the Radical-Socialists minimised what otherwise would have been a significant electoral loss (Braunthal 1967, pp. 433–4; Mortimer 1984, pp. 231–2).

225   Braunthal 1967, p. 435; Carr 1982, p. 207. Mortimer 1984, pp. 236–7.

support of each other's candidates in the second round of balloting in the upcoming parliamentary elections. The outcome of the election in late April and early May was an enormous success for the Popular Front parties, which won a majority in the Chamber of Deputies. On 4 June 1936 Blum assumed the office of Prime Minister, heading a Socialist-Radical government. To preserve their freedom to criticise, the Communists declined Blum's invitation to participate.[226]

The results of the election soon sparked an explosion of discontent within the French working class. In early May the French metallurgical industry erupted in a series of strikes and factory occupations. By early June the movement had swelled until nearly two million workers in all industries were on strike. From the beginning the leaderships of both the SFIO and PCF attempted to resolve the crisis as quickly as possible. Two days after assuming office, Blum invited workers' and employers' representatives to participate in negotiations. On 11 June, at a meeting of the Parisian membership of the PCF, Thorez urged Communists to use their influence to end the strike, arguing, 'While it is important to lead well a movement for economic demands, ... it is also necessary to know how to end it. There is at present no question of taking power'.[227] In reply to Marceau Pivert of the SFIO left who had just declared, 'Now everything is possible for those who are bold enough', Thorez responded, 'No, everything is not possible at the present'.[228] Together, the PCF and SFIO were able to terminate most strikes by early August.[229]

The Seventh Congress of the Comintern, which convened in Moscow on 25 July 1935, embraced the French Popular Front strategy, extending it to the entire world. In his report to the congress, Georgi Dimitrov called first for a 'proletarian united front' with Social Democratic parties and reformist trade unions against the class enemies of the proletariat, promising that Communists would not attack its allies in the front. Beyond that, he advocated an 'antifascist People's Front' that would include parties controlled by the 'agents of big capital'. Going further than the PCF, he announced that Communists were prepared to share responsibility for forming a Popular Front government. Finally, he even proposed the eventual unification of Social Democratic and Communist parties.[230] Aside from the Popular Front, the Seventh Congress also addressed the struggle against war. In his report on this question Palmiro

226 Braunthal 1967, p. 435. Claudin 1975a, p. 200.
227 Quoted in Claudin 1975a, p. 203.
228 Quoted in ibid.
229 Brower 1968, pp. 152–4.
230 Dimitroff 1975, pp. 9–93.

Togliatti appealed for a struggle against the main threats to peace, German fascism and Japanese militarism, through a united front of 'all those who want to defend and preserve peace'. In particular, Togliatti urged Communists to unite with the 'pacifist masses', while continuing to expose their 'pacifist illusions'.[231]

Trotsky denounced all of these policy initiatives from the left, concluding that they revealed that Stalinism now played an actively *counterrevolutionary* role in the world arena. Following his break with the Comintern, in late 1933 Trotsky had asserted that the Soviet Union had 'completely squander[ed]' its significance as an 'international revolutionary factor'.[232] He now clarified and concretised that analysis, depicting Stalinist policy as social patriotic, Menshevik, and worse than traditional opportunism, and describing the Comintern as essentially social democratic. This change was facilitated by his recent characterisation of the bureaucracy as Bonapartist rather than centrist, for that revision reopened the question of where Soviet policy fell on a left-right continuum. For Trotsky, that question was now answered by the similarities he perceived between Stalinist policy and the policies of social democracy.

Although in early 1935 Trotsky noted indications that the PCF was beginning to back away from its traditional 'revolutionary defeatism', he was shocked by the Stalin-Laval communiqué. To Trotsky, this was 'an act of treason in the fullest sense of the word, signed and notarized'.[233] He explained his reaction in an open letter to the world proletariat on 25 May and in a letter to the workers of France on 10 June. While he had serious reservations about the value of the treaty for the USSR, he did not criticise the agreement. Practical agreements with the class enemy, he asserted, 'may be correct or wrong, but they cannot be rejected on principle'.[234] Rather, Stalin's crime was in signing the communiqué. For the first time, Stalin had 'openly said what is'. That is, he had openly 'repudiated revolutionary internationalism and passed over to the platform of social patriotism'. Furthermore, the Comintern, by endorsing the communiqué, had become 'the diplomatic agent of Stalinism' which had taken 'the decisive step on the road to civil peace'.[235] Trotsky explained that when a proletarian party supports national militarism, by that act it transforms itself into the 'domestic beast of capital'. In fact, the Comintern's approval of the communiqué demonstrated it was 'the principal obstacle on the historic road of the working class'.

231   Ercoli 1968, p. 1257.
232   Trotsky 1972g, p. 102. See also Trotsky 1972g, p. 124.
233   Trotsky 1963f, p. 120.
234   Trotsky 1971b, p. 309. See also Trotsky 1971b, p. 298.
235   Trotsky 1971b, p. 291.

He concluded that the Stalinists stood at the 'extreme right wing of the working-class movement' and were even more harmful than traditional opportunists because they cloaked themselves with the authority of the Bolshevik Revolution.[236]

With the formation of the Popular Front, Trotsky also condemned the PCF's alliance with the Radicals, reiterating and amplifying upon his previous arguments. The contemporary Communist authors Monty Johnstone and Giuliano Procacci have both argued that, in condemning the policy of the PCF, Trotsky abandoned his previous perspective on the need for a defensive united front against fascism.[237] This suggests that the French Popular Front was consistent with Trotsky's demands for Germany. However, even while urging a German united front, Trotsky had stressed its necessary *limits*. It was to be a defensive alliance, composed of working-class organisations, which would retain their autonomy, including their freedom to criticise each other and to lead independent campaigns.[238] For Trotsky, even the French united front of 1934 violated these conditions, for it embraced 'almost the entire activity' of the PCF and SFIO, while excluding their 'reciprocal struggle to win the majority of the proletariat'. For this reason, Trotsky explained in October 1934, he was advancing an offensive programme for the French front, since 'a purely defensive bloc against fascism' would have sufficed only if the two parties had 'preserved complete independence' in other respects.[239]

Subsequently, the inclusion of the Radicals in the alliance, as well as its redefinition as an electoral bloc, only completed its divergence from Trotsky's united front perspective. Against claims in *Pravda* that the Radicals were a 'bloc between the middle and petty bourgeoisie', he argued in an article of 28 March 1936 that the Radicals were actually the democratic party of French imperialism.[240] While the masses were abandoning the Radical Party, the Socialist and Communist leaders were trying to save it by limiting their activities to actions consistent with the Radical programme. In fact, according

---

236 Trotsky 1971b, pp. 305–6, 312. See also Trotsky 1963f, pp. 141–2.
237 See Johnstone 1975a, pp. 309, 310–11, 313; Procacci 1963, pp. 62–9. For discussions of the differences between Trotsky's united front and the Comintern's popular front strategies, see Deutscher 1963, pp. 276–7; Mandel 1995, pp. 121–4; Mandel 1979, pp. 95–8; Molyneux 1981, p. 136.
238 See Trotsky 1971c, pp. 138–9, 164, 179. All of these conditions were included in the 'Theses on Comintern Tactics' adopted by the Fourth Congress of the Comintern in December 1922 (Adler 1980, pp. 395–7).
239 Trotsky 1979c, pp. 59–60.
240 Trotsky 1979c, p. 145.

to Trotsky the entire purpose of the Popular Front was to put '*a brake upon* the mass movement, directing it into the channels of class collaboration'.[241]

Trotsky similarly denounced the Comintern congress's extension of the 'opportunistic turn' of the PCF to the rest of the world.[242] On 23 August 1935 he asserted that the congress, while generalising the French experience on the Popular Front and the question of war, had 'liquidated Lenin's teaching, making an abrupt about-face to opportunism and patriotism'.[243] In particular, it had rejected Lenin's views that the proletariat could not take power within the framework of bourgeois democracy, that even the most 'left' bourgeois parties served finance capital, that the real culprit in imperialist war was imperialism itself, and that revolutionary defeatism was the appropriate policy within all imperialist countries. Nothing, Trotsky claimed, now distinguished Communists from Social Democrats 'except the traditional phraseology'.[244]

As far as the source of the French Popular Front orientation was concerned, Monty Johnstone and Ian Thatcher have claimed that Trotsky depicted it as entirely Soviet.[245] Actually, however, he ultimately held the Soviet leadership and the PCF leadership as *jointly* responsible. In an article dated 23 August 1935 he asserted that, following the riot of February 1934, PCF leaders who previously denounced Radicals and Social Democrats as fascists, 'completely lost faith in themselves and in their banner' and decided – 'at the direct bidding of Moscow, of course' – to seek an alliance with both parties.[246] Similarly, on 28 March 1936 he argued that, after the events of February 1934, the French Communist leadership 'scurried to the right' in the 'normal reflex action of the scared phrasemongers'. This shift, he noted, conveniently corresponded 'with the new international orientation of Soviet diplomacy'. He described Soviet thinking as follows:

> Under pressure of the danger threatening from Hitler's Germany, the policy of the Kremlin turned towards France. Status quo – in international relations! Status quo – in the internal relations of the French regime! Hopes for the social revolution? Chimeras![247]

241 Trotsky 1979c, pp. 129–30, 142, 143.
242 Trotsky 1977a, p. 126.
243 Trotsky 1977a, p. 87.
244 Trotsky 1977a, pp. 86–9, 93.
245 Johnstone 1975a, pp. 310–11; Thatcher 2003, p. 202.
246 Trotsky 1977a, p. 90.
247 Trotsky 1979c, pp. 141–2.

As the upsurge of June 1936 unfolded, Trotsky excitedly followed French developments by radio from a Norwegian village. On 9 June he proclaimed 'The French revolution has begun'! To coordinate the offensive, he called for the creation of *'soviets of workers' deputies'*.[248] For Trotsky, the difference between this perspective and that of the PCF was a measure of how far Stalinism had fallen from revolutionary politics. Reviewing the record of the strike in July, he asserted that if the 'Communist' party had been genuinely communist, it would have broken with the Radicals, called for the creation of factory committees and soviets, and proceeded to establish dual power. In his sharpest criticism of French Stalinism to date, he denounced the PCF as 'merely one of the tools of French imperialism'.[249] Regarding the international role of Stalinism as a whole, he argued,

> The Stalinist bureaucracy is a far more threatening and treacherous obstacle on the road of the world revolution than the autocratic czar once was. The Comintern covers a policy of social patriotism and Menshevism with the authority of the October Revolution and the banner of Lenin.[250]

One final development that for Trotsky revealed the contrast between Stalinism and Leninism was Stalin's interview on 1 March 1936 with Roy Howard of the Scripps-Howard newspaper chain. In that interview Stalin had reiterated the Marxist maxim that the cause of war was capitalism. However, Trotsky observed that as soon as Stalin passed 'from dim theoretical recollections to real politics', he began speaking of 'evil-minded cliques', and arguing that the 'friends of peace', utilising such instruments as the League of Nations, were growing stronger against the 'enemies of peace'.[251] When referring to imperialist countries, Trotsky remarked, it would have been more appropriate to speak of the 'friends and enemies of the status quo', which oppressed the majority of humanity. Furthermore, as the Bolshevik program of 1919 had observed, the League was merely one of the tools by which capitalists exploited the world. By duping workers with its recent statements, Trotsky asserted, both the Soviet government and the Comintern had been converted into the *political agency of imperialism in relation to the working masses*. Focusing then on the best-known aspect of the interview, Trotsky noted Stalin's denial that the Soviet

---

248 Trotsky 1979c, pp. 162, 166–7.
249 Trotsky 1979c, p. 178.
250 Trotsky 1979c, pp. 180–1.
251 Trotsky 1977a, p. 272. See Stalin 1968 p. 488.

Union ever had any plans for world revolution and his characterisation of the contrary view as a 'tragicomic' misunderstanding. For Trotsky, these remarks were entirely 'inappropriate and indecent'. In fact, he suggested, it would have been far more convincing if Stalin had simply admitted 'Your comical misunderstanding...consists in the fact that you take us for the continuators of Bolshevism, whereas we are its gravediggers'.[252]

Consistent with his new theory, Trotsky explained these rightward shifts and initiatives in international policy largely in terms of the autonomous actions of a conservative Soviet bureaucracy pursuing its own narrow interests. This was especially evident in Trotsky's discussion of the betrayal of the international proletariat, which he perceived in the Stalin-Laval communiqué.[253] Trotsky specifically attributed this betrayal to the bureaucracy's lack of confidence in, and even its hostility to, world revolution. These were attitudes which he believed were directly derived from the bureaucracy's material interests. Thus, in his open letter of 10 June he argued:

> The betrayal of Stalin and of the leadership of the Communist International is explained by the character of the present ruling stratum in the USSR; it is a privileged and an uncontrolled bureaucracy, which has raised itself above the people and which oppresses the people...The Soviet bureaucracy, above all, fears criticism, movement and risk; it is conservative; it greedily defends its own privileges. Having strangled the working class in the USSR, it has long since lost faith in the world revolution. It promises to build 'socialism in one country', if the toilers shut up, endure and obey.[254]

Fearing that the workers might frighten its new allies, the bureaucracy had decided 'to put a brake upon the class struggle of the proletariat in the "allied" countries'. Thus, for Trotsky the ultimate source of Stalin's betrayal was 'the national conservatism of the Soviet bureaucracy, its outright hostility to the world proletarian revolution'.[255]

7.6.3   Repression, Party Purges, and a New Constitution

In early 1935 the Soviet leadership continued the repression initiated after the Kirov assassination, extending it to broader strata of Soviet society. In March,

---

252   Trotsky 1977a, pp. 273, 274, 275–7. See Stalin 1968, p. 489.
253   Trotsky 1971b, p. 291.
254   Trotsky 1971b, p. 309. See also Trotsky 1971b, p. 299.
255   Trotsky 1971b, p. 309.

thousands of former aristocrats, civil servants, officers, and business people, as well as workers and their families were sent from Leningrad into exile or to prison camps in Siberia. Then, in the early summer of 1935, Zinoviev and Kamenev were brought back to Moscow to stand trial with more than 100 others for an alleged Kremlin plot against Stalin. Two of the defendants were shot and others received prison camp sentences of five to ten years. Kamenev received a sentence of an additional five years. One member of the elite affected by the reprisals was Avel' Enukidze, secretary of the Central Executive Committee of the Soviets, who was accused of assisting the Kremlin plotters. On 7 June the CC voted to expel him from that body and the party.[256]

Meanwhile, in October 1934 the party leadership decided to conduct a general registration of party membership, the Verification [proverka] of Party Documents. The original impulse for the campaign was the extreme disorganisation in party membership records, especially in local party organisations, revealed by the 1933 chistka. However, in the wake of the Kirov assassination the leadership also portrayed the administrative confusion as a security threat. A 13 May 1935 letter from the CC to local party organisations alleged that party cards had fallen into the hands of adventures, enemies of the party, and foreign spies; and it outlined procedures for verifying party documents and expelling members with invalid or unsupported credentials.[257] In his final report on the proverka in December 1935 N. Ezhov announced that 177,000 members, or 9.1 percent of the party membership, had been expelled. The majority had been dropped for apparently nonpolitical reasons such as lying to the party, having false documents, or corruption. Approximately 2.9 percent of the expelled, or a little over 5,000 members, were removed as Trotskyists or Zinovievists.[258]

Immediately after the proverka the party leadership undertook another administrative campaign, the 1936 Exchange of Party Documents [obmen partdokumentov]. In part, this was a response to the discovery in the proverka that party documents were badly worn and in need of replacement. Additionally, the obmen was initiated to reconsider questionable cases of membership that

---

256   Ciliga 1979, pp. 71, 296–8; Conquest 1973, p. 133; Getty and Naumov 1999, pp. 147, 160–1;
         Khlevniuk 2009, p. 130; Knight 1999, pp. 243–4; Serge 1980, p. 314; Serge 1996, pp. 199–200;
         Tucker 1990, pp. 305, 314. For a recent account of the Enukidze case, see Getty and Naumov
         1999, pp. 160–77. Older accounts include Ciliga 1979, p. 71; Conquest 1973, p. 133; Serge 1996,
         p. 202.
257   Getty 1985, pp. 54, 58–61; Service 2004, 216–17; Ward 1999, p. 109.
258   Getty 1985, pp. 66, 68–9; Getty and Naumov 1999, pp. 198–201, 205; Tucker 1990, pp. 311–13;
         Ward 1999, p. 109. See also Trotsky's conclusions, based on press reports, in Trotsky 1977a,
         pp. 235–6, 237–9, 281–2. Oleg Khlevniuk gives as the figure expelled in this campaign
         250,000 (Khlevniuk 2009, p. 130).

had arisen in the *proverka*. In particular, the CC urged party organisations to redirect their focus from enemies to members who did not actively participate.[259] Thus, the announced goals of the exchange were less political than those of the *proverka*. Nevertheless, in a reversal of previous instructions, an editorial in *Pravda* on 15 March 1936 asserted that the purge should be directed mainly against 'enemy and alien elements'.[260] By the end of 1936 the portion of those expelled as 'Trotskyists' or 'Zinovievists' in 1935–6 had risen to 5.5 percent.[261]

Despite these developments, news reports of preparations for a new constitution were raising hopes for political liberalisation. On Stalin's motion in February 1935 the CC established a constitutional commission with the goal of 'further democratizing' the Soviet system – a step justified on the grounds of the Soviet advance toward socialism. A draft of the constitution, approved by the Politburo on 15 May 1936 and by the CC in early June, was published on 12 June for national discussion. In his interview with Howard in March 1936 Stalin outlined some of the most important provisions: suffrage was to be universal in contrast with the previous disenfranchisement of employers and clergy; it was to be equal, replacing the system of differential representation of workers and peasants; it was to be direct instead of the previous tiered election of higher soviets by lower; and in contrast with the former system, voting was to be secret. Stalin further explained that, since there were 'no classes', and 'a party is part of a class', no parties aside from the AUCP were to be permitted. However, 'all sorts of public, non-Party organizations' would be able to nominate candidates.[262]

In his analyses Trotsky portrayed all of these policies as designed to promote Bonapartist regime characteristics: that is, either the 'domination of the bureaucracy over the country' and especially over the proletariat, or 'Stalin's domination over the bureaucracy'. Reiterating his argument of January 1935, in the succeeding months Trotsky characterised the ongoing post-assassination repression as directed against the left in order to implement Stalin's turn to the right. On 15 February, in reference to the decision to grant *kolkhoz* households the right to own livestock, Trotsky recorded in his diary, 'At the present time, the retreat is proceeding at full speed. For this very reason Stalin is once again

---

259   Getty 1985, pp. 86–7, 89.

260   Quoted in Tucker 1990, p. 313.

261   Getty and Naumov 1999, pp. 197–202; Getty 1985, pp. 87–91; Tucker 1990, pp. 311–13; Ward 1999, p. 109.

262   Carr 1950–3, vol. 1, p. 152; Cohen 1980, pp. 356–7; See Nicolaevsky 1965, pp. 26–7; Stalin 1968, pp. 492–3; Tucker 1990, pp. 305, 353–4.

forced to cut down everyone and everything that stands to the left of him'.[263] Similarly, on learning of the termination of Soviet aid for Communist propaganda in Britain and its dominions, Trotsky wrote on 4 April, 'The turn to the *right* in the sphere of both foreign and domestic policies forces Stalin to strike out at the *left* with all his might: this is his insurance against an opposition'.[264]

More specifically, Trotsky believed that the primary target of the repression was the vanguard of the proletariat, the Left Opposition. In these months he repeatedly predicted that the leadership would attempt a new amalgam against the Bolshevik-Leninists to compensate for the previous failure.[265] Indications along these lines soon appeared in *Pravda*, which on 20 March reported the prosecution of 1,074 former aristocrats, etc. for 'activity against the state in the interest of foreign nations'.[266] Five days later an amended description of the arrested denounced the 'foul dregs of the Trotskyists, the Zinovievists, the old princes, counts, gendarmes, *all this refuse*' directed by 'foreign information bureaus'.[267] From this, Trotsky concluded that the leadership had resolved 'to prepare new bloody repressions against the Oppositionists'. Since no terrorist act was available, *Pravda* had linked this to the arrests of the old proprietors, etc.[268]

However, in light of the absurdity of the charges Trotsky also speculated in his diary that perhaps the amalgam was really directed against 'some third element, not belonging to either the princes or the Trotskyists'. Consistent with his theory, he identified the likely targets to be 'liberal tendencies' within the bureaucracy. Suggesting that Stalin was preparing a coup to provide 'juridical sanction' for his personal power, on 29 March Trotsky concluded darkly, 'Some new stage is being prepared, by comparison with which Kirov's murder was only an ominous portent'.[269] Along the same lines, he suggested on 20 June that the expulsion of Enukidze was directed at Kalinin. On the basis of that event and the campaign against the Trotskyists and Zinovievists he observed, 'Stalin's dictatorship is approaching a new frontier'.[270]

---

263   Trotsky 1963f, pp. 20–1. See also Trotsky 1963f, pp. 16, 90; and Trotsky 1971b, p. 313, where
       Trotsky implied that the repression was in anticipation of the pact with Laval.

264   Trotsky 1963f, p. 66.

265   See Trotsky 1971b, pp. 151, 219; Trotsky 1963f, p. 131.

266   Quoted in Trotsky 1971b, p. 235.

267   Quoted in Trotsky 1971b, pp. 235–6.

268   Trotsky 1971b, p. 236. See also Trotsky 1963f, pp. 52–3, 60–2.

269   Trotsky 1963f, p. 53.

270   Trotsky 1963f, p. 144. In the following year Trotsky noted further evidence that the main
       targets of repression were the Bolshevik-Leninists in the accounts of Oppositionists who

At the same time Trotsky perceived the verification and exchange campaigns of 1935 and 1936 as directed against the Bolshevik-Leninists. In an article of 11 January 1936 he noted the diversity, indicative of another 'Thermidorean amalgam', of the categories of members expelled. He explained that part of the reason the Trotskyists were listed first was that the 'Bolshevik-Leninists were and remain the most irreconcilable enemies of the bureaucracy'.[271] Beyond that, he believed it was due to the fact that they were the largest group numerically. From local figures reported in *Pravda*, he mistakenly calculated that at least 5 percent, or perhaps 10,000 to 25,000 individuals, had been expelled as 'Trotskyists' or 'Zinovievists'.[272]

From these estimates Trotsky concluded that the Bolshevik-Leninists were experiencing remarkable growth. Guessing that no more than 'tens' or 'hundreds' of those purged had participated in the Opposition in the 1920s, he judged that these must be 'new recruits', especially from the youth, and concluded, 'If not as a doctrine, then as a mood, as a tradition, a banner, our tendency has a mass character in the USSR, and today it is obviously drawing to itself new and fresh forces'. Despite all of the persecutions and capitulations, the Fourth International still had *'its strongest, numerically largest, and most tempered section in the USSR'*.[273] Viewed from the standpoint of his theory, this was not unexpected. As he explained a few months later, there was no doubt that proletarian opposition groupings were 'revived precisely by the new pressure upon the workers, accompanied with new and monstrous privileges for the bureaucracy and the "best people"'. Also, in contrast with groups like the Workers' Opposition and Democratic Centralists, the Bolshevik-Leninists were growing rapidly because the 'advanced workers' supported their position on the class nature of the USSR.[274]

Trotsky similarly anticipated that the Exchange of Party Documents would be aimed at Bolshevik-Leninists. On 11 January 1936 he commented, 'Perhaps six months later we shall learn how many new Bolshevik-Leninists will... be

---

had endured years of imprisonment and internal exile. For Trotsky's summaries of these stories, see Trotsky 1977a, pp. 117, 245, 324–5.

271   Trotsky 1977a, pp. 236, 239.
272   Trotsky 1977a, pp. 236, 237–9. For repetitions of the 10,000 figure, see Trotsky 1977a, p. 255; Trotsky 1979b, pp. 635, 638, 642, 648. Shortly afterwards, on the basis of the prominent place accorded to Trotskyists and Zinovievists in reports of the expulsions in Moscow and Leningrad, he amended this estimate, asserting that 'not less than 10,000' from these two categories 'were expelled in the two capital cities alone' (Trotsky 1977a, pp. 281–2). See also Trotsky 1977a, p. 314.
273   Trotsky 1977a, pp. 240, 241.
274   Trotsky 1977a, pp. 281, 282.

promoted from the party to the concentration camps'.[275] Two months later, he
saw evidence in *Pravda* that the leadership was using the exchange to target
Bolshevik-Leninists. Noting again that the 'Trotskyists' occupied first place in
the categories of the expelled, he explained, 'This means that the heaviest
blows are directed against them'. [276]

For Trotsky, the announced provisions of the new Soviet constitution again
revealed the Bonapartist cleavages both between Stalin and the bureaucracy
and between the bureaucracy and the country. In an article of 16 April 1936
he asserted that the justification for the constitution in terms of the 'socialist' character of the USSR was contradicted by the absence of any mention of
the withering of repression.[277] Still, he believed that the leadership had important reasons for introducing reforms. One was to combat corruption within
the state apparatus. Stalin had explained that secret suffrage would be 'a whip
in the hand of the population against the organs of government which work
badly'. Trotsky perceived this as an admission that 'Stalin's autocratic rule' had
created a system of corruption that threatened the Soviet state as a source of
bureaucratic power and privilege. He concluded that the Kremlin chiefs were
turning to the population for help in cleansing the administrative apparatus.[278]

Nevertheless, Trotsky noted important limits on the participation that was
to be tolerated. One of these was the continuing ban on opposition parties,
justified by Stalin in terms of the 'classless' character of Soviet society.
According to that reasoning, Trotsky observed, there was no need for even a
single party. Nor was Trotsky impressed by Stalin's promise to allow 'all sorts of
public, nonparty organizations' to participate in nominating candidates, for all
of these organisations were dominated by 'representatives of the privileged
summits' and by the party, 'the political organization of the ruling stratum'.
Consequently, he concluded, the participation of nonparty organisations
would do nothing but promote rivalry between bureaucratic cliques within

275   Trotsky 1977a, p. 239.
276   Trotsky 1977a, pp. 285–6. Shortly afterwards, Trotsky noted an even more explicit and omi-
       nous threat in an editorial in *Pravda* of 5 June that warned of 'the remains of the counter-
       revolutionary groups', including '*especially the Trotskyists and Zinovievists*', and that
       promised to 'strike down and *destroy the enemies of the people, the Trotskyist vermin and
       furies*, however skillfully they may disguise themselves' (quoted in Trotsky 1977a, p. 342).
       Again, Trotsky explained that the bureaucracy, 'in the struggle for the maintenance of
       its power and privileges', was 'destroying a group which is trying to express the protest
       and discontents of the toiling masses' (Trotsky 1977a, pp. 342, 343). See also Trotsky 1977a,
       p. 358.
277   Trotsky 1977a, p. 302.
278   Trotsky 1977a, pp. 304–5. See also Trotsky 1977a, p. 310.

the limits set by the leadership. In fact, according to Trotsky this was the whole point of this reform. The summit hoped to utilise inter-bureaucratic competition 'to learn secrets . . . and to refurbish its regime' without allowing a political struggle that could threaten its own rule.[279]

However, Trotsky thought that an even more important constitutional objective than administrative reform was the leadership's desire to prevent the soviets from ever again becoming institutions of proletarian power. Although the soviets had lost their significance years before, they might have revived with the growth of social antagonisms. To forestall this, the constitution was, in effect, abolishing the soviets, 'dissolving the workers into the general mass of the population'.[280] The equalisation of representation was designed to smother proletarian opposition to inequality under the weight of the peasantry. In this regard Trotsky noted that Bonapartism 'always leans upon the village as against the city'.[281] The elimination of factory representation was intended to reduce workers to atomised citizens, voting 'each one for himself'.[282] Finally, the introduction of direct voting was to transform elections into plebiscites in which citizens could vote only '*For* or *against* the Leader'. By these measures, Trotsky concluded, the constitution was designed to create the legal sanction for Bonapartism that Stalin had sought since the Kirov assassination. It would 'liquidate juridically the outworn Soviet system, replacing it by *Bonapartism on a plebiscitary basis*'.[283]

In July 1936 this view of the new constitutional provisions reinforced Trotsky's recent conclusion that a political revolution would be required to overthrow the bureaucracy. Although in October 1933 he had recognised that force would be necessary to remove the bureaucracy, he had avoided speaking of 'revolution', insisting that only measures of a 'police character' would be needed. However, his revision of the Thermidor and Bonapartism analogies in 1935 promoted a further modification of Trotsky's position. In part, it constituted a new milestone in his recognition of the autonomy of the bureaucracy. At the same time, his argument that Thermidor, though not a social counterrevolution, still represented a counterrevolution of sorts, suggested the possibility of a revolution that was not a social revolution. Trotsky first outlined his new position on this question in a letter of 1 January 1936. Utilising the old

---

279   Trotsky 1977a, pp. 307–8.
280   Trotsky 1977a, p. 310.
281   Ibid.
282   Trotsky 1977a, p. 300.
283   Trotsky 1977a, p. 311.

Marxist distinction between a social and a political revolution, he now suggested that a political revolution would be necessary:

> What perspective opens before us? Very probably a new revolution. This
> will not be a social evolution, but a *political* revolution. In its evolution
> the bourgeoisie too has known of 'great' revolutions, i.e., social revolu-
> tions, and purely political revolutions which took place on the basis of
> already established property.[284]

For Trotsky, the announced provisions of the new constitution provided additional justification for this position. In a resolution for the first International
Conference for the Fourth International, he argued on 8 July that the new constitution, by sealing 'the dictatorship of the privileged strata' over the masses,
was blocking the possibility of a peaceful withering of the state, while opening
legal roads for capitalist restoration. With this 'last possibility of legal reforma-
tion' removed, the struggle necessarily became revolutionary: 'For the further
development of socialism a *political revolution* has become inevitable, i.e., the
violent overthrow of the political rule of the degenerated bureaucracy while
maintaining the property relations established by the October Revolution'.[285]

7.7   Conclusion

During the years 1933–6, Trotsky's understanding of the problem of Soviet
bureaucracy experienced a revolutionary transformation. In response to the
failure of Comintern policy in Germany, Trotsky emulated Lenin's reaction to
the failure of social democracy at the outbreak of the First World War by breaking with the Comintern. Trotsky's behaviour also curiously paralleled Lenin's
on a more abstract theoretical level. Shortly after concluding that the Second
International was dead as a revolutionary organisation, Lenin began taking
extensive notes on Hegel's *Science of Logic* – motivated, as Michael Löwy has
suggested, either by 'a simple desire to return to the sources of Marxist thought',
or by an intuition that the methodological weakness of the Second International
was its 'non-comprehension of the dialectic'. Whatever the reason, Lenin's
view of the dialectic and his political positions were profoundly altered by the

---

284   Trotsky 1977a, pp. 224–5. For earlier Marxist statements on political revolution, see for
     example, Marx 1974a, pp. 232–4; Avineri 1968, pp. 185–201; Kautsky 1907, pp. 8–9, 22, 26, 34,
     35. On Trotsky's call for a political revolution, see also Hofla 1985, p. 28.
285   Trotsky 1977a, pp. 358–9.

experience.[286] Similarly, soon after calling for a break with the Comintern, Trotsky began taking notes on Hegel's *Science of Logic*.[287] It is not clear if his theory of Soviet bureaucracy was directly affected by this reading. However, one passage from June 1934 stands out for its applicability to the development of his theory in these years:

> Historically humanity forms its 'conceptions' – the basic elements of its thinking – on the foundation of experience, which is always incomplete, partial, one-sided. It includes in 'the concept' those features of a living, forever changing process, which are important and significant for it at a given moment. Its future experience at first is enriched (quantitatively) and then *outgrows* the closed concept, that is, in practice negates it, by virtue of this necessitating a theoretical negation. But the negation does not signify a turning back to tabula rasa...This recognition [of the unsoundness of the concept] is tantamount to the necessity to construct *a new concept*, and then it is inevitably revealed that the negation...affected only certain features of the first concept...
>
>   Thus, in the domain of thinking..., the quantitative changes lead to qualitative ones, and then those transformations...are accompanied by *breaks in gradualness*, that is, by small or large intellectual catastrophes. In sum, this also means that the development of cognition has a *dialectical character*.[288]

As we have seen, the concept of Soviet bureaucracy formed by Trotsky in the 1920s initially appeared to enrich his understanding of reality. However, with the Soviet policy shifts of 1928–32, reality seemed to outgrow his earlier concept. In 1933 Trotsky was compelled to recognise that the failure of Comintern policy in Germany negated his reform perspective 'in practice'. In turn, this ultimately resulted in a 'theoretical negation' through the construction of a new concept that emphasised the autonomy of the bureaucracy as a social formation. Although Trotsky retained features of the old theory, in one 'large intellectual catastrophe' he revised his position on a whole series of theoretical

---

286   Löwy 1995, p. 192. See also Löwy 1981, p. 60. The most extensive discussion of Lenin's reading of Hegel appears in K. Anderson 1995, pp. 28–97. See also Harding 1996, pp. 77–8, 113–14.

287   Philip Pomper has explained that Trotsky's purpose in taking notes on Hegel was to prepare for writing an appendix devoted to Max Eastman's views on dialectics for his projected biography of Lenin (Pomper 1986, pp. 41–5). It is also possible that he was consciously retracing Lenin's steps.

288   Trotsky 1986, pp. 99–101.

issues. Then, in the following year and a half additional developments, including especially the repression following the Kirov assassination, provoked a series of smaller 'catastrophes' in Trotsky's thinking.

The final product of this theoretical revolution was most fully articulated in Trotsky's *The Revolution Betrayed*. The general theory presented in that book will be discussed in the next chapter. Here, it might be useful to examine a few of the strengths and weaknesses of Trotsky's analyses of specific policies during the years 1933–6. In each area these included exaggerations and errors, but also important insights – some of which were clearly derived from his emerging theoretical perspective.

Trotsky's estimation of the impact of the leadership's economic policies in this period on the Soviet working class was generally perceptive, though sometimes imprecise. In particular, his fear in early 1935 that the termination of rationing would negatively influence proletarian living standards turned out to be well founded, for the abolition of rationing resulted in serious hardship, especially among the lower strata of workers.[289] However, his views of the Stakhanovite movement were more problematic. In light of the large number of workers who were only 'occasional Stakhanovites', contemporary historian Lewis Siegelbaum has reasonably questioned whether this entire grouping can be considered a distinct social stratum. Furthermore, given the fact that perhaps a quarter of all industrial workers were ultimately included among their ranks, he has suggested that the 'aristocracy' label was inappropriate.[290] In fact, it would have been more accurate for Trotsky to have reserved that term for the far smaller and more privileged layer of 'leading Stakhanovites'.[291] Beyond that, it is clear that the relationships between Stakhanovites, the broader layers of industrial workers, and the leadership were more complex than depicted in Trotsky's brief statements on the subject. Consistent with his

---

289 See Filtzer 1986, p. 125; S. Davies 1997, pp. 28–31.

290 Siegelbaum 1988, pp. 168, 155–6, 179–83. On the numbers of Stakhanovites see also Filtzer 1986, pp. 188–9. Writing in December 1935, Sedov clearly did not anticipate how large the movement would soon grow: 'It would be absurd to think that the majority, or even a considerable portion of the working class can become Stakhanovist' (Markin 1936, p. 12). By August 1936 Trotsky recognised that 'hundreds and thousands of workers are suddenly numbered among "Stakhanovists"' (Trotsky 1937, p. 84). By that point, the number of workers enrolled in the movement was already in the hundreds of thousands.

291 See Siegelbaum 1988, pp. 179–83. Siegelbaum also suggests that the historical origins of the labour aristocracies of the West on the basis of 'unique skills' that enhanced their 'bargaining powers vis-à-vis employers' differed dramatically from the origins of the Stakhanovites (Siegelbaum 1988, pp. 168–9). However, for Trotsky it was the function of the movement, not its origins, which was relevant to the analogy. For a broader critique of the concept of 'labor aristocracy', see Post 2010.

analysis, Western research has confirmed the frequent hostility of Soviet workers to the privileges of the Stakhanovites, and it has vindicated Trotsky's prediction that the ranks of the Stakhanovites became an important recruiting ground for the bureaucracy.[292] Nevertheless, it has also documented statements of support for the Stakhanovite movement and for Stakhanovites themselves by non-Stakhanovite workers, as well as manifestations of working-class solidarity organised by Stakhanovites.[293]

Trotsky's analyses of Soviet agricultural policy in this period were even more uneven. It was perhaps reasonable for Trotsky to attribute the introduction of market reforms in agriculture to loosely defined peasant 'pressure' – at least in the form of the low productivity of the collective farms.[294] Also, he was correct in predicting that the reforms would promote the differentiation within and between *kolkhozy* that he had been warning about for years – though his concerns about this continued to be excessive. On the other hand, he was quite mistaken in his belief that the reforms marked the beginning of a far deeper shift to the right, under pressure from the growing layer of well-to-do peasants. In this respect he continued to exaggerate the power of the relatively affluent peasants as well as the leadership's responsiveness to alien class influence.

Regarding international policy, one of the more controversial aspects of Trotsky's thought in this period was his assessment of the French Popular Front. As previously noted, Monty Johnstone and Ian Thatcher are simply mistaken in their assertion that Trotsky depicted the Popular Front as originating entirely in Moscow. Nevertheless, they are right that Trotsky *emphasised* the role of Soviet pressure in bringing about the policy change. In doing so, we now know, he did not fully appreciate the degree to which Thorez independently pressed for the alliance with the Radicals, even against resistance from a section of the Comintern leadership.[295]

Additionally, Johnstone has accurately asserted that 'few historians would agree with Trotsky's portrayal of the Popular Front "lulling the workers and

---

292   On worker hostility to Stakhanovites, see Davies and Khlevniuk 2002, p. 882; S. Davies 1997, pp. 32–4; Filtzer 1986, pp. 200–5; Siegelbaum 1988, pp. 91–3, 190, 196–9, 201. On the importance of the Stakhanovite movement as a source of recruitment for the bureaucracy, see Filtzer 1986, p. 205; Siegelbaum 1988, pp. 266–77.

293   S. Davies 1997, p. 34; Siegelbaum 1988, pp. 192–3; Thurston 1993, pp. 144–6.

294   Sheila Fitzpatrick has characterised these reforms as demonstrating a 'conciliatory spirit towards the peasantry' and as a 'compromise with the peasantry' (Fitzpatrick 1994, pp. 121, 126).

295   See Carr 1982, p. 199; Jackson 1988, p. 37. However, as Haslam notes, Dimitrov, Manuilsky, and perhaps Togliotti were not opposed to the alliance with the Radicals on principle, but only because they viewed it as premature (Haslam 1979, pp. 688–9).

peasants with parliamentary illusions and paralysing their will to struggle" '.[296] He observes that the electoral victory of the Popular Front in 1936 encouraged the strike wave of May to June, Communists played a leading role in organising the strikes – to which the PCF initially 'gave its full support', and in this period the PCF grew dramatically.[297] However, it is also the case that few historians would *disagree* with Trotsky's conclusion that, for the sake of the Popular Front, the PCF did its best to moderate and dissipate the strike movement in June.[298]

A larger question concerns the validity of Trotsky's overall assessment of Comintern and Soviet foreign policy – an assessment closely related to his broader theory of Soviet bureaucracy. Trotsky's claim that the Soviet government and Comintern had been transformed into the '*political agency of imperialism in relation to the working masses*' was an exaggeration that seems inconsistent with his own growing emphasis on the autonomy of the bureaucracy. Yet, the pronouncements by Soviet and Comintern leaders on questions such as French armament, the League, and alliances with bourgeois parties really *were* striking departures from the earlier positions of the Communist International.[299] And while some may have perceived the deferral of revolution as necessitated by the overarching threats of war and fascism, this approach itself represented a major deviation from the traditions of Bolshevism. In fact, the perspective espoused by the Soviet and Comintern leadership in these years resembled in many respects the positions associated with social democracy that the Bolsheviks had similarly denounced as betrayals.

Trotsky's most interesting writings related to the regime in this period included his analysis of the Kirov assassination. In these articles Trotsky produced an account that combined some of the strongest arguments that have been raised on both sides of the contemporary debate regarding Stalin's complicity. That is, he highlighted both the circumstantial evidence that suggested top-level involvement in the assassination, but also the absence of any evidence of significant political differences between Kirov and Stalin. However, it should be noted that Trotsky's analysis was also vulnerable to criticisms that

---

296   Johnstone 1975a, p. 315.

297   Ibid. Johnstone 1975b, p. 349. See also Thatcher 2003, p. 203. On the role of the PCF in the 1936 strike, see for example, Braunthal 1967, p. 436; Brower 1968, pp. 140, 143–7; Claudin 1975a, pp. 201–2; Jackson 1988, pp. 89–92.

298   See, for example, Brower 1968, pp. 147–54; Claudin 1975a, pp. 203–7; Danos and Gibelin 1986, pp. 106–9, 151–4, 170–1; Mortimer 1984, pp. 261–2; Jackson 1988, p. 95.

299   In fact, according to the 'Conditions on Admission' adopted by the Comintern in 1920, the failure to unmask displays of 'social-patriotism' and 'social-pacifism', or to expose such illusions regarding disarmament and the League, were grounds for exclusion (Adler 1980, p. 94).

have been levelled by each side in this debate. (For example, if Nikolaev broke free from NKVD control, why was he not intercepted by Kirov's bodyguards at the Smolnyi? On the other hand, if NKVD officials were part of a conspiracy sanctioned at the highest levels, how could they have been allowed to live for years afterwards when they might have implicated Stalin?)[300] More importantly, simply on the face of it Trotsky's hypothesis of a phoney assassination plot that accidentally succeeded was implausible enough to require far more evidence than Trotsky was able to provide.

In line with his theory, during this period Trotsky portrayed virtually all of major developments related to the state and party regime as largely political in nature, and as directed specifically against the left. In fact, it is now clear that a large majority of those expelled in the party's organisational operations during these years were removed for *nonpolitical* reasons. Still, in their totality the purges matched Trotsky's characterisation of them as 'amalgams' that included both nonpolitical and political categories. And to the extent that the campaigns were politically motivated, the 'Trotskyists' and 'Zinovievists' were important targets. While Trotsky's estimate of the numbers from those two groups that were expelled was high, by the end of 1936 reality had caught up with his calculations.[301] Also, from the emphasis given those groups in official and press reports, it is clear that at least part of the leadership viewed them as far more significant than their numbers suggested.[302] Along these same lines, Trotsky was obviously right that much of the repression following the Kirov assassination was directed against 'Trotskyists' and 'Zinovievists'.

Nevertheless, there is no evidence to support Trotsky's contention in January 1936 that Soviet Trotskyism was attracting a 'mass' of 'new recruits', or that the Fourth International had its 'numerically largest' section in the USSR. In fact, Victor Serge, who was in a better position than Trotsky to evaluate the expulsions, disagreed with him on this point, arguing in May 1936:

> The classifications scarcely have any resemblance to reality. Viewed from close quarters, the vast majority of these so-called Trotskyists are absolutely worthless: informers, alcoholics, part philistine. We certainly

---

300   See Getty 1985, pp. 207–8.

301   Getty and Naumov 1999, pp. 198, 202, 275. By comparison, it seems the number of oppositionists expelled in the 1933 *chistka* was relatively small (Getty and Naumov 1999, p. 127; Getty 1985, pp. 53–4). However, it is worth noting Trotsky's assertion in January 1936 that 'since 1924 the Stalinist clique has preferred to expel Oppositionists as "moral degenerates" and even "White Guards"' (Trotsky 1977a, p. 238).

302   Getty 1985, pp. 66, 68–9; Getty and Naumov 1999, pp. 198–201, 205; Tucker 1990, pp. 311–13; Ward 1999, p. 109. See also Trotsky's conclusions based on press reports, in Trotsky 1977a, pp. 235–6, 237–9, 281–2.

have genuine reserves as big or bigger elsewhere in the party and even outside the party.[303]

Rather, it seems that Trotsky was closer to the mark in his previous suggestion that Soviet 'Trotskyism' in these years was less a matter of 'doctrine' than a 'tradition' of resistance.[304]

Trotsky frequently asserted that the leadership's motive for the repression was to facilitate its 'rightward' shifts in policy. It hardly seems likely that in these years the leadership would have believed that repression was needed to implement its moderating initiatives in either agricultural or international policy. However, the argument was more plausible in relation to the elimination of rationing. Contemporary research demonstrates that there was significant working-class dissatisfaction, and there were even public protests, related to this change.[305] It was reasonable to suggest that the leadership was directing repression against groups that might have mobilised or capitalised upon such discontent.

Trotsky's dismissive attitude toward the 'democratic' provisions of the constitution of 1936 is shared by most contemporary commentators. However, while the tendency of recent analysis has been to emphasise the propagandistic purposes of the document, Trotsky was more inclined to stress its practical implications.[306] For example, he perceived the introduction of the secret ballot and non-party nominations as an attempt by the 'Bonapartist' leadership to reform state institutions against the resistance of lower levels of the bureaucracy. Interestingly, this is consistent with evidence offered by J. Arch Getty that the top leadership's promotion of 'grass roots participation' in the 1937 elections to the Supreme Soviet was resisted (successfully) by local soviet officials.[307] Perhaps the most controversial aspect of Trotsky's constitutional analysis was his criticism of the equalisation of the representation of workers and peasants in the soviets. Trotsky may have been right that peasants would have been more inclined than workers to support social inequality. However, his conviction that the motive of the leadership was to smother proletarian resistance to inequality is dubious. It seems more likely that the salient consideration of the leadership in this regard was propagandistic.

---

303   Serge and Trotsky 1994, p. 60.

304   Trotsky 1977a, p. 240. For appreciative popular statements about Trotsky from this period, see for example, S. Davies 1997, pp. 31, 112, 118, 180, 216n38; Fainsod 1958, pp. 302, 322; Goldman 2007, p. 60.

305   S. Davies 1997, pp. 14, 28–31; Rimmel 1997, pp. 481–99.

306   For accounts that emphasise the propagandistic character of the 1936 constitution, see for example, Tucker 1990, pp. 353–4; Unger 1981, p. 83. An exception is Getty 1991, pp. 18–35.

307   Getty 1991, pp. 28–32.

The Final Theory

From 1933–6, the successive modifications of Trotsky's perspective completely overturned his previous understanding of the problem of Soviet bureaucracy. In its place these changes introduced elements of a new theory, largely based on the Marxist analysis of Bonapartism, which stressed the autonomy of the bureaucracy in relation to all social classes. In August 1936 Trotsky assembled all of these pieces into a coherent whole in *The Revolution Betrayed*, his most comprehensive statement on the problem of Soviet bureaucracy. The theory elaborated in that work would be the one he would continue to uphold until his death in 1940. Trotsky would apply it in a variety of contexts, but most importantly in analysing the Moscow Trials of 1936–8.

8.1   *The Revolution Betrayed*

In the summer of 1935 Trotsky's American publisher suggested to Trotsky, living in exile in Norway, that he write a new preface for a projected one-volume edition of his *History of the Russian Revolution*. Under financial pressures and at the urging of his American translator Max Eastman, he reluctantly agreed. His initial plan was to spend two to three months on the preface, utilising it to summarise his recent writings on USSR. However, in early 1936 he found himself consumed by the project. As he recalled in a letter to his former secretary Sara Weber, 'I became the prisoner of the subject ... I became more and more engrossed in the theme – with frenzy and desperation'.[1] By the time he completed the work in August, it had grown into a book-length manuscript entitled *Chto takoe S.S.S.R. i kuda on idet?* [*What Is the USSR and Where Is It Going?*]. Ultimately, at the suggestion of his French publisher, Trotsky adopted *The Revolution Betrayed* as its final title, demoting the original name to a subtitle.[2]

In terms of its influence as an analysis of Soviet history and politics, the significance of the book can hardly be exaggerated. In 1963 Isaac Deutscher eulogised it as a 'profound political treatise' and as a 'classic of Marxist

---

1   Trotsky 1979b, p. 714.
2   On the history of *The Revolution Betrayed*, see Deutscher 1963, pp. 296, 298; Law 1987a, p. 161; Trotsky 1979b, pp. 664, 714; S. Weber 1972, p. 190.

literature'.[3] In 1977 Robert McNeal described the book as 'a pioneer work in describing the emergence of a new elite in Stalin's Russia', and David Katz depicted it as 'a seminal study which influenced a whole generation of Sovietologists'.[4] Marxist scholar Perry Anderson asserted in 1984 that it 'remains a topical masterpiece to this day'.[5] On the fiftieth anniversary of its publication Richard Day characterised it as still 'an indispensable starting point for any attempt to address the question posed by its subtitle: *What Is the Soviet Union and Where Is It Going?*[6] Furthermore, even since the collapse of the Soviet Union it has remained a popular title in libraries, and has continued to be cited frequently in academic literature.[7]

As far as Trotsky's thinking on the problem of Soviet bureaucracy is concerned, the significance of the work is more ambiguous. In that respect too, writers as diverse as John Plamenatz, C.L.R. James, Baruch Knei-Paz, John Molyneux, Robert Wistrich, David Lovell, and Ian Thatcher have emphasised its importance, depicting it as Trotsky's 'best', 'most complete', 'most comprehensive', 'most sustained', and 'fullest' analysis of the Soviet Union under Stalinism.[8] Yet, scholars such as Siegfried Bahne, David Law, and Ian Thatcher have all insisted that, to a large extent, *The Revolution Betrayed* merely summarised Trotsky's observations from previous years.[9]

In fact, both sets of evaluations are correct. It is true that much of the work restated for a general audience views that Trotsky had expressed since 1933 in the international Trotskyist press. These included a description of the Soviet bureaucracy as a caste, a functional account of the origins of the problem of bureaucracy, the application of the concepts of Thermidor and Bonapartism to the Soviet experience, the portrayal of the bureaucracy's privileges as parasitic, the depiction of the broader privileged layer in the USSR as a labour aristocracy, the characterisation of Soviet international policy as counterrevolution-

---

3 Deutscher 1963, pp. 298, 322.

4 McNeal 1977, p. 35; Katz 1977, p. 294.

5 P. Anderson 1984, p. 124.

6 Day 1987, p. 4.

7 A search of the OCLC WorldCat database on 6 July 2013 turned up 1593 library holdings of all English language editions of *The Revolution Betrayed*, indicating this is a popular title for libraries, according to the 'brief test' methodology devised by Howard White (H. White 1995, pp. 123–9). A search of the ISI Web of Science databases on 6 July 2013 reported 452 citations of English language editions of *The Revolution Betrayed* in 433 scholarly articles during the years 1993–2013.

8 Plamenatz 1954, p. 289; James 1964, p. 25; Knei-Paz 1978, p. 382; Molyneux 1981, p. 114; Wistrich 1979, p. 170; Lovell 1985, p. 36; Thatcher 2003, p. 191.

9 Bahne 1962, p. 40; Law 1987a, pp. 161–2; Thatcher 2003, p. 191.

ary, a revised justification for continuing to describe the USSR as a workers' state, the assertion that the removal of the bureaucracy from power would require a political revolution, and the conclusion that a new party would be required to organise such a revolution.

However, *The Revolution Betrayed* was also a landmark in the development of Trotsky's thinking in a number of respects. Most significantly, it was the first systematic and comprehensive presentation of his views on Soviet bureaucracy since the late 1920s, codifying his recent insights that portrayed the bureaucracy as a highly autonomous social formation. Beyond that, it included a number of important new ideas and emphases. More clearly than before, Trotsky defined and stressed the socio-economic context of Soviet bureaucratisation. In turn, this provided him with a framework for redefining the functional origins of bureaucratic power, for evaluating Soviet policy in all areas, and for sketching the alternative futures confronting the USSR. Other elements introduced at this time included a recognition of the corrupting effects of policies and practices adopted in the early years of the revolution, a closer examination of the essential features of the bureaucratic caste, a description of the Soviet regime as totalitarian, a new explanation of how bureaucratic rule was leading to capitalist restoration, and an attempt to define the programme for the coming revolution.

8.1.1 *Context and Conception*

Perhaps the most significant innovation in *The Revolution Betrayed*, and the most consequential for Trotsky's overall theory, was a discussion of the socio-economic context of Soviet bureaucratisation. The Soviet Union, Trotsky now repeatedly emphasised, was an economically backward society, transitional between capitalism and socialism. Of course in previous years he had commented frequently upon both aspects of this description.[10] However, he never placed these elements so squarely in the centre of his analysis as he did now. He arrived at this new approach through his reflection upon the dynamics of

---

10   For example, one entire volume of Trotsky's collected works published in the Soviet Union was devoted to the '*Culture of the Transitional Period*'. Various statements by Trotsky in the early and mid-1930s on the transitional character of the period and/or Soviet society, can be found in Trotsky 1973c, pp. 204, 205; Trotsky 1973d, p. 278; Trotsky 1972f, pp. 215–16; Trotsky 1972g, pp. 113–14; Trotsky 1971b, pp. 118, 119, 170. During the 1920s the two most famous contributions on the transitional period were Bukharin's 1920 work, *The Economics of the Transition Period*, and Preobrazhenskii's *New Economics* in 1926. For a brief summary of Bolshevik views on the transitional period in the 1920s, see Samary 1999, pp. 153–4.

the Russian Revolution and in response to recent characterisations of Soviet society by the Stalinist leadership.

It is clear that Trotsky's enhanced emphasis on Soviet backwardness was largely inspired by his original effort to write a preface to *The History of the Russian Revolution*. One theme of that work was how a socialist revolution could first occur in a backward country.[11] Trotsky recapitulated his explanation in the first chapter of *The Revolution Betrayed*, depicting the triumph of the Russian proletariat in terms of the laws of 'uneven and combined development'. He argued that uneven international economic development had created a bourgeoisie too weak to resolve Russia's democratic tasks. Consequently, socialisation of the means of production had become necessary 'for bringing the country out of barbarism'. However, backwardness ultimately had exacted its revenge, for the Soviet Union was still attempting, nearly two decades after the revolution, to solve problems of technique and productivity that had been resolved long before by capitalism in the more advanced countries.[12]

This was not to say that the USSR had failed to make substantial gains since 1917. On the contrary, Trotsky again noted the monumental achievements of the first two five-year plans. But he insisted that a balanced view required comparing the productivity of labour attained in the USSR with the levels prevalent in the advanced capitalist countries. Doing so revealed that the Soviet Union still lagged far behind the West.[13] Beyond that, Trotsky emphasised the even greater gap between Soviet productivity and the productivity required for a communist society. In this regard he reaffirmed the traditional Marxist view that economic development under communism should be so high 'that productive labor, having ceased to be a burden, will not require any goad, and the distribution of life's goods, existing in continual abundance, will not demand ... any control except that of education, habit and social opinion'.[14] Of course, Marx had mentioned a lower stage of communism, called 'socialism' by Lenin. However, Trotsky noted that for Marx even such a society would stand 'higher in its economic development than the most advanced capitalism'. Consequently, recent Stalinist claims that the USSR had attained socialism were false. Rather, the Soviet Union remained, as Bolsheviks had traditionally characterised it, a *'preparatory* regime *transitional* from capitalism to socialism'.[15]

---

11   See Trotsky 1977b, pp. 25–37.
12   Trotsky 1937, pp. 5, 6. See also Trotsky 1937, p. 300.
13   Trotsky 1937, pp. 9–20.
14   Trotsky 1937, pp. 45–6.
15   Trotsky 1937, pp. 45–7. The 1918 constitution of the RSFSR described itself as 'designed for the present transition period' during which socialism was to be established (Unger 1981, p. 28).

Trotsky also drew upon the Marxist classics in his definition of the essential nature of the problem of Soviet bureaucracy. He recalled how Lenin had antici-pated in *The State and Revolution* that the proletarian revolution would 'abol-ish the necessity of a bureaucratic apparatus raised above society – and above all, a police and standing army'. On seizing power, the proletariat would 'shat-ter the old bureaucratic machine and create its own apparatus out of employ-ees and workers'. To prevent these workers from turning into bureaucrats, the proletarian state would institute the practical measures outlined by Marx and Engels: election and recall of officials, reduction of their salaries to the level of workmen's wages, and universal participation in the tasks of control and supervision. From its inception then, the dictatorship of the proletariat was to cease being a 'state' in the old sense – a special apparatus for subjugating the majority. Rather, power would be exercised by workers' organisations, and the state apparatus would begin 'to die away on the first day of the proletarian dictatorship'.[16]

For Trotsky, the contrast between this vision and the actual Soviet state could not be more striking. Instead of dissolving in a system of mass participa-tion, the bureaucracy had become a 'hitherto unheard of apparatus of compul-sion' and 'an uncontrolled force dominating the masses'.[17] Never before had 'a bureaucracy achieved such a degree of independence from the dominating class', even in fascist Italy or Germany.[18] 'In this sense', he admitted, it was actu-ally 'something more than a bureaucracy.' It was 'in the full sense of the word the sole privileged and commanding stratum in the Soviet society'.[19]

8.1.2   *Causes*
The socio-economic context sketched in *The Revolution Betrayed* provided Trotsky with a framework for a revised interpretation of the causes of the prob-lem of Soviet bureaucracy. In part, this included a reformulated version of his recent functional argument. In part, it was a recapitulation – with important new emphases and additions – of his historical account of the victory of the bureaucracy over the proletariat in its struggle for political hegemony.

Since 1933 Trotsky had explained the origins of the problem largely in func-tional terms, contending that bureaucratic power was rooted in the struggle of 'each against all' over necessities and articles of consumption. Representing social interests, the bureaucracy had been called upon to harmonise these

---

16   Unger 1981, pp. 49–51. See Lenin 1960–70, vol. 25, pp. 386–7, 395–6, 419–21, 441, 463, 473–4, 481.
17   Trotsky 1937, p. 51.
18   Trotsky 1937, p. 248.
19   Trotsky 1937, p. 249.

conflicts, but had then utilised this responsibility to enhance its own power and privileges. In doing so it had exacerbated social tensions, creating even greater need for regulatory intervention.[20] In *The Revolution Betrayed* Trotsky repeated, 'The social demand for a bureaucracy arises in all those situations where sharp antagonisms require to be "softened", "adjusted", "regulated" (always in the interests of the privileged, the possessors, and always to the advantage of the bureaucracy itself)'.[21]

However, Trotsky now amplified upon this explanation, relating it more directly to the specific functions of a proletarian dictatorship in a backward, transitional society. He explained that the 'fundamental mission' of any proletarian dictatorship was to construct a society 'without classes and without material contradictions'. An additional ' "incidental" task' was the preparation for its own dissolution. Both goals had been implied by Engels in his *Anti-Dühring*: 'When, together with class domination and the struggle for individual existence created by the present anarchy in production, those conflicts and excesses which result from this struggle disappear, from that time on there will be nothing to suppress, and there will be no need for a special instrument of suppression, the state'.[22] The problem, Trotsky observed, was that socialisation of production does not automatically eliminate 'the struggle for individual existence'. Even a socialist state in America, basing itself on the most advanced capitalism, could not immediately provide what everyone needed, and would initially be forced to spur production through the inequities of wage labour. That was why Marx had recognised that 'bourgeois law' would be inevitable in the first phase of the communist society, and why Lenin had asserted that 'under Communism not only will bourgeois law survive for a certain time, but also even a bourgeois state without the bourgeoisie'![23]

From these premises Trotsky reasoned that *any* proletarian dictatorship would have a dual character from its inception: 'socialistic' in its defense of social ownership of production, but 'bourgeois' in its distribution of goods 'with a capitalistic measure of value'.[24] Furthermore, experience had demonstrated that this dual function inevitably affects the structure of the state. Since 'the majority cannot concern itself with the privileges of the minority', to

---

20   Trotsky 1972g, pp. 167, 226–7; Trotsky 1971b, pp. 117–20, 170–1; Trotsky 1979b, pp. 523–4.
21   Trotsky 1937, pp. 49–50.
22   Quoted in Trotsky 1937, p. 52. See Engels 1939, pp. 306–7.
23   Quoted in Trotsky 1937, p. 53. See Marx 1974d, pp. 346–7; Lenin 1960–70, vol. 25, p. 471.
24   Trotsky 1937, p. 54.

defend bourgeois law the workers' state must create 'a "bourgeois" type of instrument – that is, the same old gendarme, although in a new uniform'.[25]

If such 'tendencies towards bureaucratism' would be present in *any* proletarian dictatorship, then they were especially strong in a backward one. Again, Trotsky found an anticipation of this insight in the classics. In *The German Ideology* Marx had asserted, 'A development of the productive forces is the absolutely necessary practical premise [of Communism], because without it want is generalized, and with want the struggle for necessities begins again, and that means that all the old crap must revive'.[26] Trotsky believed that Marx had failed to develop this idea because he did not foresee the possibility of a socialist revolution in a backward county. Even Lenin had been unable to draw all the necessary conclusions because he had assumed that the Russian Revolution would quickly receive assistance from socialist Europe.[27] It was only in the light of experience that Trotsky was able to draw the necessary implications from Marx's warning:

> The basis of bureaucratic rule is the poverty of society in objects of consumption, with the resulting struggle of each against all. When there is enough goods in a store, the purchasers can come whenever they want to. When there is little goods, the purchasers are compelled to stand in line. When the lines are very long, it is necessary to appoint a policeman to keep order. Such is the starting point of the power of the Soviet bureaucracy. It 'knows' who is to get something and who has to wait.[28]

Acknowledging that this explanation suggested that rising material and cultural levels should have undermined privilege, Trotsky offered two reasons for why the reverse had occurred. First, although the early Soviet regime had been far more egalitarian than the regime of 1936, this had been an 'equality of general poverty'. Only later economic growth had made it possible to provide

---

25   Trotsky 1937, p. 55.

26   Trotsky 1937, p. 56. See Marx and Engels 1998, p. 54.

27   Trotsky 1937, pp. 56, 58–9.

28   Trotsky 1937, p. 112. It seems the first person to note the significance of Trotsky's new functional account of the origins of the problem of Soviet bureaucracy was Victor Serge, who was translating Trotsky's manuscript into French. In a letter to Trotsky on 10 August 1936 Serge remarked, 'I was pleased with your radically new formulation on the question of the state. It is a major contribution to theory' (Serge and Trotsky 1994, p. 9) 2. On 19 August Trotsky replied, 'I am very glad about your comments on the theory of the state. I had a feeling myself that I succeeded in clearing up certain points' (Serge and Trotsky 1994, p. 95; for another translation, see Trotsky 1979b, p. 683).

significant privileges for a minority. Second, there had been 'the parallel political factor in the person of the bureaucracy itself'. That is, the bureaucracy had
actively sought to enhance its own privileges:

> In establishing and defending the advantages of a minority, [the bureau-
> cracy] of course draws off the cream for its own use. Nobody who has
> wealth to distribute ever omits himself. Thus out of a social necessity
> there has developed an organ which has far outgrown its socially neces-
> sary function, and become an independent factor and therewith the
> source of great danger for the whole social organism.[29]

In conjunction with this functional account, Trotsky again offered a political
and historical description of the Thermidorian process. Reviewing the history
of Soviet policy debates, he noted the apparent contradiction between the success of the Stalinists and the defeat of 'the more penetrating group', the Left
Opposition. However, he explained that a 'political struggle is in its essence a
struggle of interests and forces, not of arguments'. Underlying the contest in
the party had been shifts 'in the relations between classes', and in the 'psychology of the recently revolutionary masses'.[30] Once more he observed that every
revolution in history had been followed 'by a reaction, or even a counterrevolution', due to the effects of prolonged revolutionary upheaval on the consciousness of the insurgent class.[31] Beyond that, he suggested that the laws of uneven
and combined development had enhanced this tendency in the USSR.
Although backward in many respects, Soviet workers had accomplished 'an
unprecedented leap from a semifeudal monarchy to a socialist dictatorship'.
But when the revolution ran into obstacles, backwardness had reasserted itself
in an inevitable reaction within the proletariat.[32]

   Trotsky reiterated that the reaction had begun as early as the civil war when
leading representatives of the proletariat were either killed or were lifted up
into the bureaucracy. This period of tension, hopes, and illusions ultimately
gave way to 'weariness, decline and sheer disappointment'.[33] Then Lenin's sick-
ness and death eliminated an important adversary of the bureaucracy.
Meanwhile, the introduction of NEP was infusing new confidence into the
petty bourgeoisie, encouraging the bureaucracy to perceive itself as a 'court

---

29   Trotsky 1937, pp. 112, 113.
30   Trotsky 1937, pp. 86–8.
31   Trotsky 1937, pp. 88–9.
32   Trotsky 1937, p. 89.
33   Ibid.

of arbitration' between the classes. At the same time, the bureaucracy's policies were generating a whole series of defeats for the world revolution and wave upon wave of disappointment for the Soviet masses. Relying on the consequent passivity of the advanced workers, as well as the support of backward workers and its petty bourgeois allies, the bureaucracy defeated the Opposition.[34]

An important new element in Trotsky's historical account of the reaction was his emphasis on the negative impact of policies adopted in the first years after the revolution. Leszek Kolakowski has claimed that Trotsky never conceded that his own actions ever contributed 'in the smallest measure to the establishment of a bureaucratic regime', and that he consistently maintained that the banning of oppositional parties and dissident party factions had 'in no way infringed the healthy foundations of proletarian democracy'.[35] Similarly, David W. Lovell has asserted that 'Trotsky saw no inherent dangers in the existence of one-party states'.[36] This is simply wrong. As early as August 1934 Trotsky suggested that the bureaucratisation of the soviets was a 'result of the political monopoly of a single party'.[37] His thinking at that time about the role of political parties may have been stimulated by his recent decision to call for a new party in the Soviet Union. Now it was clearly the official sanctification of one-party rule in the draft constitution of the USSR that led him to emphasise this point.

In *The Revolution Betrayed* Trotsky observed that, despite their original intention to preserve 'freedom of political struggle' within the Soviets, in the civil war the Bolsheviks ended up proscribing oppositional parties in what they viewed as an 'episodic act of self defense'. Then, in a statement that clashed sharply with his ringing defence of one-party rule as a necessary element of proletarian dictatorship in 1920–21, he pointedly noted that this policy was 'obviously in conflict with the spirit of Soviet democracy'.[38] At the same time he recalled how, when 'underground oppositional currents' subsequently began to exert pressure on the only legal party, the Bolsheviks responded with the 'exceptional' and temporary measure of a ban on factions. This too, Trotsky

---

34   Trotsky 1937, pp. 89–92, 96–7.

35   Kolakowski 2005, pp. 942, 943. Kolakowski further asserts that in an article of December 1939 Trotsky reiterated the *correctness* of the ban on oppositional parties. In fact, what Trotsky did in that passage was declare his readiness 'to bear responsibility' for the Bolshevik's actions in proscribing oppositional parties (Trotsky 1973e, p. 133).

36   Lovell 1985, p. 3.

37   Trotsky 1971b, p. 524.

38   Trotsky 1937, p. 96. For his earlier defence of one-party rule, see Trotsky 1972c, pp. 107–8; RKP(b) 1963, p. 351.

admitted, 'proved perfectly suited to the taste of the bureaucracy'.[39] He now recognised that the dynamic had been a destructive one:

> The prohibition of oppositional parties brought after it the prohibition of factions. The prohibition of factions ended in a prohibition to think otherwise than the infallible leaders. The police-manufactured monolithism of the party resulted in a bureaucratic impunity which has become the source of all kinds of wantonness and corruption.[40]

8.1.3   Characteristics: Size, Privileges, Consciousness

Trotsky's detailed examination of the problem of Soviet bureaucracy in *The Revolution Betrayed* provided him with the opportunity to explore internal characteristics of the bureaucracy that he had only touched upon in the past. These included its size, the extent of its privileges, and various aspects of its consciousness.

Although for many years Trotsky had deplored the enormous size of the bureaucracy, his previous estimates had always been quite vague. In 1927 *The Platform of the Opposition* described the 'layer of "administrators" – in the party, the trade unions, the industrial agencies, the cooperatives and the state apparatus' as numbering 'in the tens of thousands'.[41] By the early 1930s Trotsky's estimates were higher, but no less hazy, including references to the 'millions of people' in the Stalinist apparatus, to the 'few million' functionaries, to the 'many millions' in the 'ruling stratum', to the 'multimillioned bureaucracy', and to the 'millions of bureaucrats' who supported the Stalinist tendency.[42] Now, in an effort to provide a more comprehensive analysis, he attempted a more precise estimate.

According to official Soviet figures, as of 1 November 1933 there were 55,000 directing personnel in the central state apparatus. However, Trotsky noted that the state apparatus had grown considerably since then, and that the official number had excluded various departments, the governmental apparatuses of the republics, and the 'the general staffs' of institutions such as the party and trade unions. Making the appropriate adjustments, he concluded that the 'commanding upper circles' of the USSR and its republics numbered between 400,000 and half a million people.[43] Below this layer was a 'heavy administra-

---

39   Trotsky 1937, p. 96.
40   RKP(b) 1963, pp. 104–5.
41   Trotsky 1980b, p. 356; Fel'shtinskii 1988, vol. 4, p. 150 (translation modified).
42   Trotsky 1973c, p. 63; Trotsky 1971c, pp. 213, 215; Trotsky 1973d, p. 227.
43   Trotsky 1937, p. 136.

tive pyramid' that included administrators at all levels of Soviet society: the executive committees of provincial town and district soviets; corresponding bodies in the party, trade unions, Komsomol, military, and secret police; and the administrative and technical personnel of enterprises and of party and trade-union organisations throughout the economy. By Trotsky's calculation then, 'This whole stratum, which does not engage directly in productive labor, but administers, orders, commands, pardons and punishes...must be numbered at five or six million'.[44] This was the bureaucracy in its entirety. Closely bound to this bureaucracy was the other social layer he had begun to focus upon: the 'labor and collectivized peasant aristocracy'. To arrive at an estimate of the portion of the population whose interests were represented by the top leadership, he added the figures for the bureaucracy and the aristocracy and then, treating this entire group as analogous to a social class, also included estimates for their families. From this, he concluded that twenty to twenty-five million people, or 12 to 15 percent of the Soviet population, constituted 'the authentic social basis of the autocratic ruling circles'.[45]

As far as the income of the bureaucracy was concerned, Trotsky believed that it was impossible to calculate this with any precision. In part, this was because even the legal incomes of bureaucrats were carefully hidden. Beyond that, he noted that an accurate figure would have to include the 'immense gifts' received by its members, the funds they embezzled at all levels, and the bureaucracy's 'almost monopolistic enjoyment' of such amenities as theatres and resorts. However, including all of these, he guessed roughly that 15 to 20 percent of the Soviet population enjoyed about the same amount of wealth as the remaining 80 to 85 percent.[46]

Related to its privileges was the bureaucracy's consciousness or psychological makeup. In the context of Soviet poverty, Trotsky suggested, the opportunities for bureaucratic self-enrichment available had generated a common set of attitudes. Among these he once more included acquisitiveness, caste solidarity, fear of the masses, and subservience to Stalin.[47] Again, he also alluded to the 'moral decay of the uncontrolled apparatus'. Citing articles by Rakovskii and Sosnovskii, he observed in this regard that the bureaucracy had acquired distinctly non-proletarian tastes for luxury and for young bourgeois

---

44   Trotsky 1937, pp. 136–8.
45   Trotsky 1937, p. 139. David Lovell is mistaken in asserting that, for Trotsky, the 'families of bureaucrats' formed 'part of the bureaucracy' (Lovell 1985, p. 46).
46   Trotsky 1937, pp. 140–2.
47   Trotsky 1937, p. 139.

women, and had become accustomed to treating the masses with a 'lordly ungraciousness'.[48]

Beyond that, in light of the size and diversity of the bureaucracy he noted variations in the consciousness of its diverse layers and divisions. In this regard he suggested that the contrast between the lifestyles of bureaucrats at the bottom of the pyramid and those at the top, analogous to differences between the habits and patterns of consumption of petty and big bourgeoisie in capitalist countries, had produced corresponding disparities in 'habits, interests and circles of ideas'. He also perceived similarities between the outlooks of the bureaucratic occupational groupings within the USSR and their counterparts in the West. For example, he noted that Soviet trade union leaders exhibited the 'same scornfully patronizing relation to the masses, the same conscience-less astuteness in second-rate maneuvers, the same conservatism', etc. as Western trade-union bureaucrats, and that Soviet diplomats had borrowed not only the tailcoats, but also the 'modes of thought' of Western diplomats.[49]

8.1.4   Characteristics: Policies

Considering an even broader range of issues than in previous years, Trotsky attempted to demonstrate again the divergence of contemporary Soviet behaviour from ideal socialist policy and/or from previous Bolshevik practice. Framing this discussion with his new analysis of the socio-economic context, Trotsky conceded that in each area the deviation had been partially necessitated by the backwardness and transitional character of Soviet society, but part he attributed to efforts by the bureaucracy to maintain and enhance its own power and privileges.

In his discussion of economic policy Trotsky devoted special attention to the issue of inequality. In light of the low level of Soviet productivity and the transitional nature of Soviet society, he admitted that some inequality was unavoidable. For that reason, just as the Bolsheviks had been compelled to retreat from 'socialist distribution' to NEP, the Stalinists had been forced in 1935 to retreat from planned distribution to trade, with its consequent growth of inequality.[50] However, he also insisted that much of the inequality in the Soviet Union had been introduced only to feed the enormous privileges of

---

48   Trotsky 1937, pp. 100–5.

49   Trotsky 1937, pp. 139–40.

50   Trotsky 1937, p. 115.

the bureaucracy. Consequently, Soviet society was 'divided into a secure and privileged minority, and a majority getting along in want'.[51]

Aside from the distinction between the bureaucracy and the masses, Trotsky also noted the growing income disparities within the proletariat. At one extreme were the unskilled workers living in a 'regime of destitution'; at the other were Stakhanovites who received incomes and privileges twenty to thirty times the incomes of lower categories of workers. In terms of inequality in the payment of labour, he asserted, the Soviet Union had actually 'far surpassed the capitalist countries'![52] While conceding that at least some inequality was necessary to spur production, he insisted that the bureaucracy had instituted these extreme material differences only to divide the proletariat.[53]

Even more pronounced was the inequality within the agricultural sector. Although superficially it seemed that 'collective tendencies' had triumphed over 'individualistic' in the collective farms, Trotsky contended that the struggle persisted within the *kolkhozy* themselves. He perceived bourgeois tendencies in the recent transfer of land to the collective farms for their 'eternal' use, in the restoration of private plots, and in the increasingly common – though illegal – renting of land. Together with differences in climate, soil, etc., these all had contributed to differentiation within the village and to the growth of 'a species of bourgeois collectives, or "millionaire collectives"'.[54] Once more, Trotsky conceded that some disparities were necessitated by backwardness: 'To attack the kulak collectives and members of collectives would be to open up a new social conflict with the more "progressive" layers of the peasantry, who are only now, after a painful interruption, beginning to feel an exceptionally greedy thirst for a "happy life"'.[55] However, he insisted that much of the differentiation had been introduced to buttress bureaucratic rule with the support of "Stakhanovists of the fields".[56]

Regarding international affairs, Trotsky asserted that the dangerous situation in which the USSR now found itself had been created by a combination of objective factors (backwardness and isolation) and subjective factors, including the demoralisation of the world proletariat. Of the two, he clearly perceived the subjective as more significant.[57] He placed the primary blame for the

51   Trotsky 1937, p. 116.
52   Trotsky 1937, pp. 124–5.
53   Trotsky 1937, pp. 81, 127–8.
54   Trotsky 1937, pp. 128–34.
55   Trotsky 1937, p. 134.
56   Trotsky 1937, pp. 134–5.
57   Trotsky 1937, p. 190.

deterioration of the subjective factors on the bureaucracy, which 'had brought nothing but misfortunes to the workers' movement of the world'.[58]

Trotsky reiterated that recent Soviet policy in the international arena had been characterised by concessions and compromises with imperialism – some dictated by necessity, but others that were simply unprincipled. Again, he recalled that shortly after the revolution the Soviet government had signed treaties with bourgeois governments.[59] Nevertheless, he maintained that it would never have occurred to the early leadership to portray its capitalist allies as 'friends of peace', or to suggest that Communist parties vote for bourgeois governments.[60] By painting up the episodic allies of the USSR, Trotsky repeated, the Comintern had become 'in reality a political agent of the imperialists among the working classes'.[61] Here he explained this shift in terms of the evolving mentality of the bureaucracy:

> Having betrayed the world revolution, but still feeling loyal to it, the Thermidorian bureaucracy has directed its chief efforts to 'neutralizing' the bourgeoisie. For this it was necessary to seem a moderate, respectable, authentic bulwark of order. But in order to seem something successfully and for a long time, you have to be it. The organic evolution of the ruling stratum has taken care of that.[62]

Concerning the Soviet regime, the largest part of Trotsky's discussion was devoted to the new draft constitution. While much of this simply replicated his comments from recent months, his new observations seem to have been largely inspired by his focus upon the backwardness and transitional character of Soviet society. Of all the provisions of the constitution, he perceived Article 10, which guaranteed personal property, as 'of greatest practical significance in the economic sphere'. Its legitimate purpose, he suggested, was to stimulate labour productivity by defending the property of the masses from seizures by individual bureaucrats. More significantly, it was designed to protect the far greater accumulations of the bureaucracy.[63] Turning to the new election procedures, Trotsky described these as 'an immense step back from socialist to bourgeois principles'. As such, they were not only an obstacle to the revival of soviets; they also created – by 'juridically reinforcing the absolutism of an

58   Trotsky 1937, p. 191.
59   Trotsky 1937, pp. 187–8.
60   Trotsky 1937, p. 188.
61   Trotsky 1937, pp. 193–6, 198.
62   Trotsky 1937, p. 192.
63   Trotsky 1937, pp. 259–60.

"extra-class" bureaucracy' – the political premises for 'the birth of a new possessing class' – that is, for a transition back to capitalism.[64]

In *The Revolution Betrayed* Trotsky depicted the Soviet regime most generally as 'Bonapartist'. In part, this characterisation indicated the large measure of autonomy that the ruling caste had attained; in part, it alluded to the source of that autonomy in the bureaucracy's mediating role, and in part it referred to the extreme concentration of power in the hands of one individual:

> Caesarism, or its bourgeois form, Bonapartism, enters the scene in those moments of history when the sharp struggle of two camps raises the state power, so to speak, above the nation, and guarantees it, in appearance, a complete independence of classes – in reality, only the freedom necessary for a defense of the privileged. The Stalin regime, rising above a politically atomized society, resting upon a police and officers' corps, and allowing of no control whatever, is obviously a variation of Bonapartism – a Bonaparatism of a new type not before seen in history.[65]

Elaborating, Trotsky explained that Stalinism was a variety of Bonapartism, based on 'a workers' state torn by the antagonism between an organized and armed soviet aristocracy' and the 'unarmed toiling masses'.[66] A new element worth noting here was Trotsky's redefinition of 'Stalinism'. Whereas he previously had utilised that term in reference to doctrines and policies, he now applied it to the entire political system characterised by the extreme autonomy of the bureaucracy.[67]

At the pinnacle of this system sat the leader who had acquired enormous autonomy for himself by a process analogous to the emergence of bureaucratic autonomy. Just as the various classes of Soviet society had found it necessary to cede regulatory powers to the bureaucracy, the bureaucratic caste, torn by internal contradictions, had required its own mediator, 'an inviolable super-arbiter, a first consul if not an emperor'.[68] In defence of the interests of the ruling aristocracy, this Bonapartist figure also was 'compelled from time to time to take the side of "the people" against the bureaucracy – of course, with its tacit consent'.[69]

---

64   Trotsky 1937, p. 272.
65   Trotsky 1937, pp. 277–8.
66   Trotsky 1937, p. 278.
67   See Twiss 2010, p. 557.
68   Trotsky 1937, p. 277.
69   Trotsky 1937, p. 271.

An alternative label for the system introduced in *The Revolution Betrayed* was *totalitarian*. That term had been in use for some time, having been coined in the early 1920s by the Italian fascist philosopher Giovanni Gentile. By the late 1920s and early 1930s the popular press and social scientists had begun to employ it in reference to both fascist and socialist parties and regimes.[70] It seems that the first application of the term to the USSR by a partisan of the far left was in a letter by Victor Serge, written shortly before his arrest on 1 February 1933 and published soon afterwards in the French paper *La Révolution prolétarienne*.[71] Trotsky may have picked it up either from the popular press or from a reconsideration of Serge's article.[72]

On a few previous occasions Trotsky had compared aspects of the Soviet regime to those of fascist Italy and Nazi Germany.[73] Besides noting again the 'deadly similarity' between Stalinism and fascism, in *The Revolution Betrayed* he employed the term *totalitarian* [*totalitarnyi*] five times in reference to the Soviet Union.[74] Describing the 'unlimited hierarchy of party secretaries' that reigned in the party, the state, etc., he charged that the 'regime had become "totalitarian" in character several years before this word arrived from Germany'.[75] He observed that, instead of withering, the Soviet state had 'acquired a totalitarian-bureaucratic character'.[76] And, asserting that Stalin's faction had subjected the party to its own apparatus and to the apparatus of the state, he remarked, 'Thus was created the present totalitarian regime'.[77] He did not explicitly define the term, but these passages suggest some of the features he had in mind, including the concentration of enormous powers in

---

70   See Spiro 1968, pp. 106–7; Fine 2001, p. 15791; Linz 2000, pp. 51–2.

71   Weissman 2001, p. 141. In fact, Serge later claimed to be 'the first person to define the Soviet State as a totalitarian State' (Serge 1980, p. 281).

72   The term does not appear in the correspondence between Serge and Trotsky in 1936. See Serge and Trotsky 1994.

73   In his article 'The Class Nature of the Soviet State' on 1 October 1933 Trotsky compared the parasitism of the Italian and German fascist bureaucracies to that of the Soviet bureaucracy (Trotsky 1972g, p. 119). On 20 January 1934 in an article about the Seventeenth Party Congress he remarked that 'in the last period the Soviet bureaucracy has familiarised itself with many traits of victorious fascism, first of all by getting rid of the control of the party and establishing the cult of the leader' (Trotsky 1972g, pp. 223–4). Similarly, on 22 May 1936 in an article on the repression of Oppositionists he observed, 'The concentration camps are now spread over the whole periphery of the country and are imitations of the camps in Hitler Germany' (Trotsky 1977a, p. 325).

74   On the 'deadly similarity', see Trotsky 1937, p. 278.

75   Trotsky 1937, p. 100; Trotsky 1972h, p. 83.

76   Trotsky 1937, p. 108; Trotsky 1972h, p. 89.

77   Trotsky 1937, p. 279; Trotsky 1972h, pp. 229–30. See also Trotsky 1937, pp. 183, 276.

the hands of a single individual, the abolition of popular control over the leadership, the use of extreme repression, and the elimination of contending loci of power. One additional similarity noted by Trotsky was that both Stalinism and fascism shared the same ultimate wellspring: 'the dilatoriness of the world proletariat in solving the problems set for it by history'.[78]

While concentrating his analysis in *The Revolution Betrayed* on economics, international affairs, and the regime, Trotsky also expanded his focus to a broader range of social policies, including policies related to women and the family, Soviet nationalities, and the sciences and arts. These were issues he had last addressed in 1923 and 1924.[79] He now portrayed the reaction that had taken place in each of these arenas as partially necessitated by the backward character of Soviet society, but as more significantly dictated by the interests of the ruling caste.

In the early years of the revolution, Trotsky recalled, the Bolsheviks had attempted to liberate women through a variety of measures, including the socialisation of the traditional housekeeping and child-rearing functions of

---

78   Trotsky 1937, p. 278. Later statements by Trotsky included additional features and alternative formulations. For example, in an article of 1 January 1937 his list of totalitarian characteristics included 'the suppression of all freedom to criticize; the subjection of the accused to the military; examining magistrates, a prosecutor and judge in one; a monolithic press whose howlings terrorize the accused and hypnotize public opinion' (Trotsky 1978, p. 63). In an article of 17 August 1940 he explained that the 'Kremlin oligarchy' was *totalitarian* in character, i.e., subjugates to itself all functions of the country's social, political, and ideological life and crushes the slightest manifestations of criticism and independent opinion' (Trotsky 1973e, p. 348). It is clear that Trotsky's conception of totalitarianism was not the same as that utilised by Sovietologists after the Second World War. For example, Trotsky's concept was far less clearly defined than the best-known model of totalitarianism developed in Friedrich and Brzezinski (1965). Furthermore, it did not share all of the core assumptions of that model. For example, Trotsky would have stressed the importance of ideology far less than Friedrich and Brzezinski, he would have rejected the argument that totalitarianism played a transformational role, and he would have denied that 'central control and direction of the entire economy' was applicable to fascism. Additionally, of course, Trotsky would have rejected the anticommunist perspective of Friedrich and Brzezinski, as well as their characterisation of Leninism as totalitarian, their tendency to depict 'totalitarian' societies as politically monolithic, and their view that totalitarianism is inherently static. Similarly, Weissman 2001, p. 9 has noted the differences between Serge's use of the term *totalitarian* and the understanding of that term as it was employed by the later totalitarian school.

79   In *The Revolution Betrayed* see chapter seven, 'Family Youth and Culture' Trotsky 1937, pp. 144–85. For Trotsky's writings on these questions in 1923 and 1924, see articles in Trotsky 1973a.

the family. In doing so it had run up against the constraints of poverty.[80] However, in more recent years, Trotsky asserted, the reaction in this area had gone much further than necessary. Lacking the resources to provide safe abortions, the Stalinist state had banned them altogether, and then had made a virtue of necessity by extolling the 'joys of motherhood'. At the same time it had initiated a campaign against easy divorces and had begun to glorify the family as the 'sacred nucleus of triumphant socialism'. According to Trotsky these extreme forms of reaction were inspired by bureaucratic interest: 'The most compelling motive of the present cult of the family is undoubtedly the need of the bureaucracy for a stable hierarchy of relations, and for the disciplining of youth by means of 40,000,000 points of support for authority and power'.[81]

Regarding nationalities policy, Trotsky recognised the inevitability of occasional contradictions between the cultural demands of the non-Russian nationalities and the requirements of economic construction during the transition period. Still, he was convinced it was possible, with the 'actual participation' of the nationalities, to reconcile these by distinguishing 'between the legitimate demands of economic centralism and the living gravitations of national culture'.[82] Yet that was precisely where the problem had arisen. Instead of collaborating with the national groupings to establish policy, the bureaucracy had approached 'both economy and culture from the point of view of convenience of administration and the specific interests of the ruling stratum'.[83]

Turning to the sciences and the arts, Trotsky declared that a transitional regime necessarily establishes 'severe limitations upon all forms of activity, including spiritual creation'. Still, he noted that the Bolsheviks had viewed such restrictions as temporary and had never presumed to pass judgment on artistic and scientific questions, even during the civil war.[84] In more recent years the bureaucracy had taken the different approach of conscripting all aspects of culture to justify the regime, the leader, and the latest policies. Regarding art, the bureaucracy's central concern was to present its interests in a manner that would make it attractive to the masses. Predictably, Trotsky observed, the end product was less than impressive: 'In reality, in spite of individual exceptions, the epoch of the Thermidor will go into the history

80   Trotsky 1937, pp. 144–50.
81   Trotsky 1937, pp. 150–3.
82   Trotsky 1937, pp. 170–1.
83   Trotsky 1937, p. 171.
84   Trotsky 1937, p. 180.

of artistic creation pre-eminently as an epoch of mediocrities, laureates and toadies'.[85]

8.1.5   *Consequences*

Since the early 1920s, the fear that had haunted Trotsky was that bureaucratisation could result in capitalist restoration. He emphasised this concern once more in *The Revolution Betrayed*. Again he asserted that the USSR remained a workers' state. Nevertheless, he insisted that neither the proletarian character of the Soviet state nor the transitional character of the Soviet society guaranteed a successful transition to socialism. 'In reality', he concluded, a 'backslide to capitalism is wholly possible'.[86] Specifically, he now suggested that restoration might occur through a Soviet defeat in the coming war or through the efforts of a section of the bureaucracy.

As in the past, Trotsky continued to argue that the Soviet Union was still a workers' state. After repeated modifications of his position, he was now left with just one central justification for this conclusion: property relations as codified by law remained those established by the Bolshevik Revolution. Trotsky explained,

> The nationalization of the land, the means of industrial production, transport and exchange, together with the monopoly of foreign trade, constitute the basis of the Soviet social structure. Through these relations, established by the proletarian revolution, the nature of the Soviet Union as a proletarian state is for us basically defined.[87]

Along the same lines, even though he viewed the bureaucracy as extraordinarily autonomous he insisted that it was not a ruling class for it had 'not yet created social supports for its domination in the form of special types of property'.[88]

In defence of this view Trotsky responded once more to the position that was most popular among critics to his left: that the Soviet Union was now state capitalist. Theoretically, he conceded, it was possible to imagine a system in which an entire bourgeoisie constituted itself as a stock company that owned and administered a national economy through the state. However, such a

---

85   Trotsky 1937, p. 185.
86   Trotsky 1937, p. 254.
87   Trotsky 1937, p. 248.
88   Trotsky 1937, p. 249.

system could never exist in the real world because of the inevitable contradictions that would arise among the proprietors, and because such a state would be 'too tempting an object for social revolution'. Furthermore, he argued that the state capitalist designation clearly did not apply to the USSR where the bureaucracy owned neither stocks nor bonds, where its members were recruited as administrators, where the bureaucratic offspring were unable to inherit the right to exploit the state apparatus, and where the bureaucracy was forced to conceal its income and its very existence as a group.[89]

Still, for Trotsky it was all too possible that capitalism in its traditional form might be reinstated. One route though which this might occur would be through foreign intervention in the coming war. In light of the overwhelming economic and military superiority of imperialism, he predicted that if the war remained only a war a Soviet defeat would be inevitable. And because the existing property forms were so much more advanced than the level of economic development, the result of such a defeat would be a change in property relations. Yet, he professed optimism about the chances of the Soviet Union surviving the conflict, given the 'probability, and even the inevitability' of revolution in a world war.[90]

At the same time, Trotsky pointed to domestic forces that were working toward restoration. In the late 1920s and early 1930s he had believed that the main capitalist threat was the pressure exerted upon the bureaucracy by alien class elements. In contrast, he now saw this danger as arising within the regime itself. To the extent that the regime developed the productive forces, he asserted, it was 'preparing the economic basis of socialism', but to the extent that it promoted bourgeois norms of distribution for the sake of an upper stratum, it was 'preparing a capitalist restoration'.[91] Viewing the situation from this angle, Trotsky concluded that the balance within the USSR was shifting toward capitalism.

An important new insight in this regard was an analysis of how bureaucratic autonomy was subverting the development of labour productivity. Trotsky noted that in an earlier period the bureaucracy had fostered development by imitation, borrowing techniques from the West. 'But the farther you go', he observed, 'the more the economy runs into the problem of quality, which slips out of the hands of a bureaucracy like a shadow'. He explained that in a nationalised economy, 'quality demands a democracy of democratic participation of consumers and producers, freedom to criticise, and initiative'. However, all of

89   Trotsky 1937, pp. 245–6, 249–50.
90   Trotsky 1937, pp. 226–7, 230.
91   Trotsky 1937, p. 244.

these prerequisites were banned as incompatible with a 'totalitarian regime of fear, lies, and flattery'. Thus, Soviet bureaucratism was destroying 'the creative initiative and the feeling of responsibility without which there ... cannot be qualitative progress'.[92] Another factor retarding productivity, according to Trotsky, was the growth of consumerism among the more privileged sectors of Soviet society. He commented that economic progress had been sufficient to stimulate explosive 'petty bourgeois appetites', but inadequate to satisfy them. Consequently, the Soviet Union was now devoting enormous resources to meeting these demands instead of utilising them to enhance productivity.[93]

At least for the time being, Trotsky believed, the bureaucracy was compelled to defend state property both 'as the source of its power and its income' and out of fear of the proletariat. However, in the absence of legally sanctioned property rights, the privileges of the bureaucracy were unstable, and they could not be transferred by inheritance. Consequently, the bureaucracy would eventually 'seek supports for itself in property relations'. If successful, it would become 'a new possessing class' – that is, a new capitalist class.[94]

Trotsky sketched how the process of restoration might appear, both from above and from below. On coming to power, a bourgeois party would need to remove fewer people from the existing bureaucracy than would a revolutionary party. Immediately, it would proceed to promote capitalist relations in agriculture and to denationalise industry:

> First of all, it would be necessary to create conditions for the development of strong farmers from the weak collective farms, and for converting the strong collectives into producers' cooperatives of the bourgeois type – into agricultural stock companies. In the sphere of industry, denationalization would begin with the light industries and those producing food. The planning principle would be converted for the transitional period into a series of compromises between state power and individual 'corporations' – potential proprietors, that is, among the Soviet captains of industry, the émigré former proprietors and foreign capitalists. Notwithstanding that the Soviet bureaucracy has gone far toward preparing a bourgeois restoration, the new regime would have to introduce in

---

92   Trotsky 1937, pp. 275–6.
93   Trotsky 1937, pp. 235–6.
94   Trotsky 1937, pp. 249, 251, 254. In his 1938 work, *The Transitional Program*, Trotsky asserted, 'Each day added to [the bureaucracy's] domination helps rot the foundations of the socialist elements of the economy and increases the chances for capitalist restoration' (Trotsky 1973g, p. 145).

the matter of forms of property and methods of industry not a reform, but a social revolution.[95]

At the same time, Trotsky revived a description he had offered on earlier occasions of how a restoration would appear from the level of an individual enterprise following the disintegration of the regime:

> A collapse of the Soviet regime would lead to the collapse of the planned economy, and thus to the abolition of state property. The bond of compulsion between the trusts and the factories within them would fall away. The more successful enterprises would succeed in coming out on the road of independence. They might convert themselves into stock companies, or they might find some other transitional form of property – one, for example, in which the workers should participate in the profits. The collective farms would disintegrate at the same time, and far more easily. The fall of the present bureaucratic dictatorship, if it were not replaced by a new socialist power, would thus mean a return to capitalist relations with a catastrophic decline of industry and culture.[96]

8.1.6   *Cure*

However, Trotsky still remained convinced that the regime was also continuing in various ways to stimulate the development of forces favourable to socialism. On one hand, the improved economic situation in recent years had increased the self-respect of workers while making it possible for them to devote more attention to 'general problems of politics'.[97] On the other, the process of bureaucratisation had generated growing discontent among the masses:

> The bureaucracy is not only a machine of compulsion but also a constant source of provocation. The very existence of a greedy, lying and cynical caste of rulers inevitably creates a hidden indignation.[98]

For the time being, Trotsky conceded, proletarian struggle against the bureaucracy remained muted. To a large degree that was because the Soviet working class feared that an attempt to remove the bureaucracy might open the door to

---

95   Trotsky 1937, p. 253.
96   Trotsky 1937, pp. 250–1. See also, for example, Trotsky 1970b, p. 300; Trotsky 1973c, pp. 220–1; Trotsky 1972g, pp. 117, 316.
97   Trotsky 1937, p. 285.
98   Trotsky 1937, pp. 284–5.

restoration. However, he predicted that as soon as the workers were able to see an alternative they would rise up to throw out the bureaucracy. For that to occur, it was first 'necessary that in the West or the East another revolutionary dawn arise'.[99] Again, he suggested that the struggle within the USSR might begin as a legal battle, made possible by the constitutional reforms against 'badly working organs of power'. However, for it to succeed it would have to become revolutionary, since 'no devil ever yet voluntarily cut off his own claws'.[100] To prepare and lead that assault required a revolutionary vanguard organisation – the Soviet section of the Fourth International. Although he now admitted that the Soviet section was weak and driven underground, he noted that 'the illegal existence of a party is not nonexistence', and he optimistically proclaimed that violence against a vanguard could never save a caste that had outlived its usefulness.[101]

Trotsky would not predict the precise programme of the coming revolution, which he insisted would depend upon such factors as its timing, the level of economic development the Soviet Union had attained at that point, and the international situation. However, he provided a general outline that combined democratic, economic, and cultural demands:

> Bureaucratic autocracy must give place to Soviet democracy. A restoration of the right of criticism, and a genuine freedom of elections, are necessary conditions for the further development of the country. This assumes a revival of freedom of Soviet parties, beginning with the party of Bolsheviks, and a resurrection of the trade unions. The bringing of democracy into industry means a radical revision of plans in the interests of the toilers. Free discussion of economic problems will decrease the overhead expense of bureaucratic mistakes and zigzags. Expensive playthings – palaces of the Soviets, new theaters, show-off subways – will be crowded out in favor of workers' dwellings. 'Bourgeois norms of distribution' will be confined within the limits of strict necessity, and in step with the growth of social wealth, will give way to socialist equality. Ranks [in the military] will be immediately abolished. The tinsel of decorations will go into the melting pot. The youth will receive the opportunity to breathe freely, criticize, make mistakes, and grow up. Science and art

---

99   Trotsky 1937, p. 286. See also Trotsky 1973g, p. 145.
100   Trotsky 1937, p. 287. See also Trotsky 1973g, pp. 145, 184.
101   Trotsky 1937, p. 288.

will be freed of their chains. And finally, foreign policy will return to the traditions of revolutionary internationalism.[102]

Most significant, and consistent with Trotsky's admission of the corrosive effects of the ban on opposition parties, was his new demand for 'a revival of freedom of Soviet parties'.

8.2   Applying the Theory

The *Revolution Betrayed*, Trotsky's most comprehensive statement on Soviet bureaucracy, marked the essential completion in the development of his thinking on that topic. Of course, it was not Trotsky's final word on the subject of Soviet bureaucracy. Until his assassination in 1940 he continued to defend the theory articulated in *The Revolution Betrayed*, and to utilise that theory to comprehend new developments within the USSR and in Soviet policy. In this regard, perhaps his most important and most interesting writings were those in which he attempted to discern the meaning and motivations behind the Moscow Trials and the Great Terror of 1936–8.[103]

8.2.1   *The Trials and the Terror*
On 19 August 1936 the trial of the 'Trotskyite-Zinovievite Terrorist Centre' convened in the October Hall of the House of Unions in Moscow. In addition to Zinoviev and Kamenev, the defendants included the former Zinovievists G.E. Evdokimov and I.F. Bakaev; the former Trotskyists I.N Smirnov, S.V. Mrachkovskii, and V.A. Ter-Vaganian; and nine others. All were accused of participating in a terrorist conspiracy headed by Trotsky. Allegedly, the centre had organised the assassination of Kirov and had plotted the assassinations of Stalin and other leaders in an attempt to seize power. In this trial, as in all of the Moscow Trials, the prosecution's case was based on the confessions of the accused. Key testimony was provided by E.S. Gol'tsman who recounted how in November 1932 he had met with Leon Sedov in Berlin and with Trotsky and Sedov in the lobby of the Hotel Bristol in Copenhagen. There, Trotsky allegedly instructed him to 'remove' Stalin. On 25 August the Prosecutor Andrei

---

102   Trotsky 1937, pp. 289–90. See also Trotsky 1937, pp. 252–3. For other economic and political demands, see Trotsky 1973g, pp. 145–6.

103   See, for example, Trotsky 1973g, pp. 142–4; Trotsky 1977a, pp. 410–12, 413; Trotsky 1978, pp. 102–3, 121, 188–9, 201–2, 330–31, 336, 348–9, 357, 393; Trotsky 1976b, pp. 28, 112, 204–5, 276, 303; Trotsky 1974, pp. 346–7; Preliminary Commission of Inquiry 1968, pp. 580–5.

Vyshinskii concluded his summary speech with the demand that 'we shoot the mad dogs – every single one of them'. The following day all sixteen defendants were found guilty and were executed. Trotsky and Sedov were convicted *in absentia* for directing the terrorist acts. [104]

Even during the first of the show trials, it was evident from the names implicated that another proceeding would be forthcoming. The trial of the 'Anti-Soviet Trotskyite Centre' opened in Moscow on 23 January 1937 with seventeen defendants. Former leaders of the Trotskyist Opposition among the accused were Piatakov, until recently the Deputy Commissar of Heavy Industry; Radek; L.P. Serebriakov; N.I. Muralov; Ia.N. Drobnis; and M.S. Boguslavskii. Also charged was G. Ia. Sokol'nikov – previously the Zinovievist Finance Commissar of the USSR and then the Deputy Commissar of Light Industry. Most of the other defendants had occupied important positions in the economy and industry, but had never been associated with any dissident political current.

According to the prosecution, this second group, acting on Trotsky's instructions, had established a 'parallel center' distinct from the 'united center', which had directed the sabotage of industry and transport and had plotted to assist a German and Japanese defeat of the Soviet Union with the goal of seizing power and restoring capitalism. The defendants claimed that Trotsky had transmitted most of his instructions to them through Sedov and through letters that were subsequently burned. However, the *Izvestiia* correspondent V.G. Romm also confessed that he had met with Trotsky in Paris in late July 1933, and Piatakov admitted that in December 1935 he had flown from Berlin to meet Trotsky in Oslo. All were found guilty on 30 January 1937. Thirteen were shot the following day; the other four, including Radek and Sokol'nikov, received sentences of eight to ten years.[105]

In a departure from public show trials, a few months later the prosecutions were extended to the Soviet military. In late May M.N. Tukhachevskii, Deputy Commissar of Defense, Ia. B. Garmarnik, chief of the political administration of the armed forces, and several other prominent generals were charged with working as spies for Germany in a conspiratorial bloc led by Trotsky, Rykov, Bukharin, and CC member Ia. E. Rudzutak. All but Gamarnik, who had committed suicide, were convicted in a closed trial on 11 June and were executed the same night. Within nine days of the trial, 980 additional military commanders and high ranking officers were arrested and charged with participation in

---

104   For accounts of this trial, see Report of Court Proceedings 1936; Rogovin 1998, pp. 14–25; Tucker 1990, pp. 367–72.

105   On the second of the Moscow trials, see Report of Court Proceedings 1937; Rogovin 1998, pp. 113–29; Tucker 1990, pp. 394–404, 406–7.

the conspiracy. By the end of 1938, three of out of five of the 1936 marshals of the Soviet Union, all of the commanders of the first and second rank but one, approximately two-thirds of the corps commanders, about 60 percent of the divisional commanders, and roughly half of the brigade commanders were dead.[106]

The series of political trials culminated in early March 1938 in the trial of the 'Anti-Soviet Bloc of Rights and Trotskyites'. The defendants in this proceeding were the most numerous, the most recognizable, and the most politically diverse of all the show trials. Especially prominent among the twenty-one accused were the 'rightists', Bukharin and Rykov. Former Left Oppositionists in the dock included Khristian Rakovskii and the diplomat N.N. Krestinskii. Others charged were faithful Stalinists such as G.G. Iagoda, who had been replaced in 1936 as Commissar of Internal Affairs by N.I. Ezhov; the recent commissars for Agriculture, Finance, Foreign Trade, and the Timber Industry; and the former secretaries of the Belorussian and Uzbek party organisations. The allegations in this trial were also the most fantastic in scope, involving a web of conspiracy that spanned factional boundaries as well as continents, and that stretched decades backward in time. Once more it was claimed that the defendants – under Trotsky's direction and working with Britain as well as Germany and Japan – had established a terrorist group committed to the military defeat of the USSR, the restoration of capitalism, and the dismantling of the USSR. Again, the accused were charged with organising sabotage, a plan to subvert Soviet defenses during a German invasion, and the attempted murders of the top Soviet leaders. Additionally, the prosecution charged that the centre had plotted to arrest all the delegates to the Seventeenth Party Congress in 1934, had murdered the Stalinist leaders V.R. Menzhinskii in 1934 and V.V. Kuibyshev in 1935, and had killed the writer Maksim Gor'kii in 1936. Also, it was now revealed that Bukharin and Trotsky had conspired to kill Lenin in 1918, and that Trotsky had been working for German intelligence since 1921, and for Britain since 1926. All of the accused were convicted on 13 March 1938. Rakovskii and two others were sentenced to extended terms of imprisonment; the remaining eighteen were executed.[107]

Meanwhile, the discovery of 'conspiracies' had unleashed a widening storm of repression throughout the country. In late 1936 large numbers of party members had been expelled for any past association with oppositional groups, and 'Trotskyists' suspected of terrorist activities were shot. In 1937 purges of the

106 Kuromiya 2005, p. 124; Rogovin 1998, pp. 425–47; Tucker 1990, pp. 433–8; Ward 1999, p. 117.
107 On this trial, see Report of the Court Proceedings, 1938; Cohen 1980, pp. 372–81; Rogovin 2009, pp. 39–78; Tucker 1990, pp. 492–503.

state and party apparatuses begun the previous year escalated dramatically. As a consequence, nearly all commissars and regional party secretaries were arrested and shot in the years 1937–40. Additionally, workers were encouraged to denounce the oppositional associations and wrecking activities of their factory managers and union leaders. Large numbers of these officials and of their worker and peasant family members also fell victim to the deepening terror. Beyond that, the repression assumed an even broader scale in the summer of 1937 when, on Stalin's instructions, the NKVD identified a whole series of potentially unreliable groups – including former kulaks, members of 'anti-Soviet parties', former Whites, bandits, criminals, religious activists, clergy, wives of counterrevolutionaries, and various ethnic groups – and set quotas for their arrest. The 'most active' of these elements were to be shot; the 'less active' were to be incarcerated in concentration camps or prisons for periods of eight to ten years.[108] Altogether, according to the best available evidence, during the years 1937–8 approximately two and half million were arrested in the Soviet Union, and close to 700,000 were executed.[109]

8.2.2   *Trotsky's Response*

Since the trial of those accused of killing Kirov, Trotsky had anticipated that there would be further judicial amalgams. In March 1935 he had written, 'Some new stage is being prepared, by comparison with which Kirov's murder was only an ominous portent'.[110] Still, the sweep and the horror of the 'new stage' that emerged in August 1936 exceeded even his darkest expectations. He first learned of the forthcoming trial of Zinoviev and Kamenev on 4 August, shortly after completing *The Revolution Betrayed*. Immediately branding the entire affair *'one of the greatest falsifications in the history of politics'*, he flatly denied participation in any kind of terrorist plot, and insisted that he had not even communicated with anyone in the USSR since his arrival in Norway. At the same time, he called for the creation of an international labour commission and a Norwegian government commission to investigate the charges, pledging his full cooperation with both in advance.[111] However, instead of creating an investigatory commission, the Norwegian government demanded

---

108   For relatively recent accounts of the repression, see Getty 2002, pp. 113–38; Getty and
        Naumov 1999, pp. 272–4, 282, 294, 331–3, 468, 471–9; Goldman 2007, pp. 163–203; Khlevniuk
        1995, pp. 158–76; Khlevniuk 2009, pp. 180–6.
109   Getty, Rittersporn, and Zemskov 1993, pp. 1022–23. For somewhat higher recent estimates,
        see Ellman 2002, pp. 1151–72.
110   Trotsky 1963f, p. 53.
111   Trotsky 1977a, pp. 383–5.

that he cease interfering in the politics of other countries, and then placed him under house arrest when he refused to comply.[112]

Ultimately, Trotsky was liberated by an offer of asylum from the Mexican government. Once settled in Coyoacán in early 1937, he unleashed a torrent of articles, interviews, and a book – *Les crimes de Staline*, responding to the accusations from Moscow, denouncing the trials, and analysing these latest developments. He also promoted the formation of a commission that could investigate the charges, promising that if it concluded he was '*guilty in the slightest degree*', he would place himself '*voluntarily in the hands of the executioners*'.[113] The projected 'counter-trial' materialised in hearings conducted in Coyoacán from 10 April to 17 April 1937 by a Commission of Inquiry headed by the eminent American philosopher, John Dewey.[114]

In his testimony before the Dewey Commission and in other statements during this period Trotsky provided airtight alibis regarding his own activities. He demonstrated that he could not have met Gol'tsman and Sedov at the Hotel Bristol in Copenhagen in November of 1932, since that hotel had burned down in 1917.[115] Against the assertion that he had conspired with Romm in Paris in late July 1933, he proved that he had been closely monitored at that time by doctors and police several hundred kilometers from the French capital.[116] Also, in response to Piatakov's confession of a meeting with Trotsky in Norway in December 1935, Trotsky was able to show that no foreign planes had arrived in Oslo between 19 September 1935 and 1 May 1936.[117] At the same time, Trotsky challenged the essential plausibility of the charges. He noted the prosecution's failure to explain precisely how his alleged terrorism and sabotage were sup-

---

112   See Deutscher 1963, pp. 330–45.

113   Trotsky 1972a, p. 280.

114   On the hearings of the Dewey Commission, see especially Preliminary Commission of Inquiry 1968; Deutscher 1963, pp. 371–82; Poole 1974, pp. 205–471. For other discussions of Trotsky's response to the trials, see Deutscher 1963, pp. 332, 336, 361–82, 386–7, 410–13; Law 1987a, pp. 183–206; Poole 1982, pp. 469–92; Rogovin 1998, pp. 139–46; Rogovin 2009, pp. 111–17.

115   Preliminary Commission of Inquiry 1968, pp. 146, 167–72, 516, 520; Trotsky 1977a, p. 497; Trotsky 1978, p. 97; Trotsky 1972a, pp. 286–7. After the Danish paper *Sozialdemokraten* first published this revelation, the Comintern press discovered a confectioner's shop named 'Bristol' contiguous to the 'Grand Hotel of Copenhagen'. In response, Trotsky quipped, 'Now, where did the meeting really take place? In the vestibule with the "Bristol" or in the "Bristol" without the vestibule'? (Preliminary Commission of Inquiry 1968, p. 520).

116   Preliminary Commission of Inquiry 1968, pp. 189–90, 549–53, 569–70.

117   Preliminary Commission of Inquiry 1968, pp. 210–19, 221–3, 229–30, 534, 563–7, 570; Trotsky 1972a, p. 288.

posed to bring him and his supporters to power.[118] He offered his own volumi-
nous writings and correspondence as evidence of his commitment to socialism,
his hatred of fascism, his continuing defence of the USSR, and his opposition
to individual terrorism.[119] Furthermore, he ridiculed the entire notion that a
serious conspirator would have dedicated so much time to activities intended
merely as a cover, while devoting apparently so little effort to the conspiracies
themselves.[120]

All of this inevitably raised the question of why the accused had dishon-
oured and doomed themselves with such self-accusations. In reply to this
question, Trotsky suggested that the basic premise was faulty, for only those
who had confessed had been allowed to appear in public tribunals. Regarding
those who *did* confess, he did not exclude the possibility that some had been
drugged or tortured – though he considered this unlikely. Rather, he emphasised that they had been subjected to prolonged isolation, interrogations last-
ing days on end, and 'mental torment' inflicted over years. Also, they had
confessed under the threat of certain death for resistance, and with the hope
of salvation for themselves and their family members if they cooperated.[121]

One other factor, according to Trotsky, had been the outlook of the accused.
In general, he dismissed the hypothesis later popularised by Arthur Koestler
that the defendants had offered their confessions as a 'last service' to the
party.[122] Instead, he emphasised that repeated capitulations by the defendants
had weakened their powers of resistance.[123] Beyond that, he blamed the confessions on the inability of the defendants to develop a critical political orientation such as that provided by his own theory of bureaucracy: 'Those on trial
were isolated from the external world, they were not strong enough theoretically to analyze the situation, they lost every perspective, and . . . those on trial
said to themselves, what can we do in this situation'?[124]

---

118   Trotsky 1978, p. 52; Trotsky 1972a, p. 283.

119   See, for example, Preliminary Commission of Inquiry 1968, pp. 257–61, 267–8, 272–3, 277,
      282–9, 310, 313–14, 368–9, 476, 514–15.

120   Preliminary Commission of Inquiry 1968, pp. 577–80.

121   Preliminary Commission of Inquiry 1968, pp. 390, 394; Trotsky 1977c, p. 169; Trotsky 1977a,
      pp. 389, 476, 494–5; Trotsky 1978, pp. 57–8, 96–7, 101, 103, 130, 131, 363–5; Trotsky 1976b,
      pp. 192–3, 205, 249.

122   See Koestler 1941. One possible exception to this, Trotsky speculated, was the civil war
      hero Muralov who, unable to communicate with his former leader, might have concluded
      that his 'critique of the ruling caste' was compromising the defence of the Soviet Union
      (Preliminary Commission of Inquiry 1968, pp. 395–6).

123   Trotsky 1977a, pp. 476–7, 494; Trotsky 1978, pp. 58, 131, 365.

124   Trotsky 1978, p. 365.

Five months after the conclusion of its hearings, the Dewey Commission issued its conclusion that Trotsky and Sedov were 'not guilty' of the charges. Additionally, it concurred with Trotsky that the trials had been 'frame-ups' designed to serve 'not juridical but political ends'.[125] Aside from his direct responses to the charges, most of Trotsky's statements about the trials and the terror were devoted to explaining what those political aims were.

8.2.3 Trotsky's Analysis of the Repression

For the most part, in his analysis of the repression during these years Trotsky focused on the Moscow Trials rather than the larger terror. It is likely that, as the foremost defendant *in absentia*, this would have been his emphasis even if he had been more aware of what was happening. But, as various writers have emphasised, he *could not* have known.[126] Only in later years did outside observers get a sense of the magnitude of the terror. And only since the opening of Soviet archives have we gotten a sharper picture of the repression, including of the social categories that were targeted.[127] Still, as Isaac Deutscher remarked, 'Trotsky knew better than anyone that only a small part of the terror revealed itself through the trials; he surmised what was happening in the background'.[128] Consequently, in August 1937 Trotsky referred to the 'blood purge' through the Soviet Union, and of 'mass shootings, wiping the revolutionary generation from the face of the earth'.[129] And in May 1939 he observed,

> How many have been shot, thrown into jails and concentration camps, or exiled to Siberia, we do not definitely know. But undoubtedly hundreds of thousands of party members have shared the fate of millions of non-party people.[130]

On the most superficial level Trotsky viewed each of the trials as an attempt by the leadership to correct the technical flaws of its previous frame-ups. It had been because the proceedings related to the Kirov assassination had failed to implicate the Left Opposition that Trotsky had repeatedly predicted new amal-

125 Commission of Inquiry 1972, p. 394.
126 Carmichael 1975, pp. 422–3; Deutscher 1963, p. 419; Poole 1982, p. 483.
127 In fact, most current estimates of the extent of the repression are far higher than Trotsky would have imaged, but lower than the highest estimates provided in the years before the opening of the Soviet archives. For discussions of these estimates, see, for example, Getty, Rittersporn, and Zemskov 1993; Ellman 2002; Ward 1999, pp. 132–4.
128 Deutscher 1959, p. 419.
129 Trotsky 1978, pp. 377–8.
130 Trotsky 1974, p. 319. See also Trotsky 1974, p. 346.

gams against the Bolshevik-Leninists. Along the same lines, in August 1936 he depicted the case of the 'Trotskyite-Zinovievite Centre' as 'a new and corrected version of the January 1935 trial'.[131] Subsequently, the flaws in Gol'tsman's account of his alleged meeting with Trotsky and Sedov in Copenhagen convinced Trotsky that another proceeding would soon be needed – a prediction he saw confirmed in January 1937.[132] Shortly after that, he similarly concluded that Stalin would need to organise an additional trial 'to cover up the fatal story' of Piatakov's plane.[133] For Trotsky, that prophecy was fulfilled in 1938 in the case of the 'Anti-Soviet Bloc of Rights and Trotskyites'. Summarising the entire series of hearings, he remarked that Stalin, 'a victim of his own politics', had been 'forced to drink salt water in order to quench his thirst'.[134]

On a deeper level Trotsky more frequently explained the trials and the larger repression in terms derived directly from his theory of the Soviet bureaucracy. In the past he had identified several sets of social and political cleavages directly related to bureaucratic rule, including antagonisms between the bureaucracy and the masses, the fault lines between diverse sectors within the bureaucracy, and the conflicts between the dominant Stalinist clique and the majority of the bureaucratic caste. He now enlisted each of these in his analysis of the repression.

Most generally, Trotsky portrayed the trials and broader terror of this period as directed against the Soviet masses by the ruling bureaucracy in defence of its caste interests. For example, in an interview in July 1937 he stated that 'the very fact of the Moscow Trials is a very important social, historical symptom of sharp conflict between the new bureaucracy and the people'.[135] The following month he wrote, 'The bloody purges, undermining defense, demonstrate above all the ruling oligarchy has entered into irreconcilable conflict with the people, including the Red Army'.[136] Two years later, he reiterated that the 'purges' reflected 'the unbearable tension in relations between the Soviet bureaucracy and the people'.[137]

According to Trotsky, it was this antagonism that ultimately accounted for the targeting of 'Trotskyists' and for the nature of the accusations. As in the *Revolution Betrayed*, he again conceded that the Left Opposition now had no

---

131   Trotsky 1977a, p. 387. See also Trotsky 1977a, pp. 410, 425, 429.
132   See Trotsky 1977a, p. 429; Trotsky 1978, pp. 111, 123, 133.
133   Trotsky 1978, p. 188.
134   Trotsky 1976b, pp. 186, 188.
135   Trotsky 1978, p. 363.
136   Trotsky 1978, p. 393.
137   Trotsky 1974, p. 351. See also Trotsky 1978, p. 378; Trotsky 1976b, pp. 302–3; Trotsky 1973e,
       p. 19.

real, mass following in the USSR. In fact, in January 1937 he wrote only of the 'hundreds of genuine Trotskyists' in the Soviet Union, all of whom were in prison or internal exile.[138] However, he perceived that in the language of the bureaucracy the term 'Trotskyism' had become a 'catchall concept, encompassing everything deserving extermination'.[139] As the privileges of the ruling caste grew, he explained, the bureaucracy had found it increasingly necessary to suppress the growing popular aspirations for freedom and equality most clearly articulated by the Opposition. Since it could not punish its critics explicitly for raising these demands, it had charged the Opposition with crimes against the people in order to compromise all of its opponents in the eyes of the masses.[140] In some statements Trotsky also contended that the accusations of sabotage were designed to divert mass dissatisfaction over industrial catastrophes caused by the excessive speedups associated with Stakhanovism and bureaucratic mismanagement.[141] At other times he painted the conflict between the bureaucracy and the masses on an international canvas, arguing that the trials were directed against the movement for a Fourth International because its successes were undermining Stalin's 'political authority before the workers' and the appeal of the Comintern as a tool of 'the new privileged caste'.[142]

After the first of the trials, growing numbers of officials who never had been associated with any dissident grouping began to appear in the dock. At that point Trotsky increasingly began to attribute the trials and the broader terror to conflicts between different bureaucratic groupings located on a left-right continuum. He explained to Max Shachtman in March 1938, 'Very important are the internal antagonisms in the bureaucracy; the trials are a direct expression of that; part of the bureaucracy exterminated another part'.[143] On the basis

138   Trotsky 1978, p. 112. In a discussion with American supports in March 1938, Trotsky spoke of the 'Trotskyist' tendencies among the masses that were directed against the bureaucracy. However, he noted that, although their attitude coincided with that of the Opposition, these were 'not real Trotskyists' (Trotsky 1976b, p. 304). Also, in April 1938 he admitted that 'as an organization, ... "Trotskyism" is extremely weak in the USSR' (Trotsky 1973g, p. 144).

139   Trotsky 1978, p. 347. See also Trotsky 1978, p. 280.

140   Trotsky 1977a, pp. 473–4; Trotsky 1978, pp. 102, 121; Trotsky 1976b, p. 57; Trotsky 1974, p. 347; Preliminary Commission of Inquiry 1968, pp. 581–2. In this respect, he noted, its accusations closely paralleled the charges by French Thermidorians against Robespierre and his supporters (Trotsky 1972a, pp. 292–3).

141   See Trotsky 1978, pp. 150, 169, 171, 172; Trotsky 1976b, p. 396.

142   Trotsky 1977a, pp. 410–11, 478. See also Trotsky 1977a, pp. 480–1; Preliminary Commission of Inquiry 1968, p. 583.

143   Trotsky 1976b, p. 303.

of political positions adopted by a number of high-level defectors, Trotsky discerned 'a rainbow of all political colors' within the bureaucracy: revolutionary elements, which he saw as 'a small minority'; bourgeois democrats; and fascists, a current he perceived as 'growing uninterruptedly'.[144] As he described it, these groupings had arisen in response to both extra-bureaucratic pressures and internal bureaucratic impulses. In March 1938 he argued that popular dissatisfaction had given rise to one current advocating concessions and another opposing them.[145] The following month he asserted that the few 'revolutionary elements' within the bureaucracy reflected 'the socialist interests of the proletariat', while the increasing numbers of fascist and counterrevolutionary elements represented 'the interests of world imperialism'.[146] At the same time, in line with his recent analysis in *The Revolution Betrayed*, Trotsky suggested that the rightist current sought capitalist restoration out of self-interest. Although he perceived Stalin's clique as fearful of the rightist section of the bureaucracy, he viewed it as allied with that current 'in the interests of self-preservation' against all of the groupings to its left.[147]

A third set of cleavages that Trotsky perceived as relevant was the antagonism between the mass of the bureaucracy, or sections of it, and the small Stalinist clique at the summit. In the past he had observed that Stalin – acting either in his own interests, or on behalf of the bureaucracy – occasionally came into conflict with the majority of the bureaucracy. At times, he had suggested, Stalin even sided 'with the people' in these conflicts. Along these lines, he explained in February 1937 that in the second Moscow trial Stalin, fearing his own isolation from the bureaucracy, had begun 'terrorizing the bureaucracy itself', while 'trying to play the people along' with 'demagogic trials'.[148] Directed against a section of the bureaucracy was the trial of the generals – organised because Stalin feared that 'from the midst of the bureaucracy itself, especially from the army, opposition to his Caesarist plans will arise'.[149] Yet another

---

144   Trotsky 1976b, pp. 275–6, 302–5; Trotsky 1973g, p. 143. The Bolshevik-Leninist position was
       represented for Trotsky by Ignace Reiss, a defector from the NKVD, who was communicat-
       ing with Leon Sedov at the time of Reiss's assassination. Trotsky also described Aleksandr
       Barmin, previous Soviet *charge d'affairs* in Greece, as 'friendly' to the Fourth International.
       He viewed Val'ter Krivitskii, former chief of Soviet military intelligence in Western Europe,
       as a bourgeois democrat. Fëdor Butenko, a Soviet diplomat who had been stationed in
       Rumania, he characterised as a 'fascist'.
145   Trotsky 1976b, p. 303.
146   Trotsky 1973g, p. 143.
147   Ibid.
148   Trotsky 1978, p. 189.
149   Trotsky 1978, p. 349. See also Trotsky 1978, pp. 330–1; Trotsky 1976b, pp. 205, 444–5.

example was the 'bloody crusade against all the "nationalist" heads of all the Soviet republics' in late 1937. This time, it seems it was the repressed section of the bureaucracy that was aligned with the people, for Stalin had 'decapitated' the republics out of fear that their populations would 'give political expressions to their discontent' in the upcoming elections to the Supreme Soviet.[150] A final indication of Stalin's conflict with the bureaucracy was a warning directed by Vyshinskii in early 1939 against local party secretaries, investigating magistrates, prosecutors, and judges who had engaged in 'illegal persecutions' and 'forced confessions'. According to Trotsky, the problem for the Stalinists in this case was simply that local officials had imitated Stalin, 'democratizing' the frame-up system and utilising it for their own purposes. In so doing, they had exposed Stalin's methods to the entire public.[151]

In an argument that combined all three sets of cleavages, Trotsky frequently depicted the trials as an assault upon the revolutionary traditions of Bolshevism. During the first Moscow trial, noting that every member of Lenin's Politburo except Lenin and Stalin had been charged with terrorism and conspiracy, he concluded, 'The political objective of this trial is the complete extermination of the old Bolshevik Party, its traditions, and its program'.[152] Even more sharply, after a year of show trials and executions he asserted, 'The present purge draws between Bolshevism and Stalinism not simply a bloody line but a whole river of blood'.[153] In other writings he referred to the 'extermination of the old generation of Bolsheviks', the wiping of 'the revolutionary generation from the face of the earth', the 'direct *civil war* against Bolshevism', and the exterminating of 'the old generation of Bolsheviks, and from the subsequent generations all those who were morally connected with the tradition of the Bolshevik Party'.[154] As Trotsky perceived it, for the bureaucracy as a whole the problem with Bolshevism was that its ideals continued to fuel popular discontent. 'Even within the narrow ranks of the bureaucracy', the 'old traditions' had contributed to the development of 'friction and criticism'. For Stalin, the heritage of Bolshevism rendered 'thousands upon thousands' of bureaucrats 'less and less suitable' as his supporters.[155] Additionally, Trotsky noted that the USSR's association with Bolshevism was proving to be an obstacle to Stalin's projected alliances with imperialism.[156]

---

150 Trotsky 1976b, p. 46. See also Trotsky 1976b, p. 130.
151 Trotsky 1974, pp. 214–15.
152 Trotsky 1977a, p. 406.
153 Trotsky 1978, p. 423.
154 See Trotsky 1978, pp. 280, 377–8, 424; Trotsky 1974, p. 347. See also Trotsky 1976b, p. 132.
155 See Trotsky 1978, pp. 348, 378; Trotsky 1976b, pp. 132, 205.
156 Trotsky 1977a, pp. 410–11, 414.

Regardless of the motivation, for Trotsky the social and political consequences of the Moscow Trials were enormous. In June 1937 he speculated upon the impact the proceedings were having upon the Soviet economy:

> The engineers in the planning institutions, the directors of trusts and factories, the skilled workers, are all in mortal fear. No one wants to assume responsibility. Everybody is afraid to show any initiative.[157]

In the same article he suggested that the trials were discrediting the government internationally, especially in Berlin and Tokyo where it was immediately understood that the charges were fabricated and where it was recognised that the Soviet leadership, 'waging internal warfare', was 'therefore incapable of external resistance'.[158] The following year he also observed that, by relying on careerists while executing dedicated revolutionaries, Stalin had greatly weakened 'the moral strength of the resistance of the country as a whole'.[159]

Trotsky was convinced that the ultimate victim of the trials would be the Stalinist regime. Soon after the second trial he expressed a conviction he would repeat several times: 'It is the beginning of the downfall of Stalinism'.[160] However, he was uncertain about just how this would occur. In his more optimistic statements he predicted that the trials would provoke an intensification of the struggle of the masses against the bureaucracy – a contest in which *'victory will inevitably go to the people'*.[161] On the other hand, he believed that the extermination of the Old Bolsheviks and younger revolutionary elements had disrupted 'the political equilibrium still more in favor of the right, bourgeois wing of the bureaucracy'.[162] If this development facilitated the birth of a new property-owning class, then the rising forces of counterrevolution could turn on Stalin because of his past ties with Bolshevism. In the process, Stalin might even find himself charged with 'Trotskyism'.[163]

A final development in Trotsky's thinking precipitated by the Moscow Trials was his revision of his position regarding the significance of the old right wing of the party. Beginning in the late 1920s, he had depicted the rightists as transmitters of bourgeois influence into the party. For that reason he had repeatedly

---

157   Trotsky 1978, p. 325. See also Trotsky 1973e, p. 200.
158   Trotsky 1978, p. 326. See also Trotsky 1979b, p. 735.
159   Trotsky 1976b, p. 262.
160   Trotsky 1978, p. 208. See also Trotsky 1978, pp. 189, 282, 331–2, 336, 349; Trotsky 1976b, pp. 252, 264; Trotsky 1972a, pp. 293–4.
161   Trotsky 1976b, p. 205. See also Trotsky 1976b, pp. 101, 264, 271; Trotsky 1978, pp. 304, 330.
162   Trotsky 1973g, p. 144.
163   Trotsky 1978, pp. 330–1. See also Trotsky 1978, p. 429; Trotsky 1976b, pp. 100, 252.

pledged his readiness to unite with the Stalinists to defeat them. Now he concluded that, as representatives of the old Bolshevism under assault by the bureaucracy, these 'rightists' were actually closer to the Left Opposition than were their persecutors. In April 1938 he wrote,

> The latest judicial frame-ups were aimed as a blow *against the left*. This is true also of the mopping up of the leaders of the Right Opposition, because the right group of the old Bolshevik Party, seen from the viewpoint of the bureaucracy's interests and tendencies, represented a *left* danger.[164]

Although this shift was caused most immediately by the trial and execution of Bukharin and Rykov, it was also consistent with Trotsky's general understanding of the problem of Soviet bureaucracy in the mid-1930s, which viewed the greatest threat of restoration as emanating more from the 'interests and tendencies' within the bureaucracy than from external class pressures.

8.3   Conclusion

Trotsky's *The Revolution Betrayed* represented the culmination of the development of his thinking on the problem of Soviet bureaucracy, and contained the most complete and coherent statement of his later views on the subject. The concluding chapter of this book will attempt an evaluation of the general theoretical perspective presented in that work. This section will briefly consider some of the strengths and weaknesses of Trotsky's attempts to apply his final theory to the Moscow Trials and the Great Terror. In terms of both predictive and explanatory power, his analysis of those events was impressive, but uneven.

Remarkably, in statement after statement Trotsky managed to foretell each of the major show trials. However, it should be noted that all of these predictions were based primarily on technical failures he perceived in the preceding frame-ups, rather than on a more general political analysis. Even in his 1935 warnings about the 'new stage' of Stalinism and the approaching 'new frontier' of Stalin's dictatorship, there was no premonition of the magnitude or horror of the coming storm. Furthermore, despite its subtitle, *The Revolution Betrayed* – completed on the eve of the first trial – contained no real anticipa-

---

164   Trotsky 1973g, p. 143.

tion of where the USSR was going in this regard.[165] On the other hand, Trotsky's theory provided him with a number of important insights that proved useful for analysing the trials and the larger repression once these had begun. In fact, some of Trotsky's insights have been incorporated into Western studies of the Great Terror only in recent decades.

Among Western scholars, contributions to the study of the repression of the 1930s have been dominated by two approaches: the analyses of the 'totalitarian school', and those of the 'revisionists'. Beginning in the 1950s, proponents of the totalitarian school attributed the terror entirely to Stalin as the only actor of significance, who instituted the repression out of a lust for power or paranoia. Also, they commonly depicted the terror as grounded in the ideology and traditions of Bolshevism. In reaction to this camp, during the 1980s and 1990s 'revisionist' scholars developed an approach that emphasised the complexity of the terror, the role of diverse groups in promoting it, the relevance of the social and political climate in shaping the perceptions and actions of these groups, and even manifestations of popular initiative or participation in the process.[166]

Perhaps partly due to Trotsky's use of the term *totalitarian* to characterise Stalinism in this period, a number of writers have equated a 'Trotskyist' analysis of the trials and terror with accounts provided by the totalitarian school. For example, J. Arch Getty and Roberta Manning have contended that, consistent with the totalitarian school's approach, for 'Trotskyists' an 'omniscient and omnipotent Stalin' explained 'their political defeat at the hands of an incredibly cunning dictator'.[167] Similarly, Wendy Goldman has asserted that, along with proponents of the totalitarian school, 'Trotskyists' have argued that 'the terror was strictly a top-down affair, launched and managed by Stalin'.[168] In fact, Trotsky's own writings on the trials and terror do not fit comfortably in either the 'totalitarian' or the revisionist camp. However, the differences between his approach and that of the totalitarian school are especially striking, and in a number of respects, his analysis anticipated interpretations more recently offered by the revisionists and their successors.

---

165   Trotsky 1963f, pp. 53, 144.

166   Two of the more significant works on the Great Terror by members of the totalitarian school include Armstrong 1961; and Conquest 1973. A similar approach is taken in Solzhenitsyn 1974–78. Important revisionist works on the terror include Getty 1985; Rittersporn 1991; and contributions in Getty and Manning 1993.

167   Getty and Manning 1993, p. 14.

168   Goldman 2011, pp. 4–5. Goldman specifically cites Rogovin 2009. See also Ward 1999, p. 124.

Of course, Trotsky would have perceived as absurd the suggestion by proponents of the totalitarian school that the terror was related to the principles of Marxism-Leninism. Furthermore, like the contemporary revisionists, Trotsky offered an interpretation which portrayed the terror as a multifaceted phenomenon with diverse social origins. It is true that he stressed Stalin's role in initiating the repression. This was an estimation that has been largely confirmed by evidence from the Soviet archives.[169] However, he also argued that the trials and aspects of the terror were instituted not only in Stalin's interest, but also on behalf of a variety of social and political groups, including the bureaucracy as a whole, the Stalinist layer at the pinnacle of power, bureaucratic currents on the right of the political spectrum, and groupings of officials at the base of the political system. At times, Trotsky even perceived elements of popular support for the repression – hence the 'demagogy' of the trials.

Although Trotsky's analysis of the Moscow Trials and Great Terror was multilayered, complex, and often insightful, aspects of his interpretation were clearly quite flawed. In part, this may have been due to his lack of information, but it can also be explained by the distorting effects of his theory. First, there is no evidence that the supporters of the repression within the state and party apparatuses viewed the prospect of capitalist restoration more positively than did many of its victims. In fact, the selection of former kulaks and former Whites as main targets for elimination suggests just the opposite. One source of this error on Trotsky's part seems to have been his continuing inclination, even after his theoretical revisions of 1933–6, to perceive increases in repression as directly related to rightward shifts in policy or rightist tendencies within the leadership. A second error was Trotsky's assertion that the trials represented a response by the bureaucracy to the successes of his movement for a Fourth International. The repression of the 1930s was certainly introduced by the leadership to counter a variety of oppositional threats. However, it was simply implausible to suggest that events as momentous as the Moscow Trials were specifically designed to combat Trotsky's tiny organisation – which, despite modest successes, numbered no more than a few thousand adherents.[170] At least in part, it was the importance attached to that movement by Trotsky's theory that led him to exaggerate its practical significance. A third apparent error was his contention that 'the old generation of Bolsheviks' was a

---

169   See, for example, Getty and Naumov 1999, pp. 444–90, 571–86.

170   Isaac Deutscher reports that, at the time of the founding of the Fourth International in
       1938, its eleven sections 'consisted of a few dozen, or at most, a few hundred members
       each', and that 'this was true even of the American section, the most numerous of all
       [which had a membership between 800 and 2,500]' (Deutscher 1963, p. 420).

specific target of the repression. If by this he meant 'Old Bolsheviks' – that is, individuals who joined the Bolshevik party before 1917 – he seems to have been mistaken. Contemporary studies based on the available statistical evidence suggest that Old Bolsheviks were not targeted specifically *as* Old Bolsheviks.[171] On this point Trotsky, along with many other observers then and since, may have been misled by the large numbers of Old Bolsheviks who appeared as defendants in the Moscow Trials and by the numbers of party members who were purged because of their previous dissident views or because of their rank in the bureaucracy, rather than because of their status as Old Bolsheviks.[172] Beyond that, in Trotsky's case this error was no doubt reinforced by his earlier conclusion that Stalinism was the sworn enemy of true Bolshevism.

A final deficiency of Trotsky's analysis of the repression was related to its complexity. While his writings on this subject contained numerous insights, including a rich appreciation of the complex processes and motivations at work, these were never drawn together into one coherent whole that explained which processes and motivations were paramount for which aspects of the terror, why a specific process or motivation was important at any given time, or how these diverse elements were related to one another. In this regard, Thomas R. Poole has appropriately observed, Trotsky 'did not bring to "full conclusion" or completely join together his many observations on Stalin and the purge'.[173]

---

171   See Getty and Chase 1978, p. 108; Chase and Getty 1989, pp. 205–6, 221; and Getty and Chase 1993, pp. 235–6. However, if Trotsky was referring more generally to those who joined before the end of the civil war, the same evidence suggests he was more correct.

172   For international observers who concluded at the time that the Old Bolsheviks were a target, see the sources cited by Flewers 2008, p. 254n247. For a list of some contemporary writers who assert this, see Getty and Chase 1978, p. 106 n1.

173   Poole 1982, p. 487.

Reconsidering Trotsky's Theory

Over the years, Trotsky broadly defined the problem of Soviet bureaucracy in three different ways: as one of inefficiency in military supply and the economy, in terms of the independence of the state and party apparatuses from proletarian control and their responsiveness to alien class pressures, and as a distinct social formation that had attained a high degree of autonomy from all social classes. At each point his understanding of the issue was shaped by his own major concerns at the time, by his previous image of bureaucracy, and by his analysis of current events. At the same time, throughout these years his political activities as well as his analysis of Soviet politics, society, and history were largely guided and shaped by his evolving understanding of the general nature of the problem of bureaucracy.

9.1   The Development of Trotsky's Views

In the years immediately after the revolution, most Bolsheviks derived their conception of bureaucracy from the primary popular understanding of that term, and from the traditional Marxist analysis of that concern. Consequently, they viewed the problem of Soviet bureaucracy in terms of the alienation of political institutions from the masses and as directly related to the presence of bourgeois influence in the state apparatus. In that period, Trotsky perceived the problem quite differently. Largely preoccupied with the effective operation of the war machine and of the economy, and drawing upon popular secondary meanings of the term, he defined the problem of bureaucracy almost exclusively as one of inefficiency. During the civil war and immediately afterwards, he focused especially on the phenomenon of *glavkokratiia* – an inefficient system characterised by an excessive concentration of economic power in the industrial *glavki* and *tsentry* and by the inadequate coordination of those bodies. This understanding influenced his policy choices and his political behaviour in several important ways. Most immediately, it led him to emphasise the importance of economic planning – a concern that would become a lifelong preoccupation – and to support an increase in the autonomy permitted to enterprises and local economic organs. Additionally, it impelled him to dismiss the value of Lenin's primary institutional solution for the problem of bureaucracy, the Workers' and Peasants' Inspectorate. However, it also helped bring him into an anti-bureaucratic alliance with Lenin in late 1922.

Beyond that, Trotsky's emphasis on economic planning as a means of eliminating *glavkokratiia* contributed greatly to his development of a new understanding of the problem of bureaucracy in 1923. Facing continued opposition by the leadership majority to enhanced economic planning, even after it had been endorsed by the Twelfth Party Congress, Trotsky began to see this resistance as a manifestation of political alienation. The problem, he argued, was that market forces and alien class pressures, as well as the specialisation of officials, were pushing the state and party leadership to the right. The danger was that the increasing separation of the party leadership from the control of the rank and file would further promote this rightward drift. Again, his analysis of the problem played a major role in guiding his political behaviour, leading him in late 1923 into oppositional activity on behalf of party democracy, largely as a means of changing economic policy.

Although he was defeated in that struggle, Trotsky returned to the political and theoretical offensive in 1926–7 with the formation of the United Opposition. In those years his perception that the party regime had continued to deteriorate and that both economic and international policy had moved further to the right increasingly convinced him of the direct relationship between bureaucratisation and the responsiveness of the state and party apparatuses to alien class pressures. In line with this, he put forward a comprehensive and coherent theory of Soviet bureaucracy based entirely upon that understanding. Even more sharply than before, he asserted that a shift in the balance of class forces had pressured the leadership into implementing rightist policies while repressing workers' democracy. Ultimately, he warned, this process could culminate in capitalist restoration – most likely by a gradual and phased 'Thermidorian' route. Only the Opposition, he argued, representing the proletarian vanguard, could reform the party by pushing it back to the left and compelling a restoration of workers' democracy.

In late 1927 the Opposition was beaten and thousands, including Trotsky, were sent into internal exile. However, this was followed, not as Trotsky had anticipated, by a strengthening of the party right and the restoration of capitalism, but by a series of 'leftist' initiatives in economic and Comintern policy and by the defeat of the right wing of the party leadership by the Stalinist centre. Continuing to insist upon the validity of his theory, Trotsky attempted to reconcile the contradictions between theory and reality by means of a series of ad hoc theoretical modifications and strained interpretations of events. While increasingly emphasising the autonomy of the state and party apparatuses, he tended to downplay the significance of the policy changes, and to explain these in terms of proletarian and/or Oppositional pressure. Furthermore, his theory led him to predict that, unless the left turns were supplemented by additional Oppositional pressure, they would quickly collapse.

Still, between late 1929 and early 1933 Trotsky perceived an even sharper shift to the left in the leadership's dramatic acceleration of industrialisation, its mass collectivisation and dekulakisation campaigns, and its deepening of the Comintern's Third Period line. He also noted that, while repressing dissidents of all persuasions, the leadership had inaugurated a cult of public adulation for Stalin. Trotsky denounced all of these innovations as sharply as he had criticised the policies of earlier years. At the same time, even more than before, he was compelled to stretch the limits of his old theory by ad hoc theoretical modifications that emphasised the bureaucracy's autonomy. Nevertheless, he continued to assert the responsiveness of the bureaucracy to alien class pressures. The result was an analysis that seemed both increasingly divorced from reality and increasingly incoherent.

The event that precipitated a radical revision of Trotsky's perspective was Hitler's conquest and consolidation of power – a development that for Trotsky represented a failure of Comintern policy as profound as the capitulation of the Second International at the outset of World War I. Trotsky's consequent break with the KPD initiated a chain reaction that overturned or modified a whole series of his other positions, in each case reinforcing his appreciation of the autonomy of the bureaucracy. Subsequently, Trotsky utilised these insights to analyse new shifts in Soviet economic and international policy, new developments in the party regime, and the wave of repression unleashed by the leadership following the Kirov assassination. Reciprocally, these interpretations of policy developments led him to initiate another round of theoretical modifications that in 1936 culminated in his call for a political revolution in the USSR.

Trotsky's new theory of bureaucracy ultimately received its most complete expression in his major theoretical work on the subject, *The Revolution Betrayed*. In that book Trotsky defined the bureaucracy as a social entity that had attained unprecedented independence from society as a whole, as well as from all social classes. His most important innovation was a discussion of the problems of a backward, transitional society. That notion provided a context for his reformulated account of the functional origins of bureaucratic power, a framework for evaluating Soviet policies in all spheres, and a basis for his stark identification of political revolution and capitalist restoration as the two alternatives confronting the USSR. Until his death in 1940, Trotsky utilised this theory to analyse a number of new developments, but most importantly to explain the sources and dynamics of the Moscow Trials.

9.2   Evaluating the Theory

A thorough evaluation of Trotsky' final theory of Soviet bureaucracy would require another volume at least as large as this one. Nevertheless, a few observations might be appropriate as a contribution to that discussion. Although Trotsky's ultimate theory contained a number of important deficiencies and weaknesses, it represented a significant advance over his earlier views. Virtually every aspect of the theory was both more plausible and more developed than his perspective in the late 1920s and early 1930s. In fact, in many respects Trotsky's final theory remains an important tool for understanding both Soviet history and the realities of post-Soviet Russia.

9.2.1   *Conception*

Trotsky's remarks concerning *glavkokratiia* and other forms of bureaucratic inefficiency in the first years of Soviet power had been useful for identifying specific problems in the organisation of military supply and the economy. However, they were largely irrelevant to the deeper political issues already confronting the Soviet Union. Even worse, they were advanced largely in *opposition* to the critical observations of other Bolsheviks more immediately concerned with the phenomenon of political alienation as described in the Marxist classics. Trotsky's redefinition of the issue in those terms provided him with a framework for evaluating a wide range of policies from a critical perspective. But his attempts from 1927–33 to link the alienation of Soviet political institutions from the masses directly with the problem of alien class influence proved to be constraining and disorienting. In contrast, his later theory – depicting the bureaucracy as a highly autonomous social formation comparable to a 'Bonapartist' state – was far more flexible and considerably more persuasive.

However, some writers have criticised Trotsky precisely for basing his later theory on the notion of political alienation. To a large degree they have done so because that approach differs substantially from Max Weber's analysis of bureaucracy, which is still utilised by many contemporary social scientists. In his sociological writings Weber defined bureaucracy as a form of organisation distinguished by principles of fixed jurisdiction, office hierarchy, management by written documents, expert training, the full-time employment of officials, and management according to general rules.[1] As Martin Krygier has noted, in contrast to Weber, Trotsky was not attempting 'to refer neutrally to a particular form of organizational structure'.[2] Proceeding from that recognition, Peter Beilharz has argued that Trotsky's definition of bureaucracy in a 'pejorative

---

1   M. Weber 1946, pp. 196–8.
2   Krygier 1978, p. 46.

sense alone', rather than in terms of Weber's 'bureaucratic principles of organisation', was a serious 'analytical error', and one that explains 'his political inability to combat or control Soviet "bureaucracy"'.[3] Similarly, David W. Lovell has asserted that Trotsky 'did not explain how complex administration could be non-bureaucratic'. Additionally, he has argued that 'a "ruling bureaucracy"...is a contradiction *in adjecto*', and has asked, 'How can we say that a bureaucracy "rules"'?[4]

Yet, Trotsky's utilisation of an understanding *different* from Weber's sociological analysis, despite its pejorative connotations, was hardly an 'analytical error'. As we have seen, the conception of bureaucracy employed by Trotsky represented a far older and more established tradition than Weber's. In fact, the 'rule of the bureaus' was both the original and the literal meaning of the term. Furthermore, of the two approaches, Trotsky's seems to have been more immediately relevant to the Soviet Union of the 1930s. From what we know of the political apparatuses of the USSR at that time, they hardly fit the model of precision, stability, reliability, and rationality depicted by Weber.[5] On the other hand, the notion of a privileged and authoritarian ruling elite clearly made sense to the Soviet workers and peasants who frequently articulated such an understanding themselves in their discussions of Soviet politics in the middle and late 1930s.[6]

9.2.2   *Cause*

As explained in Trotsky's later writings, the ultimate origins of the extreme alienation of Soviet political institutions from the masses were to be found in the isolation, backwardness, and transitional character of Soviet society. He argued that in terms of labour productivity the USSR was backward – not only in relation to the ultimate goals of socialism, but also in relation to the leading capitalist countries. However, he also perceived the USSR to be advanced as a societal form in the early stages of the transition from capitalism to socialism.

---

3   Beilharz 1987, p. 64. Beilharz also asserts that Trotsky viewed bureaucracy in terms of 'the bad habits of his political enemies'. But of course Trotsky explicitly repudiated the view that bureaucracy was reducible to the 'bad habits of officeholders' as early as 1923 (Trotsky 1975b, p. 91).

4   Lovell 1985, pp. 41, 66, 67. See also Lovell 1985, p. 45.

5   See M. Weber 1968, vol. 1, p. 223. For a description of the party apparatus of these years that contrasts sharply with Weber's ideal type of a bureaucracy, see Getty 1985.

6   On critical popular perceptions of the ruling elite within the Soviet Union at the time, see S. Davies 1997, pp. 124–44. On the writings of various Marxists on Soviet bureaucracy then and since, see Linden 2007. For summaries of academic analyses of the 'Soviet bureaucracy' since Trotsky's time, see Hough 1977, pp. 49–70; and Lane 1971, pp. 175–8.

This contradiction necessitated the intervention of a bureaucracy to mediate conflicts between classes by regulating the distribution of scarce resources. At the same time, according to Trotsky, the popular constraints on bureaucratic power were diminished by a variety of factors – many again related to Soviet backwardness – that contributed to the weakening and demoralisation of the Soviet proletariat.

Although it has been argued that Trotsky exaggerated the *extent* of the gap between Soviet and Western labour productivity, there is no doubt that the USSR lagged far behind the more advanced countries of the capitalist West.[7] A more questionable aspect of Trotsky's theory for many has been his characterisation of the USSR by reference to the classical Marxist ideal of socialism – defined as a society of abundance, equality, and withering coercion. Isaac Deutscher has accurately observed that much of this will seem 'doctrinaire' to the non-Marxist; yet, it was an essential component of Trotsky's analysis, for 'it stripped Stalinism of "ideological" pretensions [that socialism had already been achieved] and dissociated Marxism from Stalin's practices'.[8] Beyond that, Trotsky clearly took the Marxist vision seriously, even making it seem quite realistically attainable when he defined it in such prosaic terms as these from *The Revolution Betrayed*:

> The material premise of communism should be so high a development of the economic powers of man that productive labor, having ceased to be a burden, will not require any goad, and the distribution of life's goods, existing in continual abundance, will not demand – as it does not now in any well-off family or 'decent' boardinghouse – any control except that of education, habit and social opinion. Speaking frankly, I think it would be pretty dull-witted to consider such a really modest perspective 'utopian'.[9]

Still, for Trotsky that vision was not – as Peter Beilharz and Michael Lustig have both claimed – teleological in nature.[10] That is, it was not a predetermined endpoint guiding historical development. In fact, Trotsky repeatedly emphasised that it was far from inevitable that the transition would be achieved in the USSR.

However, the question of teleology can also be raised in connection with Trotsky's explanation that bureaucratic power originated in the 'necessity to

---

7   See Shapiro 1987, pp. 59–63.

8   Deutscher 1963, p. 301.

9   Trotsky 1937, pp. 45–6.

10   Beilharz 1987, p. 63; Lustig 1989, p. 40.

appoint a policeman to keep order'.[11] Such passages as these might be challenged by many contemporary philosophers of social science who argue that functional accounts essentially attempt to explain social phenomena by their consequences, and who reasonably insist that functional explanations are impermissible unless buttressed by causal mechanisms analogous to natural selection in evolution.[12] We cannot know how Trotsky would have responded to such a criticism, but he might have asserted that his claim regarding the distributive role of the bureaucracy was not really functional in this sense. Rather, he might have insisted, what he meant to suggest was the intentionalist argument that the Soviet leadership had *consciously* created and promoted a bureaucracy *in order* to fulfil the task or function of distributing scarce goods.

Leaving aside Trotsky's precise meaning on that question, various writers have again contrasted his account of the origins of bureaucratisation with Weber's. In this regard they have objected that Trotsky's explanation in terms of backwardness and scarcity is inconsistent with Weber's argument that bureaucracy is directly related to modernity and development. Along these lines Peter Beilharz has asserted that 'after Weber, the symbiotic relationship between modernity and bureaucracy is generally recognized', and that 'Trotsky fails altogether to register the relationship between modernization and bureaucratization'.[13] Martin Krygier also has observed that in claiming that the growth of bureaucracy 'varies directly with economic backwardness, scarcity and social dislocation, and inversely with equality and affluence', Trotsky stands Weber, as well as Tocqueville and Hegel, 'on their heads'.[14] Similarly, David Lovell has complained that 'Trotsky did not respond to the idea that with the increasing complexity of life and specialization there is an inexorable tendency to bureaucratization in most areas of social life'.[15]

As already suggested, it is difficult to compare Trotsky's and Weber's analyses of bureaucracy directly since Trotsky's understanding of *biurokratiia* and Weber's notion of *Bürokratie* were so radically different. Nevertheless, it is likely that Trotsky would have disputed Weber's contention that the demands of rational organisation in modern economic and political institutions inevitably entail a specialised body of expert officials. In this regard he probably would have agreed with Lenin that in economically developed societies popular participation in administration can be achieved through the conscious

11   Trotsky 1937, p. 112.
12   See, for example, Elster 1994; Elster 1985, pp. 27–37.
13   Beilharz 1987, pp. 63, 64.
14   Krygier 1978, p. 56; Krygier 1979a, p. 92.
15   Lovell 1985, p. 41.

simplification of administrative procedures, as well as by promoting the education and leisure time of workers. The jury is still out on that question.

However, the relationship between modernity and the *rule* of officials –
Beamtenherrschaft for Weber – is a separate issue. Weber's position on that
question was actually somewhat ambiguous. In his most important sociological work, *Economy and Society*, he described the 'power position' of a fully developed bureaucracy as normally 'overtowering', and he argued that it would be
enhanced by the elimination of private capitalism. But he also asserted that it
was 'an open question whether the *power* of bureaucracy' is 'increasing in modern states', since the fact that it is 'technically the most highly developed power
instrument . . . does not determine the weight that bureaucracy as such is capable of procuring for its opinions in a particular social structure'.[16] Even if we
assume that a specialised body of officials is necessary in a post-revolutionary
society, it seems that for socialists the important question is whether or not
the working class can contain the political power of such an administrative
apparatus by the countervailing power of its own institutions. Trotsky's argument that its ability to do this in the USSR was limited by Soviet backwardness
remains compelling.

One of the more interesting aspects of Trotsky's discussion of the factors
that weakened proletarian resistance in the Soviet Union was his recognition of
the corrosive effects of early Bolshevik practice. In *The Revolution Betrayed* he
clearly portrayed the banning of opposition parties and party factions as having
played an important role in bureaucratisation. He reiterated the same points
even more forcefully in subsequent statements. For example, in August 1937
he asserted, 'It is absolutely indisputable that the domination of a single party
served as the juridical point of departure for the Stalinist totalitarian system',
and in July 1939 he proclaimed, '*Whoever prohibits factions thereby liquidates
party democracy and takes the first step toward a totalitarian regime*'.[17]

Still, it should be recognised that Trotsky was hardly *sufficiently* critical of
Bolshevik practices – including his own – in the first years after the revolution.
There was, for example, a lingering ambiguity in his writings about whether or
not the Bolsheviks were *wrong* in viewing the restrictions on oppositional parties and factions as necessary emergency measures. In August 1937 he asserted
that 'if the revolution had triumphed' internationally, 'the need [*nadobnost'*]
to prohibit the other Soviet parties would immediately have fallen away'.[18]

---

16   M. Weber 1968, vol. 1, pp. 223–5; M. Weber 1968, vol. 3, p. 991. See also Krygier 1979c,
      pp. 66–71.

17   Trotsky 1978, p. 426; Trotsky 1979c, p. 228.

18   Trotsky 1978, p. 426; *Biulleten' oppozitsii*, 58–9 (September–October 1937), p. 15.

Equally ambiguous was his August 1939 statement regarding the Bolshevik prohibition of factions: 'One can argue whether or not this was correct'.[19] For that reason it is not clear that his remarks on this topic were the 'unmistakable self-criticism' perceived by Ernest Mandel and others.[20] Furthermore, Trotsky did not fully acknowledge the negative impact of a variety of other practices in the early years of Soviet power, including the frequent use of appointment to fill state positions, Trotsky's own militarisation of labour, and his 'shake-up' of the trade unions.[21] It may be true that some of these practices were necessitated by the circumstances – though they were defended in more general and sweeping terms at the time. But as Mandel has noted, it is undeniable that they all 'contributed, through their effects on the level of workers' self-activity, to a consolidation of the process of bureaucratization'.[22]

9.2.3   Characteristics

The most important aspect of Trotsky's discussion of the characteristics of the bureaucracy was his critique of the Soviet policies related to the economy, international affairs, and the regime. During the years from 1917 until his death in 1940, it was his disagreement over those policies that most stimulated his thinking on the problem of bureaucracy. In turn, much of his writing about Soviet bureaucracy throughout that period was devoted to analysing those policies. Although a great deal of his analysis was insightful, in each area there were important deficiencies. These were largely related to his tendency to exaggerate the immediacy and consistency of the counterrevolutionary implications of the policies under consideration.

With important exceptions, much of Trotsky's later critique of Soviet economic policy is persuasive.[23] Along with most other international observers of the time, he was appropriately impressed by the achievements of Soviet industrialisation. More significantly, he accurately predicted that this early

---

19   Trotsky 1979c, p. 231.

20   See Mandel 1995, p. 82. See also Bellis 1979, p. 80; and Chattopadhyay 2006, pp. 539–40.

21   For what seems to be an implicit recognition of the negative effects of his trade union policies in 1920, see Trotsky 1972f, p. 218.

22   Mandel 1992, p. 118. Similarly, Mandel has asserted, 'From 1920–21 the strategy of the Bolshevik leadership hindered rather than promoted the self-activity of the Russian workers. What is more, the theoretical justification and generalization of this "substitution" made the situation even worse' (Mandel 1995, p. 82). For two important explorations of these issues, see Farber 1990; and Marik 2009, pp. 369–496.

23   As one economist concluded in 1987 regarding *The Revolution Betrayed*, 'Trotsky's appreciation of economic trends in the Soviet Union, positive and negative, was generally acute' (Shapiro 1987, p. 65).

period of rapid growth would soon come to an end.[24] Again, he may have exaggerated the gap between the labour productivity in Western Europe and in the Soviet Union. Nevertheless, he was correct in emphasising the importance of this issue, in his anticipation that it would become a serious problem for the Soviet Union in the long run, and in his observation that it was related to the low quality of Soviet goods produced both for consumers and industry.[25]

Regarding inequality, the economist Judith Shapiro has noted some exaggeration and inconsistency in Trotsky's comparisons of wage differentials in the USSR with those the West. Despite this, she has concluded that, consonant with Trotsky's account, 'all of the limited evidence currently available testifies to very sharp internal differentiation in the working class, and, in the most revealing discussion in Soviet journals of the time, there is clear evidence that the size of the inequality was intended'.[26] Corresponding to that, statements preserved in Soviet archives indicate that many workers in the mid-late 1930s also believed that much of the inequality was excessive and only benefitted the privileged elite.[27] Furthermore, as various authors have noted, Trotsky's characteriations of the inequality and corruption of the Stalin era retained their relevance even in more recent periods when his observations were echoed in journalistic and sociological accounts of Soviet society.[28]

Clearly, the single greatest weakness of Trotsky's critique of Soviet economic policies in the late 1930s was his perception that they were leading toward the *imminent* restoration of capitalism. If there were indeed pro-capitalist groupings developing within and outside of the party and state apparatuses of the Soviet Union in the 1930s, their power seems to have been contained by a Stalinist leadership dedicated to maintaining dominance over a nationalised economy. By focusing so sharply on questions related to the transition to socialism and the dangers of counterrevolution, Trotsky's theory provided

---

24   In line with this, after the period of recovery from World War II, annual economic growth rates began to drop significantly from one decade to the next until the catastrophic decline of the 1980s. See, for example, Brown 1996, pp. 134–5; Hutchings 1982, pp. 272–3, 308–9.

25   This point is made in P. Anderson 1984, p. 125. For discussion of this issue, see for example, Gorbachev 1987, pp. 19–21, 53–4, 92–5; Hewett 1988, pp. 52, 54–5, 78–86.

26   Shapiro 1987, p. 64. In *The Revolution Betrayed* Trotsky claimed at one point that the scope of inequality in wages had 'far surpassed the capitalist countries'! But at another point he asserted that the distribution of goods in the USSR was 'incomparably more democratic' than in the West (Trotsky 1937, pp. 125, 143).

27   See S. Davies 1997, pp. 138–44.

28   On this point, see for example, P. Anderson 1984, p. 125; Day 1987, p. 13.

a perspective that was insightful in the long term, but that often proved to be disorienting in the short run.

In attempting to describe the Stalinist regime in his later writings, Trotsky most frequently depicted it as 'Bonapartist'. That characterisation, derived from classical Marxism, was theoretically rich, implying a large measure of autonomy on the part of the political apparatus, a great deal of autonomy on the part of the central leader, and sources of the autonomy of both the bureaucracy and the leader in their respective mediating roles. The complexity of that concept permitted Trotsky to explain a variety of diverse and sometimes apparently conflicting policies – for example, repression that appeared to advance the interests of the bureaucracy as a whole, repression that seemed to benefit only sections of the bureaucracy, and repression that apparently served only the interests of Stalin.

Nevertheless, it must also be acknowledged there were important weaknesses in Trotsky's general analysis of the Soviet regime. These largely paralleled the deficiencies in his more specific analysis of the Moscow Trials. We have noted Thomas Poole's remark that Trotsky 'did not bring to "full conclusion" or completely join together his many observations on Stalin and the purge'.[29] The same can be said about his observations regarding the regime in general. Having suggested a variety of contending sources for the formulation of policy – the bureaucracy as a whole, groupings within the bureaucracy on a left-right continuum, and the Stalinist clique – Trotsky never explained how or why one or another of these emerged as dominant at any given time. A more significant problem was his repeated explanation of increases in repression in terms of rightward shifts in policy. Aside from his analysis of the trials, this approach was apparent in his suggestion that the repression in 1935 was related to the granting of the right to own livestock to collective farmers and to the decision to terminate aid to British Communists. There is no evidence that there was such a connection. Once more, an apparent source of this mistake on Trotsky's part was his tendency to revert to an approach more typical of his previous theory of bureaucracy. A further error related to his analysis of the regime was his occasional exaggeration of the strength of his own political movement. Again, this error seems to have been inspired to a large degree by the importance assigned to that movement in his theory. In more sober statements he acknowledged that the real organisation of his supporters was actually quite weak within the USSR, and that the bureaucracy was

---

29   Poole 1982, p. 487.

simply utilising 'Trotskyism' as a 'catchall concept, encompassing everything deserving extermination'.[30]

Perhaps the most problematic aspect of Trotsky's analysis of Stalinism, as Perry Anderson has correctly emphasised, was his assessment of its international role. On one hand, Soviet policy after *The Revolution Betrayed* in many respects closely resembled his description of it as non-revolutionary or even counterrevolutionary. For example, for the sake of military alliances Soviet leadership pressured the Communist Party of Spain (PCE) and the Spanish Republic to resist the anti-capitalist demands of workers in the Spanish civil war, and it marginalised and repressed anarchist and socialist organisations to the left of the PCE.[31] Subsequently, Stalin displayed a continuing readiness to subordinate the needs of the revolution abroad to foreign policy considerations by such measures as his dissolution of the Comintern in June 1943, his urging of moderation upon the Yugoslav Communists throughout World War II, his pressing of a policy of national unity upon the French and Italian Communist Parties at the end of the war, his acquiescence in Britain's intervention against the Greek resistance in 1944–5, and his attempts to subordinate the Chinese Communist Party to the Guomindang from 1937 through 1946.[32] Examples of comparable Soviet policies from the post-Stalin era are perhaps even more numerous.

Nevertheless, Stalinism was not *simply* counterrevolutionary. Rather, as Anderson has noted, it was 'profoundly contradictory in its actions and effects abroad, just as it was at home'.[33] This was demonstrated during Trotsky's lifetime in September 1939 when the Soviet Union occupied eastern Poland while Germany invaded the west. Even at the time he correctly predicted that the Soviet bureaucracy, incapable of sharing power with the Polish ruling classes, would expropriate the landowners and carry out the 'statification of the means of production'. Although he denounced in advance the 'military-bureaucratic' character of this expropriation and the repression of independent mass activity that he expected, he also described the 'statification of property' in the occupied territories as in itself 'a progressive measure' that

---

30   Trotsky 1978, p. 347. See also Trotsky 1978, p. 280.

31   For Trotsky's comments on the Soviet role in Spain, see for example Trotsky 1973f, pp. 251–2, 311–14, 319, 347. For sources that support this assessment from a variety of perspectives, see for example, Claudin 1975a, pp. 210–42; L. Fischer 1969, pp. 273–4; Radosh, Habeck, and Sevostianov 2001, pp. 1–7; and Ulam 1974, pp. 243–6.

32   See, for example, Claudin 1975a, pp. 15–45; Claudin 1975b, pp. 374–81, 445–9, 551–63; Deutscher 1966, pp. 515–17; Löwy 1981, pp. 108–11, 121–2.

33   P. Anderson 1984, p. 125.

should be supported by partisans of the Fourth International and defended against Hitler's attempts to overturn it.[34] After the war, of course, the Soviet Union implemented comparable expropriations and 'statifications' on an even vaster scale throughout Eastern Europe. The inconsistency between these actions and the promotion of the revolutionary consciousness and self-activity of the working class is evident. However, in each case the assault upon capitalism indicates that it was inadequate to depict Soviet international policy simply as 'counterrevolutionary', or the Soviet Union and Comintern as 'the political agency of imperialism'.[35] Likewise, as Anderson observes, a number of other aspects of the external role of the Soviet Union were also (unevenly) progressive. These included the leading Soviet role in the destruction of European fascism and promotion of decolonisation, and its military and economic assistance to socialist and national liberation movements. All of these testify 'to the contradictory logic of a "degenerated workers" state, colossally distorted, yet still persistently anti-capitalist, which Trotsky wrongly suspended at the Soviet frontier-posts'.[36]

9.2.4 Consequences

For Trotsky, the greatest problem with the policies of the bureaucracy was that they enhanced the likelihood of capitalist restoration. One way in which they did this was by subverting the world revolution, which for Trotsky provided the only ultimate defence of the USSR. Along these lines he anticipated in *The Revolution Betrayed* that, unless a proletarian revolution in the West intervened, imperialist armies would 'sweep away the regime which issued from the October revolution'.[37] Nevertheless, although the Western socialist revolution envisioned by Trotsky never materialised, the Soviet Union emerged victorious from the war. Clearly, despite his assertion that the October revolution had

---

34 Trotsky 1970d, pp. 18–20. When the Soviet Union invaded Finland in December 1939 Trotsky anticipated similar expropriations (Trotsky 1970d, p. 57).

35 For a history of the discussion on this question and alternative views, see for example, Linden 2007, pp. 99–158; Callinicos 1990, pp. 27–38; McNeal 1977, pp. 41–2; National Education Department, Socialist Workers Party 1969.

36 P. Anderson 1984, pp. 126, 127. Anderson also correctly notes Trotsky's failure to anticipate the possibility of a Stalinist movement playing a revolutionary role, as in China and Vietnam.

37 Trotsky 1937, p. 227. In an interview in Coyoacán on 23 July 1939 he predicted with certainty that the Stalinist political regime would be destroyed in the war – if not by political revolution, then by invading imperialism (Trotsky 1973e, p. 18).

'a great power of resistance', Trotsky underestimated the power of resistance of the Soviet state.[38]

The alternative path to restoration for Trotsky was through a domestic counterrevolution led by a Soviet bureaucracy seeking support for its privileges in capitalist property relations. As a number of scholars have noted, Trotsky's predictions in this regard seem to have been strikingly confirmed in the early 1990s. In 1991 the economic historian R.W. Davies remarked,

> Until a year or two ago, Trotsky's prediction...that state bureaucrats might be transformed into private capitalists seemed to have been completely falsified by history...[However,] Trotsky's prediction has unexpectedly turned from a wild misjudgement into an imaginative prophecy.[39]

Similarly, in 1995 M.I. Voyeikov, professor of economics at the Russian Academy of Sciences, observed that 'in *The Revolution Betrayed* in the mid 1930s' Trotsky 'described with remarkable accuracy that which took place in our country in the early 1990s'.[40] And in 2005 the political scientist Allen C. Lynch depicted the transition immediately before and after 1990 as 'the final stage in a process of increasingly proprietary assertion by the Soviet nomenklatura that had been...anticipated by Leon Trotsky in the 1930s'.[41]

Along with Trotsky's general predictions about the tendencies toward capitalist restoration, some of his more specific expectations about the process of collapse have also been realised in post-Soviet Russia. One of these was his forecast in November 1937 that a counterrevolutionary government in power in the USSR 'for a lengthy period would have to base itself upon the nationalized economy'.[42] Another was his anticipation that if a bourgeois party came to power, 'it would find no small number of ready servants among the present bureaucrats, administrators, technicians, directors, party secretaries and privileged upper circles in general'.[43] Yet another was his repeated prediction

---

38   Trotsky 1937, p. 252.
39   R. Davies 1992, p. 69.
40   Voyeikov 1998, p. 6.
41   Lynch 2005, p. 77. See also S. White 2000, p. 291. For similar statements by Trotskyists, see C. Edwards 1998; Miles 1994–5; Miles 1998; Woods 2001. For an analysis of the process by which substantial sections of the party and especially the state bureaucracies were transformed into proponents of capitalist restoration, see Kotz and Weir 2007, pp. 105–25.
42   Trotsky 1976b, p. 63.
43   Trotsky 1937, p. 253.

that the counterrevolutionary state would be highly authoritarian – though until now the brutally repressive fascist state anticipated by Trotsky has not yet materialised.

Still, there are ways in which the downfall of the Soviet system did not match Trotsky's expectations. Most importantly, it occurred far later than he expected. Again, he may have underestimated the extent to which the Stalinist leadership of the 1930s was inclined or able to control restorationist tendencies out of self-interest. Another error pointed out by Alan Woods and Ted Grant was Trotsky's prediction that the process of restoration would begin with the breaking up of the *kolkhozy* and the creation of individual, private farms. As Woods explains, this has not occurred because the 'rural proletariat' in Russia, consisting mainly of older people, is not interested in becoming a class of small proprietors, but prefers instead the collective system which provides a certain amount of security.[44] Also erroneous were Trotsky's predictions about the major civil war that would accompany the counterrevolution. It is true that the downfall of the USSR inaugurated a series of armed conflicts in the territory of the former Soviet Union, including the struggle between Yeltsin and the Russian Parliament in 1993, and civil wars in Abkhazia and South Ossetia, Chechnya, Ingushetia, Nagorno-Karabakh, Tajikistan, Transnistria, and Ukraine. However, until now none of these has corresponded in scale or character to the sort of class war Trotsky anticipated. In part, this may have been because the ideal of socialism has been so compromised and the working class so demoralised that it has been impossible for it to mount a concerted resistance.

Of course, Trotsky's predictions about restoration presumed that the Soviet Union remained a workers' state. After February 1935 he based this assessment entirely on the fact that the Soviet Union continued to defend the property forms established by the Bolshevik Revolution. Only once, in the course of a debate within the American Trotskyist organisation the Socialist Workers' Party (SWP), did he allow himself to seriously consider an alternative view. In 1939 a minority within the SWP, challenging Trotsky's 'degenerated workers' state position', argued that a new 'bureaucratic collectivist' class had come to power in the USSR.[45] In a contribution to that discussion Trotsky entertained

---

44   Woods 2001; Grant 1997, p. 460.

45   It seems that Trotsky first used the expression 'degenerated workers' state' in his February 1935 article 'The Workers' State, Thermidor and Bonapartism'. There it was presented as the formulation of a critic of his position (Trotsky 1971b, p. 172). Although Trotsky frequently spoke of the 'degeneration' of the Soviet Union, he did not use the phrase 'degenerated workers' state' to define his own position until later. In November 1937 he described the USSR as a 'degenerating workers' state' and wrote of the '*degeneration* of the workers'

the theoretical possibility that a world war might result in a decline of the proletariat internationally, and that this could lead to the spread of totalitarianism
worldwide, and to the growth of a new exploiting class. Another theoretical
possibility was that proletarian revolutions in the West would be followed by
the rise of ruling bureaucracies. In either case, he conceded, it would be necessary to recognise that the 'USSR was the precursor of a new exploiting regime
on an international scale'.[46] Although Trotsky later denied that he had said
anything new in these comments, his critics justifiably noted that this was his
first admission that the *existing* property forms in the USSR could support a
new ruling class.[47] However, he never elaborated upon this conjecture, and
the circumstances that he believed would require a revision of position never
materialised.[48]

Among socialists, the issue of the class nature of the Soviet Union remains
the most contentious aspect of Trotsky's theory. Powerful arguments have been
advanced for a variety of positions on that question, and there is little that
can be said here that will add anything new or persuasive to the discussion.[49]
Nevertheless, it may be useful to note at least a few considerations that seem
relevant at this point.

Of all the arguments that have been levelled against Trotsky's position on the
class nature of the Soviet state, one stands out as unquestionably the strongest.
That is the recognition that it was simply counterintuitive to depict the USSR
as a 'workers' state, when, as Trotsky recognised, the working class itself was
unable to control the state in any way or to reform it.[50] Related to this, Trotsky's
critics have also noted that direct control is even more important in a workers' state than in capitalist or pre-capitalist societies because in those societies

---

state' (Trotsky 1976b, pp. 64, 67). In his *Transitional Program* in April 1938 he asserted
that, despite its 'terrific contradictions', the USSR remained '*a degenerated workers' state*'
(Trotsky 1973g, p. 142). See also Trotsky 1970d, pp. 5, 28, 52.

46   Trotsky 1970d, p. 9.

47   Trotsky 1970d, p. 31; Shachtman 1962, p. 40. On this point, see also Krygier 1979a,
       pp. 99–100; Krygier 1978, pp. 60–1.

48   Various authors have contended Trotsky was arguing that the *only* theoretically possi-
       ble outcomes in the coming war were a world revolution against both capitalism and
       Stalinism, or the rise of bureaucratic collectivism (Deutscher 1963, p. 516; Callinicos 1990,
       pp. 29–30). It is not at all clear this was his intent.

49   For a review of the various positions, see Linden 2007.

50   For Trotsky's recognition that this was the 'most widespread, popular, and, at first sight,
       irrefutable argument' against his position, see Trotsky 1972g, p. 103. For later examples of
       this argument, see for example, Cliff 1993, pp. 318–19; Hallas 1984, p. 43; Shachtman 1962,
       pp. 167–8.

class domination can take indirect forms, but a workers' state requires the conscious and direct participation of the working class.[51] In response to these arguments, Trotsky acknowledged that the deviations described by his critics clearly demonstrated that the dictatorship of the proletariat in the Soviet Union was a 'sick dictatorship'. But he insisted that to claim that they disqualified the Soviet Union as a workers' state was to substitute an idealistic, normative method for a dialectical one.[52] However, Trotsky's response inevitably begged the question of just how far a 'proletarian dictatorship' could deviate from the programmatic norm before one could conclude that the 'quantitative change' had become 'qualitative'. Was that line not crossed, for example, with the execution of hundreds of thousands of workers and peasants and with the incarceration of millions?

Another criterion for a workers' state that has been proposed has involved the question of the material interests of the working class. Along these lines David W. Lovell has argued that to say a social class is dominant is to say it 'derives some direct benefit from its position', but that for the working class such benefit 'did not obtain under the rule of the Stalinist bureaucracy (nor earlier)'.[53] Trotsky does not seem to have addressed this question directly. However, in *The Revolution Betrayed* he asserted that a return to capitalist relations would involve 'a catastrophic decline of industry and culture', suggesting he foresaw a simultaneous, precipitous decline in the standard of living of workers.[54] We cannot know if that would have been the effect of a collapse of the Soviet Union in the late 1930s, though it is noteworthy that such a decline *did* occur in the 1990s. More clearly, Trotsky insisted that the bureaucracy's defence of nationalised production and planning were of enormous *potential* benefit to the working class. In a response to critics in November 1937 he wrote,

> If the proletariat drives out the Soviet bureaucracy *in time*, then it will still find the nationalized means of production and the basic elements of the planned economy after its victory. This means it will not have to begin from the beginning. That is a tremendous advantage![55]

---

51   See, for example, Trotsky 1972g, p. 104. For a recent statement of this argument, see Post 1999, p. 143.

52   See Trotsky 1972g, pp. 105–7; Trotsky 1976b, pp. 64–9.

53   Lovell 1985, p. 51.

54   Trotsky 1937, p. 251.

55   Trotsky 1976b, p. 69.

An additional important challenge to Trotsky's position since his death has involved the length of time that the bureaucracy ruled the Soviet Union. In 1939 Trotsky cautioned his opponents in the SWP, 'Might we not place ourselves in a ludicrous position if we affixed to the Bonapartist oligarchy the nomenclature of a new ruling class just a few years or even a few months prior to its inglorious downfall'?[56] As the years piled up into decades, Trotsky's critics began to turn the argument of time back on him. In 1977 Robert McNeal argued that 'the Trotskyist tradition has been unable to confront the possibility that [Stalinism] could be a solidly founded or long-term phenomenon'.[57] In 1981 John Molyneux asserted,

> It is an inescapable fact that Trotsky's predictions...about the future of the Soviet Union were completely falsified by the march of events. Trotsky predicted that the Soviet Union would move forwards to socialism or backwards to capitalism (meaning private ownership). Over forty years later it has done neither.[58]

Even more strongly, in 1987 Peter Beilharz insisted, 'Trotsky is unable to perceive the USSR as a new society whose present form is permanent'.[59] However, it seems that this particular argument has been resolved in Trotsky's favour with the dissolution of the 'permanent' form within Russia and throughout Eastern Europe in the late 1980s and early 1990s.

Additionally, it is worth noting some of the consequences of the downfall of the Soviet Union that appear to support Trotsky's position that it remained a workers' state. One of these was the 'jubilation...among capitalists worldwide' that accompanied the demise of the USSR and that has been noted by Kunal Chattopadhyay. As he suggests, this response seems inconsistent with the theory of some of Trotsky's Marxist critics that the Soviet Union was just another variety of capitalist state.[60] Another development that challenged the state capitalist perspective was the severe economic crisis experienced by Russia in the 1990s. The economist David Kotz has argued, 'Were Russia simply shifting from one variant of capitalism to another, it would be difficult to understand the depth of the crisis produced in Russian society'.[61] Finally,

---

56   Trotsky 1970d, p. 14.

57   McNeal 1977, p. 51.

58   Molyneux 1981, p. 126.

59   Beilharz 1987, p. 61. See also Beilharz 1987, p. 63.

60   Chattopadhyay 2006, p. 541.

61   Kotz 2001, p. 160.

there were the apparent effects of the transformation on the world socialist movement. Aside from the disintegration of Communist parties around the world, these involved a shifting of Social Democratic parties to the right and a noticeable decline throughout the world in support for far-left organisations – including even Trotskyist organisations that anticipated the transformation. All of these developments seem consistent with the view that we were witnessing the aftereffects of a serious defeat for the world working class – such as might be generated by the death of a workers' state.

9.2.5 Cure

For Trotsky it was not foreordained that capitalism would be restored. Rather, as he explained in his draft programme for the Fourth International in April 1938, there were two alternatives: 'Either the bureaucracy,... will overthrow the new forms of property and plunge the country back into capitalism; or the working class will crush the bureaucracy and open the way to socialism'.[62] Throughout his final years he remained optimistic that it was the second alternative that would materialise in response to a new revolutionary upsurge abroad. In *The Revolution Betrayed* he wrote of 'the inevitability of a new revolution', explaining, 'The first victory of a revolution in Europe would pass like an electric shock through the Soviet masses, straighten them up, raise their spirit of independence, awaken the traditions of 1905 and 1917, undermine the position of the Bonapartist bureaucracy, and acquire for the Fourth International no less significance than the October revolution possessed for the Third'.[63] The same revolutionary optimism was evident in his September 1939 contribution to the internal discussion of the SWP: 'We steer our course toward the world revolution and by virtue of this very fact toward the regeneration of the USSR as a workers' state'.[64]

Of course, this was another of Trotsky's predictions that failed to materialise. Again, there were a number of factors that Trotsky did not take into account. Among these, the most obvious was that the revolutionary conflagration in the advanced capitalist West that Trotsky believed was essential for igniting the Soviet revolution never appeared. Furthermore, the Great Terror, which was far worse than even Trotsky imagined, had a devastating impact on any potential resistance or dissent. Additionally, Perry Anderson has suggested that the durability of the system was enhanced by the upward mobility that was actively promoted among sectors of the working class by the Soviet

---

62   Trotsky 1973g, p. 142.
63   Trotsky 1937, pp. 284, 290.
64   Trotsky 1970d, p. 15.

leadership.[65] Nevertheless, as noted by Ernest Mandel, the broad perspective of political revolution seems to have been supported as a realistic option by a series of explosions outside of the Soviet Union in the decades after World War II, including the revolts that occurred in Hungary in 1956, in Czechoslovakia in 1968–9, in Poland in 1980–1, and to some degree in China, as well as the GDR, Czechoslovakia, and Romania in 1989.[66]

In conclusion, then, despite its deficiencies – and these were significant – Trotsky's final theory of Soviet bureaucracy represented a remarkable intellectual and political achievement. It included a richly detailed examination of Soviet politics, society, and history. Yet it interpreted all of these within a relatively simple framework, imaginatively derived from the categories of classical Marxism. It was realistic in its portrayal of the Soviet Union, but it measured Soviet realities against the expansive ideals of socialism. It was devastating in its conclusions, yet it was politically balanced – bending to neither Stalinism nor Stalinophobia.[67] It encouraged the critical thinking of those who were already Marxists, while reopening a path to Marxism for those who were critically minded. It was both a tool for understanding and a weapon for struggle. Even though the Soviet Union and much of Stalinism has passed away, it remains a useful starting point for comprehending both today.

---

65   P. Anderson 1984, p. 125.

66   See Mandel 1992, p. 195.

67   On the strengths of Trotsky's theory in term of its historical sweep, its sociological richness, and its political balance, see P. Anderson 1984, pp. 123–4.

Bibliography

Adler, Alan (ed.) 1980, *Theses, Resolutions, and Manifestos of the First Four Congresses of the Third International*, translated by Alix Holt and Barbara Holland, London: Ink Links.

Albrow, Martin 1970, *Bureaucracy*, New York: Praeger Publishers.

Aleksandrov, A. 1899, *Polnyi anglo-russkii slovar'*, St. Petersburg: V Knizhnom i Geografichenskom Magazinie izdanii Glavnago Shtaba.

—— 1909, *Polnyi anglo-russkii slovar'*, Berlin: Polyglotte.

Alexander, Robert Jackson 1991, *International Trotskyism, 1929–1985: A Documented Analysis of the Movement*, Durham, N.C.: Duke University Press.

Anderson, Kevin 1995, *Lenin, Hegel, and Western Marxism: A Critical Study*. Urbana, IL: University of Illinois Press.

Anderson, Perry 1984, 'Trotsky's Interpretation of Stalinism', in *The Stalinist Legacy: its Impact on Twentieth-Century World Politics*, edited by Tariq Ali, Harmondworth, Middlesex, England: Penguin Books.

Andreevskii, I.E. et al. (eds.) 1890–1904, *Entsiklopedicheskii slovar'*, St. Petersburg: F.A. Brokgauz, I.A. Efron.

Angress, Werner 1963, *Stillborn Revolution: The Communist Bid for Power in Germany, 1921–1923*, Princeton, NJ: Princeton University Press.

Anweiler, Oscar 1974, *The Soviets: The Russian Workers, Peasants, and Soldiers Councils, 1905–1921*, translated by Ruth Hein, New York: Random House.

Armstrong, John Alexander 1961, *The Politics of Totalitarianism: The Communist Party of the Soviet Union from 1934 to the Present*, New York: Random House.

Arthur, C.A. 1972, 'The Coming Soviet Revolution', in *Trotsky: The Great Debate Renewed*, edited by Nicolas Krasso, 151–91, St. Louis, MO: New Critics Press.

Aulard, Alphonse 1910, *The French Revolution: A Political History, 1789–1804*, in four volumes, vol. 4, *The Bourgeois Republic and the Consulate*, New York: Charles Scribner's Sons.

Avineri, Shlomo 1968, *The Social and Political Thought of Karl Marx*, Cambridge: Cambridge University Press.

—— 1972, 'The Hegelian Origins of Marx's Political Thought', in *Marx's Socialism*, edited by Shlomo Avineri, New York: Lieber-Atherton.

Avrich, Paul 1970, *Kronstadt 1921*, New York: W.W. Norton and Co.

—— 1984, 'Bolshevik Opposition to Lenin: G.T. Miasnikov and the Workers' Group', *Russian Review* 43: 1–29.

Azrael, Jeremy R. 1966, *Managerial Power and Soviet Politics*, Cambridge, MA: Harvard University Press.

Bahne, Siegfried 1962, 'Trotsky on Stalin's Russia', *Survey* 41: 27–42.

Bailes, Kendall 1978, *Technology and Society under Lenin and Stalin: Origins of the Soviet Technological Intelligentsia*,

1917–1941, Princeton: Princeton University Press.

—— 1980, 'Stalin and the Making of a New Elite: A Comment', *Slavic Review* 39, 2: 286–9.

Bealey, Frank 1999, *The Blackwell Dictionary of Political Science: A User's Guide to its Terms*, Oxford: Blackwell Publishers.

Beilharz, Peter 1987, *Trotsky, Trotskyism and the Transition to Socialism*, Totawa, NJ: Barnes and Noble Books.

Bellis, Paul 1979, *Marxism and the U.S.S.R.: The Theory of Proletarian Dictatorship and the Marxist Analysis of Soviet Society*, Atlantic Highlands, NJ: Humanities Press.

Bensaïd, Daniel 1988, *The Formative Years of the Fourth International (1933–1938)*, Notebooks for Study and Research, 9, Amsterdam: International Institute for Research and Education.

Benton, Gregor 1996, *China's Urban Revolutionaries: Explorations in the History of Chinese Trotskyism, 1921–1952*, Atlantic Highlands, NJ: Humanities Press.

Bergman, Jay 1987, 'The Perils of Historical Analogy: Leon Trotsky on the French Revolution', *Journal of the History of Ideas*, 48, 1: 73–98.

Bettelheim, Charles 1976, *Class Struggles in the USSR. First Period: 1917–1923*, translated by Brian Pearce, New York: Monthly Review Press.

—— 1978, *Class Struggles in the USSR. Second Period: 1923–1930*, translated by Brian Pearce, New York: Monthly Review Press.

Biulleten' oppozitsii (bol'shevikov-leninrsev) 1973 [1929–41], reprint edition, New York: Monad Press.

—— 2002 [1929–41], Iskra Research, available at http://web.mit.edu/fjk/www/FI/BO/index.shtml.

Boulding, Kenneth 1956, *The Image: Knowledge in Life and Society*, Ann Arbor: The University of Michigan Press.

Brandt, Conrad 1958, *Stalin's Failure in China 1924–1927*, Cambridge, MA: Harvard University Press.

Braun, Eileen 1993, 'The Prophet Reconsidered: Trotsky on the Soviet Failure to Achieve Socialism', PhD dissertation, George Washington University.

Braunthal, Julius 1967, *History of the International*, in three volumes, vol. 2, *1914–1943*, translated by John Clark, New York: Frederick A. Praeger.

Breitman, George 1979, *The Rocky Road to the Fourth International 1933–1938*, New York: Pathfinder Press.

Broué, Pierre 1963, *Le parti bolchévique; histoire du P. C. de l'U.R.S.S.*, Paris: Les Éditions de Minuit.

—— 1980, 'Trotsky et le bloc des oppositions de 1932', *Cahiers Leon Trotsky* 5: 5–37.

—— 1988, *Trotsky*, Paris: Fayard.

—— 1989, 'Party Opposition to Stalin (1930–1932) and the First Moscow Trial', in *Essays on Revolutionary Culture and Stalinism: Selected Papers from the Third World Congress for Soviet and East European Studies*, edited by John W. Strong, Columbus, OH: Slavica Publishers.

—— 2005, *The German Revolution, 1917–1923*, Brill: Leiden.

Brower, Daniel Roberts 1968, *The New Jacobins: The French Communist Party and the Popular Front*, Ithaca, NY: Cornell University Press.

Brown, Archie 1996, *The Gorbachev Factor*, Oxford: Oxford University Press.

Bukharin, Nikolai Ivanovich 1966 [1928], 'Bukharin on Three Periods of Postwar Development and the Tasks of the Communist International', in *Soviet Foreign Policy 1928–1934, Documents and Materials*, in two volumes, vol. 1, edited by Xenia Joukoff Eudin and Robert M. Slusser, University Park, PA: The Pennsylvania State University Press.

—— 1982, *Selected Writings on the State and the Transition to Socialism*, translated and edited by Richard B. Day. New York: M.E. Sharpe.

Bullock, Alan 1952, *Hitler: A Study in Tyranny*, New York: Harper and Brothers.

Buranov, Yuri 1994, *Lenin's Will: Falsified and Forbidden*, Amherst, NY: Prometheus Books.

Burkett, John P. 1987, 'Soviet Socioeconomic Development: A Fold Catastrophe?', *Comparative Economic Studies* 29, 3: 70–93.

Calhoun, Daniel Fairchild 1976, *The United Front: The TUC and the Russians 1923–1928*, Cambridge: Cambridge University Press.

Callinicos, Alex 1990, *Trotskyism*, Minneapolis: University of Minnesota Press.

Cannon, James P. 1954, 'Trotsky or Deutscher?', *Fourth International*, 15: 9–16.

Carmichael, Joel 1975, *Trotsky: An Appreciation of His Life*, New York: St. Martin's.

Carr, Edward Hallett 1950–3, *The Bolshevik Revolution: 1917–1923*, in three volumes, *A History of Soviet Russia*, Baltimore: Penguin Books.

—— 1954, *The Interregnum: 1923–1924*, *A History of Soviet Russia*, New York: Macmillan.

—— 1958–64, *Socialism in One Country, 1924–1926*, in three volumes with four parts, *A History of Soviet Russia*, New York: Macmillan.

—— 1971–8, *Foundations of a Planned Economy, 1926–1929*, in three volumes with six parts, vols. 2 and 3, *A History of Soviet Russia*, New York: Macmillan Publishing Co.

—— 1982, *Twilight of the Comintern, 1930–1935*. New York: Pantheon Books.

Carr, Edward Hallett and Robert William Davies 1969, *Foundations of a Planned Economy, 1926–1929*, in three volumes with six parts, vol. 1, *A History of Soviet Russia*, New York: Macmillan Publishing Co.

Caute, David 1966, The *Left in Europe since 1789*, New York: McGraw-Hill.

Chase, William 1990, *Workers, Society, and the Soviet State: Labor and Life in Moscow, 1918–1929*, Urbana: University of Illinois Press.

Chase, William and John Archibald Getty 1989, 'The Soviet Bureaucracy in 1935: A Socio-Political Profile', in *Essays on Revolutionary Culture and Stalinism*, edited by John W. Strong, Columbus, Ohio: Slavica Publishers.

Chattopadhyay, Kunal 2006, *The Marxism of Leon Trotsky*, Kolkata: Progressive Publishers.

Ch'en Tu-hsiu 1976 [1929], 'Appendix', in *Leon Trotsky on China*, Leon Trotsky, edited by Les Evans and Russell Block, New York: Monad Press.

Chernenko, K.U. and M.S. Smirtiukov (eds.) 1967–88, *Resheniia partii i pravitel'stva po khoziaistvennym voprosam*, in 16 volumes. Moscow: Izdatel'stvo politicheskoi literatury.

Ciliga, Ante 1979 [1938, 1950], *The Russian Enigma*, translated by Fernand G. Fernier, Anne Cliff, Margaret and Hugo Dewar, London: Ink Links.

Clark, Roger 1983–84, 'The Development of the Marxist Position on the Aristocracy of Labor', *New International*, 1, 2: 59–94.

Claudin, Fernando 1975a, *The Communist Movement: From Comintern to Cominform, Part One: The Crisis of the Communist International*, translated by Brian Pearce, New York: Monthly Review Press.

—— 1975b, *The Communist Movement: From Comintern to Cominform, Part Two: The Zenith of Stalinism*, translated by Brian Pearce, New York: Monthly Review Press.

Cliff, Tony 1974, *State Capitalism in Russia*, London: Pluto Press.

—— 1991, *Trotsky: Fighting the Rising Stalinist Bureaucracy, 1923–27*, London: Bookmarks.

—— 1993, *Trotsky: The Darker the Night the Brighter the Star, 1927–1940*, London: Bookmarks.

Cohen, Stephen Frand 1977, 'Bolshevism and Stalinism', in *Stalinism: Essays in Historical Interpretation*, edited by Robert C. Tucker, New York: W.W. Norton and Company.

—— 1980, *Bukharin and the Bolshevik Revolution: A Political Biography, 1888–1938*, New York: Vintage Books, Random House.

Commission of Inquiry into the Charges Made against Leon Trotsky in the Moscow Trials 1972 [1938], *Not Guilty: Report of the Commission of Inquiry into the Charges Made against Leon Trotsky in the Moscow Trials*, New York: Monad Press.

Connor, Susan 2004, *The Age of Napoleon*, Westport, CT: Greenwood Press.

Conquest, Robert 1973, *The Great Terror: Stalin's Purge of the Thirties*, New York: Collier Books.

—— 1986, *The Harvest of Sorrow: Soviet Collectivization and the Terror-Famine*. New York: Oxford University Press.

—— 1989, *Stalin and the Kirov Murder*, New York: Oxford University Press.

Dal', Vladimir 1994 [1903], *Tolkovyi slovar' zhivogo velikorusskago iazyka v chetyrekh tomakh*, reprint edition, Moscow: Izdatel'skaia gruppa 'Progress' 'Univers'.

Daniels, Robert Vincent 1960, *The Conscience of the Revolution: Communist Opposition in Soviet Russia*, New York: Simon and Schuster.

—— (ed.) 1984, *A Documentary History of Communism*, revised edition, in two volumes, vol. 1, *Communism in Russia*, Hanover, New Haven: University Press of New England.

Danilov, Viktor et al. (eds.) 2000, *Tragediia sovetskoi derevni: kollektivizatsiia i raskulachivanie: dokumenty i materialy v 5 tomakh, 1927–1939*, vol. 2, *November 1929 to December 1930*, Moscow: Rossiiskaia polit. entsiklopediia.

Danos, Jacques and Marcel Gibelin 1986, *June '36: Class Struggle and the Popular Front in France*, translated by Peter

Fysh and Christine Bourry, London: Bookmarks.

Davies, Robert William 1957, 'The Inadequacies of Russian Trotskyism', *Labour Review*, 2, 4: 111–15.

—— 1980a, *The Socialist Offensive: The Collectivization of Soviet Agriculture, 1929–1930, The Industrialisation of Soviet Russia*, Cambridge, MA: Harvard University Press.

—— 1980b, *The Soviet Collective Farm, 1929–1930, The Industrialisation of Soviet Russia*, Cambridge, MA: Harvard University Press.

—— 1981a, 'Introduction' to 'The Five Year Plan in Crisis', by Christian Rakovsky, *Critique: A Journal of Soviet Studies and Socialist Theory*, 13: 1–7.

—— 1981b, 'The Syrtsov-Lominadze Affair', *Soviet Studies*, 33, 1: 29–50.

—— 1989, *The Soviet Economy in Turmoil, 1929–1930, The Industrialisation of Soviet Russia*, Cambridge, MA: Harvard University Press.

—— 1992, 'Gorbachev's Socialism in Historical Perspective', in *Stalinism: Its Nature and Aftermath: Essays in Honour of Moshe Lewin*, edited by Nick Lampert and Gábor T. Rittersporn, 16–76, Armonk, NY: M.E. Sharpe, Inc.

—— 1996, *Crisis and Progress in the Soviet Economy, 1931–1933, The Industrialisation of Soviet Russia*, Houndsmills, Basingstoke, UK: Macmillan Press.

Davies, Robert William and Oleg Khlevniuk 2002, 'Stakhanovism and the Soviet Economy', *Europe-Asia Studies*, 54, 6: 867–903.

Davies, Sarah 1997, *Popular Opinion in Stalin's Russia: Terror, Propaganda and Dissent, 1934–1941*, Cambridge: Cambridge University Press.

Davis, Kathryn 1977, *The Soviets at Geneva: The U.S.S.R. and the League of Nations, 1919–1933*, reprint edition, Westport, Connecticut: Hyperion Press.

Day, Richard 1973, *Leon Trotsky and the Politics of Economic Isolation*, London: Cambridge University Press.

—— 1987, 'Democratic Control and the Dignity of Politics: An Analysis of *The Revolution Betrayed*', *Comparative Economic Studies*, 29, 3: 4–29.

Day, Richard and Daniel Gaido (eds.) 2009, *Witnesses to Permanent Revolution: The Documentary Record*, Leiden, Boston: Brill.

Degras, Jane (ed.) 1953, *Soviet Documents on Foreign Policy*, in three volumes, vol. 3, *1933–1941* London: Oxford University Press.

—— (ed.) 1965, *The Communist International, 1919–1943: Documents*, in three volumes, vol. 3, *1929–1943*, London: Oxford University Press.

Deutscher, Isaac 1950, *Soviet Trade Unions: Their Place in Soviet Labour Policy*, London: Royal Institute of International Affairs.

—— 1954, *The Prophet Armed: Trotsky: 1879–1921*, New York: Vintage Books.

—— 1959, *The Prophet Unarmed, Trotsky: 1921–1929*, New York: Vintage Books.

—— 1963, *The Prophet Outcast, Trotsky: 1929–1940*, New York: Vintage Books.

—— 1966, *Stalin: A Political Biography*, New York: Oxford University Press.

Dimitroff, Georgi 1975, *The United Front: The Struggle Against Fascism and War*, San Francisco: Proletarian Publishers.

Dmytryshyn, Basil 1978, *USSR: A Concise History*, New York: Charles Scribner's Sons.

Dobb, Maurice 1966, *Soviet Economic Development Since 1917*, New York: International Publishers.

Draper, Hal 1962a, 'Marx and the Dictatorship of the Proletariat', *New Politics*, 1, 4 (summer 1962): 91–104.

—— 1962b, 'Marx and the Dictatorship of the Proletariat', *Études de marxologie*, 6: 5–73.

—— 1970, 'The Death of the State in Marx and Engels', *The Socialist Register*, London: Merlin Press.

—— 1977, *Karl Marx's Theory of Revolution*, in four volumes, vol. 1: *State and Bureaucracy*, in two books, New York: Monthly Review Press.

—— 1978, *Karl Marx's Theory of Revolution*, in four volumes, vol. 2: *The Politics of Social Classes*, New York: Monthly Review Press.

—— 1987, *The 'Dictatorship of the Proletariat' from Marx to Lenin*, New York: Monthly Review Press.

Drucker, Peter 1994, *Max Shachtman and His Left: A Socialist's Odyssey through the 'American Century'*, Atlantic Highlands, NJ: Humanities Press.

Edwards, Chris 1998, 'Leon Trotsky and Eastern Europe Today: An Overview and a Polemic', in *The Ideological Legacy of L.D. Trotsky: History and Contemporary Times*, edited by Marilyn Vogt-Downey, New York: International Committee for the Study of Leon Trotsky's Legacy.

Edwards, Theodore 1958, *The Soviet Union: What It Is—Where It Is Going: A Guide to the Study of Leon Trotsky's The Revolution Betrayed*. New York: Pioneer Publishers.

Egan, Thomas 1973, 'Leon Trotsky: His Political Philosophy in Opposition', PhD dissertation, Florida State University.

Ellman, Michael 2002, 'Soviet Repression Statistics: Some Comments', *Europe-Asia Studies*, 54, 7: 1151–72.

Elster, Jon 1985, *Making Sense of Marx*, Cambridge: Cambridge University Press.

—— 1994, 'The Nature and Choice of Rational-Choice Explanation', in *Readings in the Philosophy of Social Science*, edited by Michael Martin and Lee Macintyre, Cambridge, MA: MIT Press.

Engels, Frederick 1939 [1878], *Herr Eugen Dühring's Revolution in Science (Anti-Dühring)*, New York: International Publishers.

—— 1972 [1884] *The Origin of the Family, Private Property, and the State*, New York: Pathfinder Press.

Ercoli, M. (pseudonym for Palmiro Togliotti) 1968 [1935], 'The Communist International and the Fight for Peace', *The Communist International*, Greenwood Reprint, 12, 17–8: 1248–59.

Eudin, Xenia Joukoff and Robert Slusser 1966, *Soviet Foreign Policy 1928–1934: Documents and materials*, in two volumes, vol. 1, London: Pennsylvania State University Press.

Evans, Michael 1975, *Karl Marx*, Bloomington: Indiana University Press.

Evans, Richard John 2004, *The Coming of the Third Reich*, New York: Penguin.

Evgen'eva, Anastasiia (ed.) 1981, *Slovar' russkogo iazyka*, in four volumes, vol. 1, Moskva: Izdatel'stvo 'Russkii iazyk'.

Fainsod, Merle 1958, *Smolensk under Soviet Rule*, New York: Vintage Books, Random House.

Farber, Samuel 1990, *Before Stalinism: The Rise and Fall of Soviet Democracy*, London: Verso.

Fel'shtinskii, Iurii (ed.) 1988, *Kommunisticheskaia oppozitsiia v SSSR, 1923–1927: iz arkhiva L'va Trotskogo v chetyrekh tomakh*, Vermont: Chalidze Publications.

—— (ed.) 1990, *Kommunisticheskaia oppozitsiia v SSSR, 1923–1927*, in four volumes, 'TERRA', available at: <http://lib.ru/HISTORY/FELSHTINSKY/>.

—— (ed.) 1999–2002, *Arkhiv Trotskogo*, in four volumes, Kharkov: OKO, available at: <http://www.felshtinsky.com/books/6.pdf>, <http://www.felshtinsky.com/books/7.pdf>, <http://www.felshtinsky.com/books/8.pdf>, <http://www.felshtinsky.com/books/9.pdf>.

Filtzer, Donald 1986, *Soviet Workers and Stalinist Industrialization: The Formation of Modern Soviet Production Relations, 1928–1941*, London: Pluto Press.

Fine, Robert 2001, 'Totalitarianism: Impact on Social Thought', in *International Encyclopedia of the Social and Behavioral Sciences*, edited by Neil J. Smelser and Paul B. Baltes, Amsterdam: Elsevier.

Fischer, Conan 1991, *The German Communists and the Rise of Nazism*, Basingstoke: Macmillan.

Fischer, Louis 1969, *Russia's Road from Peace to War: Soviet Foreign Relations, 1917–1941*, New York: Harper and Row.

Fitzpatrick, Sheila 1974, 'Cultural Revolution in Russia 1928–32', *Journal of Contemporary History*, 9, 1: 33–52.

—— 1979a, *Education and Social Mobility in the Soviet Union 1921–1934*, Cambridge: Cambridge University Press.

—— 1979b, 'Stalin and the Making of a New Elite, 1928–1939', *Slavic Review*, 38, 3: 377–402.

—— 1982, *The Russian Revolution, 1917–1932*, Oxford: Oxford University Press.

—— 1994, *Stalin's Peasants: Resistance and Survival in the Russian Village after Collectivization*, New York: Oxford University Press.

Flewers, Paul 2008, *The New Civilization? Understanding Stalin's Soviet Union 1929–1941*, London: Francis Boutle Publishers.

Fowkes, Ben 1984, *Communism in Germany under the Weimar Republic*, London: Macmillan Press Ltd.

Foxcroft, Helen Charlotte 1938, 'The Revolution Betrayed', *The Quarterly Review*, 535: 1–14.

Frank, Pierre 1979, *The Fourth International: The Long March of the Trotskyists*, translated by Ruth Schein, London: Ink Links.

Friedrich, Carl Joachim and Zbigniew Kazimierz Brzezinski 1965, *Totalitarian Dictatorship and Autocracy*, 2nd edition, revised, New York: Frederick A. Praeger.

Getty, John Archibald 1985, *Origins of the Great Purges: The Soviet Communist Party Reconsidered, 1933–1938*, Cambridge: Cambridge University Press.

—— 1986, 'Trotsky in Exile: The Founding of the Fourth International', *Soviet Studies*, 38, 1: 24–35.

—— 1987, 'Reply to Thomas Twiss', *Soviet Studies*, 39, 2: 318–19.

—— 1991, 'State and Society Under Stalin: Constitutions and Elections in the 1930s', *Slavic Review*, 50, 1: 18–35.

—— 1993, 'The Politics of Repression Revisited', in *Stalinist Terror: New Perspectives*, edited by John Archibald Getty and Roberta Thompson Manning, Cambridge: Cambridge University Press.

—— 2002, ' "Excesses are not Permitted": Mass Terror and Stalinist Governance in the Late 1930s', *Russian Review*, 61, 1: 113–38.

Getty, John Archibald and William Chase 1978, 'The Moscow Party Elite of 1917 in the Great Purges', *Russian History/Histoire Russe*, 5, 1: 106–15.

—— 1993, 'Patterns of Repression Among the Soviet Elite in the Late 1930s: A Biographical Approach', in *Stalinist Terror*, edited by John Archibald Getty and Roberta Thompson Manning, Cambridge: Cambridge University Press.

Getty, John Archibald and Oleg V. Naumov 1999, *The Road to Terror: Stalin and the Self-Destruction of the Bolsheviks, 1932–1939*, translated by Benjamin Sher, New Haven: Yale University Press.

Getty, John Archibald, Gabor T. Rittersporn, and Viktor N. Zemskov 1993 'Victims of the Soviet Penal System in the Pre-War Years: A First Approach on the Basis of Archival Evidence', *The American Historical Review*, 98, 4: 1017–49.

Getty, John Archibald and Roberta Thompson Manning (eds.) 1993, *Stalinist Terror: New Perspectives*, Cam-bridge: Cambridge University Press, 1993.

Glotzer, Albert 1989, *Trotsky: Memoir and Critique*, Buffalo, NY: Prometheus Books.

Goldman, Wendy 2007, *Terror and Democracy in the Age of Stalin: The Social Dynamics of Repression*, Cambridge: Cambridge University Press.

—— 2011, *Inventing the Enemy: Denunciation and Terror in Stalin's Russia*, Cambridge: Cambridge University Press.

Gorbachev, Michail 1987, *Perestroika: New Thinking for Our County and the World*, New York: Harper & Row.

Grant, Ted 1997, *Russia: From Revolution to Counter-revolution*, London: Wellred Publications.

Gregor, Richard (ed.), 1974 *Resolutions and Decisions of the Communist Party of the Soviet Union*, in five volumes, vol. 2, *The Early Soviet Period, 1917–1929*, Toronto: University of Toronto Press.

Gusev, Aleksei 1996, 'Levokommunisticheskaia oppozitsiia v SSSR v kontse 20-kh godov', *Otechestvennaia istoriia*, 4, 1: 85–103.

—— 2008, 'The "Bolshevik Leninist" Opposition and the Working Class', in *A Dream Deferred: New Studies in Russian and Soviet Labour History*, edited by Donald Filtzer et al., Bern: Peter Lang.

Hallas, Duncan 1984, *Trotsky's Marxism*, London: Bookmarks.

Hamilton, Anne Wing 2007, 'Radishchev's Hundred-Headed Monster Lives! The Role of the Bureaucrat Symbol in State-Society Relations in Russia', *The Russian Review*, 66: 256–72.

Hansen, Joseph 1974 [1973], 'Introduction' in *Ten Years: History and Principles of the Left Opposition*, by Max Shachtman, Education for Socialists, New York: National Education Department, Socialist Workers Party.

Harding, Neil 1983, *Lenin's Political Thought: Theory and Practice in the Democratic and Socialist Revolutions*, in two volumes, Highlands, New Jersey: Humanities Press.

—— 1996, *Leninism*, Durham, N.C.: Duke University Press.

Harman, Chris 2003, *The Lost Revolution: Germany 1918 to 1923*, Chicago: Haymarket Books.

Harrison, James Pinckney 1972, *The Long March to Power: A History of the Chinese Communist Party, 1921–72*, New York: Praeger Publishers.

Haslam, Jonathan 1979, 'The Comintern and the Origins of the Popular Front 1934–1935', *The Historical Journal*, 22, 3: 673–91.

—— 1983, *Soviet Foreign Policy, 1930–1933: The Impact of the Depression*, New York: St. Martin's Press.

—— 1984, *The Soviet Union and the Struggle for Collective Security in Europe, 1933–39*, New York: St. Martin's Press.

—— 1992, *The Soviet Union and the Threat from the East, 1933–41: Moscow, Tokyo and the Prelude to the Pacific War*, Pittsburgh: University of Pittsburgh Press.

Hatch, John 1989, 'The "Lenin Levy" and the Social Origins of Stalinism: Workers and the Communist Party in Moscow, 1921–1928', *Slavic Review*, 48, 4: 558–78.

Hegel, Georg Wilhelm Friedrich 1973 [1820], *Hegel's Philosophy of Right*, translated and edited by T.M. Knox, London: Oxford University Press.

Hewett, Ed 1988, *Reforming the Soviet Economy: Equality versus Efficiency*, Washington D.C.: The Brookings Institution.

Hinks, Darron 1992, 'Support for the Opposition in Moscow in the Party Discussion of 1923–1924', *Soviet Studies*, 44, 1: 137–51.

Hobsbawm, Eric 1970, 'Lenin and the "Aristocracy of Labor"', *Monthly Review*, 21, 11: 47–56.

—— 1982, 'Marx, Engels and Politics', in *Marxism in Marx's Day*, vol. 1 of *The History of Marxism*, edited by Eric J. Hobsbawm, Bloomington: Indiana University Press.

Hobson, Christopher, and Ronald Tabor 1988, *Trotskyism and the Dilemma of Socialism*, New York: Greenwood Press.

Hofla, Chester 1985, 'When "Political Revolution" Replaced "Political Reform"', *Bulletin in Defense of Marxism*, 17: 25–9.

Holmes, Larry 1990, *For the Revolution Redeemed: The Workers Opposition in the Bolshevik Party 1919–1921*, 82, The Carl Beck Papers in Russian and East European Studies, Pittsburgh: University of Pittsburgh Center for Russian and East European Studies.

Hosking, Geoffrey 1993, *The First Socialist Society: A History of the Soviet Union from Within*, Cambridge: Harvard University Press.

Hough, Jerry 1977, *The Soviet Union and Social Science Theory*, Cambridge, MA: Harvard University Press.

Hough, Jerry and Merle Fainsod 1979, *How the Soviet Union Is Governed*, Cambridge, MA: Harvard University Press.

Houn, Franklin 1967, *A Short History of Chinese Communism*, Englewood Cliffs, NJ: Prentice-Hall.

Hubbard, Leonard 1939, *The Economics of Soviet Agriculture*, London: Macmillan and Co.

Hunt, Richard 1974, *Marxism and Totalitarian Democracy*, vol. 1 of *The Political Ideas of Marx and Engels*, Pittsburgh: University of Pittsburgh Press.

—— 1984, *Classical Marxism, 1850–1895*, vol. 2 of *The Political Ideas of Marx and Engels*, Pittsburgh: University of Pittsburgh Press.

Hutchings, Raymond 1982, *Soviet Economic Development*, New York: New York University Press.

Imperatorskaia akademiia nauk 1982 [1891–1929], *Slovar' russkago iazyka*, London: Flegon Press.

Institute of Marxism Leninism of the Central Committee of the CPSU 1972, *Against Trotskyism: The Struggle of Lenin and the CPSU Against Trotskyism, A Collection of Documents*, Moscow: Progress Publishers.

Isaacs, Harold Robert 1961, *The Tragedy of the Chinese Revolution*, Stanford: Stanford University Press.

Jackson, Julian 1988, *The Popular Front in France: Defending Democracy, 1934–38*, Cambridge: Cambridge University Press.

James, Cyril Lionel Robert 1937, *World Revolution, 1917–1936: The Rise and Fall of the Communist International*, New York: Pioneer Publishers.

—— 1964, 'Trotsky's "Revolution Betrayed"', *International Socialism* 16: 25–9.

Jasny, Naum 1961, *Soviet Industrialization, 1928–1952*, Chicago: The University of Chicago Press.

Jenkins, Brian 2006, 'Historiographical Essay: The *Six Fevrier* 1934 and the "Survival" of the French Republic', *French History*, 20, 3: 333–51.

Johnstone, Monty 1975a, 'Trotsky and the Popular Front', Part I, *Marxism Today*, 308–16.

—— 1975b, 'Trotsky and the Popular Front', Part II, *Marxism Today*, 346–54.

Joint Opposition 1973, *The Platform of the Joint Opposition [1927]*, London: New Park Publications.

Katz, David 1977, 'Trotsky's *The Revolution Betrayed*: A Reappraisal', *Midwest Quarterly*, 18, 3: 287–97.

Kautsky, Karl 1907, *The Social Revolution*, translated by Algie Martin and May Wood Simons, Chicago: Charles H. Kerr and Co.

—— 1971 [1899], *The Class Struggle (Erfurt Program)*, translated by William Bohn, New York: W.W. Norton and Co.

—— 1972 [1925], *Foundations of Christianity: A Study in Christian Origins*, New York: Monthly Review Press.

Khlevniuk, Oleg 2009, *Master of the House: Stalin and His Inner Circle*, translated by Nora Seligman Favorov, New Haven: Yale University Press.

—— 1995, 'The Objectives of the Great Terror, 1937–1938', in *Soviet History, 1917–53: Essays in Honour of R.W. Davies*, edited by Julian Cooper, Maureen

Perrie, and E.A. Rees, New York: St. Martin's Press.

Kimball, Alan 1998, 'The Tsarist State and the origins of Revolutionary Opposition in the 1860s', presentation to the Northwest Scholars of Russian and Soviet History and Culture, Seattle Washington, available at: <http://www.uoregon.edu/~kimball/stt&pbl.htm>.

Kirilina, Alla 1993, *Rikoshet, ili skol'ko chelovek bylo ubito vystrelom v Smol'nom*, St. Petersburg: Ob-vo 'Znanie' Rossii.

Knei-Paz, Baruch 1978, *The Social and Political Thought of Leon Trotsky*, Oxford: Oxford University Press.

Knight, Amy 1999, *Who Killed Kirov?: The Kremlin's Greatest Mystery*, New York: Hill and Wang.

Koenker, Diane 1985, 'Urbanization and Deurbanization in the Russian Revolution and Civil War', *The Journal of Modern History*, 57, 3: 424–50.

Koestler, Arthur 1941, *Darkness at Noon*, translated by Daphne Hardy, New York: Macmillan.

Kolakowski, Leszek 2005, *Main Currents of Marxism: The Founders, The Golden Age, The Breakdown*, translated by P.S. Falla, New York: W.W. Norton and Company

Kollontai, Alexandra 1977, *Selected Writings of Alexandra Kollontai*, translated by Alix Holt, New York: W.W. Norton and Company.

Kotz, David 2001, 'Is Russia Becomimg Capitalist?', *Science and Society*, 65, 2: 57–181.

Kotz, David and Fred Weir 2007, *Russia's Path from Gorbachev to Putin: The Demise of the Soviet System and the New Russia*, New York: Routledge.

KPSS 1970a, *Kommunisticheskaia Partiia Sovetskogo Soiuza v rezoliutsiiakh i resheniiakh s"ezdov, konferentsii i plenumov TsK*, in 14 volumes, vol. 2 1917–1924, edited by P.N. Fedoseev and K.U. Chernenko, Moscow: Izdatel'stvo Politicheskoi Literatury.

—— 1970b, *Kommunisticheskaia Partiia Sovetskogo Soiuza v rezoliutsiiakh i resheniiakh s"ezdov, konferentsii i plenumov TsK*, in 14 volumes, vol. 4 1927–1931, edited by P.N. Fedoseev and K.U. Chernenko, Moscow: Izdatel'stvo Politicheskoi Literatury.

—— 1971, *Kommunisticheskaia Partiia Sovetskogo Soiuza v rezoliutsiiakh i resheniiakh s"ezdov, konferentsii i plenumov TsK*, in 14 volumes, vol. 5, 1931–1941, edited by P.N. Fedoseev and K.U. Chernenko, Moscow: Izdatel'stvo Politicheskoi Literatury.

—— 1975, *XVII s"ezd Vsesoiuznoi kommunisticheskoi partii (b): 26 ianvaria–10 fevralia 1934 g.: stenograficheskii otchet*, Nendeln, Liechtenstein: Krays-Thomson.

Krieger, Joel, et al. (eds.) 1993, *The Oxford Companion to Politics of the World*, New York: Oxford University Press.

Kropotkin, Peter 1971 [1909], *The Great French Revolution, 1789–1793*, translated by N.F. Dryhurst, New York: Shocken Books.

Krygier, Martin 1978, '"Bureaucracy" in Trotsky's Analysis of Stalinism', in *Socialism and the New Class: Towards the Analysis of Structural Inequality within Socialist Societies*, edited by Marian Sawer, APSA Monograph 19, Sidney, Australia: Australasian Political Studies Association.

—— 1979a, 'The Revolution Betrayed? From Trotsky to the New Class', in *Bureaucracy: The Career of a Concept*, edited by Eugene Kamenka and Martin Krygier, New York: St. Martin's Press.

—— 1979b, 'State and Bureaucracy in Europe: The Growth of a Concept', in *Bureaucracy: The Career of a Concept*, edited by Eugene Kamenka and Martin Krygier, New York: St. Martin's Press.

—— 1979c, 'Weber, Lenin and the Reality of Socialism', in *Bureaucracy: The Career of a Concept*, edited by Eugene Kamenka and Martin Krygier, New York: St. Martin's Press.

—— 1979d, 'Marxism and Bureaucracy', PhD dissertation, Australian National University.

Kuhn, Thomas 1970, *The Structure of Scientific Revolutions*, Chicago: University of Chicago Press.

Kuromiya, Hiroaki 1988, *Stalin's Industrial Revolution: Politics and Workers, 1928–1932*, Cambridge: Cambridge University Press.

—— 2005, *Stalin: Profiles in Power*, Harlow: Pearson Education Limited.

Lane, David 1971, *Politics and Society in the USSR*, New York: Random House.

Laurat, Lucien 1931, *L'Économie Soviétique: Sa dynamique, Son mécanisme*, Paris: Librairie Valois.

—— 1932, *Économie planée contre économie enchaînée*, Paris: Librairie Valois.

—— 1940, *Marxism and Democracy*, translated by Edward Fitzgerald, London: Victor Gollancz Limited.

Law, David 1982, 'Trockij and Thermidor', in *Pensiero e azione politica di Lev Trockij: atti del convegno internazionale per il quarantesimo anniversario della morte*, edited by Francesca Gori, vol. 2, Firenze: Leo S. Olschki.

—— 1987a, 'Trotsky in Opposition: 1923–1940', PhD dissertation, University of Keele.

—— 1987b, 'Trotsky and the Comparative History of Revolutions: the "Second Chapter"', *Sbornik*, 13, Study Group on the Russian Revolution, 4–15.

—— 1995, 'The Left Opposition in 1923', in *The Ideas of Leon Trotsky* edited by Hillel Ticktin and Michael Cox, London: Porcupine Press.

Le Blanc, Paul 1990, *Lenin and the Revolutionary Party*, Atlantic Highlands, NJ: Humanities Press International.

Lenin, Vladimir Il'ich 1958–65, *Polnoe sobranie sochinenii*, in 55 volumes, Moscow: Gosudarstvennoe izdatel'stvo politicheskoi literatury.

—— 1960–70, *Collected Works*, in 45 volumes, Moscow: Progress Publishers

—— 1970, *On the Paris Commune*, Moscow: Progress Publishers.

—— 1978 [1972], *Marxism on the State: Preparatory Material for the Book* State and Revolution, Moscow: Progress Publishers.

Lenin, Vladimir Il'ich and Leon Trotsky 1975, *Lenin's Fight against Stalinism*, edited by Russell Block, New York: Pathfinder Press.

—— 1979, *Kronstadt*, New York: Monad Press.

Lenoe, Matt 2002, 'Did Stalin Kill Kirov and Does It Matter?' *The Journal of Modern History*, 74, 2: 352–80.

Lewin, Moshe 1968, *Russian Peasants and Soviet Power: A Study of Collectivization*, New York: W.W. Norton and Company.

—— 1970, *Lenin's Last Struggle*, translated by A.M. Sheridan Smith, New York: Vintage Books.

—— 1973, 'The Disappearance of Planning in the Plan', *The Slavic Review*, 32, 2: 271–87.

—— 1985, *The Making of the Soviet System: Essays in the Social History of Interwar Russia*, New York: Pantheon Books.

Liebach, Andre 1982, 'On the Origins of a Marxist Theory of Bureaucracy in the Critique of Hegel's "Philosophy of Right"', *Political Theory*, 10, 1: 77–93.

Liebman, Marcel 1975, *Leninism Under Lenin*, translated by Brian Pearce, London, Merlin Press.

Lih, Lars T. 1995a, *Deferred Dreams: War Communism 1918–1921*, Washington DC: The National Council for Soviet and East European Research.

—— 2007, ' "Our Position is in the Highest Degree Tragic": Bolshevik "Euphora" in 1920', in *History and Revolution: Refuting Revisionism*, edited by Mike Haynes and Jim Wolfreys, London: Verso.

Lih, Lars, Oleg Naumov, and Oleg Khlevniuk (eds.) 1995, *Stalin's Letters to Molotov, 1925–1926*, translations by Catherine A. Fitzpatrick, New Haven: Yale University Press.

Linden, Marcel van der 2007, *Western Marxism and the Soviet Union: A Survey of Critical Theories and Debates Since 1917*, Leiden: Brill.

Linz, Juan 2000, *Totalitarian and Authoritarian Regimes*, Boulder, CO: Lynne Rienner Publishers.

Lockwood, David 2002, 'Rival Napoleons? Stalinism and Bonapartism', *War and Society*, 20, 2: 57–8.

Longuet, Isabelle 1994, 'L'opposition de gauche en URSS 1928–1929', *Cahiers Léon Trotsky*, 53: 33–61.

Lovell, David 1987, *Trotsky's Analysis of Soviet Bureaucratization: A Critical Essay*, London: Croom Helm.

Löwy, Michael 1981, *The Politics of Combined and Uneven Development: The Theory of Permanent Revolution*, London: Verso Editions and NLB.

—— 1995, 'From the *Logic* of Hegel to the Finland Station in Petrograd', in *The Ideas of Leon Trotsky*, edited by Hillel Ticktin and Michael Cox, London: Procupine Press.

Lubitz, Wolfgang and Petra 1999, *Trotsky Bibliography: An International Classified List of Publications about Leon Trotsky and Trotskyism, 1905–1998*, Munich: K.G. Saur.

Lustig, Michael 1989, *Trotsky and Djilas: Critics of Communist Bureaucracy*, New York: Greenwood Press.

Luxemburg, Rosa 1970, *Rosa Luxemburg Speaks*, edited by Mary-Alice Waters, New York: Pathfinder Press.

Lynch, Allen 2005, *How Russia Is Not Ruled: Reflections on Russian Political*

Development, Cambridge: Cambridge University Press.

Malle, Silvana 1985, *The Economic Organization of War Communism, 1918–1921*, Cambridge: Cambridge University Press.

Mandel, Ernest 1971, 'Introduction' in *The Struggle against Fascism in Germany*, by Leon Trotsky, New York: Pathfinder Press.

—— 1979, *Trotsky: A Study in the Dynamic of His Thought*, London: NLB.

—— 1984, 'What is Bureaucracy?', in *The Stalinist Legacy: Its Impact on Twentieth-Century World Politics*, edited by Tariq Ali, Harmonsworth, Middlesex, England: Penguin Books.

—— 1992, *Power and Money: A Marxist Theory of Bureaucracy*, London: Verso.

—— 1995, *Trotsky as Alternative*, London: Verso.

Marik, Soma 2009, *Reinterrogating the Classical Marxist Discourses of Revolutionary Democracy*, Delhi: Aakar Books.

Markin, N. (pseudonym for Leon Sedov) 1936, 'The Stakhanovist Movement', *The New International*, 3, 1 (February): 9–13.

Marot, John Eric 2006, 'Trotsky, the Left Opposition and the Rise of Stalinism: Theory and Practice', *Historical Materialism*, 14, 3: 175–206.

Marx, Karl 1935, *Selected Works* in two volumes, vol. 1, Leningrad: Co-operative Publishing Society of Foreign Workers in the U.S.S.R.

—— 1966 [1871], *The Civil War in France*, Peking: Foreign Languages Press.

—— 1970 [1843], *Critique of Hegel's 'Philosophy of Right'*, translated and edited by Annette Jolin and Joseph O'Malley, Cambridge: Cambridge University Press.

—— 1974a, *Early Writings*, translated by Rodney Livingstone and Gregor Benton, New York: Vintage Books, Random House.

—— 1974b, *The Revolutions of 1848*. vol. 1 of *Political Writings*, edited by David Fernbach, New York: Vintage Books.

—— 1974c, *Surveys from Exile*, vol. 2 of *Political Writings*, edited by David Fernbach, New York: Vintage Books.

—— 1974d, *The First International and After*, vol. 3 of *Political Writings*, edited by David Fernbach, New York: Penguin Books.

Marx, Karl and Frederick Engels 1962, *Karl Marx and Frederick Engels on Britain*, Moscow: Foreign Languages Publishing House.

—— 1972a, *The Marx-Engels Reader*, edited by Robert C. Tucker, New York: W.W. Norton and Company.

—— 1972b, *The Communist Manifesto of Karl Marx and Frederick Engels*, Calcutta: Radical Book Club, B. Mitra.

—— 1998, *The German Ideology: Including Theses on Feuerbach and An Introduction to the Critique of Political Economy*, Amherst, NY: Prometheus.

Mavrakis, Kostas 1976, *On Trotskyism: Problems of Theory and History*, translated by John Mcgreal, London: Routledge and Kegan Paul.

McNeal, Robert 1961, 'Trotsky's Interpretation of Stalin', in *Canadian Slavonic Papers*, 5, 87–97, edited by G.S.N. Luckyj, Toronto: University of Toronto Press.

—— 1966, 'Trotsky's Interpretation of Stalin', in *Stalin*, Great Lives Observed, edited by T.H. Rigby, Englewood Cliffs, NJ: Prentice-Hall.

McNeal, Robert H. (ed.), 1974 *Resolutions and Decisions of the Communist Party of the Soviet Union*, in five volumes, vol. 3, *The Stalin Years, 1929–1953*, Toronto: University of Toronto Press.

—— 1977, 'Trotskyist Interpretations of Stalinism', in *Stalinism: Essays in Historical Interpretation*, edited by Robert C. Tucker, New York: W.W. Norton and Company.

—— 1982, 'Trockij and Stalinism' in *Pensiero e azione politica di Lev Trockij*, vol. 2, 377–87, edited by Francesca Gori, Florence: Leo S. Olschki.

Medvedev, Roy 1973, *Let History Judge: The Origins and Consequences of Stalinism*, translated by Coleen Taylor, edited by David Joravsky and George Haupt, New York: Vintage Books.

—— 1985, *All Stalin's Men*, translated by Harold Shukman, Garden City, NY: Anchor Books.

Medvedev, Zhores 1987, *Soviet Agriculture*, New York: W.W. Norton and Company.

Mercier, Louis-Sebastien 1999, *Panorama of Paris: Selections from Le Tableau de Paris*, edited by Jeremy D. Popkin, University Park, Pennsylvania: The Pennsylvania State University Press.

Merl, Stephen 1993, 'Social Mobility in the Countryside', in *Social Dimensions of Soviet Industrialization*, edited by William G. Rosenberg and Lewis H. Siegelbaum, Bloomington and Indianapolis: Indiana University Press.

Meyer, Alfred 1967, 'Lev Davidovich Trotsky', in *Problems of Communism*, 16, 6: 30–40.

—— 1978, 'The War Scare of 1927', in *Soviet Union/Union Sovietique*, 5, 1: 1–25.

Michail, Loizos 1977, 'Trotsky's Revolution Betrayed', *Socialist Europe*, 3: 3–7.

Michels, Robert 1962, *Political Parties: A Sociological Study of the Oligarchical Tendencies of Modern Democracy*, translated by Eden and Cedar Paul, New York: The Free Press, McMillan Publishing.

Milenkovitch, Deborah Duff 1987, 'Trotsky's The Revolution Betrayed: A Contemporary Look', *Comparative Economic Studies*, 29, 3: 40–69.

Miles, Jim 1994–5, 'How Trotsky Foretold the Collapse of the Soviet Union', *Bulletin in Defense of Marxism*, 12, 10: 29–31, 45–53.

—— 1998, 'Trotsky on the Collapse of the USSR', in *The Ideological Legacy of L.D. Trotsky: History and Contemporary Times*, edited by Marilyn Vogt-Downey, New York: International Committee for the Study of Leon Trotsky's Legacy.

Miliband, Ralph 1972 'Marx and the State', in Marx's Socialism edited by Shlomo Avineri, New York: Lieber-Atherton.

Mill, John Stuart 1994 [1848, 1879], *Principles of Political Economy and Chapters on Socialism*, edited by Jonathan Riley, Oxford: Oxford University Press.

Molyneux, John 1981, *Leon Trotsky's Theory of Revolution*, New York: St. Martin's Press.

Moore, Harriet 1945, *Soviet Far Eastern Policy, 1931–1945*, Princeton: Princeton University Press.

Mortimer, Edward 1984, *The Rise of the French Communist Party, 1920–1947*, London: Faber and Faber.

Murphy, Kevin 2001, 'Opposition at the Local Level: A Case Study of the Hammer and Sickle Factory', *Europe-Asia Studies*, 53, 2: 329–50.

—— 2005, *Revolution and Counterrevolution: Class Struggle in a Moscow Metal Factory*, New York: Berghahn Books.

—— 2008, 'Strikes during the Early Soviet Period, 1922 to 1932: From Working-Class Militancy to Working-Class Passivity?' in *A Dream Deferred: New Studies in Russian and Soviet Labour History*, edited by Donald Filtzer, Wendy Z. Goldman, Gijs Kessler, and Simon Pirani, Bern: Peter Lang.

N. 1928, 'Stalin's Left Course and the Tasks of the Opposition', April 1928, unpublished translation of 'Stalins Linderkurs und die Aufgaben der Opposition', *New Yorker Volkszeitung*, 19 August 1928.

National Education Department, Socialist Workers Party 1969, *Class, Party and State and the Eastern European Revolution*, Education for Socialists. New York: National Education Department, Socialist Workers Party.

Nicolaevsky, Boris 1965, *Power and the Soviet Elite: 'The Letter of an Old Bolshevik' and Other Essays by Boris I. Nicolaevsky*, edited by Janet D. Zagoria, Ann Arbor: University of Michigan Press.

Nicolaus, Martin 1970, 'The Theory of the Labor Aristocracy', *Monthly Review*, 21, 11: 91–101.

Nove, Alec 1976, *An Economic History of the U.S.S.R.*, Middlesex: Penguin Books.

—— 1979, *Political Economy and Soviet Socialism*, London: George Allen and Unwin.

—— 1981, 'New Light on Trotsky's Economic Views', *Slavic Review*, 40, 1: 92–4.

—— 1982, 'Trockij, Collectivisation and the Five Year Plan', in *Pensiero e azione politica di Lev Trockij*, edited by Francesca Gori, vol. 2, Firenze: Leo S. Olschki.

O'Malley, Joseph 1970, 'Editor's introduction' in *Critique of Hegel's 'Philosophy of Right'*, by Karl Marx, translated and edited by Annette Jolin and Joseph O'Malley, Cambridge: Cambridge University Press.

Pantsov, Alexander 2000, *The Bolsheviks and the Chinese Revolution, 1919–1927*, Honolulu: University of Hawaii Press.

Pasvolsky, Leo 1921, *The Economics of Communism: With Special Reference to Russia's Experiment*, New York: Macmillan Company.

Pavlenkov, Florentii 1913, *Entsiklopedicheskii slovar*, St. Petersburg: Tip. Spb. T-va Pech. i Izd. diela 'Trud'.

—— 1918, *Slovar' inostrannykh slov, voshedshikh v sostav russkago iazyka/sostavlen po Entsiklopedicheskomu Slovariu F. Pavlenkova*, New York: Izdatel'stvo M.N. Maizelia.

Peng Shu-tse 1976, 'Introduction' in *Leon Trotsky on China*, by Leon Trotsky, edited by Les Evans and Russell Block, New York: Monad Press.

Pietsch, Walter 1969, *Revolution und Statt: Instiutionen als Träger der Machtin der Sowjetrussland (1917–1922)*, Cologne: Verlag Wissenschaft und Politik.

Pipes Richard (ed.) 1996, *The Unknown Lenin: From the Secret* Archive, New Haven: Yale University Press.

Pirani, Simon 2008, *The Russian Revolution in Retreat, 1920–24: Soviet Workers and the New Communist Elite*, London: Routledge.

Plamenatz, John 1950, 'Deviations from Marxism', *Political Quarterly*, 21, 1: 40–55.

—— 1954, *German Communism and Russian Marxism*, London: Longmans, Green, and Co.

Pomper, Philip 1986, 'Notes on Dialectics and Evolutionism', in *Trotsky's Notebooks, 1933–1935*, by Leon Trotsky, translated by Philip Pomper, New York: Columbia University Press.

Poole, Thomas Ray 1974, ' "Counter-Trial": Leon Trotsky and the Soviet Purge Trials', PhD dissertation, University of MA.

—— 1982, 'Stalin's Trials as Trockij's Test', in *Pensiero e azione politica di Lev Trockij*, edited by Francesca Gori, vol. 2, Firenze: Leo S. Olschki.

Popov, Nikolaï 1934, *Outline History of the Communist Party of the Soviet Union*, in two volumes, vol. 2, New York: International Publishers.

Popper, Karl 1968, *The Logic of Scientific Discovery*, New York: Harper and Row.

Post, Charles 1999, 'Ernest Mandel and the Marxian Theory of Bureaucracy', in *The Legacy of Ernest Mandel*, edited by Gilbert Achcar, London: Verso.

—— 2010, 'Exploring Working-Class Consciousness: A Critique of the Theory of the "Labour-Aristocracy"', *Historical Materialism*, 18: 3–38.

Poulantzas, Nicos 1975, *Political Power and Social Classes*, translated and edited by Timothy O'Hagan, London: NLB.

Preliminary Commission of Inquiry 1968 [1937], *The Case of Leon Trotsky: Report of Hearings on the Charges Made Against Him in the Moscow Trials*, New York: Merit Publishers.

Procacci, Giuliano 1963, 'Trotsky's View of the Critical Years, 1929–1936', *Science and Society*, 27, 1: 62–9.

Radosh, Ronald, Mary Habeck, and Grigory Sevostianov (eds.) 2001, *Spain Betrayed: The Soviet Union and the Spanish Civil War*, New Haven: Yale University Press.

Rakovsky, Christian 1973 [1929], 'Pis'mo Kh. G. Rakovskogo o prichinakh perozhdeniia partiia i gosudarstvennogo apparata', in *Biulleten' oppozitsii (bol'shevikov-lenintsev)*, Monad Press, 6: 14–20.

—— 1980, *Selected Writings on Opposition in the USSR 1923–30*, edited by Gus Fagan. London: Allison and Busby.

—— 1981, 'The Five Year Plan in Crisis', *Critique: A Journal of Soviet Studies and Socialist Theory*, 13, 10: 7–54.

Rees, Edward Arfon 1987, *State Control in Soviet Russia: The Rise and Fall of the Workers' and Peasants' Inspectorate, 1920–34*, New York: St. Martin's Press.

Reichman, Henry 1988, 'Reconsidering ' "Stalinism" ', *Theory and Society*, 17, 1: 57–89.

Reiman, Michael 1987, *The Birth of Stalinism: The USSR on the Eve of the 'Second Revolution'*, translated by George Saunders, Bloomington: Indiana University Press.

Remington, Thomas 1984, *Building Socialism in Bolshevik Russia: Ideology and Industrial Organization, 1917–1921*, Pittsburgh: University of Pittsburgh Press.

Report of Court Proceedings 1936, *In the Case of the Trotskyite-Zinovievite Terrorist Centre*, Moscow: People's Commissariat of Justice of the U.S.S.R.

—— 1937, *In the Case of the Anti-Soviet Trotskyite Centre*, Moscow: People's Commissariat of Justice of the U.S.S.R.

—— 1938, *In the Case of the Anti-Soviet 'Bloc of Rights and Trotskyites'*, Moscow: People's Commissariat of Justice of the U.S.S.R., 1938.

Rigby, Thomas Henry 1968, *Communist Party Membership in the U.S.S.R., 1917–1967*, Princeton, NJ: Princeton University Press.

—— 1979, *Lenin's Government: Sovnarkom 1917–1922*, Cambridge: Cambridge University Press.

Riggs, Fred 1979, 'Introduction: Shifting Meanings of the Term "Bureaucracy"', *International Social Science Journal*, 31, 4: 563–84.

Rimmel, Lesley 1997, 'Another Kind of Fear; The Kirov Murder and the End of Bread Rationing in Leningrad', *Slavic Review*, 56, 3: 481–99.

Rittersporn, Gábor 1991, *Stalinist Simplifications and Soviet Complications:*

Social Tensions and Political Conflicts in the USSR, 1933–53, Chur, Switzerland: Harwood Academic publishers.

RKP(b) 1959, *Vos'moi s''ezd RKP(b), Mart 1919 goda: Protokoly*, Moscow, Gosudarstvennoe Izdatel'stvo Politicheskoi Literatury.

—— 1960, *Deviatyi s''ezd RKP(b), Mart–Aprel' 1920 goda: Protokoly*, Moscow: Gosudarstvennoe Izdatel'stvo Politicheskoi Literatury.

—— 1961, *Odinadtsatyi s''ezd RKP(b), Mart-aprel' 1922 goda: Stenograficheskii otchet*, Moscow: Gosudarstvennoe Izdatel'stvo Politicheskoi Literatury.

—— 1963, *Desiatyi s''ezd RKP(b), Mart 1921 goda: Stenograficheskii otchet*, Moscow: Gosudarstvennoe Izdatel'stvo Politicheskoi Literatury.

—— 1968, *Dvenadtsatyi s''ezd RKP(b), Stenograficheskii otchet*, Moscow: Izdatel'stvo Politicheskoi Literatury.

—— 1972, *Deviataia konferentsiia RKP(b), Sentiabr 1920 goda: Protokoly*, Moscow: Izdatel'stvo politicheskoi literatury.

Rogovin, Vadim 1998, *1937 Stalin's Year of Terror*, Oak Park, MI: Mehring Books.

—— 2009, *Stalin's Terror of 1937–1938: Political Genocide in the USSR*, translated by Frederick S. Choate, Oak Park, MI: Mehring Books.

Rossman, Jeffrey 2005, *Worker Resistance under Stalin: Class and Revolution on the Shop Floor*, Cambridge, MA: Harvard University Press.

Rothschild, Joseph 1959, *The Communist Party of Bulgaria, Origins and Develop-*

ment, New York: Columbia University Press.

Rykov, A. 1928, 'Tekushchii moment i zadachi partii', *Pravda*, Pravda Digital Archive, East View Information Services, 163: 3–4.

—— 1970 [1926], 'The Results of the Joint Plenary Meeting of the C.C and of the C.C.C. of the C.P.S.U.', *International Press Correspondence*, London: World Microfilms, 6, 57: 949–56.

Saccarelli, Emanuele 2008, *Gramsci and Trotsky in the Shadow of Stalinism: The Political Theory and Practice of Opposition*, New York: Routledge.

Sakwa, Richard 1988, *Soviet Communists in Power: A Study of Moscow during the Civil War, 1918–1921*, New York: St. Martin's Press.

Salvadori, Massimo 1979, *Karl Kautsky and the Socialist Revolution, 1880–1938*, London: NLB.

Samary, Catherine 1999, 'Mandel's Views on the Transition to Socialism, in *The Legacy of Ernest Mandel*, edited by Gilbert Achcar, London: Verso.

Sanderson, John 1963, 'Marx and Engels on the State', *Western Political Quarterly*, 16: 951–3.

—— 1969, *An Interpretation of the Political Ideas of Marx and Engels*, London: Longmans.

Sawer, Marian 1977, 'The Genesis of *State and Revolution*', *The Socialist Register*, London: Merlin Press.

Schapiro, Leonard 1971, *The Communist Party of the Soviet Union*, New York: Vintage Books.

—— 1977, *The Origin of the Communist Autocracy: Political Opposition in the*

Soviet State–First Phase, 1917–1922, Cambridge, MA: Harvard University Press.

Serge, Victor 1972 [1930], *Year One of the Russian Revolution*, translated and edited by Peter Sedgwick, Chicago: Holt, Rinehart and Winston.

—— 1980 [1951], *Memoirs of a Revolutionary, 1901–1941*, translated and edited by Peter Sedgwick, Oxford: Oxford University Press.

—— 1996 [1937], *Russia Twenty Years After*, translated by Max Shachtman and edited by Susan Weissman, Atlantic Highlands, NJ: Humanities Press.

Serge, Victor and Leon Trotsky 1994, *The Serge-Trotsky Papers*, edited by D.J. Cotterill, London: Pluto Press.

Serge, Victor and Natalia Sedova Trotsky 1975 [1951], *The Life and Death of Leon Trotsky*, New York: Basic Books.

Service, Robert 1979, *The Bolshevik Party in Revolution: A Study in Organizational Change, 1917–1923*, New York: Barnes and Noble.

—— 1995, *Lenin: A Political Life*, in three volumes, vol. 3, *The Iron Ring*, London: Macmillan.

—— 2004, *Stalin: A Biography*, Cambridge, MA: The Belknap Press of Harvard University Press.

—— 2009, *Trotsky: A Biography*, Cambridge, MA: The Belknap Press of Harvard University Press.

Shachtman, Max 1962, *The Bureaucratic Revolution: The Rise of the Stalinist State*, New York: Donald Press.

—— 1965, 'The Struggle for the New Course', in *The New Course and the*

Struggle for the New Course, Leon Trotsky and Max Shachtman, Ann Arbor: University of Michigan Press.

—— 1974 [1933], *Ten Years: History and Principles of the Left Opposition*, New York: National Education Department, Socialist Workers Party.

Shapiro, Judith 1987, 'On the Accuracy of Economic Observations of *Chto Takoe SSSR* in Historical Retrospect', *Comparative Economic Studies*, 29, 3: 45–69.

Shirer, William 1960, *The Rise and Fall of the Third Reich: A History of Nazi Germany*, New York: Simon and Schuster.

Shliapnikov, Alexander 2004 [1921], 'Theses of the Workers' Opposition', Marxists', Internet Archive, available at: <http://www.marxists.org/archive/shliapnikov/1921/workers-opposition.htm>.

Siegelbaum, Lewis 1992, *Soviet State and Society Between Revolutions, 1918–1929*. Cambridge: Cambridge University Press.

—— 1988, *Stakhanovism and the Politics of Productivity in the USSR, 1935–1941*, Cambridge: Cambridge University Press.

Sinclair, Louis 1989, *Trotsky: A Bibliography*, in two volumes, Aldershot: Scolar Press.

Siriani, Carmen 1982, *Workers' Control and Socialist Democracy: The Soviet Experience*, London: Verso Editions.

Smith, Jeremy 1998, 'The Georgian Affair of 1922: Policy Failure, Personality Clash or Power Struggle?' *Europe-Asia Studies*, 50, 3: 519–44.

Solzhenitsyn, Aleksandr 1974–8, *The Gulag Archipelago, 1918–1956: An Experiment in Literary Investigation*, in three volumes, translated by Thomas P. Whitney, New York: Harper and Row.

Sontag, John 1975, 'The Soviet War Scare of 1926–27', *Russian Review*, 37: 66–77.

Soucy, Robert 1995, *French Fascism: The Second Wave, 1933–1939*, New Haven, CN: Yale University Press.

Spiro, Herbert 1968, 'Totalitarianism', in *The International Encyclopedia of the Social Sciences*, edited by David L. Sills, New York: Macmillan.

Stalin, Joseph 1933, *Leninism*, in two volumes, vol. 2, New York: International Publishers.

—— 1950, *On the Draft Constitution of the U.S.S.R.: Constitution (Fundamental Law) of the Union of Soviet Socialist Republics*, Moscow: Foreign Languages Publishing House.

—— 1952–5, *Works*, in thirteen volumes, Moscow: Foreign Languages Publishing House.

—— 1968 [1936], 'Stalin-Howard Interview', interview by Roy Howard, *The Communist International*, Greenwood Reprint, 13, 4: 487–93.

—— 1974, *On the Opposition (1921–27)*, Peking: Foreign Languages Press.

—— 1976, *Problems of Leninism*, Peking: Foreign Languages Press.

Stokes, Curtis 1982, *The Evolution of Trotsky's Theory of Revolution*, Washington, D.C.: University Press of America.

Swabeck, Arne 1977, 'Visiting Trotsky at Prinkipo', *Studies in Comparative Communism*, 10, 1 and 2: 152–9.

Tarasov, Aleksandr n.d., 'Biurokratiia kak sotsialnyi parazit', *Skepsis: Nauchno-*

prosvetitel'skii zhurnal, available at: <http://scepsis.ru/library/id_1581.html>.

Thatcher Ian 2003, *Trotsky*, New York: Routledge.

—— 2009, 'Trotskii and Lenin's Funeral, 27 January 1924: A Brief Note', *History*, 194, 314: 194–202.

Thurston, Robert 1993, 'The Stakhanovite Movement: Background to the Great Terror in the Factories, 1935–1938', in *Stalinist Terror: New Perspectives*, edited by J. Arch Getty and Roberta T. Manning. Cambridge: Cambridge University Press.

—— 1996, *Life and Terror in Stalin's Russia, 1934–1941*, New Haven: Yale University Press.

Ticktin, Hillel 1995a, 'Leon Trotsky and the Social Forces Leading to Bureaucarcy, 1923–29', in *The Ideas of Leon Trotsky*, edited by Hillel Ticktin and Michael Cox, London: Porcupine Press.

—— 1995b, 'Leon Trotsky's Political and Economic Analysis of the USSR, 1929–40', in *The Ideas of Leon Trotsky*, edited by Hillel Ticktin and Michael Cox, London: Porcupine Press.

Timasheff, Nicholas 1946, *The Great Retreat: The Growth and Decline of Communism in Russia*, New York: E.P. Durron and Co.

Trotsky, Leon Davidovich 1919, *From October to Brest-Litovsk*, New York: The Socialist Publication Society.

—— 1923, 'Mysli o partii', *Pravda*, Pravda Digital Archive, East View Information Services, 56: 3.

—— 1929a, *Chto i kak proizoshlo? Shest' statei dlia mirovoi burzhuaznoi pechati*, Paris: H. Vilain.

—— 1929b, *La révolution défigurée*, Paris: Rieder.

—— 1937, *The Revolution Betrayed: What Is the Soviet Union and Where Is It Going?*, translated by Max Eastman, Garden City, NY: Doubleday, Doran and Co.

—— 1941, *Stalin: An Appraisal of the Man and His Influence*, edited and translated by Charles Malamuth, New York: Harper and Brothers.

—— 1958 [1923], 'Leon Trotsky on the National Question', *International Socialist Review*, 19, 3: 99–103.

—— 1963a [1925, 1927] Nasha pervaia revoliutsiia, vol. 2 of *Sochineniia*, 2 parts, Moscow: Gosudarstvennoe izdatel'stvo, Cleveland, OH: Bell and Howell.

—— 1963b [1924], *Ot oktiabria do Bresta* Part 2 of *1917*, vol. 3 of *Sochineniia*, Moscow: Gosudarstvennoe izdatel'stvo, Cleveland, OH: Bell and Howell.

—— 1963c [1925], *Osnovnye voprosy proletarskoi revoliutsii*, vol. 12 of *Sochineniia*, Moscow: Gosudarstvennoe izdatel'stvo, Cleveland, OH: Bell and Howell.

—— 1963d [1927], *Khoziaistvennoe stroitel'stvo Sovetskoi Respubliki*, vol. 15 of *Sochineniia*, Gosudarstvennoe izdatel'stvo, Cleveland, OH: Bell and Howell.

—— 1963e [1927], *Kul'tura perekhodnogo perioda*, vol. 21 of *Sochineniia*, Moscow: Gosudarstvennoe Izdatel'stvo, Cleveland, OH: Bell and Howell.

—— 1963f, *Trotsky's Diary in Exile, 1935*, translated by Elena Zarudnaya, New York: Atheneum.

—— 1964–71, *The Trotsky Papers, 1917–1922*, in two volumes, edited by Jan M. Meijer, The Hague: Mouton and Co.

—— 1969 [1906, 1930], *The Permanent Revolution and Results and Prospects*, New York: Merit Publishers.

——1970a, *Leon Trotsky on the Paris Commune*, New York: Pathfinder Press.

—— 1970b [1929], *The Third International After Lenin*, New York: Pathfinder Press.

—— 1970c [1930], *My Life: An Attempt at an Autobiography*, New York: Pathfinder Press,

—— 1970d, *In Defense of Marxism Against the Petty-Bourgeois Opposition*, New York: Pathfinder Press.

——1971a [1932], *The Stalin School of Falsification*, translated by John G. Wright, New York: Pathfinder Press.

—— 1971b, *Writings of Leon Trotsky (1934–35)*, edited by George Breitman and Bev Scott, New York: Pathfinder Press.

—— 1971c, *The Struggle against Fascism in Germany*. New York, Pathfinder Press, 1971.

—— 1972a, *Leon Trotsky Speaks*, edited by Sarah Lovell, New York: Pathfinder Press.

—— 1972b [1908], *1905*, translated by Anya Bostock, New York: Vintage Books, Random House.

—— 1972c [1920], *Terrorism and Communism: A Reply to Karl Kautsky*, Ann Arbor: University of Michigan Press.

—— 1972d, *The First Five Years of the Communist International*, in two volumes, vol. 2, New York: Monad Press.

—— 1972e, *The Position of the Soviet Republic and the Tasks of Young Workers*, translated by R. Chappell, London: Young Socialists.

—— 1972f, *Writings of Leon Trotsky [1932–33]*, edited by George Breitman and Sarah Lovell, New York: Pathfinder Press.

—— 1972g, *Writings of Leon Trotsky [1933–34]*, edited by George Breitman and Bev Scott, New York: Pathfinder Press.

—— 1972h [1937], *Chto takoe S.S.S.R. i kuda on idet?*, Paris: Edité par la IVe Internationale Rouge.

—— 1973a [1924], *Problems of Everyday Life and Other Writings on Culture and Science*, New York: Monad Press.

—— 1973b, *Leon Trotsky on Britain*, New York: Monad Press.

—— 1973c, *Writings of Leon Trotsky [1930–31]*, edited by George Breitman and Sarah Lovell, New York: Pathfinder Press.

—— 1973d, *Writings of Leon Trotsky [1932]*, edited by George Breitman and Sarah Lovell, New York: Pathfinder Press.

—— 1973e, *Writings of Leon Trotsky [1939–40]*, edited by Naomi Allen and George Breitman, New York: Pathfinder Press.

—— 1973f, *The Spanish Revolution (1931–39)*, New York: Pathfinder Press.

—— 1973g [1938], *The Transitional Program for Socialist Revolution*, edited by George Breitman and Fred Stanton, New York: Pathfinder Press.

—— 1974, *Writings of Leon Trotsky [1938–39]*, edited by Naomi Allen and

George Breitman, New York: Pathfinder Press.

—— 1975a [1922], *Social Democracy and the Wars of Intervention in Russia (1918–21) (Between Red and White)*, London: New Park Publications.

—— 1975b, *The Challenge of the Left Opposition (1923–25)*, edited by Naomi Allen, New York: Pathfinder Press.

—— 1975c, *Writings of Leon Trotsky [1929]*, edited by George Breitman and Sarah Lovell, New York: Pathfinder Press.

—— 1975d, *Writings of Leon Trotsky [1930]*, edited by George Breitman and Sarah Lovell, New York: Pathfinder Press.

—— 1976a, *Leon Trotsky on China*, edited by Les Evans and Russell Block, New York: Monad Press.

—— 1976b, *Writings of Leon Trotsky [1937–38]*, New York: Pathfinder Press.

—— 1977a, *Writings of Leon Trotsky [1935–36]*, edited by Naomi Allen and George Breitman, New York: Pathfinder Press.

—— 1977b [1932–3], *The History of the Russian Revolution*, translated by Max Eastman, London: Pluto Press.

—— 1977c, *Portraits: Political and Personal*, edited by George Breitman and George Saunders, New York: Pathfinder Press.

—— 1978, *Writings of Leon Trotsky [1936–37]*, edited by Naomi Allen and George Breitman, New York: Pathfinder Press.

—— 1979–81 [1923–4], *How the Revolution Armed: The Military Writings and Speeches of Leon Trotsky*, in five volumes, translated by Brian Pearce, London: New Park Publications.

—— 1979a, *Writings of Leon Trotsky: Supplement (1929–33)*, New York: Pathfinder Press.

—— 1979b, *Writings of Leon Trotsky: Supplement (1934–40)*, edited by George Breitman, New York: Pathfinder Press.

—— 1979c, *Leon Trotsky on France*, edited by David Salzner, New York: Monad Press.

—— 1980a, *Report of the Siberian Delegation (1903)*, London: New Park Publications.

—— 1980b, *The Challenge of the Left Opposition (1926–27)*, edited by Naomi Allen and George Saunders, New York: Pathfinder Press.

—— 1981, *The Challenge of the Left Opposition (1928–29)*, edited by Naomi Allen and George Saunders, New York: Pathfinder Press.

—— 1985, *Stalin*, edited by Iu. G. Fel'shtinskii, Benson, VT: Chalidze Publications.

—— 1986, *Trotsky's Notebooks, 1933–1935, Writings on Lenin, Dialectics, and Evolutionism*, translated by Philip Pomper, New York: Columbia University Press.

—— 1989, *Dnevniki i pis'ma*, edited by Iu. G. Fel'shtinskii, Tenafly, NJ: Ermitazh.

—— 1990 [1932], *Stalinskaia shkola fal'sifikatsii: popravki i dopolneniia k literature epigonov*, edited by P.V. Volobuev et al., Moscow: 'Nauka'.

—— 1991a [1923–4], *Kak vooruzhalas revoliutsiia: na voennoi rabote*, three volumes in five parts, Moscow: Vysshii voennyi revoliutsionnyi sovet, 1923–

1925, Microfiche, Minneapolis, MN: East View Publications.

—— 1991b [1930], *Moia zhizn': opyt avto-biografii*, Moscow: 'Panorama'.

—— 1995, *Pis'ma iz ssylki 1928*, edited by Iu.G. Fel'shtinskii, Moscow: Izdatel'stvo gumanitarnoi literatury.

—— 2004 [1923], 'Novyi kurs', Marxists' Internet Archive, available at: <http://www.marxists.org/russkij/trotsky/1924/newc.htm>.

—— 2009, 'Introduction to Ferdinand Lasalle's Speech to the Jury [July 1905]', in *Witnesses to Permanent Revolution: The Documentary Record*, edited and translated by Richard B. Day and Daniel Gaido, Leiden, the Netherlands: Brill.

Tsuji, Yoshimas 1989, 'The Debate on the Trade Unions, 1920–21', *Revolutionary Russia*, 2, 1: 31–100.

Tucker, Robert 1969, *The Marxian Revolutionary Idea*, New York: W.W. Norton and Co.

—— 1973a, 'Marx as a Political Theorist' in *Marx's Socialism*, edited by Shlomo Avineri, New York: Lieber-Atherton.

—— 1973b, *Stalin as Revolutionary, 1879–1929: A Study in History and Personality*, New York: W.W. Norton and Co.

—— 1987, *Political Culture and Leadership in Soviet Russia: From Lenin to Gorbachev*, Brighton, Sussex: Wheatsheaf Books.

—— 1990, *Stalin in Power: The Revolution from Above, 1928–1941*, New York: W.W. Norton and Co.

Twiss, Thomas 1987, 'Trotsky's Break with the Comintern: A Comment on J. Arch Getty', *Soviet Studies*, 39, 1: 131–7.

—— 2009, 'Trotsky and the Problem of Soviet Bureaucracy', PhD dissertation, University of Pittsburgh, available at: <http://d-scholarship.pitt.edu/7502/>.

—— 2010, 'Trotsky's Analysis of Stalinism', *Critique*, 38, 4: 545–63.

Ulam, Adam 1973, *Stalin: The Man and His Era*, New York: Viking Press.

—— 1974, *Expansion and Coexistence: The History of Soviet Foreign Policy, 1917–73*, New York: Praeger Publishers.

Unger, Aryeh L. 1981, *Constitutional Development in the USSR: A Guide to the Soviet Constitution*, New York: Pica Press.

Van Heijenoort, Jean 1969 [1941], 'Lev Davidovich', in *Leon Trotsky: The Man and His Work*, edited by Joseph Hansen et al., 44–6, New York: Merit Publishers.

—— 1973 [1944], 'How the Fourth International Was Conceived', in *Towards a History of the Fourth International Part II*, New York: National Education Department, Socialist Workers Party.

—— 1978, *With Trotsky in Exile: From Prinkipo to Coyoacán*, Cambridge, MA: Harvard University Press.

Van Ree, Erik 2001, '"Lenin's Last Struggle" Revisited', *Revolutionary Russia*, 14, 2: 85–122.

Vilkova, Valentina (ed.) 1996, *The Struggle for Power: Russia in 1923*, Amherst, NY: Prometheus Books.

Viola, Lynne 1996, *Peasant Rebels under Stalin: Collectivization and the Cul-*

ture of Peasant Resistance, New York: Oxford University Press.

Viola, Lynne et al. (eds.) 2005, *The War against the Peasantry, 1927–1930: The Tragedy of the Soviet Countryside*, translated by Steven Shabad, New Haven, Yale University Press.

Volkogonov, Dmitri 1991, *Stalin: Triumph and Tragedy*, edited and translated by Harold Shukman, New York: Grove Weidenfeld.

—— 1996, *Trotsky: The Eternal Revolutionary*, translated and edited by Harold Shuckman, New York: The Free Press.

Voyeikov 1998, 'The Relevance of Trotsky's Ideological Legacy' in *The Ideological Legacy of L.D. Trotsky: History and Contemporary Times*, edited by Marilyn Vogt-Downey, New York: International Committee for the Study of Leon Trotsky's Legacy.

Wade, Terence 1996, *Russian Etymological Dictionary*, London: Bristol Classical Press.

Ward, Chris 1990, *Russia's Cotton Workers and the New Economic Policy: Shop-floor Culture and State Policy, 1921–1929*. Cambridge: Cambridge University Press.

—— 1999, *Stalin's Russia*, 2nd ed., London: Oxford University Press.

Warth, Robert 1985, 'Leon Trotsky and the Comparative History of Revolutions', *Consortium on Revolutionary Europe 1750–1850: Proceedings*, 13: 196–209.

Weber, Max 1968 [1922], *Economy and Society: An Outline of Interpretative Sociology*, in three volumes, edited by Guenther Roth and Claus Wittich, New York: Bedminster Press.

—— 1946, *From Max Weber: Essays in Sociology*, translated, edited and with an introduction by H.H. Gerth and C. Wright Mills, New York: Oxford University Press.

Weber, Sara 1972, 'Recollections of Trotsky', *Modern Occasions*, 2,2 (Spring): 181–94.

Weissman, Susan 2001, *Victor Serge: The Course Is Set on Hope*, London: Verso.

White, Howard 1995, *Brief Tests of Collection Strength: A Methodology for All Types of Libraries*, Westport, CT: Greenwood Press.

White, Stephen 2000, *Russia's New Politics: The Management of a Postcommunist Society*, Cambridge, UK: Cambridge University Press.

Wieczynski, Joseph 1980, *The Modern Encyclopedia of Russian and Soviet History*, Gulf Breeeze, FL: Academic International Press.

Winsbury, Rex 1977, 'Jacob Blumkin, 1892–1929', *History Today*, 27, 11: 712–18.

Wistrich, Robert 1979, *Trotsky: Fate of a Revolutionary*, New York: Stein and Day.

Woods, Alan 2001, 'The Revolution Betrayed–a Marxist Masterpiece', available at: <http://www.trotsky.net/revolution_betrayed.html>

Zaleskii, A. 2000, *Imperiia Stalina: biograficheskkii entsiklopedicheskii slovar'*, Moscow: Veche.

Zentner, Christian and Friedemann Bedürftig (eds.) 1991, *The Encyclopedia of the Third Reich*, New York, Macmillan.

Zhelieznov, Vladimir et al. (eds.) 1993 [1910–36], *Entsiklopedicheskii slovar'*

Tovarishchestva 'Br. A. i I. Granat i Ko', in 58 volumes, Moscow: Vasanta.

Zinoviev, Gregory 1984 [1916], 'The Social Roots of Opportunism' in *Lenin's Struggle for a Revolutionary International: Documents: 1907–1916, The Preparatory Years*, edited by John Riddell, New York: Monad.

Index